MW01036416

WERNER HERZOG
A Guide for the Perplexed

Paul Cronin is the editor of Alexander Mackendrick's *On Film-Making: An Introduction to the Craft of the Director* and *Lessons with Kiarostami*. He has made films about Amos Vogel, Peter Whitehead and Haskell Wexler's *Medium Cool*. His website is www.herzogperplexed.com.

Werner Herzog
A Guide for the Perplexed

Conversations with
Paul Cronin

FABER & FABER

First published as *Herzog on Herzog* in 2002
by Faber & Faber Ltd
Bloomsbury House
74–77 Great Russell Street
London WC1B 3DA
This substantially revised and updated edition first published in 2014

Typeset by Ian Bahrami
Printed and bound in the United States of America

All rights reserved
© Werner Herzog, 2014
Commentary and "Visionary Vehemence" © Paul Cronin, 2014
Foreword © Harmony Korine, 2014
"Shooting on the Lam" © Herbert Golder, 2014
Afterword © Lawrence Krauss, 2014
All photos © Werner Herzog Filmproduktion courtesy of the Deutsche
Kinemathek, except: page 8 (bottom image) © Alan Greenberg; page 15
© Helaine Messer; page 21 © Estate of Amos Vogel; pages 28, 29, top of 30
and 32 © Lena Herzog

The right of Werner Herzog and Paul Cronin to be identified as authors
of this work has been asserted in accordance with Section 77 of the
Copyright, Designs and Patents Act 1988

*This book is sold subject to the condition that it shall not, by way of trade or
otherwise, be lent, resold, hired out or otherwise circulated without the
publisher's prior consent in any form of binding or cover other than that
in which it is published and without a similar condition including this
condition being imposed on the subsequent purchaser*

A CIP record for this book
is available from the British Library

ISBN 978-0-571-25977-9

2 4 6 8 10 9 7 5 3

Contents

v

Foreword
by Harmony Korine

werner herzog hates chickens. this is a fact. this is a consistent theme throughout his films. it is clear to me that he hates chickens, and this is one of the reasons why he has always been my favorite film director. i too hate chickens. the first time i saw even dwarfs started small i knew i wanted to make films. i had only experienced this once before, when as a boy i watched a w. c. fields movie marathon next to a man dying of emphysema. i could not imagine what type of human being could come up with such insane ideas. i could not understand how these dwarfs could laugh so intensely throughout the film. after getting to know the great man it is obvious where he gets his ideas. he gets them from a deep place where formal logic and academic thinking need not exist. he is a pure artist and maniac and there will never be another one like herzog. he has invented his own cinematic universe where out of chaos and detritus come moments of pure poetry and the deepest enlightenment. herzog's influence cannot be denied. he is a true icon of cinema. he is a foot soldier. he is not a chicken.

Visionary Vehemence
Ten Thoughts about Werner Herzog

"Life is about oneself against the world."
Paul Bowles

"Assiduity is the sin against the holy spirit.
Only ideas won by walking have any value."
Nietzsche

"An artist is a creature driven by demons. He doesn't know
why they choose him and he's usually too busy to wonder why."
William Faulkner

"The only way to stop smoking is to stop smoking."
Werner Herzog

I met Werner Herzog for the first time in the plush sitting room of a stylish central London hotel. We spent a couple of hours circling each other, in discussion about collaboration on an interview book. I returned the following morning, to continue our chat over breakfast. Would Herzog go for the idea? "All things considered," he said slowly but firmly, before carefully placing his buttered toast onto his plate, pausing for half a minute, taking an unhurried mouthful of coffee, and looking me squarely in the eye, "it's best I co-operate with you." A sigh of relief. "But there is one thing I want to do while I'm in town this week."

"Anything."

"I want to see Arsenal play."

The next day I enter new territory, wander down some dark alley, and scalp a handful of tickets. A week later I am in a pub in Upton Park drinking Guinness with Werner and Lena, his wife, having just seen West Ham play the Gunners (I don't remember who won). "Number 26 is a very intelligent player," says Werner. "Who is he?" This is not a question I am able to answer, so Werner turns to the portly, slightly inebriated gentleman and his mates standing next to us, and asks again. "That's Joe Cole," we are told. "One of the best there is. Only eighteen years old." "Yes," says Werner.

"He really knows how to use the space around him, even when he doesn't have the ball. He'll be playing for England soon." Which goes to show that Werner's understanding of football runs just as deep as that of all things cinematic: not long after this match Joe Cole was, indeed, playing for the national team.* A few weeks later, one bright early morning, Werner and I are sitting in the living room of his modest, airy Los Angeles home, tucked away in the Hollywood Hills, watching Bayern Munich play AC Milan on television. It's a crucial match for both. Tension is high. Werner chain-smokes nervously and we snack on Doritos. Munich equalise with the last touch of the game. It bodes well for the first of our conversations that will become this book.

It isn't easy to say if the following – the closest we'll get to a Herzog autobiography – does Werner's life and work justice. I have often thought about how this book might read if I had interviewed him every couple of years from the start of his career (practically speaking, not possible, since I wasn't born until about a decade in). How differently would Werner appear on paper? Memory being what it is, would these pages be filled exclusively with anecdotes about filming amidst this or that landscape rather than, as many usefully do, focusing on perennial ideas and principles? Does the distance that time has given Herzog from much of his work (it's more than fifty years, sixty films and a handful of books since *A Lost Western*) make for a more contemplative overview?

I can definitely say two things. First, Werner's memory is a good one. His most conspicuous acting job, and one of his most recent, was in the 2012 Tom Cruise shoot-'em-up *Jack Reacher*, filmed in Pittsburgh. One afternoon during production, Werner rented a car and took the time to drive several miles out into the nearby countryside where, fifty years earlier, he spent a few months. Despite not having been in the city since the early sixties, and though it involved a complicated route from downtown, he immediately found the house he was looking for. "I recognised it all," says Werner, "to the point where I was struck by

* Herzog's favourite British player of all time: Bobby Charlton, "a genius who brought football back to its basic simplicity." Glenn Hoddle – "an earthquake in a stadium" – comes a close second.

a new configuration of concrete stairs that curved down to the garage." Herb Golder, professor of classics at Boston University and trusted confidant on several Herzog films, recalls a production meeting for *Wings of Hope* at a hotel in Lima. "Werner drew from memory a map of the territory that pertained to the story, an area of the densest jungle imaginable, which he hadn't seen in twenty-seven years, including the crash site and the Pachitea tributary, snaking off to the Sungaro and Shebonya, feeding the Yuyapichis. When we compared Werner's map with an actual map the next day, we discovered that his reconstruction of the topography was almost perfect. I still have that sketched map of his, and look at it now and again, as I consider it a blueprint of the feeling for landscape and sense of space necessary for great filmmaking."

Second, a complete understanding of the irrepressible Werner Herzog is only possible if one has (a) regularly climbed inside his head to see exactly where his ideas come from, then observed him at close quarters as he makes a number of consecutive films (fiction and non-fiction); and (b) stood in his garden, *Weissbier* in hand, watching him, aproned-up, frying a lamb chop on the barbecue, or supping with him and his wife Lena on her Siberian mushroom soup as Fats Domino, their corpulent cat, roams. Regret to inform I have done only one of these things, and have yet to meet anyone who has experienced both, which leads to my own verdict on *A Guide for the Perplexed*: it's the best we've got.

Whenever Werner Herzog deploys his abilities, we can expect the unexpected, a matchless, coruscating take, those lapidary turns of phrase. The interview presented here attempts to capture his exaltation of the landscapes, objects, books, art, poetry, music, literature, cinema, ideas and people that surround us, alongside his own pastimes, convictions and judgements, with "agitation of mind" as shorthand for what this book hopefully delivers. While Hölderlin transmuted the world around him into words, Herzog has consistently transformed his experiences into sounds and images. It is, however, incidental that the subject of this book is an indispensable man of cinema. More important for our purposes is that he is an edifying and transformative conversationalist.

Over the years this book – the first iteration of which appeared in 2002, as *Herzog on Herzog* – seems to have contributed in a small way to the construction of Werner's public persona, and has become something of an eccentric self-help volume. People tell me how weighty, invigorating and (Herzog dislikes the word, feeling it makes him sound "too much like a preacher") inspirational they find it. One fellow called the book "scripture," while *Newsweek* raved, calling it "a required text for every film school in the country." We do, of course, have plenty to learn from Werner about cinema. A lifetime of filmmaking means that when it comes to the logistical battles of production, he is able to point out in which directions lie the paths of least resistance, to show us how best to minimise our weaknesses and play to our strengths. But you won't learn much about focal lengths, lighting and story structure from these pages. Werner's explication of film grammar, for example, doesn't involve details of film stock, shot size and editing techniques, rather a pithy commentary on why cowboys never eat pasta. Nor does what follows include intricate theoretical analysis that might inspire the ever-increasing number of academics aiming their eyes and brains at Herzog's work. Werner has always resisted interpretation (Hölderlin: "Man is a god when he dreams, a beggar when he reflects"), and from the start I knew better than to ask. Instead, with clarity and elegance, he describes his process, making clear that any competent investigation of his films has to be rooted in an understanding of how and where they were made, under what conditions, and by whom.

During one of our final sessions together when preparing this book, Werner called my attention to several paragraphs, all of which were comprised of material where (presumably during moments of weakness) he offered up vague explanations of his films. As we worked through the manuscript, Werner intuitively zeroed in on these lines and – as if they threatened to contaminate the entire book – trimmed. So uninvolved is he in what his films and the characters that populate them might "mean" that when Herb Golder once showed him a full-length published study of his work, Werner quickly deposited the book into the nearest dustbin, announcing, "This has nothing to do with me." On his shelves sit a host of art books (Hieronymus Bosch, John Martin, Albrecht Altdorfer), alongside select texts by the small number of authors important to him (Hölderlin, Kleist, Kuhlmann, Montaigne, Thucydides, Virgil), plus twenty volumes of the *Oxford English Dictionary* and Anderson/Dibble's multi-volume edition of the *Codex Florentino*. He has copies of some of his own books. He has none of the books about his work.

Werner told me he once met a champion ski jumper from Norway who one season beat all his adversaries. "He was also an architecture student and the following year wrote his thesis on the construction of ski ramps. He thought so much about those damned things that during the next season he lost every competition he entered." For Herzog, the moment such meditation enters the equation, when he delves too deep and starts explaining himself, imbalance sets in and creativity is forced aside, or at least clouds over. As far as he is concerned, cinema – like music – is more deeply connected to imagination than pure reason, and though indubitably respectful of the rationalists of the world, unadulterated intuition is a brighter guiding light for Werner than analysis will ever be. In other words, the new film always takes precedence over talking about old work. "Interviews make very little sense," he said in 1979. "They are not helpful, either to the audience or to myself. I prefer audiences that take a very straight, clear, open look at what they see on the screen." I am sometimes asked by colloquium organisers if Werner would attend were they to assemble a round table to discuss his films and praise him for past glories. There's a slim chance, I say, so long as he isn't working that day.

2 PERSEVERANCE

Although his place in film history is assured, Werner's work has always been a by-product of his furious "extra-cinematic" inquisitiveness and infatuations. He has forever been nourished by a wondrously eclectic range of interests that might have propelled him equally in the direction of mathematics, philology, archaeology, history, cookery, ant wrangling (see page 260), football or (as the Afterword by Lawrence Krauss suggests) science. The fact that it's cinema the multifarious Herzog has involved himself with is, to a certain extent, irrelevant to our tale, one of dedication, passion and determination. This book is the story of one man's constant and (almost) always triumphant confrontation with a profound sense of duty to unburden himself, and for that reason alone it's worth our attention.

Werner's work ethic and drive, impressive decades ago, remain formidable, and his ability to maintain creative integrity and generate new ideas is exhilarating. There is a wonderful moment in *Conquest of the Useless*, the published version of his journal, written – Walser-like – in microscopic script during production on *Fitzcarraldo*. While playing in an imaginary football match in Lima, Werner struggles to distinguish between players on his team and his competitors. When the referee refuses to halt play so one side can exchange its jerseys for those of a less confusing colour, Werner concludes that "the only hope of winning the game would be if I did it all by myself . . . I would have to take on the entire field myself, including my own team." When it comes to his films, this energy is perpetually generated by, as he calls them, "home invaders," those ideas that steal inside his head, to be wrestled to the ground in the form of a screenplay, film or book. Herzog's film-making has never given him consolation as such. It's a blessing and a burden. He never has to worry about whether a good idea for the next film will reveal itself because, like it or not, the throb is there long before the one at hand is complete. When Herzog writes that the image of a steamship moving up the side of a mountain seized hold of him with such power it was like "the demented fury of a hound that has sunk its teeth into the leg of a deer carcass," we presume there isn't a project he has involved himself with over the past fifty years that has taken hold with any less urgency. As David Mamet has written, "Those with 'something to fall back on' invariably fall back on it. They intended to all along. That is why they provided themselves with it. But those with no alternative see the world differently."

Nearly fifteen years ago, when I started work on this project, Werner hadn't attained the godlike status the world now accords him. For the past twenty years he has lived on the West Coast of the United States, most recently a few miles from Hollywood, where he is his own master. While some folks wait bleary-eyed for calls from their agent, Werner rarely picks up for his own ("For decades I didn't even have an agent and even today don't really need one"), and has forever preferred the company of farmers, mechanics, carpenters and vintners to filmmakers. In California he is free from European rigidity, even if he still feels a powerful intellectual and emotive connection to his homeland. In 1982, a year before her death, Herzog's mentor Lotte Eisner wrote that Werner is

> German in the best sense of the word. German as Walther von der Vogelweide and his love poem "Under the Lime Tree." German as the austere, fine statues of the Naumburg cathedral, as the Bamberg horseman. German as Heine's poem of longing "In a Foreign Land." As Brecht's "Ballad of the Drowned Young Girl." As Barlach's audacious wood statues, which the Third Reich sought to destroy. And as Lehmbruck's "Kneeling Woman."

Today, studio executives adventurous enough to try and entice Werner into more conventional enterprises show up at his door, though the issue, as Anthony Lane has written, "is one not of Herzog selling out but of Hollywood wanting to buy in." Werner's comrade Tom Luddy, co-founder of the Telluride Film Festival (where the Werner Herzog Theater opened in 2013), describes him as a "pop icon." Having outlived countless trends, Herzog has moved into the primary currents and is celebrated worldwide, as he suggested would happen. "I think people will get acquainted to my kind of films," he said in 1982. Werner feels no shame in admitting that the respect of those he respects somehow keeps him going, or, at least, temporarily lessens the burden. But his belief in his abilities has never seriously wavered, which means details of the peaks and troughs of his career – which essentially speak to his treatment at the hands of professional reviewers and the ticket-buying public – are barely touched on throughout the pages of this book. Herzog pays little attention to the chorus. And why should he? It isn't antagonism he feels towards such folk so much as indifference. His ferocious need to make films and write books will forever trump everything, regardless of the obstacles.

By offering up the background to each of his films and how they were made, Herzog offers details of form, structure and – indirectly – meaning. As he articulates his techniques, ideas and principles in the conversations that follow, his way of looking at the world is made clear. His "credo," as he puts it, "is the films themselves and my ability to make them." Truffaut once explained that making a film is like taking a boat out to sea, the director at the helm, forever attempting to avoid shipwreck (in his Hitchcock book he describes the process as a "maze of snares"). Being tossed about on the waves is the very nature of filmmaking, a state of affairs only an amateur would whine about. ("I'm not into the culture of complaint," Herzog says. To his fictional son in *julien donkey-boy*: "A winner doesn't shiver." Physicist Lawrence Krauss: the universe doesn't exist to make us happy.) In short: you're always asking to be sunk. Or, per Herzog, who describes himself as a product of his cumulative humiliations and defeats, filmmaking "causes pain." In discussing the day-to-day experiences and hard graft of the cinema practitioner, in stressing how vital it is for each of us to follow our own particular channel, in acknowledging that the name of the game is faith, not money, *A Guide for the Perplexed* furnishes the reader with an oblique ground plan to help navigate the rocks and manage the daily calamities.

Not coincidentally, these are the same ideas that underpin and flicker steadily throughout the three days of Herzog's extemporizing at his irreverent and sporadically executed three-day Rogue Film School. Nietzsche tells us that "All writing is useless that is not a stimulus to activity." Similarly, Herzog declaims that his ultimate aim with Rogue is to be useful rather than explicitly didactic, something I suspect he succeeds in, much to the delight of all those youthful, awestruck participants. His rousing description of the filmmaker and how he needs to move through the world, confronted at every turn by obstructions, paints him as an ingenious, brazen, indefatigable problem-solver, with forgery and lock-picking as metaphor. "This man has no ticket," says Molly in the opening minutes of *Fitzcarraldo*, as she and Brian crash into the lobby of the opera house in Manaus after having rowed for two days and two nights from Iquitos. Yet, insists Molly, Fitzcarraldo has a moral right to enter the auditorium, see his hero Caruso in the flesh, and hear him sing. In this spirit, Herzog believes, the natural order would be disrupted if a misdemeanour didn't occasionally intrude into the life of a working filmmaker. To help jump the hurdles, he suggests, purloin that which is absolutely necessary. It has always been Werner's own particular long-term survival strategy.

Over the Rogue weekend, as Herzog responds to his audience, telling story after story from memory, a repository filled with decades of filmmaking tales, this idea becomes ever clearer. I find in my handwritten notes, taken at Rogue in June 2010, the following: "Raphael talks about some rule he broke when filming at Chernobyl. Werner exclaims: 'That was a very fine and Rogue attitude.'" It might all have something to do with the exquisite Herzog line recorded by Alan Greenberg on the set of *Heart of Glass*: "There is work to be done, and we will do it well. Outside we will look like gangsters. On the inside we will wear the gowns of priests." What I can decisively say is that Herzog and the Rogue participants I met have been mutually forgiving of each other, considering the former is wholeheartedly dismissive of traditional film schools, and the latter a self-selected group which, if truly Herzogian in temperament, would gently throw the offer of a place at film school back in their hero's face.

Rogue – where the emphasis is more on surveying one's own "inner landscapes" than anything else – is a strong stimulant, the pedagogic equivalent of being doused with ice water. It affirms that Herzog's stupendous curiosity and love of the world, his explorations into uncharted territory across the planet, his insatiability for inquiry and investigation, his voracious appetite and intensity of belief, his attraction to chaos in its many iterations, have never been stronger. With his makeshift film school, a summation of many years' work, Werner has seized hold of ideas that appear in interviews stretching back forty years, acknowledged their contemporary relevance, then recalibrated and brushed them down. By doing so, he has left behind previous incarnations. The stalwart of New German Cinema has long been displaced. The accused of any number of *Fitzcarraldo* controversies is in the past. The director of five features with Klaus Kinski (the last one made more than a quarter of a century ago) is more or less gone. What remains is the resourceful, optimistic filmmaker, still going strong, shepherding us into action, showing us how to outwit the evil forces, leading by example. "I have fortified myself with enough philosophy to cope with anything that's been thrown at me over the years," says Herzog. "I always manage to wrestle something from the situation, no matter what."

Werner's fine-tuned sympathies are those of a thoughtful, exacting and studious polyglot poet who, when translating his work and that of others, is aware of the delicate nuances of one word over another, not just in German, but also English and other languages, including ancient Greek. Herbert Achternbusch has written that Herzog has an "addiction to words," and Werner himself wonders in this book whether "I might be a better writer than I am a filmmaker." This is the same Werner Herzog who, during a 1988 public conversation at the National Film Theatre in London, spontaneously told his audience, after rejecting the more ludicrous claims about the production of *Fitzcarraldo*, "If you don't believe me, we can go out into the street and fight it out. I have no proof but my physical body." Werner's approach to everything is that of a fearless pioneer, an intrepid seeker who, as he explained in a 1982 interview, doesn't "want to live in a world where there are no lions anymore." At the age of seventy he remains extraordinarily agile, and gallops rather than strolls. All things tactile and corporeal are pre-eminent. His engagement with the world is experiential, not ideological. For Herzog, film is athletics, not aesthetics. (Cameraman Ed Lachman: "What is strongest is the content of the images, not a formalistic attitude about what an image is.")

Never has Herzog lived vicariously through others. The sedentary life has never been for him. Ready to pack his bag at any moment, he usually doesn't know where he will be next month. A joy of geographical inquiry has forever characterised his existence, even before he ever picked up a camera. This is something the Germans have a word for: *Fernweh*, which could be translated as "a yearning for distant lands." (Herzog may be right in claiming to be the only person to have filmed on all seven continents.) Remote peoples and faraway places, however inhospitable, are a crucial source of inspiration, and there is no reason to doubt Werner when he says that if a one-way journey of exceptional exploration were offered, if the opportunity arose to leave the stratosphere and go in search of untainted images, he would jump at the chance. With his ability to sniff out the lyrical and extraordinary, which is usually there for all to see ("We thank NASA for its sense of poetry," Werner tells us at the end of *The Wild Blue Yonder*, perhaps laying to rest once and for all the notion that irony is beyond him), the visceral experiences are imbibed, after which the stories, characters and scenarios take shape, and the images pour out with an exactitude and urgency that make Herzog more a transcriber than an author per se. The scripts – often unconventional in format, part of Werner's quest to establish a new form of literature – are prepared only for the purpose of fund-raising. Their author has never needed them to realise his ideas. Wrote Wagner of his process: "The detailed musical treatment is more of a calm and considered finishing-off job, which the moment of real creation has preceded."

The legend is that in his travels, the never-tentative Herzog seeks the strongest currents and most treacherous waters ("That slope may look insignificant," says Fitzcarraldo, "but it's going to be my destiny"). His long-time cameraman Peter Zeitlinger insists that "Werner never takes the paved road, always the dirt track," adding that he has, "probably from mid-puberty, been trying very hard to die a grand, poetic death." According to Zak Penn, who has directed Herzog as an actor in two films, "Werner fulfils the important role of a physical adventurer. We live vicariously through him, wishing we had his courage and nerve. He's a paragon, a mythic hero." (Pauline Kael's description: a "metaphysical Tarzan.") It's up for debate whether the unflappable Herzog is being truthful when insisting he is no reckless risk-taker, but what we can be certain of is that he seeks what Robert Walser called a "very small patch of existence," a non-hierarchical and self-governed land without profanity, absolutism, servility, mendacity, sorcery, demagoguery, dogma, ossification and unnecessary rules and regulations, devoid of repressive political manipulation and slavery, free from rampant, gratuitous commodification, welcoming of poets and contrarians, with a minimum of bureaucracy, where self-determination, inquiry and pluralism can flourish, and a secular community is offered the chance to thrive under its own humane guidelines. "To be honest," he told me last year, "I wish I didn't have to travel so much these days, but if you want to make a film in Antarctica, you have to get on an aeroplane."

Werner offers counsel at his Rogue Film School, but I can't imagine he himself has ever asked anyone for advice. Errol Morris has spoken of a line from an interview with Gabriel García Márquez, who, after having read Kafka's *Metamorphosis* for the first time, said to himself, "I didn't know anyone was allowed to write things like that." It was the same line Errol muttered to himself upon exiting the Pacific Film Archive, having just seen Werner's *Fata Morgana* for the first time. We know what he means. In his 1977 review of *La Soufrière*, Amos Vogel described Herzog as "the most important director now working in Germany. One of the great film talents of our time, not even at the peak of his creative life, Herzog is a person who will not compromise, who deliberately remains 'unclassifiable,' hence attacked by those who must classify." Perhaps this is why Herzog's films, even those made forty years ago, don't appear to have aged one bit.

The stories in this book and Herzog's improvising at Rogue make clear that he has chased his deepest fascinations since his earliest days. Some films might have been adapted from literary sources or inspired by real-life events, but with their unique view of the world every one is created *ex nihilo*, predicated on his singular imagination. At a point in his career when many would have run out of ideas – a moment when accolades and retrospectives are flowing thick and fast – Werner has in the recent past become a beacon of hope for neophytes everywhere, looked upon by many as someone who has forever risen unblinkingly to the challenge. "I encourage myself, since nobody else encourages me," he wrote in 1974.

After working closely with a number of filmmakers – big and small, famous and unknown, living and dead – I feel confident in telling people there's no point in comparing Herzog to anyone. It isn't that he's a non-conformist, responding to his surroundings and actively setting himself apart. He just naturally is apart, which makes it foolish for anyone to try to emulate him. Rogue – where the concept is all his, where he maintains full control – is the result of his avoidance of institutions of any kind. While he isn't unhappy, throughout this book, to ally himself to a small number of people with whose centuries-old work he feels a vigorous concordance, Herzog really is his own startlingly original man, and his repeated insistence that his films can't be categorised as part of the Romantic tradition reflect his disregard for any club that might have him as a member. For Herzog, there was never a question of film school or an apprenticeship. Instead, he burst upon us, fifty years ago, almost fully formed as a filmmaker, ready to share his personal fantasies at any cost. Werner is one of those few figures who have created a body of work worthy of sustained investigation, yet one so disassociated from the world of cinema around him – so "cut off from every web of film history," as Hans Schifferle has written – that knowledge of such things might actually get in the way of appreciating his films.

5 STORYTELLING

At the Opéra Bastille in Paris, during dress rehearsals for Herzog's 1993 production of *The Flying Dutchman*, the electronics malfunctioned. "The mammoth iceberg was drifting towards the orchestra pit and sometimes we couldn't even open the curtain," says Werner. "It turned out that all these problems were triggered by a special kind of signal, a taxi call frequency. If a cab drove past the opera house, this state-of-the-art computer equipment went haywire. I insisted we use more primitive techniques instead. Anything else was dangerously inadequate." For Herzog, analogue will almost always win out over digital. Although he has an abiding passion for every stage of the filmmaking process and is happy to experiment with the latest piece of equipment, technology has never been Werner's thing. He is a primeval sophisticate of great erudition who yearns nostalgically for a pre-literate, pre-electric (or post-literate and post-electric) existence, where the primitive wisdom of the uninstructed and those able to memorise stories and poems, then recite them free of all props, predominates.

6 THE HOLY FOOL

There are few filmmakers who don't tell stories of people in trouble, struggling to overcome obstacles, humiliated, wracked with anxiety and confusion, adrift, at odds with the world, called upon to fight against adversaries. The outsider and rebel is a dramatic trope that stretches back to the beginnings of storytelling. But Herzog's protagonists – extremists all – are of a particular persuasion. Amos

Vogel wrote that the Holy Fool inhabits the films, the figure who "dares more than any human should, and who is therefore – and this is why Herzog is drawn to him – closer to possible sources of deeper truth though not necessarily capable of reaching them." In his monograph on Herzog's *Nosferatu*, S. S. Prawer suggests there are two characters ubiquitous in Werner's world: "outsiders in a society where they can never feel at home, and which in the end destroys them; and rebels who try, by violent means, to realise what their lives refuse them, but also ultimately fail." The wide and colourful variety of these individuals, the sheer number in both his documentaries and fictions – represented always with empathy and compassion – make clear that they all somehow reflect their creator's innermost enthusiasms. It is never incongruous to see Herzog on screen, responding and interacting.

Some of these figures (Aguirre, Fitzcarraldo, Walter Steiner, Reinhold Messner, Francisco Manoel, Graham Dorrington, brazen all) seek overwhelming challenges, while others (Fini Straubinger, Adolph Ratzka, Kaspar Hauser, the premature baby of *Stroszek*, the anguished Woyzeck, Michael Goldsmith, Jared Talbert, the victims of *From One Second to the Next*) have burdens thrust upon them. We are repeatedly confronted with dispossessed outcasts and eccentrics, estranged loners, struggling overreachers and underdogs who live *in extremis*, at the limits of experience, isolated and fraught with problems of communication and assimilation, railing against sometimes stifling social conventions, often foolhardy and spirited enough to embark on undertakings they know are futile, thus providing a series of vivid definitions of the human condition, alongside some level of insight into the society, even the entire historical era, in which they live. "The existential dimension of his characters always seems to take precedence over any social issue against which they might revolt or from which they might suffer," writes Thomas Elsaesser.

The titular strongman hero of the ironic *Herakles* – who takes on the twelve labours, assuming tasks he can't possibly succeed in – is the quintessential Herzog anti-hero. To clean the Augean stables he has to empty out an enormous garbage dump, while resisting the Stymphalian birds means being confronted by the might of the United States Air Force. Stroszek, from *Signs of Life*, is caught in a hermetically sealed circle of repetition and inevitability, unable to break out except by force of sheer violence. He extends himself far beyond his means, pushing his limits and exceeding his own capabilities. The failure of his titanic struggle is preordained, but in the face of overwhelming oppression Stroszek never stops trying anyway. It isn't unlike the other Stroszek – played by Bruno S. a few years later – who finds himself standing in the freezing cold as his repossessed mobile home is loaded onto a truck and driven away. Stroszek wants to rob a bank, but it's closed, so he holds up the local barbershop instead. ("I think it's the saddest robbery I have ever seen on screen," Werner says.) The little people of *Even Dwarfs Started Small* know it makes no sense to rebel against bourgeois table manners, that this is a lost cause, but they do it anyway. The delusional Aguirre – searching for something (El Dorado) that doesn't even exist – defies nature to such an extent that nature inevitably hits back. His was a suicidal mission from the start. *Fitzcarraldo* – a film that retains a powerful hold on audiences more than three decades after it was released – is a projection of Herzog's almost unattainable fantasies, though he had no choice but to ensure that reality caught up with the imaginary events swarming through his mind. The most poignant moment in *Invincible* is the return of Zishe Breitbart to the shtetl where he grew up, desperately warning his fellow villagers of the impending Nazi threat ("We have to get strong. We shall need a thousand Samsons"). To abdicate ambition and cast aside unrealised hopes and dreams means to encounter a heavier burden. "Even a defeat is better than nothing at all," says the voiceover during the final seconds of *The Unprecedented Defence of the Fortress Deutschkreuz*.

Listen, in the opening minutes of *Handicapped Future*, to the gloriously optimistic wheelchair-bound young girl who ran out of things to dream about at the age of five and wants nothing more than to walk, visit America, and meet the Indians of her favourite western. Consider the dignified Aborigines in *Where the Green Ants Dream*, with their moral claim to ancient lands, up against the deranged officialdom of the white man's courts. Watch Reinhold Messner weeping at the thought of telling his mother her other son is dead. All are in some form a representation: the benign minds of Fini and Vladimir Kokol; the chronic back pain of the Bad Lieutenant; the maniacal fury of Gene Scott, ecstatic frenzy of Brooklyn preacher Huie Rogers and murderous impulses of

Carlo Gesualdo; Bokassa in Bangui feasting from his vast refrigerators, and death-row inmates chatting behind the bulletproof glass windows of Texas prisons; flying into the abyss with Steiner, and frolicking with Timothy Treadwell and the bears of Alaska; inside the comforting cockpit with Dieter Dengler, and struggling through the terrorising jungle with Juliane Koepcke; standing over the only person left on a deserted island about to explode, and swimming under the dream-like Ross Ice Shelf; sweeping over speechless children amidst the oblivion of post-war Kuwait, and listening to melancholic ballads sung by young Miskito Indians in Nicaragua; encountering the inhabitants of the undulating dunes of the Sahara and the cast of characters at the inaccessible McMurdo Station, then moving down into a cave adorned with immaculately preserved Palaeolithic art and up to the vertiginous Cerro Torre; bearing witness to the authority of exiled film historian Lotte Eisner and the self-reliant, snowbound hunters of Siberia; marvelling at those seeking some form of religious salvation, be they fervent pilgrims, half a million peripatetic Buddhists, or figures crawling on ice in search of a lost city.

There is also Herzog's own implacable autodidactic nature and knowledge that the entire world is on offer should we be able to muster the requisite excitement; his never-ending *Bildung* (self-improvement, personal transformation), refusal to sing in public, and mythical final moments, walking – alone and unbound – until no road is left; his attempts to nurture a community on the fringes of Germany's most important film festival, to create a utopia in South America, to construct a modern-day atelier, brimming with collaborating artisans, where communal working methods can blossom far from the commercial excesses of Hollywood. Consider also a perfect football match while walking across mountains of sugar beet from Munich to Paris (see *Of Walking in Ice*); the excesses of African slavery; the hypnotic state of a doomed, archaic society; a plague-ridden city rejoicing in its disintegration; a small-scale, close-knit and well-functioning film crew; imbecilic aliens who land on Earth and get nothing right; travelling on foot to pull together a divided nation (and, en route, saving a young Albert Einstein from choking); space exploration; the ability to fly. Herzog seeks nothing but freedom. Reinhild Steingröver tells us that both nature and culture are presented in Herzog's work as "inescapably hostile realms." Werner can do nothing but try to elude the potential menace nonetheless.

7 SURVIVAL

Werner lives a life of austerity, asceticism, authenticity. In an interview recorded more than thirty-five years after Herzog made his first film, his friend and collaborator Florian Fricke said: "Werner Herzog is one of the few friends that are very famous and have, regardless of their fame, not changed at all. He is in no way different from the way I knew him twenty-five years ago. He still drinks his beer from the bottle." (I have taken a number of subway rides with Werner in New York after a taxi ride was deemed extravagant.) Herzog has always had respect for audiences, aware that the admirers of his films have for years put food on the table, insisting he doesn't lead the life of an "artist," claiming instead the title of "soldier" or "craftsman." Debatable perhaps, but probably something we can live with. After all, as Walter Gropius told us nearly a century ago, "The artist is an exalted craftsman." What is certain is that while both German states of the second half of the twentieth century might have been "crassly materialistic" (as Günter Grass once described them), Werner never has been. He recognised at an early age that money would never get him what he wanted (though it might someday become, he said in 1976, "a concomitant of my work") and has long since chosen the hands-on existence of someone whose living space is manifestly conjoined with his professional life. Happy to integrate himself into mainstream film culture whenever the right opportunity arises – whether it be working with Twentieth Century Fox on *Nosferatu* or, as a director for hire, thirty years later, on *Bad Lieutenant* – there have been no major deviations in Werner's life. When the abyss stares up at him, Werner looks fixedly back, then moves on. "A comedy with Eddie Murphy," he says, "would be my way of pulling back from the edge."

8 RELIGION

Herzog is a humanist, a materialist awe-inspired by scientific exploration and progress, disdainful of the supernatural, but with an appreciation more profound than most of the ethereal, of what

Christopher Hitchens would describe as "the numinous, the transcendent or – at its best – the ecstatic." Organised religion plays no part in Werner's life. But the divine and the sacred and the ineffable always have.

9 POLITICS

Politics are rarely mentioned explicitly in *A Guide for the Perplexed*, but unpack Werner's thoughts about (a) "the lack of adequate imagery" as an incalculable danger to society, and (b) our failure to lob grenades into television stations, and it becomes difficult to divorce these two issues from their wider context. Both ideas reflect Amos Vogel's work as an historian, author and curator, the belief that most of the images around us, suffused with commercialism, are worn out and pernicious in their banality, that television chokes off and impoverishes (*"Es verbloedet die ganze Welt"*). Both are intertwined with the animosity felt by some towards those diabolical bureaucrats who – with robust corporate backing – reap vast fortunes via the time-wasting, conformist, escapist sounds and pictures with which they regularly assault the world. Both could be dubbed "political" ideas, as per Orwell's definition: "Desire to push the world in a certain direction, to alter other people's idea of the kind of society that they should strive after." To paraphrase Orwell, the deprivations of cinema have political and economic causes, and are not due simply to the "bad influence" of individual filmmakers. When "civilization is decadent," the images it reflects "must inevitably share in the general collapse." We are, all of us, in this day and age, at the mercy of overwhelming and impersonal historical, economic and environmental forces, so it's unlikely that the tide of stagnant cinema will ever be beaten back. There are, fortunately, some willing to confront the corrupted, debased, stale, adulterated, ready-made and cliché-ridden images that surround us. The actions of an enlightened individual or vanguard few, ready to kick back no matter what the odds, those striving for the ideal, can inspire regeneration. Werner has long recognised that he can't change the world through his films, but he can help us better understand certain things.

Although ideology is always handled in Herzog's films and interviews with, as he might describe it, "a pair of pliers," even if the timeless – not the topical – is what he has always been consumed by, and though his "visionary" stance means his work is "unmediated by historical or socio-political concerns" (as Eric Rentschler writes), it could never be argued that Herzog is an apolitical figure. Werner's anti-despotic verve, for example, is active indeed and given the right circumstances would surely define his very existence. He once told me – without a hint of bluster or bravado – that he would never bear witness to a regime like the Third Reich on home soil for the simple reason that he would stand and fight, surely dying in the process. In an unpublished recording of a conversation with Amos Vogel from 1970, Werner suggested an important lesson needed to be learnt by those in charge, and that he hoped the United States would "lose the war in Vietnam." Referencing events at the Cannes and Oberhausen Film Festivals, in an article written for a German film magazine in 1968 – a politically and socially convulsive year for many countries around the world – Herzog wrote that

> In a climate of radical political activities, it becomes impossible to communicate anything based on a personal decision, because any pronouncement is reduced to fit a lopsided friend-or-foe construct . . .
>
> The lesson I have learned from the events at Oberhausen and Cannes is that a filmmaker cannot and must not keep his films out of the political debate. For such a standpoint, the situation in the field of cultural politics has become far too serious. In these times of upheaval it is no longer possible to try and rescue one's film and shelter it in the safe corner of neutrality. A filmmaker can no longer remain neutral, nor can he make the excuse that it is really everybody else who has turned his film into a political statement.
>
> The politicising of film, however, is fraught with dangers. This is to say that as soon as a crucial political moment is reached, what is expected of a film is automatically reduced. Film can no longer develop its full potential with regard to content and style because everybody's interest will be focused on some palpable results to be gleaned from it. Instead of gaining an awareness of issues and developing questions, people will – according to the film's political stance – primarily read or even force arguments out of it. That is why I have always sought to

declare *Signs of Life* apolitical, though the film has as its theme an individual's radical rebellion.*

Jean-Pierre Melville wrote that a filmmaker "must be a witness to his times." Werner is just that, though he has always observed and participated on his own terms. For him, poetry and abstraction will naturally overwhelm the prosaic nature of commonplace politics. Never hesitant to ridicule the more wrongheaded political activity of the 1968 era, Herzog suggests that today, should the zealous *soixante-huitards* take a look at the abstract *Even Dwarfs Started Small* – with its pint-sized insurgents and their disorganised, fragmented, misplaced, futile but still respectable revolutionary fervour – "they might see a more truthful representation of what happened in 1968 than in most other films."

10 ACCOUNTANCY

"When he was in school," Herzog's mother once explained, "Werner never learnt anything. He never read the books he was supposed to read, he never studied, he never knew what he was supposed to know, it seemed. But in reality, Werner always knew everything. His senses were remarkable. If he heard the slightest sound, ten years later he would remember it precisely, he would talk about it, and maybe use it some way. But he is absolutely unable to explain anything. He knows, he sees, he understands, but he cannot explain. That is not his nature. Everything goes into him. If it comes out, it comes out transformed." I once spoke to Herzog about the techniques behind his more stylised documentaries. If everything were explained, he said, "the charm of fabrication would disappear. I have no problem being a magician who doesn't let his audience in on how his tricks are done." Although we find in the pages below plenty of examples of this mischievous sleight of hand – Werner's creative, often ingenious methods of unmasking, of liberating "truth" from its submerged depths, of showing us what we could not otherwise perceive – there are presumably many more we will never know about.

How important, Herzog asks in his essay "On the Absolute, the

* Translated by Martina Lauster. From "Mit den Wölfen Heulen" (see Bibliography, p. 496).

Sublime and Ecstatic Truth," is the factual? "Of course, we can't disregard the factual; it has normative power. But it can never give us the kind of illumination, the ecstatic flash, from which truth emerges." Reality has always been too obscure and unknowable for Werner to tackle head on. Mere facts – the "accountant's truth" – have a shameful sterility about them, which is why he constantly plays with such things. He knows we respond more intensely to poetry than reportage and actuality, that the poet is able to articulate a more intensified, condensed, elevated and mysterious truth, that the artist is – wrote Amos Vogel – the "conscience and prophet of man." Last year Dr Graham Dorrington, who was closely involved in the production of *The White Diamond* and appears as a central character in the film, wrote to me. "What is and was always clear to me is that Werner was never making a strict documentary. It was a film, carefully crafted with deliberate and remarkable style. What still amazes me is that gullible viewers (who wrote to me), or even some critics, assume that *The White Diamond* is a documentary that attempts to portray factual truth. That is why I don't think my exposition of such truths is necessarily useful, i.e., I have accepted any necessary misrepresentation (or distortion), in the same way that a portrait by (say) Picasso, Jan van Eyck or Hieronymus Bosch is not a photographic likeness of anyone." (Abbas Kiarostami's version: "Every filmmaker has his own interpretation of reality, which makes every filmmaker a liar. But these lies serve to express a kind of profound human truth." Even simpler, from Fellini: "Fiction may have a greater truth than everyday, obvious reality.")

Dorrington's comments lead to thoughts about a concept that appears throughout this book, most emphatically in Chapter 9. Werner's attack on what he calls "cinéma-vérité" requires an elaboration. He frequently uses the term – always disparagingly – and it lies at the heart of his Minnesota Declaration (see p. 476), so it is worth introducing three interlocking ideas. First, film theory, in its many renderings, has never been Werner's thing, and he readily admits to a lack of interest in cinephilia, so there is no good reason why he would know the differences between *cinéma-vérité* and Direct Cinema. The former evolved in the fifties in France and necessarily involved a level of intrusion by filmmakers – who had no compunction about making clear their presence – in whatever was being recorded. The latter is a form of non-fiction cinema that

emerged not long afterwards in North America, whereby incon-
spicuous and unobtrusive cameramen were more or less forbidden
to interfere with the supposed actuality they were faced with, where
events were not to be altered for the sake of the film (no voiceover, no re-enactments, nothing staged, etc.). In simplified terms, it's
the difference between instigating something and capturing it by
chance. Worth pondering is the notion that Werner's criticisms of
cinéma-vérité ("a malady, an endless reproduction of facts") make
more sense when aimed at Direct Cinema. Vérité filmmakers, wrote
James Blue in 1965, "intervene, probe, interview, provoke situations that might suddenly reveal something. There is an attempt
to obtain from the subject a kind of creative participation." In
other words, more or less what Herzog does with what he calls his
"manipulations." He even hails Les maîtres fous, by pre-eminent
vérité practitioner Jean Rouch – who always brought some layer
of calculated artifice to his work – as one of his favourite films. For
Rouch, the camera was a catalyst, "an incredible stimulant for the
observed as well as the observer."

Second, when it comes to this kind of non-fiction filmmaking, the
word "truth" is a red herring, and always has been. If the poetry
of Direct Cinema (or cinéma-vérité, or whatever you choose to call
it) seems to appear by passing chance, it is an affirmation of the
filmmakers' artfulness. Direct Cinema – albeit often sociologically
framed, in the tradition of reportage – was masterfully, deliberately
produced in such a way as to penetrate what Werner would name
the "deeper truth." Even when the cameramen filmed quotidian
reality, their work was anything but the fly's view from the wall.
There was always an active point of view, though all to the good if
people believed this was "reality" up there on the screen. The best
of the classic Direct Cinema films, if a touch less imaginative and
"ecstatic," if occasionally populated by characters more humdrum
than Herzog's and usually not quite so rehearsed, are no less truthful. The virtuosos of all forms of documentary cinema seek to draw
audiences' attention to particular details (through camerawork and
editing, as they subjectively reorder material to meet the demands
of the film), rarely claiming objectivity or outright truth. They don't
deny having interpreted events around them in varying degrees when
they deem it necessary by exercising control, projecting themselves,
creating a structure, imposing a "theme," all without compromising

the integrity of the footage. "We express ourselves in an indirect fashion by expressing ourselves through what we find to be interesting around ourselves," explained Direct Cinema cameraman Al Maysles in 1971. If Emerson was right when he told us that "Fiction reveals truth that reality obscures," on closer examination there isn't much of a philosophical divide between Werner's "ecstatic" filmmaking and the foundational works of Direct Cinema, whose directors left a somewhat lighter mark on their end result – one not so fanciful or glaringly apparent – than Werner does on his.

Third, Herzog's Minnesota Declaration isn't to be taken as gospel. It's more a provocation than anything else. He knows full well there is no such thing as absolute transparency in non-fiction cinema, that a truly neutral image doesn't exist, that only the surveillance cameras record objectively and impassively. The point is that Werner doesn't dismiss *vérité* out of hand so much as use it as what Guido Vitiello describes as "a rhetorical device for establishing his own poetics by contrast." For Herzog, it is an instrument of combat that allows him to position himself and define his approach within a sea of verisimilitude-obsessed bilge. (He isn't alone here. "*Cinéma-vérité*" is a term of convenience that lacks any nuance and doesn't begin to speak to the variety of film practices it encapsulates.) For Werner, that collection of twelve aphorisms, first articulated in 1999 at the Walker Art Center in Minneapolis before an enthusiastic audience, remains a way of mobilising support against the meretricious product being pumped out in every direction, those heinous crimes – indiscreet reality shows, pious and "unflinching" save-the-world rants, dreary talking heads, pseudo-anthropological didacticisms, sanctimonious and pre-digested feel-good weep fests ("the impossible triumph of the human spirit"), tawdry reconstructions, noxious filler between television commercials and/or film-festival parties (David Mamet calls it "the cheetah overpowering the same old antelope") – committed in *cinéma-vérité*'s name by those preoccupied more with facts than "truth," for whom veracity is obtainable only through the most conventional means. You other filmmakers out there, willing to do the hard work, Herzog admonishes, don't turn a blind eye. Push back.

Considering that on the opening and closing pages of this book we are told he doesn't consider filmmaking a "real profession" and looks upon his job "with great suspicion," Werner has weathered the past fifty years with grace and skill. I respect him – recalcitrant by nature, an unyielding opponent of sacred cows – in equal measure for his individuality, grace, candour, fortitude, natural authority, apparent effortlessness, discipline, tolerance, joyousness, single-mindedness, adaptability, plain-spokenness, unpretentiousness, practical sensibility and what Lotte Eisner called "visionary vehemence." There is no complacency, self-pity, torpor, abstruseness and diffidence in Herzog's world. Hats off to the uncompromising Werner also for the fact that it's a point of pride for him that he has no office, personal assistant or secretary, that his inbox always runneth over, that he does it all himself. He has always been out there working hard, with the required confidence, even if the eyes of the entire crowd were fixed on players at the other end of the pitch. I applaud his thoughts on conceptual art, the preponderance of indiscretion, bicycle helmets and hand sanitizers, his acceptance of the personal sacrifice that filmmaking necessarily involves, his (misplaced) fear of outliving his welcome as a filmmaker, his deep love of Bavaria, his dismay at how too many of us seek insulation from adversity. He's good company too, these days happy with himself. Werner is stoical, but also sentimental. Bruce Chatwin's description is on the button: "immensely tough, yet vulnerable, affectionate and remote, austere and sensual."

Herzog would never dream of displaying the multitude of awards accumulated over the years proudly on his mantelpiece. He knows the value of the never-ending search for novelty, even if he is someone who will sit in silence for as long as it takes, who appreciates the peace and quiet of home life, of "an easy chair with a cup of tea," who deletes unlistened-to phone messages when there are too many to handle ("Everything of importance eventually reaches me anyway"). He is principled too, a man of his word. In 1984, cameraman Ed Lachman said that "Werner once told me that if he said he'd be at a certain place on a certain street and on a certain day in 1990, he'd be there." Admiration also flows in the direction of Herzog for moving so effortlessly between fiction and non-fiction, and as the entrepreneurial film producer for having maintained financial control of almost the entirety of his body of work. Herzog the *kinosoldat* is unshakable, forceful but not strident, able to withstand it all, bowing only when he chooses to. While at work on this book, Werner explained he wanted something done a particular way. I suggested to him that "the publisher doesn't usually do that." He absorbed what I told him, paused, then said softly, "I'm not interested in how things are usually done. I want it done *this* way."

I thank Werner for his time on *A Guide for the Perplexed*, which inevitably means less to him than any one of his films. "As someone who has given literally thousands of interviews over the years, as well as filmed many conversations for my own films," he told me, "it has been forever clear to me that journalists who rely on tape recorders inevitably get the story wrong, but those who sit, listening carefully, writing down the odd word, taking in the bigger picture, have a better chance of getting the story right." I do have hours of recordings that document some of my time with Herzog, but he is nonetheless tolerant of this book, even if he feels – probably correctly – that its tone sometimes fails to capture his true self with enough precision. "Too verbose," was the frequent charge Werner laid on the book. He immediately knew what was important. The chat-show-like elements – the boring, flippant, vague bits – were removed, a blade taken to the overwritten passages, certain "overcooked" ideas, those where Werner "endlessly pontificated," scaled back.

Years ago, shortly before publication of the first edition, as Werner ploughed through a rough draft, he actually made it quite clear he had regretted ever agreeing to co-operate. This is, after all, someone who by his own admission lives with as little introspection as possible, who would rather embark on a thorough exploration of the world's jungles, deserts, fields, cities and mountains than look inside. ("Oceans have always eluded me, both in life and in my films, even if I can appreciate them and even if I feel I understand men of the sea.") Fortunately, Werner considered this second edition respectable enough to give considerable time to, including twelve intense days as we refined the manuscript together, working through it line by line, reaching for the thesaurus, chuckling at the possibilities, reading entire chapters out loud to each other. I particularly appreciated the moment when, before one of our final meetings, Werner opted out of pain relief during a trip to the dentist so he could be clear-headed during an afternoon session.

I am often asked how I met Werner, so please permit an aside, concerned with how I came to edit this book, which is itself a representation of the themes it expounds. If *A Guide for the Perplexed* is a roundabout treatise on how to spark dormant curiosities we never knew we had, immobilise evil forces forever raining down on the filmmaking process, neutralise the surrounding stupidity, clear the decks, wrench from the deepest recesses the requisite courage, flush away all obstacles (internal as well as physical), reclaim dignity (or, at least, adjust to there being none), accept the hardships, stomach the dejection and angst, counteract the self-doubt, brush yourself off after the kicks and slaps, and just get down to work, then it's the best example in my life. Time spent on work you believe in is never wasted.

I first became aware of Herzog at a screening of *The Great Ecstasy of Woodcarver Steiner* and *La Soufrière* at the Institute of Contemporary Arts in London. I was about sixteen years old and remember feeling that these were some of the most intriguing films I had yet encountered. My interest in Herzog was sealed when (sitting behind Susan Sontag and Wallace Shawn) I saw *Lessons of Darkness* at the Film Forum in downtown New York. Years later I found myself up against a wall, so wrote a hubris-packed letter to Walter Donohue – who still handles film books at Faber and Faber – explaining I had something to offer. At the time I was assisting Ray Carney with his *Cassavetes on Cassavetes*, doing research in European archives and offering French translations, so had minor credentials and a flimsy connection to Faber. Walter called me, explaining that his second-in-command was about to leave for the Cannes Film Festival, and suggesting I spend unpaid time at the Faber office and see the operation from the inside. Less than a week later I was in the office of the man who might give the go-ahead to the one book I knew I wanted to do and felt the world needed to read. (There was a gaping and – as far as I could determine – inexplicable gap on bookshop shelves between Howard Hawks and Alfred Hitchcock.) I turn to that other Herzog – Mr Bellow's – for as concise an explanation as possible of my reasoning behind what has turned into years of work: I was (and remain) "overcome by the need to explain, to have it out, to justify, to put in perspective, to clarify." And to put it all in one place.

After a week of answering phones amidst the stimulating, sedate atmosphere of Faber's Queen Square office, I asked Walter why *Herzog on Herzog* didn't exist. It seemed a natural fit in their inter-view-book series. Walter told me he had received various proposals over the years but hadn't liked the approaches they had taken, suggesting they had been too academically orientated. I asked if I could do the book. Walter told me to put my ideas down on paper and he would take them to the editorial board. Word soon came down: move ahead with the project. Now all I had to do was persuade Herzog. I went home, wrote a short letter and faxed it to his office in Munich. A week later a reply arrived: "I have never circled around my own work. I do not like to do self-scrutiny. I do look into the mirror in order to shave without cutting myself, but I do not know the color of my eyes. I do not want to assist in a book on me. There will be no *Herzog on Herzog*." I reached for my original letter, which turned out to be overly formal and uptight. My next one, considerably longer, laid out, in simple, emotive terms, who I was and why this was a worthy project, adding that I felt the final result would surely find an appreciative audience. A few days later a fax arrived. "Thank you very much for your good letter which puts you as a person in a new and different perspective," Werner wrote. "I will be in London in September. This seems to be the best opportunity to meet and talk things over."

I tell you all this, dear reader, because – at the risk of sounding like a cheap self-help guru – it's worth sticking to your guns, pursuing what you want, taking that leap of faith. I could easily have junked the entire project after receiving that first fax, but instead stuck with it. Werner is the first person I ever interviewed, but for some reason I felt I could make it work. The result is, I believe, the straight dope, a volume of uncluttered prose, not unlike Herzog's films. "My stories are never deeply complicated and intellectual," he explains. "Children everywhere can understand them."

Nothing is imprecise in Herzog's world. The characters in his films might occupy liminal positions, but Werner – an intensely instinctive filmmaker – never does. He does nothing by half. In the poetic *Conquest of the Useless*, we find this: "If I were to die, I would be doing nothing but dying." He frequently took me to task when it came to my working methods, insisting it was all becoming stale ("When will the book be ready? Do the five-day version. It needs life! Leave the gaps in it, leave it porous. Shake the structure out and write it. Let's get the motherfucker over and done with") and accusing me of being an "endless fiddler" (guilty as charged). The line from Preston Sturges's *Unfaithfully Yours* was written about him: "If you ever want anything done, always ask the busy man. The others never have time."

There is lucidity in this book, there is a wonderful stubbornness and iron determination, there is conviction, compulsion and some obstinacy, there is a crystal-clear understanding of priorities, there is perhaps hyperbole. It is all apodictically (one of Werner's favourite words) not stale. Even if it probably contains a few benign contradictions, I have great confidence in this book, which is the result of someone exercising his daunting powers of storytelling. *A Guide for the Perplexed* is, as Herb Golder once told me, "Werner on everything, from outer space to our inner lives." A friend of mine describes it as "a truly passionate encounter, like an absorbing conversation that you stumble across in the back room of a party, where real ideas and personalities are being laid bare, away from all the noise and pretentious prattle in the kitchen." While sleepless nights and being mired in duplicity (Going Rogue) became the norm over the years, a creeping and burdensome sense of responsibility caught up with me. The decade-long chase – which invited persuasive trips to Sachrang, Neuschwanstein and Skellig – provided a hearty, rewarding challenge. Fortunately it's been that long, as things are only now starting to make sense. The immersion has confirmed two things: first, exploring Herzog's body of work has served as an object lesson in how lifeless and superficial the interpretive/theoretical approach too often is, how so many resort to the pointless rehash. Second, it's downhill from here for me. As someone who on occasion interviews people of cinema, Werner is the top of the pile. The raw material doesn't get any better.

Since the first version of this book appeared, a desire emerged to make it a thing in itself, not just commentary. As such, its contents have been rewritten/augmented with – wrote Moses Maimonides of his similarly titled tome – "great exactness and exceeding precision, and with care to avoid failing to explain any obscure point." The interview here has been consciously inflected in certain ways, carefully pushed in various directions, coloured with specific ideas. Everything in its proper place. Structure, rhythm and tempo were painstakingly imposed upon the Herzog in these pages, after the fact, with Werner's words edited into single, often lengthy responses to prompts and questions that were, for the most part, written afterwards. ("You should let the readers know this. I

sound so talkative in the book, but I'm really not that garrulous.")
Take this portrait of an individual, this carefully calibrated provocation, with the caution it deserves. This official version is no less
of a construct than any of the multitude of Herzogs that populate
cyberspace and elsewhere, those complementing and competing
"doppelgängers," as Werner calls them. There was no other way of
presenting this much material so efficiently.

The notion of "perplexity" has been vaguely appropriated
from Maimonides – Jewish philosopher, physician, mathematician, astronomer and mystic. Writing in the twelfth century,
Maimonides addressed his tome to those respectful of science but
struggling to balance that knowledge with a devotion to divine law,
metaphysical beliefs and "profound mysteries." Within his book,
wrote Maimonides, are solutions to the big issue of his age: the
problem of religion, which is "a source of anxiety to all intelligent
men." Werner's attempts to address more contemporary concerns
and answer the sharp questions that today hang in the air are documented below. How, for example, to put food on the table when a
desire for self-expression is so overwhelming? Is individuality possible in such a homogenised world? Can the requisite tenacity and
steadfastness be mustered when confrontations with unfavourable
odds inevitably occur? How exactly do you hypnotise a chicken?
By chronicling so clearly his own liberation from the impediments
and strictures of our culture; by showing how to transcend the
bankrupt world into which we are sinking, one choked with anti-
intellectualism, cynicism, consumerism, fear, cowardice, vulgarity,
extremism, laziness and narcissism; by articulating an untram-
melled and distilled commentary on life and cinema, Herzog – our
persistent, knowing and sceptical guide, his anarchic streak glowing – offers tough-love wisdom to bewildered doubters everywhere,
those intimidated by the uncontrollable waves of information
washing over humanity, caught in the violent seas of indifference
that this godless, technology-ridden, semi-literate age has wrought.

Werner's thoughts in his *Guide for the Perplexed* are part of a
decades-long outpouring, a response to the clarion call, to the fervent requests for guidance. He presents us with his personal ethos,
talks of himself and his work, and by so doing – by laying bare his
pragmatism and righteousness – offers support and reinforcement,
assisting each of us in the construction of our own personalised

bastion. Herzog the wayfarer is a dynamic and open-minded chaperone on the path, accessible to all. He is the honest showman providing us with something like an instruction manual, with tools for living, a much-needed shot in the arm, a map to the resting point. To paraphrase Maimonides: those readers who have not studied cinema will still derive profit from many a chapter, but those who attempt creative and imaginative endeavours of any kind will surely derive benefit from every chapter. How greatly will he rejoice! How agreeably will these words strike his ears! Let the truth and right by which you are apparently the loser be preferable to you to the falsehood and wrong by which you are apparently the gainer.

The conversations in *A Guide to the Perplexed* take a chronological approach, with each film – from *A Lost Western* (1957) to *From One Second to the Next* (2013) – discussed in turn. Interjections have been kept to a minimum (there was never any "systematic questionnaire" or "long list of intricate questions" brought to bear, to quote Truffaut on his work with Hitchcock), and are presented as stepping stones more than anything else. (Wanting to listen to your own voice can be a deadly trait in an interviewer.) Conscious of the fact that there are few people who have seen every Herzog film, the interview is presented in such a way that even when the reader hasn't seen the work under discussion, there will still hopefully be something immediate and tangible to appreciate.

Towards the end of this volume, readers will find a selection (made, initially, by me) of images drawn primarily from Herzog's archive at the Deutsche Kinemathek in Berlin, new translations of his poetry (originally published in 1978), a journal written in 1982 during his walk around Germany, the legendary "The Minnesota Declaration" from 1999, and Herb Golder's "Shooting on the Lam" (extracted and edited from an unpublished book-length manuscript), from which we learn that filmmakers with an intellect are able to fortify, educate and invigorate in ways that institutionalised theorists and academics, in thrall to obfuscating sensibilities, can only dream about. This essay – which says more in a few pages than most pieces about Herzog's films fail to say in a hundred – serves as a bulwark against theoretical utterances about the films.

Take it with a pinch of salt and don't be one of those who ignore the self-mockery and humour Werner's films and interviews are full of (one reason to search out some of the many readily available recordings of him). How best to transcribe the following with the playfully sardonic tone with which it was told? "I once had a public discussion with the diminutive Agnès Varda, who seemed to take offence at my postulation that a filmmaker, rather than having this or that quality, should be able to clear his or her own height. She didn't like that very much." Herb Golder recalls the production of *Wings of Hope* and *My Best Fiend*: "I remember a particularly gruesome species of tree we often encountered in the Amazon whose entire trunk was covered in thorns the size of small spikes." Remarked Werner: "Let the tree-huggers try this one."

This book is dedicated to the memory of a true *mensch*, Werner's friend ("The Last Lion") and mine too, a man who lived for great purpose, restless and always on guard, able to perceive the enemy and explain it to us, forever in search of fresh forms of visual expression, who urged us to keep our eyes on and minds alert to the complexities and banalities exploding around us, eternally willing to offer support to anyone seeking to heighten awareness and extend the borders of the possible, who inspired and galvanised generations of filmmakers and cineastes, who never made inferences from insufficient data, who – with creativity and rectitude – sought unfailingly to mould public taste and facilitate a shift in consciousness, who favoured knowledge over information: Amos Vogel, "one of the most profound connoisseurs of the cinema, endowed with an unerring instinct for new talents," as Werner once wrote of his mentor. I miss his resilience, being able to peruse his bounteous library, hearing the clicks of those five-drawer filing cabinets and exploring the wonders within, and the strolls through Washington Square Park with my surrogate grandfather. Long may his ideas burn through society, dissolving what needs to be eradicated, devoured by those agitated rogues in search of adequate imagery who refuse to avert their eyes.

Now be a man and quit that moody brooding.

Paul Cronin
New York
February 2014

Facing the stark alternative to see a book on me compiled from dusty interviews with all the wild distortions and lies, or collaborating – I choose the much worse option: to collaborate.

Werner Herzog
Los Angeles
February 2002

1

The Shower Curtain

Before we start, can you offer any general insights for your readers so they might sleep easier at night?

Let me say this, something for human beings everywhere, whether they be filmmakers or otherwise. I can answer your question only by quoting hotel mogul Conrad Hilton, who was once asked what he would like to pass on to posterity. "Whenever you take a shower," he said, "always make sure the curtain is inside the tub." I sit here and recommend the same. Never forget the shower curtain.

When did you realise that filmmaking was something you were going to spend your life doing?

From the moment I could think independently. Unlike most people, I didn't have the privilege to choose my profession. I didn't even ask myself whether I could do it, I just pushed on with things. This became clear to me within a few dramatic months at the age of fourteen, when I began to travel on foot and converted to the Catholic faith. It was my first real escape from home life. My father – a militant atheist – was furious, though my mother seemed to think I did it only because the local priest played football. I was fascinated by the historical tradition of Catholicism and its attention to ritual, and intrigued about how so much Bavarian folklore was rooted in religion. The Calvinistic rigour and austerity of Christianity never attracted me; I was always drawn to its more exuberant and baroque elements. If I had grown up in the north of Germany, where almost everyone was Protestant, perhaps I would have been more interested in that denomination instead.

I

I wanted to go to Albania, which at the time was a mysterious country closed off to the rest of the world and controlled with an iron fist by hardcore Maoists who wouldn't allow anyone in. I went instead, by foot, as far as the Adriatic, keeping close to the Albanian/Yugoslavian frontier, maybe a couple of hundred feet at most; I never dared try and enter Albania. On several occasions I travelled by foot to northern Germany and a couple of times got caught out, in the freezing cold, several miles from the nearest town. I was always able to open up one of the nearby holiday chalets using the few lock-picking tools I had with me, and eventually became quite adept at getting into these places without leaving a trace. They were often full of excellent wines, and I would sometimes finish a crossword puzzle. Before leaving I would make the bed and clean up like a good Boy Scout, even leaving a thank-you note. One time I was asleep when suddenly the house was full of light and I heard voices downstairs. I climbed out of the window and leapt onto the garage roof, where a family was unloading their car. Everything in the garage stopped when I thumped down, and I heard a woman's voice say, "That must be the cat." In such weather conditions, taking shelter in these homes was a natural right, and if the police had discovered me I'm sure all they would have done was give me a mug of hot tea. I would never pay for the wine, though, and from there it was a small step into filmmaking, which to this day I have problems seeing as a real profession.

What do you mean, "a real profession"?

I don't take myself too seriously, and at my age should probably find more dignified work than filmmaking. At the same time, cinema has made a stronger impression upon us than any other form of imagery ever invented. Films contain the most intensive chronicle of the human condition, just as painting used to have such high standing. Most people wouldn't be able to name the most important Dutch writers of the seventeenth century, but they know several Dutch artists of that period. Just as during the high Middle Ages architecture had some kind of privileged status, in years to come we will look to cinema as the most coherent representation of society, of our achievements and failures, in the twentieth century.

Talk more about this period of organised religion.

Many adolescents of that age have instances of momentous decision-making, when something explodes with energy inside of them, though perhaps not with the intensity I experienced. There was a dramatic condensation of everything in my life at the time and a need to connect to something sublime, but my interest in religion dissipated and dwindled away fairly quickly. I left it behind without even noticing, after which came a period of radical disinterest in God – a feeling that might still be with me. I remember feeling furious at the nonsensical nature of the universe and its flaws that seem to have been built into the fabric of things from the very start, at the fact that every one of the creatures who live in the jungles and oceans and mountains of the world don't care about us one bit. Religion is clearly an important part of our inner being. It offers consolation to many people and has a certain value to the human race, so I would never dismiss it out of hand, and having been baptised – which according to the dogma of the Catholic Church is an indelible mark on my soul – I will always be a Catholic. But ever since my close encounter with organised religion I have known it isn't for me, though to this day there is something of a religious echo in my work. The scientific basis of reality will always be more important. There should never be an ideology standing between us and our understanding of the planet. The facts are facts.

I should note here my admiration for the early Christian Stylites, who would perch atop a pillar, stubbornly refusing to come down for years. It's the ultimate form of exile and solitude. There were cases of two of them screaming from pillar to pillar, each accusing the other of being a heretic. Sometimes I envy people able to find consolation in religion.

What do you mean by "sublime"?

Start with its Latin origin: *sublimus*, meaning uplifted, lofty or elevated. A door has a threshold down below and a raised lintel, the horizontal support overhead. It is elevated above us as we walk through the door. It is beyond us and outside us and larger than us, yet not wholly abstract or foreign.

Do you believe in God?

"I cannot imagine that God created everything out of nothing," says Kaspar Hauser. If he does exist, I'm content to think of God as being as foolish, confused, contradictory and disorientated as man. As for the Devil, I believe in stupidity, which is as bad as it gets.

You travel constantly.

It isn't easy to explain why I shoot films so far from home, but I do know that a healthy imagination needs space; the great works of cinema weren't made while standing at the kitchen sink. For me, every film is a ticket into the world and the business of living. What I'm looking for is an unspoilt, humane spot for man to exist, an area worthy of human beings where a dignified life can be led, something alluded to in my films. In *Fitzcarraldo*, Huerequeque recounts that the forest natives have been wandering for three hundred years, one generation after another, in search of a place where there is neither sorrow nor pain. For Ingmar Bergman, the starting point of a film seems to be the human face, usually that of a woman. For me, it's a physical landscape, whether a real or imaginary or hallucinatory one. I know that by staying in one place I'll never find what I'm looking for. The search is unremitting. In *Incident at Loch Ness* you see my wife – who is from Siberia – and me sitting quietly. It's a Russian custom. Before you go on a trip, after all the running around and packing, stop for a moment so you leave from a point of complete stillness. It makes for a safe and pleasant journey.

Even before officially leaving school in Germany, I spent a few months in Manchester because my first real girlfriend had moved to the city, where she was studying English. I followed a few weeks later with a little money, and bought a run-down house in the slums of the city together with a handful of people from Bengal and Nigeria. I paid my share and had a room, where I lived with my girlfriend. It was one of those nineteenth-century terrace houses; the backyard was strewn with debris and garbage, and the house was full of mice. Manchester is where I picked up a lot of English, on the streets talking to the locals. I didn't have a job, and one time, out of curiosity, joined my girlfriend in class. The chubby teacher made every student repeat – in unison, ten times – a single

4

sentence, which to this day is engraved on my mind: "He mumbled and grumbled because he was troubled." At that point I fled.

In 1961, at the age of nineteen, after my final school exams, I met some people transporting used trucks from Munich down to Athens and the island of Crete. I invested what little money I had in a share of one of these vehicles, and made some cash by joining a small convoy. From Crete I took a boat to Alexandria in Egypt, with the intention of travelling to the former Belgian Congo. I never made it, which I'm eternally glad about. I later learnt that of those who had reached the eastern Congolese provinces at the time, almost all perished. Congo had just won its independence, and the deepest anarchy and darkest violence immediately set in. Every trace of civilisation disappeared, every form of organisation and security was gone, and there was a return to tribalism and cannibalism. I'm fascinated by the notion of civilisation as a thin layer of ice resting upon a deep ocean of darkness and chaos, and by observing Africa hoped to better understand the origins of Nazism in Germany, how it could have happened that the country lost every trace of civilisation in the course of only a few years. To all appearances Germany was a civilised, stable nation, with a great tradition in many fields – philosophy, mathematics, literature and music – when suddenly, during the era of the Third Reich, everything overwhelmingly dangerous in the country was brought out into the open. Strange that at the centre of Europe is a nation that, deep in its heart, is still barbarian.

Where did you go after Alexandria?

Along the Nile to Sudan, but on the way to Juba, not far from eastern Congo, I became very sick. I knew to survive I had to get back home as quickly as possible, and luckily made it up to Aswan, where the dam was still under construction. The Russians had built the concrete foundations, and there were German engineers working on the electrical intestines. I don't know how long it was after I took refuge in a tool shed that I was discovered. I had a serious fever and have only blurred recollections, though I do recall endlessly sorting out my small number of possessions and placing them carefully into my duffel bag, as if I were putting my affairs in order. I was hallucinating about being eaten by a shark, and when I awoke discovered that rats had bitten me on my elbow and armpit. Apparently they wanted to use the wool from my sweater for a nest, because when I stretched out I discovered a huge hole. One rat bit me on the cheek before scurrying away into a corner. The wound didn't heal for many weeks. I still have the scar.

Eventually I made it back to Germany, where I made my first couple of films. Once in a while I showed up at Munich University, where I was supposed to be studying history and literature, but I can't claim to have been very serious about it all; I maintained my student status mainly because it enabled me to buy inexpensive train tickets. I did, however, very much appreciate listening to one professor, Ingrid Strohschneider-Kohrs, who taught German literature and had an extraordinarily lively intelligence. I was immediately aware of the precision with which she applied certain ideas to these texts. Her classes – where she spoke about writers like Georg Büchner – were so demanding that I was rarely able to follow them for very long. She told me about the time she travelled to the Black Forest and met with Heidegger, to whom she wanted to pose a series of detailed and intricate philosophical questions, but all Heidegger wanted to do was walk with her through the forest and discuss mushrooms. Although I was only in my first year as an undergraduate, Professor Strohschneider-Kohrs invited me into a postgraduate seminar, and suggested I do a doctorate under her supervision, but she moved to Bochum University and I would have had to follow her there. The truth is, I hadn't the faintest idea what I would have done with a doctorate. Anyway, I've always been more interested in teaching myself. If I want to explore something, I never think about attending a class; I do the reading on my own or seek out experts for conversations. Everything we're forced to learn at school we quickly forget, but the things we set out to learn ourselves – to quench a thirst – are never forgotten, and inevitably become an important part of our existence.

How did your parents react to your plans to become a filmmaker?

We should speak primarily of my mother because my father was rarely around. I never knew him very well, and he played only a small role in my childhood.

My mother, Elizabeth, was a biologist with a doctorate who had studied with Karl von Frisch. She and my father met when they were both students at university in Vienna. My paternal grandfather's house was full of books, but we weren't there very often; I never really explored his library and didn't grow up in a particularly intellectual household. Raising three boys on her own in West Germany and having been somewhat left behind by the *Wirtschaftswunder* ["economic miracle"] because her Austrian qualifications weren't recognised, my mother was obliged to become a very down-to-earth and practical woman. For a time she worked as a cleaning lady, and to this day, at any moment if needed, I would have no problem sweeping streets to earn a crust. My mother – who divorced my father in 1948 – remains the most courageous and adventurous person I have ever met. At the age of seventy she started to learn Turkish because she had friends in Munich who spoke very little German, and even took trips to eastern Anatolia.

When it came to filmmaking, she took a sensible approach, trying to give me a realistic idea of what I was getting myself into and what might be a wise move. She explained what was going on economically in West Germany, and in her letters asked me to think carefully about my future. "It's too bad we never talked about it in detail," she wrote. But my mother was always supportive and never tried to guide or coach me into a career or profession. She wouldn't know where I was when I ran away and disappeared for weeks at a time, but sensing I would be gone for a while, realising I was one of those who shouldn't be kept in school indefinitely, she would immediately write a letter to my school saying I had pneumonia. I always felt a stranger there because, compared to my classmates, I had other goals and interests. I distrusted the textbooks given to us, and when it came to mathematics questioned the solutions offered to basic formulae. Wasn't it possible that someone would eventually come up with a different way of doing things? Though teaching is undoubtedly a noble profession, I never felt comfortable in school and have never trusted teachers. In fact, I hated school with such intensity that I hatched a plan to burn the place to the ground one night, though never followed through with it. When I think back, perhaps the one important thing I got from school was during history class, when we often read primary sources, not textbooks. To this day I wouldn't trust a book on a particular subject written long after the events in question. I still have on a bookshelf my childhood copy of *The Odyssey*, in ancient Greek, full of scribbled pencil annotations.

In August 1961, my mother sent me two letters – on consecutive days – that I received when I was on Crete. In them she wrote that my father was anxious to dissuade me from becoming a film director. Before leaving Munich I apparently made some pronouncements that upon my return I was going to do just that. At the age of about fourteen I started writing screenplays and submitting proposals to producers and television stations. In her letters, my mother tried to convince me to return to Germany from Crete so I could start an apprenticeship in a photographer's lab, which she thought would be a good prospect for me. For her, the rush was on; I had to get back by September so as not to miss another year. She had spoken to an employment expert who told her filmmaking was a difficult profession to break into and that because I had only high-school exams I should start in a lab; he said this would be the basis of becoming an assistant director in a film company. I clearly had something else in mind and couldn't be persuaded. A few years later my mother set about assembling every article, review and interview about my films she could find, and pasted everything into a series of huge scrapbooks that for years sat on a bottom shelf, collecting dust, in my Munich office. It was partly because she was proud, but also because she could see I was never going to collect such things myself. She told me I might need them one day.

German women of my mother's generation were grandiose. In 1945, at the end of the war, they rolled up their sleeves, cleared away the rubble and began rebuilding. My mother was no exception; she always guided us children by setting a good example. One day my brother and I bought a motorcycle, and after a series of minor accidents – at least one a week – she casually stubbed out her cigarette and said, "I think you should get rid of your motorcycle because I just got rid of my last cigarette." The following week we sold it, and though she had smoked for many years, my mother never smoked again. For a short time in the early days she thought the Nazis were a force for good in Germany, perhaps because she had grown up in Vienna, born into a military family of nationalists from Croatia – a country with a strong tradition of fighting for its identity – and in her youth had been political herself. Two of her relatives were apparently involved in the assassination of

8

King Alexander I of Yugoslavia in Marseilles in 1934, and she was briefly in prison herself before the war. In 1933, the year Hitler assumed power, many people were deeply connected to their sense of national identity, probably more than they are today, and this impetus for independence occasionally morphed into support for fascism. My paternal grandmother was different. Although I never discussed politics with her, it was obvious she didn't care for Hitler at all. She thought he was a buffoon, that there was something not quite right about him.

Dietrich, my father, was of French Huguenot descent, also with a PhD in biology. He had fought in the war, though I don't think he ever saw combat, and was held captive in France for nearly two years. He was a walking encyclopaedia and could speak several languages, including Japanese and some Arabic, but was forever trying to dodge his responsibilities. He refused ever to involve himself in even the slightest productive work and would often talk about a vast, universal scientific theory he was working on. He maintained that one day it would be finished, though we all knew he hadn't written a thing. His insistence that it had to be completed conveniently meant he could avoid getting a real job to earn a living and support his family, so it was forever up to my mother to take charge and look after everyone. One time, while he was ranting about this mammoth text, I touched his shoulder and said, "But you haven't written anything." He looked at me and somehow acknowledged I was right, but five minutes later was raving about his non-existent book again. It took years for my father to be convinced of the catastrophic impact the Nazi regime had on Germany, though I think for him it was partly a question of cultural supremacy. Lots of English words entered the language after the war thanks to the American Forces Network radio. American culture became a major part of German life, but my father looked back to seemingly better times. Over the years I have learnt from his deficiencies, about how not to be a father. Even at the time I knew it was a blessing he wasn't around when I was growing up.

You came of age during the reconstruction of post-war Germany.

A couple of days after I was born, in September 1942, the house next door to us in Munich was destroyed by a bomb and our place was damaged. We were lucky to get out alive. Apparently my mother found me in my cradle, covered with debris and glass shards, but unhurt. She moved my older brother and me out of the city to Sachrang, a small, remote mountain village less than a mile from the German–Austrian border, about an hour's drive from Munich and surrounded by forests, like something out of a fairy tale. We stayed there for the next eleven years before moving back to Munich. The Kaisergebirge in the Austrian Tyrol and around Sachrang were one of the last pockets of resistance in Germany at the end of the war. At that time the Werewolves – the fanatical SS troops of the Third Reich who led the last-gasp resistance against the Allies – were on the run and passed through the village, hiding their weapons and uniforms under the farmers' hay before grabbing civilians' clothes and taking refuge in the mountains. One night a man sat in front of a raging fire at the creek behind our house, his eyes and face reflecting the flames. I was aware of the dividing line between Germany and Austria because my mother would often take my brother and me across to Wildbichl in Austria; she used the two of us to help smuggle back home various things not so easily found on our side of the border. She would use sand to clean the pans and dishes, so one time for her birthday my brother and I filled a large sack with sand from a nearby riverbed and gave it to her as a gift. It took us nearly a day to carry it back to the house because it was so heavy. I don't remember ever seeing her so happy.

Parsifal is a character I understand because as a child I had no knowledge of the outside world; we were totally disconnected. On our way to school in the village we had to cross a forest that I was convinced was haunted by witches. Even today, when I pass this spot, I still get the feeling there is something eerie about it. Sachrang was such an isolated place at the time that I didn't know what a banana was until I was twelve, and I didn't make my first telephone call until the age of seventeen. A car was an absolute sensation; we would all sprint after it just to look at the thing, and there is still something exciting to me about watching hundreds of vehicles swishing around on a system of interconnected freeways. I have always felt most comfortable in remote mountains, and part of me has never really adjusted to modern technology; I jump whenever the telephone rings. Our house had no running water or proper mattresses, so my mother would stuff dried ferns into a linen bag for us to lie on; she sewed all our clothes from the thickest material she could find. During the winter months I would awaken to find a layer of ice on my blanket. The outside toilet was frequently covered in snowdrifts, and there was so much snow blocking the front door we had to climb out of the window. Sometimes we went to school on skis. During the summer we children went without shoes for months, wearing nothing but lederhosen.

We were always full of imagination, constantly inventing our own toys. I remember the feeling of flying through the air on the swing attached to the huge tree behind our house. The guns and arms caches we found – remnants of the SS soldiers – became things to play with, and one time we blew up a small sewage pipe with some explosives. I was part of the local gang of about a dozen children, including one girl who we all respected because she was so tough. Together as a group we invented a kind of flat arrow made from beech wood. I didn't know anything about aeronautics but somehow figured out how to make it fly some distance; I would throw this thing with a whip-like action, which made it sail through the air more than 400 feet. After lunch my mother would send my brother and me outside no matter how cold it was – summer or winter – and wouldn't let us back in for several hours. She thought it was good for our constitution. I spent a lot of time alone when I was young, and developed a strong sense of self-reliance.

Everyone thinks growing up in the ruins of the destroyed German cities must have been a terrible experience, and no doubt for parents who lost everything it was, but for us children it was glorious, the most marvellous of times. Munich wasn't as badly destroyed as some other cities in Germany, though there were huge gaps where once had been buildings. Truckloads of debris, headed to the outskirts of the city, where vast mountains of rubble piled up, would pass by our apartment window. We children took over whole bombed-out blocks and discovered the most amazing things in cellars strewn with rubble. The remnants of buildings and factories were our playgrounds where great adventures were acted out. It was a surreal environment, and everyone I know who spent their early years in the ruins of post-war Germany raves about that time. With no fathers to listen to and no rules to follow, it was anarchy in the best sense of the word. We invented everything from scratch.

Some years ago I saw a film comprised entirely of footage shot in Leningrad before, during and after its siege during the Second World War.* Everything appears so peaceful, with no sign of imminent drama. People stroll through the streets, they chat in sidewalk cafes, and children play in parks. Nothing in their faces points to a looming disaster. Then the bombardment starts, followed by mass starvation. Death stalks those very same streets, cafes and parks with unspeakable horror. When I look back on my childhood, it's clear that Europe is currently going through a period of tranquillity rarely seen in human history.

What are your earliest memories?

One night my mother wrenched my brother and me out of bed and carried us – one in each arm, wrapped in blankets – up the slope behind our house. In the distance we saw an entire sky pulsating orange and red; it's one of those indelible, unforgettable images of childhood. "I took you out of bed because you must see this," she said to us. "Rosenheim is burning." Rosenheim, which for us was the big city at the end of the world, was being bombed. Sachrang sits in a valley, eight miles from Aschau, where there was a hospital and train station. Beyond that lies Rosenheim, which as a young child was somehow the limit of my universe.† I also have a memory of seeing Our Lord himself, when I was about three years old. It was on *Nikolaustag*, when the holy St Nicholas appears with a book listing all your misdeeds of the year, accompanied by Krampus, a demon-like figure. I was absolutely terrified, fled under the couch and peed my pants. As if coming to my rescue, the door opened and a man stood there. He was wearing brown overalls and no socks, and his hands were covered with oil. I was sure it was the Lord himself, there to save me from Krampus, but it turned out to be someone from the electricity company who happened to be passing.

When I was five or six I fell quite ill. There was no point in

* *Blockade* (2005), directed by Sergei Loznitsa.
† Rosenheim (birthplace of Hermann Göring) burnt on the night of 18 April 1945, less than two weeks before Hitler killed himself in Berlin. Herzog was about two and a half years old. That evening, in an attempt to destroy enemy transport systems, 148 American B-17s dropped more than 400 tonnes of bombs on the town's marshalling yards.

calling an ambulance because we were too deeply snowed in, so my mother wrapped me in blankets, tied me on a sleigh and dragged me through the night to Aschau, where I was admitted to hospital. She visited eight days later, coming on foot through deep snow, and was amazed that I was without complaint. I had pulled a single piece of thread from the blanket on the bed and played with it for all that time. I wasn't bored. This strand was full of stories and fantasies for me.

Do you ever get bored?

The word is not in my vocabulary. I astonish my wife by being capable of standing and staring through the window for days at a time. I may look catatonic, but not so inside. Wittgenstein talked about looking through a closed window of a house and seeing a man flailing about strangely. You can't see or hear the violent storms raging outside and don't realise it's taking great effort for this man even to stand on his own two feet. There are hidden storms within us all.

American soldiers occupied Sachrang at the end of the war.

We lived in one of the last places the occupying American soldiers moved into. The GIs arrived in jeeps with one leg dangling and chewing gum non-stop; I thought it was all the Americans in the whole world. For the first time I saw a black man, and I was completely mesmerised because I had only heard about black people from fairy tales. I ran to my mother and said, "I just saw a pitch-black Moor!" He was a big, wonderful man with a tremendous voice, which I can still hear today. My mother asked how I communicated with him. "We talk in American," I said. He gave me a piece of gum which I kept for a whole year, until my older brother found where I hid it every night and stole it. Another early flash of memory is of the white flags hanging from the windows of the houses in Sachrang. On the day the Americans rolled into town, every house had a white flag or bed sheet on view. This was a sign it was friendly, not resistant to the American occupation and not harbouring Werewolves or Nazis. I remember playing on the balcony of our house and letting this sheet fall to the ground. The scolding we got was particularly intense, like nothing I have ever experienced, which was understandable because our games meant the house could have come under immediate gunfire.

For a time my father worked as a supply officer in the army and sent food packages home whenever he could, but we were constantly hungry and looking for things to eat, forever hanging on our mother's skirt, crying. "Children," she once told us, "if I could cut a piece of flesh from my own ribs, I would." She was constantly searching for food and would sometimes skim the cream from the top of the milk churns when the farmers weren't looking. Anything that helped fill our stomachs. Once the farmers had harvested their nearby fields we would go in and collect the small potatoes they left behind. On the way to school we tried to catch trout in the creek with our bare hands. If we got one, we would put it in a tiny pond near by and pick it up after school. To this day I know the value of food and have always had great respect for whatever is on my plate. One time I stumbled across some workers who had shot a crow and were cooking it in a pot on the side of the road. For the first time in my life I saw fat floating on the surface of a soup; it was a sensation for me. Later I tried to shoot a crow, using one of the sub-machine guns we found in the forest, but I was thrown to the ground by the recoil. I was surprised that my mother wasn't angry. She took me into the forest and shot a single round into a thick beech log, causing splinters to fly out the other side. "This is what you should expect from a gun," she said to me. "You must never point even a toy gun at anybody." I was so stunned by this violence that I was immediately cured of my preoccupation with such things. She showed me how to secure and unload the weapon, telling me I could keep it so long as I learnt how to carry it safely.

What were you like as a child?

I was a taciturn and hot-tempered loner, usually withdrawn and known to brood for days on end, after which I would erupt in violent fits of rage. It took me a long time to get my behaviour under control, notably after an unspeakable disaster when I attacked my older brother with a knife. When I was eleven we moved back to Munich, where I learnt to concentrate because the whole family lived together in a single room. There were four of us in this tiny place, everyone doing their own thing. I would lie on my back on the floor reading for hours, no matter how much talking and activity was going on around me. Often I would read all day, incredibly focused, concentrating on my book, and eventually look up to discover everyone else had left hours ago. One of the first books I owned was a copy of *Winnie the Pooh*, which arrived in an American care package. It's still one of my favourites, and along with cornflour was an excellent way to pull Germany back into the civilised world. Many considered cornflour chicken feed, but my mother was able to fool us by saying it had lots of egg yolk in it, and all of a sudden we found it delicious. Long live the Marshall Plan. All these years later I remain full of gratitude and have held America in high esteem ever since. Later, during my adolescence, the American influence in West Germany was strong, but not for me. I never wore jeans and was never that interested in Elvis, though I did go to see the first of his films released in Munich. In the middle of the screening everyone got up and calmly shook the rows of seats until they came loose from the floor. Eventually the police were called to restore order.

It was my brother Tilbert – who is a little more than a year older than me – who took charge once we moved to Munich. He was very smart, always the leader of the gang and epicentre of mischief. He was thrown out of school after a couple of years and immediately started in business, rising like a comet. At the age of fourteen he became an apprentice at a firm that imported tropical wood, and by sixteen was the primary breadwinner in the family. It was because of him I was able to continue in school, though I would work myself whenever I could. I owe a great deal to Tilbert; even today he remains the boss of the family. My younger brother Lucki is someone with whom I have worked closely over the years. We have different fathers but for me he is a full brother. He had great musical talent as a youngster but quickly realised he wasn't good enough to compete with all the other pianists out there, so he also went into business, also rising quickly through the ranks. I think that shook him up because he quickly took off for Asia, visiting India, Burma, Nepal and Indonesia. I wrote him a letter asking for help making *Aguirre*, and he crossed the Pacific, making it to Peru to give us much-needed assistance. Eventually Lucki started working with me full time, and for several decades has run my production company. He was always better than me when it comes to the financial aspects of filmmaking.

Is Herzog your real name?

It's my father's name. My parents divorced when I was five or six, at which point my legal name became Stipetić, which was my mother's maiden name. I always felt much closer to my mother but chose to work under the name Herzog in part because it means "duke" in German. I thought there should be someone like Count Basie or Duke Ellington making films. It's hostile and murderous out there in the universe; what looks friendly to us is actually two hundred thousand atomic explosions every second. The sun is a tiny grain of sand and there are many even nastier suns out there. Down here, we humans are living proof that things have gone warped. Perhaps changing my name has somehow protected me from the overwhelming evil of the universe.

What were the first films you saw?

I didn't know cinema existed until I was eleven years old and a travelling projectionist for remote provincial schools showed up with a selection of 16mm films. Although I was stunned such a thing was possible, I wasn't particularly taken with the first film I saw, about Eskimos constructing an igloo. It had a ponderous commentary and was extremely boring. Having had to deal with a lot of snow as a child, I could tell the Eskimos weren't doing a very good job; they were probably just actors, and bad ones at that. There and then I learnt that the worst sin a filmmaker can commit is to bore his audience and fail to captivate from the very first moment. The second film, about pygmies building a liana bridge across a jungle river in Cameroon, was better. The pygmies worked well together, and I was impressed with their ability to construct such a well-functioning suspension bridge without any real tools. One pygmy swung across the river on a liana like Tarzan and hung from the bridge like a spider. It was a sensational experience for me.

Later I watched Zorro, Tarzan and American B-movies. A Fu Manchu film I saw was a revelation for me. A man was shot and fell sixty feet from a rock, did a somersault in mid-air, then a little

kick with his leg. Ten minutes later, because of this little kick I recognised the same shot when it appeared in another gun battle; they
had recycled it and thought they could get away with it. I spoke
to friends about this and asked how it was possible the same shot
had been used twice, but none of them had even noticed. Before
this I thought it was some kind of reality I had been watching, that
the film was something like a documentary. All of a sudden I saw
how it had been narrated and edited, how tension and suspense
were established, how a logical sequence of scenes had been pieced
together to create a story. At that moment I became fascinated by
cinema. In Munich I would steal empty milk bottles from school-
yards and use the deposits to see as many films as possible.

When I was about twenty-one, a young American named
P. Adams Sitney came to Germany and brought with him a selection of experimental films, things like Stan Brakhage and Kenneth
Anger.* That there was a group of young filmmakers using this
vocabulary and grammar of cinema was exciting to me. I respected
these fascinating films, so different from what I was already used
to, even though I knew they weren't the kinds of images I wanted
to work with myself. Just seeing there were people out there doing
such bold and unexpected things, making films that ran counter to
the standard textbook accounts of cinema history, intrigued me so
much that I wrote about them and asked a film magazine to publish
the article.† What particularly excited me was that the range and

* From December 1963 to August 1964, P. Adams Sitney was curator
of the International Exposition of American Independent Film, which
travelled to several cities including Munich (January 1964), Amsterdam,
Stockholm, Paris, London and Vienna. The trip was organised by
Lithuanian-American filmmaker and curator Jonas Mekas, who later
established Anthology Film Archives, one of America's leading venues for
non-mainstream cinema.
† "Rebellen in Amerika," *Filmstudio*, May 1964. In this essay, Herzog
describes a screening in Munich of films by Robert Breer, Dick Higgins,
Jonas Mekas, Stan Brakhage, Ken Jacob, Ed Emshwiller and Kenneth
Anger. "Tellingly," he writes, "German film reviewers – alarmed by the
implications of such an event or, conversely, so fossilized as to be incapable
of any sort of arousal – have until now virtually ignored the intensive
efforts, evolving over the past decade, of the American avant garde, those
filmmakers who have continued rigorously where Surrealist experiments
left off."

depth of their work came not necessarily from an understanding of film and art, but from a lifetime of reading. The first time I met Stan Brakhage, years later at the Telluride Film Festival, he had a copy of Spenser's *The Faerie Queene* in the original archaic English. He explained how important a text it was for him and asked if I wanted to hear some lines from it. "Of course," I said, at which point he closed the book and recited five minutes of beautiful poetry from memory.

Have you written poetry yourself?

As a youngster I entered a competition in Munich for young authors where there were ten awards available for the ten best poems. I submitted five under five different names, all posing as poets who lived together in a commune, and four of them won. What caused a stink was me outing myself by showing up and reading all four winning entries. I remember a couple of names I used; one was "Wenzel Stroszek," the other was the very Scandinavian "Erika Holmehave." Years later I published a small number of poems in a German magazine.* I did once start a novel when I was on the island of Kos for the first time, at the age of fifteen. I rediscovered the manuscript not long ago when I was clearing things out and realised how similar it is to *Signs of Life*, which I made a few years later. I might still have a couple of novels in me, but great focus is needed for such a project and these days I don't have the time. A screenplay can be written quickly and a detective story can be knocked out in three weeks, while no one should spend more than a month on a doctoral dissertation. A novel, however, takes longer. For a while I have contemplated writing a book about battles that never took place because the armies missed each other. I might get around to that one day.

It's surprising how few films you have heard of, let alone seen.

I love cinema, but unlike some filmmakers who spend their lives watching other people's films – Martin Scorsese, for example, who has his own library of film prints, and for whom cinema is the joy of his life and constant point of reference – I don't feel the necessity to see three films a day. Three good ones a year are enough for me.

* See "Ten Poems," p. 439.

I average maybe one film a month, and that's usually at a festival, where I see them all at once. I'm not a compulsive film-goer, and compared to most directors am hardly what you would call cinematically literate. I can't imagine my work would be any better or worse if I crawled into a darkened room and spent days watching other people's efforts.

Cinema is the strongest fascination in my life. I feel overwhelmed when I see a great film. I might recall something I saw years ago and ache with pain about its beauty, though such things have forever remained a mystery to me. I don't think I could ever put my finger on what constitutes true poetry, depth and illumination in cinema. I have always wondered how Kurosawa made something as good as *Rashomon*; the equilibrium and flow are perfect, and he uses space in such a well-balanced way. It's one of the small handful of truly great films ever made. The sins, on the other hand, are easy to name. The bad films have taught me most about film-making. Seek out the negative definition. Sit in front of a film and ask yourself, "Given the chance, is this how I would do it?" It's a never-ending educational experience, a way of discovering in which direction you need to take your own work and ideas. *Herakles*, my first blunder, taught me certain important lessons, and from then on I had a much stronger sense as to how I should go about my business. It was good to have made that small film first, rather than jump into something more meaningful.

You set up your own production company at an early age.

I was seventeen when I received a call from some film producers who were interested in a proposal I submitted to them. I had avoided meeting with any of these people because I was so young and felt I wouldn't be taken seriously. The reactions I usually got from producers were probably because my puberty was late; I looked like a child until I was sixteen. I would write letters or speak to them on the phone instead – some of the first calls I ever made – until finally, after a series of conversations, two producers seemed willing to accept me as a first-time director.

When I walked into their office, I saw the two of them sitting behind a huge oak desk. I remember it second by second. I stood there as they looked beyond me, waiting, as if the father had come into town with his child. The first one shouted something so abusive I immediately wiped it from my memory, while the other slapped his thigh and laughed, shouting, "Aha! The kindergarten is trying to make films nowadays!" The entire encounter lasted fifteen seconds, after which I turned and left the office, knowing full well I would have to become my own producer. The meeting was the culmination of many setbacks and humiliations, and proved to be a pivotal moment for me. "What makes these idiots producers?" I thought to myself, realising then and there that until the end of my days I would be confronted by this kind of attitude if I wanted other people to produce my films. Not long after this meeting, my mother took me to see the husband of a friend of hers, a wealthy industrialist, who she said would explain to me how to set up a production company. He started talking in a ridiculously loud voice and ended up shouting at me for nearly an hour. "This is completely foolish! You idiot! You've never been in business before! You don't know what you're doing!" Two days later I filled out the necessary paperwork, paid the few dollars to register the company, and founded Werner Herzog Filmproduktion.

Establishing my own company when I so young meant I didn't really have a proper childhood. I skipped over everything expected of someone my age, like finishing school and becoming an apprentice or attending university. Instead – not even twenty years old – I assumed certain responsibilities that most people confront only at the age of thirty. I probably didn't live my teenage years in any kind of traditional way either. A few years later, when I made *Signs of Life*, my first feature, I was still only about twenty-five and looked even younger, but had a certain authority about me. I was always very firm about my ideas and knew exactly what I wanted, which meant the actors – many of whom were older than me – never doubted who was in charge. When the film was released, people who saw it thought I was in my forties or fifties. They were convinced it was the work of an older, more mature director, and found it inconceivable I was so young.

You are hardly a typical Hollywood mogul.

My company was formed as an emergency measure because no one else would organise and finance my films, and to this day it has only ever produced my own work. For years I lived with my mother in her Munich apartment on Neureutherstrasse, which is where I edited many of the early films, though when my eldest son was born my wife and I moved to our own small apartment. Up until the time of *Nosferatu* I worked out of this place with a telephone and typewriter. There was no clear division between private and professional life; my son was raised amidst a film-production office. Instead of a living room we had an editing room, where my wife and I would sleep. I had no secretary and only family to help with paperwork, bookkeeping and contracts. I did as much as possible myself; it was an article of faith, a matter of simple human decency to do the dirty work as long as I could. Inevitably, by the late seventies, as my work reached larger international audiences and there were more retrospectives being organised and too many people to stay in touch with, as well as more formidable productions being planned, it became difficult to operate that home office on my own, so for years I had a small office in Munich run by my brother and a full-time assistant. Three things – a phone, computer and car – are all you need to produce films. Even today I still do most things myself. Although at times it would be good if I had more support, I would rather put the money up on the screen instead of adding people to the payroll.

Years ago Twentieth Century Fox was interested in working with me on *Nosferatu*. The studio executives asked me to travel to Hollywood for a meeting and offered me the use of a mansion so I could sit and write the script. I didn't particularly want to go, so I invited them to Munich instead. It was almost a test to see how serious they were about the project. One freezing winter morning I met four men – all wearing suits and ties and carrying fancy briefcases – at the airport, and after squeezing them into my Volkswagen drove into the Bavarian countryside. They talked about "financing" a number of screenplays. I didn't understand what they were talking about. "How much do you need?" they asked. "It will take me a week and cost $1.50 for a hundred sheets of paper," I said. "Perhaps another dollar for a few pencils." They looked at each other in bewilderment.

You paid for your early films yourself.

During my final two years at high school I worked the night shift as a welder in a steel factory. I did *Punktschweissen*, the kind of electrical welding that doesn't require the precise skills of a welder, which is much trickier and takes years to master. Much of what I did was menial assembly work, though occasionally I operated a high-pressure hydraulic machine to shape pieces of metal. I can scarcely remember my last two years at school; I was so tired, working every night until six in the morning, saving every penny. They threatened to throw me out because occasionally I would sleep through class. "It would be justified if you kick me out because I can't translate a phrase from Latin," I told my teachers, "but it would be a scandal if you did so because I'm working harder than anyone else."

The best advice I can offer to those heading into the world of film is not to wait for the system to finance your projects and for others to decide your fate. If you can't afford to make a million-dollar film, raise $10,000 and produce it yourself. That's all you need to make a feature film these days. Beware of useless, bottom-rung secretarial jobs in film-production companies. Instead, so long as you are able-bodied, head out to where the real world is. Roll up your sleeves and work as a bouncer in a sex club or a warden in a lunatic asylum or a machine operator in a slaughterhouse. Drive a taxi for six months and you'll have enough money to make a film. Walk on foot, learn languages and a craft or trade that has nothing to do with cinema. Filmmaking – like great literature – must have experience of life at its foundation. Read Conrad or Hemingway and you can tell how much real life is in those books. A lot of what you see in my films isn't invention; it's very much life itself, my own life. If you have an image in your head, hold on to it because – as remote as it might seem – at some point you might be able to use it in a film. I have always sought to transform my own experiences and fantasies into cinema.

The owl carved out of a walnut in *Signs of Life*, the one with a live fly inside, and the mummies at the start of *Nosferatu* I first saw fifteen years before I filmed them, when I lived for a few months near Guanajuato in Mexico. Around the turn of the century there was no more space to bury anyone, so the authorities excavated the bodies in the local cemetery. It turned out that many had become mummified. There was a nearby underground tunnel where these mummies were placed in long rows, leaning on opposite walls with their mouths open, giving the impression of screaming or singing, which is why I chose choral music to accompany the images. It was an image that kept on coming back to haunt me and I knew it would fit perfectly in *Nosferatu*. By the time I went back to make the film, the mummies had been placed inside glass cases. I bribed the nightwatchman, who removed them from their transparent coffins so I could shoot them exactly as I remembered them all those years before.

For *Herakles*, my first real film, I needed a good amount of cash, relatively speaking, because I wanted to shoot on 35mm, not 16mm. For me, filmmaking could only ever be 35mm; everything else was amateurish. It was also a format that had the capacity to reveal – more than any other – whether or not I had anything of substance to offer. "If I fail," I said to myself before starting production, "I will fail so hard I can never recover." At the time I was peripherally involved with a group of filmmakers; there were eight of us, most of whom were slightly older than me. Of the films we planned, four never went into production because the most basic hurdles couldn't be overcome. Another three were shot but never finished because of sound problems. Mine was the only completed project. It was instantly clear to me what the key to filmmaking was. They have a beautiful expression in Peru: "Perseverance is where the gods dwell."

Money has nothing to do with it?

It was faith, not money, that pulled the boat over the mountain in *Fitzcarraldo*. I was once asked about what an interviewer called the "disastrous" production of that film. I stopped him in mid-sentence and said, "It was not disastrous. It was glorious, a genuine achievement." I never made the mistake of thinking that the problems I encountered in the jungle could be resolved with dollar bills. When I went to the Cannes Film Festival and first spoke to producers about *Fitzcarraldo*, one of them – a friend of mine who would open a fresh bottle of champagne if the one we were drinking from wasn't cold enough – became excited and asked how much money

I needed for pre-production. "A million dollars," I told him. With a grand gesture he handed over a cheque for that amount, which I pinned to the wall of my office because I knew that was all it was good for. My encounter with this man was a sign that money wasn't necessarily going to help me get the project off the ground.

You ended up producing Fitzcarraldo *independently.*

"Independent cinema" is a meaningless term. It's a myth. Real independence is a state of mind, nothing more. To call someone "independent" is to give Hollywood too much credit; studios aren't the navel of filmmaking or the baseline of anything. There has always been a dependent relationship between financiers, directors and distributors, which means there's no such thing as true "independent" cinema, with the exception of home movies made for the family album or footage shot with a cellphone at a spring-break beach party in Florida. No one makes films completely alone; audiences and filmmakers have always been reliant on each other, though some – and I include myself here – have perhaps forged a greater degree of self-reliance than most. I have always been ready to roll up my sleeves and take care of whatever needs to be done. From the start I had a strong urge to do things for myself.

Years ago I was shooting in New York and showed up with a van at an equipment-rental place. "You aren't allowed to pick up anything yourself," the man who worked there told me. "A union truck has to deliver it." We had an endless debate until I grabbed what I needed, put it in my van – which was ten feet from the door of this place – and drove off. I once even considered setting up my own actors' union. A friend recently asked if I would record a couple of lines for a film he made, but the Screen Actors Guild told me it wasn't allowed unless I was paid the standard rate and his company was registered with the union, which my friend couldn't afford. I found it all completely ridiculous; it's the kind of mentality that stops emerging filmmakers dead in their tracks. At the time I contemplated establishing a competing labour union for actors. For me the questions were simple. Could I, a German, form a union in America, and how many Founding Fathers would I need? Four, forty or four thousand? There are too many rituals and hierarchies in Hollywood; to be independent means to be free of such things.

The union caught up with us during production on *Stroszek* and announced they were going to send a representative to the set. I told them to meet us in Death Valley, a couple of thousand miles away from where we were shooting. I never heard from them again.

You have a reputation as someone who goes to extremes.

If you give a piece of an unknown metal alloy to a chemist, he will examine its structure by putting it under great pressure and exposing it to great heat; this gives him a better understanding of what that metal is composed of. The same can be said of human beings, who often give insight into their innermost being when under duress. We are defined in battle. The Greeks had a saying: "A captain only shows during a storm." Shooting under a certain amount of pressure and insecurity injects real life and vibrancy that wouldn't otherwise be there into a film. But I wouldn't be sitting here if I had ever risked anyone's life while making a film. I'm a professional who never looks for difficulties; my hope is always to avoid problems.

During filming on Mount Erebus in Antarctica, I wanted to be lowered down into the live volcano with a camera, but quickly realised how stupidly dangerous it was. However curious I was personally, I knew there wasn't any good reason to get those shots when it came to the film I was making. I don't believe in fate and destiny, but I have great faith in probability; I make sure that whatever I do puts me firmly on the side of safety. Perhaps mountaineers are motivated to seek out the most difficult routes, but not me. As a filmmaker, such an attitude would be wholly unprofessional and irresponsible, and being my own producer means it's especially in my interests to work as efficiently as possible. When it came to *Fitzcarraldo*, I knew there would be certain inevitable problems to overcome, which meant it was inevitable I wasn't going to shy away from them. Some challenges can't be shirked. But in heading directly into such things, I'm only doing my duty. I have never gone out seeking inhospitable terrain to film in, nor have I ever taken idiotic risks, as a blind, stupid daredevil would do. I'm aware of my reputation of being a ruthless madman, but when I look at Hollywood – which is a completely crazed place – it's clear to me that I'm the only clinically sane person there. As my wife will convincingly testify, I am a fluffy husband.

Surely you've taken a few risks as a filmmaker.

Perhaps, but only in a calculated and professional way. Generally it's me who tests the waters before everyone jumps in. As the leader of a platoon, the obligation to walk out front, with everyone following, is yours. I'm the one ultimately responsible for everyone's safety, and I would never ask anything of an actor or technician I wouldn't do myself. A director has to be on an equal footing with those around him, and by doing so establish a sense of solidarity. There is a scene in *Signs of Life* where the soldiers are playing with fireworks; that's my hand in the close-up as the rocket – which really was full of gunpowder – is being lit. I tested the rapids of the raging river during production on *Aguirre* before anyone else went down there, and walked ahead of the cameraman into a minefield in Kuwait during production on *Lessons of Darkness*. It was cold while we were filming the sequences of *Nosferatu* with the rats, so when we released thousands of them onto the streets of Delft they all clustered together to keep warm. I ran in to try and disperse them, and was bitten at least twenty times. When you see rats crawling over naked feet in the film, that's also me; no one else wanted to do it. Years ago, when I was staging an opera, I thought about having a stuntman crashing down from the rigging about fifty feet above the stage, as if a mountain climber had fallen from a rock face and disappeared into the clouds below. He had to hit a narrow space – an opening in the floor with a large air cushion underneath – and it wasn't easy to achieve this from such a height. We couldn't afford a stuntman, so I decided to test the fall myself. I was hoisted up incrementally, trying it from various different heights, beginning at ten feet. Eventually, at a height of about thirty-five feet, I jumped down and got severe whiplash in my neck. I realised it was ridiculous to try from fifty feet, and immediately scrapped the whole idea.

In the jungles of Guyana, making *The White Diamond*, I wanted footage from above the jungle canopy, but knew that the test flight of the electrically powered dirigible might be the only time it ever flew. I couldn't ask our cameraman to go up because a few years earlier a cameraman had died while filming something similar on the maiden flight of a prototype airship, so I insisted on shooting it myself, though the aerospace engineer Graham Dorrington – who designed and built the dirigible – was resistant. For a shot in *Rescue Dawn* I wanted the actors to run across an old rope-and-plant bridge that spanned a stretch of flowing water. Christian Bale rightly insisted the bridge be checked before he made his move, which I did myself. When we filmed the scene of Christian and Steve Zahn moving downstream on the raft, I was in the water with them for hours. During the scene where Dieter eats a plate of wriggling maggots, I told Christian I would also eat some, but he let me off the hook. "Just roll the camera," he said. My first question to him when we met to discuss the film was: "How do you feel about sleeping in the jungle at night and waking up covered in leeches? Are you prepared to bite a live snake in half and eat it?" When he said, "Yes," it was clear we would be able to work together. I also told Christian – who spent months losing nearly sixty pounds under medical supervision – that I would lose half as much weight as he had to for the role, and ended up something like thirty pounds lighter. It would have been counterproductive if I showed up on set as emaciated as him.

How did you lose the weight?

It had nothing to do with dieting. Just eat less and move more. Let me add something about risk by mentioning two individuals who fascinate me. Quirinus Kuhlmann was a virtually unknown baroque poet, deeply, dangerously into the essence of life. He staged the last crusade by criss-crossing Europe on foot while preaching – he called it a divine mission – and eventually set off with two hysterical women, a mother and daughter, for Constantinople, where he attempted to set up a Jesus Kingdom. The women abandoned him in Venice, absconding with some sailors, and the ship left without him, so he jumped into the water and almost drowned. He was hoisted aboard and taken to Constantinople, where he was imprisoned after trying to convert the Sultan. He eventually arrived in Moscow, where he incited some sort of religious riot – which was misunderstood by the authorities as a political one – was imprisoned again and then, together with his books, burnt at the stake. For a time I had a vague idea about making a film with Kinski about Kuhlmann's life and ecstasies. Joseph Plateau was a Belgian physicist, the first person to study the principle of persistence of

vision, the afterglow of light on the retina, which is the fundamental principle of moving images in cinema. I consider Plateau to
be one of the most significant explorers who ever lived. His tests
rendered him blind because he stared directly into the sun for too
long. He's a hero; the man sacrificed his eyes for cinema. Was it
worth it? Perhaps, because he helped give meaning to our existence. There is nothing wrong with perishing in the travails and
tribulations of life.

*You recently uncovered your first effort as a filmmaker, made in
1957, when you were fifteen.*

One of my friends, Tony Fischer, was a tall, handsome guy who
kept telling me he was better looking than Gary Cooper and could
act him off the screen, so one day I decided to put him to the test.
My older brother was working in a trading company that had a
cafeteria, and we got permission to film there one weekend. That
was our western saloon. We put in swing doors, then nailed up
a "WHISKY" sign and a "WANTED" poster. The result was a
primitive silent, about six minutes long, on 8mm. There isn't much
to it; it was the joy of kids making a film. We wore the most basic
cowboy costumes we could get our hands on, played cards, swigged
from a whisky bottle and got into a bar fight. Today I call it *A Lost
Western*. It turned out that Tony did look as good as Gary Cooper,
but was abysmally bad as an actor. A few years ago I was at the
film museum in Turin and saw one of the first films ever made,
Nain et géant, by Georges Méliès, from 1901. At the time there
was a retrospective of my work in town and I was able to watch,
back-to-back, *A Lost Western* and this early piece of cinema. What
struck me was how similar my first film is to the Méliès short. It's as
if, like those pioneers, I too was inventing cinema in my own way.

You have said Herakles *was more an experiment in editing than
anything else.*

Looking at the film today I find it rather pointless, though at the
time *Herakles* was an important test for me. It was some kind of
an apprenticeship; I felt it would be better to make a film than go
to film school. I was friendly with the boss of a company who gave
me several shots from the newsreels he produced, all for free. I took

various pieces of this material and intercut it with footage I filmed myself of bodybuilders, including Mr Germany 1962. It was fascinating to edit such seemingly disconnected and diverse material, all these images and sounds that wouldn't normally fit comfortably together. A special spirit invades cinema when you marry together elements usually kept apart. One of the most interesting things in the film is a shot of a policeman at the Le Mans racetrack in 1955, immediately after a horrific accident that killed more than eighty people, when burning fragments of a car flew into the spectators' stand. He is so stunned by what has happened that he has no idea what to do, and just stares into the camera. There is a beautiful saying: "The best description of hunger is a description of bread." In the same way, the best description of a catastrophe is the blank stare of this policeman.

The film focuses on the strongman, a figure that resonates throughout your work.

I have always felt a close affinity to strongmen. "Strongman" is a word that reverberates beyond mere physical abilities; it encompasses intellectual strength, independence of mind, confidence and perhaps some kind of innocence. I make a distinction between strongmen and bodybuilders. I don't like the quasi-beauty ideal that has emerged from bodybuilding; the complete opposite is actually more compelling. Many years ago the author Herbert Achternbusch and I talked about establishing a publishing company. Nothing came of it except our name, Fehler-Pferd, which literally means "All-Malady-Horse," and the logo we designed, which was adapted from an image issued by a major American pharmaceutical company that produced various drugs for horses. It was of a horse suffering from every conceivable illness and visible disease, just to show what can go wrong: a drooping lip, multiple hernias, a sagging, broken back, malnutrition, splintered hoofs. A truly wretched sight, the negative definition of beauty. We never published a single book, though the idea remains alive in my mind.

My fascination with strongmen probably stems from my childhood heroes when I lived in Sachrang. One of them was an old farmhand called Sturm Sepp ["Stormin' Joe"]. He must have been about eighty years old and was more than six feet tall, though you couldn't tell because he was always bent over. He was a strange, almost biblical figure with a full beard and long pipe, and was always silent; we never got him to say so much as a word about himself, or utter a single sound. We would taunt him when he was out mowing in the field, and he would go after us, swinging his scythe. I vividly remember watching Sturm Sepp, stark naked, washing himself with a bunch of roots, underneath the freezing, thundering waterfall in the ravine behind the house where I grew up. The story told to us children was that at one time he had been so strong that when his mule collapsed as it was pulling some tree trunks, Sepp loaded several enormous logs onto his shoulders and carried them down the mountain. Because of this feat of strength, he had been bent over at the waist ever since. There was also a legend that during the First World War Sepp single-handedly took an entire squad of French soldiers prisoner, twenty-four men in all. He was so quick at running across the hills, popping up again and again in different places, that the French – encamped in a small hollow down in the valley – thought they were surrounded by a massive detachment of Germans. I can still picture the scene in my mind.

My other childhood hero was Siegel Hans. He was a lumberjack, a brave, daring young chap with rippling Mr Universe muscles, and the first person in the village to own a motorcycle. We truly revered and admired him. Once, when the milk truck broke through a wooden bridge, Siegel Hans was fetched to help. He climbed down into the stream, took off his shirt, revealing his bulging muscles for all to see, and tried to heave the truck back up again with his bare hands. He didn't succeed, but the fact that he even attempted it was enough to inspire in us an awe that I am unable to comprehend today. It's an image I used decades later in *Invincible*. Siegel Hans was involved in a local smuggling operation, where a load of coffee was brought across the border with the collusion of customs offic-ers. When the police came for Siegel Hans, he leapt out of a win-dow and fled straight up the nearest mountain, the Geigelstein. At the summit he blew on his trumpet and the police set off in pursuit. When they arrived at the peak they suddenly heard Siegel Hans's trumpet from the opposite mountaintop. And so it went on, to and fro, for days. The whole village revered him for this; we went into positively religious ecstasies over him. In the end he gave himself up. I remember thinking that to evade the police in the valley for so long he had actually run around the entire German border. It's like shooting a bullet from a powerful rifle that will ultimately hit you in your own back because it orbits the entire planet.

When I was growing up, these kinds of tales – of mythological heroes and lumberjacks getting into bar-room brawls, which you see in *Heart of Glass* – were ever present. The farmer next to our little house was another very strong guy called Beni, and for a couple of years Siegel Hans was always challenging him to a fight. These two bull-headed men would sit in the pub, beer steins in hand, staring at each other, then all of a sudden do something violent. To this day I can look at two Bavarians enjoying themselves at the Oktoberfest and know whether in the next ninety seconds they are going to start fighting. The signs are subtle, but I can read them. There is actually a law in Bavaria stating there must be two grooves on either side of a stein handle so it breaks off easily, otherwise too many skulls would be fractured. One day a fight erupted while I was in the pub. Siegel Hans eventually got Beni's head down into the urinal as the entire village cheered them on, shouting, "We have to know who is the strongest in the village!"

Soon after finishing Herakles, *you won the Carl Mayer Award for your screenplay* Signs of Life.

My behaviour at the time was ridiculous, but I was so convinced of my abilities that I arrogantly told my brothers I didn't need to read the other scripts I was competing against; I knew mine was the best. The jury held its session in Munich, and when one of its members rang at my door late one night with great excitement to tell me I had won the award – worth about $7,000 – I looked at him and said, "You don't have to wake me past midnight to tell me that. I already knew." Although the film wasn't made for a few years, the award was a step forward. At the time I felt it gave me real momentum and would carry me for a decade.

My next film was *The Unprecedented Defence of the Fortress Deutschkreuz*, financed by money I got from the screenplay award. The basic expenses were for raw stock, lab fees and something for the four actors. It's a short film about a group of men protecting an abandoned castle from imaginary attackers, the same story

I worked with a few years later in *Signs of Life*. They barricade themselves inside a fortress and wait aimlessly for an enemy they know will never show up, then leave and take a wheat field by storm. At the start of the film the voiceover sounds like a commentary on the action, then emerges as deranged chatter that does nothing to clarify the situation, completely disconnected from what is happening on screen. This unreliable narrative gives the film a hallucinatory feeling. It isn't even clear whether these four men inside the fortress are playing a game or if they really are at war.

You made a film between Herakles *and* The Unprecedented Defence of the Fortress Deutschkreuz.

Game in the Sand, which was more of a proper film than *Herakles*, but actually only a few people have seen it. I was careful to take it out of circulation almost immediately after finishing it, though at the time I did show it to friends. It's the one film I will never publicise in my lifetime; I might even destroy the negative before I die. It was filmed in the Burgenland province, in southeast Austria, and when Volker Schlöndorff saw the footage he decided to shoot his first film, *Young Törless*, in the same village. *Game in the Sand* is about four children and a rooster. During shooting I had the feeling things were moving out of control; the boys involved in the filming became violent, and I did nothing to stop them. When I look back, the film should probably not have been made at all, though I did incorporate elements of it into *Signs of Life*, when Meinhard walks along the beach and comes across a heap of sand out of which is sticking the head of a rooster. Fortunately, something useful came out of my experiences, which is that I was able to establish – firmly and with absolute certainty – my own personal ethical boundaries. I learnt how important it was to set the parameters within which I would work as a filmmaker and ensure I had control over every situation. I learnt this by accident, by making a mistake.

You visited the United States for the first time.

There were offers from producers who wanted to buy the screenplay for *Signs of Life* and make the film, but I turned them all down; I knew I had to direct it myself. I couldn't find anyone to finance the film, even after shooting those early shorts and winning the screenplay award, so in 1964 I applied for and was awarded a scholarship to study in the United States. It gave me free choice about where to go, but I didn't want to head to a fancy city like New York or Los Angeles, so I chose Pittsburgh, a place populated by real working people, by welders. It was a world I understood. I took the boat from Bremerhaven, not long before transatlantic flying became the norm, and remember sailing for ten days, enjoying the anticipation of arrival. What I didn't know was that by the early sixties Pittsburgh was in heavy decline; the steel mills were shutting down and life for many people was falling apart. My plan was to study at Duquesne University, but I had no idea there was such a difference in quality between American universities, and quickly felt Duquesne wasn't the right place for me. Three days after I arrived I returned my scholarship and ended up penniless, with no host family and no passage home.

I was a drifter in Pittsburgh for a few weeks before being picked up from the side of the road by the Franklin family. Evelyn, the widowed mother, had six children between the ages of seventeen and twenty-seven, as well as her own ninety-three-year-old mother. I owe them so much, this wonderful, crazy family who let me stay in the attic of their house near Fox Chapel, where I lived for almost six months. The youngest children were twin seventeen-year-old girls. Billy, the eldest son, was a failed rock star who would spend his nights playing gigs in bars. Grandma, hoping he would one day lead a virtuous life, tried to wake him every morning at seven, banging on his door and reciting Bible verses. Billy would eventually emerge, stark naked, at around four in the afternoon, talking wildly to his cocker spaniel in an invented language and theatrically pounding his chest, bemoaning his sinful life to Grandma. The twin girls would come home from school at around the same time, with a couple of friends in tow, who would screech and flee at the site of the naked Billy. Another brother had fallen from a moving car as a child; his speech had been slow and slightly slurred ever since. He had served part of his military service at Ramstein Air Base, not far from Frankfurt, and from him I took the line "*Was ist los? Der Hund ist los*" and used it in *Stroszek*. It was the only German phrase he picked up in two years. The father – an alcoholic – had died a couple of years before I showed up. It was extraordinary how Evelyn ran this wild bunch, having added "The Kraut" into the family mix; I gave the mayhem added colour. That's mostly what they called me, though it changed depending on Grandma, because every second day she would ask me what my name was. "Werner," I said. "Ah, Wiener," she would say. Her hearing wasn't good and she was rather gaga. Actually, the name stuck, and even today, when he writes to me, my brother Lucki addresses his emails to Wiener. My son Rudolph calls me Wiener and to my granddaughter Alexandra I am Pappous Wiener. A few days later Grandma would call me something like "Urfan" or "Urban," so the twin girls sometimes called me "Urban Wiener, the Kraut." At the time I was good at high-jumping and the only one who could reach the ceiling of the living room with my head, which occasionally made me "The Leaping Kraut."

The twins introduced me to the Rolling Stones, and sometime in 1964 we all went to a concert in Pittsburgh. When it had finished, I noticed that rows of plastic seats were steaming; many of the screaming teenage girls had peed themselves. That's when I knew this was something big.

How did you make a living?

I heard about a film producer who worked with WQED in Pittsburgh. He was planning a series of films on advanced, futuristic, rocket-propelled systems for NASA, and suggested I make a film about plasma propulsion, which involved me going to Cleveland to talk to scientists and visit what at the time was one of the world's most powerful magnets. Journalists are always writing that I made films for NASA and abandoned a promising career as a scientist – even an astronaut – to become a filmmaker. The truth is that because they had a high-security atomic reactor in Cleveland, everyone who worked there had to be cleared through intensive security checks. I had access to certain restricted areas and talked to the scientists, but just before I was about to start work on the film it was discovered that I didn't have a permit to stay in the country unless I was a student. I had violated my visa status, and soon afterwards was summoned to the immigration office in Pittsburgh.

It was obvious I was about to be thrown out of the country and shipped back to Germany, so I drove an old Volkswagen to New

York during an extremely bitter winter, where I planned to look for work. I lived in the car for a few weeks, though its floor was rusted through and I had a cast from my ankle up to my hip because I had fractured my leg a few weeks earlier while playing around with the Franklin twins in Pittsburgh. They had a habit of ambushing me with the cheapest perfume they could find and soaking me with it. One day I decided to jump out from the third-floor bathroom window and tackle them from behind, but that hadn't gone as anticipated. I couldn't move my toes properly in the cast and they nearly froze, so I wrapped wads of newspaper around them to make sure I didn't lose anything to frostbite. At night, when it got exceptionally cold, the homeless of New York – who live almost like Neanderthal men – would gather together on some empty, desolate street and stand huddling around fires kindled in metal trash cans, all without speaking a word. I didn't make a particularly good impression on potential employers because I was in such bad shape, so I eventually cut the damned cast off with a pair of poultry shears and fled across the border to Mexico, near Guanajuato and San Miguel de Allende, then down to San Cristóbal de las Casas in the south.

Mexico is where you learnt Spanish.

And where I developed my love and fascination for Latin America. While I was down there I struggled to make a living, until I discovered a weak spot on the border, across the Río Grande from Reynosa in Mexico to McAllen in Texas. Every day thousands of day-labourers would commute across the border and return home at night because they had a special sticker on their windshield. I stole one, bought some television sets for people who wanted them down in Mexico – where they were expensive – and resold them. It was, I suppose, smuggling of a sort, though I ended up with only pocket change. One time a rich ranchero asked me to get him a Colt pistol made of silver because he wasn't able to find one in Mexico, so I bought one and took it down there. I was able to support myself on these indiscretions, though from this years later came the legend I worked as a gun-runner.

I spent a couple of weekends as a rodeo rider in a *charreada*. They had three cowboys, or *charros*, in the ring who would catch the bulls by using lassos to pull the animal to the ground and then tie a rope around its chest. Then I would squat on it, at which point the bull would explode with rage. I saw some of them jump clear over a six-foot stone wall. I had no idea how to ride a horse, something that soon became patently clear to the spectators, so I appeared under the name El Alamein, which after Stalingrad was the biggest defeat of the German forces in the Second World War. I was injured every time I went out there in front of the crowd, which loved cheering on the idiot. One time I was in the ring with a bull that got on its feet and stood there staring at me. "*BURRO!*" I screamed. "YOU DONKEY!" I can still hear the crowd screaming. The bull became rather angry and tried to pin me to the stone wall. My leg – the one I had fractured in Pittsburgh – got caught and I sustained an injury that was so bad I quit there and then. Today it all sounds funny and I can look back at my time in Mexico with some humour, but it was rather banal and occasionally quite miserable, even if it was *pura vida* – the raw, stark-naked quality of life – as the Mexicans say.

I drove back to Pittsburgh and spent a few weeks with the Franklins, though I was in hospital for much of that time because I picked up hepatitis in Mexico. Eventually I flew back to Europe and travelled around for another few months before returning home, where almost immediately I started pre-production on *Signs of Life*. I still wasn't taken seriously, even after the Carl Mayer Award and my short films, which by now had been screened at the Oberhausen Short Film Festival and other places. At the time Munich was the cultural centre of West Germany, and I was able to make contact with other filmmakers, including Volker Schlöndorff, who was about to make *Young Törless* and showed up at my door one day. He has been helpful ever since, the most loyal of all the friends I have among filmmakers, though his films are so different to mine. He defended me with great passion during some of my darkest hours, and more recently spoke the French voiceover for *Cave of Forgotten Dreams*.

This was also when I encountered Fassbinder for the first time. Rainer was always a solid comrade in our battle to plough fields that hadn't yet been worked over. This pimply, chubby twenty-two-year-old showed up at my door one evening – it must have been around 1967 – and slammed down prints of his first short films. He looked like a peasant, though was actually quite sophisticated and streetwise; I immediately sensed there was something forceful about him, that here was real talent. "Watch these, now! I want you to produce my films," he told me. "For God's sake, Rainer," I said, "do it like me. You must produce your own work." I explained to him I wasn't a producer like any other, that I didn't make films on a mercantile basis by acquiring a project and then hiring a director. My company was established to make only my films. "You must have the guts to set up your own production company," I told him. "Just go for it." Later he was grateful I threw him out, and said I had shown him possibilities he never knew existed.

You have lived outside of Germany for years, but have you retained your German sensibilities?

You can't stand on one leg in Hollywood; you have to be all there or else you'll never belong. It was the dream of some German film-makers to move to Hollywood and make American films, which meant leaving their own culture behind. That never interested me. Decades after leaving Germany, it doesn't matter where my films are physically made; they are still very much Bavarian in spirit. I can leave my land but not my culture. Some Irish write in English, but they are still Irish. Today I function very much in English, but I'm still a Bavarian. Historically speaking, Bavarians have never considered themselves part of Germany. My first language was a Bavarian dialect; my own father sometimes couldn't understand me, and one time he turned to my mother and asked her to translate. It was a culture shock when I went to school in Swabia for a few months, where everyone spoke a different language. I was teased because I spoke with such a thick accent, and at the age of about eleven had to learn *Hochdeutsch* – proper German, the language established by Martin Luther – for the first time.

Down in Bavaria there's a different approach to doing things, a way of life I am inextricably intertwined with. Being Bavarian means as much as it is to be Scottish in the United Kingdom. Like the Scots, Bavarians are hard-drinking, hard-fighting, warm-hearted and imaginative. The difference between a German and a Bavarian film is the difference between Kaiser Wilhelm of Prussia and King Ludwig II. Wilhelm was excellent at co-ordinating armies and starting wars, while Ludwig possessed an extraordinarily fertile mind and was a patron of Richard Wagner, to whom he was almost religiously devoted. He was completely mad and caught up in his own fantasies, but as a young man ended up as king because his brother Otto was even crazier. Ludwig designed a cable car suspended from a gas balloon that could carry him over the Alps, and nearly bankrupted the country by building a series of castles full of quintessential Bavarian dreaminess and exuberance, which became models for the ones you find in Disneyland. Wilhelm could never have come up with something like Ludwig's extraordinary castle at Neuschwanstein, incomplete at his death in 1886, which is full of frescoes that portray scenes from Wagner operas. His Linderhof Palace was technologically ahead of its time, and contains a fantastical grotto full of dynamos that provided an array of lighting effects. It was constructed for a single private performance of Wagner's *Tannhäuser*; Ludwig even designed the boat in which he personally rowed Tannhäuser to land. He was often up all night and would go out on an ornate sleigh he had designed himself, travelling through the winter forest with a couple of footmen, knocking on the doors of startled local peasants at four in the morning. He would ask for a glass of water, and in exchange hand over his most precious gold and diamond jewellery. Ludwig led a tragic life and was eventually forcibly removed from power; he died a mysterious death when he and his physician were found drowned in the shallowest part of Lake Starnberg. He's the only person who could have made *Fitzcarraldo* apart from me. You see this kind of baroque imagination in Fassbinder's films, the kind of unstoppable, roughly hewn and ferocious creativity he had. Like his work, my films aren't ideological constructs, thin gargling water instead of thick stout, which we saw too much of in West German cinema throughout the seventies.

What do you miss about Bavaria?

An interviewer once asked me what my favourite season is. "Autumn," I told him. For years I have lived in southern California, where there are no seasons to speak of. I yearn for them. And I could murder someone for a steaming pretzel fresh from the oven, covered with butter, and a beer. That's what being Bavarian is all about. Living abroad means I rarely get to listen to the genuine

Bavarian dialect, which I miss more than anything. A few years ago I was awarded the *Bundesverdienstkreuz*, Germany's Order of Merit. I had no plans to accept, and attended the ceremony only after my brother called me to say that he had been asked by journalists, "The President has bestowed Herr Herzog with this honour, but he won't show up. Why does he hate Germany so much?" Of course I don't hate Germany, and especially not Bavaria, though not every development has been particularly enlightened. Today I look at Munich and see a city empty of all significance, invaded by Prussians and stripped of its Bavarian spirit.

You have spoken about happiness as being something you aren't particularly interested in.

I find the notion of happiness rather strange, and do sometimes wonder why I seem to be different from many Americans, who even wrote the "right" to happiness into their Declaration of Independence. It has never been a goal of mine; I just don't think in those terms. I barked at a Hare Krishna disciple one time at Miami airport because he insisted I take the book he was offering. "Aren't you interested in happiness?" he asked. "NO!" A sense of justice is more important to me, and certainly more valuable than money and acclaim. I can't tell you how many honorary degrees I have politely declined from universities that are reckoned to be the best on the planet, including Cambridge and a big one in New York. I'm not interested in decorating my hat with such things. I'm after something else instead.

What?

I try to give meaning to my existence through my work. That's a simplified answer, but whether I'm happy or not really doesn't count for much. I have always enjoyed my work. Maybe "enjoy" isn't the right word; I love making films, and it means a lot to me that I can work in this profession. I am well aware of the many aspiring filmmakers out there with good ideas who never find a foothold. At the age of fourteen, once I realised filmmaking was an uninvited duty for me, I had no choice but to push on with my projects. Cinema has given me everything, but has also taken everything from me.

Is it true you don't understand irony?

It's a serious communication defect, one I have wrestled with my whole life, ever since I was able to think independently. I have no sensory organ for irony and am forever falling into its traps. I feel close to Kuhlmann because of this. Apparently he took everything literally, and around 1700, while the alchemists were searching for the philosopher's stone, he dug for it in the ground with a spade in Silesia. A few weeks ago I received a phone call from a painter who lives in the neighbourhood. He told me he wanted to sell me some of his paintings, and because I lived nearby he said he could make me a deal. He started to argue with me, saying I could have this or that painting for only $10, or even less. I tried to get him off the phone. "Sir, I'm sorry," I said, "but I don't have paintings in my apartment. I don't have art on my walls, only maps. Sometimes a family photo, but never a painting." He kept on and on until all of a sudden he started to laugh. "I know this laughter," I said to myself. The painter didn't change his voice when he announced that he was my friend, Harmony Korine.

Let me offer another example. I am unable to distinguish a gay man from a straight man unless he shows up in drag and make-up. For me, a man is a man. Not long ago I was with film director John Waters – who I have known for forty years – on stage at an event. A single, blinding spotlight shone down on him, and sixteen hundred eyes stared out from the darkness. I stepped aside and from arm's length looked at John with an intensified focus. I turned to my wife and whispered, "Could it be that John is gay?" Such a bold filmmaker, a man very dear to my heart. I admire his audacity, but I was truly oblivious to the fact that he is gay. I always just took him for John Waters.

After it was announced I was to receive the *Bundesfilmpreis* for *Signs of Life*, I got a call from the Ministry of the Interior. It was the minister's personal assistant who called me. "Are you Werner Herzog? The minister would like to have a conversation." I was then connected to the minister, who started stuttering and said, "Ah well, Mr Herzog. We have publicised the news that you have won the *Bundesfilmpreis* but . . . ahem . . . I have to personally take the matter in hand and humbly apologise. I regret to say that in reality it was not you who won the award, rather someone else." I

40

remained stunned yet composed, and replied, "Sir, how could this have happened? You as Minister of the Interior are responsible for many things, including internal security and the safety of our borders. In what kind of a state is your house? This letter in my hand has not only your signature, it has two others. I accept what you're saying, but how could it have happened?" It went on like this for ten minutes, when suddenly the minister started to roar so hard with laughter that I recognised the voice of my friend Florian Fricke. "Florian, you bastard," I said. He hadn't even used a different voice when he was playing the minister's personal assistant, but I still took them for two different people. That's how bad my communication defect is. When it comes to irony, there are things common to almost everyone that are lost on me.

Compared to other filmmakers – particularly the French, who are able to sit around in cafes, nursing their coffee and waxing eloquent about their work – I'm a brooding, squatting Bavarian bullfrog, a country bumpkin incapable of discussing art with people. The French love to play with their words, so to master their language is to be a master of irony. Technically I can speak French; I have the vocabulary and know the grammar, but will do so only when forced to. Only twice in my life has this happened. One time, while we were shooting *Fata Morgana* in Africa, I was arrested. I was surrounded by drunken soldiers who aimed a rifle at my head, another at my heart and a third at my balls. I started to explain who I was, when the commander screamed at me, "*ON PARLE QUE LE FRANÇAIS ICI!*" They pointed at one of our microphones and asked what it was. I made the sound of an electric razor because our equipment would have been immediately confiscated if I had told them the truth. Then they wanted to open our cans of undeveloped film, so I spoke to them in French before handing over three sealed cans, all full of wet sand. I insisted they find a darkroom before opening them, and we smuggled the real footage out of the country. The second occasion I spoke French was when we were making *La Soufrière* on Guadeloupe, which is French-speaking, though almost the entire population is African. We found the man we were looking for, the only person who had refused to be evacuated from the island, asleep under a tree. I woke him up and we talked. So under pressure I will speak the language, but only when there is a real necessity, otherwise I withdraw and become a denizen of the crag.

You might not understand irony, but you do have a sense of humour.

Of course. A magazine in Germany once ran an article on me with the headline "This Man Never Laughs" under a photo of me looking as serious as some people expect. "Laugh! Laugh!" the photographer said. "Why don't you ever laugh?" I was feeling more and more uncomfortable, and eventually told him, "I never laugh once a camera is pointed at me." Naturally they left out the second part of what I said.

There's a big difference between irony and humour. I can understand humour and laugh at jokes, even if I've never been very good at telling them myself; my face just isn't made for laughing. Often overlooked is the humour in my films, from *Even Dwarfs Started Small* to *Bad Lieutenant*. My audiences laugh all the time, and an audience that laughs is always in the right; that's a law of nature. They even chuckle at *Aguirre*, when one of the soldiers is hit by an arrow and says, "Long arrows are coming back into fashion," before falling down dead. Seeing audiences laugh at my films has always been important to me, though being unable to comprehend irony is an obvious defect of mine.

An endearing defect.

Not if you saw me sitting in a Parisian cafe.

2

Blasphemy and Mirages

You benefited from the film-subsidy system in West Germany.

I belonged to a generation of post-war Germans many of whom were attempting to express themselves in new ways cinematically, which isn't surprising when you think of West German cinema in the fifties. There were production companies in existence when we started out, but none of us wanted to have anything to do with them. Almost everything they produced was somehow tainted with Nazism, like the *Heimat* films, steeped in blood and soil; none of it felt right to my contemporaries and me. Even an acclaimed film like *Die Brücke* seemed outdated and old-fashioned, though it is anti-Nazi in spirit.

What was clear by the early sixties was that we West German filmmakers needed to grow up and take our destiny into our own hands. This went further than just production; I'm talking about creating our own festivals and distribution systems, and establishing relations with television stations willing to fund our work. I consider Alexander Kluge to be the spiritual and ideological force behind West German cinema of the period, including the film-subsidy laws that created an environment within which many of us were able to work, and the Oberhausen Manifesto, issued in 1962, the year after the Berlin Wall went up, declaring the arrival of a new generation of West German filmmakers. Kluge and Edgar Reitz – both ten years older than me – saw some of my early films and asked if I wanted to work through their company and the film school in Ulm they had founded [*Institut für Filmgestaltung*]. When I told them I was going to be my own producer, they offered me the use of their equipment, and I spent time on their machinery transferring various recordings I had made. Kluge and Reitz's support was important to me because at the time I was an absolute unknown. It was through Reitz that I met Thomas Mauch, who was the cameraman on several of my films, including *Aguirre* and *Fitzcarraldo*.

For a time the country had probably the most subsidised film industry in Europe, if not the world, but it was still never easy to make films there. There was an organisation called the *Kuratorium junger deutscher Film* [Committee of New German Cinema], devised and created by filmmakers, which gave a first start to many young West German directors.* You had to submit your script and see if your film would be one of the few they decided to give money to. It was a decent amount of cash – about 300,000 DM for each film, around $200,000 – though you had to have the rest of the funding in place before they accepted your application. I had made three short films, each of which in some way caught the attention of the media and film festivals, and the screenplay for *Signs of Life* had won the award a couple of years earlier. Although I already had some money to make *Signs of Life* and felt myself to be an ideal candidate, I was denied *Kuratorium* money for two years, probably because at the time there was nobody at the age of twenty-two who had produced and directed a feature film. I was just too young and inexperienced.

I did eventually benefit from the subsidy system, and acknowledge that the money it generated served as the cornerstone for several of my films, but I never felt it was the healthiest way to run things. It was decision-making by committee, some kind of artificial respiration, which has certain inbuilt weaknesses. Too many people were slaves to handouts, forever trying to fulfil the wishes of the boardroom, which is why so many of them made only one film, then gave up. They were too busy filling out paperwork. As soon as it became more difficult to qualify for subsidy money, many of these people dropped away; they weren't able to stand

* The not-for-profit *Kuratorium*, funded by the Ministry of the Interior, was established to put the proposals of the Oberhausen Manifesto into practice. Submitted scripts were read by film reviewers. Between 1965 and 1968 the *Kuratorium* assisted in the financing of twenty films by providing interest-free loans.

on their own two feet. When it comes to the kind of filmmaking I do, the free market is a harsher but more vibrant structure to function within. It's where the real battle is fought. If you can leave the respirator and submit yourself to the roughness of the market, you should. At the time I appreciated how lucky I was to be given certain opportunities, but felt I had to learn to walk on my own two feet as quickly as possible.

Around the time of your first feature, Signs of Life, *what became known as New German Cinema emerged.*

So-called New German Cinema didn't have much significance for me because I started making films before the Oberhausen Manifesto was issued. There was a real culture of short films at the time, and I showed some of my work at the Oberhausen Film Festival, but never involved myself with the manifesto, which I was asked to sign. I found the whole thing too derivative of the French New Wave and considered the signatories a bunch of mediocre and insignificant epigones. Look at the list and you'll see that apart from Kluge and Reitz, only a tiny handful made any lasting impact as filmmakers. Most disappeared completely. Even experts in German cinema would have to dig deep into their encyclopaedias to find reference to these people. There was undoubtedly a rebirth of German cinema in the late sixties and into the seventies, but it's a myth that we were a coherent group, either stylistically or in terms of subject matter and theme. Everyone was producing very different films, and a few of us barely knew each other. I had loyalties to no one and felt distinctly alienated from some of my contemporaries and their work, like those doctrinaire political films that endlessly and stupidly postulated world revolution. They never had any mass appeal to audiences in West Germany, and rightly so. By the late sixties I had already produced a handful of films, and from my earliest days had spent time outside of Germany, so I could never realistically be seen as a spokesman for New German Cinema, which more than anything was a convenient construct of American and perhaps French journalists. Today I have no problems about being included because there was enough good work being done for me not to be embarrassed by it all. But I know I don't truly belong.

We were individuals making films independently of the main-stream industry in the country; that was the one crucial thing unit-ing us, not the films themselves. There was a highly active, collective excitement of the mind, a pragmatic solidarity between filmmakers, and several of us would assist each other logistically if we were able to. Having said that, when Schlöndorff and I would meet we would usually talk about women, and if I encountered Fassbinder at a film festival, with a glass of champagne in hand, some of his entourage thought I was gay because we gave each other a fleeting, rather shy hug. In public Rainer and I would be discreet about the things that mattered. When journalists expected some profound statement about cinema from either of us, I would point and say, "I like your tie." Our most intense discussions took place in his kitchen, deep into the night, fuelled by beer. Because he was so unruly – a sweaty, grunting wild boar crashing through the underbrush, leaving gaps wide open for others to walk through – and because of the reckless-ness of his private life, the media mistakenly labelled him a revolu-tionary, but I never considered him as such.

When I was doing pre-production for *Aguirre* in Peru, without Fassbinder knowing I took his film *Katzelmacher* down along with some of my own – and prints of Jean-Marie Straub's *The Chronicle of Anna Magdalena Bach*, Werner Schroeter's *Eika Katappa* and Peter Fleischmann's *Hunting Scenes from Bavaria*, all of which I had subtitled into Spanish – and held a mini-retrospective in Lima. These screenings, in a cinema I rented, were a big success, though at the time West German cinema was completely unknown down there. Later, when Fassbinder learnt that I had grabbed a print of his film and taken it with me, he was appreciative. I had the feeling that two or three of his films in a row weren't so good and I would lose heart; he made them so quickly, sometimes three or four a year. But then he would come out with a great one – like *The Bitter Tears of Petra von Kant* or *The Merchant of Four Seasons* – and I would tell myself not to lose faith in the man.

German filmmakers came in waves. The first was the Oberhausen Manifesto people, who were generally older than people like Fassbinder, Wenders and me; I was part of the early second wave. Actually, Fassbinder and Wenders came a little later; they are almost the third wave. There were others who came after us with some fine films but who never persevered. They either dropped away entirely or started working exclusively in television, where there was more security.

It took a while for the rest of the world to catch on to West German cinema.

You might say that by the time most people outside the country realised there was good work being done in Germany, New German Cinema was subsiding. For a brief moment a small number of West German filmmakers were able to screen their films internationally. You could see some Fassbinder, Schlöndorff and Wenders abroad, but never anything of Achternbusch or Werner Schroeter, who was one of the truly important filmmakers working in West Germany at the time. He had an extraordinarily innovative mind, though he was desperately underappreciated at home and elsewhere. In 1969, as a jury member at the Mannheim Film Festival, I insisted that his *Eika Katappa* be given an award, against much cowardly opposition from the other jurors. The problem was that West German cinema had a tendency to be too provincial; it never occurred to some directors that they should try reaching international audiences. From my beginnings as a filmmaker I looked further than Germany's borders and was always hopeful my work would be distributed and appreciated overseas. It's gratifying to me that *Aguirre, the Wrath of God* and *The Enigma of Kaspar Hauser* can be screened to audiences in London, Kiev and São Paulo, or to Native Indians in Peru, and be appreciated. I quickly realised that West German cinema wouldn't survive if it remained so insular.

Years ago I pulled up to a gas station in America's Deep South driving a car with Pennsylvania plates. The mechanic at the pump called me a Yankee and flatly refused to sell me any gas. A century and a half after the end of the Civil War, northerners still smell bad to southerners. Some people feel the same way about Germany today. Starting in 1945 there were two jobs of reconstruction: the cities had to be rebuilt physically, but just as important was the need to rebuild Germany's legitimacy as a civilised nation. The slow pace at which the collective consciousness changes is maybe one reason why recent German filmmakers had such a hard time exhibiting work outside their country so many years after the war. It isn't easy to say when German writers, painters and filmmakers will be able to retake their place, fully and freely, within international culture.

Did you have any contact with the distribution company Filmverlag der Autoren?

I was invited to be a part of the group when it started in 1971, but turned them down. The concept was good: filmmakers who had no access to distribution companies would create their own. But I didn't like the concoction of personalities at Filmverlag; there was something disparate about it that didn't feel right to me. If it had been just Fassbinder and a couple of others and me, then perhaps I would have trusted the operation, but there were some people involved who had an agenda and seemed disunited in their work. Later they distributed some of my early films, but I'm usually wary of collectives. They get watered down when mediocre people climb on board and the ship inevitably sinks. My advice is to find the best people and keep it exclusive.

Signs of Life, *inspired by a short story by Achim von Arnim, was your first feature film.*

At the time I was reading about the Seven Years' War and issues of military strategy. I discovered a journal from 1807 that contained a short article about an incident in Marseille during the war in which a man became insane and locked himself up in a tower. It turned out von Arnim had used this same event when writing his story "Der tolle Invalide auf dem Fort Ratonneau," written in the early nineteenth century.* Von Arnim's story is a wonderful tale about an old colonel sitting by the fireplace who gets so involved in telling a story he fails to notice that his wooden leg has caught fire. It's one of the few occasions – as with *Woyzeck* and *Cobra Verde* – when a piece of literature triggered a screenplay in my mind.

My travels to Greece when I was fifteen were the strongest influences on *Signs of Life*. I had spent time following in the footsteps of my paternal grandfather, Rudolph, investigating what he had

* Translated as "The Mad Veteran of the Fort Ratonneau" in *The Blue Flower: Best Stories of the Romanticists*, edited by Hermann Kesten (Roy, 1946).

48

done years before as an epigrapher and archaeologist on Kos. At a young age he ditched everything – he already had a university chair in Classics – and set off to become an archaeologist. He did his life's work on Kos, starting around 1902, carrying out important excavations for a few years; in the fortress where I shot *Signs of Life* you can see inscriptions on stones that are the actual ones my grandfather translated and published more than sixty years earlier. Later he became insane, and I only got to know him when he was an old man. It was sad to see someone who had been so intuitively connected to the world suddenly so disorientated. For years, when he would read a book he would underline certain passages, but towards the end of his life he would carefully mark up page after page, until every line in the book was underscored. I loved my grandfather very much, though as children we were sometimes terribly cruel to him. We would hide behind the bushes in the garden and make fun of him by calling out nasty rhymes, like *"Herr Professor, Herr Professor, Menschenfresser!"* ["Mr Professor, Mr Professor, cannibal!"], before climbing up the nearest tree, where he couldn't reach us. One time my grandmother used a wooden cooking spoon to give me the hardest spanking of my life.

Every evening my grandfather would pack his belongings into crates and stack up the furniture because he was convinced someone was going to arrive at the house with a truck, pick everything up and have him evicted. My grandmother endured a great deal. Every morning she would unpack his bags and put the table and chairs back in place. I can still hear her saying, "I have lived with him and loved him for so long that only over my dead body will he leave our home." One night my grandfather dressed for dinner, sat at the table, gently put his cutlery aside, folded his napkin, stood, bowed and said to my grandmother – who he no longer even recognised – "Madam, if I weren't already married I would ask you for your hand. How did I come to make your acquaintance?" It's a line I borrowed for *Nosferatu*. Although he was drifting into the night, my grandfather would often speak eloquently and coherently of his excavations as an archaeologist. He died when was I ten years old.

While in Greece, riding a donkey on Crete, I stumbled across the Lasithi Plateau. I was travelling over a mountain pass and looked down into a valley. Beneath me lay ten thousand revolving windmills; it was a field of spinning flowers gone mad. The squeaking noise alone was astonishing. My heart stood still and I had to sit down. "I have either gone insane or have seen something very significant," I said to myself. It turned out these frenzied windmills were real, pumping water for irrigation. I knew as I stood there I would return one day to make a film, and years later this cosmic image became a pivotal one in *Signs of Life*. My attention has always been drawn to the screams that emanate from certain images, and if something cries out so loudly and insistently, I respond. Had I never seen the windmills, I wouldn't have made the connection between this unimaginable ecstatic landscape and the von Arnim story, which I read later on.

Signs of Life *is set during the Second World War.*

The story takes place during the Nazi occupation of Greece, so some people inevitably think it's an historical drama. But the facts of the occupation never interested me in this context, and there is absolutely nothing in the story that makes any direct reference to the Second World War. If a pedantic historian were to look carefully, doubtless they would find many falsehoods. I used a truck dating from the mid-fifties in the film, which was much cheaper than anything I could find from the forties, and when I show the soldiers they are almost always barefoot or shirtless and they never salute. When the captain has them fall in, one of the soldiers is munching on a roll. This has nothing to do with the Third Reich. How often do you see German soldiers acting as decently as this in a war film? Shakespeare based *Hamlet* on events that took place hundreds of years before his time, yet the story's relevance is there not only for his time, but ours as well. *Signs of Life* concerns itself not with a particular era or military conflict, but with the idea of putting instruments of war into the hands of individuals.

Did Signs of Life *have a smooth production?*

As a filmmaker, dependent on so many things outside my control, making *Signs of Life* was an important lesson for me. Things never go exactly as you hope. Whatever potentially can go wrong will eventually go wrong, and there's no point in fuming about it. I quickly learnt that this was the very nature of filmmaking, something that hit me harder and earlier than it did most of my colleagues. Throughout the shoot it became clear that I – as a filmmaker – attract certain troubles. It was as if a curse weighed on me. There were problems during the making of *Signs of Life* that paved the way for what happened later with *Fata Morgana* and *Fitzcarraldo*.

I secured permission to shoot where I wanted to, but three weeks before we were due to start filming a military *coup d'état* took place in Greece. It was a dramatic moment, with multiple arrests of politicians, the immediate suppression of civil rights and suspension of the constitution. I was unable to contact anyone; telephone lines were down, airports were closed and trains were stopped at the border. I drove by car non-stop to Athens and discovered I wasn't allowed to shoot on Kos because the authorities were afraid of the military. My filming permits had become invalid overnight. The problems eventually died down, but then, well into the shoot, the lead actor, Peter Brogle, had an absurd accident and broke his heel bone. He had originally been a tightrope walker, so I suggested we shoot a sequence in the fortress where he walks from one wall to a small tower. He fixed the rope himself but fell about eight feet, and we were forced to suspend shooting for five months. It was unclear whether we would ever finish the film. When we all returned for a final ten days of filming it wasn't easy to find our rhythm again, especially because we could shoot Brogle only from the waist up; he had to wear a brace that kept his broken heel off the ground. When it came to the final sequences of the film, the military forbade me to use fireworks, though they were essential to the story. "You'll be arrested," an army major told me. "Then arrest me," I said, "but know that I will not be unarmed tomorrow, and the first man who approaches will drop dead with me." The next day there were fifty policemen and soldiers standing around watching me work, plus a few hundred people from the town who wanted to see the fireworks. None of them dared come close. My threat to carry a gun was an empty one, of course, but they weren't to know.

What exactly is it that causes the main character, Stroszek, to go mad?

He can't find the words to express himself or make himself understood, and is inhibited because of this. His eventual response is shooting fireworks at the sun, meeting absurdity with absurdity, violence with violence. I always felt Stroszek is actually quite sane.

There are some mysterious moments in the film, but I couldn't really tell you how they explain Stroszek's actions. In one scene he sits on the quay with some boys, one of whom says – for no apparent reason – "Now that I can talk, what shall I say?" before staring directly into the camera. Another moment is very important to me, when the two soldiers are on a reconnaissance mission. They meet a shepherd who lives in a remote house and gives them some water to drink. A young girl sits in the doorway. The shepherd explains that because her mother is out with the sheep all day and he works through the night, the girl rarely hears spoken words and hardly ever talks. "It's beautiful up here in the mountains, but there are no children here for her to talk to," he says. "Sometimes she picks up a few words down in town when she's with her aunt." The father then asks her to recite a poem to the soldiers. I wrote a text about ninety-eight sheep wandering around the Lasithi mountains, one of which gets lost, but purposely didn't give the girl much time to learn it and hid the entire crew behind the camera so she couldn't look around for help from anyone. As she starts to recite the poem she gets stuck and twists her skirt in despair. On her second attempt she got through the whole text beautifully, but I knew it was the first version that should be in the film.

Never in *Signs of Life* did I want to concentrate on Stroszek's psychological state. Before his disintegration, the film is a series of scenes spread over weeks, but once he barricades himself in the fortress, laying siege to an entire town, the story is condensed into only a couple of days. At the moment he might become interesting to psychologists, we see him from a thousand feet away. In fact, we basically don't see him at all in the last twenty minutes of the film; his explosive responses and actions take over as he fires rockets across the bay, sets a chair on fire and shoots a donkey dead. Everyone – including Peter Brogle – asked me why I didn't move in for a close-up at this point. He told me it was important he be allowed to express his character's insanity on screen, then piped up with some drivel about how the human face is the most fascinating landscape on God's earth. "It is not," I told him. "You'll be more fascinating to the audience if they see you as big as an ant in the landscape." I have always preferred keeping a distance between camera and actors. Moving too close to a face is intrusive, almost a personal violation of whoever is in front of the camera. Close-ups aren't necessarily the apotheosis of psychological intimacy; you won't find many in my films. I prefer wide-angle shots because I want audiences to be aware of the physical space the characters inhabit. During the emotional moments in *Nosferatu* – like the scene when Jonathan says goodbye to his wife – I filmed the actors from behind; we don't even see their faces. I have never wanted to see an actor weep. I want to make the audience cry instead.

What did the public think of Signs of Life?

They were unimpressed. The film won the annual *Bundesfilmpreis* [National Film Award] in West Germany, which meant money for my next production plus a trophy and handshake from the Minister of the Interior, and was awarded the Silver Bear at the Berlin Film Festival. Word spread, so there was some level of public awareness. I was invited to a screening in Wiesbaden after a local newspaper published an article about the film, and got to the place to find only nine people in the auditorium. It's the kind of shock I still feel in my bones. I have forever struggled to get audiences' attention in Germany; my films have never been as well received there as they have almost everywhere else in the world, by both reviewers and audiences. The fact is that Germany has never been a nation of film-goers; it's full of passive television viewers instead. For decades there has been insecurity among audiences, which is understandable as Germany was the cause of the two biggest catastrophes of humanity of the past hundred years. This has continued to make post-war generations very cautious. Whenever somebody sticks their head out too far from any kind of obscure or marginal trench – trying to draw attention to themselves or show their work to the world – the rest of the country is immediately suspicious.

The Germans have never liked their poets, at least not the living ones. Compare this to Ireland. I once stayed at a tiny guesthouse in Ballinskelligs, on the southwest coast. The landlady asked me what I did, and off the top of my head – I don't know why – I said, "I'm a poet." She opened her doors and gave me the room for half price. In Germany they would have thrown me out into the street. Years ago I had the good fortune to be able to descend eight floors into a nuclear-proof bunker under the state bank in Reykjavik, where the *Codex Regius* is stored, a piece of literature that defines the Icelandic soul, similar in importance to the Dead Sea Scrolls for Israel. For three hundred years the Danes had owned this little wrinkled parchment, until it was returned to Iceland by Denmark's largest warship, accompanied by a submarine. Half of Iceland's population celebrated for five days and nights. When they discovered I had held the actual manuscript in my hands, I was treated like a king. Such things are inconceivable in Germany. Around the time of *Aguirre* I was at a press conference in Cannes talking about the renaissance of West German cinema when I heard a laugh from the corner of the room where the Germans were sitting. People don't believe me when I tell them the ratings board hated *Aguirre* and refused to acknowledge it had any cultural value, which meant there were no tax incentives for cinemas in West Germany to screen the film and it was treated like a hardcore porno. Years later it stunned me when *My Best Fiend* was embraced by both the German press and audiences. I felt it was the first time they had truly accepted my work.

How did the short Last Words *come about?*

The film was a departure into unknown terrain, as if there were no history of cinema preceding it. It has an utter disregard for the narrative "laws" that traditional cinema uses to tell stories. *Signs of Life*, by comparison, is conventional indeed. Without *Last Words* I don't think *Fata Morgana* would have happened, nor would I have developed subsequent narrative stylisations in my work. I shot the film on Spinalonga, a little island off the coast of Crete, in two days and edited it in one. Everything about it was so evident and clear-cut to me that it has been a source of encouragement ever since.

The idea behind *Last Words* is of a decaying island that has been evacuated because of an outbreak of leprosy. Bizarre stories are told about its former inhabitants, like the man with no legs and the woman with no arms who marry each other out of necessity. One man who has clearly lost his mind and believes himself to be king refuses to leave the island. He is forcibly brought to the mainland by the police, but remains defiant of the forces of society, even of the rules of language. Back living a so-called respectable life, the man continues to fight against the world and refuses to speak or go out, except at night, when he plays on his lyre. Not all of this is explained in the film; we get only glimpses and compulsive repetitions – for example, the man who tells the tale of the last Turk's last footprint. He jumped from a cliff into the sea and left a footprint behind him in the rock, and the Greeks have constructed a chapel on the spot. The man has scarcely finished telling this tale when he starts it again from the beginning, then retells it a third time. There are also the two policemen, to whom I said, "When you make a film you always do a scene over and over again, so please repeat the words ten times and I'll use the best version." They stand there together, in front of the camera, saying the same thing over and over again: "We got him from over there, we saved him," and "Hello, how are you doing?" By hearing these stories – again and again in quick succession – the language of these people takes on a strange quality, and despite the compulsion they are locked into, through their torment you get an inkling of who these people are. The lyre player was fascinating to me. All he recites for minutes on end is, "No, I'm not saying a word. Not a single word. Absolutely nothing. I won't even say no. You won't hear a word from me. I'm saying nothing. If you tell me to say no, I'll refuse to do even that."

Precautions Against Fanatics *is set at a racetrack where various individuals feel it necessary to protect the animals from various "fanatics."*

I went to the racetrack on the outskirts of Munich, where a number of prominent media figures and actors were taking part in an annual race, and when I saw them in training immediately decided to make a film. Like *Last Words*, it's a bold short in its narrative structure and has a strange humour to it, though that might not be immediately evident to those who don't understand German. At the time audiences roared with laughter because all the people in the film are celebrities, like director Peter Schamoni, actor Mario Adorf and the sensational Serbian goalkeeper Petar Radenković, who played for Die Löwen [The Lions], a team from Munich. He was a loose cannon, a real eccentric who during a game would spot a duck at the side of the field and run after it. He was also known to dash out of his area and sprint towards the ball if a player got through the defence. The crowd would go wild whenever he made his way into the opponents' half of the pitch.

I talked Kodak into giving me some raw colour stock for free; it had been returned to them after apparently having been exposed to extreme heat in Africa and was also long beyond its expiration date. Under no circumstances can raw stock like this be sold, though apparently Kodak were interested in discovering if it could survive such disadvantageous conditions. They gave me about ten rolls only after I signed a letter of indemnity stating they had warned me it was unusable and weren't responsible for the results. I gladly took the stock and shot the film not knowing if I would end up with anything. I figured that if decades after Scott had died near the South Pole his negatives had been successfully developed, then this Kodak film was bound to be okay. We lost not a single frame, though the colours are a little off, which gives the images a strange quality. Sometimes I think about getting my hands on all the out-of-date stock out there and making a film or two.

You went to Africa, where you interwove the filming of Fata Morgana, Even Dwarfs Started Small *and* The Flying Doctors of East Africa.

The Flying Doctors, filmed in Tanzania and Kenya, is what I call a *Gebrauchsfilm*, a "utility" film. It's more a *Bericht* – a report – made as a gift to the doctors than a film, and it earned them a fair amount of money, enough to purchase two small aeroplanes. I was asked to work on the project by a woman who raised funds for the doctors, and went with them into the field where they performed surgery, to places where people had never seen doctors before. While I was out with the flying doctors, they were primarily doing preventative medicine, in particular vaccinations and lectures, in this case against trachoma. Prevention is cheap and easy; the disease is caused by a lack of hygiene. I was allowed to fly on their tiny aeroplanes and shoot things I wouldn't otherwise have been able to film, material that was later incorporated into *Fata Morgana*, like the beautiful aerial footage of Lake Nakuru, full of millions of pink flamingos.

Though I made *Flying Doctors* with a specific purpose, it does offer some unusual observations. The most interesting scenes stem from my interest in vision and perception, the process of recognising images and how the brain sorts through and makes sense of them. One of the doctors in the film talks of showing a poster of a fly to the villagers, who had never seen photographs or images of any sort. "We don't have that problem," they said. "Our flies aren't that big." It was a response that fascinated me, so we took the posters – one of a man, one of a human eye that filled an entire piece of paper, another of a hut – and conducted an experiment. I asked if they could identify the human eye, and most of the villagers couldn't; the images were just abstract compositions to them. One man thought the window of the hut was an eye, and another pointed to the eye and said, "This is the rising sun." It was clear that certain elements of visual perception are in some way culturally conditioned, that these people were processing images differently to how Westerners might. There were other things that emerged, like the fact that – perhaps because of some ancient taboo – members of the Maasai tribe were extremely reluctant to enter the mobile medical unit. The trailer was elevated just two feet off the ground, but only a few eventually braved this obstacle and climbed the steps.

In *The White Diamond*, decades later, Graham Dorrington tells Marc Anthony Yhap that when he first landed his airship, he had the feeling that local Amerindian children weren't able to see it, as if the airship was so inconceivable to them that it was invisible. He explains that when Captain Cook first landed on a Pacific island, the native Maoris apparently didn't see the boats because the concept of such a thing was beyond their bounds of perception. They couldn't comprehend the existence of such a thing. It's a wonderful idea, but doesn't sound very likely. After all, the Aztecs could clearly see the Spanish fleet of Cortés, and in the *Florentine Codex* there are accurate descriptions and illustrations of a sighting of distant galleons and the landing of ships. However unfamiliar the concept of a galleon was to them, the Aztecs could still see them. Human figures in ancient Egyptian art are shown only in profile, but the fact that the Egyptians didn't represent perspective doesn't mean they couldn't recognise and understand it in real life.

There is an image in The Flying Doctors of East Africa *of five Irish doctors.*

We see them from head to toe, staring into the lens, as they sur- reptitiously start to shuffle about as a group. "I don't want to move the camera towards you because I don't have a dolly and the shot would be too shaky," I explained, "but perhaps you can move imperceptibly towards me, as if you're floating." They were half embarrassed and half bemused, but as they start edging forward, an instantaneous empathy develops between them and us.

During the filming of *Flying Doctors* I shot some sequences for *Fata Morgana* in Tanzania and Kenya with cameraman Thomas Mauch. Then we went to Uganda with the intention of filming with John Okello, the man who a few years before had staged a rebel- lion in Zanzibar and declared himself field marshal and president. I had read wild stories about him in various newspapers; he was also the mastermind behind the atrocities committed against the Arab population there. I never did find Okello, though I corresponded with him for a time because he wanted me to translate his book into German and publish it,* something I never did, though a cou- ple of years later I named a character in *Aguirre, the Wrath of God* after him because the film owes something to his hysterical and atrocious fantasies. He would deliver incredible speeches from his aeroplane directly through to the radio, things like, "I, your field marshal, am about to land. Anyone stealing so much as a piece of soap will be slung into prison for 225 years." The tone of Okello's rants was a strong influence on the language that Aguirre uses. Near the end of his journey through the jungle, he warns his troops that anyone who eats so much as a single extra grain of corn will be locked up for 155 years, and whoever thinks about deserting will be cut into 198 pieces, then trampled on until his body can be used to paint walls.

Did you go to the desert with a script for Fata Morgana *or was your plan just to document whatever you found?*

I never look for stories to tell; instead they assail me, and I knew there was something I needed to film in Africa. To me, those

---

* *Revolution in Zanzibar* (East African Publishing House, 1967).

primordial and archetypal desert landscapes, strewn with debris, look completely unreal, as if from another planet; they had fascinated me since my first visit to the continent. But *Fata Morgana* soon became an extremely difficult ordeal, something that rubbed off on the general feel of *Even Dwarfs Started Small*, which was made almost immediately afterwards. Although I was cautious in Africa, things always went wrong for me there. I'm not one of those Hemingway Kilimanjaro nostalgia types who tracks animals through the underbrush with an elephant gun while being fanned by natives. Africa is a place that has always left me nervous, a feeling I will probably never be able to shake off due to my experiences there as a young man. What I experienced on the shoot of *Fata Morgana* was no different.

We shot the film in bursts, starting at the end of 1968, then returned in the middle of 1969 and December of that year, and finally went back the following year during the summer. At no point was there a script; we filmed with no coherent sense of what we might do with the footage once we got home. My original idea was to go to the southern Sahara and shoot a science-fiction story involving aliens and ancient astronauts from the planet Uxmal in the Andromeda Nebula who arrive on Earth with a camera and film the planet and its inhabitants. They want to prepare a report for folks back home, but their spacecraft crashes. In the debris we humans discover their footage and edit the material into a kind of investigative film, a report of a strange, unknown planet, which enables us to see how aliens perceive us and our world.

On the first day of shooting I decided to scrap this idea. The visionary aspects of the desert landscape that had taken hold of me were much more powerful than any ideas I had brought with me, so I junked the story, opened my eyes and ears, and filmed the desert mirages. I asked no questions; I just let it happen. My reactions to what I was seeing around me were like those of an eighteen-month-old baby exploring the world for the first time. The film is like those moments when you are half asleep in the early morning and a series of wild, uncontrollable things flow through your mind. These are rarely orderly thoughts and images, yet they belong to you and have a mysterious coherence to them. It was as if I had woken up after a night of drunkenness and experienced a moment of real clarity. All I had to do was capture what I was seeing and I would have my film. Every night when I slept in the desert, I forgot about what I had shot the previous day. I worked as if in a dream or hallucination, never asking myself questions during the shoot or thinking about how to structure the material I was gathering. I went to sleep in the sand without the faintest idea of what I was going to film the following day. Interestingly, there does remain in *Fata Morgana* a distant echo of science fiction, with its imagery of the beauty, harmony and horror of a world that is obviously our own, even though it seems like a distant alien planet.

What is a Fata Morgana?

A mirage, one which you can actually film in the desert. You can't capture hallucinations – which are only in your own mind – on celluloid, but mirages are something different. A mirage is a mirror reflection of an object that exists and that you can see. It's similar to you taking a photograph of yourself in the bathroom mirror. You aren't really there in the reflection, but you can still capture the image of yourself on celluloid. The best example is the sequence of the bus on the horizon, which was shot with a long telephoto lens. The vehicle seems to be almost floating on water, and it looks as if the people are gliding alone. We filmed much of *Fata Morgana* in the afternoon, when the heat – which that day was truly beyond belief – creates a strange hallucinatory quality. We were extremely thirsty and knew some of the buses had supplies of ice and cooled water on board, so immediately after filming we all rushed over there. From a distance the bus looked as if it were no more than a mile away, but we couldn't find a single trace of anything. No tyre tracks, no tracks at all. There was nothing there, nor had there ever been anything there, and yet we had been able to film it. There must have been a bus somewhere – maybe twenty or a hundred or three hundred miles away – which was visible to us because of the heated strata of air that reflected the image of this vehicle.

The opening sequence was filmed at Munich airport one hot summer's day and is comprised of eight shots of eight different aeroplanes landing one after the other, starting early in the morning. The hotter the air became, the more the heat shimmered and distorted the images. Eventually something visionary sets in – like fever dreams – and it remains for the rest of the film. The more aeroplanes that land, the stronger the sense of unreality. I had the feeling that audiences who were still watching by the sixth or seventh landing would stay to the end of the film; the opening sequence lays out the challenge of what is to come. The first three minutes allow viewers to acclimatise themselves to *Fata Morgana*'s unusual tone. They divide the audience into those who walk out, those who fall asleep and those whose eyes remain affixed.

You filmed in the Sahara.

Deserts are mysterious places. The Sahara is so unreal it's like being in a perpetual dream or on another planet. It isn't merely a landscape, it's a way of life. The solitude is the most overwhelming thing; a hushed quality envelops everything. At night the stars are so close that you can harvest them with your outstretched hands. Although we were driving, the spirit of our journey was like one made on foot, something only people who have travelled through the desert can truly understand. My time there was part of an ongoing quest.

There were four of us: me; Hans Dieter Sauer, a mountain climber who had studied geophysics and had already crossed the Sahara several times; photographer Gunther Freyse; and cameraman Jörg Schmidt-Reitwein. The whole thing started rather unfortunately. On our first day, barely out of Munich, I accidentally banged the hood of one of the cars down on Schmidt-Reitwein's hand. The bones in one of his fingers were smashed and he needed special steel wire to fix everything in place. We drove down to Marseilles in two cars, which we also slept in because we couldn't afford hotels, and from there to Africa. Once we reached the desert there were real technical problems. The emulsion on raw stock doesn't take heat well, and at one point it was more than 120°F in the shade. During sandstorms it was impossible to keep the cameras totally sealed and free of sand; we spent days cleaning them and finding ways to keep the raw stock cool. You don't notice how much you sweat in the desert – particularly a salt desert – because it evaporates immediately, so drinking a minimum of eight litres of water is imperative. Freyse was so thirsty he started fantasising about wells and declared he was going to jump, ass first, into the next one we found. Fortunately I checked before he leapt. It was more than two hundred feet deep, and empty.

I looked at various books beforehand and had a vague idea of where I wanted to go. We visited the salt flats of Chott el Djerid, before heading south to the Hoggar mountains in the Algerian desert, then to the Republic of Niger, where we ran straight into a sandstorm that took several days to recover from. By the time we reached the southern Sahara it was the start of the rainy season, and the sudden flash floods became the most serious problem. More people die in the Sahara from flooding than from dehydration. I still remember the thunderstorms and lightning that lit up the sky with such intensity that you could have stood outside, in the middle of the night, and read a newspaper. We planned to arrive during the hottest time of year because that was the best moment to film mirages, so we had no choice but to accept these fierce challenges of nature and particularly difficult conditions. After that we drove to Côte d'Ivoire to film in a lagoon, which is where the procession and chants I used in *Even Dwarfs Started Small* were shot. I wanted to go back to Uganda to film up in the Ruwenzori mountains – where there is a kind of prehistoric landscape with unusually mysterious and luxurious vegetation ten thousand feet up – but we weren't able to cross Nigeria because of the raging civil war. Eventually we decided to head to the Congo, and ended up travelling to Cameroon by boat, then heading northeast overland.

Almost immediately after arriving in Cameroon, things got completely out of hand. There had been an abortive *coup d'état* in the country a few weeks before we arrived. All four of us were arrested because Schmidt-Reitwein had the bad luck of having a name similar to that of a German mercenary the authorities were looking for and who had been sentenced to death *in absentia*. They were convinced they had caught a wanted man, so we were thrown into a narrow cell with no water, food or light and sixty other men. For many it was standing room only, and someone in there was close to death after having been badly beaten. Whenever anyone used the toilet bucket in the corner, everyone would shout and sing obscene songs, but when I sat on the bucket the whole place went dead silent. I fervently prayed for them to make noise. I don't want to go into details, but we were no longer in control of the situation. Schmidt-Reitwein and I both contracted malaria and bilharzia, a blood parasite. We were unable to contact the German embassy, and when we finally got out, quite ill, there was still a warrant out for us – either on purpose or because the slovenly officials had forgotten to withdraw it – so we were arrested again. We stopped shooting only when we were too sick to continue. On arrival in Bangui, in the Central African Republic, we took an aeroplane back to Germany. We had been in the desert for three months.

Fata Morgana was a difficult film to make, but I learnt how to wrestle something creative from a bad set of circumstances and come up with something clear, transparent and pure. Two months later I was in Lanzarote, in the Canary Islands, to start work on *Even Dwarfs Started Small*, which is where I finished shooting *Fata Morgana*.

Who are the people in the film?

We stumbled across them, including the woman on the piano and the guy with goggles playing the drums who play some of the saddest music I have ever heard. I gave him the goggles and stuck black paper over them so he couldn't see anything. We shot that scene in a brothel in Lanzarote during production on *Even Dwarfs Started Small*; she's actually the madam and he's a pimp. He was in charge of discipline and would beat any prostitute who hadn't pleased her client. In some way the film is about ruined people in ruined places, and that sequence spoke of a terrible sadness and despair. There is one rather strange image in the film which I shot on Lanzarote, amidst its bizarre rock formations, where grapes for Malvasia wine are grown. We encountered a busload of Western tourists, who I asked to climb down into the holes in the ground and go as crazy as they could, flailing about. I think it was in the Republic of Niger where we met the nurse who stands in the puddle with the children, teaching them to say "*Blitzkrieg ist Wahnsinn*" ["War is madness"]. I found a boy with a pet fennec fox and asked him to hold it up to the camera. I promised he would be well paid if he didn't move or blink. He stood absolutely still for ten minutes, then walked away.

To this day I find the man who reads the letter he takes from his pocket very moving. He was a German who lived in great poverty in Algeria, a former foreign legionnaire who fought on the side of the French against the Algerian revolutionaries, but at one point during the war he had deserted and switched sides. I liked the attitude of the villagers who took care of him; the Muslim world deals with people like this with great dignity. By the time we met him he had basically lost his mind and was carrying a letter that had been written by his mother probably fifteen years before. You can see it's in tatters; he had kept it under his shirt all this time. He proudly read the letter to us on camera, but I always felt that he wasn't actually reading it, just inventing something. I think he had forgotten how to read and write. There is great sadness here; it's obvious he'll never get home again. The man wearing goggles with the reptiles was from Switzerland and had clearly been out in the sun too long. He owned the little hotel where we stayed during the shooting of *Even Dwarfs Started Small*; at the time it was the only one on the island, inconceivable now when you see what the place has become after the infection of tourism. Under the cliffs of Bandiagara in Mali we filmed an old man with his medals – probably awarded for his service with the French army – standing next to a boy carrying a radio, then walking slowly towards the camera. He spoke to us in a Dogon dialect. To this day I have never asked anyone to translate it.

The long tracking shot of the sand dunes was done from the roof of our VW van. It took real work because we spent days smoothing out the terrain before we filmed. Vast areas needed to be cleared up – something we did ourselves under incredible heat – because I felt that one six-minute shot would be more interesting than a series of short shots. Schmidt-Reitwein was on the roof of the car with the camera, and I was driving, with one eye on the dunes. It was important to understand how to move with the rhythm and sensuousness of the landscape, so I was constantly slowing down and speeding up. All the strange machinery you see in the film, these absurd and desolate fragments of civilisation simmering under the sun, was part of an abandoned Algerian army depot. We would find things lying in the middle of the desert – a cement mixer or something like that – a thousand miles from the nearest major settlement or town. Was it ancient astronauts who placed these things there? Were they man-made? If so, what purpose could they possibly serve? These are the embarrassed landscapes of our planet, the kinds of images that appear throughout my work, from *Fata Morgana* to *Lessons of Darkness* and beyond.

The structure of the film was conceived during editing.

There were no opportunities to look at rushes while we were shooting, and once we finished filming I had no clear idea what had been shot, so the editing of *Fata Morgana* was a more important process to me than it had been on my work up to that point, though in a strange way the film's rhythm was still established during shooting. We brought the footage home and ploughed through everything. The film has a three-part structure: "Creation," "Paradise" and "The Golden Age." During editing I looked at every shot and said, "This belongs to the first part and this to the last." Some of the images I organised, some organised themselves.

As I sat watching the footage, I felt that a Mayan text I had stumbled across when living in Mexico – the sacred book of the Quiché Indians, *Popol Vuh*, one of the most beautiful things I have ever read – corresponded to the images I was looking at. *Popol Vuh* consists of long passages on the heroic exploits of the first migrations, and I decided to adapt the Creation myths at the beginning of the book for the voiceover of "Creation," the film's first third, in which we see a wrecked aeroplane, piles of machinery, empty oil drums, the flames of a refinery and the carcasses of rotting animals. In *Popol Vuh* we learn that the initial creation of the earth was such a failure that the gods started again – I think it was four times – and by the end they had entirely wiped out the people they had originally created. I found all this particularly interesting because I never felt connected to the Christian concept of Creation I had grown up with, one that culminates in a planet of equilibrium and beauty. There is something primordial and anarchic about Mayan myths that goes beyond our Western way of thinking. They remind me of Hieronymus Bosch's triptych *The Garden of Earthly Delights*, in the first part of which he shows us Paradise, in which something dark and ominous, almost cannibalistic, lurks; we see a creature that has caught something in its mouth, but Adam and Eve are oblivious. Murder and disaster are implanted in part one of the painting and inevitably spread into the other two panels. According to Bosch, Hell – on the right side of the triptych – is inevitable because during Creation, on the left side, God made so many mistakes. The other two sections of the film – "Paradise" and "The Golden Age" – use texts that I mostly wrote myself. "Paradise," in which the voiceover announces that "The gates of Paradise are open to everybody," is full of damaged people, like the impoverished quarry workers covered head to toe in slaked lime. There is also a bizarre, unfinished factory being constructed in the middle of the desert, hundreds of miles from any human habitation. No one could tell us what it was for or who was building it.

Fata Morgana remains close to my heart because two remarkable people assisted me with the film. One was Lotte Eisner, who did the original German voiceover and about whom I will talk later. I travelled to her Paris apartment with a Nagra and recorded it in a single take, with no rehearsals. The other was historian Amos Vogel, who refined the English translation I did of the voiceover. Amos was a remarkable man, a true visionary and great film scholar who was a mentor to me for decades. He grew up in Vienna and escaped with his family from Austria before the Holocaust, eventually arriving in New York, where he established the film club Cinema 16. Later he was instrumental in creating the New York Film Festival, which he ran for several years. I first met Amos at the Oberhausen Film Festival in the mid-sixties, where he stood up for a film of mine that had been derided by the crowd. "Do whatever you want," he said. "Boo and hiss as loud as you can. This film will outlive us all." He was a deeply impressive man, the person who one day, out of the blue, said to me, "You look like someone who should have children." I named my first son after him: Rudolph Amos Ahmed Herzog. The name Ahmed comes from the last surviving workman from my grandfather's excavation on Kos; he was seven years old when my grandfather took him in and gave him a job. Ahmed was overjoyed that I made the journey to Kos, at the age of fifteen, so many decades later, and took me on a tour of the site where my grandfather had worked. He opened all the empty drawers and cupboards in his house, proclaiming, "This is all yours!" Ahmed appears briefly in *Signs of Life*, and even today I find seeing his dignified presence on screen a moving experience. The Greek children would make fun of him because he was a Muslim who prayed so many times a day. He even wanted me to marry his granddaughter. I politely declined, but promised I would have children one day and name the first of them after him. So my first son ended up with three names.

The music in Fata Morgana *always fits the images.*

The tracking shot of the dunes felt like a feminine landscape, and by playing a recording of a women's choir singing Mozart's *Coronation Mass* audiences are seized more powerfully by the shot. Some images become clearer and more understandable when a particular piece of music is playing behind them. They don't physically change, but their inner qualities are exposed and new perspectives opened up. Music is able to make visible what is latent; it reveals new things to us, helps shift our perception and enables us to see deeper into things. We perceive what we would otherwise be oblivious to. An image might not be logical in a narrative sense, but when music is added – even if it somehow disrupts and undermines that image – certain qualities might all of a sudden become transparent that were previously unknown. This can work the other way round, when a piece of music is transformed and resonates with new meaning if juxtaposed with a specific image.

Look at the opening moments of *The Enigma of Kaspar Hauser* with the boat, the tower and the washerwoman. Some of those shots were filmed with a telephoto lens, on top of which I mounted a wide-angle lens, which gives an eerie quality. These images might not make strict sense in terms of the story, but they acquire a dynamic internal logic when accompanied by an aria from Mozart's *The Magic Flute*. Listen carefully to the soundtrack during the lengthy shot of the windmills in *Signs of Life*, which is as important as the imagery. I started by taking the recording of nearly a thousand people clapping at the end of a concert, then distorting it electronically until it sounded like pieces of wood clacking together. I added another sound, what you hear when you put your ear on a telegraph pole and the wind passes through the wires. As children we called it "angel song." This constructed soundtrack doesn't physically alter the thousands of windmills or the landscape, but it does change the way we look at them. This is what I have always tried to render in my films: a new perspective, one that touches us deeper than realistic sounds and images. Such things are beyond verbal explanation; combining images with music is a wholly intuitive process. The point is that there is no such thing as background music in my films. It's always an integral part of the whole.

There are very few directors who truly understand the possibilities of music in cinema. Two exceptions come to mind, both of whom are extraordinarily lucid in their use of music: Satyajit Ray and the Taviani brothers. I doff my hat to them. In the Taviani brothers' *Padre Padrone* the music suddenly starts up and builds until an entire landscape appears to be in mourning. The film won the Palme d'Or at Cannes, but the television network in West Germany that co-produced the film said it wasn't going to release it theatrically and would screen it only on television. "No matter what your contract might say," I told the television executives, "this film will be released in cinemas." The next day Volker Schlöndorff and I, along with several other filmmakers and my young son, chained ourselves to the gates of a cinema in Munich in protest. The film is about a shepherd, so we brought a sheep with us. The press reports of this stunt somehow triggered various people to ask the fundamental question: why can't we see *Padre Padrone* on the big screen? Eventually the film – which remains one of my favourites – was released in cinemas, and I reviewed it for a newspaper.*

You chose not to release Fata Morgana.

Today I can see elements of the film in my more recent work, like *The Wild Blue Yonder* and *Encounters at the End of the World*, with the images of the Ross Ice Shelf and tunnels under the South Pole and the frozen sturgeon. But immediately after finishing *Fata Morgana* I had a feeling it was inaccessible to audiences, that they would ridicule it. It seemed dangerously fragile, like a cobweb, and I didn't consider it a robust or releasable piece of work. Sometimes it's better to keep things under wraps, passing them from friend to friend, never making them public. Only after several generations

---

* "Vom Ende des Analphabetismus," *Die Zeit*, 24 November 1978. In his review, Herzog compares the Taviani brothers' film to two other recent books published in Germany, all "cases of village illiterates who, through appalling suffering, liberate themselves from backwardness and isolation by their own strength. At the same time these books illuminate something else, the fact that the phenomenon of illiteracy has another side to it. It is a form of experience and intelligence which is necessarily being lost in our civilisation, a cultural asset disappearing from the Earth." Translated by Martina Lauster.

should a film be released. I held on to *Fata Morgana* for almost two years without showing it, but was deviously tricked by my friends Henri Langlois, founder of the Cinémathèque Française, and Lotte Eisner, who worked there as a curator. They borrowed a print and screened it at the Cannes Film Festival. When I saw the public's reaction, I knew the film could be shown in other places too, including the New York Film Festival. It was eventually released and considered by some people as one of the first European art-house psychedelic films, a genre with which it has absolutely no connection. Today, more than forty years later, *Fata Morgana* is very much alive to audiences; it's like nothing they have ever seen before, and everyone comes away with their own understanding. Perhaps more than any other of my films, it needs to be completed by those who watch it, which means all feelings, thoughts and interpretations are welcome.

Why dwarfs in Even Dwarfs Started Small?

German culture is full of them, from the earliest fairy tales through to Wagner and *The Tin Drum*. The dwarfs in the film aren't freaks; these are well-proportioned and beautiful midgets. If you are only two feet tall, it's the world around you that's completely out of proportion: motorcycles are monstrous, beds and door handles are huge, the world of commerce is grotesque, and education, table manners and religious education are all horrific abnormalities. Even flowerpots have the strangest of dimensions. If the film has a "message," it's that we and the society we have constructed for ourselves – with oppressive and institutionalised violence, rules and regulations – are monstrous, not the dwarfs. We all have something dwarfish, inadequate, impotent and insignificant inside us, as if there is an essence or concentrated form of each of us screaming to escape, a perfectly formed representation of who we are. Think about the laughter we hear at the end of the film, which is laughter that can never be surpassed. A very real nightmare for some people is knowing that deep down they are a dwarf. Sometimes, when I was working on the film, I woke up in terror and had to feel about with my arms and legs. Was I still as big as I was when I went to sleep? Reactions to *Even Dwarfs Started Small* seem to depend on people's feelings about their inner dwarf.

Where did you find the actors?

When you find one midget you find several, so for a year I went from one to the next, hiring everyone. They were happy to make the film, and I would always ask their opinions about what was or wasn't suitable. For the first time they were able to reveal their real personalities to the world. If the dwarfs are good in the film, it's because they express genuine humanity, and by doing so affirm their dignity. A deep relationship formed between the actors and the crew, and after a week of working with them I completely forgot they were so tiny. They really got into the spirit of things. The one up on the roof of the car as it goes round in circles was truly a bold little guy, and he was actually run over by this automobile. I thought he was dead, but he scrambled to his feet, proud of having done something that would usually have been entrusted to a stuntman. Later in the film, when the dwarfs burn the flowerpots, they really did water them with gasoline. All of a sudden this same dwarf caught fire. The crew stood there, looking at him as he burned like a Christmas tree, so I ran over and smothered him beneath me to extinguish the flames. Fortunately only his ear was singed.

Incidents like these led to a little side event being reported in almost every biography of me. As I have already explained, being on equal terms with the crew and actors is vital. A director should never be safe behind the camera while everyone else is alone out there. The day this little guy caught fire, I told everyone, "If all of you get out of this film unscathed, if you're unhurt at the end, I will jump into that field of cacti. Get your 8mm cameras ready. I'm going to do the big leap into the plants for you." I thought I should give them something for their family album, the way kids on snowboards leap up into the air and strike a pose. I put on some goggles to protect my eyes and jumped from a ramp, but miscalculated. I can tell you that getting out is more difficult than jumping in. Any old idiot can make the leap, but it takes great skill to extricate yourself from something like that. The spines were the size of my fingers. I don't think there are any left embedded. The body seems to absorb them eventually.

Where is the film set?

In the published script it says the story takes place near San

Cristóbal, in Chiapas, Mexico, at an institution for juvenile offenders. But I couldn't say for sure.

We filmed for five weeks, and were especially careful with the sound because I knew it was important to record all the dialogue live. Hombre's unique high-pitched voice is the reason you could never dub a film like this into another language. On the first day of shooting I discovered he had an extraordinarily shrill laugh, so I would grab and tickle him when he wasn't expecting it. "Your laughter is more important than any spoken words in this film," I told him. I found his laughter – which he would secretly rehearse – so astonishing that I decided it would carry the end of the film, with the shot of him and the dromedary as he literally laughs himself to death. In the final frames it's almost as if he is screaming for help. That one sequence sums up the whole film. "Give it your best laughter," I told him. "This is your big moment. Go wild. We'll shoot it only once, but make sure you give the ultimate performance. You'll be the last thing in the film." He gave it everything he had and even started to cough, but kept on going. If I had gone back three weeks later, he would have still been there. Eventually the moment came when I couldn't take it any longer. "This really is too much," I said to myself. "Let's go home. End of film."

The scene with the car that drives round in circles – an image you also see at the end of *Stroszek* – was inspired by a real experience of mine. When I was a teenager I had an absurd job as a parking attendant at the Oktoberfest. There was an area filled with Ferris wheels and other rides next to a gigantic meadow, which was used as a parking lot, and every night I had to cope with two thousand drunkards. The Bavarian police weren't much help; they would let people drive off unless they were half unconscious. Some were so far gone I confiscated their keys and hoisted them from their cars. They wouldn't even bother getting up and just fell asleep there and then. Sometimes I would take an automobile, lock the steering wheel in place, step out and let it drive around in circles until it ran out of gas.

Where does the opening music come from?

I asked a young girl, perhaps eleven years old, from Lanzarote to sing a local song, which I recorded in a cave, gaving it a strange, unique sound. "Sing until your soul departs," I said. "Sing your lungs out of your body." What she did has something wild and ecstatic about it, and corresponds perfectly with the rest of the film. *Even Dwarfs Started Small* also has music that I originally recorded for *Fata Morgana*: a thousand-person choir in a cathedral at Grand Lahou in Côte d'Ivoire. I had gone there because someone claiming to be the Messiah had created his own little state where a group of people lived; he would preach in the cathedral and perform miracles for the locals. We went there on a Sunday and encountered an extraordinary procession and beautiful singing. If you look carefully, you'll find other things from *Fata Morgana* that seeped into *Even Dwarfs Started Small*, like the goggles the two blind dwarfs wear. In many ways the films intermingle.

How different do you think Even Dwarfs Started Small *would have been if your experiences in the desert had been less harrowing?*

When I returned to Lanzarote I was still much affected by sickness and the hardships of the production of *Fata Morgana*. The resulting film became much more radical than I had originally planned, and when I look back, it's clear I made *Even Dwarfs Started Small* to free myself from recent bad memories; *Aguirre* looks like kindergarten in comparison. Somehow I had the feeling that if Goya and Bosch had the guts to do their gloomiest stuff, why shouldn't I? There was such pressure inside me that I felt the necessity to share these visions. Up until that point my other films had been quite discreet, but *Even Dwarfs Started Small* screams loudly at audiences. When it was first screened in cinemas, I asked projectionists to turn up the volume because I felt the film's impact would be diminished if it weren't loud enough. It all sounds so gloomy when I talk about it here, but the film has a genuinely playful tone and is actually a comedy. Destroying everything they can find and turning everything upside down has been a truly memorable day for the midgets; you can see the joy in their faces. Audiences walk out aching from laughter.

The film wasn't widely seen.

In West Germany at the time we had something called *Freiwillige Selbstkontrolle*, which was essentially voluntary censorship. After the Nazi era, the West German constitution refused to accept any sort of censorship, though the film industry had a self-imposed set of rules. You weren't legally obliged to submit your films to the censorship board, and if you chose to bypass it there were no penalties per se, but distributors generally wouldn't touch films that hadn't been passed, and most cinemas refused to screen them. I submitted *Even Dwarfs Started Small*, and the board banned it from the first to the last minute. I appealed the decision and said they would be forever ashamed if the film went unseen in West Germany, then rented a handful of cinemas in a couple of towns to screen it myself. Eventually it was released uncut, and I got several death threats. A white-supremacist militia from Bavaria called every week to tell me I was second on their "to kill" list. To this day the film has never been broadcast on German television.

Even Dwarfs Started Small was accused of being anarchistic and blasphemous, which I suppose it is. The film certainly breaks a number of taboos, though none of the criticisms bothered me because time always somehow allocates the correct significance to things. The animal-rights people were furious at the scene in which the monkey is tied to the cross and paraded about, though we used soft wool to hold the creature down. The religious song the dwarfs sing meant the Catholics were also breathing down my neck, and the final scene caused problems because a rumour went around that to get the dromedary on its knees for so long I cut its sinews. I quickly learnt that you can't kill a rumour with a fact; you kill it only with an even wilder rumour. I immediately issued a statement explaining that I had actually nailed the dromedary to the ground. That shut everybody up. In reality the creature was a docile and well-trained animal whose owner was standing two feet outside the frame giving it orders. He was trying to confuse the dromedary by constantly giving it conflicting orders by hand: sit down, stand up, stand still. Not knowing what to do, the animal defecated in despair, something that looks exquisite on screen.

The only film I can think of that has a similar quality to *Even Dwarfs Started Small* is Tod Browning's *Freaks*, which, with its exceptionally dark vision, I consider to be one of the greatest films ever made. I hadn't actually seen *Freaks* when I made my film, but after finally watching it I was overjoyed to discover that forty years before me there was a filmmaker doing something comparable.

Although the monsters in *Freaks* are portrayed with real tenderness, it seems that Browning was apologetic about his film, and maybe never knew what a great piece of work he had created.

You have described your films as "the articulation of collective dreams."

The images in my films are your images too. Somehow, deep in your subconscious, you find them, dormant, lurking, like sleeping friends; they correspond with the inner landscapes inside us all and strike directly into the soul of man. Occasionally – perhaps only a dozen times throughout my life – I have read a text, listened to a piece of music, watched a film or studied a painting and felt that my existence has been illuminated. Even if centuries are being bridged, I instantly feel I'm not so alone in the universe. Watching one of my films is like receiving a letter announcing you have a long-lost brother, that your own flesh and blood is out there in a form you had never previously experienced. This is one reason why so many people around the world seem to connect with my films, which represent the universal visions buried within us all. None of my work is subject to trends or historical movements.

In no way would I compare myself to the man, but allow me to cite his name to make a point. I once went to the Vatican to see Michelangelo's frescoes in the Sistine Chapel. I was overwhelmed by the feeling that before he started painting, no one had articulated and depicted human pathos with such clarity. Pathos had always existed, but Michelangelo was the first to really express it. Since then we have been able to understand ourselves that much deeper. The purpose of the filmmaker is to record and guide, as chroniclers of past centuries did. Like many people who express themselves through images or writing, I am seeking some insight into human nature. There's nothing exceptional about this; most painters and writers with any skill are working away at the same thing. It isn't that I'm particularly inventive, only that I am able to awaken certain feelings and thoughts inside of you. I can see, on the horizon, unpronounced and unproclaimed images. I can sense the hypnotic qualities of things that to everyone else look unobtrusive, then excavate and articulate these collective dreams with some clarity.

74

Apparently you never dream at night.

Every morning upon waking I feel a deficit. "Again! Why haven't I dreamt?" This might be one reason why I make films. Maybe I want to create images for the screen that are so obviously absent from my head at night. Perhaps my films are a way of filling this void. Please note, however, that I constantly daydream.

You really never dream?

It's very much a singular event for me, perhaps once every couple of years. And my dreams – always in monochrome – are very prosaic, something like me eating a sandwich. Do the psychoanalysts really want to spend time on that?

3

Adequate Imagery

Do you have an ideology, something that drives you beyond mere storytelling?

"Mere storytelling," as you put it, is enough for a film. Steven Spielberg's films might be full of special effects, but audiences appreciate them because at the centre of each is a well-crafted story. Spielberg deserves the position he is in because he understands something that those who are concerned only with the fireworks of flashy visuals don't. If a story in a narrative film doesn't function, that film won't function.

My films come to me very much alive, like dreams, without explanation. I never think about what it all means. I think only about telling a story, and however illogical the images, I let them invade me. An idea comes to me, and then, over a period of time – perhaps while driving or walking – this blurred vision becomes clearer in my mind, pulling itself into focus. I see the film before me, as if it were playing on a screen, and it soon becomes so transparent that I can sit and write it all down, describing the images passing through my mind. I don't write a script if I can't see and hear the entire film – characters, dialogue, music, locations – in my head. I have never written a screenplay for anyone else because I see my stories in a certain way and don't want anyone else to touch them. When I write, I sit in front of the computer and pound the keys. I start at the beginning and write fast, leaving out anything that isn't necessary, aiming at all times for the hard core of the narrative. I can't write without that urgency. Something is wrong if it takes more than five days to finish a screenplay. A story created this way will always be full of life. I saw the whole of *Even Dwarfs Started Small* as a continuous nightmare in front of my eyes and was extremely disciplined while typing so I wouldn't make any mistakes. I just let it all pour out and didn't make more than five typos in the entire screenplay.

People sense I am well orientated, that I know where I have come from and where I'm headed, so it's understandable that they search for some guiding ideology behind my work. But no such thing exists as far as I'm concerned. There is never some philosophical idea that guides a film through the veil of a story. All I can say is that I understand the world in my own way and am capable of articulating this understanding through stories and images that are coherent to others. I don't like to drop names, but what sort of an ideology would you push under the shirt of Conrad or Hemingway or Kafka? Goya or Caspar David Friedrich? Even after watching my films, it bothers some audiences that they are unable to put their finger on what my credo might be. Grasp this with a pair of pliers, but the credo is the films themselves and my ability to make them. This is what troubles those people who have forever viewed my work with tunnel vision, as if they were looking through a straw they picked up at McDonald's. They keep searching. No wonder they get desperate.

Some of these milkshake-drinkers have located themes running throughout your work.

Apparently so, but don't ask me to do the same. A film is a projection of light that becomes something else only when it crosses the gaze of the audience, with the viewer able to connect what he is looking at with something deeper within himself. Everyone completes images and stories in a different way because everyone's perspective is unique, so it's never been a good idea for me to explain what my films might mean. The opinion of the public, however different from my own, is sacred. Whenever anyone asks me if Stroszek kills himself at the end of *Stroszek*, I tell them they're free to choose the ending that best works for them. If anyone is expecting a statement from me on such matters, it would be best if they put this book down right now and poured themselves a glass of wine. Consider this line from Walt Whitman: "Behold I do not give lectures or a little charity. When I give I give myself." None of my films were made following deep philosophical contemplation. My way of expressing certain ideas – our deep-rooted hopes and gnawing fears – is by rendering them visible on screen.

Those hordes who write about cinema have often been trained to think in certain ways, to analyse a body of work and investigate apparent connections, to bring certain rigid, fashionable theories to bear and show off everything they know while doing so. They read their own intellectual make-up and approach to life into my films, apparently deciphering things that for me don't need to be deciphered, and by churning out page after page of unappealing prose actually obscure and confuse. It doesn't mean they're right, it doesn't mean they're wrong. They function in their world, and I in mine. I want to appeal to people's instincts before anything else. When I present an audience with a new film I hope they bring only their hearts and minds, plus a little sympathy. I ask for no more than that. Film isn't the art of scholars but of illiterates. It should be looked at straight on, without any prefabricated ideas, which is something Henri Langlois knew all too well. At the Cinémathèque Française he would screen films from around the world – in Bengali, Chinese, Japanese, Portuguese – without subtitles. It means audiences had to cultivate a kind of intelligence and intensity of vision that has little to do with rational thought. They almost developed their own sense of illiteracy, tapping into an innate but usually long-dormant facility.

You must be able to see some connections between your films.

People say I'm an outsider, but even if everyone finds me eccentric, I know I'm standing at the centre. There is nothing eccentric about my films; it's everything else that's eccentric. I never felt that Kaspar Hauser, for example, was an outsider. He might have been continually forced to the sidelines, he might have stood apart from everyone, but he's at the true heart of things. Everyone around him, with their deformed souls, transformed into domesticated pigs and members of bourgeois society, they are the bizarre ones. Aguirre, Fini Straubinger and Stroszek all fit into this pattern. So do Walter Steiner, Hias in *Heart of Glass*, Woyzeck, Fitzcarraldo, the Aborigines of *Where the Green Ants Dream* and the desert people of *Fata Morgana*. Look at Reinhold Messner, Jean-Bédel Bokassa,

Nosferatu and even Kinski himself, or Vladimir Kokol, the young deaf and blind man in *Land of Silence and Darkness* who connects with the world only by bouncing a ball off his head and clutching a radio to his chest, much like Kaspar, who plays with his wooden horse. None of these people are pathologically mad. It's the society they find themselves in that's demented. Whether dwarfs, hallucinating soldiers or indigenous peoples, these individuals are not freaks.

I have always felt that my characters – fictional or non-fictional – all belong to the same family. It isn't easy to put my finger on exactly what binds them together, but if a member of the clan were walking about town, you would intuitively and instantly recognise them. If you were to sit and watch all my films in one go, you would see the cross-references, the relationships and similarities between characters. They have no shadows, they emerge from the darkness without a past, they are misunderstood and humiliated. If you turned on the television and saw ten seconds of something, you would immediately know it must be one of mine. I look at my films as one big story, a vast, interconnected work I have been concentrating on for fifty years. Like the separate bricks that make up a building, taken together they constitute something bigger than their individual parts.

Does investigation of these individuals tell us anything about their surroundings?

We learn more about the buildings, streets and structures of an unknown city by climbing to the top of an overlooking hill than by standing in its central square. Looking in from the outskirts, we come to understand the environments in which these characters live.

How close do you feel to the characters in your films?

I have a great deal of sympathy for these people, to the point where Jörg Schmidt-Reitwein joked that I should play everyone in my films myself. I function pretty well as an actor and in several of my films could have played the leading character if necessary. I could never make a film – fiction or non-fiction – about someone for whom I have no empathy, who fails to arouse some level of appreciation and curiosity. In fact, when it comes to Fini Straubinger in *Land of Silence and Darkness*, Bruno S. in *The Enigma of Kaspar*

Hauser or Dieter Dengler, these people are points of reference not just for my work, but also my life. I learnt so much from my time with them. The radical dignity they radiate is clearly visible in the films. There is something of what constitutes them inside me.

Do you watch television?

One of the great achievements of communal life is our ability to create narratives, something we have been doing since Neanderthal times. We should cherish this flame we all have inside of us and get on our knees to thank the Creator for having endowed us with the gift of storytelling, something cavemen huddled around campfires understood and appreciated. Instead, today, with television and its incessant commercials, our consumer culture has destroyed any semblance of dignity we might have once had. We are fragmenting and fracturing stories for the sake of business. We grow up enveloped by fifteen-second storytelling and are conditioned by filmmaking at breakneck pace. Decades from now, our great-great-grandchildren will look back with amazement at how we could have allowed a precious achievement of human culture like storytelling to be so disrespected, infected, then shredded by advertisements. It will be the same amazement we feel today when we look at our ancestors, for whom slavery, capital punishment, the burning of witches and the Inquisition were acceptable everyday events. We will be blamed for having not thrown hand grenades into television stations and laying waste to their institutionalised cowardice, for not taking up arms and occupying such debased places which venerate that single, pernicious god: the *Einschaltquote*, the ratings. It has always been their Golden Calf. It has nothing to do with me or my films.

Our culture today, especially television, infantilises us. The indignity of it kills our imagination. May I propose a Herzog dictum? Those who read own the world. Those who watch television lose it. Sitting at home on your own, in front of the screen, is a very different experience from being in the communal spaces of the world, those centres of collective dreaming. Television creates loneliness. This is why sitcoms have added laughter tracks which try to cheat you out of your solitude. Television is a reflection of the world in which we live, designed to appeal to the lowest common denominator. It kills spontaneous imagination and destroys our ability to entertain ourselves, painfully erasing our patience and sensitivity to significant detail.

Just when I think television can't get any more sordid and unadventurous, it does. Years ago the executive from the station that paid for *Little Dieter Needs to Fly* saw the film for the first time, and immediately asked where the men's room was because he said he needed to vomit. "This is unquestionably the worst film I have ever seen in my life," he said, before shifting it from a prime-time slot and burying it late at night, when hardly anyone was even awake, let alone watching his station. When the film won awards and received positive reviews, he told me that perhaps it wasn't so bad. One of my most recent experiences working with a television station was *Encounters at the End of the World*, which was a big success with audiences. There is a line in the voiceover where I speak about "the abomination of aerobic studios and yoga classes" down at McMurdo Station in Antarctica. The network executives insisted on cutting it because they didn't want to insult the housewives who might be watching, and washed their hands of the film by selling it for a tenth of what they had originally invested. It might also have been the word "evolution" – which one of the scientists uses in the film – that the network was unhappy with. Darwinism is a concept that's anathema for half of the United States' population. I hammer home to the participants of my Rogue Film School that they must brace themselves for such attitudes.

I sound so negative about all this, but fortunately there is another side to it. Television specialises in those early-morning satellite experiences, like the Muhammad Ali/George Foreman fight and the moon landing. I was so excited I almost had a heart attack before those. Over the last decade standards have risen when it comes to storytelling on television. It's wonderful to see audiences immersing themselves in such intelligent narratives that play out over a period of years. Many of these series are expertly written, acted and directed, with a great sense of pace and long-range timing.

Tell me about what you describe as the "inadequate imagery" of today's civilisation.

Our inability and lack of desire to seek fresh imagery means we are surrounded by worn-out, banal, useless and exhausted images, limping and dragging themselves behind the rest of our cultural evolution. When I look at postcards in tourist shops and the images and advertisements in magazines, or turn on the television, or walk into a travel agency and see huge posters with those same tedious images of the Grand Canyon, I sense that something dangerous is emerging. Just as a person without a memory will struggle to survive in this world, so will someone who lacks images that reflect his inner state.

We are, as a race, aware of certain dangers that surround us. We comprehend that global warming and overcrowding of the planet are real dangers for mankind. We have come to understand that the destruction of the environment is another enormous danger, that resources are being wasted at an extraordinary rate. But I believe that the lack of adequate imagery is a danger of the same magnitude, as serious a defect as being without memory. I'll repeat it again as long as I'm able to: we will die out like dinosaurs if we don't develop adequate images. We need to learn to adapt our visual language to new and unforeseen situations. If our ingenuity isn't up to the task, if we aren't able to create fresh images, we will be stunted in our growth, unable to face the unforeseen challenges charging at us. All too many images are at a standstill, and consequently meaningless. Look at the depiction of Jesus Christ in Western iconography, unchanged since the kitsch of the Nazarene school of painting in the late nineteenth century. Representations like this are sufficient proof that Christianity is moribund. Why doesn't anyone ever paint a chubby or laughing Jesus? Look at France in the 1870s, by which time the Industrial Revolution had transformed the country, yet its art still depicted the Napoleonic era. The Impressionists weren't describing the future, they were updating things. You see the same thing with language. In Latin America they speak a lively Spanish compared to formal Castilian Spanish, as if the conquest of the New World paralysed language back home, creating some kind of impasse that has yet to be overcome. When a language becomes immobile, unable to adapt, the culture that created it disappears into the abyss of history.

We need images in accordance with our civilisation and innermost conditioning, which is why I appreciate any film that searches for novelty, no matter in what direction it moves or what story it tells. Years ago I saw an astonishing four-hour film by

Theo Angelopoulos. Everyone said it was too long, but the images awoke new ideas in my mind, so to me it felt much too short. The struggle to find unprocessed imagery is never-ending, but it's our duty to dig like archaeologists and search our violated landscapes. We live in an era when established values are no longer valid, when prodigious discoveries are being made every year, when catastrophes of unbelievable proportions occur weekly. In ancient Greek the word "chaos" means "gaping void" or "yawning emptiness." The most effective response to the chaos in our lives is the creation of new forms of literature, music, poetry, art and cinema.

Who is willing to take the necessary risks?

I would never complain about how difficult it is to get images that belong to the recesses of the human heart, that show unexpected things we have never seen or experienced before, that are clear, pure and transparent. I would go absolutely anywhere; that's my nature. Down here on Earth it's hardly possible any more. I wouldn't hesitate for a second if given the chance to venture out with a camera to another planet in our solar system, even if it were a one-way ticket. It's frustrating to me that astronauts never take advantage of the photographic possibilities available to them. On one of the Apollo missions they left a camera on the moon, slowly panning from left to right, then right to left, for days. I yearned to grab the damned thing. There are so many possibilities up there for fresh images, and I always thought it would be better to send up a poet instead of an astronaut; I would be the first to volunteer. I did actually once seriously consider applying to NASA to be on one of their missions. Space travel is unfinished business for me, though these days I wouldn't be allowed. You need a complete set of teeth to get inside a spaceship.

Do you ever tire of travelling?

Jet lag is no friend of mine, believe me, and the cultural shock of moving from one place to the next is hard to absorb. I'll be at home in Los Angeles one day, then on an island off the coast of Panama the next. From there to Paris, the tropical jungles of Thailand, the desert terrain of North Africa and the mountains of South America, then back to the cold winds of Berlin. Living the way I do, having a real home is vital. It's essential I can wake up in the middle of the night and know where the light switch is. I would never travel without a book that requires great attention; it becomes my home into which I immerse myself. The truth is I am continually drained by travelling, but never tire of it. It has forever energised me.

Why does Land of Silence and Darkness *resonate so strongly?*

In contrast to *Even Dwarfs Started Small*, there's a lot of serenity in the film. *Land of Silence and Darkness* is particularly close to my heart; if it didn't exist there would be a hole in my life. Fini Straubinger – the fifty-six-year-old deaf and blind woman at the centre of the film – helped me understand something about loneliness to an extent I never had before.

Fini was outside of society and history. When I asked what she remembered about the Second World War, she explained that because she wasn't able to hear or see, the destruction barely registered for her. The only thing she perceived was hunger and the physicality of being led down into the cellar during bombing raids to take refuge from the explosions. In her case loneliness was taken to unimaginable limits, and I have the distinct impression that anyone seeing the film asks themselves, "What would be left of my life if I were deaf and blind? How could I live, overcome loneliness, make myself understood?" The question of how we learn concepts and languages is woven deep into *Land of Silence and Darkness*, with its deaf and blind characters who make visible the difficulty of human communication. The film is about the terror of sometimes not being able to make ourselves understood, and our subsequent isolation. If you were to knock on Fini's door, she wouldn't hear you, and if you were to switch on a light, she wouldn't see it. When you rang her doorbell, a small ventilator turned itself on so that Fini would feel a draught and know there was a visitor. It meant she could prepare herself for the fact that someone was arriving from the outside world and would be laying their hand on her shoulder. She had all these practical ways to prevent fright and shock. Once I rang her bell and nothing happened; it turned out the ventilator was broken. I went in anyway, found her sitting at a table, and asked myself how I should best approach her and make my presence known.

The film was made by only three people.

Yes, and the ratio of footage shot to what you see in the final film is probably two to one. The film is an hour and a half, but we shot about three hours of footage in total. Not only that, but the film cost only $30,000. It was me recording sound, Schmidt-Reitwein on camera and Beate Mainka-Jellinghaus, who edited the film. We had absolutely nothing, yet came up with a film still watched forty years later. This should be a lesson to filmmakers today with inexpensive digital technology at their disposal. You need only a good story and guts to make a film, the sense that it absolutely has to be made. Every able-bodied filmmaker out there today should be able to raise the pittance needed to make a film like *Land of Silence and Darkness*. Don't wait for the system to finance such things. Rob a bank if you need to. Embezzle if necessary.

There was no preconceived structure before we started shooting; things fell into place very easily, and the resulting film is some of the best work I've ever done. Look at the sequence at the end with Herr Fleischmann, the deaf man who became blind when he was thirty-three years old and lived for six years in a cowshed just to experience the warmth of other living beings. I consider him to be one of the most important characters in any of my films. He lived with his mother in a retirement home because she was the only person he wasn't afraid of. She explained to us that five years before, after a heavy snowstorm, when she opened the window, took his hand and put it into the snow, he said, "Snow." It was the last word he ever uttered. The shot where Herr Fleischmann walks away from the group of people and approaches a tree, feeling its shape by gently touching – almost embracing – the branches, is unforgettable; it's an entire human drama played out in two minutes, and one of the deepest moments audiences will ever encounter in a film. If you were to show that scene to someone who hadn't seen the whole film, it would seem insignificant. What's happening on screen at that moment is startlingly simple, and anyone who tuned into the film would think, "It's just a shot of a man touching a tree." But this is an image that requires the preceding one and a half hours for audiences to be sufficiently receptive to its power. If this were the opening sequence of *Land of Silence and Darkness*, it would be meaningless, and nor would it make sense if you showed

85

it apart from the rest of the film. As with *Little Dieter Needs to Fly* and *Stroszek*, for an hour before the end of the film the inner rhythm inexorably leads us to the final sequence, and as soon as I saw Herr Fleischmann under that tree I knew I had the last scene of the film. It was one of those things that occasionally fall into my lap and that I wonder if I really deserve.

I had my arm around Schmidt-Reitwein and gently turned him towards Herr Fleischmann. He understood that there was something he hadn't noticed, turned to pick up on this solitary figure walking slowly away, then zeroed in on him under the tree. You can feel the tender approach we took in the camerawork of *Land of Silence and Darkness*. I wanted the characters to come across in the most direct way possible, and told Schmidt-Reitwein that if he used a tripod, we would end up with fixed, lifeless images. I wanted him to let the camera beat as if it were part of his own heart, and by extension that of the people he was filming. It was clear that if the camera were sitting on his shoulder – even when he wasn't moving – it would make a tremendous difference. I told him that wherever possible he shouldn't use the zoom, but instead move towards people with his whole body.

How much freedom do you give the cameraman at moments like these?

I have always had a symbiotic and physical relationship with the cameramen I work with. I move step by step in contact with them; we're like a pair of ice skaters. From behind, I put one arm around their chest or my hand on their belt, and if I see something unforeseen and interesting I push them towards it with a nudge or whisper. The cameraman's peripheral vision is restricted when he looks through the lens, so an important part of my job at moments like this is to provide an additional set of eyes and guide him in certain directions. But this is never the sighted leading the blind. The cameraman is always searching with his other eye for the next thing to film.

Peter Zeitlinger, with whom I have worked for the past few years, is the only cameraman ever to put the camera down in the middle of a take and say, "Werner, this scene has no rhythm." In his youth Peter played ice hockey for Sparta Prague, which means in his hands a camera is more fluid than a Steadicam. Along the slopes of Mount Erebus in Antarctica, steam has created a series of bizarre ice corridors and chimneys, some reaching two storeys in height. During production on *Encounters at the End of the World*, Peter and I descended down into the ice and moved along a fuma-role, which is a long tunnel, at points only twenty inches high. There is a beautiful shot in the film where you see me crawling, as if exploring the unknown. Then, suddenly, the tunnel opens out into a blue grotto of pure fantasy, with intense light shining through the ice. Peter was on his belly behind me, and with extraordinary agil-ity was holding the camera stretched out with one hand in front of him. He has always understood how physical his job is, and in one sequence for *Encounters* managed to control a moving snowmobile with one hand while filming with the other. In *Little Dieter Needs to Fly*, when Dieter is tied up and runs through the jungle with his captors, Peter was running after everyone, the camera to his eye, skilfully avoiding the trees and roots that covered the path. At one point he crossed a creek using a fallen tree as a narrow bridge. Watch the scene again and you'll notice that a third of the way across is a wooden branch sticking up out of the mud. Peter had placed it there himself in preparation for being able to balance his body so that he could get a smooth shot as he moved from one side of the creek to the other. I never liked the system in America where a distinction is made between the cinematographer and camera operator. A real cinematographer operates his own camera.

Where did you first meet Fini Straubinger?

I was asked to make a film about victims of the West German equivalent of thalidomide, and produced a film called *Handicapped Future*. The film isn't as stylised as some of my other documentaries because, like *The Flying Doctors of East Africa*, it was proposed by someone else, in this case by a young man whose friend was in a wheelchair. The initial suggestion was that I do a film on him alone, but after some investigation I felt there was more to the subject, so I made *Handicapped Future*, an attempt to tackle basic issues about how physically disabled people functioned in West Germany. I gave the film – which is another example of a "utility" work – to several institutions that took care of the physically handicapped, and they used it to raise public awareness of their cause.

Beyond the fundamental practicalities – like the lack of ramps in public spaces and sidewalks inaccessible to wheelchairs – the more deep-rooted problem was that many handicapped people felt isolated from society. There were more than four million of them in West Germany at the time, including nearly half a million of school age, but the treatment of these people was mediaeval, and according to surveys the majority of Germans didn't want to live anywhere near them. What opportunities could their communities and government usefully offer them? I became interested in the community facility that was built in Munich in 1968 where, for the first time, handicapped people could live with their families in specially furnished apartments instead of being isolated in institutions, as was mostly the case; it was the equivalent to assisted-living facilities for the elderly. There were two schools, medical amenities and a gym where physical training could take place, including the balancing exercises you see in the film. People with no arms have different perceptions of balance and their bodies than everyone else. *Handicapped Future* is probably my most politically aware film because I wanted to explore the development of legislation emerging from the United States that was providing assistance to the handicapped and which later trickled across to West Germany and other European countries. I went out to the UCLA campus in California and filmed with Adolph Ratzka, a young German university student who some years before had been paralysed by polio. He spoke of the "pompous stairways" common in German buildings, compared to the mandatory facilities for wheelchair users in public buildings in California.

I don't know if I like the film today. It tries to maintain some kind of friendly attitude, and seems dangerously conventional and well behaved. If I were to work on a similar project today, it would have a harsher tone when it came to the lack of acceptance of disabled people in general. Still, the film was one of the first voices to let it be known that changes were needed in West Germany, and it helped trigger a shift in awareness of these issues, eventually leading to new legislation. More importantly, it was somehow a predecessor to *Land of Silence and Darkness* and led directly to that project. During filming, Schmidt-Reitwein and I went to hear a speech by Gustav Heinemann, the president of West Germany, which is where I met Fini. The first time I encountered her was captured on film; it's the scene about halfway through *Land of Silence and Darkness*, when she is at Heinemann's talk, sitting with a companion who is describing to her what is being said by use of an extraordinary tactile language. We were filming the president when I turned and saw this man tapping with his fingers onto the hand of the woman sitting next to him. I immediately sensed this was something big and that I should take note, so I gently nudged Schmidt-Reitwein, who slowly moved his camera around and filmed the two of them.

I was instantly fascinated by Fini. As a nine-year-old child she had fallen down a staircase and landed heavily on her head, but because she was worried about her mother being angry, she kept quiet about it and felt sick for months. The doctor thought it was because she was growing, but after one or two years she became blind, then as a nineteen-year-old became deaf. Adding to this misfortune she was addicted to morphine – prescribed to alleviate her constant pain – and was bedridden for thirty years. Because she couldn't hear herself, Fini talked very slowly and carefully. For her, history stopped around 1920 because she had lived for so many years surrounded by pious nuns in a convent and spoke an anachronistic German from the previous century. The day I saw Fini for the first time was the day I decided to make a film about her.

How easy was it to persuade her to be filmed?

I was able to establish an immediate trust with her and learnt the tactile language fairly quickly; it takes about as long as it does to learn how to type. I was eventually tapping onto Fini's toes and the sole of her foot, and using her left hand instead of her right, which is like writing in reverse. I would speak to Fini as straight-forwardly as I would to anyone else, and once told her that the sweater she was wearing didn't match her skirt, suggesting she put on a different one instead. Nobody had ever told her anything like that before, and she immediately went to change. Fini allowed me to make *Land of Silence and Darkness* because she understood that the film wouldn't be just about her, but also the community in which she lived and the people she surrounded herself with. Happiness or unhappiness never played a role in Fini's existence.

She experienced complete isolation having been bedridden for so many years, unable to see and hear, but there were things that were more important to her. She knew her life had meaning because she was such a support for other deaf and blind people. We filmed, on and off, for more than a year, following her to various events, meetings and special occasions.

For her birthday one year I organised a ride in an aeroplane, the first time she had ever flown; she loved feeling the jolts and shifts of air as the aircraft bounced along. I knew Fini had always wanted to go to the zoo and that the other deaf and blind people she spent time with had also never been there, so I persuaded the director of the local zoo to let them feed the elephants and hold the chimpanzees. We also went to a local arboretum, where they handled various cacti. Away from the cameras I did things with Fini that nobody else would ever do, like have her cook me a meal. She had been prevented from making mischief for such a long time, so I took her out into the countryside on my motorcycle to poach pheasants. It was exhilarating for Fini when she fired my small-calibre rifle, which she would hide under her coat because I had no hunting licence. Later, when she plucked the pheasants, Fini was still delighting in the mischief we had made together, and the bird tasted twice as good. When I would have her over for dinner, she could tell whether my roast was ready just by the smell. It was one sensual, visceral experience after another. I even asked Fini to babysit for my son Rudolph, who was only a year old; nobody had ever entrusted her with such responsibility. My mother became close to Fini and learnt the tactile language so they could communicate with each other. For my mother and me, our contact with Fini went far beyond the film.

You filmed with children born deaf and blind.

I thought it was important to show another side to the story, and these sequences came naturally. Fini became deaf and blind when she was a teenager, which makes a difference to the kind of contact she had with the outside world. She knew language and what things looked like. There are well-known cases, like the American Helen Keller, who became deaf and blind at an early age and wrote several books; her story raises questions about innate human emotions and how these children think about abstract concepts. But it isn't easy to know what children born deaf and blind think about the environment they inhabit because there is no easy way to communicate with them. Contact rarely surpasses the palpable essentials, things like, "This is heat. Do you need food?" It seems certain they feel and understand emotions like anger and fear as anyone else would, but how do they cope with their anonymous fears within? Although their brains are normal, they have no conception of language or their environment. Without the ability to see and hear, it's difficult for their minds to be fully awakened. The children we filmed seemed to experience moments of deep fear that related only to what was happening inside their own heads.

We discovered some other extraordinary cases. Else Fährer was a deaf and blind woman, about fifty years old. The only person she was able to communicate with was her mother, but she had died and no institution in Germany would accept Else, so she was placed in a psychiatric hospital where the nurses had no idea how to look after her. Else knew she didn't belong in this place, surrounded by such unstable people. She could read Braille and was able to speak and write, but after her experience in this psychiatric institution she retreated into herself so much that she wasn't able to communicate with anyone. There is a scene in the film where Fini goes to meet Else. She tried to make contact in any number of ways, but was never able to. Words appear on screen: "When you let go of my hand, it is as if we were a thousand miles apart."

Land of Silence and Darkness was rejected by television stations for more than two years, so I threatened the executives by telling them I would buy their stations in twenty years' time, when I was rich, then fire everyone. Eventually they tested the waters by screening the film late at night, and it got such a favourable response from the public that it was repeated twice shortly afterwards and became a great success. Some reviewers – primarily in Germany – accused me of exploitation. Thankfully several people jumped to the film's defence and gave it the backing it needed, including Oliver Sacks, the neurologist and author of *Awakenings*, who loved the film. Somehow word spread that it was a worthy project.

Aguirre, the Wrath of God was your first international success, a film regarded as one of the great achievements of post-war German cinema.

Perhaps, but hardly anyone wanted to see the film when it got its first limited release, and it was difficult to find money to even make it. The budget came from the small amount of revenue I had received from my previous films, plus a loan from my brother Tilbert, plus money from Hessischer Rundfunk, a German television station, which had the right to screen the film the very evening it was released in cinemas, so naturally it was hardly a box-office success. This was before the *Film/Fernsehen Abkommen* [Film/ Television Agreement, 1974], which opened up opportunities for co-productions with the networks and put in place a rule that films released theatrically wouldn't be screened on television for at least two years. When I made *The Enigma of Kaspar Hauser* a couple of years later I made sure the contract stipulated there would be a substantial delay between the film's cinema release and its television premiere. We struggled to sell *Aguirre* at first, but it was finally picked up by a small French distribution company and sold out a couple of Paris cinemas of about a hundred seats each for more than two years. Eventually the rest of the world took notice.

Aguirre *is about a little-known sixteenth-century Spanish adventurer who went in search of El Dorado.*

From one point of view, as I look back on it, *Aguirre* could be viewed as an adventure story that on the surface has all the characteristics of the genre, but on a deeper level contains something new and more complex. It really is a genre unto itself.

The film isn't about the real Aguirre. As with *The Enigma of Kaspar Hauser* a couple of years later, I took the most basic facts known about the man and spun my own tale. By chance, at a friend's house I found a book for adolescents about adventurers – Alexander the Great, Roald Amundsen, Columbus, people like that – with a few lines on Lope de Aguirre, a Spanish conquistador who threw himself into a search for the lost city of El Dorado and called himself "the Wrath of God." He initiated a revolt, made himself leader of the expedition, declared the king of Spain overthrown, and went down the entire length of the Amazon. After reaching the Atlantic, half starved, he sailed north and attacked the Spanish garrison at Trinidad, completely underestimating the forces there, before finally being captured and put on trial. These few lines in this book fascinated me and I tried to find out more about Aguirre, but little is known about his life; there are only a few remaining documents about the man. History is generally on the side of the winners, and Aguirre is one of its great losers. There are, however, several pieces of literature – novels and memoirs – that discuss him in legendary terms. Years after I made the film I read Aguirre's letter to King Philip II of Spain, which is actually rather boring.

Aguirre fascinated me because he was the first person who dared defy the Spanish crown and declare the independence of a South American nation, though the film – which is set during the first few weeks of 1561 – never dwells on Machiavellian politicking per se, only the madness of such things. I invented a wildly defiant tone for him, a fury and absolute fanaticism, as he rebels not just against political power, but nature itself. He curses the king, dethrones and strips him of all rights, proclaims himself the new emperor of El Dorado and New Spain, then insists, "When I, Aguirre, want the birds to drop dead from the trees, then the birds will drop dead from the trees. I am the Wrath of God. The earth I walk upon sees me and trembles." By the end of the film it isn't just Aguirre who is mad; the whole situation is demented. There is a powerful sense of menace surrounding the characters. We feel them slipping further and further into trouble as the story progresses, and because of this the movement of time in *Aguirre* is more important than in any of my other films. What interested me was how these Spanish conquistadors set off in search of El Dorado and gradually all drift to their deaths. There is an army of a thousand people at the start, but by the end this is a small and pathetic group of the sick and wounded, a military force that has lost all sense of direction, eventually grinding to an almost complete standstill. At a certain imperceptible moment, a feeling sets in that everyone is futilely revolving in circles, that there can be no happy resolution to this story. This is one reason why *Aguirre* was shot in sequence, because the chronology of the story is so linked to the film's rhythm.

It wasn't my original plan to have a voiceover, but during editing I felt the film needed a more precise tempo. A voiceover also allowed me to introduce specific dates and emphasise the passing of time, underlining just how long these soldiers have been in the jungle. By creating the impression of time dragging on, we get the sense it's running out for them. The text you hear is an invented diary of the monk on the voyage, though a real monk with the same name – one of the first to have travelled down the Amazon – did actually exist and wrote a diary of a totally different expedition. Historians are always asking me where I found the documents; I tell them it was in this and that book, but unfortunately can't remember the title. Some of the other characters were invented, or if they did exist weren't on the expedition as portrayed in the film. Gonzalo Pizarro, for example, the brother of the conquistador Francisco Pizarro, died a few years before the story takes place. I made up characters based on the names I read in the handful of real documents I could find. The script is pure invention. It's my interpretation of history, like Brecht's retelling of Galileo and Shakespeare's *Henry V*.

Real events acquire unreal qualities.

There is an inner flow to most of my films, one that can't be followed with just a wristwatch. In *Aguirre* things steadily move into delirium and become hallucinatory, as if the audience is being taken directly into the interior of things. You certainly experience this by the time of Aguirre's revolt against Ursúa. Watch the scene of Don Fernando de Guzman's "coronation" and you'll see a brief tableau, a highly stylised shot, where all the characters look directly into the camera, like in a nineteenth-century photo. This is similar to the shot of the Irish doctors in *Fata Morgana* and the image in *Nosferatu*, with Renfield wearing a straitjacket and two guards standing on either side of him as he leaps crazily up and down. There is also a similar shot in *Signs of Life*, at the wedding, when the couple and their parents pose for the photographer and stare into the camera. Look again and you'll notice Peter Brogle gasping for breath. I made him race me as fast as he could for a mile in the suffocating heat; everyone was ready to roll while we ran at top speed back to the set. I quickly tossed Peter a towel for him to dry his face and made him line up with the others, telling him, "Stare at the lens and try to suppress your heavy breathing. Don't let on that you're panting." He stood there, his face contorted.

There is an image in *Aguirre* that comes immediately after the opening sequence, a minute-long shot of the raging waters of Río Urubamba, below Machu Picchu. The waters are so violent, almost boiling with rage, completely out of proportion to what a human being might be able to withstand. Three seconds of this would have been sufficient, but a minute of it prepares the audience for an approaching fever dream in the jungle. A filmmaker carefully sows, then harvests. After having seen this image, we are better prepared to accept the disproportion to come, the outrageousness of Aguirre, his grandiose failure to conquer an entire continent with thirty starving and ill-equipped soldiers.

These frozen moments don't necessarily have any significance for the story per se; they connect more deeply, to the film's inner narrative. *Aguirre* almost holds its breath as the multiple threads of a story moving in all directions are tied in a knot for one brief moment. Images like this have more to do with music – with pace and rhythm – than with cinema. It's like knowing how long audiences can be confronted with absolute silence in a concert hall or opera house before they start squirming in their seats. While making *The Transformation of the World into Music* I spoke to James Levine, who was conducting *Parsifal* at Bayreuth; he's the one in the film who always conducts with a neatly folded towel over his left shoulder. During the fermata, after the first few bars of the overture, he would signal for the musicians to stop, then take the towel from his shoulders, mop his brow, put it back on his shoulders and wait. The orchestra would look at each other nervously, thinking there was a problem. Only then would he start up again. James told me he wanted the silence to continue until the audience began to wonder if the conductor had dropped dead in the orchestra pit or run off because his house was on fire.

By the time Aguirre is standing on the raft staring into the face of a monkey, the surreal qualities and fever dreams of the jungle have infiltrated his fantasies. What we see on screen might be a delirious hallucination. Even the way the soldiers die is done in an operatic way. Ursúa's wife has been wearing a blue dress throughout the film, but when she walks into the jungle – presumably never to be seen again – suddenly she's wearing a beautiful golden royal gown, in perfect condition, though everything around her is rotting away. Logic plays no part in such things; grandiose stylisations have taken over. When audiences see the brigantine up in the tree they wonder if it really is there or if it's just a fantasy of the soldiers. The image might appear unreal to us, but for those on the raft – who have long since lost their sense of reality – it doesn't seem so strange. For that scene I wanted a slightly stylised feeling, so we waited for the heavy atmosphere that emerges during the rainy season, when ominous clouds appear about an hour before it starts to pour with rain. We constructed the boat in five sections, built an enormous scaffold around the tree and hoisted it up. It took twenty-five workmen a full week to reassemble it. The thing had no bottom, so it couldn't float, but it had a mast and sails, and a canoe dangling from its stern. Who knows, it might still be up there.

You spoke earlier of the "rhythm and sensuousness" of the desert. Can the same be said of jungle landscapes?

Absolutely. Jungles and deserts are at the extreme ends of the landscapes this planet has to offer, and both have enormous visual force. They also both hit back at idiots like me who challenge them by wanting to make films there.

As a Bavarian I have an affinity for the fertility of the jungle, the fever dreams and physical exuberance of the place. For me, jungles have always represented an intensified form of reality, though they aren't actually particularly difficult challenges. A jungle is just another forest; it's the myth of travel agencies that they are dangerous places. I really wouldn't even know what hazards are out there. Like deer, snakes usually flee as fast as they can crawl. It isn't as if the jaguars are all lined up to eat you, and piranhas won't bother you unless you do something stupid. I used to catch them with a fishing line and eat them, and right after I pulled one out would jump into the water and take a swim. There's no danger so long as you stay away from stagnant water. I have a strong memory of the cobalt-blue butterflies, attracted by the sugar-cane brandy we would drink at night. I would be awoken by the screeching monkeys on the other side of the river and find five butterflies had settled on my hand, slowly opening and closing their wings. It was an inexplicably beautiful moment. There is something glorious about people lying all day in their hammocks on the riverbank, endlessly watching the river passing by. Everyone does what they want because no coherent authority exists. It's complete anarchy out there, a world away from the established order of the city. Outsiders have to adapt or leave, like a girl wearing a bikini in Munich during winter who quickly enough realises what needs to be done.

I never present literal landscapes in my films. What I show instead are landscapes of the mind, locales of the soul. Just as there is no such thing as background music in my films, landscapes aren't picturesque or scenic backdrops as they are in Hollywood, nor merely representations of physical space. Most directors exploit landscapes only to embellish what is happening in the foreground, which is one reason why I like some of John Ford's films. He never used Monument Valley as just a backdrop; for Ford it signified the American soul and the very spirit of his characters. Westerns are all about our basic notions of justice, and when I see Monument Valley I somehow start to believe in American justice. For me landscapes are active members of the cast, like the desert in *Fata Morgana* and the burning oil fields of Kuwait in *Lessons of Darkness*. During the opening credits of *Signs of Life* the camera holds for an unusually long time on a single image of a mountain valley in Crete, allowing audiences to climb deep inside the landscape. The jungle of *Aguirre* is never some lush, beautiful environment there for decoration, as it might be in a television commercial. It's a representation of our most intense and forceful dreams, our deepest emotions and nightmares. With its madness and confusion, the place becomes a vital part of characters' inner landscapes, taking on almost human qualities.

When I write a script, I often describe landscapes I have never seen. Although I had never been to Peru before I started making *Aguirre*, I imagined the atmosphere with a strange precision, and when I arrived in the jungle for the first time everything was exactly as I had pictured it. It was as if the landscapes had no choice; they had to fit my imagination and submit themselves to my idea of what they should look like. Although sometimes I struggle to find actual environments that match those in my head, I'm good at reshaping physical landscapes and making them operative for a film. They always somehow adapt themselves to the situations required of them. Often I try to introduce a certain atmosphere into a landscape, using sound and vision to give it a definite character. The fact is that I can direct landscapes, just as I do actors and animals.

Where does this ability come from?

Perhaps my grandfather, Rudolph. As I said, he was a self-taught archaeologist, an unusually bold and distinguished man with a real instinct for terrain. He could look at a landscape and determine where a temple now deep under the ground had been constructed two thousand years before. On Crete, the remains of Knossos had been known about for centuries because columns were sticking out of the ground for everyone to see. On the island of Kos, by contrast, there was no visible trace of any ancient ruins. Archaeologists there had already spent years searching for the Asklepieion, which was some sort of centre of healing and resort dedicated to Asklepios, the god of medicine. My grandfather read about it in a text by Herondas when he was a classics teacher, immediately quit his job, proposed to and married my grandmother – who was nineteen years old – and went in search of the Asklepieion. Like Heinrich Schliemann, who excavated Troy, my grandfather set out with only a spade and started digging. Other archaeologists had carried out excavations in different spots on Kos without finding anything, but for reasons known only to himself my grandfather chose to dig in the middle of a field that was covered in trees and vineyards, and promptly discovered a Roman bath.

What preparation did you do for filming in the jungle?

The calibre of some films is decided by pre-production, and pre-production on *Aguirre* was meticulous. Before I took the crew into the jungle I bought the most primitive and cheapest of cameras – some tiny Super 8 plastic thing with a wide-angle lens which I couldn't even focus – and went to Peru, where I scouted locations. It was the first time I had ever been in the jungle. I did reconnaissance on a small steamboat, then had a nimble balsa raft constructed. For several weeks an oarsman and I drifted down the Urubamba, Nanay and Huallaga tributaries, sleeping on hammocks and rarely leaving the raft. From the first to the last tributary was a distance of nearly fifteen hundred miles. I was trying to develop a feeling for the river's currents, searching for those that looked spectacular but weren't too dangerous. Several stretches were clearly too hazardous for a film crew. At one point the raft struck some rocks and was split in two. The half we were on became caught in a whirlpool; what saved us was getting stuck in a strong current and being swept several miles away. It would have been a disaster to have made the film without having gone down there beforehand to test things out. It was crucial to be in physical contact with the rapids before I started filming, not unlike a few years before, when I took the actors and crew around the fortress before we shot *Signs of Life*. I had to create some tactile connection to the place, and wanted everyone to be familiar with the environment before we started filming. "We aren't going to pull out the equipment for at least two days," I said, and asked them to walk around, touching the walls and feeling the smooth surfaces, which is how I had experienced the fortress myself when I first encountered it as a teenager.

Peru was governed by a military dictatorship at the time we made *Aguirre*, but a left-wing one that had nationalised various industries and instituted a vast land-reform programme. President Juan Velasco Alvarado was of Native Indian descent and controlled a regime very different to those of people like Stroessner in Paraguay and Pinochet in Chile. We weren't offered much assistance by the Peruvian government, though the army supplied us with an amphibian aircraft and established a radio station, which meant we could be in contact with the nearest big city, providing the electricity didn't fail. Shooting permits were needed, otherwise showing up at conspicuous places like Machu Picchu would have been problematic. The government representatives we worked with appreciated that the strongest force in *Aguirre* is the Native Indians with their ancient heritage, fighting the imperialist invaders. They are the ones who ultimately survive, not the plundering Spanish conquistadors.

Once production started, we built an encampment for 450 people on Río Urubamba, including the 270 Indians from the mountains who acted as extras. It was so big I decided it needed a name, so I called it Pelicula o Muerte [Film or Death], which is a joke version of the Cubans' cry of "*Patria o muerte*" at the Bay of Pigs. For a time I slept in a nearby hut owned by a hunchback dwarf, her nine children and more than a hundred guinea pigs, which crawled all over me. We eventually moved to Río Huallaga, but with a much smaller group of extras because throughout the story so many characters drop away like flies. Filming took about six weeks, including a whole week lost when we took the cast and crew from one tributary to another, a distance of more than a thousand miles.

Once we arrived at Río Nanay we lived on rafts that had been especially built. There were less than ten in total, and on each was a small hut with a thatched roof and hammocks inside. We weren't able to set foot on dry land because in the flat lowlands the jungle was flooded for miles around, so at night we tied the rafts to overhanging branches. They floated in a convoy about a mile behind the one we were shooting on, which meant we could film the river without having any other rafts in shot. Once filming was done for the day, we would tie up and wait for this floating village to arrive, including the raft that was used exclusively as a kitchen.

In one scene the rafts pass through the rapids.

It took only two minutes, or even less, and we absolutely had to get those shots the first time around. The wooden rafts were extremely solid, constructed by the Indians, who were expert builders, and we also had several excellent rowers. Having said that, sometimes they were drunk and had no control over where they were going. With *Aguirre* the audience can feel the authenticity of the situations the actors are in, but there was never any danger because everyone – including the Indian rowers – was attached by cords, which you can see if you look carefully. Cameraman Thomas Mauch and I were the only people moving freely.

The scene where the soldiers get caught in the whirlpool and are found dead the following morning was especially difficult to shoot because the flow of the river was so fast and violent. At the end of the day we lowered ropes down to the actors from the cliff above, which they attached to themselves, and we pulled them up. The next morning the raft was still there, wrestling with the fierce counter-current. The extras – who were paid more than everyone else – were proud of themselves once they reached safety, though they were vomiting because of the raft's incessant spinning. At one point I was standing on the cliff looking down at the water; the rocks were slippery, so I grabbed a branch to stop myself from sliding. I could see it was covered in fire ants, but stupid as I am I swung my machete to chop the thing off. All that did was shake it violently, and hundreds of these ants rained down on me. I was bitten all over and ended up in bed for two days with a serious fever.

Later, at a much calmer bend on Río Urubamba, we found a

cable strung across the river, with a primitive platform attached to it. The rope needed to pull the platform to either side was missing, so my production co-ordinator Walter Saxer and I decided to swim across, carrying a rope with us. We also wanted to explore the other side of the river, which looked like an especially beautiful spot. I jumped in and almost immediately saw a whirlpool coming at me. It was moving quickly in a semi-circle and gave off a loud, strange slurping sound. I managed to swim to the other side of the river and then, with the rope in my mouth, swung my arms and legs over the cable and pulled myself towards the platform in the middle of the river. I had a beautiful gold watch in my pocket, one of my most prized possessions at the time, a gift from my first great love. As I was clambering across I felt it slipping, and watched helplessly as it dropped into the water. I was very upset, but at the same time I knew that all these rivers carry gold deposits. "Oh well," I remember thinking to myself. "Gold back to gold."

How much trouble were the monkeys in the final sequence?

That scene was different from the one written in the screenplay, but during my initial scouting of the rivers I befriended a little monkey who would sit on my shoulder. He became a good comrade and I named him after one of my two favourite football players, Di Stéfano, the brilliant Argentinian. Unfortunately Di Stéfano perished because of a stupid mistake I made. I tied him to a metal post because I had to go on land and take care of some things. When I returned three hours later, he was dying because he had wrapped his leash around the post and was dangerously exposed to the sun. He died later that day because of my negligence, so I thought I should honour my little friend with the scene at the end of the film. My other favourite football player of all time, by the way, is Garrincha, a brilliant dribbler.

I hired local Indians who captured hundreds of savage little monkeys – the ones who overrun the raft – but gave them only half the money up front because I knew if I paid full price, the guy organising everything would run off with the cash. Even so, the animals never arrived on set, so we drove out to the airport as quickly as possible. It turned out they had all been resold to an American businessman and were already on an aeroplane waiting to be shipped out to a dealership in Miami. "I'm the veterinarian!" I yelled to the cargo handlers, making use of the kind of subterfuge that has always been an indispensible element to my filmmaking. "Stop immediately! Where are the vaccination documents for the monkeys?" They were caught completely off guard and admitted they had no papers, so we unloaded the animals from the aeroplane, put them into our truck and sped off. When it actually came to shooting the sequence, the monkeys had some kind of panic attack and bit me all over. I couldn't cry out because we were shooting live sound at that point. Another jumped onto the shoulder of the cameraman Thomas Mauch and started viciously biting his ear. His mouth was wide open but no scream came out. He just kept on filming, endearing himself to me beyond description.

Where did the Indian extras come from?

From a single village high up in the mountains. I travelled there to explain what the film was and what I needed from them, and we ended up hiring almost the entire population, a conscientious group unafraid to carry out the sometimes difficult work. They were well paid compared to what they usually earned. One time, after filming in the mud and swamps, I noticed the Europeans were exhausted and wanted to call a halt for the day, but the Indians asked me why we were stopping. They said it would be even more difficult to continue later on, so why not carry on now and finish the job? I can't say I ever truly understood the Indians, but we were all aware of something we had in common: a mutual respect for work. They were part of a socialist co-operative at Lauramarca, with a real knowledge both of their own history and the current political situation, and understood that their time on the film wasn't useful only for themselves, but for the Indians' cause as a whole.

One of the extras was a man I encountered at the main square in Cusco, where he would drum on tin cans and play a pan flute, and occasionally make money by selling pairs of scissors. I never knew his real name and I'm not sure he even knew it himself, so everyone called him Hombrecito, which means "Little Man." I liked him so much I asked him to come with us for the shoot. I explained I would pay him well, more than what he would earn in ten years sitting there playing for people. At first he refused, saying that if he were to stop playing in the square, everyone in Cusco would die. He wore three alpaca sweaters at the same time, even when it was unbearably hot and humid, and refused to take them off because he thought they would be stolen. He said they protected him against "the bad breath of the gringos." Hombrecito seemed to carry all the humiliation, oppression and despair of his people on his shoulders. I persuaded him to join us, and he became the crew's mascot; you can see him in the film playing his pan flute. He would take his sweaters and place them carefully in a plastic bag which he hid in the jungle so no one would steal it. Every evening the crew had to hunt around for the bag because Hombrecito could never remember where he put it. Once filming was over, he went back to Cusco's main square, this time wearing three jackets, one on top of the other, which he had bought with his wages.

We shipped in costumes and props from a rental company in Spain. Jungle transportation wasn't easy to organise because we had to squeeze everything – including all the camera equipment and even the horse – into one big amphibian aeroplane. In the sequence where the soldiers go on shore and raid a village is a single shot of a mummy. My brother Lucki found a real one and flew it in from Lima. It was so fragile he had to buy a separate seat for it, so for the entire journey had this ferocious-looking thing sitting next to him wearing a seatbelt.

Did you write the script for Klaus Kinski?

I don't need to hole myself up in a monastery or retire to a quiet spot for months on end to write. Most of the screenplay was written on a bus going to Italy with the football team from Munich I played for. By the time we reached Salzburg, only a few hours into the trip, everyone was drunk and singing obscene songs because the team had drunk most of the beer we were bringing as a gift for our opponents. I was sitting with my typewriter on my lap. In fact, I typed the whole thing almost entirely with my left hand because with my right I was trying to fend off our goalie sprawled on the seat next to me. Eventually he vomited over the typewriter. Some of the pages were beyond repair and I had to throw them out of the window. There were some fine scenes lost because I couldn't recall what I had just written. They're long gone. That's life on the road for you.

Later on, in between football games, I wrote furiously for three days and finished the script. It was written so fast and so spontaneously that I didn't think about who might play the part, but the moment I finished it I knew it was for Kinski and sent it to him immediately. A couple of days later, at three in the morning, I was awoken by the telephone. At first I couldn't figure out what was going on; all I heard were inarticulate screams at the other end of the line. It was Kinski. After about half an hour I managed to filter out from his ranting that he was ecstatic about the screenplay and wanted to play Aguirre.

My first choice for the role was actually Algerian president Houari Boumediene. Take a look at photos of him from when Algeria won its independence and you'll see why he intrigued me; his physical presence was powerful indeed. Ahmed Ben Bella became president in 1963, but Boumediene was the man behind everything, including running the military. Later he ousted Ben Bella in a *coup d'état* and became president. I never pushed the script on him as I figured he had other things to take care of, but if he had been removed from office himself before we started filming I would have offered him the role.

How was Kinski in the jungle?

He arrived with a load of alpine equipment – tents, sleeping bags, crampons, ice axes – because he wanted to expose himself to the wilds of nature. But his ideas about the jungle were rather insipid; mosquitoes and rain weren't allowed in his world. The first night after setting up his tent it started to pour and he got soaked, which set off one of his raving fits. The next day we built a roof of palm fronds above his tent, and eventually moved him and his wife into the only hotel in Machu Picchu. We all drank river water, but Kinski had a constant supply of bottled mineral water.

He had just cut short his infamous *Jesus Christus Erlöser* tour, scenes of which you can see at the start of *My Best Fiend*. His plan was to take the show around the world, but the first performance, in Berlin, ended in mayhem after about ten minutes. Kinski was playing the kind of ferocious, revolutionary Jesus who chased the merchants from the temple with a whip, not the kind, tolerant and benevolent Son of God. He lived by styling himself to excess and would adopt the personae of various people. For a time he was

François Villon, whose poetry he recorded; later Dostoyevsky's idiot; and in the years before his death he portrayed himself as Paganini. When he arrived in Peru to start filming *Aguirre* he identified so strongly with his role as a derided, misunderstood Jesus that he would sometimes answer questions in character and scream at me in biblical verse. Every day Kinski could see the problems I was having, yet he continued to create scandals or explode if so much as a mosquito appeared.

I knew of his reputation, that he was probably the most difficult actor in the world to deal with; working with Marlon Brando must have been like kindergarten in comparison. While filming a scene he nearly killed an actor when he struck him on the head with his sword. Thankfully the man was wearing a helmet, though he carries a scar to this very day. One evening a group of extras were in their hut; they had been drinking and were making too much noise for Kinski. He screamed and yelled at them to stop laughing, then grabbed his Winchester and fired three bullets through the thin bamboo walls. There were forty-five of them crammed together in this small room, and one had the top of his finger shot off. It was a miracle Kinski didn't kill any of them. I immediately confiscated his rifle, which is one of my big souvenirs. During filming he would insult me every day, sometimes for hours. Kinski had seen *Even Dwarfs Started Small*, so to him I was the "dwarf director." He screamed in a high-pitched voice in front of everyone, saying it was an insult I would even think about talking to him, the great actor. He insisted he could do everything himself, that being directed by me was like working with a housewife, and shrieked that David Lean and Brecht had left him alone to do his job, so why shouldn't I? "Brecht and Lean?" I said. "Never heard of them." That upset him even more. I was forced to put up with his behaviour, but Kinski never reckoned with my determination to see the job through. No one tamed him as well as I did.

Kinski and I agreed on nothing without a struggle. Temperamentally he was forever on the verge of hysteria, but I managed to harness this and turn it to productive ends. Sometimes other methods were necessary. On one occasion, towards the end of the shoot, he was looking for a victim to jump on; it was probably because he didn't know his lines. Suddenly Kinski started shouting like crazy at the sound assistant. "You swine! You were grinning!"

He insisted I fire the guy on the spot. "I'm not going to do that," I said. "The whole crew would quit out of solidarity." Kinski immediately left the set and started packing his bags, saying he was going to find a speedboat and leave. I went up to him and said, very politely, "Mr Kinski, you will not do this. You will not leave before we are finished here in the jungle. Our work here is more important than either our personal feelings or private lives." Quitting like that would have been a gross violation of his duty to the film, so I told him – quietly and calmly – that I would shoot him if he left. "I have had time to ponder the unthinkable," I said, "and have already made up my mind about this. After months of deliberation I know precisely what line I will not permit you to transgress. I don't need a single second longer to know what must be done. Leaving now is something you will not survive." I told him I had a rifle – it was actually his Winchester – and that he would only make it as far as the next bend in the river before he had eight bullets in his head. The ninth would be for me. Although I didn't have a gun in my hand at that particular moment, he knew it was no joke and screamed for the police like a madman, though the nearest police station was at least three hundred miles away. The police would never have done anything anyway. Over there the laws of the jungle are what count; a few bottles of whisky and a couple of hundred dollars would have been sufficient to dissuade the locals from investigating or have them put the incident down to an unfortunate hunting accident. For the remaining ten days of the shoot Kinski was extremely well behaved. The press later wrote that I directed him from behind the camera with a loaded gun. A beautiful image, but complete fiction.

Kinski was known for breaking contracts and walking away from a film if he felt like it. During a performance of Goethe's *Torquato Tasso* he stopped in the middle of a speech, hurled insults at the audience, threw a lit candelabra into the auditorium and wrapped himself in the carpet that was lying on stage. He remained coiled inside until the audience was cleared from the theatre. Before *Aguirre* he had to have a check-up for insurance reasons. I took him to see a doctor, who asked routine questions about allergies and hereditary diseases, and then: "Mr Kinski, have you ever suffered from fits of any kind?" "YES, EVERY DAY!" screamed Kinski at the highest pitch possible, before laying waste to the doctor's office. At one point during filming I reached up to move a strand of hair that was hanging down over his face. "Pardon me, Mr Kinski," I said, gently brushing it aside. He immediately exploded. "HAVE YOU GONE CRAZY? NOT EVEN MY BARBER IS ALLOWED TO TOUCH MY HAIR. YOU'RE AN AMATEUR!" The tabloid press adored him, and whenever he appeared on a talk show everyone in the audience would sit on the edge of their seats waiting for him to deliver the scandal. It never took more than a few minutes.

You admire his performance in the film.

Absolutely. He was an excellent actor and truly knew how to move on screen. I wanted to give Aguirre a vicious little hump, like a tumour on his shoulder, the size of a fist. I felt there should be some differentiation between Aguirre's physicality and everyone else's; the character had to have some kind of inner distortion that would be apparent on the surface. It was Kinski's idea that Aguirre should have a kind of pigeon chest with a slight protrusion, and he decided to make one of his arms appear longer than the other so he would walk lopsidedly. His left arm became so short that his sword wasn't around his waist; it was higher up, almost up into his armpit. He introduced these physical aberrations into the film gradually and precisely, and by the final scene the character is even more deformed. Kinski did it all perfectly, moving almost like a crab walking on sand. As an actor he knew all about costumes, and I learnt a great deal as I watched him oversee every buttonhole and stitch. He wanted a dagger as a prop, as long and thin as a knitting needle. "When I stab someone," he told me, "it has to be malicious. No blood should be shed. My victims bleed to death internally." In the screenplay, to spare her the shame of his defeat, the original idea was that Aguirre kills his daughter with this dagger.

Having said that, he was a complete scourge and didn't care if *Aguirre* was ever finished or released. He was interested only in his salary, and once shooting was over he refused to come to Munich and re-record some of his dialogue. About 20 per cent of what we recorded in the jungle was unusable because of the noise from the roaring rapids. What he actually said was: "I'll be there, but it will cost you a million dollars." He was absolutely serious about this, so I had no choice but to hire an actor – who had a lengthy career dubbing Humphrey Bogart into German – to dub Kinski's entire part. He did it with great skill, and years later I heard Kinski raving about how good he was in the German version of *Aguirre*. For the next film we did together I put into the contract that he was obliged to do a few days of re-recording, though Kinski insisted I could kidnap him, drag him to the studio, sit him in front of a microphone and handcuff him, and he would only sing his lines. Although for a couple of years afterwards he said he hated the film, I know he eventually liked it very much. At times it was clear he recognised and respected the work we did together, and understood that he and I were out to capture things beyond our individual existence, even beyond our collective existence. The man was a complete pestilence and a nightmare, and working with him became about maintaining my dignity under the worst conditions. It's also true that I call every grey hair on my head Kinski. But who cares about such things now? What's important is that the work was done and the films were made.

What was the film's budget?

Three hundred and seventy thousand dollars, a third of which went to Kinski, so I couldn't afford to take many people with me into the jungle; the entire crew numbered less than ten and we shot only a very small amount of footage in total. Although Kinski later insisted that I dined on caviar every night, sometimes I had to sell my boots just to get breakfast. I was the one who would take a boat out at four in the morning and go downriver to buy some chicken, eggs and yucca, or ate nothing if there wasn't enough food to go around. Like *Fitzcarraldo* a few years later – where I traded unopened bottles of shampoo and aftershave I had bought in Miami for sacks of rice – *Aguirre* was a barefoot film, so to speak, a child of poverty. Some of the actors and extras sensed this might be one of the film's virtues, so they never took their costumes off, even though they were full of mould because of the humidity. There is something authentic about the jungle that can never be fabricated, and if we had filmed in a studio I would have burnt through the entire budget in three days.

Was the spectacular opening shot in the script or did you stumble across the mountain?

I originally planned a scene on a glacier, 17,000 feet up, which started with a long procession of four hundred altitude-sick pigs tottering and staggering towards the camera. After a few minutes of following this line of animals, the audience would realise they are part of a Spanish army of adventurers, accompanied by hundreds of Indians. I tried things out with various pigs during pre-production, but none of them became altitude sick. Later a veterinarian in Austria did some tests, but after injecting a pig it became aggressive rather than woozy, so I ditched the whole idea, especially when several of the crew – some very tough men – became altitude sick up on this glacier. Taking all those people and animals that high up clearly wasn't feasible.

We ended up filming the opening sequence at a much lower altitude near Machu Picchu, on the side of a mountain that had a sheer vertical drop of 2,000 feet. It's thick vegetation up there, though the Incas had dug out a narrow staircase in the rocks, which is the trail the hundreds of people in the shot are using as they emerge from the clouds. We started transporting everyone at two in the morning – plus horses, pigs, llamas and cannons – and when I finally arrived at the top of the mountain there was indescribable chaos. It was pouring with rain and extremely slippery, there was dense fog and the whole valley was completely enshrouded by grey clouds. The Indian extras came from an altitude of 14,000 feet, but many of them still got vertigo, and we had to secure them with ropes during shooting. I spent much of the time trying to persuade everyone not to go home, begging them to be patient. I must have run up and down those steps three or four times instructing people what to do. I didn't want to use a megaphone; such things have to be done in direct contact with people. I somehow managed to convince them this was something special and extraordinary, and a couple of hours later was relieved that everyone was still in place as the fog and clouds suddenly opened up. We shot it only once, this line of people with the fog on one side, the mountain on the other. When the camera rolled I had a profound feeling, as if the grace of God were with this film and me.

Kinski eventually realised he would be a mere dot in the landscape, not the centre of attention, and wanted to act in close-up, leading the entire army with a grim face. I explained he wasn't yet the leader of the expedition, and in the end removed him entirely from the shot because I had the feeling the scene would be far more powerful if there were no human faces in it. Our concepts of the landscape differed profoundly. Kinski wanted the shot to embrace all of scenic Machu Picchu, including the peak and the ruins, which would have looked like a postcard or television commercial. I had in mind a very different framing of the landscape, an ecstatic one.

Is Aguirre *a metaphor for Nazism?*

Because their work is often seen explicitly in light of their nation's history, there are misunderstandings lying in wait around every corner for Germany's artists, writers and filmmakers. Even today Hitler's legacy to the German people has made us hypersensitive. Like many Germans I am acutely aware of my country's history, and apprehensive even about bug spray; I know there is only one step from insecticide to genocide. With *Aguirre* there was never any intention of creating a metaphor for Hitler.

You worked with Thomas Mauch previously on Signs of Life *and* Even Dwarfs Started Small. *Was your approach to filming in the jungle any different?*

Not really. I wanted to use a hand-held camera for most of *Aguirre* because the physical contact the camera had with the actors was an important element of the film. I never needed to explain to Mauch what I wanted; he intuitively knew. The final shot – with the camera circling and swooping around the raft – had to be as smooth as possible. A helicopter would have been too expensive for us, so Mauch and I boarded a speedboat and drove it around the raft several times. I manoeuvred it myself, just as when I drove the van through the desert in *Fata Morgana*. When a speedboat approaches a raft at forty miles an hour it creates an enormous wake, which meant we moved through the waves we were creating. I rehearsed with the boat, going faster and slower; the whole thing was done with great precision. I had to feel with my whole body what the water around us was doing.

We shot the entire film with a single camera, which meant we were forced to work rather crudely during production; it added to the authenticity and spirit of the film. There was none of the glossy multi-camera sophistication you find in expensive Hollywood productions. Perhaps this is why *Aguirre* has survived for so long. It's such a basic film; you really can't strip it down any more than it already is. The camera I used was actually stolen from the predecessor to the Munich Film School. They had a lot of equipment – including editing tables and a row of cameras sitting on a shelf – but never let young filmmakers use any of it. I wanted them to lend me a camera but had to endure an arrogant refusal. One day I found myself alone in this room next to the unlocked cabinet, saw a couple of cameras smiling down at me, and decided to liberate one of these lazy machines for an indefinite period. It was lying there looking up at me, a basic 35mm silent Arriflex, the camera I ended up using to make my first dozen or so films. I never considered it theft. For me, it was truly a necessity. I wanted to make films and needed a camera, so I had some kind of natural right to this tool. It was expropriation. If you are locked in a room and need air to breathe, take a chisel and hammer and break down the wall. When you have a good story to tell, by dint of destiny or God knows what, you gain the right to do such things. I helped this camera fulfil its destiny.

At one point Aguirre screams at a horse so maniacally that it collapses.

The idea was that he would shout at the animal and it would pass out in terror. We visited various veterinarians and tried all sorts of methods to make a horse topple over as if unconscious, but the animals would just get drowsy and eventually fall asleep. The solution was an injection directly into the carotid artery that would make a horse collapse in twelve to fourteen seconds. We gave the animal the shot and rolled the camera. Kinski started his dialogue, then turned and shouted at the horse, which dropped to the ground; it was all timed to the second. I had originally intended a scene where Aguirre shouts at a huddle of pigs and they all drop dead, but it was a logistical nightmare. A few years later we shot a scene that was cut from *Nosferatu* in which the vampire is standing in front of some horses in a meadow. At the moment when he slowly raises his arm an explosive went off behind the camera and the animals bolted. It looked good, but in the end I felt it was too much like a circus trick.

Many of my films contain animals, like jellyfish, which show up in several scenes, but I have no abstract concepts to offer that might explain how a particular animal signifies this or that. All I know is that animals have an enormous weight in my work, and some of the most hilarious performances I have ever seen are by animals, including those wacky television programmes where people send in videos of their crazy cat or piano-playing hamster. People always remember the dancing chicken at the end of *Stroszek*. I encountered that freak show about fifteen years before I made the film, at a Cherokee reservation in North Carolina, and couldn't get it out of my head; I knew that one day I had to return and film it. It's also where I heard Sonny Terry's harmonica music for the first time, which lingered in my mind. There was no doubt it had to be used at the end the film, and also, decades later, in *Bad Lieutenant*. It was too good not to recycle. I asked the owners of the chickens, which were in Alabama for the winter, to start special training months before we were due to film. Usually the animals would dance the barnyard shuffle for only five seconds and pick up a grain of corn after a quarter was deposited into the machine, but I needed this to go on as long as possible, so the owners set about intensively preparing the creatures for their big moment. It's a very bleak image, accompanied by the rather miserable feeling that if you came back a year later, the animal would still be there, dancing away. But as with the last sequence of *Land of Silence and Darkness*, you know it fits perfectly, including the manic rabbit jumping on a toy fire truck and the duck playing the drums. *Stroszek*'s small crew of about ten people all found the scene very stupid and embarrassing; everyone asked whether we were really going to shoot such rubbish after spending so much time on this stupid film. "Please," I said to Thomas Mauch, "just point the camera, press the button and let it roll until the film runs out. This is something very big. It's unobtrusive when you look at it with the naked eye, but can't you see there is something big about it?" Perhaps a great metaphor too, though for what I couldn't say. It's like those perfect goals you score from a theoretically impossible angle. Such things are beyond me.

Chickens obsess you.

Chickens in some forms – roasted, for example – are perfectly acceptable to me, but look into their eyes while they are alive and bear witness to genuine, bottomless stupidity. They are the most horrifying and nightmarish creatures in this world. During production on *Even Dwarfs Started Small* I watched a group of chickens trying to cannibalise a one-legged comrade, and in *Signs of Life* and *The Enigma of Kaspar Hauser* I show audiences how to hypnotise them, which is ridiculously easy. Hold the bird to the ground and using a piece of chalk draw a straight line away from its head. Do that and they don't budge an inch. You can also draw a circle around the animal and it will run in a loop until it drops from exhaustion.

Many years ago I became fascinated by a rooster named Weirdo, who weighed over thirty pounds. His offspring, Ralph, was even bigger. The man who had raised these extremely aggressive animals had been forced to singe off their spurs with a blowtorch. Then I found Frank, a miniature horse, specially bred from sixteenth-century Spanish stock, who stood less than two feet high. I told Frank's owner I wanted to film Ralph chasing Frank – with the tiniest midget riding him – around the biggest sequoia tree in the world, more than a hundred feet in circumference. It would have looked extraordinary because horse and rider together were still smaller than Ralph the rooster. Unfortunately Frank's owner refused. "My horse isn't going to show up for that," he said. "It will make him look stupid."

4

Athletics and Aesthetics

For you, filmmaking is athletics, not aesthetics.

It would be misleading to boil things down to a maxim like that, but let's try to shed some light on it. Everyone who makes films has to be an athlete to a certain degree. Cinema doesn't come from abstract academic thinking; it comes from knees and thighs, from being prepared to work twenty-hour days. Anyone who has ever made a film knows this. I have always appreciated a physical connection to my tools, from using the camera on location through to carrying prints of my films, each of which can weigh up to forty-five pounds, from my car into the projection room. What a relief to feel this weight, this substance, then let the heaviness drop away. It's the final stage of the physical act of filmmaking. A coward in body is often also a coward in mind. I will continue making films only as long as I am physically whole. If I were to lose a leg tomorrow, I would stop directing, even if my mind and sight were still solid. Let me offer a metaphor: all my films have been made on foot.

Have you always had this appreciation of all things physical?

For years I played with a bottom-division football team in Munich. Although almost everyone else was a faster or more technically skilled player, I was able to read the game better than anyone and often ended up in the right place at the right time, the spot where the ball would land, which meant I would regularly score goals. I'm still something like number three in the list of the all-time highest scorers for the club, even though some people spent twenty years playing for the team. Knowing what was going to happen next on the pitch and how to use the space around me was my only quality as a footballer.

I'm an excellent map reader and am rarely lost. You could take me down into the subway, lead me through the tunnels and spin me around three times, and I would still know which way was east. This ability to orientate myself has decided many important battles for me. When shooting interiors I always work closely with the set designer. Together we might move heavy furniture – perhaps the piano and bookshelf into this or that corner – to see how it feels. Physically rearranging objects in a room provides the knowledge necessary to operate within that space. With all this taken care of, I quickly work out where to place the actors in front of the camera. No time is wasted. Any aesthetic pattern that emerges within a shot always comes from a physical understanding of the environment in which the filming is taking place. I could never work competently in a space – interior or exterior – that I hadn't experienced with my body.

In the death scene of *The Enigma of Kaspar Hauser*, with all the characters arranged around Kaspar's bed in a tableau, there is a perfect balance within the space. Even with two days to move the actors about, no one would have succeeded in filling that space more effectively. There is a short scene earlier in the film shot in a garden where we worked for six months during pre-production. Before we got there it was a potato patch, so I planted strawberries, beans and flowers myself. Not only did this patch start to feel like the landscaped gardens of the era, but when it came to filming I knew exactly where every plant and vegetable was. I usually have no patience for these kinds of things, but in this case it was vitally important.

Why did you make The Great Ecstasy of Woodcarver Steiner?

I have always felt close to ski flyers. I grew up on skis and, like all children in Sachrang, dreamt about becoming a great ski flyer and national champion. I was in serious training until a friend of mine had a horrifying accident. He hit some rocks at sixty miles an hour, fracturing his skull, and was so badly injured that I was convinced he would die if I moved him even an inch. I ended up carrying him back to the village a mile and a half away, down a steep slope. My friend was in a coma for three weeks but miraculously recovered. This experience was the instantaneous end of my hopes of being a ski flyer. Then, in 1973, I saw the Swiss ski flyer Walter Steiner – the best of his generation – compete at Oberstdorf in Bavaria, where he jumped so far that he landed only thirty feet short of the flat. I had finally encountered the living embodiment of my dreams, someone who could move like a bird. It was almost as if it were me flying out there.

Ski flying at the level Steiner practised is fantastically dangerous. The speeds reached on the slope mean the slightest gust of wind or patch of bad snow can cause a serious crash landing. God help the athlete who tumbles off the end of the ramp and is projected uncontrollably into the air, which is comparable to falling off a speeding express train. The other danger is flying too far and landing on the flat, which would be like hitting the ground after jumping from the Empire State Building. I knew just what Steiner must have been going through before each jump, and would joke with him, saying, "Walter, if I had continued to jump, I would have been your only true rival." He was also a woodcarver and would leave his art on trees hidden up in the mountains, many of which remain undiscovered.

Though Steiner is an introverted, taciturn man, we had an instant rapport and he immediately understood my intentions. I told him that when I saw him in competition as a seventeen-year-old, trailing far behind all the others, I turned to my friends and said, "That's the next world champion." A few years later I was proved right. During production even the television network I made the film for kept reminding me that in the previous events Steiner had come in almost last, asking if perhaps I might rather choose a different jumper for the film. But I knew this man was the greatest of them all. Much of *The Great Ecstasy* was shot at Planica in Yugoslavia, where Steiner outflew everyone and even had to start lower down than everyone else, otherwise he would have landed on the flat again. Most ski ramps were truly lethal for someone with Steiner's skill, and in the film he talks about the thousands of spectators down in the valley out for his blood, though he asked me to edit out the line. "Don't put it in the film, for heaven's sake," he said. "I'll never be able to compete in Yugoslavia again." I told him it was important to include his thoughts on the subject, that people should have an idea of what it means to be up there against such inhumane demands. Steiner's experiences in Planica actually helped facilitate an eventual change in the construction of ski ramps.

You appear in the film.

People who accuse me of self-promotion point to *The Great Ecstasy* as proof, but it was actually a requirement that I be in the film. The German television network in Stuttgart had a series called *Grenzstationen* [*Border Stations*], which included some remarkably good work. I knew there must be one person behind all these films, so I called the station and asked who was responsible for the series. I met with him and explained I had an idea that would fit perfectly, and half an hour later we had a deal. Any film I made for this particular series would have to conform to the network's rules, one of which was that the filmmaker appear on camera. I never felt particularly comfortable with being physically present in the film, but because ski flying is so close to my heart I knew I could act as a competent commentator. When I finished *The Great Ecstasy*, I came to understand that if a film needed a voiceover commentary, it would be best that I spoke it myself; it's more credible that way. I have the feeling my presence can give a film a certain authenticity, something you don't necessarily get from listening to a well-trained actor with a polished voice. I realised there was value in me being the chronicler of events and presenting my own viewpoint on things. My work is never anonymous, and these days I would feel alienated from a film if I didn't record the voiceover myself, including English versions, which make for a stronger connection to my original intentions than audiences reading subtitles. I'm aware that my voice has an interesting cadence and tone to English speakers; they seem to like hearing me talk. The same is true for Germans because, with its Bavarian inflections, my voice is similarly unusual.

What is the "great ecstasy"?

The word comes from the Greek "*ekstasis*", meaning "to step outside oneself," like the mediaeval mystics did, experiencing faith and truth in an ecstatic, visionary form. Ecstasy in this context is something you would know about if you had ever been a ski jumper. You can see it on the flyers' faces as they sweep past the camera, mouths agape, with their extraordinary expressions.

Ski flying isn't just an athletic pursuit; it's also spiritual, a question of how to master a fear of death. Those jumpers who thought they could beat Steiner only through athletic means never stood a chance. There is a profound solitude in what these men do. These are lonely people who train for ten years to prepare themselves for a few seconds in the air, when they step outside all we are as human beings. It's as if they fly into the deepest, darkest abyss there is, in flagrant defiance of gravity, chasing one of mankind's oldest dreams: to move through the air without a machine. Overcoming this mortal fear and deep anxiety is the striking thing about ski flyers. You rarely see muscular athletic men up there on the ramps; usually these are young kids with deathly pale, pimply faces and an unsteady look in their eyes. They dream about flying, about stepping into the ecstasy that pushes against the laws of nature. I don't particularly care for gravity, so I suppose it's no coincidence that several of my films – *Little Dieter Needs to Fly*, *Wings of Hope* and *The White Diamond* – are about people who dream of flying, are punished for it and crash to earth. I always saw Steiner as a brother of Fitzcarraldo. Both defy the laws of gravity in their own way.

We had five cameramen and special cameras on either side of the ski ramp that could shoot in extreme slow motion, at something like four or five hundred frames a second. Filming at this speed is a challenge because the entire reel shoots through the camera in only a few seconds, and enormous physical force is placed on the celluloid. For this short moment of acceleration the cameramen follow the trajectory of the jumper through the air, trying to keep him in frame and focus. The result is slow-motion shots of these men endlessly floating down to earth. Once seen, these images are never forgotten.

Steiner tells the story of his raven.

I went through his family album and found a picture of him as a kid with a raven. I asked him about it, but he turned the page and wouldn't say anything. It took three more attempts on different days before he agreed to tell the story. You can see how uncomfortable he is in the film when he explains that when he was twelve, his only friend was a raven that he reared on bread and milk. Both the raven and Steiner were embarrassed by their friendship, so the raven would wait for him far away from the schoolhouse, and when all the other children were gone it would fly onto his shoulder and together they would ride on his bicycle. When the raven started losing its feathers, other birds began pecking it almost to death, and it was eventually so badly injured that Steiner was forced to kill it himself. "It was torture to see him being harried by his own kind because he couldn't fly any more," he says in the film. From that scene I cut to Steiner flying in slow motion, a shot that lasts more than a minute. A written caption appears, taken from a text by Robert Walser: "I should be all alone in this world, I, Steiner, and no other living being. No sun, no culture, I, naked on a high rock, no storm, no snow, no streets, no banks, no money, no time and no breath. Then I wouldn't be afraid any more."*

The story with the raven made such an impression on me that a couple of years later I borrowed it for a short film called *No One Will Play with Me*, made at a school for problem children in Munich. No one will play with Martin because, say his classmates, he stinks. He tells Nicole, a girl in his class, about his talking crow called Max, and they both visit it. Nicole then invites Martin to her home, where Nicole's mother takes care of the bruises and cuts on Martin's feet. It turns out he has been beaten repeatedly by his father and eats only popcorn because his mother is bedridden and dying of cancer. The conclusion I came to after making *No One Will Play with Me* is that there is no such thing as problem children, only problem parents. As with *The Flying Doctors of East Africa*, what interested me were questions of human perception, and before filming I spent time with the children, showing them prints of various paintings. One was of a city with castles, a harbour, a fish market and hundreds of people unloading ships; there were all sorts of things going on. I projected a slide of the picture for maybe ten seconds before turning it off, then asked the children, "What have you seen?" Four or five of them shouted in one voice, "A horse! A horse!" "Where on earth is the

* Adapted from the last lines of Walser's "Helblings Geschichte" (1914): "*Ich sollte eigentlich ganz allein auf der Welt sein, ich, Helbling, und sonst kein anderes lebendes Wesen. Keine Sonne, keine Kultur, ich nackt auf einem hohen Stein, kein Sturm, nicht einmal eine Welle, kein Wasser, kein Wind, keine Strassen, keine Banken, kein Geld, keine Zeit und kein Atem. Ich würde dann jedenfalls nicht mehr Angst haben.*"

horse?" I thought to myself. I put the slide back on and searched. "Down there!" they all shouted, pointing. Hidden in the corner of the picture was a single horseman with a lance, standing next to a horse. Then we watched an American film, and I asked them to talk about what they had seen. Several said they liked the soldier leaning in a doorway. I couldn't understand where they had seen this figure, but then replayed the scene and noticed that at one point the prince and princess leave the castle and a solitary soldier is standing guard. No adult would even have noticed this minor character, but for some of the children it was the thing most strongly imprinted on their minds. It makes me think to this very day.

Do you make a point of reading the reviews of your films?

Rarely. A positive review doesn't make a film better, nor does a negative one make a film worse. I've never been interested in circling around my own navel; I try to avoid myself. I might glance at some of the more important reviews because they can influence box-office takings, but generally none of it has anything to do with me. Audience reactions have always been more important than those of professional film-goers. When it comes to other people's work, I trust the professional even less; urgent recommendations are what I prefer. Some reviewers – like John Simon – have hated almost all my films, but that's okay. I never minded Simon dunking me underwater for as long as he could, and actually like him for his hostility and all-pervading vitriol. He is dismissive of a film from beginning to end. The man is not apathetic.*

He wrote that The Enigma of Kaspar Hauser *is historically inaccurate because Bruno S. – a forty-year-old man – played a sixteen-year-old boy.*

When it comes to that film, age doesn't matter. Bruno looked like a sixteen-year-old and is so unbelievably good on screen; he radiates

---

* On *Aguirre*'s photography, for example, which "never transcends mere adequacy," Simon wrote: "If this was a matter of insufficient funding, my condolences to Herzog; if a deliberate notion of minimal art, the back of my hand to him." "German and Gimcrack," in *Something to Declare*, p. 334.

such profound tragedy and radical, unblemished human dignity as no one else ever has. He's the finest actor I have ever worked with, and at the time I insisted he win the Academy Award for his performance. I remain convinced he gives one of the greatest performances ever on film; no other actor in the world has moved me so deeply. As with some of the situations in *Aguirre* that were genuinely dangerous for everyone involved, when you see Bruno on screen you aren't watching an actor merely playing a role and pretending to suffer. Some filmmaking is all about stylisation, but Bruno's fundamental identity as a human being was untouched in *The Enigma of Kaspar Hauser*. Watch the film and witness genuine human suffering, not theatrical melodrama. Anyway, who cares about the man's age? I'm a filmmaker, a storyteller, not an accountant of history. Whether Bruno was forty or seventy or fifteen years old isn't important. Criticism like this comes from the knowledge that audiences bring with them, and has nothing to do with the film per se.

Some reviewers compared it to Truffaut's film *L'Enfant sauvage*, which had been released a few years before and is about the doctor who cared for the Wild Boy of Aveyron, a young child who was found in a forest, unable to speak or walk properly. Truffaut's film is about a child raised by wolves who has some kind of social system instilled in him, even if it was that of wild animals. But Kaspar has no nature whatsoever, not that of bourgeois society, nor of wolves. He is, simply, human. Over time there have been several documented cases similar to the one in Truffaut's film, but Kaspar's story is unique. Nobody could tell exactly how old the real Kaspar was, though there are plausible guesses that he must have been about sixteen or seventeen when he was pushed out into the open as a foundling, unable even to walk.

Who was Kaspar?

Nobody had any idea where he came from or who he was when he showed up in Nuremberg in 1828. When the townsfolk tried to communicate with him, it turned out he had spent his entire life locked away in a dark dungeon, tied to the ground with his belt. Like many of the characters in my films, Kaspar emerged from the blackest night. He arrived never having had any contact with or understanding of human beings; food was pushed into his cell every night while he was sleeping. He was unable to walk properly, had no idea what a house was, knew nothing about table manners and thought the belt around his waist was a natural part of his anatomy. It's fascinating to read some of Kaspar's own writings, where we learn he was even frightened by birdsong. His mind was unable to co-ordinate what it was hearing because he had no conception of the world. A couple of years after being taken in by the town, and once he had learnt language, word got out that Kaspar was writing his autobiography. Soon after came the first attempt on his life, followed by his murder. It was about two and a half years since he had been found in the town square. To this day no one knows who killed him.

When we hear the story of Kaspar Hauser, we think about how civilisation manipulates and remodels, always bringing us into line. His problems are our problems, the anxiety and difficulties we all have in adapting to the world, in connecting and communicating with others. Kaspar is the most intact person in this unnamed town; he has the kind of genuine intelligence you sometimes find in illiterates. But everything spontaneous in him is systematically deadened by this philistine society. Kaspar is propelled into the world as a young man who hadn't experienced society in any way, and is doomed from the instant he arrives in town. The stultifying and staid existence of the people surrounding Kaspar reveals itself very potently within the historical setting of the Biedermeier era, the most intensively bourgeois period of German history, with its interminable rituals and rules. There's a scene in the film when a young child holds a mirror up to Kaspar's face; it's the first time he has ever seen his reflection, and he immediately feels confused and shocked. This is what Kaspar is doing to everyone around him: forcing them to confront their day-to-day existence with new eyes. He is the stumbling block over which society trips.

At one point Kaspar spontaneously starts weeping after being given a baby to hold, then says, "*Ich bin von allen abgetan*" ["I am so far away from everything"]. In another scene, a professor of logic tests him by explaining there is one village inhabited by people who tell only the truth and a second where people tell only lies. A man is walking between the two villages. What is the only question, the professor asks Kaspar, that can be asked of this man to determine whether he is from the village of truth-tellers or the village of liars? In terms of strict logic, the only solution to the professor's problem is the one he gives Kaspar, but Kaspar's answer – that you can ask the man if he is a tree frog – is also correct. In the autopsy scene, the townspeople are like circling vultures as they feverishly attempt to find some physical aberration in Kaspar, and are overjoyed to discover that apparently he has a malformed brain. Finding this physical difference between themselves and Kaspar makes them feel better about how they treated him when he was alive. There is an inevitability about someone as uncivilised and uncultured as Kaspar not being able to survive that environment, and if the real Kaspar hadn't been murdered, I would have killed him at the end of the film anyway. In terms of a coherent cinematic narrative, he has to be finished off.

How much historical research did you do?

When the film came out, I was asked if I used Jakob Wassermann's novel *Caspar Hauser* as the basis of the story, though to this day I've never read it. I did look at Peter Handke's play *Kaspar*, about the origins and distortions of language, and there is also a beautiful poem by Verlaine called "Gaspard Hauser chante". I took time to read a volume of original documents and essays that included the first part of Anselm von Feuerbach's report, alongside the poetry and autobiographical fragment Kaspar wrote, and details of his autopsy. Various things in the film – like Kaspar's toy wooden horse, him being carried to a hilltop where he is taught to walk, his extremely tender feet, him spitting out food in disgust but delighting in bread and water – come from this source, as well as the text of the letter found in Kaspar's hand read by the cavalry captain and Kaspar's own beautiful line, *"Ja, mir kommt es vor, dass mein Erscheinen auf dieser Welt ein harter Sturz gewesen ist"* ["Well, it seems to me that my coming into this world was a terribly hard fall"]. The Kaspar Hauser archives are in Ansbach, the town where he was killed, but I never went there. A thousand books and more than ten thousand articles and research papers about Kaspar have been published; I asked myself whether I really needed to involve myself with such extraneous scholarship. The vast majority of this material focuses on the criminal case and frames the facts as a detective story or a police thriller, or digs into Kaspar's origins, speculating on whether he was Napoleon's illegitimate son. A film version of the story even suggested Kaspar was a prince from the royal house of Baden,* a theory disproved when a German magazine did a DNA test on the blood from the shirt Kaspar was wearing when he was killed and compared it to blood taken from a living member of the house of Baden. It's everything beyond these things that is truly interesting about Kaspar.

As with *Aguirre, The Enigma of Kaspar Hauser* doesn't purport to be a factually correct retelling of history. The film tries to reach a more profound truth than that of everyday reality, something made clear with the visualisations of Kaspar's dreams. Only the most basic factual elements of his life as we know them are contained within the story; the rest is invented. As far as we know, he was never exhibited in a circus, he never talked to a professor of logic and never spoke about the Sahara. The real Kaspar – having escaped the attempt on his life – said that he had, in a flash, recognised the assassin as the man who had brought him from the cellar and taught him to walk, which is why I used the same actor in both roles.

Like Fata Morgana, The Enigma of Kaspar Hauser *has elements of science fiction to it.*

If you strip away the story and look only at the dream sequences, you would be left with something that feels like *Fata Morgana*, just as if you strip away the story of *Signs of Life* and keep the shot of the windmills. I always felt that *The Enigma of Kaspar Hauser* is almost *Fata Morgana* with a narrative. The tale of this boy is almost a science-fiction story similar to the idea of aliens arriving on our planet, as with the original conception of *Fata Morgana*. They have no human social conditioning and walk around confused and amazed. The real question is perhaps anthropological: what happens to a man who has crashed onto our planet with no concept of the world, no education or culture? What does he feel? What does he see? What must a tree or horse look like to him? How would he be treated? What interested me was the story of someone who was uncontaminated by society and outside forces. There is a moment

* *Kaspar Hauser* (1996), written and directed by Peter Sehr.

when Kaspar sits calmly as a swordsman lunges at him, because he has no understanding of danger. In another scene he burns himself on a flame because he has never seen fire before. When Kaspar was first found by the townspeople, he spoke only a few words and a handful of phrases he clearly didn't understand, including, "*Ich möchte ein solcher Reiter werden wie mein Vater einer war*" ["I want to be a gallant horseman the way my father was"]. He spoke the sentence like a parrot.

Some of the shots in the film are held for an unusually long time, like the one near the beginning of the rye field blowing in the wind. I want audiences to empathise with Kaspar by looking anew at certain things and seeing them through his untainted eyes. The music – Pachelbel's *Canon* – represents Kaspar's awakening from his slumber. What contributes to the power of this moment are the words that appear, from Büchner's *Lenz*: "Don't you hear that horrible screaming around you, the screaming men call silence?"

The literal translation of the film's German title is "Every Man for Himself and God Against All."

The evening I finished the screenplay I watched a Brazilian film called *Macunaíma*, directed by Joaquim Pedro de Andrade, in which one of the characters says, "Every man for himself and God against all." I jumped out of my seat because I knew it was the perfect title for Kaspar's story. I wrote a sequence for the film but never shot it, a discussion between the priest and Kaspar after the first attempt on his life in which Kaspar says, "When I look around at people, I truly have the feeling God must have something against them."

Is casting something you always do yourself?

It has always been an essential part of my work. When you have a good screenplay and a good cast, you barely need a director. Whoever said that casting was 90 per cent of the director's job was right. I am extremely careful when casting even minor roles; whoever steps in front of my camera is royalty. You can't throw actors together and expect a film to coalesce; they have to complement each other and create a certain chemistry and – at times – friction. One lousy performance can contaminate the entire film.

Sometimes there are difficulties in persuading others that your choice is the right one. My efforts to cast Bruno S. in *The Enigma of Kaspar Hauser* are a good example. I first encountered him in *Bruno the Black*, a film by a young student called Lutz Eisholz about marginal figures – street performers and singers – in Berlin. It was a lucky coincidence for me, because after writing the screenplay I had no idea who I might find to play Kaspar. When I saw Bruno on screen I was immediately fascinated by him, and literally found myself getting up out of bed and standing in front of the television set, staring intensely. The next day I asked Eisholz to put me in touch with Bruno, and the following week we both went to his apartment. He was mistrustful of everyone he met, and when he opened the door wouldn't even look me in the eye. It took about half an hour before he would even make eye contact with me and start to confide certain things, but once we had established a rapport we maintained it throughout the production. Our conversations were always complex and invigorating, and on several occasions I put into the film things I heard him say, like the line, "The people are like wolves to me."

Everyone doubted whether Bruno would be able to play the lead character in a feature film. They all told me it was impossible to direct a man like that, so I did something I had never done before and have never done since: I assembled a full crew and a 35mm camera to shoot a screen test, on a lake near Berlin, with Bruno in full costume alongside another actor. Immediately things were uncomfortable, and I had a feeling it would all end up in embarrassment because Bruno was so stiff and nervous. But when I looked at the footage I only saw my mistakes, not Bruno's, and realised exactly how to handle him in the future. When I showed the screen test to ZDF [Zweites Deutsches Fernsehen], the television network that was putting up much of the budget for the film, I sank deeper and deeper into my chair. The lights went up in the screening room and there was a nasty silence hanging in the air. The network executive stood up and said, "I'm against Bruno for the part. Who is with me?" The hands of everyone – all thirty people – shot up into the air. I sensed there was a hand not raised next to me. It was Jörg Schmidt-Reitwein, my cameraman. "Jörg," I asked, "are you for Bruno?" He grinned and nodded. His inner fire had somehow prevailed.

I'm not in favour of numerical democracy in voting, so I looked at these people against Bruno, then turned to Schmidt-Reitwein and said, "We have won the ballot." It was like in mediaeval times, when, if a group of monks were against some innovation or a reform of monastic life because of indifference, and only a couple of them had the feverish knowledge that these changes had to be made to advance the cause of faith, then out of the enormity of their wish these two would declare themselves the *melior pars* – the "better part" – and win the ballot. Intensity wins the battle, not strength in numbers. "Bruno is going to be the one," I announced to everyone in the room, and asked the ZDF executive to declare himself either with me or against me. He looked into my face for a long while, then said, "I'm still on board." His name is Willi Segler, and I love him for his loyalty. It was a great moment for me. In situations like this, dig in your heels and budge not a single inch. We went into production almost immediately.

Why did you choose to keep Bruno's identity secret?

He asked us to, and he was right to do so. When he was four years old, his mother, a prostitute, beat him so hard he lost his speech and used this as a pretext to put him into an asylum for retarded and insane children. Bruno told me about his time in an institution during the Nazi era, something he talks about in *Stroszek*, the second film we made together. If he wet his bed at night, he had to stand with his arms stretched out holding the sheet in front of the other children, until it was dry. If he lowered his arms, he was beaten. Eventually, at the age of nine, he escaped and spent the next twenty-three years of his life in and out of institutions and prisons. He also picked up a number of minor criminal convictions for things like vagrancy and public indecency.

Bruno was aware that the film we made together was as much about how society had destroyed him as it was about how society had killed Kaspar Hauser. Maybe for this reason he wanted to remain anonymous, and for many years I called him the "Unknown Soldier of Cinema." *The Enigma of Kaspar Hauser* is his monument; I even considered calling the film *The Story of Bruno Hauser*. I felt he shouldn't be removed from his environment for long, nor should he be exposed to the press or regaled as a film star, but he was excited when he heard about the Cannes Film Festival and said, "*Der Bruno* wants to transmit [*durchgeben*] his accordion by playing to those people." He referred to himself in the third person, and never said "act" or "do," always "transmit." I was wary about taking him to the meat market out there, but he really wanted to go. "My whole life I was excluded," he said. "I could never involve myself in anything. Now we have done something beautiful, I want to be a part of it." The press is so intrusive at Cannes, but he was extraordinarily grounded when confronted by them, pulling out his bugle and giving a signal. One time he stood up in front of an audience with his accordion and said, "I will now play all the nuances of the colour red." He drew so much attention, yet remained completely untouched by it and wasn't the least bit concerned by the hordes of photographers. At the press conference for the film Bruno impressed everyone. He said he had come to look at the sea for the first time, and marvelled at how clean it was. Someone told him that, in fact, it wasn't. "When the world is emptied of human beings," he said, "it will become so again." If you watch him in certain scenes in *Stroszek*, you can hear the extraordinary sweetness in his voice. Although he had been systemically trampled upon throughout his life, Bruno was a genuinely warm-hearted man.

How did he acclimatise to being on a film set?

Without the mutual trust quickly established between the two of us, I wouldn't have stood a chance. With Bruno there was always physical contact. He liked it when I held his wrist; not his hand, just his wrist, as if I had my fingers on his pulse. But he could also be unruly, and whenever he would talk about the injustices of the world I tried to give him the space to say whatever he wanted. I got angry with a soundman who, after a few minutes of ranting, opened a magazine and started to read. "You're being paid to listen," I told him. Eventually Bruno would see that everyone was looking at him, and say, "*Der Bruno* has talked too much. Let's do some good work now." I repeatedly said to him, "Bruno, when you need to talk and speak about yourself, do it. It's not an interruption for us. It's very much a part of what we're doing here. Not everything needs to be recorded on film."

Bruno liked the character of Kaspar so much that he refused

to take his costume off. One day he overslept for breakfast, so I knocked on his door. There was no answer. I pushed it open and it immediately banged into something. It was Bruno, sleeping on the floor, right next to the door, fully clothed, with a pillow and blanket. In a split second he stood upright in front of me, wide awake, and said, "Yes, Werner, what is it?" It really broke my heart when I saw this. "Bruno, you've overslept," I said. "Did you really sleep here on the floor?" "Yes," he said, "*Der Bruno* is always sleeping next to the escape." That's where he felt safe. In the past, whenever Bruno would break out of a correctional institution he would go into hiding, and because of this was always on high alert, ready to be recaptured.

Shooting the film was tiring for him, and whenever Bruno was exhausted he would say, "*Der Bruno* is going to take that one," before having a nap for a couple of minutes between takes. It was his way of removing himself for short periods of time. At the end of each shot we would record a minute of ambient sound. Every interior and exterior has its own atmosphere and tone of silence, and for continuity in editing it's always useful to get a recording. But with Bruno around this wasn't always possible because five seconds after calling "cut" he would be snoring. Sometimes I had to cut in the middle of a scene because he was farting so loudly. Much of the dialogue was written while I was sitting on set, literally as the lights were being positioned, because at that point the actors needed something to say. Giving them their dialogue at the last minute obviously meant they weren't able to learn anything by heart, which I came to realise was important when it came to working with Bruno. About a week before we were due to shoot Kaspar's death scene, I talked him through the moment when he is mortally stabbed, and he immediately started making notes to himself. A few days later he said, "Werner, finally I know what to transmit." He stood there and said, very seriously, "I will transmit the cry of death!" before screaming wildly like a bad theatre actor, then thrashing about and falling to the ground. Bruno envisioned himself playing the scene that way, so twenty minutes before shooting I did a rewrite. It would have been too difficult to persuade him otherwise, and in the film you see Kaspar stumbling into the garden having already been stabbed. From then on I went out of my way to make sure that Bruno wasn't able to mull over the script in advance.

Something else to deal with was the fact that Bruno didn't speak pure German, or even grammatically correct German, rather a dialect from the Berlin suburbs. In the end we were able to take advantage of this because his slow and careful recitation of dialogue somehow elevates the acting to a level of stylisation. It adds to the power of Bruno's performance because his speaking voice and articulation produced a beautiful effect, as if he is discovering language for the first time.

Did Bruno become more confident as the shoot progressed?

He was an intelligent and streetwise man, not at all defenceless, even if the character he played was fundamentally unable to protect himself from the world. I made it clear to him before we started work that on the most primitive level this was to be an exchange of services. "You act in the film and I'll pay you," I explained. "But there's more to it than that, because you'll be able to fill this character with more convincing life than anyone else in the world. There is a considerable responsibility on your shoulders." It was a challenge he accepted without hesitation. He quickly became used to how we did things on set and worked hard, which included refusing to eat lunch because he said it disturbed his concentration. For the scene where Kaspar learns to walk, it was Bruno's idea to put a stick in the hollow of his knees, then sit for two hours and numb his legs, after which he was unable to stand.

Bruno also had moments of real distrust of us all, especially me. He was always going into bars, throwing his money around and getting drunk, so I suggested we open a bank account for him, which would be a hurdle to him spending money so easily. He was immediately convinced there was a conspiracy to steal his wages. No one – not even the bank manager – could persuade him it was impossible for me to take money from his account unless I had his personal authorisation in writing. He even accused me of hiring a stooge to play the manager. But the times when he did trust what we were doing were important and quite moving. He would talk incessantly about death and wrote a will. "Where shall I put it?" he asked me. "My brother will kill me, or I will kill him if I see him. I can't trust my family. My mother the whore is dead, my sister the whore is dead." I told him to put it in a safe in the bank or to give it to a lawyer. "No, I don't trust them," he said. Two days later he handed me the will and asked me to take care of it.

We found an old-fashioned, genuine autopsy table made of solid marble for the death scene. Bruno was so fascinated with death and this table that once shooting was over he desperately wanted to have it. "The name of this table is Justice," he would say in a strange tone of voice. "This is where the rich and poor end up." He wanted to take the table, but I explained that we had rented it as a prop from an antique shop. I think I even suggested it probably wasn't the kind of thing he wanted to own. "No, *Der Bruno* must have it!" he said. "When I saw myself lying on this table, I knew that the cause of death was *Heimweh* [homesickness]." I took his request seriously only when he gave me some paintings he had done of the table, which were basically self-portraits of him lying on this thing. A speech bubble from his mouth had the words "Cause of death: *Heimweh*." A few months later I asked him if he wanted any stills from the film or photographs taken on the set. "The only one I want," he said, "is a photo of the scene of the autopsy. The table is Justice." After that I felt he should have the table after all. I bought it from the shop and gave it to him.

Our work together gave Bruno a certain confidence, and helped him within his own social milieu. People who lived in his Berlin neighbourhood would drag him into the pastry shop and buy him a treat, and the local barber would give him a free haircut and shave. I was careful to ensure that he held onto his job as a forklift driver in a steel factory; we filmed during his vacation, and because he got only three weeks off every year I asked for additional unpaid holiday time for him. He had been treated like a freak there, but after the film was released I called the factory and asked to speak to Bruno. The secretary would say, "Sorry, our Bruno isn't on the factory floor at the moment." Before they would never have used the word "our," but now they were genuinely proud of him. Apparently every employee of the factory went to see the film. People took him seriously and he was given real responsibilities.

I was aware that none of this could solve the fundamental problems Bruno's catastrophic life had showered on him. During shooting he would sometimes express utter despair about his life and what had happened to him. I told him what he already knew, that working together for five weeks could never repair the damage so many years of imprisonment and catastrophe had caused. I know that in the long term his involvement with the film helped Bruno come to terms with his experiences. It was a unique opportunity for him to reflect on his own life, though there were things he still didn't understand. Why, when he walked down the street, dirty and neglected, did the girls have no time for him? He would grab one of them and cry, "Why don't you kiss me!" Bruno earned a good sum of money for his work, which we helped him put to good use, so on the primitive level of economics Bruno benefited from the experience. When I first met him, his apartment was a single room piled high with rubbish. By the time we made *Stroszek*, he was living in a bigger place, which he proceeded to fill with things he pulled out of the garbage.

I had the feeling that *The Enigma of Kaspar Hauser* was some kind of summing up after so many years of work, and several characters from earlier films appear in various scenes: Hombre the dwarf sitting on a throne; Walter Steiner as a drunken peasant; composer Florian Fricke as a piano player, the same role he plays in *Signs of Life*; and Hombrecito from *Aguirre*, played by Kidlat Tahimik, a Filipino director, speaking in Tagalog. There's also a young Mozart, the remnant of a project I never got off the ground. It was as if I were drawing a line with the scene, summarising my work up until that moment, seeing where I should go from there. I felt as if I were exploring new directions without constraints, which I continued to do with *Heart of Glass*.

For which you hypnotised the actors.

Cinema per se has a hypnotic quality to it. I often find myself in an almost unconscious state on the film set, having to ask the person doing continuity what scenes have already been done and what work remains. What a shock to be told it's already the third week of filming. "How is this possible?" I ask myself. "Where has all the time gone? What have I actually achieved here?" It's as if I were at a drunken party and somehow arrived home without being aware of it. The next morning three policemen are standing at my bedside, accusing me of having killed someone the night before.

The story of *Heart of Glass* was loosely adapted from a chapter of a novel called *Die Stunde des Todes* [*The Hour of Death*] by Herbert Achternbusch, who played the chicken hypnotiser in *The Enigma of Kaspar Hauser*. The book was based on an old folk legend about a peasant prophet in Lower Bavaria who – like Nostradamus – made predictions about the cataclysmic end of the world. The story is about an inventor of a special kind of ruby glass who has died, taking his secret with him to the grave. No details can be found in his home, and after a smelter tries in vain to recreate the formula, the local factory owner sends for the herdsman Hias, known for his prophetic gifts. Hias proves to be of little help, and the factory owner eventually comes to believe that the blood of a young virgin must be added to the glass mixture, so he stabs his housemaid to death. When he announces he now has the knowledge to formulate ruby glass, a euphoric, crazed celebration breaks out in town. Hias has apocalyptic visions because he is able to see further into the future than anyone around him. In his trances he imagines a new world; he foresees the people around him becoming insane and the destruction by fire of the town's glassworks. The owner burns his own factory down, as prophesised, and the glassblowers search for a culprit. They mistake the prediction of evil for its origin, and Hias is blamed for the fire.

Although at the time I knew very little about hypnosis and it had never crossed my mind to use it in a film, I started to think about the story I had before me, this tale of collective madness, of people aware of an approaching catastrophe yet who do nothing. After all, the idea of people walking into a foreseeable disaster is an unfortunately familiar situation in German history. I wondered how I could stylise the actors, creating sleepwalkers with open eyes, as if in a trance. I wanted performers with fluid, floating movements, which meant the film would depart from commonplace behaviour and gestures. I wanted it to have an atmosphere of hallucination, prophecy and collective delirium that intensified towards the climax. The identities of the actors would remain intact under hypnosis, but they would be stylised. Maybe the title *Heart of Glass* makes more sense in this light; for me, it refers to a sensitive and fragile inner state, one that has a kind of transparent glacial quality. I wondered if a hypnotised person could open their eyes without waking up, and if people under hypnosis would be able to communicate with each other. Both turned out to be possible. In fact, if you put two hypnotised people in a crowded room, they are intuitively drawn to each other, and learning dialogue is easier because in many cases memory functions better while under hypnosis.

Two films encouraged me to push on with my ideas. One was *The Tragic Diary of Zero the Fool*,* featuring a theatre group from a lunatic asylum in Canada; the other was Jean Rouch's *Les Maîtres fous*, shot in Ghana and featuring the annual ceremonies of the Hauka tribe, who – while in trance and heavily under the influence of drugs – enact the arrival of the English governor and his entourage. Rouch's boldness and depth of insight into human nature have forever stayed with me; I consider *Les Maîtres fous* one of the greatest films ever made. It virtually stopped my heart the first time I saw it, and has forever inspired me to venture into the abyss of the human soul in ways most people would never dare.

Did you do the hypnosis yourself?

During pre-production I put an ad in a newspaper asking for people who wanted to take part in a film project involving hypnosis, and about six hundred people responded. I spent more time on casting *Heart of Glass* than for any other film I've made, before or after; there were sessions once a week for six months. We selected about forty people according to the types needed for the story, and also, crucially, based on their receptivity to hypnosis. We were careful to choose individuals who were emotionally stable and genuinely interested in what we were doing. Being hypnotised isn't about just sinking into the unconscious, it's about concentration. There is a certain proclivity for being hypnotised; just as some people can ride a bicycle without any training, some are able to be hypnotised very easily. Everyone's susceptibility is different. Some people immediately slip into an apathetic state and become wholly disorientated; they lose much of their ability to control themselves physically, so obviously we didn't select them. Others are so normal in their reactions that you can hardly distinguish them from the non-hypnotised. Everyone is different, and one of the actors

---

* *The Tragic Diary of Zero the Fool* (Canada, 1969), directed by Morley Markson, who describes the film as "an experimental improvisation. I remember entering it into the Toronto Film Festival but it failed to qualify for entry because, they said, it's simply 'not a movie.' I liked that a lot." See *Monthly Film Bulletin*, March 1971.

we selected – the old man playing the factory owner who laughs throughout the film – had no interest in waking up once he had been hypnotised, resisting whenever I tried to bring him out of it.

We had a hypnotist who was supposed to act as some kind of assistant director, but he turned out to be a New Age creep who claimed hypnosis was a cosmic aura that only he, with his special powers, could attract and radiate. His whole approach disgusted me; he would babble on about how hypnosis was a direct link to the supernatural. Years later I put some of these more ridiculous ideas into the script of *Invincible*, when Hanussen is performing on stage. The neurological difference between being awake and being asleep, and being asleep and being under hypnosis, is more or less the same. Hypnosis is surrounded by an aura of mystery, but it's really an ordinary phenomenon; science just hasn't yet furnished us with a sufficient explanation of the exact physiological processes at work when someone is under hypnosis. It has nothing to do with metaphysics or any kind of evil power, even if the country-fair hypnotist has forever tried to convince his audience otherwise. The way hypnosis works is by the hypnotist giving life to the act of self-hypnosis via mind and speech rituals. It's all about auto-suggestion. The fact is that anyone with natural authority and a certain intensity of suggestion can become a hypnotist, and after two rehearsal sessions I ended up doing it all myself.

Did some people suspect it was just a gimmick?

Of course, but there was a very clear purpose to it. The potential for visionary and poetic language is revealed through hypnosis. I wanted to provoke poetic language from people who had never before been in touch with such things, just as the nightmarish *Even Dwarfs Started Small*, the ecstatic *Woodcarver Steiner* and the films I made with Bruno S. and Fini Straubinger were attempts to render on screen, for everyone to see and experience, certain inner states.

The aim of rehearsals was to work out a catalogue of suggestions that would result in the kind of stylised somnambulism you see in the film. What counted was the way things were suggested to the actors, and soon they were able to feel non-existent heat so intensely they would break out in a sweat. They could hold conversations with imaginary people, and two hypnotised actors could even talk coherently to a third imaginary person. I hypnotised one woman and told her she was no longer able to speak. When I woke her she had such difficulty talking, even asking for a glass of water, that I hypnotised her again and told her, "You are slowly regaining the gift of speech. When you wake up, you will be able to speak like a great orator." She immediately began to talk with great eloquence. The timing of the movements and speech of the actors was often very peculiar, and once they had been brought out of their states many had only a vague recollection of what they had been doing. If there were a pause of more than two minutes between takes, I would wake them up because it isn't healthy to keep someone under hypnosis for very long. After working with the actors for several weeks, it usually took only ten or fifteen seconds to put them back under again.

Rather than give specific directions per se, it was more important to get the actors into the right mood. Instead of asking them to walk across a room, I said something like, "You move as if in slow motion because the whole room is filled with water. You can breathe easily, like a scuba diver. You are drifting, floating." Or, "You see your partner but look through him, as you look through a window," and "You are an inventor of great genius working on an insane, beautiful invention. When I put my hand on your shoulder, tell me what this thing is and how it works." I wanted each actor to write a poem, but what they came out with depended on the quality of the suggestion, so I never asked someone just to write a poem. Instead I told them, "You're the first one for centuries who has set foot on a foreign island. It's overgrown with jungle and full of strange birds. You come across a gigantic cliff, and on closer inspection discover the rock is actually green emerald. Hundreds of years ago a monk took a chisel and hammer and engraved a poem into the wall. You open your eyes and are the first one to see it. Read out loud what you see." One actor with no formal education whose day job was tending the horse stables of a Munich police squad stood there and apologised. "I didn't bring my glasses," he said. I told him to move closer, then everything would be in focus. He stepped forward and in a strange voice said, "Why can we not drink the moon? Why is there no vessel to hold it?" On it went, a very beautiful reading. Sometimes, of course, hypnosis triggers only banalities. I told the same story to one young man – a law student who had dropped out of his studies – who took one look at the wall and said, "Dear Mother, I'm doing fine. Everything is all right. I'm looking to the future now. Hugs and kisses, Your Son."

The only actor in the film not put into trance was Josef Bierbichler, who played Hias, the only clairvoyant among the townsfolk. The workers in the glass factory, who were all authentic, professional glassblowers, also weren't under hypnosis because it would have been too dangerous, as liquid glass has a temperature of more than a thousand degrees. They were also drinking a fair amount of beer because of the heat. It's intensive work; they literally have no tools except a long pipe and a pair of pliers. Certain things they do could never be achieved with mechanical devices. One particular shot – a glassblower creating a figurine of a horse – is truly extraordinary to watch. I have never met anyone who understands physical materials as these people do. Nothing is more rewarding than observing real artists working at close quarters.

During the scene in the bar, with all the men sitting around, every time I told the cameraman Jörg Schmidt-Reitwein to take one step to the left, all the actors did too. I ended up using two voices with different intonations during shooting: one for the technical crew, the other for everyone in front of the camera. Years later, on the set of *Invincible*, I trained Tim Roth in hypnosis for the part of Hanussen. At one point during filming I looked up and saw cameraman Peter Zeitlinger staggering backwards. He was so close to Tim – who in the film has a wonderful demonic quality to him and was speaking almost into the lens of the camera – that he had become semi-hypnotised himself.

Was it important for audiences to know the actors were hypnotised?

I never made a fuss about it and hoped the whole thing could be done as unobtrusively as possible; it was only the media who dug their teeth in. They made certain statements I felt I should respond to, and at one point a journalist showed up at a rehearsal without making himself known to me and proved to be a disruptive force. It was suggested by the press that I was using hypnosis because I wanted more control over the actors, but I certainly wasn't looking for a bunch of performing puppets for the film. It's a common mistake to assume that someone under hypnosis can be manipulated in certain ways, but this absolutely isn't the case because their hard core remains untouched. Murder under hypnosis is a myth; if I ask a hypnotised person to take a knife and kill his mother, he would refuse. Hypnotised people also have a tendency to lie, which means my plans had nothing to do with a desire for control. Another misconception about the power of hypnosis is that it can reconnect people to their former lives. During the first few days of casting, the creepy hypnotist put some of the participants into a trance and told them they lived in ancient Egypt. Some of them spoke in a strange language about their former lives in eras long ago; one woman even described living in Alexandria as a dancer on a high platform from which she could see the Nile. But it was all obvious nonsense. No branch of the river's delta passed near Alexandria at the time, and the language she spoke was meaningless babble, not unlike what you hear in Southern Baptist churches, with people speaking in tongues.

When I talk to people who have no idea I used hypnosis on the actors, they speak of the film's "dreamy atmosphere." The opening images of the waterfall are there almost to help put audiences into a trance. Staring directly into the moving water and listening intensely to the suggestions of the voice in German – reading the English subtitles doesn't really do the job – makes you feel as if the waterfall is standing still and it's you who are floating upwards. The experience isn't unlike staring from a bridge down into a fast-flowing river. All of a sudden the river seems to stop moving, and you start to float. There's a line from one of Hölderlin's poems: *"Man kann auch in die Höhe fallen"* ["One can even fall upwards"]. I once showed *Aguirre* to a hypnotised audience. To keep everyone under hypnosis for an hour and a half, I played a piece of music by the band Popol Vuh – one that appears in the film – before the screening. I told the audience that whenever they heard this music, they would sink into a deep hypnotic state. I spoke to some of them afterwards. One man believed himself to have been in a helicopter, flying around Aguirre, evading his gaze. A handful of people had fallen asleep, though when I questioned them about this they insisted they had seen the entire film. When I asked them to tell the story back to me, they embellished what they had missed in very imaginative ways.

It's actually possible to hypnotise someone from a screen. The original idea was for me to appear in a prologue to *Heart of Glass*

crash down onto the rock face. It wasn't easy getting the shots of the rowing men because of the violent waves and torrential rains. Whenever the cameraman Thomas Mauch was ready to shoot, the actors were vomiting over the sides, and whenever they were ready to shoot, Mauch was wretching. I was busy throwing pieces of bread into the air to attract the gannets. The locals told us we were the first people for years to make the journey in such small boats. You can still visit the original thousand-year-old monastery at the top, comprised of several buildings all in excellent condition and accessible thanks to the staircase of six hundred stone steps, expertly carved by monks.

Hias has a vision of a man standing up there, someone who still believes the Earth is a flat disc ending in an abyss somewhere far out in the ocean. For years he has stood staring out over the sea, until several men – who have also yet to learn we live on a spherical planet – join him. One day they resolve to take the ultimate risk and row out to sea in a small, fragile boat. These men are some of the few who have the courage to explore; they need to see where the world ends. They voyage into grey, open waters, battling against the waves, in search of the truth. In the last shot of the film, as music from Martim Codax plays, we see the ocean growing dark under heavy clouds.

Words appear: "It may have seemed like a sign of hope that the birds followed them out into the vastness of the sea." Did you write that?

I did. And somehow, maybe, I want to be that man seen from a distance, looking to the horizon, staring beyond the raging ocean into the unknown, who decides to set out and discover the shape of the earth for himself.

5
Legitimacy

You claim not to be part of the German Romantic tradition.

Years ago I was in Paris shortly after an exhibition of the work of German Romantic painter Caspar David Friedrich. Every journalist I spoke to seemed to have seen the exhibition and insisted on viewing my films – especially *Heart of Glass* and *The Enigma of Kaspar Hauser* – within the context of this knowledge they had suddenly acquired. Then, after a similar exhibition of German expressionism a few years later, everyone told me how many elements of expressionism could be found in my work. One year it was inconceivable to them I hadn't imbued my films from start to finish with elements of German romanticism, the next they were even more incredulous that there was no preconceived notion of expressionism in my work. Those are the only two movements in German art the French have ever heard of, so I must have been influenced by one or the other. It's a fire I have never been able to extinguish. When it comes to Americans, who have generally been good to my films over the years but have little knowledge of either romanticism or expressionism, for them the only question is, "Is this film in line with Nazism or not?" Or, occasionally, "Does this film relate in any way to Brecht's theories and principles?"

You can't get a more contrary position towards the Romantic point of view than mine. Go back and listen to what I say in *Burden of Dreams* – the film Les Blank made on the set of *Fitzcarraldo* – about nature being vile and base, lacking in harmony, full of creatures constantly fighting for survival.* Anyone who understands such things

* "The trees here are in misery and the birds are in misery. I don't think

knows those could never be the words of a Romantic. If you're interested in what I think about nature, take a look up into the night sky and consider that it's a complete mess, full of recalcitrant chaos. The overwhelming quality of the universe is monumental indifference and lack of order. It's a statistical improbability we're even on the planet, this miniscule speck surrounded by a myriad of uninhabitable, hostile and lethal stars that boil in nuclear rage. Look at the solar system from a satellite and see how utterly insignificant Earth looks. The universe couldn't care less about us, and I hope I never have to call upon it for assistance. What do they care, these stars out there, ten thousand times larger than Earth, billions of miles away? In Timothy Treadwell's footage, as seen in *Grizzly Man*, we are witness to his sentimentalising of wild nature and his idyllic portrayal of bears living in perfect harmony with their environment, something that doesn't go uncontested for a second. "Here I differ with Treadwell," says my voiceover, as I explain my views on the subject, which are diametrically opposed to his pseudo-romanticism.

While almost everything about romanticism is foreign to me, Caspar David Friedrich is someone I do have great affinity for. In his paintings *Der Mönch am Meer* [*The Monk by the Sea*] and *Der Wanderer über dem Nebelmeer* [*The Wanderer Before the Sea of Fog*] a man stands alone, looking out over the landscape. Compared to the grandeur of the environment surrounding him, he is small and insignificant. Friedrich didn't paint landscapes per se, he revealed inner landscapes to us, ones that exist only in our dreams. It's something I have always tried to do with my films.

---

they sing, they just screech in pain . . . It's a land that God, if he exists, has created in anger. It's the only land where Creation is unfinished. Taking a close look at what's around us, there is some sort of harmony. It is the harmony of overwhelming and collective murder. We in comparison to the articulate vileness and baseness and obscenity of all this jungle, we in comparison to that enormous articulation, we only sound and look like badly pronounced and half-finished sentences out of a stupid suburban novel, a cheap novel. And we have to become humble in front of this overwhelming misery and overwhelming fornication, overwhelming growth and overwhelming lack of order. Even the stars up here in the sky look like a mess. There is no harmony in the universe. We have to get acquainted to this idea that there is no real harmony as we have conceived it. But when I say this, I say this all full of admiration for the jungle. It is not that I hate it. I love it. I love it very much. But I love it against my better judgement."

What art has been most influential on you?

Matthias Grünewald, Hieronymus Bosch and Pieter Brueghel come to mind, alongside Caspar David Friedrich. There is also a seventeenth-century Dutch artist I feel close to, a virtual unknown called Hercules Segers. He was one of those clairvoyant and independent figures hundreds of years ahead of his time. Little is known about his life, and only a few of his works have survived. The man was an alcoholic and considered insane by those around him; he was so poor he printed on anything he could find – including tablecloths and bed sheets – and when he died many of his prints were used for wrapping buttered bread. Rembrandt was one of the few who took him seriously; he owned at least eight Segers prints. He also bought one of Segers's oil canvases and immediately "improved" it by adding some clouds and, in the foreground, an ox cart. It isn't unintelligently improved, but the resulting painting – which can be found in the Uffizi in Florence – is very much like the conventional paintings of the period. Segers's prints, on the other hand, feel far ahead of his time, outside of history itself. Encountering these images was as if someone had reached out with his hand across time and touched my shoulder. His landscapes aren't landscapes at all; they are states of mind, dream-like visions full of angst, desolation and solitude. Things emanate from deep underground and rocks that aren't physically there, yet seem present nonetheless. Hardly anything is recognisable; his work is so surreal it looks like an alien descended to our planet. Human figures rarely appear, and when they do show up are tiny specks, like sleepwalkers. Entire mountaintops – flying in the atmosphere – seem not to comply with gravity. Segers's images are hearsay of the soul. They are like flashlights, held in our uncertain hands, giving off a frightened beam that opens breaches into the recesses of a place only partially known to us: our selves. It's an outrage that I haven't met a single art student who has even heard of Segers.

Musical influences?

These have always been strong, maybe the strongest. People might think it strange that music could make such an impact on a film-maker, but it's quite natural to me. I like the early composers, like Monteverdi, Gesualdo, Heinrich Schütz and Orlando di Lasso. Or let's go back even further, to Johannes Ciconia, the troubadour Martim Codax, Francesco Landini and Pierre Abelard, before we arrive at Bach's *Musikalisches Opfer*.

Literature.

I find great consolation when moving through the dark with certain poets. There are works of German literature upon which I can only gaze in awe, like Büchner's *Woyzeck*, Kleist's short stories, the poetry of Hölderlin, who explored the outer limits of language. He became insane after travelling on foot from Bordeaux to Stuttgart, and spent the last thirty-five years of his life locked in a tower. He understood language to the point of self-destruction, and I find his attempts to use poetry to hold himself together deeply moving. When I read Hölderlin, I have the sensation of the Hubble telescope probing the depths of the universe. Johann Christian Günther, Andreas Gryphius, Friedrich Spee and Angelus Silesius, poets of the baroque epoch, are also important to me. I appreciate work by Peter Handke and Thomas Bernhard – though they are both Austrians – and Swiss author Robert Walser. I would rather read the 1545 Bible translation of Martin Luther than any of the German Romantics, and who can walk past Joseph Conrad's short stories or Hemingway's first forty-nine stories – especially "The Short Happy Life of Francis Macomber" – without experiencing something phenomenal? The first real modern writer in English is Laurence Sterne, particularly his wonderful *Sentimental Journey*, though I also recommend *Tristram Shandy*, which is such a thoroughly modern novel. The narrative – with its wondrous jumps and contradictions and wild ranting – still feels fresh today, two hundred and fifty years later. If I were caught on a desert island, without a doubt I would want all twenty volumes of the *Oxford English Dictionary* to keep me company. Such an incredible achievement of human ingenuity, one of the greatest cultural monuments the human race has created. Thousands of scholars have contributed to it over one hundred and fifty years.

Film.

I think about what an extraordinary cultural upheaval would have taken place throughout the world if cinema had been discovered a few hundred years earlier, if Segers, Kleist, Hölderlin and Büchner had expressed themselves through film. Of the filmmakers with whom I feel some kinship, Griffith – especially his *Birth of a Nation* and *Broken Blossoms* – Murnau, Buñuel, Kurosawa and Eisenstein's *Ivan the Terrible*, which isn't so beholden to his theories of montage, all come to mind. I always saw Griffith as the Shakespeare of cinema, though everything these men did has a touch of greatness. I like Dreyer's *The Passion of Joan of Arc*, Pudovkin's *Storm Over Asia* and Dovzhenko's *Earth*, while Mizoguchi's *Ugetsu Monogatari* contains wonderful poetry, and no one who appreciates film can fail to recognise Satyajit Ray's *The Music Room*. The opening sequence, with a wealthy aristocrat surveying his land from the roof of his crumbling palace, is astonishing. The film – completely lacking in sentimentality – could end after four minutes and we would already know everything about this character. Figures like Tarkovsky have made some striking films, but he is, I fear, too much the darling of French intellectuals, something I suspect he worked towards. I also like the aesthetic and political cinema of Cuba, especially Humberto Solás's *Lucía*, and always felt that the *Cine Nõvo* movement in Brazil, with directors like Nelson Pereira dos Santos, Ruy Guerra and Glauber Rocha, was important. I knew Rocha slightly and spent a few weeks with him in California in the early seventies. We were both staying at the home of Tom Luddy, the co-founder of the Telluride Film Festival, where he would knock on my bedroom door at three in the morning and rave about some wild idea of his.

I have rarely seen films of such power as those of Iranian director Abbas Kiarostami, which have left an indelible mark on me. In *Where Is the Friend's Home?* a boy has mistakenly taken home with him the exercise book of the lad who sits next to him in class, and does everything he can to return it. He knows the teacher has threatened to throw this other boy out of school for failing to do his homework. The boy has domestic chores to do – like buying bread and keeping an eye on the baby – but in breach of the iron discipline he lives under he runs off and disappears over the hill in search of his classmate. It's a heartbreaking and arrestingly simple film, though you immediately sense that Kiarostami's films are rooted in five thousand years of Persian poetry. Take a taxi from the airport into Tehran, and the driver will likely recite Khayyám,

Firdusi and Hafez to you. There is a scene in Kiarostami's *Close-up* – one of the best films ever made about filmmaking – where all of a sudden the narrative stops for a few seconds as we watch a spray can roll down a hill until it comes to a stop. It's audacious stuff.

Then there are essential films, things like kung fu, the car chases and smashes of *Mad Max*, a good porno – more watchable than a pretentious, artsy-fartsy film – and the ingeniousness of Russ Meyer, who captured the vilest and basest instincts of our collective dreams on celluloid. "Movie" movies, so to speak. Fred Astaire might have had the most insipid face, but his dancing is the purest in all of cinema. Buster Keaton was a true acrobat and one of my witnesses when I say that some of the best filmmakers have been athletes; he moves my heart more than anyone of the silent era. The message of all these films comes from how the moving image itself exists on the screen. I love this kind of cinema because it doesn't have the falseness and phoniness of films that try so hard to pass on a heavy idea to the audience, and has nothing to do with the fake emotions of most Hollywood product. Astaire's emotions were always wonderfully stylised, and compared to a good kung-fu film someone like Jean-Luc Godard is intellectual counterfeit money. Anyone who claims that cinema is "truth twenty-four times a second" hasn't an ounce of brain. He isn't even French, but tries to out-French the French.

Animation.

Sometimes at a festival, after five bad films in a row, an audience will rhythmically chant for Woody Woodpecker. At such dire moments I might encourage this kind of behaviour, though I'm not much into animation.

Are you an artist?

Never. All I've ever wanted to be is a foot soldier of cinema. My films aren't art. In fact, I'm ambivalent about the very concept of "the artist." It just doesn't feel right to me. King Farouk of Egypt, in exile and completely obese, wolfing down one leg of lamb after another, said something beautiful: "There are no kings left in the world any more, with the exception of four: the King of Hearts, the King of Diamonds, the King of Spades and the King of Clubs." Just as the notion of royalty is meaningless today, the concept of being an artist is also somehow outdated. There is only one place left where you find such people: the circus, with its trapeze artists, jugglers, even hunger artists. Equally suspicious to me is the concept of "genius," which has no place in contemporary society. It belongs to centuries gone by, the eras of pistol duels at dawn and damsels in distress fainting onto chaises longues.

What are your films, if not art?

Poetry. I'm a craftsman, and feel closest to the late-mediaeval artisans who produced their work anonymously – like the master who created the Köln triptych – and never considered themselves artists. To remain anonymous behind what you have created means the work has a stronger life of its own, though today, in our increasingly connected world, it's an illusion to think you can remain hidden. Along with their apprentices, artisans had a genuine understanding of and feeling for the physical materials they worked with. Every sculptor before Michelangelo considered himself a stonemason; no one thought of himself as an artist until maybe the late fifteenth century. Before that they were master craftsmen with apprentices who produced work on commission for popes or *Burgermeisters*. Once, after snow had fallen in Florence, a particularly idiotic member of the Medici family asked Michelangelo to build a snowman in the courtyard of the family villa. He had no qualms about stepping outside, without a word, and completing this task. I like this attitude of absolute defiance.

Any thoughts about film festivals?

The financial strictures under which most directors work mean a film isn't alive unless an audience sees it, and these days one of the only places many films are shown is at a film festival. But be cautious about which ones you submit your work to; there is no wisdom behind the criteria that decide which films are accepted and which win prizes. People always look upon festivals as if they were proof of a film's quality, but both *Aguirre* and *Nosferatu* were rejected by the competition at Cannes. Many filmmakers have a healthy mistrust of the incestuous festival circuit. I was head of the Berlin Film Festival jury one year, which only confirmed my belief that judging films isn't quite kosher. Out of the twenty films up for awards, fifteen were garbage. Festivals have become self-serving entities, too structured around cliques and – even worse – prizes, which have never had any importance for me, aside from the fact that they are sometimes accompanied by money. A film is never better or worse because it has or hasn't won an award; those things are best left to dog shows and cattle at agricultural fairs. I wonder if a festival will ever have the nerve to announce that not a single film is good enough to qualify for an award.

These days I find the culture of festivals irritating, especially when some young filmmaker buttonholes me and puts on a show about how exceptional they and their work are. At Sundance one year, in the middle of a conversation, the young woman I was talking to pulled out her cellphone to take a call while introducing me to her business manager and agent. I had to flee. The startling proliferation of festivals in recent years means there is an ever-growing arena for the mediocre, mundane and undeserving. There are four thousand film festivals out there and in a good year four films worth seeing. The imbalance is stunning; it's a vicious discrepancy. Don't trust in festivals and agents or reviewers, only in your own abilities. Be wary of praise offered on someone else's terms.

Even back in 1968, the first time I was at the Berlin Film Festival with one of my films, I found it ossified and suffocating. I felt the festival should be opened up to everyone and screen work in other cinemas around the city, so I took the initiative, got hold of some prints by young filmmakers and rented a cinema for a few days in Neukölln, a working-class suburb of Berlin, which at the time was populated largely by immigrants and students. The free screenings at this parallel venue were a big success and generated intense discussions between audiences and filmmakers, which were exciting to witness. The whole thing was my rebellious moment against the Establishment, which I saw as being unnecessarily exclusive. I told the festival organisers they needed to have more free screenings and open the festival up to the wider public, which shortly afterwards they did. Having said all that, I can't deny that some festivals – like Venice and Cannes – are important platforms, where it's possible to present a film on a worldwide stage and thereby overnight generate publicity that might otherwise take months. In the early years I met people at festivals who became lifelong friends. There is usually a good man behind a good film.

Do you ever go to the theatre?

Theatre has been so disappointing for me that I stopped going a long time ago. The few productions I have seen were an affront to the human spirit. I find stage acting – all that yelling and door-banging – completely unbelievable, not credible at all, somehow dead to the world. It pains me to watch the overdramatic forms and fake passion of actors on a stage, and when I watch a film I can immediately tell if an actor hails from the theatre. I always prefer to read plays – especially the work of hard-drinking Irish author Brendan Behan – than see them performed because it means I can create everything in my mind. I did once translate a play into German, Michael Ondaatje's *The Collected Works of Billy the Kid*. My sister is a theatre director and wanted to stage the play in Germany, though it's almost impossible to translate because at times Ondaatje seems to destroy grammar. Carl Hanser Verlag wanted to publish the Ondaatje novel of the same name and, because there was overlap between that text and the stage play, asked me to translate it. I asked Ondaatje what certain things meant, but in some cases even he didn't know, so like him I invented words. After watching a production of *Uncle Vanya*, I once thought about directing a play in which the actors would stand with their backs to the audience throughout the entire performance. Let me say it even more drastically: the time of theatre is over; it has exhausted itself. Theatre audiences think and function in a different way to me; you would get me watching WrestleMania before you could drag me into a theatre. I'm much more comfortable with the vulgarity of that crowd. There is more honesty in WrestleMania's fakery than in traditional theatre.

In 1992 I staged a variety performance at the Hebbel-Theater in Berlin. The composer Mauricio Kagel was celebrating his birthday and decided he wanted to have his music performed, with him conducting and various acts staged in parallel. He asked me to create a series of vaudeville performances – which included Bablu Mallick, the Indian shadow puppeteer – that corresponded to the rhythms and characteristics of the compositions. The following year some of these acts appeared in a show I staged in Vienna called *Specialitäten*. I brought together a group of phenomenal performers, the best of the best – and many with extraordinary physical agility – like British mime artist Les Bubb, whose signature act is pretending there is a balloon stuck in mid-air that he can't dislodge by even a single milli-metre. I loved what Les did so much that a few years later I cast him in *Invincible*. Other acts included the Russian comedy magicians Buba and Buka, ventriloquist André Astor, the young German jug-gler Oliver Groszer, South African trapeze artists the Ayak Brothers and Borra, "King of Pickpockets." He pretended to be an usher as the audience entered the auditorium, and then suddenly, in the mid-dle of his act while he was on stage, would say, "Mr Wilson. Yes, you in row N, seat 23. I believe it's your birthday in three days. How would I know that? Perhaps you should check your wallet." Mr Wilson would search around and discover that it had been removed from his pocket before the show had even started. "Would you like it back?" Borra would ask. Mr Wilson would walk up on stage, and while he was being handed his wallet, Borra would take Mr Wilson's wristwatch and necktie. He could steal suspenders, shoes and the glasses from someone's face without them noticing. The most ingenious performer I have ever worked with.

Ballet and dance.

All foreign to me. I also dislike concerts because I don't do much listening when sitting in front of an orchestra. I'm too interested in watching the bassist's hands shoot up and down, and never actu-ally hear what's being played. I could stare at something like that for an hour without taking my eyes off it. Although I'm a great lover of opera music, I generally dislike seeing other people's pro-ductions. I often see a whole world when I listen to an opera and am inevitably disappointed when confronted with someone else's vision. Let me put it this way: when I see an opera performed, I see images out there that are in direct contradiction to those in my head. The whole experience is miserable for me.

Museums.

They intimidate me, and anyway, nothing ever feels truly alive when hidden away under glass. There is a worrisome permanence about things in museums, and I rarely visit such places, though one time I did go to the British Museum because I wanted to see the Rosetta Stone. The decipherment of ancient Egyptian hieroglyphics was an extraordinary achievement. I have been to Athens many times, starting at an early age, but only on my most recent trip did I muster the courage to visit the Acropolis.

I hardly ever go to exhibitions and dislike the world of the *vernissage*; those crowds are the most repulsive of all. These days most art is too conceptual for me, with long descriptions pasted up on the walls of galleries. "Art" should reveal itself to audiences without written explanation. Most of what I see is garbage, sometimes literally so, like an installation with a few cardboard boxes thrown into a corner, an empty beer can and a dirty sleeping bag. This apparently represents the desperate fate of the homeless. I see an absence of dignity in contemporary art. There is too much emphasis on concept, not craft. Just as religion has been watered down by television evangelists, so has art. What makes me particularly suspicious is the speculative art market. A whole set of values is being continuously invented and manipulated, and vast amounts of real money are being paid out. A criminal conspiracy has developed between auction houses, galleries, artists, curators, museums and even those big, glossy magazines. It all reminds me of the prices attached to mediaeval relics, when fortunes were spent to acquire a nail from the True Cross of the Christ, or the bone of a saint. All this is wrapped in "art speak" – an abomination in itself – which makes the whole charade even more unbearable.

Photography.

I once had a pinhole camera, and more recently used a Deardorff – a large-format mahogany camera with bellows and plates – to take photos of ski flyers at the gigantic ramp at Kulm in Austria. This is the moment of absolute judgement for them. But generally, if something is worth photographing, I remember it in my head. None of those Japanese tourists snapping away before the aeroplane has even landed truly see the world around them. Real life – the birth of a child, for example – should never be viewed through a lens. In recent years I have developed a familiarity with photography because my wife is a professional photographer and has her own darkroom in our home. I marvel at the alchemy of the process, but generally don't look at things in still images. I see them in terms of scenes and movement.

Restaurants.

Waiters in tuxedos intimidate me. It's misery for me when being waited on; I'm literally close to panic. I would rather sit on the sidewalk munching potato chips than eat at one of those chic restaurants. I often stay in hotels on my travels, but for years avoided that world whenever I could. In Berlin I used to sleep on my son's floor rather than stay in a hotel. It had nothing to do with money or physical comfort; I lived on a raft for weeks while shooting *Aguirre*. Today, ever older, I have reconciled with hotel rooms, though the little chocolates they leave on my pillow every evening exude an aura of despair, the same feeling that overwhelms me during the presentation of the official mascot of the Olympic Games, or when a film star becomes a Goodwill Ambassador for the UN.

Zoos.

I enjoy visiting them with children, otherwise I find zoos very sad places.

Hobbies.

I have no hobbies.

How Much Wood Would a Woodchuck Chuck . . . *was shot in Pennsylvania, at the World Championship of Livestock Auctioneers.*

I was fascinated by livestock auctioneers and had the feeling that their incredibly fast speech was the true poetry of capitalism. Every system develops its own extreme language, like the ritual chants of the Orthodox Church, and there is something final and absolute about how auctioneers speak. How much further can it go? It's almost like a ritual incantation, frightening but quite beautiful at the same time; there is real music in their delivery, the sense of rhythm these people have. One of the auctioneers told me he trained himself by reciting, over and over again, "If it takes a hen and a half a day and a half to lay an egg and a half, how long does it take a broken, wooden-legged cockroach to kick a hole in a dill pickle?" Another was the only one in his family who would milk the cows, and as a young man practised out loud while sitting on a bucket in the stables. The jury of the competition was judging how wildly the auctioneers could accelerate their speech, but this was also a real auction, and at all times the auctioneers had to look carefully into the crowd for bidders. That might sound easy, but the buyers were competing among themselves. No one wanted anyone – except the auctioneer – to know they were bidding, so their gestures were minuscule, perhaps just a flick of a finger or a quick blink of an eye, and had to be recognised instantly in a sea of three hundred people. Within two or three hours on that day in June 1976, $3 million and over a thousand head of cattle changed hands. My dream ever since has been to do *Hamlet* with livestock auctioneers in under fifteen minutes. The auction takes place in New Holland, which to this day is one of the centres of cattle farming in the United States and home to an Amish community which tills the soil, raises cattle the biblical way and rejects capitalism and competition, making it the very antithesis of the auctioneers.

Is America an exotic country?

Take a look at those beauty pageants for four-year old girls and you realise it's more bizarre than exotic. What I love is the heartland of the country, the so-called "flyover" zone, like Wisconsin, where we filmed *Stroszek* and where Orson Welles was from. Marlon Brando came from Nebraska, Bob Dylan from Minnesota, Hemingway from Illinois, these middle-of-nowhere places, to say nothing of the South, the home of Faulkner and Flannery O'Connor. I like this kind of terrain, where you can still encounter great self-reliance and camaraderie, the warm, open hearts, the down-to-earth people. So much of the rest of the country has abandoned these basic virtues.

I like America for its spirit of advancement and exploration; there is something exceptionally bold about the place. The idea of everyone having an equal chance to succeed, no matter who they are, is impressive. If a barefoot Indian from the Andes had invented the wheel, the patent office in Washington would have assisted him in securing his rights. I once visited a company in Cleveland that had two thousand employees and a twenty-eight-year-old boss. That would be unthinkable in Germany. When I made *The Wild Blue Yonder* I discovered an extraordinary cache of footage shot by NASA astronauts in outer space, and was told that because it was filmed by federal employees, the material was "property of the people." I asked, "Can I, a Bavarian, be considered one of the people?" Such images, it turns out, according to American law belong to everyone on the planet. This is a unique and astounding attitude to the world. Naturally there are things in the United States I'm ambivalent about, just as there are when it comes to Germany. I could never be a flag-waving patriot. But there are many reasons why I have been in America for so many years. The country has always had a capacity to rejuvenate itself, pull itself out of defeat and look to the future. There has always been space there to create real change. I could never live in a country I didn't love.

Is Stroszek *about the decline of the American dream?*

It came out of nowhere. At the time I wanted to make *Woyzeck* and had promised the title role to Bruno S.; he didn't know Büchner's play, so I told him the story and he liked the idea. But two months before we were due to start shooting I realised this was a big mistake. It was clear to me that Kinski should play the part, so without hesitation I called Bruno to let him know. There was a kind of stunned silence at the end of the line. "I have already booked my vacation, plus some unpaid time," he said. "What am I going to do?" It was clear that being in the film meant a lot to Bruno. I was ashamed of myself and wanted to sink into the ground because of embarrassment, so out of the blue I said, "We'll do another film instead." He said, "What film?" I told him, "I don't know yet. What day is it?" "Monday," he said. "By Saturday you will have the screenplay," I said. "I will even give it a title now which sounds like *Woyzeck*. It will be called *Stroszek*." I felt relieved, but after hanging up found myself on Monday at midday with a title and the task of writing a story for Bruno, which I ended up delivering on schedule. I still consider it one of my best pieces of writing and one of my finest films. The title comes from the name of the lead character in *Signs of Life*, which in turn came from someone I vaguely knew years before. I was enrolled at university but hardly ever showed up for class, so asked a fellow student to write a paper for me. "What will you give me in return?" he asked. "Mr Stroszek," I said, "I'll make your name famous."

The character Bruno plays in the film is close to his real self.

Stroszek was built around Bruno. It reflects my knowledge of him and his environment, his emotions and feelings, and my deep affection for him. For that reason it was easy to write the screenplay, though even today it pains me to watch certain scenes of *Stroszek*. The sequence in the apartment when the two pimps beat up Eva Mattes and throw Bruno over the piano reveals how he really would have reacted to such treatment, the kind doled out to him for years when he was a child. "Don't worry," he told me before we shot the scene. "I've been hurt much worse before." There is such magnificence in his performance.

The scenes in Berlin of him singing and playing the accordion show exactly what he would do every weekend. Bruno knew the courtyards and alleyways of the city, and some of the songs he sings in the film he wrote himself. The place where he goes immediately after leaving prison is his local beer cellar, where everyone knew him, and all the props he uses in the film – including the musical instruments – were his own. Although *Stroszek* was scripted from start to finish, some scenes were improvised and based on Bruno's real life, like the one where he talks to Eva Mattes about his mistreatment as a child. "When we start rolling," I said to him, "go ahead and tell Eva about your feelings, your thoughts, your past. Do it any way you want." The less I gave Eva to work with, the better she was. All I said was, "Make Bruno stick to the point. He has a tendency to rant about Turkish guest labourers and God knows what else." She was so good in the scene because all she did was listen intently and gently encourage him. Often all she had to do was get Bruno to mention certain things and trigger specific responses. I didn't really have to direct either of them.

The idea of writing a critique of capitalism didn't enter my head. Lines like Bruno talking about being in America came about because that's where we were, though the film does reflect my experiences of Pittsburgh, where I saw the nation's underside. I say that with great affection for the place. The film doesn't criticise the country; it's almost a eulogy to the place. For me *Stroszek* is about shattered hopes, which is clearly a universal theme, and it wouldn't really matter if the characters move from Berlin to France or Sweden. I simply felt familiar enough with America to set the second part of the story there. I love the way we captured the country on screen, and when I watch *Stroszek* today it hasn't aged for me, unlike many films from that period. One of the most important scenes has nothing to do with America, when Bruno goes to the hospital and talks to the doctor, who was played by my eldest son's real doctor. I was fascinated by the fact that premature babies have an ape-like grip reflex and can support their own body weight, something the doctor demonstrates by having a baby hang from his two fingers. Apparently we lose certain instincts soon after being born, including this reflex, but premature babies retain the ability. You see a remnant of it when a baby born at nine months takes hold of your finger.

What did Bruno think of America?

He loved it. New York was a revelation for him, just as it is for everyone who experiences the city for the first time. The sequences there were all filmed in a single day because we had no shooting permit. We improvised a scene, then disassembled the camera, packed it up, carried it to the next spot, reassembled it, then filmed for a few minutes, at all times trying to dodge the police. The shots on the observation deck of the Empire State Building were quickly done by Thomas Mauch before the guards up there spotted us. From the deck we saw a boat arriving at the pier and decided to have the three characters arrive in the country like classic European immigrants, so we rushed over there and got a shot with the boat behind them, as if they had just stepped off. The shot of them driving on the New Jersey Turnpike was done with Mauch and me strapped to the hood with a rope; we didn't have another vehicle to film from. The first time the police stopped us I told them, "We're just a bunch of crazy Kraut film students," and they let us go. Half an hour later the same cop caught us again. I bamboozled him out of his wits and we avoided being arrested.

Where did you find Clemens Scheitz, the old man who appears in the film?

I needed extras for *The Enigma of Kaspar Hauser* and looked rapidly through various card indexes. I had seen more than two hundred faces when I found his. The agency suggested I choose someone else. "Although we work in the interests of our clients," they said, "we should warn you that Herr Scheitz is no longer completely right in the head." I told them I didn't mind, that I wanted him anyway. I liked Herr Scheitz so much that I kept asking him to stay for one more scene after another, to the point where he basically appears throughout the film. I even rewrote the ending so he would have the final word.

Although he was always complaining that Bruno smelt, Herr Scheitz was a charming old man, full of fantasies, able to explain in between gulps of coffee that he was in the process of writing a magnificent oratorio and at the same time working on a major scientific work that he would never write down in case it was stolen. He would talk about how he would never dare fly to Berlin, which at the time was deep inside East Germany. "Both the KGB and CIA would kidnap me and torture my secrets out of me," he insisted. Apparently he had constructed a rocket that could hit a target dead on after a thirty-thousand-mile flight, and just by writing a few numbers on a restaurant tablecloth could prove that the moon landing was faked, Einstein was a fool and Copernicus a fraud, though apparently Galileo had some useful things to say about the universe. Newton was also an imbecile because in his colour scheme green was a colour, though every five-year-old knows that green is just blue and yellow mixed together. Herr Scheitz had his own scheme where the name "green" didn't exist. I asked him what name he would give the colour, and he said, *"Feilgau,"* which is as meaningless in German as in English. It's an invented word. I tried to create his character in *Stroszek* around his eccentricities and ended up putting him in both *Heart of Glass* and *Nosferatu*. The scene in *Stroszek* where he talks about animal magnetism was my idea, but it's close to what he really believed. We were in the middle of nowhere when a couple of hunters, who had driven in from Milwaukee, pulled up. I asked if they would appear in the film. They kept saying, "But we're not actors." I told them all they had to do was listen to Herr Scheitz talking in German, and when they had heard enough get into their car and drive off. They didn't understand a word he said, but played along wonderfully. The whole scene was basically shot in real time. There was one quick change of camera position while we ran around to the other side of the car, but otherwise what you see is exactly what happened.

The two men drove off. I never knew their names and never saw them again.

Who play the pimps?

Norbert Grupe was a wrestler and heavyweight boxer who called himself the "Prince of Homburg." He lost a bout against the Argentinian boxer Oscar Bonavena in 1969, and became famous after appearing on a live sports talk show on German TV the following day. When asked by the interviewer about his crushing defeat, Grupe sat there in silence, staring ominously at this man throughout the entire broadcast. The situation became so dangerous that given one more question you knew he would have killed the interviewer; it was one of the most stunning moments I have ever seen on television.

Before we filmed *Stroszek*, Grupe would drag me around, night after night, introducing me to all his pimp friends in Berlin, showing me the darkest depths of his life. He had been in prison a few times and was very dangerous, so other pimps would bring him along to settle fights. Many of his insults in the film – like "I'm going to bury that runt up as deep as he'll go" – come directly from him. At one point during filming one of the crew was going to be celebrating his birthday. He was very into sports and we often played football together, so I said to him, "On your birthday I'm going to rent a gym with a boxing ring and go three rounds with the Prince of Homburg. As a present to you, I promise I'll still be standing at the end of round one." The Prince and I laughed about this, but two days before it was meant to happen he took me aside and said, "Werner, this is utterly stupid. You'll be knocked down within thirty seconds at most and end up in hospital. It's not worth it." He was no dummy, though sometimes a very frightening man. I'm sure he was genuinely drunk in the scene where they beat Bruno up in his apartment. The other pimp is Burkhard Driest, a writer, filmmaker and actor who started out as a law student. Two weeks before his final exam he committed a bank robbery and hid the loot in his girlfriend's apartment. She turned him in and he spent three years in prison, where he started writing. His book *Die Verrohung des Franz Blum* [*The Brutalisation of Franz Blum*] was quite successful, and by the time of his release he was a well-known character.

Once Herr Scheitz, Bruno and Eva get to America, we meet the character of Herr Scheitz's nephew, a mechanic, played by Clayton Szlapinski. Clayton, who I had encountered a year earlier, really was a mechanic. I was driving from Alaska to meet Errol Morris in Wisconsin and needed to get my car repaired, and discovered Clayton's wreckage yard about a mile and a half out of town. I immediately liked him and his chubby Native American assistant. When I returned to the area to film *Stroszek* I went straight to the garage because I wanted them both in the film, but the assistant wasn't there. I asked Clayton about this and described the young man to him, but he had no idea who I was talking about. It turned out Clayton had hired him the morning I had shown up a year before, then fired him that same evening. We eventually tracked him down and asked him to be in the film.

I don't make a distinction between "professional" and "non-professional" actors. There are only two kinds of actors: good and bad. If an audience finds a performance credible, then it's a good performance, and if an actor is good on screen then he or she is a professional. The same thing applies to technicians. A professional is anyone good at his job. I once spoke to the manager of a football team who said he could tell in sixty seconds if a player was gifted and could be of use to the team; he didn't need two weeks of training. The first thing is to see how the player runs, then what the ball does with the player, then what the player does with the ball. When I direct actors I focus on what they do to the camera as much as what the camera does to them. Interactions between "professional" and "non-professional" actors can be interesting, but in my experience things work best when the former are in some way debriefed and told to do as little as possible, and the latter are given only the vaguest instructions.

You thank Errol Morris in the opening credits of Stroszek.

Errol, at one time in his life, was deeply involved in researching mass murderers. He had collected thousands of pages of the most incredible material and was planning on writing a book. Errol had spent months in Plainfield, Wisconsin, and kept telling me about this tiny town in the middle of nowhere with less than five hundred inhabitants. What's so extraordinary about Plainfield is that, within a period of five years, five or six mass murderers emerged from the place, for no apparent reason. There was something gloomy and evil about the town, and even during filming two bodies were found only ten miles from where we were working. I felt it was one of those focal points where every thread converges and is tied into a tight knot. You have these places, these knots in the United States – Las Vegas, Disneyland, Wall Street, San Quentin prison – where dreams and nightmares come together. I count Plainfield, Wisconsin, among them.

Errol was interested in the town because it was where Ed Gein – who inspired the Norman Bates character in *Psycho* – had lived and committed his murders. Errol had spoken to the sheriff and townspeople and even to Gein himself, and had hundreds of pages of interview transcripts, but was stuck with one puzzling question. Ed Gein had not only murdered several people, he had also dug up freshly buried corpses from the cemetery, used human skin to make a lampshade and cover some chairs, and decorated his bedposts with skulls. Errol discovered that the graves he had dug up formed a perfect circle, and at the centre was Gein's mother. Errol wondered whether or not Gein had actually dug up his own mother. "You'll know only if you go back to Plainfield and dig there yourself," I said to him. "If the grave is empty, Ed was there before you." We excitedly decided to meet there with our shovels. At the time I was in Alaska, shooting a couple of sequences for *Heart of Glass*, and on my way back to New York crossed the border from Canada and headed down to Plainfield. I waited for Errol, but he chickened out and never showed up. I figured it was probably for the best. The act of asking a question is sometimes more valuable than scrambling for an answer.

I loved being in Wisconsin and went back later to film there. The scenes in *Stroszek* of Eva working at the truck stop were shot in the middle of the day at a real truck stop near Madison. I just went in there and asked if we could film. "Sure thing," the owner said. "We love having you Krauts around!" We told the truckers to be themselves, and Eva went round pouring coffee. Ed Lachman, the second cameraman, became an especially important part of the production because he explained to the townsfolk and truckers precisely what was going on and what sort of things they should say. In the film we called the town Railroad Flats because Plainfield was still kind of Errol's terrain. He even accused me of stealing his landscape, which for Errol was a serious crime indeed. In a pathetic attempt to appease him I thanked him at the start of the film. I think he's forgiven me by now.

There is an almost total absence of sex in your work.

There are only a few kisses in all my films, and some of the sexual relationships – like Bruno and Eva in *Stroszek* – are implied but never seen. All I can say is that it's better to experience sex in person, and that love between people never seemed too interesting a theme for me as a storyteller. As to the question of why there are so few women populating my work, I can offer only a vague response, which is that the characters in my films are somehow reflections of myself, so most are men. Let's say no more on the matter, though let me add here, if it even needs to be said, that I'm very fond of women; from my earliest childhood they played an enormous part in my life. I moved to the United States in 1995 for one reason only: Lena, the Siberian-born woman who became my wife four years later, was there. When I left Vienna, where I was living at the time, I gave up every one of my earthly possessions, as well as my language. A customs official at San Francisco airport wondered why I had no luggage and only a one-way ticket. He looked at me suspiciously and asked, "Did you forget to pick up your bags from the carousel?" When I told him I had only a tooth-brush, I was questioned for two hours. For the first few months in our little apartment, Lena and I had only two plates, two sets of cutlery and two wine glasses. Guests were requested to bring their own kitchenware when they came for dinner. Such was our domestic bliss.

Allow me to vent here about the prevalent image of masculinity in mainstream Hollywood films, which seems to be post-pubescence, actors like Leonardo DiCaprio and Brad Pitt. Where are the manly men of times gone by? The last one standing is Clint Eastwood, who hails from the likes of Bogart, Brando, Bronson, John Wayne, Richard Widmark and Gary Cooper. Collective female dreams have shifted significantly over the years, and today this kind of hero seems to be out of fashion, but I have no interest in the boy-men. Things will eventually revert to the manly men. Today hardly anyone has a beard, but I predict that within a few years most men will be wearing them.

La Soufrière *was filmed on a Caribbean island as you waited for an "unavoidable catastrophe."*

There is a definite element of self-mockery in the film; everything that looks dangerous and doomed ultimately ends up in utter banality. In retrospect I thank God on my knees it wasn't otherwise. Fortunately the film is missing its potentially violent climax. It would have been ridiculous to have been blown sky high with two colleagues while making a film.

I was editing *Stroszek* when I heard about the impending volcanic eruption, and discovered that the island of Guadeloupe – population eighty thousand – had been evacuated, though one person refused to leave. I immediately knew I wanted to talk to him and find out what kind of relationship this man had with death. He is the reason I headed to the island and made the film; I assure you we didn't go because we thought it would be fun to sit on an exploding volcano. I'm not in the business of suicide. I telephoned the television executive with whom I had worked on various films, including *The Great Ecstasy of Woodcarver Steiner*. He was in a meeting at the time, so I asked his assistant to drag him out of there for only sixty seconds, no matter where he was, what he was doing or how important the people he was with. "Tell him Herzog has to talk to him for one minute." Everything had to be put in place immediately because if we didn't leave within hours, the whole thing might be over; the volcano would explode and the film would be no more. In less than a minute I explained the situation to him. "Just get out of here and do it," he said. "How do we do the contract?" I asked. "Come back alive," he said, "and we'll do the contract." I love the man for his faith. Let me name the horse and rider: Manfred Konzelmann, a true believer.

Ed Lachman came from New York, and I flew from Germany with Jörg Schmidt-Reitwein. We met up in Pointe-à-Pitre in Guadeloupe, which is a twin island with a narrow isthmus between the northern and southern part. The entire southern part was evacuated. The first thing you notice in the jungle is the sound of birds, but they had all fled from the island and the place was deadly silent.

All the snakes had slithered down from the slopes of the volcano, then drowned in the ocean, and were being washed back on shore. The traffic lights were still working, switching from red to green and back again, but the streets in Basse-Terre were deserted. Even as we were driving past roadblocks up the side of the volcano I repeatedly asked Lachman and Schmidt-Reitwein if they wanted to continue, and made it clear that everyone had to make his own decision. There was no question I was going to walk to the top of the volcano. "I'm definitely going, but you have to make up your own mind," I told them. "I need a single camera, and if necessary can shoot it all myself." Schmidt-Reitwein immediately said yes; there was no doubt he was always going to come along. Ed was timid and had some initial hesitations, as any normal human being would. He thought about it for a few minutes, then meekly asked, "What will happen if the island blows up?" "Ed," I said, "we'll be airborne." This encouraged him and he picked up his camera. I love a crew bold enough to step outside the norm. We left a camera in the far distance on time lapse, clicking single frames throughout the day, so if things had gone badly there would at least have been images of us shooting upwards.

We approached the mountain from the leeward side and had a real fright when the wind changed; all of a sudden toxic fumes came wafting down towards us. We ended up standing on a deep fissure that had been ripped open right at the top of this steaming volcano. The next day Ed realised he had left his glasses up there, so we went back for them, but discovered there had been so many shockwaves that the whole landscape had been ripped apart and the mountaintop looked completely different. The glasses were now buried under thirty feet of rock and mud. Schmidt-Reitwein and I were actually rather disrespectful of the volcano. We went up to the edge and took a leak into it.

All something of a risk, wouldn't you say?

I can't deny that flying out to an island that might not exist the following morning to make *La Soufrière* was a blind gamble, as well as a transgression of normal family life. It's not the sort of thing that should be done if you have a wife and young child at home. We made our decision to travel to Guadeloupe in the knowledge that shortly before there had been a series of unbelievably power-ful earthquakes across the world. Many thousands were killed in Guatemala, a quarter of a million people died in China and a major quake hit the Philippines. Experts insisted that an explosion on Guadeloupe was guaranteed with almost 100 per cent certainty. The signals the volcano was emitting were identical to those of Mount Pelée on the neighbouring island of Martinique just before it erupted so violently in 1902, killing thirty thousand people. It was determined that La Soufrière wouldn't erupt and just spew lava everywhere. It was going to blow with the force of several Hiroshima-sized atomic bombs, so if it had gone up and we had been within a five-mile radius, there would have been absolutely nothing we could have done. For me, the whole thing was com-pounded by the fact that I was unable to move as quickly as I wanted because a few weeks before I had injured my ankle playing football and had only recently cut off the cast myself. The film's full title, *La Soufrière: Waiting for an Unavoidable Catastrophe*, suggests the absurd nature of our task.

I can laugh about it now, but all we wanted to do was get out of there with a film. There was no element of bravado about the experience, though I knew if I could escape from this one alive I would be able to joke about it afterwards. I saw myself as the captain in the joke about Italian soldiers in the First World War trenches. For weeks they're being bombarded, day after day, until their captain grabs a rifle and shouts, "Up, men! Attack!" Enemy fire cuts him down before he has gone two steps, and he falls back into the trench, stone dead. The soldiers, none of whom have fol-lowed and who are quietly sitting around smoking, immediately applaud and say, "Bravo, *capitano*!" Thankfully *La Soufrière* was one of those moments when we weren't mowed down. There was a deep sense at the time that making the film was the right thing to do, though today, looking back, I'm not so sure, and admit that with *La Soufrière* we were playing the lottery. The second we shot our last roll of film we jumped in the car and fled. You never feel as afraid of things when there is a camera in your hand; somehow it acts as a protective shield. I remember thinking that the volcano didn't feel real to me, that it was just a projection of light on a piece of celluloid.

A few years after you made the film, you told an interviewer: "I hate the whole life-insurance thing. Keeping everything secure is destroying our civilisation."

Let's face it, the world is impossibly risk-averse these days, and panics are almost always completely out of proportion to reality. Years ago, during the mad-cow crisis, it was obvious to me that more people would die crossing the road getting to the butcher than ever would from eating contaminated meat. These days six-year-old children have five different kinds of helmets: one for roller-skating, one for baseball, one for bicycling, one for walking in the garden, one for God knows what. Parents these days even send their children to the sandpit with a helmet. The whole thing is repulsive. I would never trust in a man who has had multiple helmets by the age of five. Wall-to-wall protection is devastating because children are conditioned not to be intrepid; they will never grow up to become scientists who jump across boundaries into the unknown. And every time I walk past a hand sanitiser – those bottles attached to walls everywhere across America these days – I want to tear it down. They are an abomination. I never use antibiotics and have taken maybe ten aspirin in my entire life. Such things will be the death of us all. A civilisation that uses pain relief at every turn is doomed; we can't know what it is to be truly human without experiencing some level of discomfort and physical challenge. When you read in a travel book that the author has taken a snakebite kit on his journey into the jungle, you know the paperback in your hand is fit only for feeding the campfire. Life knows no security. The only certainty is that we all die despite helmets and life-insurance policies. These days people cut their finger or graze their knee and consider it a life experience.

Your next film was a remake of Murnau's Nosferatu.

Although I have never truly functioned in terms of genres, I knew that making a film like *Nosferatu* meant understanding the basic principles of the vampire genre, then modifying and developing them. It was like my approach to adventure films when I made *Aguirre*. For me "genre" means an intensive, almost dream-like stylisation on screen, and I consider the vampire myth one of the richest and most fertile cinema has to offer. The images it contains have a quality beyond our usual experiences as film-goers; there is fantasy, hallucination, dreams and nightmares, visions and fear. Although my film is based on Murnau's, I never thought of *Nosferatu* as being a remake. It goes its own way with its own spirit and stands on its own feet as a new version. I wasn't trying to rewrite *Hamlet*. I like what Lotte Eisner said: that Murnau's film was reborn, not remade. It's like Carl Dreyer and Robert Bresson, who both made films about Joan of Arc; one is hardly a remake of the other. My *Nosferatu* has a different context and a somewhat different story.

I set out to connect the film to Germany's genuine cultural heritage, to the best of German cinema, the silent films of the Weimar era, to filmmakers of the past whose vision was brought to an abrupt end by Nazism. A filmmaker can't function without some connection to his culture. Continuity is vital. Although the Second World War shattered Germany's cultural identity, there wasn't a complete void because important literature was being published after 1945, and other forms of expression picked up pace within the ruins and debris. But cinema remained a barren desert for a quarter of a century, and to speak about German film after the war is to dig into pathetically uninteresting work. When I finished *Nosferatu* I remember thinking, "Now I'm connected. At last I've reached the other side of the river." The film acted almost as some kind of bridge for me; the ground under my feet felt much more solid. This might have all sounded incomprehensible to British, Italian and French filmmakers at the time – countries that kickstarted film production after the war with relative ease – but it was something that impacted on many young German filmmakers in the seventies. We all carried a certain weight that had to be cast off.

Coming of age in the early and mid-sixties, we young Germans looked around for a point of reference. But our fathers' generation either sided with the barbaric Nazi culture or had been chased from the country. With a few exceptions – directors like Wolfgang Staudte and Helmut Käutner – there had been no legitimate German cinema since 30 January 1933, the day Hitler came to power. As the first real post-war generation, we were orphans with no fathers to learn from; we had no active teachers or mentors, people in whose footsteps we wanted to follow. This meant it was the grandfathers – Lang, Murnau, Pabst and others – who became our points of reference. At the time I felt strongly about finding my roots as a filmmaker, and chose to concentrate on Murnau's masterpiece, knowing full well it would be impossible to better the original. This wasn't nostalgia or me trying to emulate a particular filmmaking tradition. I was just expressing my admiration for the heroic age of German cinema, one that gave birth to *Nosferatu* in 1922. Many of my generation shared a similar attitude to Murnau and his contemporaries: cinema as legitimate culture.

Lotte Eisner gave you the support you needed.

Just as Charlemagne had to travel to Rome to ask the Pope to anoint him, we couldn't just issue a self-empowering decree. In the case of German film, we were fortunate to have Lotte, who could give her blessing. She was the missing link, our collective conscience, a fugitive from Nazism and for years the single living person in the world who knew everyone in cinema from its first hour onwards. She was a veritable woolly mammoth, one of the most important film historians the world has ever seen and a personal friend of the great figures of early cinema: Eisenstein, Griffith, von Sternberg, Chaplin, Renoir, even the Lumière brothers and Méliès. She alone had the authority, insight and personality to declare us legitimate. It was an important moment when she insisted that what my generation was doing in Germany was as important as the film culture Murnau, Fritz Lang and the other Weimar filmmakers had created all those decades before. When Lang said there would never again be anything of substance in German cinema, Lotte told him to see *Signs of Life*, and even sent him a 35mm print. "You told me Germany would never have a film culture, not after Hitler," she told him. "But look at this film by a young unknown who is only twenty-five." Lang watched the film and said, "Yes, I have hope now." I always found Lang's work too geometrical, but appreciated what he said about *Signs of Life*.

For ten years it was Lotte's affirmation and support that gave me the strength to continue; she was the first person to recognise my work and offer whatever assistance she could. I met her because of her voice. Lotte gave a lecture at the Berlin Film Festival in the mid-sixties, the first time she had returned to Germany since 1933. I walked past the half-open door of this auditorium, heard her speaking, and was instantly drawn in; it was so magnetic I could do nothing but listen. She was an archaeologist by training, though she always had an interest in film and literature, and a sharp appreciation for things of substance. When Lotte was eighteen, a friend brought her a notebook that contained the draft of a play. "I met this young man and he claims to be a poet," her friend said. "You understand poetry. Read it and tell me what you think. If it's any good, I might have an affair with him." Lotte read the drama and next day said to her friend, "Have the affair. He will be the greatest poet in Germany." The drama was *Baal* and its author was Bertolt Brecht. Being outspoken and Jewish, Lotte was on the Nazi hit list. The rabid National Socialist newspaper *Der Stürmer* [*The Attacker*] insisted – even before Hitler was voted into power – that if heads were going to roll, Lotte's would be one of the first. She left the country for France weeks after Hitler became chancellor, and a gap in German film culture of thirty years opened up. When I spent time with Lotte, at her home in Paris, we would usually speak German, but sometimes we lapsed into English because the sound of her original language had become too painful for her.

A few years after I saw Lotte in Berlin, I discovered that she had seen *Signs of Life* and wanted to talk with me. "Lotte speaks so highly of you but doesn't dare meet you," a friend told me in 1969, "and you speak so highly of her and you don't dare to meet her either, so I'll get you together." One of the most memorable things about the shooting of *The Enigma of Kaspar Hauser* was that Lotte was there for some of the time.* For her to show up on the set of one of my films was a great honour, and very significant for me. She didn't ask questions or talk to many people; she just sat there with a pleased look on her face. It gave me confidence, and a few years later she visited the set of *Nosferatu*. I vividly remember sitting with Lotte in her Paris apartment at a time when I was sure there were no audiences out there for my films. "I just can't go on," I told her. In between a sip of tea, munching on a biscuit, without even looking up, she said, quite calmly, "You aren't going to quit. The history of cinema won't permit you." Then she went on about her noisy neighbours, or something like that. The casual nature of how

---

* See Eisner's essay "Herzog in Dinkelsbühl," *Sight and Sound*, autumn 1974.

she brushed off what I was saying has always been with me. It was one of the key moments of my life. Lotte encouraged me by making clear that I didn't have the right to abandon my work.

Was your script for Nosferatu *based on Murnau's film?*

I could probably have made a vampire film without the existence of Murnau's film, but there's a certain reverence I tried to pay to his *Nosferatu* – whom he called Count Orlok – and on one or two occasions even tried to quote him literally by matching the same shots he used in his version. In this respect certain elements of my film are clear homages to Murnau. I went to Lübeck – where he shot the vampire's lair – and among the few houses there not destroyed during the war, I found the ones Murnau had put in his film. They were being used as salt warehouses. Where in 1922 there had been small bushes, I found tall trees.

The reason Murnau's film isn't called *Dracula* is because Bram Stoker's estate wanted so much money for the rights, so Murnau made a few unsubtle changes to his story and retitled it. By the time I made my film, Stoker's book was in the public domain, so I changed some of the names, including turning Count Orlok back into Count Dracula. Although there are some interesting things in Stoker's book, it's a rather dull piece of writing. It was published in 1897 and is a compilation of all the vampire stories floating around from Romantic times. What I find intriguing is Stoker's foresight in somehow anticipating our era of mass communication. His epistolary novel encompasses many of the changes wrought by the Industrial Revolution of the nineteenth century, and telegrams and voice recordings on Edison cylinders play an important part in the story. There may well be something similar taking place today, with the shift to the digital age and the explosive evolution of means of communication; in both cases an uneasiness exists in society. At their heart vampire stories are about solitude. They accumulate in popular culture during times of restlessness, which is perhaps why there has been a recent resurgence of interest.

Kinski plays the vampire.

In Murnau's film the creature is frightening because he has no soul and looks like an insect, but Kinski's vampire has a real existential anguish. I tried to humanise him by presenting the vampire as an agonised, sad and lonely creature, desperately thirsty for love, but terrifying at the same time. I wanted to endow him with human suffering, with a true longing for love and, importantly, the one essential capacity of human beings: mortality. "It's cruel not to be able to die," he says. He is deeply pained by his solitude and inability to join with the rest of humanity, by his profound terror of forever remaining undead. The vampire isn't realistic, but he is human. Kinski was apprehensive about taking on the role, but once he agreed – two months before filming started – he immediately shaved his head. In the film he played brilliantly against his appendages: the long spider-like fingernails and snake-like fangs, his seven-inch heels and those pointed ears. After two minutes the audience sees beyond the horror of these things. Kinski was extraordinary at expressing utter satisfaction at drinking Lucy's blood, like a baby that has just been fed, and there's a clear sexual element when the vampire enters her bedroom. Lucy's face takes on a new expression as he bites her neck, and she almost tenderly holds on to the vampire. Thanks to her, Kinski's vampire becomes an erotic figure. Kinski wanted to shriek during his death scene, but I said, "Inhale! Suck the death and pain into you. Inhale the light that's killing you." Listen to his wheezing as the creature expires.

The character of Lucy is an ambiguous figure, at the same time attracted to and repelled by the vampire. In Murnau's version she gives herself to Dracula in the hope that her husband will be saved, but in mine Lucy's sacrifice is in vain. The plague has already devastated the town, and though she is unaware, her husband has already transformed into a vampire. The creature is also some sort of prophet of change, with victims leaving behind their bourgeois lives and sensibilities. As the plague spreads, people gather in the main square, where there is a kind of great joy in the air. From historical testimonies of the fourteenth century we know that during the last stages of the plague, a town would experience moments of jubilation in the midst of all the desolation and death; a strange freedom and euphoria – almost redemption – took over. There was dancing in the streets, wild drunken revelries, and all sense of ownership would fragment. Townsfolk happily burnt their furniture and threw money into the canal, almost in celebration.

How was Kinski to work with?

For almost the entire shoot he was happy and at ease with himself and the world, though he would throw a tantrum maybe every other day. He resisted using any make-up as the vampire, but eventually relented and would sit with Reiko Kruk, the make-up artist, for hours at a time, listening to Japanese music as she sculpted him every morning, putting his ears and fingernails on, fitting his teeth and ears, and shaving his head. Seeing him so patient was a fine sight. I would walk in and sit with him for fifteen minutes. We wouldn't talk; we just looked at each other in the mirror and nodded. He was good with the project and with himself. Although the film is close to two hours and Kinski appears for maybe seventeen minutes in total, his vampire dominates every scene. The finest compliment I can give him for his performance is that there is a palpable sense of doom and terror and anxiety even when he isn't on screen. Everything in the film works towards those seventeen minutes. We will never see a vampire like Kinski again.

Roland Topor plays Renfield.

I was at the Cannes Film Festival and heard maniacal laughter behind me, so turned around but there was nobody there, only a closed-circuit television broadcasting the press conference for the film *La Planète sauvage*. Topor – a filmmaker, actor, illustrator and novelist – was incapable of saying anything without laughing, and I kept him in mind. My original idea was to have Valeska Gert, a German cabaret artist and dancer of the grotesque, play Renfield, but she died three days after signing a contract, and I immediately remembered Topor. I showed up at his apartment in Paris with a case of German beer and persuaded him to be in the film. Topor and his family had survived the war by hiding out in the French countryside. Perhaps that was why he was unable to finish a sentence without this strange laughter, as if Creation – having required him to run for his life from the Nazis as a young boy – could be nothing other than a complete farce.

You let loose ten thousand rats loose in Delft during filming.

I was looking for a northern German or Baltic town with boats and canals. A Dutch friend of mine suggested Delft, which has remained unchanged for centuries, and as soon as I saw the town I was fascinated by it. Delft is so tranquil, bourgeois, self-assured and solid, so tidy and well ordered; it looks like a stylised film set, and I knew it would be the perfect place to shoot this story. The entire cast and crew – except Kinski, who always gravitated towards five-star hotels – lived communally in an abandoned convent. Filming in town wasn't easy because our work involved a certain amount of disruption of daily life. The two scenes shot in the town square with the rats were done early in the morning, when we had less than three hours to set everything up and film. I asked for sympathy from the citizens of Delft, and some responded positively, like the local cinema enthusiasts who organised a retrospective of my films and circulated petitions to gather support. The sequence of the boat arriving, bringing Nosferatu to town, was filmed in Schiedam, a few miles away, because there are too many bridges in Delft and the canals are too narrow.

I knew the horror and destruction of the vampire would show up most effectively in such an uncontaminated town. *Nosferatu* is about a community invaded by an anonymous terror, something signified very provocatively by rats. Our fear of the creatures probably stems from the fact that for every human being on the planet there are three rats. Before we started shooting I explained to the town council in Delft exactly what I had in mind. Many residents were nervous because the place is full of canals, and for decades there was a serious rat problem that had only recently been eradicated, so I showed them our detailed technical plans and precautionary measures to prevent a single animal from escaping. Before we released them in the town we sealed off every gully, side street and doorway. We fixed nets along the canals to prevent the rats from getting into the water, and even had people in boats down in the canal to collect any creatures that might escape. During filming in the town square we had a movable wooden wall just behind the camera and another in an alley at the end of the street. When the signal was given, both walls were pulled out of their hiding places and brought towards each other, trapping the rats in an ever narrower space so they could be caged. We never lost a single one, and I sold them once filming was over.

We stored the rats in a farmhouse just outside of town. Money was sent to the owner, who was to feed and take care of the animals, but for some reason this payment never arrived. When I went over to pick up the rats, this man was absolutely enraged. I explained that of course he would be paid immediately, but he prevented us from gaining access. There was no arguing with him, so I picked the lock and opened the barn doors. When he saw this, he went wild, started his Caterpillar and drove directly towards one of our trucks, onto which we had loaded a couple of thousand rats. I lay down in front of this massive vehicle but quickly realised that was a stupid idea because the bastard would have run me over. He drove the massive shovel of this Caterpillar through the window of our truck, at which point I grabbed an iron bar and swung it at his seat, with the intention of just missing him. "The next blow will hit you," I told him. "Give me the keys." I still have them, a kind of souvenir of the film's production.

Where did you get the rats?

From a laboratory in Hungary. Customs officials checked the medical certificates at every border, and somewhere en route one of them opened a box to check the contents and promptly fainted. When we bought the rats, they were snow white, so I decided to have them all dyed grey. There was a huge factory in Germany that produced shampoo and hair dye, and they always tested their products on rats because the texture of rat hair is similar to that of humans. I visited this place along with Henning von Gierke, a painter and art director who did the set design for the film, and Cornelius Siegel, a special-effects expert who taught at the University of Bremen. Cornelius was the one who set the glass factory on fire in *Heart of Glass* and single-handedly built the clock in *Nosferatu*, with all its moving parts. After talking to the people at this factory, Cornelius designed a massive conveyor belt. We put the rats into wire cages, dipped each cage into the dye for a second, washed every rat with lukewarm water, then dried them all using a system of hair dryers, otherwise they would have caught pneumonia. Even today there are claims floating around that the rats were mistreated and that some died while being transported to Delft, even resorting to cannibalism because they were so hungry. The fact is that we ended up with about five hundred more than when we started. There were also allegations that we submerged each rat into a bucket of boiling grey paint. I hereby offer the even wilder truth of the matter: we boiled the rats for such a long time that they volunteered to turn grey.

What language was the film shot in?

We had people of multiple nationalities on set, so English was the common language. As a filmmaker a choice has to be made, not just to ensure that communication between cast and crew is as easy as possible, but also for the sake of international distributors. As with *Aguirre* and *Fitzcarraldo*, *Nosferatu* was originally shot in English, but after a number of preview screenings it was clear that audiences were confused because of all the different English accents. We decided to dub the film into German, which for me is the most convincing version. I wouldn't dare to speak of the "better" version, but for me it's the more culturally authentic one. Pre-production took four or five months, and we shot for about eight weeks. I had final cut, but after Twentieth Century Fox – the studio that had bought the distribution rights for the United States – saw the film they asked me to shorten a few things for the American version, and I made some other minor modifications. After several previews it was clear that for some audiences the film dragged a little, so I cut it by a couple of minutes, though no one at the studio insisted on this.

Where did you shoot the sequences at the vampire's castle?

Whatever you see of Transylvania was shot in the former Czechoslovakia, much of it in Moravia at Pernštejn Castle and in the High Tatra mountains. I wanted to shoot in Transylvania proper, in Romania, but wasn't allowed to because of restrictions imposed by the Ceauşescu regime. I never actually received a direct refusal from the authorities, but did get word from some Romanian filmmakers, who advised me not to wait for permission, as it would never come so long as Ceauşescu was around. At the time Dracula was a sensitive subject for Romanians because there was a campaign to rehabilitate the historical figure of Count Dracula as an esteemed leader in the history of their country. Not much is known about him, but in the fifteenth century he was an important force against the Turkish armies. After a battle, so the legend goes, he impaled twenty thousand prisoners, which is probably where the motif in every vampire film comes from, that you can kill a vampire only by driving a stake through his heart. Parliament had bestowed upon Ceauşescu the title of the new Vlad Dracul, the historical defender of Romania, which in contemporary terms meant he was protecting the country from the Soviet empire. He heaped all sorts of honours on himself; I think he had the world-record number of honorary doctorates – something like sixty or seventy – and every school hailed him as the Great Creator of Paradise. It turned out these local filmmakers were right, that to the authorities it was unthinkable that Vlad Dracul was a vampire, so I left the country, though not before I had a wonderful time searching for locations, methodically travelling every path of the Carpathian mountains.

Five days after you finished shooting Nosferatu *work began on* Woyzeck, *with the same crew and lead actor.*

Today *Woyzeck* – which took seventeen days to film and five days to edit – seems like a little hiccup after *Nosferatu*. I would have started shooting the day after we finished *Nosferatu*, but we had to let Kinski's hair grow for the role. It was mainly for bureaucratic reasons that we continued with the same crew on a new film, because at the time obtaining shooting permits in Czechoslovakia was an endless saga. We ended up filming the second half of *Nosferatu* in Moravia and other places in the eastern part of Slovakia, and I figured it was best to continue shooting *Woyzeck* but tell the authorities we were still working on *Nosferatu*. Actually, we started filming the day after *Nosferatu* was completed. I just shot around Kinski's part.

Kinski was never an actor who would merely play a part. After *Nosferatu* he remained deep in the world we had created together, something apparent from the first day he walked onto the set of *Woyzeck*. He loved playing Woyzeck and was very much in balance with himself during the shoot, but also exhausted and somehow broken and vulnerable, which was precisely the condition required of the role. It meant his performance had a rare and profound quality. He truly captured the spirit of the part; there's a smouldering intensity to him, and from the opening scenes of the film he seems fragile. Look at the shot of him immediately after the title sequence, where he stares into the camera. Something isn't quite right with his face. When he does his push-ups during the title sequence, the drill major kicks him to the ground. The person who did the kicking is Walter Saxer, my production manager on many films, who a couple of years later was screamed at by Kinski on the set of *Fitzcarraldo*, something you can see in *My Best Fiend*. "He's not doing it right," Klaus said to me. "He has to really kick me. He can't pretend." The two of them always had an antagonistic relationship, so Saxer had no problems giving Kinski what he was asking for. Kinski was pushed so hard into the cobblestones that his face started to swell. "Klaus, don't move," I said. "Just look at me." He was panting, still exhausted from doing his push-ups, but looks into the camera with such power that it establishes the atmosphere for the rest of the film.

This was clearly a project that had been on your mind for a while.

The character had forever been burning inside me. I don't believe there is a greater drama in the German language than Büchner's *Woyzeck*; it's a work of such stunning actuality, like an undefused bomb. The first time I read it I felt as if a lightning bolt had shot through me. The play is actually only a fragment, and there has long been a debate among scholars as to which order the loose, unpaginated sheets should go in. I used an arrangement of scenes that made the most sense as a continuous story, one that is used in the majority of theatrical productions. In my opinion there is no completely satisfying English translation of the play. The film is my most direct connection to the best of my own culture, even more so than *Nosferatu*.

I structured it around a series of four-minute-long shots, the length of a roll of 35mm stock, which means there is a much greater reliance on the acting and text than on the camera. I will probably never achieve a film of such economy again. What made the whole approach exciting is that the cinematic space is created not by cuts and the camera's movement, but by the actors within the frame, by the force of their performances. It was my way of giving due deference to Büchner's words, though it wasn't easy to maintain this style because no one was permitted any mistakes.

Look at the scene where Woyzeck tries to flee from the drum major, where he moves directly into the lens of the camera and is pulled back at the last moment. In a shot like that Kinski creates a space far beyond that of the camera; he shows us there is a whole world behind, around and in front of the lens. You feel he is crawling desperately towards you, even into you. I like filmmakers willing to let their pants down, daring enough to show a whole sequence in a single shot lasting three or four minutes. Some directors move the camera about for no reason; they use flashy tricks and an excess of cuts because they know the material isn't strong enough to sustain a passive camera. It's a giveaway that I'm watching an empty film. If you want to use stylistic tricks and gimmicks, they can never be added as a whim. Embed them firmly in the storytelling.

You once said that cinema comes from the "country fair and circus," not from "art and academicism."

On the table in front of us is a pile of academic articles about my films that you brought over for me to look at. The minute you leave here today, it will all be thrown into the trash. The healthiest thing anyone can do is avoid that impenetrable nonsense. My response to it all is a blank stare, just as I respond to most philosophical writings. I can't crack the code of Hegel and Heidegger; it isn't the concepts that are alien to me, but I get my ideas from real life, not books. When I hear the kind of language used by zealots and film theorists, Venetian blinds start rattling down.

You rarely find people in universities who truly appreciate literature. At school we sliced through Goethe's *Iphigenia* and *Faust*, vivisecting and layering them with incomprehensible theoretical babbling, the kind of thing that goes on at universities today with ever more pathetic fury. It was so bad that I'm still unable to read *Faust*. My love of poetry was almost entirely eradicated when I was young, but thank God I managed to keep my genuine sense of wonder intact. The best example of agitation of the mind that literature can offer comes from my wife, who as a teenager living in Siberia wrote out in longhand a samizdat copy of Bulgakov's *The Master and Margarita* and secretly circulated it to her friends. As for film, the theoreticians have dedicated their lives to the very opposite of passion. Our feelings for cinema should be like those during an eclipse or when we see a close-up of the sun, with those protuber-ances – thousands of times larger than our own planet – shooting out, or the same fascination I felt as a child when I looked through a telescope and saw the mountains and craters of the moon, or those instances of special intensity in a piece of music, when sud-denly you hear something so startling that it rails against the most basic rules you're accustomed to. I remain in awe when I think back on those moments. Academia stifles cinema, encircling it like a liana vine wraps round a tree, smothering and draining away all life. Construct films, don't deconstruct them. Create poetry, don't destroy it. Whenever I encounter film theorists, I lower my head and charge. Thankfully cinema remains in robust shape. There has yet to be a lethal dose of intellectualism.

Reading about cinema is of little use to aspiring filmmakers, and as for those people who write about film, rather than read-ing endless books on the subject they should study something like the deciphering of Assyrian cuneiform texts or the Jacobi constant, which dates back to the nineteenth century and is concerned with the movements of objects around planets. Horizons need to be broadened at all times. I've never read a single book about cinema. Actually, I did read some chapters of Lotte Eisner's work, and when it first came out I looked at Amos Vogel's *Film as a Subversive Art*, which contains hundreds of extraordinary images. But that's it. I always felt that if you really love cinema, the healthiest thing to do is ignore books about it. I prefer the film magazines with their gar-ish colour photos, snippets of celebrity news and nauseating gossip columns, or the *National Enquirer*. That kind of vulgarity is far healthier.

6

Defying Gravity

How did you end up in Berkeley, publicly munching through your footwear, as documented by Les Blank in Werner Herzog Eats His Shoe?

In the seventies I spent time in Berkeley with Errol Morris, who was a graduate student, when we were both hanging out at the Pacific Film Archive. When you meet Errol, you immediately sense that everything around him is aflame, that he is absolutely original in his thinking, with his relentless questioning mind and extraordinarily lively spirit. He is an important comrade-in-arms, someone who has found his own unique way to explore the paths that lead as far as possible away from *cinéma-vérité* and fact-orientated film. As a young man Errol had great talent as a cellist, but he suddenly abandoned the instrument, and dropped his book project after collecting thousands of pages of conversations with serial killers. Then he said he wanted to make a film, but complained about how difficult it was to find money from producers and that all the subsidies had dried up. I made it clear that when it comes to filmmaking, money isn't important, that the intensity of your wishes and faith alone are the deciding factors. "Stop complaining about the stupidity of producers. Just start with a roll of raw stock tomorrow," I told him. "I'll eat the shoes I'm wearing the day I see your film for the first time." Eventually he made an extraordinary work called *Gates of Heaven*, about a pet cemetery in California. I'm a man of my word, so en route from pre-production of *Fitzcarraldo* in Peru I stopped off at Chez Panisse in Berkeley to pay my dues.

I could have worn light track shoes, but cowards have never

impressed me, so I made a point of bringing the same shoes I had worn when I made my vow to Errol: ankle-high Clarks desert boots, with a sole that melted away like cheese on a pizza. When I cooked them, that day Chez Panisse had duck as a main course. There was a huge pot of duck fat, which I reckoned would come to boiling point at about 140°C, a much higher temperature than water, so I thought I would be better off cooking the shoes in that rather than water. I added a red onion, four heads of garlic and some rosemary. Unfortunately, the fat caused the leather to shrink, which made it even tougher. Friends of mine seriously debated whether I should be allowed to go ahead with it at all. There was no way to eat the leather unless I used a pair of poultry shears and cut it into tiny fragments, then swallowed it down with beer. I couldn't tell you what it tasted like because I was already too drunk by the time I started eating. I do remember being up on the stage of the UC Theatre in Berkeley having consumed an entire six-pack, then staggering out of the place. But don't worry, leather is easy to digest, and Tom Luddy, who was up there on the stage with me, distributed small pieces to the audience in solidarity.

I had a tacit agreement with Les Blank that his footage of the event was something strictly for the family album. Maybe the events he documented are too personal for me to acknowledge that *Werner Herzog Eats His Shoe* should ever have been seen publicly, but Les is such a good filmmaker that I forgive him anything. Today I'm glad he captured it all on film. These days you hear about things like shoe-eating out of context and it sounds ridiculous, but to me it made perfect sense. I did it as an encouragement for anyone who doesn't have the guts to make films. And anyway, a man should eat his shoes every once in a while. Errol recently suggested that next time I should eat my foot. At the New York Film Festival screening of *Gates of Heaven* someone asked him a question, the first ever thrown to him at a press conference. "Mr Morris, I think your film would be twice as good if it were cut in half." "So would you, madam," said Errol, without missing a beat.

During pre-production on Fitzcarraldo *you made two shorts in the United States.*

I first encountered televangelist Dr Gene Scott years before I made my film about him. Whenever I was in America I would always switch on his programmes, and quickly became addicted. As wild as he might have been as a public figure, there was something heartbreaking about him that moved me. He could never have been a friend of mine, but I still somehow liked him. His was basically a one-man show, on screen for up to eight hours every day. The way he raged at his audience was extraordinary, as he insisted that "God's honour is at stake every night!" and that it was merely a case of "Six hundred miserable dollars, and you sit there glued to your chair!" He would threaten and intimidate the people at home watching him, saying things like, "I'm going to sit here in silence for the next ten minutes. If $20,000 isn't pledged during that time, I'll pull the plug!" On one day when we filmed with him, more than a quarter of a million dollars were pledged.

Scott was a controversial figure; when I made the film, there were something like seventy active lawsuits against him. The charges ranged from embezzlement and blackmail to slander and tax evasion. The authorities had seized his assets, claiming he was running a television channel, not a church, and in protest Scott barricaded himself in the studio for two days. He was a polarising force, and his audience was anything but indifferent. People either loved or hated him. He was an intelligent man but also, I felt, deeply unhappy. There was a compulsion to him; he was all alone up there, talking to the camera, day after day, and would interrupt his flow only because he needed to go to the bathroom. His singers would perform some phoney religious tune while he was backstage. How can anyone keep something like that up for so many years? I saw nothing of him once the film was finished, but heard that before he died he went completely bonkers, abandoning many of his explicit Christian teachings, and on his show would sit in a glass pyramid talking about pyramid energies. Scott somehow appeals to the paranoia and craziness of our civilisation. He took issue with the way he came across in *God's Angry Man* and asked me to change the original title, which was *Creed and Currency*.

Huie's Sermon was shot in Brooklyn, New York. I bumped into Bishop Huie Rogers and asked if I could make a film about him. The end result needs no discussion; it's a pure work about the joys of life, faith and filmmaking. There is great joy in the image of Huie as he starts completely harmlessly, gradually whipping up his flock into an extraordinary elation. He would rail against the immorality of society and man's corruption, but I always felt that with his wondrous ecstatic fervour he outdoes even Mick Jagger. I cut away from Huie to the surrounding streets a couple of times only because we had to change the magazine in the camera.

Did you expect such intense media interest when you started work on Fitzcarraldo?

What I didn't expect was walking down the street in Munich a few months after the film was released, seeing a man running frantically towards me, then watching as he leapt up into the air, kicked me in the stomach, picked himself up from the ground and screamed into my face, "That's what you deserve, you pig!"

Many of the problems we experienced during *Fitzcarraldo*'s production stemmed from the fact that there were things going on in the area where I wanted to make the film that had nothing to do with us, including a border war that was steadily building between Peru and Ecuador. All around us was an enormous and increasingly threatening military presence, and at every second bend of the river there was a chaotic military camp swarming with drunken soldiers. Oil companies were busy exploiting natural resources in the area, and they had – with great brutality against the local population – constructed a pipeline across the Indians' territory and the Andes all the way to the Pacific. When we showed up on location in the jungle, with full permission from the local Indians, all these unsolved problems somehow started to revolve around our presence. We had real media appeal because Mick Jagger was scheduled to be in the film alongside Claudia Cardinale, with Jason Robards – who I had seen in *The Ballad of Cable Hogue* – as Fitzcarraldo. I had no interest in becoming the dancing bear of the media circus, but all of a sudden here was the exotic concoction of Claudia and Jagger, plus the mad Herzog, a bunch of Native Indians, a border war and a military dictatorship. Fortunately it was easy to rubbish the claims the press made, not least because a human-rights group sent a commission down to the area and concluded there hadn't been a single violation. I was sure that the wilder and more bizarre the legends, the faster they would wither away, and after two years of being criminalised by the press that's just what happened.

Brian Sweeney Fitzgerald adores Caruso and wants to build an opera house in the middle of the jungle so he can invite the world-famous tenor to the opening night.

Years before I thought of the story, while working on another film and searching for locations, I took a drive along the Brittany coast. At night I reached a place named Carnac and found myself in a field covered with menhirs – huge prehistoric stone slabs, up to thirty feet high and some weighing six hundred tonnes – stuck in the ground. There were thousands of them, parallel rows going on for miles inland across the hills. I thought I was dreaming. I bought a tourist brochure and read that science still has no clear explanation of how, eight or ten thousand years ago, these huge blocks were brought overland to this spot and set upright, using only Stone Age tools. The brochure suggested it was the work of ancient alien astronauts. This itched me, and I told myself I wasn't going to leave until I had worked out how I, as a Stone Age man with the available tools – simple hemp ropes or leather thongs and levers and ramps – would have moved a menhir over a distance of a couple of miles.

This is what I came up with. I would need a group of men to dig a series of trenches under the menhir. Then I would push hardened oak-tree trunks into the trenches and dig away the rest of the earth, so the menhir would be resting on the trunks. Once this is accomplished, the stone could be moved on these "wheels" with ropes and levers. The real task ahead would be to construct a ramp – a mile long, almost horizontal – on an almost imperceptible incline. For that, I would need two thousand disciplined men. The ramp would lead to an artificial mound twenty feet high, with a crater dug into it. To move the menhir up the ramp would take far fewer men and could be done in only a few days. They would use levers and a primitive pulley system with turnstiles, finally tipping the stone into the prefabricated hole. Once it tilts into the crater with its pointed end down, you basically have an upright menhir, and all that needs to be done is to remove the earth, the mound and the ramp. If *Fitzcarraldo* had a passport, Carnac would be listed as its place of birth.

Years later José Koechlin, a friend of mine from Peru who had helped raise part of the budget for *Aguirre*, came to visit me in Munich and suggested I return to the jungle and make another film. "Everyone's waiting for you there," he said. I knew I couldn't go back without the right story. José then told me the true tale of Carlos Fermín Fitzcarrald, a fabulously wealthy real-life rubber baron from the late nineteenth century who had a private army of four thousand men and drowned at the age of thirty-five in a boating accident. The history of the rubber era in Peru didn't interest me, nor was Fitzcarrald a particularly compelling character; he was just another ugly businessman. It was thin stuff for a film, save for one detail José happened to mention: Fitzcarrald had once dismantled a boat into hundreds of pieces and, over a period of several months, carried it overland from the Ucayali River to the Madre de Dios River, where he set about reassembling it, which is how he was able to bypass a series of rapids and take control of a territory almost the size of Belgium. That absolutely fascinated me. Inspired by the rubber barons who built the Teatro Amazonas in Manaus just before the turn of the century, I came up with the idea of Fitzcarraldo wanting to finance the construction of his own opera house. When I wrote the screenplay and listed the characters on page one, the first name wasn't Fitzcarraldo, it was Enrico Caruso, though you only ever hear his voice in the film. I eventually pieced these three elements – Fitzcarrald, Caruso and Carnac, which became a ship moved overland – together into a single story. The question was: how do I move a steamboat, all 340 tonnes of it, in one piece for more than a mile across a mountain, in the primeval forest, several hundred miles away from the nearest town?

I was working with Twentieth Century Fox on *Nosferatu* at the time, and after reading a seventeen-page treatment the studio wanted me to sign a contract for a package deal that would have included *Woyzeck* and *Fitzcarraldo*, especially once Jack Nicholson expressed interest in playing Fitzcarraldo. I was certain that a Hollywood studio would never get involved in anything as wild as moving a steamboat over a mountain in the middle of the jungle; it was too far outside their horizon of thinking. The executives even suggested I use a miniature boat and fake mountain, and film in the botanic gardens in San Diego. But using models was out of the question for me. *Fitzcarraldo* is set in an invented geography, but I knew I had to do it for real. For months I sat through insufferable and endless meetings with financiers in Los Angeles before deciding to start pre-production with my own money, which was enough to get things moving. I knew that the way to carry through a project of this size was to pull the train out of the station so everyone could get an idea of its scale, speed and direction. Once there was some momentum, people would jump on board. The film ended up costing $6 million, much of which hadn't been secured by the time shooting began.

Even before filming started you had been in the jungle for some time.

Pre-production took more than three years. In the film you see a rusty old boat that Fitzcarraldo fixes up. We found it in Colombia, but it had sat on dry land for twenty-five years and had such huge holes in its hull that it was beyond repair. We tugged it to Iquitos in Peru with six hundred empty oil drums stuffed into its belly to keep it afloat, and used it as the model for two identical boats we set about building. One had to be constructed in such a way that it wouldn't break apart while being pulled over the mountain. While it was sitting on the mountainside, we could be shooting with the other boat in the rapids, which we had to reckon might sink. Constructing the identical twin ships was a long and arduous procedure because there wasn't a single dock in Iquitos where we could work, so we had to build a primitive wharf. We also had to construct a camp for hundreds of extras and a small crew. I spent a lot of time either in the jungle or travelling up to America or Europe to collect things we needed, or trying to raise more money, which is why pre-production took so long.

Then, once shooting finally started and we had shot about 40 per cent of the film, which took about six weeks, Jason Robards became ill with amoebic dysentery. Before shooting had begun, his lawyer had requested we install a second radio station and a heart–lung machine in the camp, then fly in an American doctor with modern medical equipment and have an aeroplane ready at all times to be able to get him out of there quickly. It was all utterly ridiculous, not least because the kind of machinery they requested would never have functioned properly in the jungle because of the humidity and unreliable electricity. Beyond that, our financial situation would never have permitted it. Robards went back to the United States, and the entire production came to a halt while we waited for him. Then, after a few weeks, his doctor categorically forbade him to return to the jungle. Although the insurance company accepted our claim, this was an absolute catastrophe for us. Practically everything we had in the can included Robards, so none of it was of any use.

In the meantime, Jagger – who played Fitzcarraldo's devoted and deranged sidekick, an English actor named Wilbur who forever spouted Shakespearean soliloquies, including the opening lines from *Richard III* – had to honour his commitment to a Rolling Stones concert tour, so I decided to write his character completely out of the story. Mick Jagger is, after all, irreplaceable. I liked him so much as a performer that anyone else in the role would have been an embarrassment. Jagger is a truly great actor, something few people have noticed. I was backstage at a Rolling Stones concert many years ago and saw him talking with someone about a particular brand of whisky he liked and that should have been in his dressing room, but wasn't. All of a sudden, in the middle of this argument, there was an announcement on the loudspeaker: "Ladies and gentlemen, please welcome the Rolling Stones!" I watched Jagger stop in mid-sentence and leap a few steps onto the stage, where, in front of a crowd of thousands, he gave the most demonic performance I have ever seen.

I appreciated Mick's attitude during the filming of *Fitzcarraldo*. On the first day of shooting there was a general strike in Iquitos, so things were at a standstill. Everyone was afraid to leave the hotel, but Mick had a car we rented for him which he insisted on using to drive actors and extras to the location. He knew how important that first day was for everyone. I liked that he knew the value of real work; he's a professional in the best sense of the word. Everything was a great adventure to him, and having to make the film without Mick is one of the biggest losses I've ever experienced as a director. Robards didn't have the intensity of Kinski; he was more of a warm-hearted Fitzcarraldo, so the two versions would have been different. I like the film today, but would also have liked the Robards/Jagger version.

With Robards gone you thought about playing the role of Fitzcarraldo yourself.

I would have played the part only as a last resort, and would have been a credible Fitzcarraldo because what he has to do in the film was almost exactly what I had to do as its director. There wasn't much of a borderline between this fictional character and me. I wouldn't have been undignified in the role, but would never have been as good as Kinski. Thank God he did it. It was actually Mick Jagger who advised me not to play the part. I flew out from the jungle, completely exhausted, and met with Kinski in a hotel in New York. I was devastated by everything that had been going on in Peru and thought he was going to scream at me, but he was very supportive and opened a bottle of champagne, saying, "I knew it, Werner! I knew I would be Fitzcarraldo! When does filming start? When can I try on my costume? When do we leave for Peru?" I had contemplated Kinski playing the role from the start, but reached a false conclusion, the same one everyone else probably had, which came from the fact that in every one of his films Kinski never showed a spark of humour. I also decided against him because I knew he had no stamina. Today, when I look back, it's unthinkable that anyone else might have been Fitzcarraldo.

I truly liked Kinski for the attitude he brought to that hotel room, though once he arrived at the site where the boat was to be pulled over the mountain and saw how steep the terrain was, his heart sank. He was convinced it couldn't be done, and became the strongest negative force on the film. At one point, when the river was swollen and I was sitting in my hut, gazing at the fast-flowing current, watching the water level rise, a small delegation arrived that had obviously been sent by Kinski. They told me to be calm, that they were here to protect me from my own madness and folly, that I should abandon the film, or at least continue to flatten out the mountainside. We had already turned a gradient of sixty degrees into one of forty. "I'm the only one who's calm," I told them. For a time not a single person was on my side. The question I kept hearing was, "Why don't you just rewrite the script and cut out this whole thing of pulling a ship over a mountain?" My response was always the same: to do so would mean losing the central metaphor of my story.

In an interview from the time you said that if you were to make a film like Fitzcarraldo *again, "there would be only ashes left of me."*

One of the cameramen asked what I would do if the entire negative were lost in an aeroplane crash. I told him I would start all over again tomorrow, that I would go through everything once more.

With Robards and Jagger gone and production halted, it was vital to get the film up and running as quickly as possible. We had already booked the opera house in Manaus, where several key sequences of the film were to be shot, and if we didn't get going immediately the boats would have been immovable because of the imminent dry period. There were other things to deal with, like making it clear to the five hundred Indians who had already spent two months working on the film that their efforts hadn't been for nothing, and the fact that our encampment was at risk of being devoured by termites. About ten days' voyage further up Río Camisea from where we were working lived the Amahuacas, a nomadic tribal group who had repelled all attempts by missionaries and the military to contact them. That season was the driest in recorded history and the river had virtually dried out. A group of Amahuacas were forced to move downriver, further than ever before, probably in search of turtle eggs. In silence and total darkness they attacked three locals who were extras in the film and who were fishing for our camp, shooting gigantic arrows through the neck and leg of one of the men, something you see in Les Blank's documentary *Burden of Dreams*. The man's wife was also hit, in her abdomen, with three arrows, leaving her in critical condition. It was too risky to transport them anywhere, so we performed eight hours of emergency surgery on a kitchen table. I assisted by illuminating her abdominal cavity with a torch, and with my other hand sprayed repellent at the clouds of mosquitoes that swarmed around the blood. Thirty of our native extras left on a retaliatory raid to push the Amahuacas back into their own territory, but they never made contact. My hut was on the edge of the camp and was the most exposed, so the Indians insisted on posting six guards with bows and arrows at the foot of my bed and beside my hammock.

There were also inevitable complications with getting the boat up the mountain, not least because every spare part – as well as everything from generators, sinks, refrigerators, an entire make-shift radio station, ovens and kitchen equipment, to material for costumes, sewing machines, food, livestock and crates of mineral water – had to be shipped in from Iquitos. Then, once we actually got the boat to the top, there was no water in the tributary on the other side, so it sat there for six months. I hired a family with five children and a couple of pigs to live inside it until we returned, at which point we spent a couple of weeks getting shots of the ship moving down the other side of the mountain. Filming in Iquitos was difficult because there was no infrastructure. Phoning long distance was practically impossible, there were power cuts twice a day, and the dirt road from town to our offices was basically a swamp, so most taxi drivers refused to make the journey. Those who did had cars which were rusted through and falling apart. We held on to the doors to keep from falling out, and instead of a steering wheel some of them used a pair of pincers to steer.

By pulling a real boat over a real mountain were you after realism?

When the boat is crashing through the rapids it jerks the gramophone, and we suddenly hear opera playing. The realistic noises fade away to reveal Caruso singing, and the whole thing becomes a dream-like event. Once the boat starts to move up the mountainside, there are fewer and fewer people in shot; it's almost as if the boat were gliding by its own force over the top of the mountain. Had we shown anyone in frame, the endeavour would have been realistic, an event of human labour. As it is, in the film the whole thing seems to have been transformed into an opera of fever dreams and pure imagination, a highly stylised and grandiose fantasy, part of the vapour sweat out by the jungle. The film challenges the most basic laws of nature; boats aren't meant to fly over mountains. Fitzcarraldo's story is the victory of weightlessness and fantasy over heaviness and reality, and the elation that follows. He defies gravity head on, and by the film's end I hope audiences feel lighter than they did two hours earlier.

You set yourself a daunting engineering task.

Some people expressed doubt about what we were doing, and one of the loudest accusations against me was that I risked people's lives during production. The fact is, I was careful about everything. I hired a team of engineers from the University of Bremen who travelled to Peru and examined the condition of the soil, the gradient of the mountain and tractive power of the boat. They made calculations and drew up plans, but their solutions – one of which was to place the ship on inflated air cushions – weren't feasible.

I then hired a Brazilian engineer who supervised the logistics of dragging the boat; he's the one in *Burden of Dreams* who says we have a 30 per cent chance of pulling the boat over the mountain. He quit the production because once in the jungle, he said that a twenty-degree angle was all the technology would allow for, insisting there was a real danger that our dead post – drilled into the ground to take the weight of the boat – would be pulled out of the ground if we went ahead. He was convinced the whole thing was a disaster waiting to happen. When he left, I took things into my own hands and halted production for two weeks. I had a much more stable hole dug for the dead post and sank a huge tree trunk about thirty feet into the ground, letting it stick out by only two feet. It isn't difficult to calculate the force of physical objects, like the boat against this post, which by the time we had finished could have comfortably held something like ten times the weight of the steamship. We also brought in a heavier and more substantial pulley system. The margin of safety was extravagant.

I wish we had recorded everything in Dolby stereo because the noises the ship made when moving over the mountain were stunning. Steel cables sound unhealthy and sick when close to breaking point; no sound engineer could ever have invented what we heard on location. An overstressed cable glows red hot inside from the pressure. The only thing to do is to release as much tension as possible and get out of the way, because when it snaps under such circumstances it becomes a gigantic, deadly whip. I was careful not to allow anyone to stand next to the ship – particularly behind it – when it was being pulled up the mountain. The Native Indians demanded that if they had to be close to this enormous object for a particular shot, then I had to be there as well, which I acceded to immediately. The rear of the ship was sealed off from the rest of the set, and if the cables holding the boat had broken, it would have slid down the mountain without harming anyone. No one was ever at risk while it was moving. No one means no actor, no technician, no extra.

We had seven hundred Indians who provided pulling force by revolving the turnstiles we had constructed, but I also imported a Caterpillar bulldozer from Texas that spent weeks clearing a path up the mountain. The power of the turnstiles operated by the Indians was real, but more symbolic than anything else; the largest amount of physical power came from this Caterpillar. There are primitive physical laws behind what we did on that mountain. Given the fact that we had a pulley system with a ten-thousand-fold transmission, theoretically speaking I could have dragged the boat over the mountain with my little finger. It would have taken very little strength, though I would have had to pull the rope about five miles to move the boat five inches. I think it was Archimedes who said it's possible to hoist the earth off its hinges if you have a pivotal point and lever sticking far enough out into the universe. The real Fitzcarrald moved a far lighter boat from one river system to the next, but he disassembled it into little pieces, then had engineers reassemble it. There was no precedent in technical history for what we did. The obvious problems were the steep inclination and landslides caused by torrential rains, which meant the boat kept on sinking into the mud. No one will ever need to do again what I did. I'm a Conquistador of the Useless. Actually, a few years ago I was in the archive of the Vatican library and discovered that the obelisk in St Peter's Square was erected in the same way I pulled the ship over the mountain. I devised my own method all those years ago, but it turns out the same ideas were being used back in 1586.

People still believe Indians were killed when the boat was dragged up the mountain.

There is a shot in *Fitzcarraldo* where the boat finally starts edging up the side of the mountain before slipping back again and crushing a couple of Indians. I'm proud the scene is so well staged that some people think the Indians really died and that I had the audacity to film their bodies, deep in the mud underneath the boat. Thankfully Les Blank got that shot he used in *Burden of Dreams*, where we see them emerging from underneath the boat, laughing, then washing themselves in the river. Some of the wilder accusations were triggered by images that looked too convincing.

Several accidents occurred during filming, but none of these were directly related to the actual shooting of the film. Many of the Indians had come from the mountainous areas and couldn't swim. I would sometimes see them taking our canoes out into the middle of the river, so I decided to move the boats up to higher ground and even chain them together. One day I was coming round a bend of the river in a speedboat and saw a great tumult on the riverbank. I immediately knew something had happened and realised that a canoe had capsized just moments before, so I dived down and tried to find the two young men who were in the water. One of them reached the shore, but the other drowned. Three days later, after consulting with the tribal chief, his fifteen-year-old wife remarried. Soon after that one of our aeroplanes was taking off from the jungle runway when its wheels tossed up a branch that became stuck in the tail section, immobilising altitude control. The aeroplane continued to climb very steeply until it stalled. Everyone survived, but some people sustained serious injuries. At our infirmary, where we had a doctor who specialised in tropical diseases, we were able to treat over a thousand locals who had nothing to do with the film, though an elderly woman and two children died of anaemia.

Naturally there are some things I have to take responsibility for. During the filming of the scene where the boat moves through the rapids, the assistant cameraman Rainer Klausmann was sitting, with a camera, on a rock in the river covered with moss and surrounded by turbulent water. It hadn't been easy to reach this spot, let alone stabilise a camera there. We got the shots we wanted, during which the boat smashed against the rocks so violently that the keel was completely mangled. Just past the rapids the boat ran aground on a sandbank, and we frantically tried to free it because the dry season was approaching and we knew the water level would sink even further, preventing any kind of rescue of the ship. We all had a lot on our minds and eventually made it back to camp for the night. Next morning at breakfast I couldn't find Klausmann, and asked if anyone had seen him last night. No one had. We had forgotten him on that rock the day before. I jumped into a boat and went over to the rapids as fast as I could, and saw him just sitting there, shivering with cold, hanging on to this rock. He was very angry, rightfully so. Klausmann had attracted bad luck even before that. Near Iquitos there was a dead branch of the river, the kind of place where normally you would find piranhas, but because all the townsfolk and children would go there to swim, we did too. One afternoon we were in the water and all of a sudden I heard a scream and saw Klausmann scrambling to shore. A piranha had bitten off the top of one of his toes. He was on crutches for weeks.

At one point I had a deep scratch on my finger; in *Burden of*

Dreams you see I have white gaffer tape wrapped around it. Soon afterwards a red streak appeared under the skin, running from the finger past my elbow all the way to the armpit. Our doctor casually asked, "Are you allergic to penicillin?" I told him I didn't know. "Let's test it," he said, and scratched my skin with a needle. Immediately I had a wild reaction; my entire body was covered in red patches the size of large coins and my ears turned purple and swelled up. He would have killed me on the spot with an injection into a vein. Later, one beautiful day I was walking on the deck of one of the boats, looking out into the jungle, and leant on a section of railing that had been recently repaired but not properly screwed back on yet. It gave way and I fell directly into the water, right in between the hulls of the two identical ships, which were about thirty feet apart. At that same moment an eddy started pushing them together. I swam out of there as fast as I could, otherwise I would have been crushed.

Claims about your treatment of locals were made during the extended period of pre-production.

Months before we had even brought the cameras down into the jungle, the press tried to link me to the military regime and make me out to be a major force in the exploitation of local Indians. In fact, the soldiers were constantly arresting us because for a time I had no official permits to move the ships along the River Marañón. I didn't have this paperwork because I felt it was better to ask the Indians who actually lived on the river, rather than the government in Lima, for permission. When we got to Wawaim – which was in the vicinity of where we wanted to pull the ship over the mountain – we talked at length to local inhabitants who were happy to help. They signed a contract that detailed what was required of them and how much each person would be paid for this basic exchange of services. They earned about twice as much as they would have working for a lumber company.

At the time there was a power struggle going on within the larger communities of Indians in the general area; there were opposing political factions, and our presence became the pretext for each side to claim areas of influence. The main opposition to us came from some distance away, from an unofficial tribal council of Aguarunas

[Consejo Aguaruna y Huambisa] that insisted it represented all the indigenous groups in the area, though many Indians where we had established our camp had no idea the council even existed, and those that did wanted nothing to do with it. There was never one voice for the Aguarunas, despite what this council said, which tried to make a name for itself by blaming us for the oil pipeline and generally being responsible for the military presence. They spread bizarre rumours, including that we planned to cut a canal between the two river systems and leave several communities stranded on an island, and wanted to take everyone back with us to Europe. They also said we wanted to do things like rape the women and use their bodies for grease. It didn't help that almost from the start the press said we were smuggling arms and had destroyed the Indians' crops during filming. But at that point we were in the early stages of pre-production, and this was all months before a single frame had been shot.

Outsiders arrived, trying to incite the Indians against you.

A political propagandist from France turned up and showed the local Indians photos of Auschwitz victims, piles of skeletons and corpses. He was one of several activists who flocked to the area, the kind of doctrinaire zealots and left-wing ideologues of the 1968 revolution who make up the Diaspora of Shattered Illusions, still hoping to fulfil their failed dreams. One of the Indian leaders showed me material given to them and explained that the Frenchman had tried to convince the Indians that this is how Germans treat everyone.

After several months of pre-production, the military build-up on the border had become scary. One time we passed downriver near one of the army's encampments and a shot was fired over our heads, so we rowed to shore and were held captive for a few hours. This was the first time I had real doubts about whether we should stay in this area; I eventually made the decision to abandon the camp we had built and find another shooting location, which meant going in search of a specific and rare configuration of geography, because I had precise requirements when it came to locations for the film. Most of the tributaries of the Amazon are something like ten miles apart, with 8,000-feet mountains in between, but

I needed two rivers that ran parallel, almost touched each other and had a mountain in between them that wasn't too big, but not too small either. We looked at aerial shots and spoke to pilots and geographers, concluding that there were only two suitable places in the whole of Peru. The first was the site we had just evacuated; the second was more than a thousand miles to the south, in the middle of the jungle, about eight hundred miles south of Iquitos, where Río Camisea and Río Urubamba are divided by an elevation more than six hundred feet high. I hadn't actually found the second location before I moved out of the first camp, but could see that our presence was becoming the focus of something unpleasant, even dangerous. We definitely didn't belong.

A few people stayed in the first camp, and I maintained our medical outpost for the locals because I felt that as long as I could pay for a doctor, one should remain there. I also hoped that by doing so things would fall into place, but after the camp was almost entirely evacuated a group of Aguarunas from the tribal council, who lived some distance away, set the place on fire. They brought press photographers along with them; it was clearly a media stunt. Around that time – I don't recall whether it was before or after – the border war between Peru and Ecuador broke out in the immediate vicinity.

A tribunal in Germany attempted to try you, in absentia, *for your crimes.*

They accused me of torturing and imprisoning Native Indians, which were such bizarre accusations that even some of the press who normally loved this kind of stuff weren't interested in what was being said. There were suggestions that we had occupied an area where Indians had never been exposed to the white man, but it was obvious to anyone who cared to look that we hadn't invaded a tribe of untouched natives. The Aguarunas were relatively sophisticated and, politically speaking, the best organised tribal group in Peru. At one point they expressed their concern to me about the film because they didn't want the world to see an outdated representation of Native Indian life. None of them was surprised by the technology we brought down there. They communicated via shortwave radio, watched kung-fu videos and smoked Lucky Strikes. Most of the men had served in the army and flown in helicopters, and a good number spoke Spanish. In *Burden of Dreams* you see some of the Aguarunas wearing John Travolta disco-fever T-shirts.

The only serious lingering allegation was that I had four Indians arrested by the military, so I went to the town of Santa María de Nieva to uncover the facts for myself. It turned out all four men existed, but none had even the remotest contact with the production of the film. One of them had been imprisoned for about a week because of his unpaid bills in every bar in town. I asked Amnesty International to look into reports of human-rights abuses, and they spread word that I wasn't the cause of any problems, though the media didn't take much notice. Typical of the climate was a report in *Der Stern* magazine. A photographer was sent to the jungle set, where he took at least a thousand pictures, none of which were published. Instead, the magazine ran photos from their archives of naked Amazon Indians spearing fish, hinting we had intruded into a sanctuary of "uncontaminated" natives. The fact is that had we been the cause of even a single arrest, I would have scrapped the whole film during pre-production.

You said earlier that the best way to fight a rumour is with an even wilder rumour.

At one point the Italian press exploded with a story that Claudia Cardinale had been run over by a truck and was critically injured. A journalist from Italy somehow reached me on the phone in Iquitos; it sometimes took forty-eight hours to place a call down there. He was hysterical, so I calmly told him I had just eaten dinner with Claudia and she was fine, but the rumour mill kept grinding and reports of her injuries started spreading globally. Two days later the same journalist reached me from Rome yet again. "Sir, please don't repeat what you've written so far," I said after a flash of inspiration. "The truth is actually much more serious than that. Not only was Claudia Cardinale badly injured when she was hit by the truck, the driver was a barefoot drunkard who raped his unconscious victim in the presence of onlookers." There were twenty seconds of silence, then he hung up, and from that moment on there wasn't another word about any of it.

Hopefully this book will help demolish certain untruths.

No, let this book serve other purposes. I can best argue against the stories with the film itself. There is a moment when Fitzcarraldo tells of a lonesome trapper and frontiersman who was the first white man to see Niagara Falls, at a time when the Pilgrims had only just arrived. Upon relating what he had seen, the man was called a liar. "What's your proof?" he was asked. His answer was simple: "My proof is that I have seen them." I – and many others – were eyewitnesses to what happened during the making of *Fitzcarraldo*. We know the truth. In almost every story the media came up with, I was acquainted with a Werner Herzog who had very little to do with the real me. So be it.

In recent years there has been a slew of these other Herzogs, sometimes dull, occasionally rather intelligent: from a fake and quite awful impersonation of me reading a children's book, to an equally fake but amusing pastiche involving me reading a letter I wrote to Rosalina, my cleaning lady. Although the recorded voice is a poor rendering and the author of this piece actually identified himself, a good number of people asked if it really was me. No matter how wild the caricature, I never deny such things – which are proliferating at speed thanks to the Internet – and in the case of the cleaning lady I explained I was actively pursuing her deportation back to Nicaragua. I feel safe from the world knowing that between the rumours and me is a strong shield of false Herzogs. The parodies and misperceptions protect and serve as unpaid bodyguards, so I do my best to keep the rumours alive. Let them sprout and grow, let the mythology mushroom. I want more of these doppelgängers, these stooges, however crazed, to do battle out there. They take the brunt while I get on with my work.

There are shots in Burden of Dreams *of you and Kinski on the boat as it moves through the rapids.*

At one point the fourteen steel hawsers broke simultaneously under the enormous thrust of the water, and the boat – with two people on board, the cook and his pregnant wife – took off through the rapids with nobody to steer it. Unfortunately no camera had been set up to film this, so over a period of several days we winched the ship back into position. We set up three cameras and filmed it careening through the rapids again, this time without anyone on board. There was no one to steer, and it crashed into the rocks left and right. I was watching from the cliffs and decided it looked safe enough to do it again with people on the ship. It was, in fact, some members of the crew who strongly suggested we do another round of filming through the rapids. Kinski was immediately eager; he always had good knowledge of what would work well on screen, and knew this was a moment he should be involved with. I was hesitant, and in this case he actually pushed me.

Seven of us got on board, with three cameras. Les Blank was also with us. We used two belts to strap Jorge Vignati and his camera to the wall behind the helm; when we hit a rock he was jolted into his straps so hard he broke a couple of ribs. Beat Presser hit his head on the second camera, which was screwed to the deck, and suffered a concussion. Thomas Mauch and I were with Kinski. One impact was so violent that the lens flew out of the camera like a bullet. I tried to hold Mauch with one arm, and with the other grabbed onto an open doorframe, but we flew through the air. Mauch was still hanging on to his camera and banged his hand down onto the deck, splitting it apart between two fingers. Two days before, all our anaesthetic had been used during emergency surgery on the two Indians hit by arrows. As we had hired a group of Peruvian lumbermen and oarsmen, we were advised by a local missionary to have two prostitutes stationed in our camp, otherwise the men would chase after the women in the next settlement. While we sewed up Mauch's hand without anaesthetic, one of these women consoled him in his agony. She buried his face between her breasts and told him how much she loved him.

Once the boat had passed through the rapids we all got off, and almost immediately it dug itself into a gravel bank. The anchor pierced the hull, and the keel twisted up like the lid of a sardine can around its key, but the boat was so solidly built – with its reinforced steel lining and protective air chambers – that it didn't sink. We tried to pry it loose from the sandbank, but had to face the fact that the boat couldn't be moved until the next rainy season, which was half a year away. We were prepared for something like this to happen because it wasn't all that unlikely the ship would sink in the rapids. The speed of the water was more than forty miles an hour and there were whirlpools everywhere. Our back-up was the second boat sitting on the mountain, which we planned to bring down the other side into the river, then continue filming with it. Unfortunately the water level had dropped to the lowest ever recorded, from forty feet to two feet, which meant we couldn't drag the ship down into the other river because there was literally no water there. All of a sudden both ships were immobilised until the next rainy season.

Why do the Indians help Fitzcarraldo?

They are on a mythic mission, one Fitzcarraldo never quite comprehends. For much of the film the audience is left in the dark about their true motivations; we never really understand why they are toiling and going to all this trouble to tow the ship over the mountain. Only when it hurtles through the rapids does everything make sense. The Indians are as obsessed as Fitzcarraldo; they just have different dreams. While his is to build an opera house, they want to rid themselves of the evil spirits inhabiting the rapids, and are convinced that sacrificing the boat by cutting it loose and sending it through the rapids will lift the curse over their land. It will be their salvation. "They know that we are not gods," says Huerequeque, "but the ship has really impressed them." The Indians win and Fitzcarraldo loses, though ultimately he rises to the occasion and – through the power of his imagination and creative spirit – converts this defeat into some kind of triumph. At the end of the film, though we know that Fitzcarraldo has bankrupted himself, it's obvious he'll be up to mischief before long. This is someone who has always stood his ground, and perhaps might finally finish his trans-Amazon railway, abandoned years before.

Did your work with the Indians have any lasting effect?

Our presence in that part of the jungle was ephemeral yet to some degree helpful because it meant attention was focused on the problems of Native Indians in the Peruvian rainforests. When we shot the film we were conscious of wanting to do more for them than just provide financial remuneration. Some wanted to be nurses, so I asked our doctor to provide training. The younger men dreamt of buying Honda motorcycles because they loved riding them when they were in the army, but there were no roads in the jungle, so that didn't seem too useful. The Indians' canoes were too small to transport crops, including their cocoa harvests, to the nearest market. Travelling merchants would buy things from the Indians at low cost and make profits reselling this merchandise downriver, so our builders and carpenters showed them how to build larger boats.

The most important thing was recognising that oil and lumber firms had started to cast a greedy eye over the Indians' land. Wholesale encroachment and plunder had to be prevented, so I sent in a surveyor to chart the territory, which had never been properly delineated, with a view to helping the locals secure their land rights. Overcoming the legal issues wasn't easy. Even after engaging lawyers and bribing everyone I could find, I became lost in labyrinthine bureaucracy. I decided to take two elected representatives of the Indians to Lima, where we had an audience with the president of the republic, Fernando Belaúnde, who promised to co-operate and do whatever he could to help them gain the title to their land, but stated he didn't accept the Indians' argument that they had lived since time immemorial in this area. He told them that legally they had no case, though it was clear their grandfathers had lived on the land; it was all hearsay as far as Belaúnde was concerned. I told him the notion of hearsay had actually been accepted into English common law, in a case from 1916 in what is now Ghana. Some white settlers had told the jungle communities that Lima didn't exist and that there was no ocean, so I took these two Indian representatives down to the beach. Mesmerised, they waded with their new blue jeans and T-shirts into the surf, tasted the water, filled an empty wine bottle with seawater, corked it and took it home as proof.

By the time I went back to shoot *My Best Fiend*, the Indians had succeeded in gaining the legal title to their land. On the other side of the river – which wasn't part of the Indians' territory – there was a camp and an airfield that belonged to the oil companies. The area contains one of the largest deposits of gas in the world, but to this day there has been no drilling on Indian land. They really do have control over it, so I feel we assisted them in a small way, though their moral and historical right to the territory was unquestionable.

Twenty years after you wrote them, you published your Fitzcarraldo *diaries.*

A decade after I made *Fitzcarraldo* I looked at the diaries, but just couldn't handle it. For a long time I was terrified to dig into those notebooks. I wrote the text in sub-miniaturised, microscopic hand-writing that no one but me could read. It can't get any smaller because no pens exist that give a finer stroke. I don't know why I wrote it like that; my longhand is of normal size. I ignored the note-books for so long because I was unable to read the tiny letters, but eventually my wife bought me a pair of magnifying glasses – the kind jewellers wear – and told me that if I didn't edit and publish the text myself, someone would do it once I was gone. I no longer had an excuse.

When I read the notebooks for the first time after so many years, I realised how much I had forgotten. I ended up cutting the text down from a thousand pages to three hundred, skipping over an entire year that was just too painful to revisit, and published it as *Conquest of the Useless*. There is a breathless urgency to the prose, and I'm convinced the book will outlive all my films. It's a diary of the film's production only in the broadest sense of the word; more than anything this is a piece of literature, a fierce and relentless look at what was going on around me at the time and my reactions to it all. At moments I run off into wild, invented fever dreams, and put down on paper the kinds of images that occurred to me in the midst of my experiences of filming in the jungle. The more duress I was under, the more frequently these types of visions appeared to me. I would invent bizarre accidents and fantasies, describing them in writing because by doing so would somehow prevent them from happening in real life. By naming the disaster I banish it, like the boat on the sleep slope that breaks loose. Like a torpedo it shoots down until it hits a crowded ocean beach, buries itself deep in the sand and flings an ice-cream stand up into the air.

When things become difficult some people find solace in music and religion, but when I read my diaries so many years after I wrote them, what became evident was that in the turmoil of production I took refuge in language. It has forever been a powerful anchor for me, and I suspect that my true voice emerges more clearly through prose than cinema. I might be a better writer than I am a filmmaker.

Why did Les Blank call his film Burden of Dreams?

Cinema emboldens us. It helps us surmount everyday life and encourages us to take our hopes and desires seriously, to turn them into reality. When things were going badly I headed back to Germany in an attempt to hold together the film's investors. They asked me if I was going to continue. "Do you really have the strength and will?" I said, "How can you ask this question? If I abandon this project, I will be a man without dreams. I live my life or I end my life with *Fitzcarraldo*." It wasn't possible for me to allow myself private feelings of doubt while making the film. I never had the privilege of despair; had I hesitated or panicked for a single second, the entire project would have come tumbling down around me. The final film ended up basically as I had always hoped it would, with the exception of the Mick Jagger character. Months later Claudia Cardinale said to me, "When you came to Rome four years ago you explained your ideas to me and all the difficulties we would have to overcome. Now I've seen the film, and it's exactly as you first described it."

If you watch *Fitzcarraldo* and have the courage to push on with your own projects, then the film has accomplished something. If one person walks outside after watching one of my films and no longer feels so alone, I have achieved everything I set out to achieve. When you read a great poem you instantly know there is a profound truth to it. Sometimes there are similar moments of great insight in cinema, when you know you have been illuminated. Perhaps, occasionally, I have achieved such heights with my own films.

Burden of Dreams *includes scenes from the original version of* Fitzcarraldo, *with Robards and Jagger.*

People are always asking me if they can visit my sets and shoot footage of me at work; I tell them they will experience nothing but an endless chain of banalities. I didn't invite Les to the jungle, but he was eager to come down and make a film. At first I was reluctant to have a camera around because there is something distasteful about making films about filmmakers. I don't like being recorded while working. When you cook a meal at home and there is someone staring at your hands, suddenly you're no longer a good cook. Everyone functions differently when being observed, and filmmakers are usually pathetic embarrassments when they appear on film. I include myself here.

Tom Luddy had shown me some of Les's films, and I loved them instantly, especially *Spend It All*, which has a scene where a man pulls his own tooth out with a pair of pliers, an image I borrowed for *Stroszek*. His films document the vanishing marginals of American life in the most vibrant ways. I also loved Les's cooking and general attitude to life. He turned out to be a healthy presence in the jungle. Most of the time he was like a southern bullfrog brooding behind a beer, unobtrusive, always knowing when he should turn on the camera and when there were significant moments to capture on film. What I really liked about Les was that he wasn't just mono-syllabic; often he was zero-syllabic. He hardly ever spoke a word and somehow managed to blend into the environment. I was also persuaded by his argument that however confident I was about finishing the film, if everything fell apart then thanks to his footage there would at least be some record of this foolhardy quest.

Les wasn't some court jester who adulated everyone, no matter what they were doing. He had an extraordinarily good eye and brought a considered subjectivity to what he was filming. He was just as interested in watching how the Indians would ferment yucca as he was documenting the production of *Fitzcarraldo*, and most of the time could be found in the camp where the natives did their cooking. One time at breakfast I explained to him that later in the day there would be a real event: for the first time in months we planned to move the boat up the mountain. "I'm not here to film events," said Les, and he didn't show up. That evening he told me he had spent the day filming an ant carrying a parrot feather. I always liked his attitude, and can look back at the diaries I wrote during production and find a world of observations completely different to what Les was documenting at the same moment.

I like *Burden of Dreams*, though certain things in the film might not project a particularly favourable image of me, and even caused problems. Les screened a few minutes of footage at the Telluride Film Festival before he had finished the film, and out of context some of my comments made me look dangerously obsessed. In the voiceover of *Burden of Dreams* it's stated that I could have shot the entire film outside Iquitos, which would have made things easier for everyone, but as explained I needed very specific terrain, and for a thousand miles in the vicinity of Iquitos there is no elevation more than ten feet; it's as flat as the ocean. At one point in *Burden of Dreams* I talk of how people had died during production, but Les chose not to include my explanation of the circumstances, so it sounds as if I risked lives and drove people to their deaths just for the sake of a film. It was a stench that followed me for a decade. Les immediately wanted to re-edit the film once I pointed these things out to him, but I told him not to bother. I've got better things to do than correct everyone's mistakes and misreadings. Les always had the final say; I never asked him to change things, even when I knew they might be damaging to me. It's worth knowing that Les was filming over a period of only five weeks, but *Fitzcarraldo* took four years to make, so he captured only a fraction of what went on during production.

I never kept any footage of Robards and Jagger; the only clips in existence are those from Les's film, scraps of celluloid he grabbed before I junked everything I didn't need for *Fitzcarraldo*. For that reason alone I'm glad Les's film exists. Sometimes it's better not to have all the facts, though *Burden of Dreams* remains the best "making of" film ever made.

Ballad of the Little Soldier *is about the struggle fought by the Nicaraguan Miskito Indians against the Sandinistas, their former allies in the revolution against Somoza.*

Allow me to correct you: it's about children fighting a war. The film was made in Nicaragua, and the dogmatic Left – for whom the Sandinistas were still a sacred cow at the time – refused to believe I wasn't in the pay of the CIA. But anyone can see that *Ballad of the Little Soldier* isn't a political document, even though after making the film I felt I should face those who I was criticising, so I accepted an invitation to Managua a few months after it was released, where I was involved in a lengthy discussion after a screening. There was no real reconciliation in our viewpoints, though I was impressed how civilised and nuanced the debate was. In Argentina a few years earlier I would have disappeared within hours.

I made *Ballad of the Little Soldier* because a friend of mine, Denis Reichle, was working on a film about child soldiers and asked for help. Reichle is a photographer, reporter and filmmaker who made a film in the Golden Triangle of Burma, Laos and Thailand about Khun Sa, the Burmese warlord and so-called "opium king." I immediately saw he was the kind of person who worked with great care to compile reports from inaccessible places. For decades Reichle travelled extensively and reported on oppressed minorities. From the age of two he lived in an orphanage, and at the age of fifteen was drafted along with his entire school into the *Volkssturm*, the battalions made up of children and older men used in the defence of Berlin during the final months of the war. He was trained to lay mines and use anti-tank weaponry before being sent to the front, an experience he was lucky to survive. After the war Reichle was held prisoner by the Russians for a few weeks before escaping back to Alsace, where he was originally from. He became a French citizen and was sent to Indochina, where he spent a few months in French uniform. All this by the age of twenty. As a photojournalist working for *Paris Match*, Reichle arrived in East Timor in 1976, just as the mass murder was starting. Nobody dared land on shore, so he swam the last half mile from a small fishing boat, holding his camera above his head. He was eventually arrested by Indonesian soldiers and deported. He escaped the Khmer Rouge in Cambodia, who captured him because they thought he was a Soviet spy, and was held hostage in the Philippines by Abu Sayyaf, an Islamic separatist group, before being exchanged for twenty-four Kalashnikovs. My favourite story of his took place in Angola, a country saturated with landmines. He was driving on a road outside of town and saw some boys sitting in the shade of a tree. As he advanced steadily towards them, he saw them plugging their ears with their fingers. Reichle slammed on the brakes and stopped ten feet from a landmine, preventing the boys from enjoying the moment of him being blown up.

Reichle is the most fearless and methodical man I know, instantly able to read the signs correctly, equally daring and prudent, which is why he has survived so much. He's one of the few people I have met in my life into whose hands I would entrust myself, so we decided to work together on a film about the Miskito Indians. From Honduras we took a small plane that brought us to the Atlantic coast, where we met up with the Miskitos in their training camp. To get into Nicaragua – where I spent nearly three months – we illegally crossed the border at Río Coco. At one point during filming we were planning to accompany some Miskito soldiers and film an attack on a convoy. Reichle asked whether a security team with a machine gun was being left in place to cover our retreat. It turned out there was no such plan, so he took me aside and flatly told me we wouldn't be going with them, that they had no clue what they were doing. It just wasn't safe.

What is the political background to the film?

Originally the Miskito Indians – who within their social structure traditionally lived a primitive form of socialism – had fought against Somoza as allies of the Sandinistas, but soon their alliance soured. A strip of Miskito land in Nicaragua, on the Honduran border, was categorically depopulated by the Sandinistas; sixty-five towns and villages were razed to the ground and violence was perpetrated against the native population. At Sandy Bay, on the eastern coast of the country, I watched six Sandinista soldiers arrive by boat, firing their Kalashnikovs into the air, acting as if they occupied the country. The entire Miskito population of the village fled into the jungle, screaming in fear. The soldiers shot the cows, then skinned them and loaded the meat onto their boat. When they left they fired a round into the air as a departing salute.

The key to the film is the human element, so to talk about it in political or military terms isn't useful. I wanted to focus on child soldiers and could have filmed in any number of countries, like Liberia, Cambodia or Iran. It doesn't matter what ideologies are in play when there are nine-year-olds – barely strong enough to handle machine guns and grenade-throwers – fighting a war. Child soldiers are such a tragedy that details of the conflict in question are unnecessary. I spoke to some of the Miskito children for hours before rolling the camera. Every one of them had volunteered for the army after a personal and traumatising experience. Many were completely silent, others responded with only one-word answers; they never elaborated. I talked to a boy in a commando unit who was clearly in a state of shock. His two-year-old brother, six-year-old brother and father had all been killed. His mother was cut in pieces before his eyes. He was still in training but wanted to go out the next day and kill. I asked him to talk more about how his brother had died. "With an M16," is all he said. Several of the children in *Ballad of the Little Soldier* were dead by the time the film was released.

In The Dark Glow of the Mountains *you speak with Italian mountaineer Reinhold Messner about walking until the world ends.*

Messner talks of his desire to walk from one Himalayan valley to the next, without looking back. He says either his life or the world will stop. "Presumably it will be that as my life ends, so will the world." I like the idea of having a group of huskies loaded up with leather saddlebags and just disappearing, turning down the path and walking until everything has been left behind, continuing until there's no road left, or just floating downriver. It's how I would like to end my life. Either that or being hit by an enemy's bullet.

In the seventies Messner was one of those young climbers who brought a new approach to the sport. He was determined to climb the Himalayas alpine-style, and succeeded in reaching the peaks of all of the planet's fourteen 8,000-metre-plus mountains without large-scale expeditions and hundreds of Sherpas. He was the first to climb the Himalayas with just a rucksack and no support camps, and the first to climb Mount Everest without oxygen – by what he called "fair means" – which was considered a great achievement in the mountain-climbing community. Cesare Maestri, a famous Italian climber of the fifties and sixties, used to scale peaks by hauling himself up inch by inch with powerful motorised sledgehammers, hooks and machine drills. It would take him weeks to get to the top. A ridiculous thing to do; I could climb the world's tallest building if I had all that equipment and three months to spare. Maestri's approach was another case of the perversion of adventurism; he shamed and embarrassed every mountain he climbed. It's the opposite of the "free climbing" approach, which emerged from California, where ropes are used only to prevent accidents. Using as little technical equipment as possible meant that Messner became the father of modern mountaineering. He's a man of great survival skills, endowed not only with extraordinary technical proficiency, but also a sense of exactly what is happening around him and a knowledge of when something isn't right. I learnt a lot from him about evaluating danger. He attempted to scale Dhaulagiri twice; once he turned back five hundred feet shy of the summit because of avalanche conditions, and another time stared for days at the south face of the mountain through binoculars, watching a series of avalanches, then went home. Finally, in 1985 he and his climbing partner Hans Kammerlander reached the summit.

The Dark Glow of the Mountains emerged from questions I was asking myself. What goes on inside the minds of mountain climbers who undertake such extreme endeavours? What drives them to scale these peaks? Why did Messner – a man who lost his brother and some of his toes on Nanga Parbat – feel the need to scale it for a second time? What motivates a man like this? I once asked him, "Don't you think you're a little deranged to keep climbing mountains?" His response was simple: "All creative people are insane." I always felt the man had the wisdom of the snake, sitting there coiled up, waiting for the opportunity to strike. One time he told me he was unable to describe the feelings that compel him to climb any more than he could explain what compels him to breathe.

The film was meant to be the predecessor of something much bigger I had in mind. I wanted to make a feature film in the zone of K2, the second-highest and most dangerous of the Himalayan mountains, and in preparation thought it would be a good idea to make a relatively small film as a test run. I could have written a script as quickly as I normally do, but felt the need to physically experience the environment myself. I wanted to test the situation and learn about the logistical difficulties of filming in such a place and what technical problems we might encounter. How feasible was it to get supplies for everyone up there? During filming we experienced temperatures so low that our raw film stock – which needs to be bent and fed into narrow loops inside the camera – broke like uncooked spaghetti. A gigantic avalanche hit the bottom of the glacier a mile away from us and, like a horizontal atomic explosion, the impact sent a cloud of snow towards us and wiped out our camp. I immediately adapted my plans for a feature film.

Messner talks about his brother's death.

Messner is a media-savvy showman who has appeared on every talk show ever seen on European television. He knew that in making the film I would be digging deep and might ask questions about his brother's death. "There will be situations in which I will go far,"

I told him, "but you can defend yourself." Messner knew there would be no mercy for him because film per se knows no mercy.

Initially it was a problem getting him to appear on camera as himself. The first thing we shot was a sequence in the shadow of Nanga Parbat. We drove through the night, and when we awoke the next morning could see mountain in front of us; it was absolutely stunning, not a cloud in the sky. I woke Messner up and set him in front of the camera. He launched into his usual media rap, and I immediately stopped the camera. "This isn't how I want to make this film with you," I told him. "I need to see deep inside your heart." Messner looked at me with a stunned expression and fell silent. He understood how close I was to junking the entire project, and towards evening said to me, "I'll give you the whole story." It was difficult to decide whether to include the sequence of him weeping, but I eventually told him, "You've done lifeless talk shows all your life. Now, all of a sudden, something personal has been brought to light. You aren't just another athlete conquering every mountain with cold perfection. This is why I'm not going to edit out the scene." Once Messner saw the finished film, he was glad we went as far as we did.

What mountain do they climb in the film?

To climb an 8,000-metre mountain is considered a feat, and Messner has done them all. To traverse a mountain using one route and then climb down the other side is considered extraordinary. But what Messner and Kammerlander did during this expedition was traverse two 8,000-metre mountains – Gasherbrum 1 and 2 – in one go, which had never been attempted before. They did it without oxygen or Sherpas, a remarkable accomplishment that hasn't been repeated since. They set off at two in the morning, in pitch darkness, at a fantastic speed because they could carry only a small amount of provisions. It was clear from the start there was no way for me to follow them with a camera, so the shots of the summit in the film are taken by Messner himself. Before they left the camp he took me aside and said, "Maybe we won't survive this one. If you don't hear from us within ten days, we must be dead. It would take twenty days for help to arrive, much too long to save us. If this happens, take over the expedition and see that the

Sherpas get paid with the money I deposited in such-and-such a place." He left without uttering another word.

I went only as far as the base camp, a little over 5,000 metres up, before encountering a Spanish expedition. They had some supply camps to clear out and allowed me to attach myself to their rope and climb with them for another 1,500 metres. The route they took was along a difficult and dangerous area of the glacier, with shifting slabs as big as office blocks separated by deep crevasses. The Spaniards moved up very quickly, and when we arrived at the camp I had clear signs of altitude sickness because I wasn't sufficiently acclimatised. The symptoms are easily recognisable: you become absurdly apathetic, and I sat down in the snow with my whole body slumped. It was extremely alarming to me, so I decided to go back down to the camp. The Spanish should have stopped me, but stupidly I made the trip on my own. I didn't follow the flags and took the most direct route instead, across a glacier covered in snow, almost breaking through a snow-covered crevasse three hundred feet deep. I seemed almost to step into a void.

Are you an adventurer?

Anyone who labels himself an "adventurer" today is a disgrace. I have never done anything adventurous for the sake of a film. There is a myth that I purposely make things more difficult for myself; it's the wrongest of wrongs. I would rather have made *Fitzcarraldo* in the middle of Central Park, the only problem being there's no jungle in the neighbourhood. I would have directed the film from an apartment window on Fifth Avenue, just as a few years later I would rather have made *Scream of Stone* in Munich, where I could have slept in my own bed. Mountaineers might be motivated to seek out the most difficult routes, but not me. I would never have finished a single film if I purposely sought out trouble. Filmmaking is difficult enough, and it's plain bad luck I'm drawn to characters like Fitzcarraldo, whose mission is to pull a boat over a mountain. I never seek adventure. I'm not irresponsible about things. I just do my job.

There is a difference between exploration and adventure. I'm a curious person, forever searching for new images and dignified places, but though often given the contemptible tag of "adventurer,"

I categorically deny the label. It applies only to men and women of earlier times, like the mediaeval knights who travelled into the unknown. The concept has degenerated since then, and today it is an ugly, pitiful embarrassment. Local mountain people, like the Sherpas, the Baltis and the Swiss, traditionally never climbed the peaks that surrounded them, thus robbing them of all dignity. They left the splendour of the mountains intact. There is a foul philosophy behind those bored English gentlemen who started climbing for the sake of it, then scampered off to make sure they were the first at the South Pole. There's nothing that interesting about the place; it's just water and drifting ice. The whole thing suggests dead fish – white, rotten, bloated, belly up – floating in dirty water, and since then the self-promoters have run the show. Modern-day adventurers speak about their travels in military terms, like "We conquered the summit," or "We returned victorious over Mount Everest." I can't stand such talk. What a big shot you were in 1910 when you came back from Africa and told the ladies how many elephants you had killed! Do the same thing at a party today and you'll have a glass of champagne tossed in your face.

I particularly loathe pseudo-adventurism, where the mountain climb becomes about exploring your personal limits. I had arguments with Messner about this because he stylised his media persona on the concept of "The Great Adventurer." I'm bracing myself for the first barefoot climber on Everest or backwards sprinter through the Sahara, the kind of nonsense the *Guinness Book of World Records* is full of. You can even book an "adventure holiday" to see the headhunters and cannibals of New Guinea. It's the kind of absurdity pervading the degenerate concept of "adventurism" that I find so feeble. On the other hand, I love the Frenchman who crossed the Sahara in reverse gear in a 2CV, and people like Monsieur Mangetout, who ate his own bicycle. I think he also tried to eat a twin-engine aeroplane. What a guy!

He's dead.

Really? Ah, well. There will surely be another like him.

7

Going Rogue

It's possible to learn to play an instrument as an adult, but the intuitive qualities needed won't be there; the body needs to be conditioned from an early age. The same could be never said for filmmaking. A musician is made in childhood, but a filmmaker any time. At the age of about fifteen I read a few pages in an encyclopaedia about things like camera lenses, microphones and how a lab functions. I learnt about optical soundtracks and perspective lines, about what will be in frame if you're using a 24mm lens and standing here as opposed to a 50mm lens over there. Everything I needed to get myself started came from those few pages. There isn't much more anyone can teach you about filmmaking.

I always knew film school wasn't for me. I had no formal training nor had I worked as someone's assistant. My early films came from my deepest commitments; I never had much of a choice. It will never be the curriculum of a traditional film school and access to equipment that makes someone a filmmaker. Who wants to spend four years on something a primate could learn in a week? What takes time to develop is a personal vision. Knowing certain technical tricks doesn't make you a filmmaker any more than knowing how to type makes you a novelist.

Tell me about your ideal film school.

Such a place would never exist, though there's nothing wrong with fantasising wildly. You would be allowed to submit an application only after having travelled, alone and on foot, let's say from Madrid to Kiev, a distance of nearly two thousand miles. While walking, write about your experiences, then give me your note-books. I would immediately be able to tell who had really walked and who had not. You would learn more about filmmaking dur-ing your journey than if you spent five years at film school. Your experiences would be the very opposite of academic knowledge, for academia is the death of cinema. Somebody who has been a boxer in Africa would be better trained as a filmmaker than if he had graduated from one of the "best" film schools in the world. All that counts is real life.

My film school would allow you to experience a certain climate of excitement of the mind, and would produce people with spirit, a furious inner excitement, a burning flame within. This is what ultimately creates films. Technical knowledge inevitably becomes dated; the ability to adapt to change will always be more impor-tant. At my utopian film academy there would be a vast loft with a boxing ring in one corner. Participants, working every day with a trainer, would learn to somersault, juggle and perform magic tricks. Whether you would be a filmmaker by the end I couldn't say, but at least you would emerge as a confident and fearless athlete. After this vigorous physical work, sit quietly and master as many lan-guages as possible. The end result would be like the knights of old who knew how to ride a horse, wield a sword and play the lute.

How do you keep your own flame burning?

That's never been my problem, though one simple way is to avoid shooting in studios, which are by definition artificial places. The spontaneity necessary for the kind of cinema I want to create is eas-ily extinguished in such sterile and controlled places. I just don't like the way they smell; I feel more comfortable waist-deep in a swamp. The green-screen shot at the end of *Invincible*, with the boy flying up into the air, and the green-screen sequence in *Rescue Dawn* of Christian Bale, as Dieter Dengler, in his cockpit are the only two moments I have ever shot in a studio. The opening sequence of *Bad Lieutenant* – where we flooded an entire set – was shot in an empty warehouse rented out for film shoots. The production before us had been set in a prison and they hadn't yet dismantled everything, so I rushed over and asked if we could make use of a few pieces. The world of the studio rarely offers surprises to the director, in part because the only people you ever run into at such places are paid to be there; hardly anyone interesting ever shows up unexpectedly. There is no environment per se, only four solid walls and a roof. I have always functioned better out in the world, where a story that looked abstract on paper is finally able to engage with real life.

The other thing I'm fiercely opposed to is storyboards, the instruments of cowards who have no faith in their imagination and no confidence in their fantasies. I can see the need for them when it comes to a scene with special effects, but otherwise storyboards turn everyone into marionettes of a pre-existing design. The only time I ever storyboarded a sequence was the crash in *Rescue Dawn*, which was a single event filmed by three cameras that needed careful planning. That really is a big chunk of fuselage impacting onto a rice paddy, followed by a stunt man being propelled by a small explosion. Nothing digital was added. Walter Saxer, the driving force behind *Scream of Stone*, insisted on preparing a series of storyboards for the more complex climbing sequences in that film, but I ignored them. You can't turn a mountain into a docile pet.

Is there a pre-planned aesthetic behind your films?

My dislike of perfectionists behind the camera – people who spend hours setting up a single shot – has been an eternal source of conflict with cameramen over the years. I once watched with great impatience as a world-famous cinematographer spent five hours lighting a scene that would have taken me five minutes. Peter Zeitlinger is always trying to sneak "beautiful" shots into our films, and I'm forever preventing it. Our friendship and respect for each other has grown because of this. On *Rescue Dawn* he wanted to do radical colour correction by turning the jungle almost black and white until the blissful moment of Dieter's rescue, when full colour would blossom for the final minutes. That's a rather drastic example; Peter and I often differ in opinion, but we always resolve our differences within twenty seconds. Things are more problematic when there is a spectacular sunset on the horizon and he scrambles to set up the camera to film it. I immediately turn the tripod 180° in the other direction. Thankfully, when we were down in Antarctica making *Encounters at the End of the World*, the sun was high in the sky twenty-four hours a day for months.

I need people who see and feel things as they are, not someone concerned with creating the most beautiful images possible. I don't give much thought to the composition of an image; I focus instead entirely on what that shot is about and how it fits into the overall story. Everything else is irrelevant. When it comes to working with cameramen, there are basic discussions about the general look of a film, but rarely about aesthetic details. I know how to articulate images on film without resorting to endless conversations about lighting or spending thousands on production design. I don't consciously reflect on aesthetics before making a film because, for me, the story always dictates such things. Of course, aesthetics do sometimes enter unconsciously through the back door, because whether we like it or not our preferences always somehow influence the decisions we make. If I were to think about my handwriting while writing an important letter, the words would become meaningless. When you write a passionate love letter and focus on making sure your longhand is as beautiful as possible, it isn't going to be much of a love letter. But if you concentrate on the words and emotions, your particular style of longhand – which has nothing to do with the letter per se – will somehow seep in of its own accord. Aesthetics, if they even exist, are to be discovered only once a film has been completed. I leave it to the philosophers to enlighten me about such things.

I'm sure you can think of several examples in your films.

There are a small number of such moments of experimentation and stylisation, but these are isolated and specific images. Think of the tower and washerwoman from *The Enigma of Kaspar Hauser*, which I talked about earlier, or the clouds in the final shot of *My Son, My Son, What Have Ye Done*, which were digitally added, or certain shots in *Heart of Glass*, where we placed an orange filter over the lens and slightly underexposed the image; then, during processing, we overexposed the film, which gave it Rembrandt-like colours. While working on *Heart of Glass*, Schmidt-Reitwein and I studied the work of seventeenth-century French painter Georges de La Tour. I wanted to capture the same atmosphere you find in his canvases, and some of the interior sequences were filmed using only candlelight. During production on *Fitzcarraldo* in the jungle there were only ten minutes every day when the sun was setting because we were so close to the equator, and sometimes we would wait for that perfect moment just before sunset when the light in the sky was exceptionally beautiful. Most of *Even Dwarfs Started Small* was shot with a relatively wide-angle 24mm lens because I wanted the characters to be in focus amidst the extraordinary landscapes.

Perhaps the best example is the trance-like dream sequences in *The Enigma of Kaspar Hauser*, showing what looks like a newly discovered foreign world. One influence here was the experimental German filmmaker Klaus Wyborny, who I brought along when I went to the Spanish Sahara, where he shot Super 16 footage of the caravan in the desert. The finest of the dream sequences was shot by my brother Lucki when he was travelling in Burma as a nineteen-year-old. He filmed what he described as a strange and shaky pan across a wide valley full of grandiose temples. I thought it was very mysterious and absolutely tremendous, so I begged him to let me use it. I modified the image by projecting it onto a semi-transparent screen from very close up, which made it the size of my palm, then filmed it with a 35mm camera from the other side, so you can clearly see the fabric of the screen. The image seems to flicker in and out of darkness because I purposely didn't synchronise the projector with the camera. I also changed the colours slightly in the lab. It's the same thing I did at the start of *Heart of Glass* with the images of the waterfall I spoke about earlier and other landscape shots just after the opening credits.

Light and darkness play an important role in Nosferatu.

That film is probably the one major exception to my lack of interest in aesthetics. I felt a certain respect had to be paid to the classical formulae of cinematic genres, in this case the vampire film. The opening shot of the bat was filmed with a camera running at several hundred frames a second, and the final image of the film is two combined shots: one of a beach in Holland, with strong winds and sand flying everywhere; the other of clouds filmed separately, in single exposures, which is why they move so fast. In post-production I flipped the shot of the clouds upside down and superimposed it on the top half of the screen so that they bulge down from a dark sky into the landscape. It gives the sequence a heavy sense of doom, as if evil were spreading out into the world from this one single point. Underneath we see Jonathan Harker – now a vampire himself – riding towards the horizon, ready to infect the landscape around him. It's a profoundly pessimistic image, and by doing it like this I can hardly deny I was attempting to create a specific stylised look for the shot. The landscapes of *Nosferatu*, especially this one, are more mythical than geographically exact. There are no credits at the end of the film because, in some way, the story continues inside of all of us. The music is Gounod's *St Cecilia Mass*, which gives an almost religious feeling to the whole thing. The cameraman Jörg Schmidt-Reitwein and I spent time discussing the placement of lights for various shots in *Nosferatu*, but that was mainly because in the film the vampire has no reflection in mirrors, which meant we needed to create a number of carefully planned lighting effects, such as when the creature enters Lucy's attic bedroom while she is sitting in front of a mirror. The first shadow that appears on the back wall was cast not by Kinski, but by someone else wearing a cape, pointy ears and claws. Kinski was standing next to the camera, and only when it pans slightly to the right do we see his true shadow on the wall, then Kinski himself. It was a complex moment to orchestrate, done without technical tricks.

I worked with Schmidt-Reitwein on *Fata Morgana, Land of Silence and Darkness, The Enigma of Kaspar Hauser* and *Heart of Glass*. He has a strong feeling for darkness and contrast, threatening shadows and gloom, I suspect in part because he experienced prison and darkened dungeons himself. Just after the Berlin Wall went up he was caught smuggling his girlfriend out of the East and placed in solitary confinement for several months. At the time the East German regime insisted that the wall had been built as a protective barrier against the fascist intruders, though trading was still going on between the two countries. The East Germans sometimes took hostages under a petty pretext and would imprison people for years, waiting until some kind of exchange could take place. Schmidt-Reitwein had worked for a single week at the television station RIAS [*Rundfunk im amerikanischen Sektor*] in Berlin, which was partially financed through the United States, so the East Germans insisted he was a CIA agent. He was swapped for a wagon full of butter after three years of imprisonment. I think this experience formed much of what the man is today; once these people emerge from under ground they see the world with different eyes.

For a while Schmidt-Reitwein and I shared an apartment in Munich and planned to establish something like a late-mediaeval guild, with workshops and apprentices. When one of the small film laboratories in Munich went bankrupt, we even contemplated buying it so we could strike our own prints. Thomas Mauch, who shot *Signs of Life*, *Aguirre* and *Fitzcarraldo*, is the cameraman I would go to when I needed something more physical and spontaneous, images with more innocent vitality to them. He has a phenomenal sense for the rhythm of what is unfolding before him. Sometimes there were difficult choices about which of these two fine cameramen to work with on particular films, but I think I made the right decisions over the years. If I had taken Schmidt-Reitwein to the jungle for *Fitzcarraldo*, the camera would probably have been more static, and certain scenes would have been stylised, with more elaborate lighting.

Do you ever plan shots before arriving on set?

Some shots are formulated and blocked beforehand: for example, in *Invincible*, when the strongman is dying in hospital and rises out of bed because he hears piano music. "My ears are ringing," he says. "Somebody must be thinking of me." The camera follows his gaze as he looks towards the window at his little brother, who gets out of his chair and pushes the curtain aside. Outside, through the window, we see his five-year-old sister looking at us. There is a shot near the end of *Signs of Life* where the camera moves forward towards a window, and through it we see fireworks exploding in the sky. The whole thing was carefully planned.

But generally I function best in the unknown, and have an intuitive sense about where to put the camera and when to turn it on. Apart from what I see in my head, I usually plan nothing visually and have no advance plan of the specific shots required that day. I don't even touch the screenplay until the first day of shooting. I might go through it quickly to establish how many locations are needed, but constantly re-reading a script suffocates the life out of it. I prefer to keep things dormant, which means that when I pick up the screenplay on set – sometimes months after last looking at it – the material is as fresh for me as it is for everyone else, and I can rediscover the story again. It's like being thrown onto a distant island that no one has ever seen before and stepping onto the shore alongside a small group of survivors. I might be disorientated for a few moments, but I quickly set about exploring my surroundings with fresh eyes, determining exactly what needs to be done.

I work closely with the cameraman to determine where the camera should be, but usually only when we're on set. When it comes to these kinds of decisions, as I said, the important thing is to know your story and what the scene is about. In *Invincible* there's a scene in the circus in which Zishe challenges the famous strongman. The person doing continuity kept asking, "How many shots are we going to do for this scene?" Eventually I looked at her and said, "At least one." I told her just to watch along with everyone else. "Let it develop. Let's see what they do and if it holds its suspense and substance." We ended up shooting four and a half minutes in a single shot; it was so good we needed only a couple of cutaways to trim it down. I explained what I wanted from the two actors, who were friends and knew each other from strongman competitions. At every moment they knew where each was leading the other and what the next move was going to be, so I let things develop naturally.

When I direct, I feel like a football coach who has given tactics to his team but knows how vital it is for the players to react to unexpected situations. Too much planning means things become stale. If a footballer worked out his every move in advance, he wouldn't be a very effective player. My approach to filming is that from the start I have a general sense of what I want, but allow the action to develop naturally without knowing precisely what camera angles and how many shots will be needed. If a scene develops differently from my original idea because of the actors or vagaries of the location, but does so without major deviation from the original story, I generally try to encompass those new elements. As a filmmaker you have to be open to opportunities, even actively encourage them. My cinema is killed stone dead without the outside world to react to. It's the same thing when I stage opera. As any theatre actor or singer will tell you, each individual performance has a life to it, and room has to be given to allow certain characteristics to emerge and develop, otherwise the vitality of the live performance dies.

There was a scene in *Aguirre* I wanted to film near the rapids, but that day I was awoken at four in the morning to discover the river was about to flood. In a matter of hours the water had risen by ten or twelve feet. Our rafts were damaged and the set was under water. A location already established during shooting no longer existed. There was no more shore; it had disappeared. If *Aguirre* had been a Hollywood production, this would all have been a major catastrophe, because it meant filming would grind to a halt. The crew would have stayed put, generating a massive bill, but nothing would be shot. I decided to find a more direct solution and immediately made the flood an integral part of the story by incorporating the high water into the script. I rewrote a scene where the conquistadors realise there is no way back for them, something that precipitates a row between Aguirre and Ursúa. There was no other way to overcome this obstacle to production. It had to be embraced and turned to our advantage, even acting as an accelerator on the film's narrative.

Filmmaking is a more vulnerable journey than other creative ventures. A sculptor has only a lump of rock to chisel away at, but filmmaking involves complex organisation, money, people, expensive equipment. There are so many intermediaries between an idea and its realisation, so many things that can go wrong. Problems will befall you at every turn. You can build a ship, cast five thousand extras, then plan a scene with your leading actors, but in the morning one of them might be ill and can't make it to the set. You might get the best shot of your life, but if the lab mixes the developing solution incorrectly or your hard drive crashes, the images are lost for ever. Your producers might insist there is enough money in the budget for something, but at the last minute an entire sequence has to be dropped. Everything is interwoven and interlinked, and if one element doesn't function properly, the whole venture is prone to damage or collapse. There is always the potential for a million catastrophes, even failure. People who moan about these kinds of things aren't suited to this line of business. It's the very nature of the medium. Your job is to overcome these problems, to cope with the mischievous realities that do everything they can to prevent you from completing your work, to think around corners and respond to unforeseen circumstances. You have to learn how to turn the forces of catastrophe in your favour. Filmmakers should be taught how to talk to a crew that's getting out of hand, how to negotiate with a bureaucrat so the right paperwork is signed, how to handle a producing partner who won't pay up or a distributor who won't advertise properly. Flexibility is the lifeblood of a filmmaker, and anyone unable to respond to whatever is being thrown won't get through their first day on the job. The film director has to be a lion tamer of the unexpected.

Do you rehearse with actors?

Only on set, never weeks beforehand in some bright, air-conditioned office in Santa Monica. The best dialogue is sometimes written on location to fit each actor's unique mannerisms and personal style of speech, as well as the physical conditions of the film set. After I hear the lines spoken, I might decide to alter them or ask how the actors would speak a particular sentence in their own words. If during this process the exact dialogue as written is modified, but the feel and spirit of the scene remains the same, I discard the original script pages. An actor might say his assigned lines and everyone cringes. In the *Rescue Dawn* screenplay, when Dieter crawls out of the hut, Duane originally said something like, "God be with you, Dieter." I looked at Steve Zahn, who had turned purple. "I know what you're thinking, Steve," I said. "What would you say?" The line became "Good luck, Dieter." Actors should always have the liberty to bring real life into a scene. When writing a screenplay I'm conscious that things might change once we start shooting, and when I make a film I always keep things open, ready for an invasion of the unexpected.

Altering dialogue is always possible, but it has to be done within a clear framework; for me improvisation isn't an open door for the actor. Spontaneity can reveal things about characters – for example, when I worked with Bruno S. – but it's not as if I set up the camera, bring in the actors and say, "Let's improvise something." Sometimes I gave Kinski more space to manoeuvre than I would other actors, and on several occasions I figured it was better just to let him step out in front of the camera without any direction. The only thing I told him about the bell-tower sequence of *Fitzcarraldo* before we shot it was that he had to be in complete ecstasy and fury, and shout down into the town that the church would be closed until he had constructed an opera house. Kinski himself didn't know exactly what he was going to say until the camera was rolling. At other times he needed precise guidance and restrictions, so I would physically block through the actions, reining him in where necessary. If anyone asked him about such things, of course, he would vehemently deny it, insisting he made every decision himself.

I knew I had to allow Nicolas Cage a certain freedom to add something extra to *Bad Lieutenant* and let him be an architect of his own character. He has the keen sense of a member of a jazz quintet who takes off and improvises with great fluidity, but keeps within the melody and rhythm of the overall piece. In the scene where he intimidates the couple outside the bar, it was Nicolas's idea to fire a shot into the air. Much of the scene in which he interrogates the two women in the nursing home was ad-libbed; the old ladies were genuinely terrified. I threw out an old Bavarian saying to Nicolas – "Turn the hog loose!" – and stood there in amazement. We actually shot two versions, one with him harassing them with the gun and one without. I rarely want a second version of a scene, but had a feeling it was over the top. During editing it was immediately clear the first version with the gun was best. It became a truly extraordinary moment, establishing some kind of secret conspiracy between audiences and the film, as if we're being given the opportunity to laugh at things we have never before been allowed to enjoy. Nicolas and I had great confidence in each other; he knew I wanted him to go to unexplored limits. Sometimes he would start a scene with something in mind, but I don't think even he knew precisely what he was going to say until the moment the words came out.

Do you ever talk to actors about "character motivation"?

Jeremy Davies is a hugely gifted and dedicated actor who insisted on half starving himself in preparation for his role in *Rescue Dawn*. He was already very skinny, but decided he wanted to lose even more weight and seemed to eat nothing during filming; he only drank water. If he had half a line to say, he would ambush me in the hotel the night before with twenty-five pages of ideas and arguments about his character's motivations. "Jeremy," I said, "I'm too tired to read all this, and even if I weren't, I still wouldn't look at it. Just read the script and you will know everything you need to know. Tomorrow we do the scene. Tomorrow you will stand and deliver." He's deeply involved in all things cerebral and psychological, always wanting to discuss his character endlessly. If he had entered into this labyrinthine way of playing the part, we would never have finished the film. Occasionally I would show up on the set and frighten him by suggesting we shoot a totally different scene to the one he had prepared for. Thankfully, however, he's nothing like the conceited, vacuous actors that often emerge from certain theatrical traditions. Let it be said here that Lee Strasberg was a skunk. Marlon Brando would have done his best work regardless of time spent with him. Any kind of methodology when it comes to acting is an embarrassment.

There are no general rules about working with actors; everyone needs to be handled differently. I don't, as a rule, have precise instructions for performers and generally avoid showing them what I want by acting things out myself, but when I do it's usually to help set the tone. I listen to the rehearsal and might say, "It has to be softer, slower. Take your time." On *Aguirre* I took Daniel Ades aside; he played Aguirre's henchman Perucho, who sings softly to himself just before he blows up the raft on the other side of the river, hangs Ursúa from a tree and cuts off the head of the soldier who is talking of deserting. Ades would put a melody into it, something like "La-la-LA-la-la," instead of "La-la-la-la-la." I told him not to sing. "Speak it, in only one level of pitch," I said. "It has to be dangerous and well timed. Do it in a single tone, like a telex machine rattling on in exactly the same monotone, and it will be much more menacing."

Your early screenplays are written differently from the average script.

I don't usually slavishly fill page after page with dialogue; in my early scripts some key speeches are there, but no more than that. Rather than having dialogue on the page word for word, the script will describe in general terms what characters are saying. Some of my screenplays – like *Signs of Life* and *Where the Green Ants Dream* – have more dialogue than others, but my first few were written in prose form, full of detailed descriptions of action that include scene titles, like "Descent into the Urubamba Valley."

I put down on paper only things seen and heard; rarely do you read about what these characters are thinking, something best left to a novel. Over the years I have been forced to write certain scripts because I was working with producers who wouldn't sign a contract unless I presented them with something in the form of a screenplay. I felt that if I had to write things down, then I should at least attempt something new with the form, so I've always tried to give my scripts a life independent from the resulting films. This is why my published screenplays appear without photos incorporated into the text, because I don't want to reference the films themselves. I have forever been trying to create a new genre of literature. Look at the opening lines of the *Cobra Verde* script: "The light murderous, glaring, searing; the heavens birdless; the dogs lie dazed by the heat. Demented from anger, metallic insects sting glowing stones." These aren't literal images; they offer a certain mood to the reader. More than anything else it's about atmosphere, rhythm and conjuring up images in the mind. In no other professional screenplay will you find prose as you do in mine.

Small film crews are best.

On *Rescue Dawn* there were times when Christian Bale, Steve Zahn, Peter Zeitlinger, the sound man and I would escape the rest of the crew and shoot a couple of scenes on our own. We had fourteen trucks full of personnel and equipment, constantly travelling down narrow jungle roads. It took them at least an hour to load everything and another half an hour just to turn around and drive to the next location, which meant I was sometimes able to grab a skeleton crew, jump into a van and rush over there before everyone else had even finished packing up. I wanted to work with this nucleus that I knew could take care of the essentials efficiently. By the time the trucks had arrived, we already had the scene in the can. I've never particularly enjoyed dealing with a clumsy apparatus like a big film crew. I can't stand having too many people on set; I find myself having to work around them. Sometimes you have to bypass certain things to stay dynamic, quick and lively, and get your work done.

There is a scene in Harmony Korine's film *Gummo* where a picture is taken down off a wall and a cluster of cockroaches crawl out from behind it. Harmony told me that apart from the cameraman, every single member of the crew was absolutely disgusted and showed up on set the next day in hermetically sealed toxic-waste outfits to protect themselves from the filth. They arrived as if they were filming in a nuclear wasteland. Harmony immediately stripped down to his Speedos. Jean-Yves Escoffier, the cameraman, was equally upset and said, "Harmony, let's throw everyone out. It should just be me, you, the actors and one fucking light bulb." That's filmmaking to me. Nothing more than the essential. I can't stand this kind of larmoyant behaviour. Don't be such a wimp.

In 1990 you made eight films for Austrian television called Film Lessons.

They offer hints about how my film school might be run. Every day at a fixed hour during the Vienna Film Festival – which I programmed in 1990 and 1991 – I invited a guest, including American magician Jeff Sheridan. I was fascinated by how he presented his magic and sleight of hand to audiences through his silent performances. Sometimes I think about becoming a magician myself, in direct physical contact with people in the street, playing out these little dramas with my bare hands. The trick to magic is diversion and misdirection, which are also the secrets of cinema. As a director you need to be able to push and pull the audience's attention in whatever direction the story demands, making sure everyone's eyes are focused on specific things at specific times. It's no coincidence that George Méliès, the great pioneer of early cinema, was a magician before he became a filmmaker. As Jeff said during his demonstration, the point of his job is to move beyond the logical and rational. Film might appear to be a representation of reality, but it's actually a complex illusion.

I recorded a discussion for *Film Lessons* with Kamal Saiful Islam, a cosmologist from Bangladesh who worked at the Max Planck Institute in Munich, entitled "Fantastic Landscapes and the Algebraisation of Unthinkable Curves and Spaces." I projected details of landscapes in paintings by Segers, Grünewald, Rogier van der Weyden and da Vinci, with his *Madonna in the Grotto*, where we see a mesmerising, ideal landscape in the distance, a bizarre flight of fancy that connects directly to our dreams. In the background of Altdorfer's *Battle of Alexander* is an invented land-scape of the mind, an island inhabited with cities, fields, harbours, ships, all teeming with life. These men were given precise orders by their patrons to paint particular religious motifs, but chose to venture far beyond. Their landscapes might be as small as my hand, but they are fantastical windows onto new worlds. I would love to publish a book of these miniature worlds of ecstasy and trance.

Kamal proved there are spaces unthinkable to our minds that can be conclusively proven algebraically; for example, a bottle with an interior but no exterior. We discussed the future directions cinema might move in, proving the existence of objects and images impossible for us to imagine today. It reminded me of what people must have thought during Columbus's time, when they were scared to travel to the other side of the earth because they were convinced they would hurtle down into empty space. Today every schoolchild can tell you why this isn't so, why the force of gravity keeps us grounded regardless of where we travel. One day a kind of cinema might be created that is as inconceivable to us today as basic gravitational physics was to contemporaries of Columbus.

It didn't matter that no more than a tiny handful of people in the audience in Vienna understood the imaginative and exotic mathematics being discussed. Kamal and I ranted and raved about questions that had intrigued me for a long time, like immovable positions within the universe. It isn't difficult to relate this to three-dimensional spaces. If you hang yourself by the neck in your attic and somebody finds your body dangling, what would this person need to do to fix you in a completely immobile position? Answer: one rope from your ankles down to the floor to prevent you from swinging and one from your belt to a wall to prevent you from spinning around your axis. I know the question isn't appropriate in a dynamic universe, but how many ropes are needed to fix yourself in a totally immovable position within the universe?

Are there any "rules" when it comes to cinema and filmmaking?

As a youngster, when I watched films I always asked myself questions. Why is Zorro dressed in black, which is normally the costume of the Bad Guy? Why do you never see chickens in westerns? In the final shoot-out, is the Good Guy shooting left to right or right

226

to left? I quickly realised there is a certain grammar of filmmaking most directors adhere to. Imagine the hero of a western lying in bed, tucked under a thick eiderdown blanket. An impossibility! He sleeps next to the campfire under the open sky, with his saddle as a cushion and a crude blanket to keep warm. The only exception to this rule would be when he walks up the saloon staircase to the pretty singer's room, where a perfectly made bed is waiting for him. He lies down on the cover – never under it – crosses his legs and props his spurred boots on the brass bedrail. When the hero shows up he always appears out of nowhere, riding on horseback, and when he leaves he disappears into the landscape, moving anonymously towards the horizon. There's a vagueness about where he comes from and where he's heading. All these things point to some deep-rooted, inherent principles that have to do with nomadic versus sedentary life.

The big question is: what exactly does a cowboy eat? Whatever it is, he rarely consumes anything indoors. He is allowed a drink or two, but it absolutely must be a whisky that comes skidding along the saloon bar. Under no circumstances can it be orange juice, which is as much a no-no as eating noodles. Can you imagine a cowboy cooking spaghetti in a warm, comfortable kitchen? Forget it. It can only be beans and bacon, cooked in a pan on a crackling outdoor fire. Frying an egg would be a clear violation of the genre's iron laws, and coffee never has milk or sugar; it's always black and strong, swilled from a tin mug. These questions aren't as ridiculous as they sound. Try to discover the hidden mechanics behind such things and you'll discover countless other rules that apply to westerns and other genres.

Your own lecture for Film Lessons *was entitled "Orientation in Film."*

For many families, when they sit down at the dinner table a natural seating arrangement automatically emerges. The same thing happens when going to the cinema; I feel comfortable only if I can seat myself slightly to the left of the centre of the screen, and if I'm sitting next to someone, they must be on my right. I feel cramped if I have to seat myself in a way that goes against my inner orientation.

"Orientation in Film" dealt with my own needs and interests, but also the unspoken requirements of audiences. The most obvious example is the invisible optical axis between two actors that the camera must never cross, otherwise – when cutting from one to the other – both actors would be looking in the same direction, instead of opposing each other on screen. This gets trickier if you have three people involved. A shot of a barman serving two guests is easy since the bar can serve as the axis, but what if there is no bar? A film like *Waterloo* is a useful example to learn from, with its shots of three armies marching from three different directions towards the battlefield; we always know exactly who is who and from which direction they're coming. Much of *Aguirre* deals with orientation; the small army moves with a clear purpose and sense of direction, but somewhere in the film it loses both, and by the end is going in circles. In the final shot all orientation is lost, and only a dizzying movement remains. The camera circles around the raft, which is more or less stationary, an image that reflects the story of a man who by this point has no hope of salvation. There were potential problems with *Aguirre* because several scenes took place on rafts that were spinning in the water. If we weren't careful when shooting dialogue between characters – taking into account the invisible axis between them – the riverbank in the background would move from left to right in some shots and right to left in the reverse angle. To avoid confusion and keep audiences orientated, the camera pans from one character to the other rather than cutting from one to the next.

During the Second World War, Goebbels gave an order to all cameramen at the front: "The German soldier always attacks from left to right." That was it, no further explanation. Sure enough, if you look at old newsreels, the Germans always advance from the left to the right of the screen. There was some logic to this when Germany attacked Russia in the east, but what about the war against France? Even in newsreels of the invasion westwards into Europe, German forces are seen to attack from left to right. The question we need to ask ourselves is: why does the direction of their movement make soldiers look so victorious and optimistic? There must be something within us, some hidden law. The same could be said about how to show vast distances covered on film. I might have imagined it, but I remember a scene in Luis Buñuel's *Nazarín* where Nazarín crosses Mexico on foot, walking a thousand miles with a cross over his shoulder. Buñuel used a mere three shots – each one not more than five seconds long – to give the audience a sense of the immense distance being covered. How does he manage to economise in this way? How does he compress weeks of walking into fifteen seconds? The trick is using the same set-up three times. The camera starts almost on the ground, pointing up to the sky, while the frame remains empty for a fraction of a second. Then the character steps into the image, and the camera twists and pans after him, watching him walk away into the distance. Five seconds of walking will do just fine. The whole process is repeated twice elsewhere and the three shots are cut together. We suddenly get the impression of Nazarín having walked a thousand miles. A remarkable phenomenon, how vast distances can be compressed by using an odd, twisted camera movement. I have no idea why it works, though I used the technique in *Heart of Glass* for the scene at the start of the film where Hias descends from the mountain and walks into the valley below.

When it comes to orientation in film, my favourite example is Jean-Pierre Melville's *Le deuxième souffle*. There's a scene where a gangster is summoned to meet his rivals, and beforehand he secretly checks out the room where the encounter is going to take place. He tests the possible seating arrangements and notes where he would be pushed if threatened with a gun. The only logical place is up against a cupboard, so he stands in front of it and raises his hands, then decides to leave his gun on top of the cupboard, inches away from where his raised hand would almost certainly be. When he leaves the building he is spotted by one of the rival gangsters, who then goes up to the room to check out what this guy might have been doing up there. He walks into the room, situates himself in various positions, and finds the gun. All of a sudden orientation – and the potential configurations within the space – becomes vitally important.

You established your own film school in 2010.

For years there has been a steady stream of young people who want to be my assistant or somehow learn from me; I seem to be a point of orientation for them. The number of people who send me things or ask for advice or a job is substantial, far more than those who get in touch with my much better known colleagues. A few years ago I spoke at a venue in London with a capacity of two and a half thousand. It sold out almost immediately, and there were still a thousand people waiting outside without tickets. There is clearly a hunger for an alternative way of doing things, of exploring avenues different from the brainless three-act structures of Hollywood storytelling. My Rogue Film School is an attempt to give a systematic response and deal with the amorphous avalanche coming at me. I have always been aware that making films is an enormous privilege, and feel I should pass on the knowledge acquired throughout my life.

I get a never-ending stream of requests from film schools to bring my Rogue seminars; buildings and facilities are offered, but I would rather head into an abandoned quarry in the Mojave desert or an open field in Ireland than link myself to an existing institution. There is no committee at Rogue to judge applications; I read every submission statement, view every film sent as part of the process and issue all invitations. I run the seminars single-handedly, and they take place sporadically – perhaps averaging one a year – over a long weekend in relatively out-of-the-way places. I assemble everyone in hotel conference rooms near Gatwick, Newark or in Koreatown in Los Angeles, instead of central London, Manhattan and Santa Monica, which would be prohibitively expensive for participants. Besides, too many people would be knocking at the door. I need only a room, a projector and fifty chairs. I could do Rogue anywhere.

What do you teach?

Nothing in particular. I don't hold myself up as Moses on the mountain, proclaiming the commandments. More than anything, my relationship to those who attend Rogue is like the late-mediaeval master carpenters or stone-cutters who surrounded themselves with apprentices. All I can usefully talk about is how I do my own work, and perhaps nudge participants in certain directions, helping them overcome their problems.

What does it mean to "go Rogue"?

The Rogue Film School is a provocation. It's about a way of life, about being bold enough to have the endurance to seize hold of your vision and the excitement that makes film possible, about giving courage to your dreams. It isn't about the technical things you need to know; for that, apply to your local film school. And it isn't for the faint-hearted. Rogue is for those with a fire burning within. It appeals to those with a sense of poetry willing to learn about lock picking and forging shooting permits, and who can tell a story to a four-year-old child and hold their attention. At one session a participant revealed himself to have worked in the wrestling business and gave us a wonderful line from former wrestler and governor of Minnesota Jesse Ventura, which serves as a perfect dictum for the Rogue Film School: "Win if you can, lose if you must, but always cheat." When the system doesn't respond, when it doesn't accept what you're doing – and most of the time it won't – you have to become self-reliant and create your own system. There will always be periods of solitude and loneliness, but you must have the courage to follow your own path. Cleverness on the terrain is the most important trait of a filmmaker.

Always take the initiative. There is nothing wrong with spending a night in a jail cell if it means getting the shot you need. Send out all your dogs and one might return with prey. Beware of the cliché. Never wallow in your troubles; despair must be kept private and brief. Learn to live with your mistakes. Study the law and scrutinise contracts. Expand your knowledge and understanding of music and literature, old and modern. Keep your eyes open. That roll of unexposed celluloid you have in your hand might be the last in existence, so do something impressive with it. There is never an excuse not to finish a film. Carry bolt cutters everywhere. Thwart institutional cowardice. Ask for forgiveness, not permission. Take your fate into your own hands. Don't preach on deaf ears. Learn to read the inner essence of a landscape. Ignite the fire within and explore unknown territory. Walk straight ahead, never detour. Learn on the job. Manoeuvre and mislead, but always deliver. Don't be fearful of rejection. Develop your own voice. Day one is the point of no return. Know how to act alone and in a group. Guard your time carefully. A badge of honour is to fail a film-theory class. Chance is the lifeblood of cinema. Guerrilla tactics are best. Take revenge if need be. Get used to the bear behind you. Form clandestine Rogue cells everywhere.

Revenge?

Sometimes you need to respond creatively to the more obnoxious people who stand between you and your work. Although I would never encourage anyone, in a published book or elsewhere, to break the law, it must be acknowledged that a certain amount of criminal energy can be useful. My weapon of choice is butyric acid, which is unbelievably pungent. Spray it into the car of an enemy and he won't want to drive it for two years. Ask a bold chemistry student to provide you with some.

Why is forgery a skill useful to the film director?

During production of *Fitzcarraldo*, soldiers were constantly denying us access to places, insisting we weren't permitted to proceed. I went to Lima and bought some old-fashioned notary paper of exceptional quality, and with great care set about piecing together an expert forgery, an extravagant four-page document full of wonderfully antiquated Spanish and covered in a series of beautiful watermarks and seals. It gave me permission to move about the country, to places I wouldn't otherwise have been able to go, areas swarming with military installations. The document was signed by the secretary of state and even the president of the republic himself, the supreme commander of the armed forces Fernando Belaúnde. We needed an ornate stamp so that the whole thing looked authentic. I used an impressive one in German that said something like, "To acquire the reproduction rights of this photo contact the author," something I knew nobody out there in the jungle would be able to decipher. This particular document, this fabrication, which did no harm to anyone, opened many doors for me. We constantly needed to navigate upriver through militarily controlled areas. When I showed the document en route to various officers and they saw *El Presidente*'s signature, everyone immediately saluted and stepped aside. *Fitzcarraldo* couldn't have been made without it.

Be prepared. Study how to forge a document. Carry a silver coin or medal with you at all times; if you put it under a piece of paper and make a rubbing, you can create a kind of "seal." Top that with a bold signature and you have something that looks official. There are plenty of obstacles in filmmaking, but the worst is bureaucracy.

Find your own way to battle that particular menace; you have to learn to neutralise and outsmart the rampant red tape and corruption of the world. Bureaucracy loves nothing more than paper, so keep feeding the machine. It will chew on those pages until it's quiet. A grotesque forgery pleases bureaucrats like nothing else if it appears on impressive-looking paper.

Lock picking?

Definitely a crucial skill, requiring sensitivity and patience, as Philippe Petit revealed during his *Film Lessons* presentation, when he showed how to pick a pin tumbler lock and escape from handcuffs. Imagine you need to get a shot of a street but a truck is blocking your view. During the filming of *Stroszek* in Wisconsin a truck stopped right in front of the camera, so I asked the driver if he would move it. "No way!" he said, and went for lunch. Without him noticing I moved the truck a couple of hundred feet away, got the shots we needed, then drove it back to the exact same spot an hour later. Perhaps one day you'll be forced to break into your home or office because your production manager is on the other side of the world with the keys in his pocket.

Filmmaking requires a certain attitude. Liberties have to be taken now and then, and occasionally we have to step beyond the strictures of the law. Philippe Petit is the only person ever to walk on a tightrope between the Twin Towers of the World Trade Center, a distance of two hundred feet, more than four hundred metres up. In Vienna we spoke of the years of planning and organisation required, about how he carried a ton of equipment to the top of the towers, of the documents and ID cards he forged in order to complete his task, about how he played the role of a homeless man, then a French journalist who was writing an article about the construction of the World Trade Center, and how to deflect suspicion and ensure that the authorities are looking the other way when you need them to. He talked about evading security guards when he was setting up the equipment he needed to make the walk from one tower to the other. He and a co-conspirator were about to be busted, so he started pushing his colleague aggressively, shouting things like, "You're doing a lousy job! What's the matter with you? I told you Tuesday, not Wednesday!" The two of them stormed off and the guard didn't dare say anything. No one wants to interfere with a man in the middle of a fight. Philippe pointed out that the opposite also works, that people won't bother you when you're laughing your heart out.

A participant at one Rogue session was a former hostage negotiator; he'll surely make a fine filmmaker. Another told us the story of a film he was making in Portugal about street kids. He had been filming for weeks with a group and got release forms signed by every child and parent but one. Once the film had been edited, he spent months tracking down this last kid whose signature was missing; the production company and television station insisted on it. The filmmaker never found the boy and had to cut him from the film. I assure you that if I had been involved, I would have grabbed a pen myself and solved this particular problem in no more than ten seconds. Release forms are a subtle form of censorship, which has shifted away from governments, production companies and television stations towards issues of insurance, risk aversion and fear of being sued. Errors and Omissions is the high priest at the altar of bureaucracy. That said, it can never be permissible to forge a signature if it incriminates anyone or puts them in jeopardy.

The original plan for *My Son, My Son, What Have Ye Done* was to film the flashback sequences in northern Pakistan, but it was too dangerous to take an American production there. We decided on Kashgar in western China instead, which had been an important intersection on the ancient Silk Road. The cattle market, where we filmed, is a vast, open space full of hundreds of people who look exactly as they did a thousand years ago. Obtaining a shooting permit was next to impossible, so actor Michael Shannon and I pretended to be tourists. The place was volatile, swarming with police and Chinese military; a few weeks later the Uighur uprising took place and several hundred people lost their lives. We were particularly conspicuous because Michael – who is six foot three inches tall – had a small video camera mounted on a protruding wooden arm strapped to his chest, which pointed directly at his face. I moved ahead of him, leading us into the densest crowds I could find, where the throng was thickest; everyone who saw us stared directly into the lens. We ended up near a line of twenty policemen. I had no idea if they were going to challenge us, so to pre-empt any trouble I walked directly towards them. In such situations a single policeman will stop you, but a crowd hardly ever does; everyone thinks someone else will take charge. Not making eye contact and mumbling to myself, I said, *"Hast du Harty gesehen?"* ["Have you seen Harty?"], and we walked straight past them. With airport customs officials I use another technique. I stride towards them with my gaze fixed in the distance, as if I've spotted a friend waiting for me. Very occasionally it works.

About halfway through shooting *Aguirre*, it looked as though everything we filmed had been lost in transit to the laboratory in Mexico, where the exposed negative was to be processed. The plan was for everything to be transported to Lima, and from there to Mexico City. Our only form of communication with the lab was a telex machine, but they insisted no negative had been received. Only my brother Lucki and I knew that everything might be irretrievably lost; we told none of the actors or crew because they would have instantly freaked out. We knew it was an absurdity to continue shooting because we had no insurance, so there was no choice but to muster our nerve and carry on with our work. I thought perhaps the lab had accidentally destroyed everything, but had a hunch there was a problem with the shipping company in Lima. They insisted the material had been sent to Mexico, so I asked Lucki to head down there and told him to enter their offices, if necessary by force. He eventually scaled a high fence and found all the footage thrown away, scattered inside the sealed-off customs area at Lima airport, baking in the scorching sun. The shipping agency had bribed various airport employees to stamp the documents, which "proved" our negative had left the country. Apparently it was too much trouble to actually send the material. Lucki grabbed everything and took it to Mexico City himself. So I tell you all now: whenever you have to, Jump the Fence. And if you can't do that, barbed wire is easy enough to get through; just set about it with wire cutters. Razor wire is something else. Find a mattress to cover it before making the leap.

What films do you screen at Rogue?

Who said anything about watching films? I tell the Rogues to read, read, read, read, read. Those who read own the world; those who immerse themselves in the Internet or watch too much television

235

lose it. If you don't read, you will never be a filmmaker. Our civilisation is suffering profound wounds because of the wholesale abandonment of reading by contemporary society.

I give the Rogues a mandatory reading list that has nothing to do with cinema. I tell them to read Virgil, Hemingway, the *Codex Regius* and Rabelais' *Gargantua and Pantagruel*, which is wonderfully debased, wild storytelling. I recommend the Warren Commission Report, the official government account of President Kennedy's assassination, an extraordinary crime story with tremendous narrative power and phenomenal, conclusive logic, one of those books that make you rush back home just so you can continue reading. I also suggest a book I discovered fairly recently: J. A. Baker's *The Peregrine*, first published in 1967, at a time when peregrine falcons were on the brink of extinction in Britain because of the prevalence of pesticides. There were very few pairs of healthy breeding peregrines left because so many had been poisoned. The intensity and precision of observation in Baker's book is startling; it's a text of great beauty. Humans hardly feature at all. Instead, he writes with delirium about the magnificence of the falcon and how it hunts, filling the book with ecstatic descriptions of the peregrine swooping down from the sky. Baker almost becomes a bird himself; it's like a religious transubstantiation. His fervent fascination, inner involvement and enthusiasm with the natural world, and the way he sees things around him so intensely – truly capturing the essence of a single brief event in such minute detail – are wondrous. It's the same attitude required of filmmakers, who need to discover and seize upon the intensity within.

There are a few films I ask Rogue participants to watch before they arrive, including *Casablanca*, *The Treasure of the Sierra Madre* and *America, America*, all examples of great Hollywood storytelling. I also recommend Pontecorvo's *The Battle of Algiers*, which I admire because of the acting, and Elia Kazan's impeccable *Viva Zapata!*. In no other film have I seen such a powerful introduction of the leading character, played by Marlon Brando. At Rogue I talk about how the ending of a story is just as important as the beginning. Consider how – after sitting for two hours in the darkness staring at the screen – your audience is catapulted back out into a world full of sunshine, noise and traffic. How do you create something that will linger in their souls and not immediately

236

dissipate? Think about the dancing chicken in *Stroszek*, which people never forget, even if they have no memory of anything else in the film.

You discuss things at Rogue that have nothing to do with cinema per se.

I encourage the Rogues to study languages, including Latin, which means to understand the genesis of our culture and the Western world. I read them "The Catalogue of Dwarfs" from the Icelandic *Poetic Edda*, an extraordinary collection of Old Norse poems compiled in the fourteenth century and probably handed down, in the oral tradition, a thousand years earlier. Rogue is about making clear the significance of the word just as much as the image.

Out of idle curiosity I have explored things like the mathematical proposition known as Zorn's lemma. I'm fascinated by the rules, paradoxes and structures that exist in numbers, but which few people can see. I've spent a lot of time thinking about things like the Riemann hypothesis, the greatest unsolved question in mathematics, which deals with the distribution of prime numbers. At Rogue I talk about the work of the brilliant polyglot British architect Michael Ventris, who in the early fifties deciphered Linear B, a script dating back to something like 1450 BC that was found on hundreds of clay tablets. The intellectual ingenuity, experimentation and guesswork that Ventris exercised in determining that Linear B must be an archaic form of Greek was astonishing. He created a series of complex logical grids, similar to those used to encrypt codes during the war, and assigned each of the eighty-seven signs found on the tablets with a phonetic value, making clear that the script is syllabic, not composed of ideograms. An entire culture and civilisation opened up to us thanks to Ventris – only in his late twenties at the time – though unfortunately the tablets deal with tedious bureaucracy and bookkeeping; none of them contain poetry, history or anything particularly interesting. We have inventories of who owed how much to whom; there are mentions of wool, livestock, spices, perfumes and weapons, the kind of work slaves did and how the Mycenaean military was organised, including chariot formations. Regardless, Ventris's work remains a phenomenal achievement of the human intellect. It's the kind of exploration I have always enjoyed engaging with. I wonder if he would have been able to decipher the example of Angelyne, who thirty years ago put photos of herself – with her endless facelifts and breast enhancements – on billboards across Los Angeles. Little is known about this woman because she had no profession as such. She wasn't a singer or a model or a film star; she was just Angelyne. In most cases fame and popularity stem from actually having done something – like being a mass murderer or a television chef or a footballer or a politician – but in Angelyne's case her prominence came from the fact that her image suddenly appeared around the city. It's unlikely any Rogue Film School participants would ever want to find out more about Michael Ventris, but that's not the point. He understood how to read the signs, something every film-maker has to be able to do. If you don't keep yourself open to these kinds of fascinations, you will never be a filmmaker.

The only criterion I use when selecting books for the mandatory reading list of Rogue is that they are titles I like to read myself. Everyone ultimately has to create their own list and discover their own intellectual curiosities to dig into, their own Linear B. What distinguishes us from the cows in the field is an inherent human desire to understand the world around us. It doesn't matter that many of my interests have never been translated directly into my film work. Everything that simmers inside of me eventually finds its expression somehow, somewhere.

You have spoken about being able to establish an instant rapport.

Filmmaking is about creating immediate and profound connections with people. I have a rather biblical-sounding axiom for you: to be a filmmaker you need to know the heart of men.

In Bodhgaya, when we were making *Wheel of Time*, I saw a monk sitting by himself, surrounded by four hundred thousand pillows, in an enclosed area where not long before had been that many people. It was a beautiful image, something like a metaphor for the concept of nothingness. I was astounded by the serious-ness of this one person still praying after so many hundreds of thousands had moved on. My instinct was to leave him in peace. I caught his eye from a hundred feet away and glanced down at our camera; it was a silent way of asking him if we could film. He nodded his permission with a slight, almost imperceptible gesture. He had such a glow that I wouldn't have done any filming around him had he not agreed to it. Ultimately his dignity was untouched by the camera, and the image of him sitting alone, sunk in prayer, is one of the most significant I have ever captured.

I filmed with Dr Franc Fallico, Alaska's chief medical examiner, for *Grizzly Man*. He was the coroner who performed autopsies on Timothy Treadwell and Amie Huguenard. I could tell he was a thoughtful man, so I said, "Today, in front of this camera, you aren't Dr Franc Fallico. We aren't in court now and I don't want you to be matter-of-fact about this. I want to know how you felt when you saw their remains. Twenty-eight pounds of Treadwell, twenty-two of Huguenard found out there in the field, and the rest of both in the stomach of a bear. I want to talk to a human being, not a coroner." He looked at me, said, "I understand what you mean," and proceeded to give a remarkable and touching performance, which is in the film..

One of the first things I did when I set about making *The Wild Blue Yonder* was meet with astronauts from the 1989 space-shuttle mission. We found ourselves in a large, empty room at the Johnson Space Center in Houston, them in a semicircle of chairs and me sitting opposite. For a minute I didn't know what to say, and an embarrassed silence hung in the air. Spontaneously I turned to Michael McCulley and said, "As a child in the mountains of Bavaria I learnt to milk cows with my hands. Ever since then I have been able to recognise someone who knows how to milk a cow." I looked him in the eye, pointed to him and said, "You, sir!" He slapped his thigh, made the gesture of milking a cow and exclaimed, "Yes! I grew up on a farm in Tennessee!" The ice was broken. I can tell from fifty feet away whether someone knows how to tug on an udder.

In Antarctica, during the filming of *Encounters at the End of the World*, I spoke with David Ainley, who had been studying penguins for twenty years. By the time I met him he didn't care much for conversations with human beings and wasn't giving anything away. I set up the camera and microphone very meticulously, procrastinating as much as possible, because I wanted to take time to warm him up and establish a rapport before we started filming. I needed more than just a muffled grunt in response to my questions, so

I asked if there were any documented cases of homosexuality in penguins. That got him going. He spoke about seeing a triangular penguin relationship, a case of prostitution involving one female and two males. Then I asked if there was such a thing as derangement among penguins. He told me he had never seen one of the animals banging its head against a rock, though sometimes the creatures become disorientated and end up a long way from the ocean. Who else had ever asked him such questions? He could see there was somebody sitting opposite with an imagination. I hadn't read a single book about penguins, but I had done some unusual thinking on the subject.

A few years later, during production on *Into the Abyss*, I had only a few minutes with Reverend Richard Lopez, the death-house chaplain, whose job is to be with prisoners in the moments before and during their execution. He immediately tapped his wristwatch, saying, "I have to be in the death house in forty minutes to assist with an execution." I had ten seconds to introduce myself before placing him in front of the camera and filming him. He immediately started speaking like a phoney, superficial television preacher, about a merciful and forgiving God, about redemption for everyone and paradise awaiting us all, about the beauty of Creation. Then he mentioned how much he loves being alone on the golf course in the morning, and how he switches off his cellphone so he can listen to the sounds of nature. He wanted to experience the dew-covered early-morning grass and watch the squirrels and deer running about and a horse looking at him with big eyes. I sensed our conversation was moving in the wrong direction, that I had to put an end to these platitudes, so I stopped him and asked something that nobody else on God's wide earth would have. From behind the camera, with a cheerful voice, I said, quite spontaneously, "Tell me about an encounter with a squirrel." Immediately, within twenty seconds, he began to unravel and completely came apart. He was so shaken to his core that he started to weep, talking about the bad choices and mistakes of the many people with whom he had been during the last moments of their life. Although he was able to stop his golf cart before it ran over a squirrel, he couldn't halt the inexorable procedures of an execution. I don't know why I asked him about the squirrel; I only knew I had to crack him open. In such situations the film director has to put aside everything that

240

is explicitly professional and rally every ounce of humanity from within.

My job as a filmmaker is to look into the deepest recesses of the soul. When it comes to such things, I have acquired the required vision thanks to certain essential experiences. What is it like to be imprisoned? To go hungry? To raise children? To be stranded alone in the desert? To face genuine danger? To walk a thousand miles? To handle a Kalashnikov? To keep a group of youngsters entertained? To be astounded by poetry? Much of what we do as filmmakers is inexplicable, but the groundwork is done without a camera and the barrier it creates. Give me the name of the film school that teaches such things.

Do you offer Rogue participants any general advice?

A few things come up again and again during our sessions.

When it comes to organising your set, it's important to maintain close physical contact with your crew at all times. There are often a dozen people hanging around, talking on their phones, paying no attention. I insist that all non-essential conversations take place far from the camera and actors, which means no walkie-talkies within a hundred feet of my set and no cellphones within three hundred feet. Once people realise they have to step away from the centre of activity to make a phone call, they inevitably decide most conversations aren't that important. During heart surgery nobody is standing on the periphery talking on the phone; everyone is present and paying close attention, or at a distance doing something else. Absolute concentration, quiet and focus are required from everyone, at every moment, on my set. The only way for someone to respond to unexpected things is to be completely aware of what everyone else is doing. The cameraman has to listen to what's going on around him before making his move; being able to attune his ears to his surroundings is as important as seeing what's happening. A dolly movement is often triggered by a line of dialogue, but I've seen a dolly operator move too early because he wasn't listening carefully enough. One way of creating this climate of absolute professionalism on day one, and making it clear to everyone how your set is going to function, is to start filming within ninety minutes of everyone arriving, no matter what. Roll the camera even if the gaffer is still in shot; he'll realise fast enough that he needs to get out of there. Your attitude should always be as if you have only two days to make the entire film. Think of Roger Corman, who wouldn't spend much more time than that shooting an entire feature.

During the shooting of a non-fiction film, don't show footage to anyone you have been filming with because they often become self-conscious and complain about how they look. My response to these requests is simple: I tell them I might throw the entire thing out or use just 10 per cent of what we recorded, so it would only be confusing and disappointing for them to look at it now. "Just leave me in peace and thank God you don't have to wrestle with this material. That's my job."

Within every film is some sort of unique inner timing that must be discovered and respected. What's important to understand is that this can never be established retrospectively while editing, only during shooting. You might be able to alter a film's pace during editing, but never its fundamental rhythm. Never delegate decisions down the line to post-production that should be handled on set during filming; by that point many problems can never be adequately resolved. Bad acting, to give the most obvious example, can never be fixed.

There is often a separate, parallel story playing out in the hearts and minds of everyone watching your film, which means an audience will collectively anticipate certain things and race ahead of the actual narrative building on screen. With a romantic comedy we intuitively jump to the end of story and hope that the lovers will overcome all obstacles and find each other. You have to pay attention to these parallel stories; if you don't understand and develop a sense for them, you'll never grasp the essence of storytelling for cinema. It's the same thing as the inaudible overtones beyond a musical chord. We don't necessarily hear them, but if you aren't able to listen, you'll never fully understand that chord.

One final thing. I carry two texts when I am about to embark on a film I know will give me trouble: Luther's translation of the Bible and Livy's account of the Second Punic War. The Book of Job acts as consolation, Livy gives me courage. His book is a description of Carthage's war against Rome, a war that Rome almost didn't survive. Livy tells the story of two of my favourite historical

242

figures: Hannibal and Fabius Maximus. Hannibal was a leader of extraordinarily bold designs, moving across the Alps with his army and elephants trained for battle. But Maximus is an equally fascinating character, someone who refused to do battle against Hannibal's armies, and because of this was considered a hesitant coward. Why did he act in this way? To save Rome. He knew that after the two most catastrophic disasters Rome had ever endured – the defeats at Cannae and Lake Trasimene – another open-field battle against Hannibal would mean the end of the republic. Fabius Maximus waged a war of attrition instead, attacking stragglers in the rearguard, devastating Hannibal's supply lines and luring him into places where there was nothing for his army to eat. There is a striking passage in the book where Hannibal, who has been leading campaigns in Italy for years, learns that his brother Hasdrusbal's supply fleet has been destroyed off the coast of Sicily. Hannibal knows he has been cut off from his ships, and after a long moment of silence utters the phrase "I know the destiny of Carthage." That was his only response to the situation. He knew Carthage was lost and would be destroyed, inevitably disappearing into the abyss of history.

Although he was vilified and derided by Roman historiography, called a coward and dubbed *Cunctator*, the delayer, the cowardly hesitant one, Maximus' far-sighted tactics are why he is the greatest among the leaders of his era. He defeated Hannibal and saved Rome not by demonstrating the kind of brainless bravery shown by his predecessors – men who lost decisive battles – but by following a different path. We owe him a great debt. If Hannibal had prevailed, today we would all be living in a very different culture; the world around us would be Phoenician and North African. Maximus is one of my idols, someone who followed a vision no matter what anyone thought of him, who refused to align himself to pre-existing traditions. When the boat was slipping back in the mud during the shooting of *Fitzcarraldo*, Fabius Maximus had a hand on my shoulder.

There is often great frustration in this work. I say this not to discourage anyone; it's just a way of life. One way to get through it is sheer discipline. This isn't about physical discipline, rather a certain psychological state. Plough on no matter how many spectacular humiliations and undignified defeats you suffer. Under normal circumstances, when a human being leaps into an abyss, he shrinks back. But when a ski jumper takes off, he leans forward, head first, into the void. If he doesn't, he rotates backwards. A downhill racer might be able to brake if he needs to, but when a jumper starts down that ramp, nothing can stop him. The same could be said of filmmaking. Learn to overcome your fears and shepherd your project to completion, no matter what. It's the essential moments of struggle over the decades that I have learnt from and which have brought to me this point. When I think back to my earliest years in this business, I see I am nothing today but a product of my defeats. When I was burnt I learnt about heat, and when I was belittled I learnt about power structures. Instead of going to film school, for me it became a process of trial and error, and for the first few years it was mostly error.

Writers and filmmakers are all alone; there is usually no one to help you, so just get off your ass and start walking. When you make a film or write a book and roll it out to audiences, be prepared to deal with either kicks to the stomach and slaps to the face or complete indifference. Most of the time no one cares about what you're doing, except you. A filmmaker's existence is different from that of a train conductor or bank teller. You have made certain choices about your life, which means you need to learn to overcome the despair and loneliness. Stay focused, quiet and professional at all times. Face what comes at you. You can never be irresolute, not for a single second. Plant yourself into the ground and move for no one. Make films only if there is a natural urge within. Switch off your Internet connection and get to work.

Has it been easy to finance your more recent films?

A natural component of filmmaking is the struggle to find money. It has been an uphill battle my entire working life. People think it's easy for me to finance my films these days, but the basis of operations is continually shrinking when it comes to distributing the kind of work I produce. Raising money might be even tougher today than it ever has been, certainly when it comes to feature films, and audiences seem to be getting smaller and smaller. But this is all unimportant. Fifty years ago, when I walked out of the office of those pompous producers and established my own production

With mother Elizabeth and brothers, Lucki (far left) and Tilbert

Signs of Life

Signs of Life

Signs of Life. With Athina Zacharopoulou and Peter Brogle

Even Dwarfs Started Small

Even Dwarfs Started Small

Fata Morgana

Aguirre, the Wrath of God

The Great Ecstasy of Woodcarver Steiner. With Walter Steiner

The Enigma of Kaspar Hauser. With Lotte Eisner

Heart of Glass

Heart of Glass

No One Will Play with Me

Stroszek

Stroszek. With Thomas Mauch

Stroszek

Stroszek. With Bruno Schleinstein

La Soufrière. With Jörg Schmidt-Reitwein

Nosferatu

Nosferatu. With Klaus Kinski

Nosferatu

Woyzeck

With Volker Schlöndorff and Rudolf Herzog

With Arnold Schwarzenegger

Lincoln Centre, New York, 1982

Fitzcarraldo

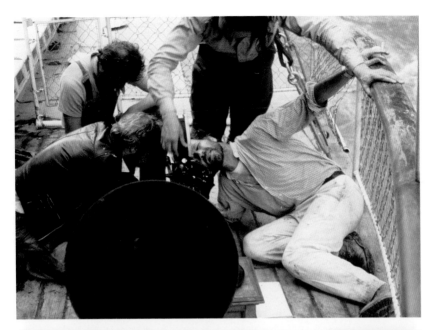

Fitzcarraldo

Fitzcarraldo. With Klaus Kinski

Ballad of the Little Soldier

The Dark Glow of the Mountains. With Reinhold Messner (left)

Cobra Verde

Cobra Verde

Cobra Verde. With Klaus Kinski

With Amos Vogel

Scream of Stone

Lessons of Darkness

Bells from the Deep. With Yuri Yurevitch Yurieff

Death for Five Voices

The Transformation of the World into Music. With Wolfgang Wagner

My Best Fiend

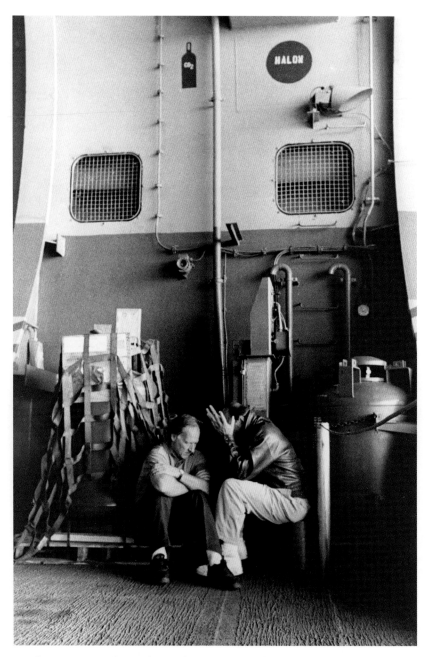

Little Dieter Needs to Fly. With Dieter Dengler

Wings of Hope. With Juliane Koepcke

Wheel of Time. With Peter Zeitlinger

Grizzly Man

The White Diamond

Rescue Dawn. With Christian Bale and Steve Zahn

Bad Lieutenant. With Nicolas Cage

Cave of Forgotten Dreams

Into the Abyss

Telluride Film Festival, 2013

company, I knew I would never shoot a single frame of film if I continued wasting my time with such people. If you want to make a film, go make it. I can't tell you the number of times I have started shooting a film knowing I didn't have the money to finish it. I meet people everywhere who complain about money; it's the ingrained nature of too many filmmakers. But it should be clear to everyone that money has always had certain explicit qualities: it's stupid and cowardly, slow and unimaginative. The circumstances of funding never just appear; you have to create them yourself, then manipulate them for your own ends. This is the very nature and daily toil of filmmaking. If your project has real substance, ultimately the money will follow you like a common cur in the street with its tail between its legs. There is a German proverb: "*Der Teufel scheisst immer auf den grössten Haufen*" ["The Devil always shits on the biggest heap"]. So start heaping and have faith. Every time you make a film you should be prepared to descend into Hell and wrestle it from the claws of the Devil himself. Prepare yourself: there is never a day without a sucker punch. At the same time, be pragmatic and learn how to develop an understanding of when to abandon an idea. Follow your dreams no matter what, but reconsider if they can't be realised in certain situations. A project can become a cul-de-sac and your life might slip through your fingers in pursuit of something that can never be realised. Know when to walk away.

Many years ago I decided I wanted to publish my screenplays and prose texts, so I approached a respected German publishing house. When they turned me down, I immediately realised there was no point spending time sending out letters to other publishers asking the same question. I set up my own publishing house, Skellig, and issued *Heart of Glass* and two volumes of screenplays. I printed a few thousand copies of each, and whenever I was invited to talk at a cinema would load a couple of hundred copies into my car so they could be sold at the box office. They cost something like $3 each to produce and I sold them for $4, so I even made a small profit. If another publishing house had produced the book and sold it in a store, it would have cost eight times as much, but I had no need of advertising and a complex system of distribution, the things that make books expensive. The technical costs of printing have always been minimal. Once it was clear how successful the books were, Carl Hanser Verlag in Munich asked if they could continue publishing the texts. I agreed, but insisted the cover had to be exactly the same as the Skellig editions – a simple design of orange lettering on a black background above a monochrome photograph – and no film stills inside.

Have your films made money for you?

I don't function in the way traditional film producers do. From the very beginning I have taken a long-range view of things, always looking beyond everyday financial arrangements. Short-term survival was never my plan. For years in Germany I worked in a vacuum with few financial returns. When *Aguirre* was screened on television the same day it was released in cinemas, and in both cases did badly, I asked myself, "How can I survive this disaster? How can I continue working in this way?" Though I still carry these questions with me, I have always had faith in my films and the belief that one day they would be seen and enjoyed. Perseverance has kept me going over the years. Things rarely happen overnight. Filmmakers should be prepared for many years of hard work. The sheer toil can be healthy and exhilarating.

Although for many years I lived hand to mouth – sometimes in semi-poverty – I have lived like a rich man ever since I started making films. Throughout my life I have been able to do what I truly love, which is more valuable than any cash you could throw at me. At a time when friends were establishing themselves by getting university degrees, going into business, building careers and buying houses, I was making films, investing everything back into my work. Money lost, film gained. Today I can earn money on films I made forty years ago by releasing them on DVD and screening them on television and at retrospectives. At an early age I understood the key to this business is being your own producer. I never thought twice about taking a salary for writing and directing when I first started out. I worked out of my small apartment, with my brother and wife as close collaborators. We cobbled money together from revenues of previous films, subsidies and pre-sales, and used it for only the bare essentials, like travel costs, raw stock, lab fees and costumes. You could see every penny up there on the screen.

In the early days I made a living, but only just. I lived with very few possessions, most of which were the tools of my trade: an Arriflex camera, a car, a typewriter, a flatbed editing machine, a Nagra tape recorder. My material needs have always been limited. So long as I have a roof over my head, something to read and something to eat, all is fine. I own one pair of shoes, a single suit, and once I finish a book I pass it on to a friend. I'm just a man from the mountains who isn't very interested in owning things. I've been driving the same car for nearly twenty years, and have to hand-crank the window and lock each door individually. A few years ago I closed down the small Werner Herzog Filmproduktion office I maintained in Munich, and around the same time my brother Lucki started methodically collecting all the audio tracks, negatives, scripts and paperwork of my work, going back to the sixties, which we gave to the Deutsche Kinemathek Museum für Film und Fernsehen in Berlin. The plan is to establish a non-profit foundation, at which point I'll no longer even own my own films. Even if I went broke, I wouldn't be able to sell anything to the highest bidder. What makes me rich is that I am welcomed almost everywhere. I can show up with my films and am offered hospitality, something you could never achieve with money alone. You saw how that stranger insisted on paying the bill for our lunch yesterday. "Thank you for *Woyzeck*," he said. For years I have struggled harder than you can imagine for true liberty, and today am privileged in the way the boss of a huge corporation never will be. Hardly anyone in my profession is as free as I am.

Have you always made films for audiences rather than for yourself?

In making *Aguirre* I purposely set out to create a commercial film for a wide audience, even if the end result was as personal as anything I had done before. The art-house circuit was a lifeline for me during my early years of filmmaking, but I never felt I belonged there, and *Aguirre* was always intended for the general public. If I could have been guaranteed an audience for *Aguirre*, perhaps I would have made it differently, rougher and less genre-orientated. As it is, the film is probably easier to follow than my previous work. The sequence of action is less subtle than in *Signs of Life* and there's a clear line of demarcation between good and bad, like in classic westerns, so the audience can choose which side they want to root for. At the time the film drew a lot of criticism from my peers, which I can still hear ringing in my ears. From a perspective of forty years it's extraordinary to think that *Aguirre* was considered a commercial sell-out, as if I had sold my soul to the Devil. People close to me turned away. "He's gone commercial," they said. It was the worst of all sins.

I never set out to make cloudy and complicated films. Every one has been born out of my deepest interests and beliefs, but at the same time every one – from the smallest television documentary to *Bad Lieutenant*, which stars some of the biggest names in Hollywood – was made for the largest possible audience. I don't have much of an idea about what audiences want because I'm so out of touch with contemporary trends and culture, but when asked I'll always customise a film to fit the television schedule; it's always been a necessary part of the process. In some cases, like *Little Dieter Needs to Fly*, I had to deliver a film of exactly forty-four minutes and thirty seconds, and decided to produce a feature-length version at the same time, which is over eighty minutes. Most people saw the film in its truncated form. I didn't mind changing the title of the television version to *Escape from Laos* because it's essentially a different film. This was all on my mind while we were making the film, which we shot simultaneously in English and German. *The Great Ecstasy of Woodcarver Steiner* was originally an hour long, but the television executives asked me to cut it down to exactly forty-four minutes and ten seconds so it would fit in their schedule. I never felt I was compromising anything by editing the film down to that length. Filmmaking is a craft, and as far as I'm concerned being a craftsman is about producing work that people will see. It has always been important for me that my films reach their audience. I don't necessarily need to hear what those reactions are, just so long as they're out there. Making a film and not releasing it would defeat the purpose. Even if my films haven't instantly found audiences, they have been on a steady upwards curve. Forty years after *Aguirre*, people around the world want to see it and talk about it. These days I get emails from seventeen-year-olds about films I made when their parents were in diapers. I have always been mainstream. The secret mainstream.

Some might call me eccentric, but by comparison it's everyone else who deserves that label. Consider someone like Peter Alexander, a wildly popular singer, actor and television star who for thirty years was one of the biggest stars in Austria and Germany, a repulsive *chanteur* and *charmeur* similar to Maurice Chevalier. He was also one of those in public life always talking about the good old days, forever in denial of the catastrophes that Germany had so recently brought to the world. Although Alexander might have stood at the centre of culture fifty years ago and appealed to the masses, today it's clear that everything he did is laughably stupid. Although millions of people watched Alexander every week, he was the master of collective insanity, and as the decades tick on he will become ever more irrelevant. Most of what we see around us is the ephemeral mainstream, mass-produced populist commercial trash, designed to go straight through us. Look instead at Robert Walser, an outsider who lived at the edge of the world and spent his final decades in a madhouse, formulating ideas in his writings that a hundred years later retain startling power and validity. Walser had a talent for penetrating the hidden anguish of those around him, and his ideas will be with us for generations to come. Someone like Kafka – who worked for years in an insurance company and was appreciated by only a tiny handful of people while he was alive – was also on the edge of things. He was so embarrassed about how unpopular his work was that he visited the bookshops of Prague and bought up copies himself. Today we acknowledge that Kafka was the secret mainstream, very much at the centre of his time.

There is a strong emphasis in Hollywood on story structure.

Things like "story structure" and "character development" all sound so stale to my ears. I know some writers stick postcards over their walls, but that's all foreign to me. I get hundreds of scripts sent to me every year, many of which are exactly 116 pages, presumably because some bloated "guru" once insisted that a script should be 116 pages, not a line longer. These screenplays are the work of writers in thrall to certain recipes; for example, that by page thirty the hero has to "know his mission" and emerge from the story a changed man. It's a misguided way of doing things. The result is a series of thoroughly unappetising dishes, the efforts of legions of industry writers who follow the pathetic postulates. I turn my back on such people. They are bedwetters, every one of them.

I am a storyteller who writes so fast he can't afford to think about the structure of the writing. There is such an urgency to tell the tale that it inevitably creates its own structure. Hollywood scripts are designed to push certain buttons at certain times, which is filmmaking by numbers. There are solid production and distribution systems in Hollywood, and very skilled technicians and craftspeople, but you hardly ever find a good story there any more. The way they do things is deranged, built around the endless rewriting of a script, bringing in one writer after another to produce a screenplay. It would be unimaginable for me to write something five times over. Too much screenwriting today is dictated by boardroom decision-making. Real storytelling will always prevail, just as it has for thousands of years. It's so much a part of our collective existence, our dreams and nightmares, that it will never be easily brushed aside. I see the role of the film director as being that of the storyteller in a busy, noisy market in Marrakech, surrounded by an excited crowd. He knows he has to hold his audience's attention at all times. Eventually, when he is finished, if the people are satisfied, he walks away with coins in his hand.

8

Reveries and Imagination

Do you still not own a cellphone?

I'm the only thinking person I know without one. I don't want to be available at all times. Permanent connectivity isn't my thing; I have always needed moments of quiet solitude for myself. There's a Chinese poem from the Tang dynasty about someone describing a boat journey along the Yellow River and leaving his friend behind, a monk on a mountain, in the knowledge that they probably won't see each other or have any contact for years. This man's return, decades later, has an indescribable substance and depth. Compare this to standing in line at the airport, chatting on your cellphone to your loved one, who is waiting in the car park. There is too much shallow contact in our lives. I prefer to be face to face; I want the person I'm communicating with to be so close I can put my hand on their shoulder. Text messaging is the bastard child handed to us by the absence of reading.

It is my firm belief that solitude will increase in proportion to the new tools at our disposal, the explosive evolution of electronic and digital communication. Technology might remove us from our isolation, but we are entering an era of solitude. When you are caught in a snowdrift in South Dakota, fifty miles from the nearest town, your isolation can be overcome with a mere cellphone, but your solitude never will be. As for "social networks," mine has forever been my kitchen table, where I cook for no more than four or five friends.

You use the Internet.

Of course. Who can avoid it? But I do so with hesitation. It has, after all, opened up a gigantic field of indiscretion, arrogance, narcissism and self-aggrandisement. Humility is scarce and mediocrity flows from every direction, with attention-seekers unleashing their innermost thoughts. I seem to be one of the few left who consider discretion a virtue, though we have to be cautious about such things because our sense of what is virtuous is forever shifting. A virtue can become obsolete – for example, chastity – and these days young men, their honour besmirched, would never challenge each other to a pistol duel. They would phone their attorneys instead. One time after Les Blank had been given a haircut he wasn't happy with, I suggested he do what any American would: "Give your lawyer a call and sue."

One morning in 1984 you left Sachrang, the village where you lived as a child, and proceeded to walk around the border of West and East Germany. Was this a political act?

Not explicitly. At the time, German reunification looked like a lost cause. The nation was in fragments, with no true centre, without a real metropolis or beating heart at its core. While the real capital city – Berlin – was a divided enclave deep in a separate country, we had to make do with Bonn, a provincial town, as our seat of government. It would be like having Ann Arbor, Michigan, as the capital of the United States. The Berlin Wall stood there, an edifice that was going nowhere without a decisive change occurring in the planet's balance of power. It was a lingering and painful wound of the Second World War, located in the spot where two political continents rubbed up against each other. Germany had become homeless within its own territory. There is, I believe, a geographical fate to nations, not only a cultural or political one. In many cases there exists an unequivocal necessity of reunification, and today we await change in Ireland and Korea; these are quests that can never be abandoned. Prominent figures like Günter Grass insisted that the two Germanys should never be brought together,* but

---

* See Grass's *Two States – One Nation? The Case Against German Reunification* (Secker and Warburg, 1990), where he writes: "We should be aware – as our neighbors are – of how much grief this unified state caused, of what misfortune it brought to others and to ourselves as well. The crime of genocide, summed up in the image of Auschwitz, inexcusable

for years the country's unification was close to my heart. I was convinced of its inevitability and felt unhappy with politicians like Willy Brandt, who, in an official statement as chancellor, declared the matter closed. Of all the German politicians I have been aware of as an adult, Brandt is the only one I ever really liked, but I found his public declarations on reunification scandalous. As far as I was concerned, there was an inevitable and irrepressible desire of the German people to reunite, so for me the question was always very much open, though I didn't think it would be solved in my lifetime, or even my children's.

The division of the country never affected me personally because I had no relatives behind the Iron Curtain, but for those who did the situation was catastrophic. I was at a train station in East Berlin about ten years after the Berlin Wall had gone up. East Germany had allowed West Berliners to cross the border on certain days, but they had to return home before midnight. There were at least five thousand people, maybe a quarter of whom were going back to West Berlin, saying goodbye to their mothers and fathers, their sisters and brothers. Every once in a while we are witness to a truly unforgettable drama, a catastrophic tragedy. At that moment, watching all these people who didn't know if they would ever see each other again, a great chasm opened up between Brandt and me.

I vividly remember the deep feeling of joy and jubilation when the Berlin Wall came down. My hope was that in an explosion of freedom everyone in East Germany would crawl out of their holes and display to the world their creative energies, though after only a week almost everyone had lapsed into a climate of complaint and self-pity. "The politicians aren't doing enough for us." "Why aren't they creating more jobs?" "Why aren't we as rich as the West?" In the early nineties there was an incessant debate about relocating the government to Berlin. How could Parliament, we were told, move and start its sessions in the new Reichstag without having offices ready for the parliamentarians? It was all so small-minded to me. A parliament can hold its session in an open field, if need be.

Back in 1982 I felt that Germany was a godforsaken country, and

---

from whatever angle you view it, weighs on the conscience of this unified state."

wondered who was capable of holding it together until reunification. I had the increasingly strong sense that the most robust connections between Germans were cultural and linguistic. If the politicians had abandoned the nation, it was the poets who remained. With a clear understanding of the historical necessity to move beyond politics, I set out from my home village of Sachrang one morning and walked west around the border. I was careful to travel clockwise, so Germany would always be on my right. My idea was to hold the country together as if with a belt. Unfortunately, after nearly a thousand miles, I fell ill and had to return, so I jumped on a train home, where I was hospitalised for a week because of an old football injury. To this day my journey – which never had any explicitly nationalistic element to it – remains unfinished business, though of course the need to complete the walk no longer exists. I later gave a public talk at the Munich Kammerspiele theatre, where I read from texts I wrote during my travels.*

Has travelling on foot always been important to you?

For too long we have been estranged from essential nomadic life. Humans aren't made to sit in front of computer screens or travel by aeroplane; nature intended something different for us. Walking great distances has never been extreme behaviour to me. It has forever helped me regain my equilibrium, and I would always rather do the existentially important things in my life on foot. If you want to propose marriage to your girlfriend and you live in England and she is in Sicily, do the decent thing and walk down there. Travelling by car or aeroplane wouldn't be right at such a moment. Making a journey like that on foot has nothing to do with being a tourist; you won't find many of them carrying binoculars, a canteen, a compass and a penknife but no camera on their travels. In fact, the dignity and identity of cultures around the world are being stripped to the bone by tourism. I have a dictum that connected me instantly with Bruce Chatwin: "Tourism is sin and travel by foot is virtue."

Travelling on foot isn't about testing your limits or exercising or hiking with a tent on your back. It's about moving through a landscape, embarking on a process of discovery, with no shelter

* See "Thinking about Germany," p. 458.

at hand. My voyages on foot – wandering out into the world unprotected – have always been essential experiences for me. For hours during my walk around Germany, sometimes even for a day or two at a time, there was no well or creek to drink from. I would knock on the door of a farmhouse and ask if I could use their faucet to fill my canteen. "Where have you come from?" the farmer would ask. "Sachrang," I would say. "How far is that?" "About eight hundred miles." "How did you get here?" he would ask. The moment I told him I had walked, there was no more small talk, only an immediate reflex of grandiose hospitality as he invited me into his home. When people take note of how far you have come on foot, they tell you stories that have been bottled up for years. One evening in a mountain hut I spoke with a retired teacher who told me a story about the final day of the Second World War in Holland. Canadian forces were advancing on him with their tanks. He had been given orders to take a group of soldiers prisoner at a farm behind the advancing line of enemy tanks. He told me that only by turning his gun on his superior officer did he manage to prevent the execution of these prisoners. Then, together with his Dutch captives, he had to overtake the advancing enemy and was eventually intercepted by Canadian tanks and taken prisoner himself.

When you come on foot you bring a certain intensity. Although I never dream at night, when walking I experience exciting voyages into my own imagination, and fall into deep reveries. Rhymes seize hold of me and I'm unable to shake them out of my mind. While on my walk around Germany I was consumed with a phrase about a Bavarian mountain: "*Der Watzmann rennt, der Watzmann rennt, holldrioh mein Holzbein brennt*" ["The Watzmann's racing, the Watzmann's racing, hey-de-ho, my wooden leg is blazing"]. I float through fantasies and find myself inside unbelievable stories while walking. I move through entire novels and films, as well as extraordinary football games, always with the best players, most wondrous action and perfect goals you can imagine. When I emerge from a story, or once I hear the whistle blow, I find myself ten miles from where I started. Exactly how I got there I don't know. The world reveals itself to those who travel on foot.

When Lotte Eisner fell ill, you refused to let her die.

We German filmmakers were still a fragile group in 1974, so when a friend called me from Paris to say that Lotte had suffered a massive stroke and I should get on the next aeroplane, I started looking for flights, before realising it wasn't the correct way to proceed. I was unable to accept that Lotte might die, and though it was the start of the onslaught of an early winter, I decided to walk from Munich to Paris. My pilgrimage was a million steps in rebellion against her death.

I stuffed a bundle of clothes and a map into a duffel bag, then set off in the straightest line possible, sleeping under bridges, in farms and abandoned houses. I made only one detour – to the town of Troyes, where I marvelled at the cathedral – and ended up walking across the Vosges mountains for about twenty miles, following the same route Büchner describes in *Lenz*. I'm not superstitious, but did feel that coming by foot would prevent Lotte's death. The Catholic Church has a wonderful term for this: *Heilsgewissheit*, the certainty of salvation. I moved with the faith of a pilgrim, convinced that Lotte would be alive when I got to Paris four weeks later. When I arrived in town I stopped at a friend's place to take shelter from the rain and sat in his office, steam coming off my clothes, utterly exhausted after having walked the last fifty miles without a break. I gave him my compass, which I no longer needed, and walked to Lotte's home. She was very surprised, but happy to see me. Years later, bedridden and nearly blind, unable to read or see films, Lotte wrote to me, asking if I would visit her. I went to Paris, where she told me, "Werner, there is still some spell cast that prevents me from dying. But I can barely walk. I am saturated with life [*lebenssatt*]. It would be a good time for me now." Jokingly, I said, "Lotte, I hereby lift the spell." Two weeks later she died. It was the right moment for her.

When you travel on foot it isn't a matter of covering actual territory, rather a question of moving through your own inner landscapes. I wrote a diary of my walk to Lotte – the story of a journey on foot – which is like a road movie that never lingers on physical landscapes. After some initial hesitation, then after excising the most private passages, I released it as a short book. *Of Walking in Ice* is literature created more by my feet than my head, and remains closer to my heart than any of my films.

You were friends with British novelist and travel writer Bruce Chatwin.

Bruce and I had an instantaneous connection because we both knew that travelling on foot is an essential part of being human. We shared the conviction that mankind's problems started the moment humans abandoned a nomadic existence, became sedentary, and began building permanent settlements.

I first met Bruce in 1984, when I was in Melbourne working on *Where the Green Ants Dream*. I read in the paper that he was in the country, so I immediately contacted his publishing company and tried to locate him. They told me he was somewhere in the desert in central Australia. Two days later they phoned back and said, "If you phone this number in Adelaide within the next twenty minutes, you can reach him before he goes to the airport." I called. "You're the one with the films!" Bruce said. I asked what his plans were. He was about to fly to Sydney and then London, but after a short conversation decided to head to Melbourne instead. How would I recognise him? "Look for a man with a leather rucksack," he said. Apparently Bruce knew some of my films and had read *Of Walking in Ice*, which he liked and said was one of the few books he always carried with him. We spent two days together, talking. For every story I told him, he would tell me three. We would sleep for a couple of hours, then wake up and carry on.

Years later, when he was ill, Bruce asked me to come and show him my film about the Wodaabe. Before I arrived I had no idea he was dying. He had the strength only to watch ten minutes at a time, but insisted on seeing the film anyway. He was lucid, but eventually became delirious, and would exclaim, "I have to be on the road again." "Yes," I said. "That's where you belong." He wanted me to come with him, so I explained we would walk together when he was strong enough. "My rucksack is heavy," he said. "I will carry it, Bruce," I told him. His bones were aching, and he asked me to shift him in his bed. He called his legs "the boys." One time he asked me, "Can you move the left boy to the other side?" He looked down and saw that his legs were so weak they were almost spindles. Then he looked at me and said, with great lucidity, "I will never walk again. I'm busy dying now." For years Bruce used a leather rucksack made by an old saddler in Cirencester. He carried it for five thousand miles on his back before giving it to me. "It's you who has to carry it now," he told me. It has always been much more than just something in which to carry things. If my house were on fire, I would first grab my children. Of all my belongings, it would be the rucksack I would throw from the window first.

Where did you get the idea for the Aboriginal drama Where the Green Ants Dream?

I first went to Australia in 1973, as a guest of the Perth Film Festival, where I saw a film by Michael Edols called *Lalai Dreamtime*, featuring Sam Woolagoodja, a saint-like, charismatic old Aborigine. I'm fascinated by the dignity and intensity of individuals and groups who have to defend themselves and their communities against the destruction of ancient traditions. I immediately decided I wanted to make a film with Sam, but he died before I got the chance. Nonetheless, the idea of setting a story in Australia, one that could feature some of the Aborigines I had met, stayed with me.

I had read several newspaper articles about a trial involving Nabalco, a Swiss bauxite-mining company in the northwest of the country, where various Aboriginal clans had lived since time immemorial, and whose sacred sites had been destroyed.* It was the first time the Aborigines had sued a mining company; they lost the case because they were unable to prove they had title to the land before 1788. At the end of the trial the judge acknowledged that the Aborigines had inhabited the territory for many thousands of years, and expressed genuine regret that Anglo-Saxon common law forced him to make a judgement in favour of the mining company. The ruling turned out to be a political victory because it raised public consciousness of the Aborigines; the case touched upon fundamental questions of identity and history, and how white Australians deal with Aboriginal culture. Several other cases eventually came to court that were mostly won by Aborigines. I was inspired to write the story of a group of Aborigines struggling to

* *Milirrpum* v. *Nabalco* (1971) 17 FLR 141 was the first litigation on land rights and native title in Australia. The Northern Territory Supreme Court ruled against the Aborigine claimants, a decision overruled by the High Court of Australia in 1992.

defend their sacred site – the place where the green ants dream – against the bulldozers of a mining company. The trial scenes in the film are based on genuine courtroom transcripts.

It was a pleasure working with the local Aborigines, although they raised a couple of objections. There was a deceased member of their community with the same name as one of the characters in the screenplay. Once someone dies their name mustn't be spoken out loud for at least ten years; the locals would talk instead of "the man who died." It meant I had to make some minor changes to the script. The other issue had to do with the sacred objects in the courtroom scene. During a case heard before the Supreme Court of the Northern Territories, the Aborigines brought with them objects that had been buried for about two hundred years, asking that all spectators in the courtroom be removed so they could show them only to the judge. They were carved wooden artefacts, completely beyond the comprehension of an Anglo-Saxon judge, though for the Aborigines they were irrevocable proof of why and how they had special connections to this territory. They asked me not to show any representations of these objects during the film's courtroom scene, and refused my offer to fabricate duplicates. These moments of the film have greater depth because audiences are forced to push their imaginations beyond what can actually be seen.

The Aborigines in *Where the Green Ants Dream* lived far from where we were filming, in a place called Yirrkala, near the Gulf of Carpentaria, in the north of the country. Most of the social structures of the Aboriginal communities throughout Australia had disintegrated, and in many parts of the country there were serious problems with alcoholism. People would get their social-security cheque on Friday morning, and by the afternoon most had already visited the liquor store. By the evening they were so drunk they had to be picked up off the streets. You see a similar phenomenon in any group of tribal people that has been abruptly thrown into a civilisation technically thousands of years ahead of its own. Many are unable to cope, like the Inuit in Alaska and the bushmen of the Kalahari. Wherever you go the problems – alcoholism, disintegration of society and criminality – are almost identical. But the group from Yirrkala was largely intact, handling the modern world with their traditional ways of doing things. I spent a lot of time talking with the lucid and dignified elders – who were able to exercise a level of control over the younger men – and explained my ideas about the story I had written.

At the time we made the film there wasn't a single Aboriginal community in the country that hadn't been in close contact with white civilisation for the past half-century. Aborigines are curious people and actively seek out the modern world; their culture might appear to be primitive, but is actually highly complex. These days very little is new to them. To say we're intruders into their society is a simplification.

What are green ants?

I respect the Aborigines in their struggle to keep their visions alive, but because my understanding of them was limited I wanted to develop my own mythology and create my own totem animal by inventing a legend that came close to their thinking and way of life. I made up the story of the green ants. It was never my intention to be anything like an anthropologist, strictly following the facts.

There's a character in the film who lives on a mountaintop because he believes there is nowhere else in Australia where the earth's magnetic field is so abnormally distorted. He explains that the green ant is the only living creature with a sensory organ attuned to magnetic fields, like a compass. They line up and all face north when a storm approaches, which is why it's said they dream about the origins of the world. In less than a day they can build six-foot termite hills hard as rock, with immense and intricate tunnel systems beneath. Once a year the ants grow wings and fly in gigantic swarms eastwards, across the mountains. There is actually a real species of ant with green tails, and we tried shooting a scene with four hundred thousand of them. I wanted them to face in the same direction, like soldiers aligned in a magnetic field, but they wouldn't behave. We came closest when they were placed in a storeroom that was at a temperature barely above freezing. They were immobilised by the cold, but as soon as the light was switched on they started to stir and move and bite; within fifteen seconds they were all over the place. If the storeroom had been half a degree colder, they would have died, so I called a halt to the whole thing. I won't be unhappy if readers come away from this book with nothing other than the fact that ants cannot be wrangled.

My understanding is that Aboriginal Dreamtime stories and myths – which were especially important to pre-colonial Aborigines – explain the origins of everything on the planet. *Where the Green Ants Dream* isn't their "dreaming"; it is, respectfully, my own, though it does come fairly close to a number of their myths. At the same time, I could never claim to make their cause my own. One of the tribesmen told me, "We don't understand you either, but we see you have your own dreaming." There are some beautiful things about the Aborigines I don't think we can ever truly comprehend; for example, how Australia is somehow covered with a network of dreams, or "songlines." The Aborigines sing songs when travelling, and through the words and rhythms are able to identify the landscapes, rocks and mountains around them. In his book about Australia, Bruce Chatwin writes about being in a car with some Aborigines who are singing in fast motion – as if you were running a tape at ten times the normal speed – because they were moving so fast. The rhythm of the song had to keep up with the landscape. Aborigines see themselves as part of the earth, so when we destroy the planet we also destroy them. "We don't own the land, the land owns us," Sam Woolagoodja told me. "We act as caretakers for our brothers. When you cut the land, you also cut me." In *Where the Green Ants Dream* the Aborigines sit in front of bulldozers that are tearing up the land, but this is no traditional sit-in; they are literally part of the rocks being removed. During the trial scene, a tribal elder asks the judge, "What would you do if bulldozers and pneumatic drills knocked down St Peter's Basilica in Rome or St Paul's Cathedral in London?"

I have to be careful when discussing these ideas because I'm no expert. I can't bear people – missionaries, anthropologists, politicians – who claim to understand Aboriginal society and culture. The Aborigines evolved during the Stone Age, something that profoundly influenced their way of life until maybe only two or three generations ago. Twenty thousand years of history separate us from them. Even if we spent fifty years living with the Aborigines and spoke their language, we would still only comprehend them marginally. Our backgrounds are different indeed; we are limited to our own thinking and culture, just as they are. People come back from a weekend trip to the outback and exclaim how magical it is, claiming an ability to feel in unison with the spirit of the native people. But no outsider – including white Australians – can ever truly understand such things.

You seem ambivalent about the film.

Where the Green Ants Dream isn't that bad, it just has a climate that these days I'm resistant to. For me the story is about protecting the spirit, traditions and mythology of the Aborigines, but the film has a slightly self-righteous tone to it, even if it does represent my thoughts and disquiet about contemporary society. It will always be important for me because the film is, in some sense, a requiem for my mother, who died just before we started shooting, and to whom I dedicated the film. I wrote the script when she was still alive, though from the start the spirit of the story had something of a requiem about it. I still appreciate the idea of the aeroplane – piloted by a mechanic who sings "My Baby Does the Hanky Panky" – that may or may not have crashed. Perhaps the Aborigines really have flown over the mountains and escaped into their dreamland, even if there are reports of an aeroplane wing having been found. I also like the shots at the beginning and end, those blurred, strange images that somehow represent the collapse of the world, even if they have nothing directly to do with the story. Jörg Schmidt-Reitwein spent weeks in Kansas, Oklahoma and Texas with scientists from a meteorological laboratory who were researching storms and chasing tornadoes. It's how I envision the collapse of the planet: a tornado wipes everything away, sucking it into the clouds. Years later I witnessed the destruction caused by Cyclone Tracy, which swept across Darwin in northwestern Australia. Among the debris I saw a water tower with a vast rectangular imprint on it. A huge refrigerator had flown through the air for a few miles and smashed into the tank a hundred feet above the ground.

You joined up with Kinski again to make Cobra Verde, *based on Chatwin's novel* The Viceroy of Ouidah.

The production was one of the worst I have ever experienced, and once filming was over it was clear I would never again work with Kinski. At the time I thought to myself, "Will somebody please step in and carry on the work with this man? Enough is enough."

Making *Cobra Verde* with him was like tracking a wild animal. If we wanted to catch the beast on film, we had to hide in the bushes for days at a time. Suddenly he would come and drink at the water-hole, but by the time we turned the camera on he had disappeared into the night. He was prone to bursts of fury, interspersed with moments of grace. It was no longer a case of rehearsing a scene or checking he was on his mark, but just rolling the camera as quickly as possible.

There was also something about Kinski's presence in the film that meant a foreign stink pervaded, and *Cobra Verde* suffers because of this. In some scenes there is a stylisation that Kinski forced on the production, one vaguely reminiscent of bad spaghetti westerns. It was a real problem holding him together during filming. He had recently married some Italian beauty queen and whenever he could find a phone line would talk for hours with her. From day one I struggled to harness his insanity, rage and demonic intensity. He was like a hybrid racehorse that would run a single mile and then collapse, but on *Cobra Verde* I was forced to carry him for five miles. At the time he was involved in an all-consuming project and had written a confused screenplay of the only film he was to direct: the life story of Paganini, with himself in the title role. For years he implored me to make the film, but I always said no; I knew this was something he had to do himself. I urge everyone to see *Kinski/Paganini* for no other reason than for years he claimed that I was a talentless imbecile and it was him who actually directed the films we made together. It will take you a long time to find a film as bad as his. See it and make up your own mind.

Every day I wondered if we would ever finish *Cobra Verde*. Kinski directed his abuse in the direction of cameraman Thomas Mauch, and terrorised him so badly I had to replace him within the first week. He wanted to stay, but unfortunately caught the brunt of Kinski early in the battle. I chose his replacement – the Czech Viktor Růžička – because I heard he was physically strong, built like a peasant and very patient. Anyone else would probably have quit within two hours. Nothing really changed once Mauch was gone, and it remains a very bitter moment for me. Abandoning my loyalty to him was one of the most difficult things I have ever done.

How was production in Africa?

Sometimes it was so hot you couldn't step outside. To find a working telephone was a major chore, there was hardly any gasoline for our vehicles and I struggled to find sufficient accommodation, transport and food for cast and crew. In northern Ghana, near Tamale, two hundred people worked around the clock for ten weeks constructing a palace out of clay and making several thousand plaster skulls. There wasn't a single kilo of plaster to be found in the entire country when we began. Félix Houphouët-Boigny, the president of neighbouring Côte d'Ivoire, had one ambition: to build the largest church on the planet, which he eventually did in his home town of Yamoussoukro. We knew there must be a lot of plaster over there, so we bribed some construction workers and drove several vans of the stuff across the border, which meant we could fabricate the skulls we needed. The entire palace collapsed about a week after filming had finished because of a particularly fierce rainstorm. All the costumes and props for the film had to be produced in a very short period of time, which caused endless headaches because everything in Africa takes much longer than it should. It isn't a question of money; even with $25 million I would have had as many problems. You have to deviate from your normal way of doing things and try to understand the tempo of the continent. A strict Prussian military type would buckle in a matter of days. In the midst of all this was Kinski, in a ferocious rage, holding up shooting because one of the buttons on his costume was loose.

We spent several weeks working with an army of a thousand young Amazon women. They were gathered together at a football stadium in Accra, where Benito Stefanelli – an Italian stunt co-ordinator who had worked on Sergio Leone's films – trained them in the use of swords and shields. They were a truly frightening bunch of ferocious, eloquent, proud, strong women. On pay day we lined them up in the inner yard of the slave fortress and opened a small gate through the main door, with the idea that they would walk through one after the other. From inside, eight hundred of them pushed against the door at the same time and squashed the ones at the front almost to death. Some of the women were already fainting, and after narrowly avoiding being torn to pieces I was able to calm the potentially fatal situation by grabbing a nearby policeman, dragging him over to the gate and having him fire three shots into the air.

When did you first read Chatwin's novel?

Around the time of *Fitzcarraldo* I read his book *In Patagonia*, the story of a long walk, and was so impressed I immediately read *On the Black Hill* and *The Viceroy of Ouidah*, the nineteenth-century story of the bandit Francisco Manoel da Silva, who is cheated of his wages as a gold miner, then travels from drought-ridden Brazil to the kingdom of Dahomey in Africa and becomes a viceroy and slave trader. It was full of fascinating characters and showed a great sensitivity for Africa, as well as being centred around the slave trade, so I immediately thought it would make a magnificent film. I'm a great admirer of Joseph Conrad – especially his *The Nigger of the "Narcissus"*, *Typhoon* and *Heart of Darkness* – and feel that Bruce is somehow in the same league. He has the touch you rarely see in literature. I let him know about my interest in the book, but added I couldn't undertake such a monstrous project right after *Fitzcarraldo*. I had to lick my wounds for a while and work on projects like *Where the Green Ants Dream*, some operas, some smaller films. I asked Bruce to let me know if someone else wanted to buy the rights to his book, and a few years later he got in touch to say David Bowie's agents had expressed an interest. Apparently Bowie was more interested in buying the rights so he could play the lead character than in directing the film, so I told Bruce to sell the book to Bowie on the condition that I direct. I felt attached to the project like a dog to a bone, and eventually bought the rights myself because I was convinced Bowie wasn't right for the role of Francisco Manoel. He lacks the mystery and savagery of the character, and has no real depth. The man is a neon light bulb.

I felt there wasn't a single Hollywood actor – dead or alive – capable of playing the part. Although he immediately came to mind, and though I tried to ignore him, the only person I could think of for the role was Kinski. If you read the published script, you'll notice that every character except Francisco Manoel is described in precise physical terms. This was because I wanted to avoid describing Kinski on the page; I didn't want to allow him to penetrate my imagination and insert himself into the film. But while I was writing the script, throughout that long week when I was working away at my typewriter, he appeared between the lines, worming his way onto the pages. The script was like a boat taking on water, with Kinski slipping in through every crack. By the time I had finished, no other possibility existed. Some facts have to be faced whether you want to or not, so I immediately called Kinski, and though he was really too old for the part, I told him, "If you don't take this role, I won't make the film."

The novel doesn't have a linear narrative.

Rather than having the structure of a cinematic work, *The Viceroy of Ouidah* captures the inner world of this character, as well as offering a rich understanding of Africa and the slave trade. The first thing I did was explain to Bruce that his book's narrative wasn't a cinematic one, which meant there would be certain technical issues in adapting it for the screen. The novel is narrated in a series of concentric circles, but I knew a film would have to proceed in a more linear way, so I told Bruce my plan was to invent things and make some changes. I let the story move through the action at its own speed and turned it into a fable, a ballad, which is made clear by the opening scene of the blind fiddler. Bruce never wanted to get mixed up with the screenplay or involve himself in the pro-duction, though he was on location with us for a few days* and before I wrote the screenplay recommended I read an obscure book from 1874 called *Dahomey as It Is*, which provided details for *The Viceroy of Ouidah*. It was written by a British biologist named J. A. Skertchly, who was studying beetles in a coastal region of Dahomey, which is now Benin. Skertchly was asked if he would travel to the king's residence and stay for a few days to instruct the palace guards in the use of their new rifles. The king began to enjoy his conversations with Skertchly so much that a week became eight months. In his book he describes in almost scientific detail time spent at the king's court – where he was treated as a prisoner – and his testimony constitutes a unique and exceptional document.

What I took from Bruce's book was the African atmosphere the text is so effective at creating. I travelled through Brazil, Mali, Ghana

* See Chatwin's essay "Werner Herzog in Ghana," in *What Am I Doing Here* (Vintage, 1998).

and Côte d'Ivoire, before deciding that Colombia and Ghana were the best places to shoot the film. Ghana was one of the first African states to become independent. Culturally speaking, it's probably the most refined nation on the continent, and the people there possess a great self-confidence. For centuries the English, Portuguese, Dutch and French colonials tried to get rid of the multitude of little kingdoms, but after independence successive governments refused to abolish them. Ghana's leaders understood the importance and usefulness of the ancient local cultural traditions.

Were you especially interested in the slavery narrative of The Viceroy of Ouidah?

Neither the film nor Bruce's novel is explicitly about slavery; I don't consider *Cobra Verde* to be an historical film, just as I never saw *Aguirre* and *The Enigma of Kaspar Hauser* as faithful representations of certain events. The story is about the fantasies and follies of the human spirit, not colonialism. I was interested in Francisco Manoel's relationship with power, though I didn't particularly want to explain why this enigmatic character becomes a bandit or describe his psychological journey from South America to Africa. He'll do anything to escape poverty, even if – as he says – it costs him his life. He becomes a slave trader in Africa after overhearing rich landowners in Brazil discussing their plan to send him to his death, because for the last ten years the king of Dahomey has killed every foreigner who has set foot on the soil of his country. It's pure defiance of what awaits him that pushes Francisco Manoel to confront the situation head on and accept the job without hesitation. He has a grander design than those of his enemies and is prepared to walk directly to his apparent doom. When he reaches west Africa, Francisco Manoel boldly demands that the slave fortress – which has long since been abandoned and looted – is turned over to him and the slave trade resumed.

Although much discussed in the United States and the Caribbean, in many African countries the wounds of slavery are still so deep that people don't speak about it in public. The subject remains taboo, I suspect, because of the well-established fact that African kingdoms were implicated in the slave trade almost as deeply as white traders. There was also a great deal of trading between the

Arab world and black Africa, and even between African nations themselves. Setting the story of *Cobra Verde* during the last days of slave trafficking means moving it beyond a simple account of an historical phenomenon. As Francisco Manoel says, "Slavery was not a misunderstanding, it was a great crime. Slavery is an element of the human heart." In other words, no amount of legislation will truly eradicate it.

Africa, not Kinski, is the star.

I was never so successful in filming the landscapes and capturing the spirit of the continent. There are some shots in the film – like the one of the crippled boy who shuffles away from the camera and stops when he reaches the steps, which he is unable to climb – that illustrate the pain slavery has inflicted upon an entire continent. It's almost as if this boy represents Francisco Manoel's guilt, and it reminds me of the sequence at the end of *Where the Green Ants Dream* with the girl sitting in the mining encampment clutching a stone as she listens to a voice on the radio screaming about a goal scored by Argentina during a football match. Both images carry great pathos and sadness, somehow summing up the heart of these films.

The South American sequences of *Cobra Verde* always felt heavy to me; the African part of the story is much more interesting. What audiences see of the continent are things they aren't used to, like court rituals and flag signals along the coast, and the wonderfully anarchic and chaotic crowd scenes have real life to them. In most films set in Africa the place is portrayed either as a crumbling, primitive and dangerous place full of savages, or with a kind of *Out of Africa* nostalgia. *Cobra Verde* deviates from all that. I set out to show things that had been ignored, like the continent's sophisticated and complex social structures, its kingdoms, tribes and hierarchies. I even managed to get His Royal Highness Nana Agyefi Kwame II, the real king of Nsein, to play the king of Dahomey. He was a wonderful and dignified man who brought three hundred members of his court with him to the set. I hadn't originally planned a scene with his entourage, but they looked so magnificent that I put them in the film. Everything and everyone you see around him is authentic; all the jesters, princes, princesses, ministers, dancers and musicians, and the traditional objects they carry. These are the kinds of characters that could never be invented. Kwame II exercised a powerful authority over everyone – even Kinski – and I could never have found anyone more convincing than him to play the king. At one point Kinski attacked a member of the crew and insulted the hundreds of Africans who had come there especially for us. He started to pack his bags, and all the king's extras were also about to leave. Kwame II explained to Kinski that filming had to continue and that he had to stay, that there were too many important things being said for the first time in the film about slavery, about Africa, about the history of the continent for anyone to allow the production to be halted. Kinski never again raised his voice against the Africans. The king literally saved the film.

I have never seen your short Les Français vus par . . . Les Gauloises.

It was made as part of a compilation film; the other directors included David Lynch, Jean-Luc Godard and Andrzej Wajda. For my contribution I purchased a $1,000 bottle of wine and brought together Claude Josse and Jean Clemente, two of the greatest living French sommeliers, then filmed them opening the wine and gushing poetic descriptions. As a contrast, I wanted to film some real Celtic people; for me they were best represented by members of the Stade Toulousain rugby team, who allowed me into their locker room before a match. I watched them spend a few hours physically menace each other and work themselves up into an absolutely berserk mood as preparation for meeting their opponents out on the field.

Could any of your films be categorised as ethnography or anthropology?

Only in so far as my goal is to use cinema to explore and chronicle the human condition and our states of mind. I don't make films using only images of clouds and trees; I work with human beings because the way they function within different cultural groups interests me. If that makes me an anthropologist, so be it. But I never think in terms of strict ethnography, going out to some distant island with the explicit purpose of studying the natives and their communities.

I understand what you're getting at with a question like that, but a film like *Wodaabe, Herdsmen of the Sun* can't be seriously considered ethnographic because it's stylised to such an extent that the audience is taken into the realm of the ecstatic. I don't deny you can learn a certain number of facts about the Wodaabe from the film, but that was never my primary intention. There is no voiceover, and even the short text at the start tells you only the barest facts about these people, that they have been around since the Stone Age and are a ragged tribe despised by neighbouring peoples. I purposefully pull away from anything that could be considered anthropological. In the opening scene of the bizarre male beauty contest, the tribesmen are rolling their eyeballs, extolling the whiteness of their teeth and making ecstatic faces. The fact that they were being filmed made no difference; they were completely immersed in the spectacle. These young men are so wildly stylised, why shouldn't I be too? On the soundtrack we hear a 1901 recording of Gounod's *Ave Maria* from an Edison cylinder, sung by the last castrato of the Vatican, which creates a strange, almost ecstatic feeling, and establishes a powerful counterpoint between music and images. A traditional ethnographic filmmaker would never dare do anything like that. Using this specific recording helps carry us out of the realm of what I call the accountant's truth; anything else wouldn't touch us so deeply. It means the film isn't a documentary about a specific African tribe, rather a story about beauty and desire. It's the same idea as when I used drumming music from Burundi in *Fitzcarraldo*, which has nothing per se to do with the Amazon jungle, and is why, at the end of *Little Dieter Needs to Fly*, you hear a piece of music sung in Malagasy that was recorded in 1931 in Madagascar. I can't tell you how many people asked me why I didn't use Laotian or Vietnamese music.

What drew you to the nomadic Wodaabe of the southern Sahara?

They are scornfully referred to by neighbouring peoples as "Bororo," a term of abuse roughly meaning "ragged shepherds." Wodaabe, the name they call themselves, means "those under the taboo of purity." They number no more than about two hundred thousand, and travel through the Sahel zone of the desert from Senegal on the Atlantic almost across to the Nile, particularly Mali and Niger. We know Wodaabe have been in the Sahara since time immemorial because the brand marks on their cattle are the same as those found on six-thousand-year-old rock engravings in the Aïr mountains. They have no concept of modern-day borders and are in strong danger of disappearing because their living space has shrunk as a result of the dramatic southwards spread of the desert. The Wodaabe don't know where they come from; their myths make vague mention of crossing a great stretch of water in the east. Since their language is unrelated to that of any other African peoples and they have light skin and sharp-featured, narrow faces, some people believe they must have come from Mesopotamia, crossing the Red Sea in prehistoric times.

The Wodaabe consider themselves to be the most beautiful people on earth. The men compete against each other in contests, while the young women assign one of themselves to select the most handsome man. She picks one out and disappears with him into the bush for a few nights. Most of the women are already married, which is why they return their booty to the bosom of his family once they are finished with him. Occasionally they keep the man for themselves, resuming their nomadic journey with him. During the preparations for their beauty contests groups of young men in the encampments joke and laugh, making themselves as beautiful as possible; they dress up and put on make-up made from natural dyes that have been pounded into powder. Some take a whole day to prepare for the festival, which starts at dawn and lasts five days. It's thought to be particularly beautiful to show as much of one's teeth and the white of the eyeball as possible, and some of the men roll their eyes upwards as if in ecstasy. A succession of complex dances and ritu-als are performed, with the men in straight lines, striding forward, grimacing ecstatically, then retreating until the moment of decision, when the winner is chosen. One of the women I filmed joked that none of the men were anything special – actually on the ugly side – and that the one she had spent the previous night with was a wimp of a lover. She was determined to find a better one.

Jean-Bédel Bokassa is the subject of Echoes from a Sombre Empire.

It was during the making of *Fata Morgana* that I first went to the Central African Republic, after having been released from prison in Cameroon. Let me say this about my time there: if you were driving a Land Rover and suddenly the vehicle was surrounded by a crowd of screaming people, the only sane thing to do was put your foot down and get the hell out of there. Bokassa had assumed power after a *coup d'état* in 1966, and in 1977 proclaimed himself emperor. He was truly bizarre; the evil sparkling of this incredible character was fascinating to me. Bokassa was completely unlike Léopold Sédar Senghor, who, before he became the first president of Senegal, had studied Western thought and philosophy. Bokassa was, alongside Idi Amin, the most African of African leaders. Film allows us to reveal the least understood truths of man. It delves into our fantasies and dreams, in this case our nightmares. Bokassa represented the kind of human darkness you find in Nero or Caligula, and *Echoes from a Sombre Empire* was an attempt to explore the dark abysses that lie at the heart of man. Some reviews inevitably said the film should have focused more on French foreign policy and history, but it isn't for me to discuss such things. I leave that to the journalists.

There was a cornucopia of stories surrounding Bokassa and his regime, most of which are well documented today. He had a number of children killed because they weren't wearing school uniforms, and spent a third of the country's national budget to pay for his coronation. He personally presided over the judicial system, had people indiscriminately thrown to the crocodiles, and apparently fathered fifty-four children. The cult of personality surrounding him was astonishing. He awarded himself a huge number of medals, all of which he would wear at public events, claimed he was bulletproof and could read people's minds, issued orders to have the ears of thieves cut off and personally beat inmates to death with his ivory-topped cane. The deeper I dug, the more I discovered tragedies worthy of Shakespeare. There is the tale of the two Martines, a film in itself. When Bokassa was a soldier in Indochina he had a child called Martine with a local woman. Once in power he decided to find his daughter and bring her to Africa, but the girl who was found and brought over turned out not to be the real Martine. When he eventually did find the genuine Martine he allowed the other one to stay, and the two women were married on the same day in a huge celebration, though soon afterwards both husbands were executed. Apparently one of them was involved in the murder of the other's newborn child. Bokassa decided to send the "fake" Martine back to Vietnam. She was put on an aeroplane that returned only half an hour later; it was obvious she had been pushed out over the jungle. Bokassa's crumbling palace represented the melancholy of his story. A building like that quickly decays in such a climate. Compare it to the seventeenth-century castles in Scotland, overgrown with ivy and moss, which have aged beautifully.

After he was deposed, Bokassa fled to France and was condemned to death *in absentia*. A few years later, however, he decided he couldn't stand the French winters, so, cold and homesick, he boarded a commercial airliner, believing he would be received like Napoleon returning from exile, his nation on its knees before him. He was immediately arrested, put on trial and condemned to death again, though his sentence was later commuted to life imprisonment, then twelve years, then house arrest. Permission came down from President Kolingba to film with Bokassa, and he wanted to meet us, but at the last minute we were expelled from the country by the minister of the interior. He was apparently implicated in several crimes from the Bokassa era, so didn't appreciate us being so nosy.

Did the man really eat human flesh?

The German ambassador to the Central African Republic told me that after an execution in front of the press and diplomatic corps, the execution squad rushed forward, ripped the liver from the body and ate it. After speaking to so many people who had stories about Bokassa, I quickly realised that when there is so much hearsay about a single man or event – when you hear the same stories from so many different people – speculation condenses into something factual. We have to believe it. The deeper truth of the situation is outside our reach, but not the facts. Bokassa was a cannibal. During his trial – which was videotaped in its entirety – there were precise witness accounts, including one from Bokassa's cook. When the French paratroopers who assisted in deposing Bokassa opened up the huge refrigerators in his palace, they found half of one of the emperor's ministers frozen solid. The other half had been eaten during a banquet.

Cannibalism is a documented phenomenon of many human societies, but when we made the film even those officials who had been in opposition to the Bokassa regime flatly denied he ever ate anyone. Such behaviour clearly breaks so many taboos, and admitting it somehow casts the whole continent of Africa in a bad light. You see the same kind of thing in Mexico, where some people still maintain the Aztecs never sacrificed human beings or practised cannibalism because they consider it so shameful. They make wild suggestions that such claims are a fabrication of the Spanish to denigrate the Aztec way of life.

Michael Goldsmith guides us through the story of Bokassa's regime.

I encountered Michael – who at the time was the head of the African branch of the Associated Press – after having read some of his published dispatches. I don't recall exactly where I first met him, but like those who have crossed the Sahara, people who have been in the Central African Republic during Bokassa's reign or the chaos of the Congo somehow find each other. I can't explain how such people connect; we just recognise one another. Michael Goldsmith was different from most journalists I had met in Africa. Many were young social climbers or ageing, cynical alcoholics, but Michael expressed a certain philosophical attitude. He had reported from around the world for decades, and I appreciated his outlook on life. From the moment I encountered him I knew he was the key to telling Bokassa's story, which is why I always saw *Echoes from a Sombre Empire* more as a journey into a personal nightmare than a documentary. In the seventies he had been accused by Bokassa of being a spy and was sentenced to death. He almost died after being beaten with the imperial sceptre by the emperor himself, then manacled to the wall of a rat-infested cell, and was saved only after his wife intervened. Years later, once Bokassa had been deposed, Michael was anxious to return to the Central African Republic.

Although he looked like a kindly librarian, Michael was a courageous man who was used to being in dangerous situations and had real insight into Africa. Soon after we finished the film he went to Liberia and was taken prisoner by a faction of insurgent rebels, most of them child soldiers. Eight-year-old children wearing rags and brandishing Kalashnikovs and M16s were shooting at everything that moved. Michael told me they were usually drunk or stoned, and one time raided a bridal store so they could dress up as bride and groom. The "bride" was an eight-year-old boy wearing a veil and a gown with high heels that were much too big for him who fired his rifle wildly, and the "groom" was naked except for a tailcoat that dragged after him. Very strange images. Michael was held captive in a building from where they had shot a passer-by; day after day he watched the body decompose. By the end dogs were carrying away the last pieces and only a dark spot remained. He managed to get home and saw *Echoes from a Sombre Empire* at the Venice Film Festival. Three weeks later he died.

Is The Eccentric Private Theatre of the Maharaja of Udaipur *another of your "utility" films?*

Sort of. I made it after receiving an invitation from André Heller, an Austrian director and creator of events who had travelled across India and appears at the start of film. He talks about the incomparable nature of the country, its extraordinary cultural diversity and the hundreds of languages spoken, and about how the arts in India are what he calls a "life-sustaining" force. André – who once created what might have been the largest fireworks display ever in Europe – asked if I wanted to film the mammoth event he had organised at the City Palace of Udaipur, on the banks of Lake Pichola in India. At the behest of the Maharaja of Udaipur, who wanted in some way to document the rich heritage of the country before "McDonaldisation" triumphed over everything, André planned to bring together a vast range of Indian performers. He had a permit from the maharaja to stage what became the events of the film, and sent out people throughout India in search of magicians, singers, dancers, snake charmers and fire-eaters, ending up with something like two thousand performers who spoke a total of twenty-three languages. I get sent a lot of screenplays that people want me to make, but I don't get many requests to make films like this, so I agreed because André's ideas were unique. The actual event took place over just a single day, but I spent a few days shooting rehearsals. I made the film for a friend and enjoyed travelling to India, somewhere I had never been. It was good to capture things that would otherwise have been ephemeral. I flavoured the film by inventing a background story – influenced by Satyajit Ray's *The Music Room* – about the palace of a fabulously wealthy maharaja which is crumbling underneath him.

Scream of Stone is reminiscent of pre-war German "mountain cinema."

Throughout the twenties German directors like Luis Trenker and Arnold Fanck produced a number of *Bergfilme* [mountain films], but unfortunately the genre later fell in step with Nazi ideology, which is probably the reason it's somewhat unexplored today. I liked the idea of creating a new, contemporary form of *Bergfilm*, like Peter Fleischmann did when he used the elements and rules of the *Heimatfilm* in his film *Hunting Scenes from Bavaria*, bringing new depth to the genre. But I would never push the idea of making a connection between *Scream of Stone* and those melodramas of the twenties – which I've never actually seen – including those featuring Leni Riefenstahl.

Scream of Stone had a problematic birth. Reinhold Messner – with whom I had worked on *The Dark Glow of the Mountains* – had an idea based on a true story about the first apparently successful attempt on Cerro Torre, a peak in Patagonia. Cesare Maestri, the Italian climber who would scale mountains with pneumatic drills, claimed to have reached the summit, but there had been instant doubt as to whether this was true, due to the fact that his climbing partner had never returned and his body never recovered. Walter Saxer, my production manager, picked up the story and developed it with a colleague. He wanted to go beyond the usual boundaries of German cinema, and from the start was the driving force behind the film. I immediately liked the ideas they came up with. There was something wonderfully physical about the story that I found interesting, but the script had many weak points, particularly the dialogue, and needed real work, so I hesitated about accepting the project because at first I didn't know how I could improve it. Finally we came to an agreement and I stepped into the film, but immediately found myself up against a brick wall when it came to making substantive changes.

Saxer was bull-headed about everything, so I can't even say that *Scream of Stone* is my film, though it does contain some impressive sequences, like the one where Stefan Glowacz climbs up a mountain vertically, then horizontally and then vertically again, all without a safety line, all in a single take, all with the most stunning landscape behind him and a gaping abyss below. It's the most extraordinary thing you'll ever see on screen, much more so than anything in a Hollywood blockbuster. At the time Glowacz was the "rock master," the world-champion free-climber, and actually did three takes of this climb before calmly saying, "No more, Werner. My arms are boiling." The character of Fingerless, played by Brad Dourif, who turns out to be one of the few climbers who actually makes it to the top of Cerro Torre, leaving a picture of Mae West there as proof, was the only character in the original script I was allowed to make changes to. He writes a hundred and sixty letters to Mae before finally getting a response: "Come back from your mountain, climber, and see me sometime. There's a hell of a mountain waiting for you." The original idea was to cast Messner in the film. After my experiences with him on *The Dark Glow of the Mountains* I felt he could handle the role, but then I met the Italian actor Vittorio Mezzogiorno and immediately knew he should play the part. I think Messner was almost relieved he had been passed over, though he would have been good in the film.

Did your previous experiences with Messner help you on Scream of Stone?

To a certain extent. Cerro Torre is the most dangerous, difficult and ecstatic peak on earth, a 4,000-feet-high needle of basalt sticking straight up into the sky. It's more a symbolic image of deadly fear than a mere mountain. For many years it was considered unclimbable; the first verified ascent was sometime in the mid-seventies. More people have climbed Mount Everest than have ever made it to the top of Cerro Torre. You can only truly understand why it strikes so much fear into the hearts of climbers when you see the peak before you. There may be higher mountains to scale, but what makes Cerro Torre particularly treacherous are the sheer cliff faces and weather conditions. Most of the time there's a pandemonium of storms that make the summit invisible. I call them storms, but we don't really have an equivalent in our language to describe the phenomenon. The winds easily reach a hundred miles an hour at the top; our tripod was cemented down but still needed five men to hold it steady. Ice fragments and stones the size of my fist get torn away and come shooting by like bullets. One time a sudden storm hit, and two of our climbers, hanging onto the rock face, immediately dumped their rucksacks so they could get back to our encampment fast enough. These bags didn't fall to the ground; they just sailed away horizontally, never to be seen again. On a mountain near Cerro Torre I saw the unforgettable sight of wind hitting a waterfall with such force that it literally flowed vertically upwards, dissipating into mist.

Were you ever on the summit of Cerro Torre yourself?

Twice, both times by helicopter, which took five minutes. The second time I landed on the summit I stepped out of the helicopter with Mezzogiorno, turned around and saw him lying as flat as he could on the ground, his nails dug as deep into the ice as he could get them. I asked what was wrong. "I want to get up but my body won't co-operate," he said meekly. "Give me a little more time." I spoke to Hans Kammerlander – the climber who appears in *The Dark Glow of the Mountains* and has a small role in *Scream of Stone* – about the ice cave that had been built at the top of Cerro Torre and stocked with eight days' worth of provisions, in case we needed to take refuge. When Kammerlander saw me walking towards it without holding on to the rope, he grabbed me and said, "If you start to slide, there's nothing anyone can do for you. You will accelerate, then be airborne for a mile." Kammerlander looked me right in the eye. "If that happens," he said, "promise me one thing: enjoy the vista."

At one point our helicopter took Stefan Glowacz, a cameraman and me up to a ridge not far from Cerro Torre's peak to prepare a sequence. Normally a team of climbers would make extensive preparations, like building an emergency shelter and taking up provisions and equipment, after which the actors and technical crew would follow. A storm had been raging for ten days, but suddenly we had a calm, crystal-clear night, followed by a beautiful morning without wind. The conditions looked so good we made the mistake of flying up there without sending a vanguard. Once we were dropped at the ridge, the three of us started walking towards our location. All of a sudden, out of the corner of my eye, I saw something absolutely outrageous, something I will surely never witness again in my life. Below us, as far as the eye could see, were clouds; they looked like motionless balls of cotton. All of a sudden everything exploded like gigantic atomic bombs. I immediately radioed the helicopter, which was still in sight, and watched as it made a loop towards us. It came as close as 150 feet before the storm hit us like a bullet. The clouds were over us, there was a gust of more than a hundred miles an hour, and the temperature fell thirty degrees. After twenty seconds my moustache was a lump of ice. The helicopter was literally tossed away and we found ourselves alone with no sleeping bags, tents, food or ropes. Nothing except two ice picks. We had to dig ourselves into the snow immediately, otherwise we would have frozen to death within a few hours.

We spent just over two days and nights in the snow hole. All we had to eat was a small piece of chocolate I had in my pocket. You can get by with nothing to eat for fifty hours, but water is something else; you have to drink at least a gallon of water a day, otherwise your toes and fingers freeze away. Ninety-five per cent of all losses of digits are the result of dehydration. After twenty hours some of my toes were turning black, and the cameraman, a very tough man, was in bad shape. He was running a temperature and having cramps. We used our walkie-talkie only every two hours for a few seconds to save batteries, and radioed down that he wouldn't survive another night. This stark message alarmed our team in the valley, and two teams of four climbers were sent out to reach us. The strongest of them became delirious, threw his gloves into the storm, then clicked his fingers, insisting on calling a waiter over so he could pay for his cappuccino. They had to guide him down back to the glacier, but an avalanche swept them down two hundred feet and they had no choice but to dig a snow cave themselves because one of them had lost his sunglasses and showed signs of snow blindness. After fifty hours, the clouds burst open for ten minutes, and with this lull in the storm the helicopter was able to pick us up. The pilot was in a panic and couldn't wait until the last person – me – had scrambled inside, so I crouched in a basket outside the helicopter and held on to a metal bar. When we finally touched down, my hand had frozen to the bar. It thawed out after one of the Argentinian climbers urinated on it.

Talk about your approach to editing.

The most important thing to say about editing is that it isn't a technical process. It comes from something much deeper, from an understanding of the vision behind the images and the story you need to tell. If you don't have that, your work will be subject to whims and continual fumbling. The danger of digital non-linear editing is the ability to create twenty parallel versions of your film, which is a meaningless act. Those who produce such things are irretrievably lost in their material.

I have always been very specific about what I film, and never shoot endless amounts of footage. Every second of celluloid costs money, so the impetus when shooting on film is to expose as little raw stock as possible. Even today, when I make a film on video I never end up with a lot of footage. If you let the tape run and run, you'll have three hundred hours of mediocrity. Some filmmakers wear the fact they have so much material as a badge of honour, but attempting to be encyclopaedic is a misguided strategy, practised only by accountants. Most filmmakers with that much footage don't know what they're doing; I know I'm talking to a spendthrift when I meet a director who tells me they worked for years editing a film.

The way I work is to look through everything I have – very quickly, over a couple of days – and make notes. For all my films over the past decade I have kept a logbook in which I briefly describe, in longhand, the details of every shot and what people are saying. I know there's a particularly wonderful moment at minute 4:13 on tape eight because I have marked the description of the action with an exclamation point. These days my editor Joe Bini and I just move from one exclamation point to the next; anything unmarked is almost always bypassed. When it comes to those invaluable clips with three exclamation marks, I tell Joe, "If these moments don't appear in the finished film, I have lived in vain." With digital technology, anything mediocre or that detracts from the story is easily junked, and the remaining material melted down to the absolutely vital moments. I can edit almost as fast as I can think because I'm able to sink details of fifty hours of footage into my mind. This might have something to do with the fact that I started working on film, when there was so much celluloid about the place that you had to know where absolutely every frame was.

But my memory of all this footage never lasts long, and within two days of finishing editing it becomes a blur in my mind.

I can identify the strongest material at great speed, and rarely change my mind once I make a decision. Usually we can piece together a first assembly of what the final film will be in less than a fortnight. We never look at what we edited the previous day; every morning we start from the point where we finished the day before. Once we have worked through the entire film, we move backwards; this keeps the material fresh and ensures that only footage of the highest calibre remains. It isn't that I have a particularly slovenly attitude to the editing process; I'm just ruthless with the decisions I make. I feel safe in my skills of navigation and never try out twenty different versions of the same sequence. On the few occasions an editor has persuaded me to go back and look at something I decided against, or to cut a sequence in a new way, it almost always turns out not to have been worth the effort. Occasionally, however, it pays dividends. One recent instance stands out, when Joe Bini and I were working on *Bad Lieutenant*. There is a sequence in a moving car where Nicolas Cage pulls out his Magnum and threatens to shoot everyone. The drug dealer appeases him by giving him a bag of heroin. In one of the takes Nicolas went beyond the script. He grinned, waved his gun and said, "I'm going to kill you all to the break of dawn!" It didn't feel right to me, but Joe thought it was great material and asked me to consider it in the context of this character's evolution. After he put together the final thirty minutes of the film I was able to see exactly how the scene fit in the story as a whole, and realised that both Joe and Nicolas were right.

Let me say something here about how time and money is wasted during post-production, in particular when it comes to documentaries. I often meet people who make detailed transcripts of the conversations they have recorded, then prepare "paper edits" of their films. I've never seen the point of all this. If you focus only on the words on the page and don't watch the actual images and listen to the people talking, you bypass the nuances, rhythms of speech and physical gestures. You'll never understand the fundamental spirit of the person and, in turn, of the conversation. Editing a film from a transcript can be misleading. You might think it's possible to cut a piece of dialogue very cleanly, when in reality the person you filmed was talking very quickly and ran one sentence into the next in the same breath. More importantly, you miss the sometimes extraordinarily powerful silences. I categorically forbid transcripts to be made until a film is finished, and only then for legal and archival reasons.

Have you ever reached the editing stage and found the footage an unworkable mess?

Never. If you have footage of real substance, it will always connect and cut together. The first version of *Invincible* was too long, so I put it aside for six weeks and tried to forget about it; I needed some distance between the film and me. After a day of condensing and tightening, I cut forty minutes. Sometimes an individual scene won't work exactly as planned. I shot an intense seven-minute sequence for *The Enigma of Kaspar Hauser* with Kaspar and an impoverished peasant who, in despair, had killed his last surviving cow. The idea was to place the scene about two-thirds of the way into the film. It made sense in the context of the story but somehow disrupted the flow of the narrative, shifting the focus of the story away from Kaspar. The scene detoured the audience too much, and it would have taken several minutes to get back into the story once it was over. Although it was one of the two or three best sequences I have ever shot, I threw it out.

Beate Mainka-Jellinghaus joined you on the set of Stroszek.

I don't particularly like confronting my footage alone, and prefer working closely with an editor. Having another pair of eyes that can help me discover qualities and elements I might have missed is always valuable. I like having collaborators around me, people with their own vision, though none of my editors over the years have had complete freedom; I'm present throughout the entire editing process. Beate Mainka-Jellinghaus edited for Alexander Kluge before working on several of my early films, including *Aguirre* and *Land of Silence and Darkness*, and was truly gifted at instantly sensing the quality of the footage in front of her, always able to identify what material worked and what didn't.

Starting with *Signs of Life*, the first film we made together, Beate always complained about how bad my films were; she thought they were so embarrassingly terrible that she never went to the opening night of any of them, with the exception of *Even Dwarfs Started Small*. We checked the first reel of *Signs of Life* on the flatbed, a 2,000-foot roll. It had been coiled the wrong way from the end, so she put it on the machine and spun it backwards, about five times as fast as it would normally be viewed. Then she grabbed the whole reel and threw it into the garbage, saying, "This is so bad I'm not going to touch it again." I was aghast, but after a couple of weeks looked at the reel again in the context of the film as a whole and realised she was right. Beate was able to spot good footage just as quickly. While some people have perfect pitch when it comes to music, she was able to express a sensibility for film material that corresponded to my own. Her grumbling about the terrible footage I was forever dumping on her doorstep was somehow a challenge; it pushed me to do the best I possibly could. I loved seeing her with those reels that she truly felt had such little value because I knew she would work harder than anyone to salvage whatever good might be in them.

For years I explained to Beate that much of what she complained about when in the editing room was due to the physical circumstances of shooting, that there were always obstacles that I struggled with on location, that every shot involved some sort of compromise. "If you don't believe me," I told her, "why not come to the set of the next film?" She came to do continuity and watch the filming of *Stroszek* in Germany and America, and hated every day of shooting even more than the time she later spent editing the film. She found the whole experience, and the story, completely disgusting, and would sometimes signal to the cameraman to stop the whole damned thing, including one take when Bruno and Eva Mattes were doing some of the best work I have ever seen. But that's life; you have to accept strong collaborators. I don't need yes-men and -women around me, a docile crew that tells me everything I do is great. What I want are people like Beate, who bring with them a strong independent spirit and attitude.

Having said that, because Beate had been on location the film was more difficult to edit, and after *Stroszek* I realised there is a certain value to keeping the editor as far away from the shoot as possible. Maintaining a distance helps preserve the purity of approach; an editor must be able to look at footage as clearly and objectively as possible. Being witness to all the trouble and effort that goes into shooting a particular scene – maybe one I'm anxious not to cut – means they might decide to keep it because of all the trouble it caused us during filming. But not wanting to remove a scene that doesn't work can never be a useful position to take. During the editing of every film you have to undergo the sometimes painful, sometimes joyous process of tearing things out and throwing them in the garbage. A film is easily ruined when a director squeezes his material into preconceived notions that have been channelled into post-production. When looking at your material, forget about the screenplay you wrote and then filmed; put aside any ideas you might have brought into the editing room about how the material should be pieced together. If a filmmaker distorts the fundamental nature of his footage by butchering the images to fit preconceived editing patterns, audiences immediately sense a patch-up job. The only thing to do is look carefully at what is sitting in front of you. Let it all overshadow you. Only one question remains: what is truly present in the footage? At every stage it's vital to allow the material to take on a life of its own. You might want your children to have certain qualities, but you will never end up with one to your exact specifications. Every film needs the chance to live its own life and develop its own character, however surprising. It's a mistake to suppress this. If material contains qualities you didn't expect, continue digging and discover the gems.

Have you thought about releasing the so-called "director's cuts" of your films?

I have been the producer of much of my work, and every film of mine has been the director's cut. As for out-takes, I have none. It's too expensive to store such things – those endless reels – and soon after the release of a film I throw out all the unused footage, everything that didn't make the final cut, including the negative and printed out-takes. A carpenter doesn't sit on his shavings. When I was in New York after the shoot of *Fitzcarraldo*, I looked through all the material and decided what was useful and what wasn't, then threw out everything I didn't want to transport back to Germany, which meant considerable savings in freight and customs charges.

I have always kept the completed, cut negatives of my films. For years they were in a state of decay, some with colours fading, because I never had the money to pay for a duplicate negative. Originally my feelings about this had to do with my belief that film has a shorter shelf life than literature, that the inevitable deterioration and decay of celluloid is a natural phenomenon. Most films made in the first years of cinema's history are no longer with us, and in the not too distant future perhaps people will read books to find out what films were being made at the turn of the millennium. All that will exist is a single photo, alongside a basic description of the story and a few lines about the director. In the last few years my attitude to film preservation has changed, perhaps against my better judgement. I can see why films are worth saving, especially because I'm glad that certain German films from the twenties are still in existence, and that much of the work of Griffith, Méliès and the Lumière brothers is in good shape and available for contemporary audiences. Our world has always been, in a manner of speaking, reflected through cinema, and when you think about people five hundred years from now trying to understand civilisation today, they will probably get more out of a Tarzan film than the president's State of the Union address. Attitudes and trends shift so radically over time that what is considered today a third-rate B-picture, ridiculed and rejected on its first release, might tomorrow be heralded a masterpiece. It means we have a responsibility to preserve even bad films.

There is something about the work I produced forty years ago that still draws people in, but I'm under no illusions: my existence on this planet is fleeting, and so, perhaps, should be the lives of my films. I would never dare predict that anyone will be watching them a hundred years from now. Anyway, I live wholly in the present and really couldn't care less about posterity. There is only forward.

9

Fact and Truth

What was the starting point of your Minnesota Declaration?

The Minnesota Declaration, written in 1999, is somewhat tongue-in-cheek and designed to provoke, but the ideas it tackles are those my mind has been seriously engaged with for many years, from my earliest documentaries onwards. After wrestling with these issues in various films, they became more relevant than ever with *Bells from the Deep*, *Death for Five Voices* and *Little Dieter Needs to Fly*. The point is that the word "documentary" should be handled with care. It seems to have a precise definition, but this comes from the lack of a more appropriate concept for a whole range of cinema, and our unfortunate need to categorise. Although they are usually classified as such, it would be misleading to call those three films documentaries. They merely come under the guise of that label.

The background to the Minnesota Declaration – subtitled "Truth and Fact in Documentary Filmmaking" – is simple. I had flown from Europe to San Francisco and back again in a short space of time, and ended up in Sicily, where I was staging an opera. Unable to sleep because of jet lag, at midnight I turned on the television and was confronted by an excruciatingly boring nature film about animals somewhere out in the Serengeti, all cute and fluffy. At two in the morning I stumbled across something equally unbearable. But then, at four o'clock, I found a hardcore porno. I sat up in bed. "My God," I said to myself. "Finally something straightforward, something real." It was the naked truth, even if it was purely physical. I had been thinking about writing some kind of manifesto, a rant against *cinéma-vérité* and my thoughts about fact and truth in filmmaking. I wanted to explore the idea of what I call "ecstatic truth," even if it's a phrase that shouldn't be interpreted too deeply; everyone should figure it out for themselves. That same night I sat for twenty minutes and wrote down the twelve points, the fundamental idea behind which is that we can never know what truth really is. The best we can do is approximate.

There is a monastery in Rome called the Santissima Trinità dei Monti. On one of the walls of the cloister is a painting of St Francesco di Paola. From a distance, looking down a corridor, the image is clearly of a saint staring up into the sky in some sort of rapture, but the closer you move to the picture, by doing so changing your perspective on it, the more distorted and incomprehensible it becomes. When you stand directly in front of it, the image has been completely transformed; the saint has disappeared and a landscape – the Strait of Messina – has taken his place. There are other examples of paintings that use anamorphosis, but I have always considered this the most interesting one. Sometimes, when you think something is understood, when you feel that the truth of an image has been grasped, the more unknown it becomes, no matter how close you get to it and how deep you explore. Truth can never be definitively captured or described, though the quest to find answers is what gives meaning to our existence.

A few days after my late-night hotel experience in Sicily, I was at the Walker Art Center in Minnesota for a retrospective of my work. In something that turned into a serene, low-key rant, I read out to the audience what I had written in that hotel room and distributed printed copies. "I have brought you a kind of manifesto," I told everyone, "and would like to call it the Minnesota Declaration. Do I have your approval? If anyone has any objections, let me know." The crowd went wild; it was the first time I had ever received unanimous public approval. These dozen points contain, in condensed form, everything that has angered and moved me over the years. And hopefully people will find it all somewhat humorous and unpretentious.*

Your conclusion about cinéma-vérité *is that it fails to penetrate the deeper truth of situations it portrays.*

As I said when we talked about *ekstasis*, some mystics lived

* See p. 476 for the Minnesota Declaration.

their faith and spirituality as if in ecstasy, allowing them to penetrate things more deeply than pure rationality does. They experienced truth in an ecstatic form by leaving behind the confines of their human essence. The word for "truth" in ancient Greek is *"aletheia,"* derived from the verb "to hide." This is a negative definition, meaning to bring something out of hiding and make it visible, and is actually a very cinematic concept because when you film something, there is a latent image on the celluloid; only when you develop that celluloid does the image emerge for all to see. My work in cinema strives for the same: to make visible those things that are latent in us.

When filmmakers explore dimensions beyond the so-called "truth" of *cinéma-vérité*, they are ploughing fertile ground. *Cinéma-vérité* is fact orientated and primitive. It is the accountant's truth, merely skirting the surface of what constitutes a deeper form of truth in cinema, reaching only the most banal level of understanding. If facts had any value, if they truly illuminated us, if they unquestionably stood for truth, the Manhattan phone directory would be the book of books. Millions of established and verifiable facts, but senseless and uninspiring. The important truths remain unknown. Do we know what all these people dream about? For whom do they cast their ballots? Why does Mr John Smith cry into his pillow at night? Too many documentary filmmakers have failed to divorce themselves clearly enough from the world of journalism. I hope to be one of those who bury *cinéma-vérité* for good.

None of us lead lives of pure logic and order, and similarly, in the best cases, cinema has a strange, mysterious and illusory quality. It isn't suited to capturing realism and daily life; it has forever been able to reach beyond formal systems of understanding. It sheds light on our fantasies and – like poetry, literature and music – can illuminate in ways we will never truly be able to grasp. It leads audiences into places where they can observe truth more deeply. I have, with every one of my films, attempted to move beyond facts and illuminate the audience with ecstatic truth. Facts might have normative power, but they don't constitute truth. Facts don't illuminate. Only truth illuminates. By making a clear distinction between "fact" and "truth," I penetrate a deeper stratum that most films don't even know exists. The truth inherent in cinema can be discovered only by not being bureaucratically, politically and mathematically correct. In other words, I play with the facts as we know them. Through imagination and fabrication, I become more truthful than the bureaucrats. I keep telling young people – sometimes hesitant to explore this kind of cinema – that manipulation, concoction and invention are what cinema is really about.

Is there, in this respect, any difference between your fiction and non-fiction films?

The line between fiction and documentary doesn't exist for me. My documentaries are often fictions in disguise. All my films, every one of them, take facts, characters and stories and play with them in the same way. I consider *Fitzcarraldo* to be my best documentary and *Little Dieter Needs to Fly* my best feature. They are both highly stylised and full of imagination.

Land of Silence and Darkness *is an important film in this respect.*

Yes, though at the time my ideas on the subject weren't so developed. I wonder if they were even conscious; it was more an instinctive approach. The line quoted at the end of that film – "If a world war were to break out now, I wouldn't even notice it" – isn't something Fini ever said; I wrote those words because I felt they encapsulated how someone like her might experience the world. The lines at the start of the film, when she talks about the ecstatic faces of the ski flyers who she says she used to watch as a child, are also by me. This is all pure invention; Fini had never actually seen a ski flyer before. I asked her to recite those words because I felt that the solitude and ecstasy of these athletes as they flew through the air was a powerful visual metaphor to represent her solitude and state of mind. No scenes were ever shot contrary to her wishes; she was happy to record what I had written for her, and showed her understanding by squeezing my hand. Different rules apply when the subject of a film is dead. With Kinski in *My Best Fiend* and Timothy Treadwell in *Grizzly Man* – both of whom weren't around to defend themselves – I was especially careful with the material I was working with and the stories I wanted to tell.

What I did with *Invincible* is an example of how I have used these ideas and applied them to a feature film. Most of the facts about the life of Polish blacksmith Zishe Breitbart in the twenties didn't interest me, so I reinvented the character, transplanting him into the early thirties, the period when the Nazis were gaining power. Everything fascinating about the relationship between Germans and Jews was exacerbated in that era, then turned into the most monstrous crime and tragedy. The "truth" about Zishe's life is brought much more into focus when we see his story through the lens of Nazi Germany.

This isn't an approach you take for all your non-fiction films.

The stylisations in my documentaries are usually subtle ones; you probably wouldn't notice them unless you were paying close attention, though even in a film like *Ballad of the Little Soldier* you can see hints. I could have made a straightforward study of the situation in Nicaragua and called it *The Children's War Against the Sandinistas*, but I used the title I did because some of the most interesting material I shot was of villagers and young soldiers singing. The Miskito Indians are a people with a great musical tradition, and I felt their songs were a powerful way of revealing their deepest beliefs. I wanted to tell the story of children who were dying in battle, and the images of them singing become a powerful way of looking into their hearts, much more so than filming them with rifles in hand. In *Cave of Forgotten Dreams* you see Maurice Maurin, a man with extraordinary olfactory talent, roaming the landscape, fantasising about the odours of thirty thousand years ago. I filmed him using his primal technique of searching for currents of air and sniffing around at the base of a mountain. This was all my invention, though at one time Monsieur Maurin really was president of the French Society of Perfumers.

Take a look at the argument I have with Graham Dorrington in *The White Diamond*. He didn't think it right that I go up in the prototype airship, and insisted that for safety's sake he make the maiden flight on his own. But if there was going to be only one flight, I wanted to be up there with a camera. The truth is that though these conversations really did take place, what you see in the film was staged, and we shot the scene several times. In *The White Diamond* is a sensational image captured by one of the cameramen, a wildlife photographer. We see a droplet of water in extreme close-up, and refracted through it is the waterfall, which appears upside down. I knew if I placed it in the right context and was inventive enough, the kitsch wouldn't show. There's a scene where Marc Anthony Yhap is out foraging for medical herbs. He stops on a ledge where there is a view of the falls and points out this droplet to the camera. Everything he says was planned, including my question to him, the most insipid New Age thing I could think of: "Do you see a whole universe in this one single drop of water?" In real life I would never ask something so stupid, but Marc Anthony slowly turns with an imperceptible smirk on his face and says, "I cannot hear what you say, for the thunder that you are." I shot this scripted line – which I borrowed from *Cobra Verde* – a few times before I got exactly what I wanted. It wasn't actually even a real droplet of water. It was glycerine, which is more translucent and has better optical properties. I placed it very carefully on the leaf myself.

At the start of *Echoes from a Sombre Empire* I appear on camera, sitting in my Munich office, reading from a letter written by Michael Goldsmith in which he explains that his experiences of Bokassa and the Central African Republic still resonate powerfully within him, and that he recently dreamt about crabs invading the earth. These large, bright-red creatures have emerged from the ocean and are crawling everywhere, eventually covering the entire planet, layer upon layer. Michael's letter was real, but it never mentioned crabs; the idea was mine, and the images of them crossing the railroad tracks came from footage I found in an archive. There is no symbolism here and I can't explain it fully, but I know these images belong in the film. There is, incidentally, no clear-cut symbolism in any of my films. I've never thought in such terms; for me, a chair is a chair, and even if it were shoved under my nose I wouldn't recognise a symbol in a painting or film. Years later I went to Christmas Island in the Indian Ocean, west of the Australian mainland, and filmed those same crabs for *Invincible*. I spent days waiting for millions of these creatures to crawl out from the jungle, head towards the sea, mate, then lay their eggs.

The final scene of *Echoes from a Sombre Empire* is set in a decrepit zoo, where we were searching for the lions that had lived in Bokassa's court. When someone was sentenced to death they were often thrown either to the lions or crocodiles. By the time we got there, almost every animal in the zoo had starved to death; we found only a leopard, a hyena and – the saddest thing I have ever seen – a chimpanzee addicted to cigarettes, thanks to the drunken soldiers who had taught it to smoke. In the film you see Goldsmith looking at this creature. He says something like, "I can't take this any longer," then asks me to turn off the camera. "Michael, I think this is one of the shots I should hold," I answer back from behind the camera. "Only if you promise this will be the last shot in the film," he says. The nicotine-addicted animal was real, but this dialogue and my use of the animal was a scripted invention. The scene – which we shot six times – was carefully planned. There was something momentous and mysterious about the chimp, and filming it in the way I did elevates *Echoes from a Sombre Empire* to a deeper level of truth. To call the film a documentary is like saying Warhol's *Campbell's Soup Cans* is a document about tomato soup.

The opening quote at the start of *Lessons of Darkness* is from Blaise Pascal: "The collapse of the stellar universe will occur – like Creation – in grandiose splendour." This may sound like Pascal, but it was invented by me. Even some scholars don't know the quote is a fake, but I would rather see people dig around and read Pascal than ask me where I found these lines. I tell everyone it comes from an obscure essay published in a journal of the period which has never been included in his complete works. This means they keep searching, which is good news for me. I have a joy of invention, and this Pascalian pseudo-quote helps elevate audiences to a higher, almost sublime level before they have even seen the first image of the film. We're immediately in the realm of poetry, which inevitably strikes a more profound chord than mere report-age. Audiences have been lifted to a level that prepares them for something momentous; they are instantaneously immersed in the cosmic. Pascal himself couldn't have said it better. Shakespeare thought the same way: "the truest poetry is the most feigning." My purpose is never to deceive or mislead. Does Michelangelo deceive us with his *Pietà*, one of the most beautiful sculptures on God's wide earth? Jesus is correctly portrayed as a thirty-three-year-old man, but his mother is sculpted as a girl of seventeen. In this context my Pascal invention is legitimate. Following the quote, *Lessons of Darkness* continues with a voiceover that speaks of "A planet in our solar system with wide mountain ranges enshrouded in mist." What I actually filmed were little heaps of dust and soil created by trucks as they drove through the desert. Those mountain ranges were no more than a foot high. Like many things in my films this isn't a lie, just an intensified form of truth.

You made Lessons of Darkness *soon after the end of the Gulf War.*

The world had been saturated night and day with images of the burning oil wells in Kuwait, but through the filter of television news. I remember watching those broadcasts and knowing I was witnessing a momentous event that had to be recorded, but in a unique way for the memory of mankind. The networks and cable channels had filmed it all wrong; that tabloid style of reporting, with its eight-second snippets, quickly inured audiences to the horrors, and all too soon everyone had forgotten about those spectacular fields of serene, pitch-black burning oil that covered the landscape. I was seeking images of another kind, something very different, something longer lasting. I wanted to see these shots play out in long, almost endless takes. Only then could the images reveal their true power.

The stylisation of horror in *Lessons of Darkness* means the images penetrate deeper than regular television news footage ever could, something that bothered audiences in Germany. When the film was shown at the Berlin Film Festival, nearly two thousand people rose up with a single voice in an angry roar. They accused me of "aestheticising" the horror, and so hated the film that when I walked down the aisle after the screening, people spat at me. I was told that *Lessons of Darkness* was dangerously authoritarian, and so – finding all this hostility rather invigorating – I decided to be authoritarian at my very best. I stood before them and said, "Mr Dante did the same in his inferno, and Mr Goya did it in his paintings. Brueghel and Bosch too. You cretins are all wrong." You should have heard the tornado of disgust. The German press found the film to be a dangerous attack on everyone's decency, though it received tremendous reviews around the world. After all, I'm hardly the first filmmaker to show this kind of stylisation on screen. Kubrick's *Dr Strangelove*, with its beautifully blossoming atomic explosions, is one of the most painful films I have ever seen. Sitting here twenty years later I would dare an assumption: if I showed *Lessons of Darkness* to audiences at the Berlin Film Festival today, they would like it.

There were criticisms about you not identifying Kuwait.

There was never a need to name Saddam Hussein and the country he attacked. If people watch *Lessons of Darkness* in three hundred years' time, it still wouldn't be necessary for them to know the historical facts behind the film. War has no fascination for me beyond its absurdity and insanity, and *Lessons of Darkness* consciously transcends the topical and the particular; this could be any war and any country. The film is about the evil that human beings are capable of, which is why it will never age. It is precisely because Iraq and Kuwait aren't named that humanity will always respond to these sounds and images.

I located the people I filmed through various organisations that were working with torture victims, and specifically set out to find individuals who had lost the power of speech after being tortured. There's an imbalance to the film because I wanted to speak with more of these victims, but the Kuwaiti authorities were constantly scrutinising what I was doing and eventually expelled me from the country. From the start they hoped I would make a film that showed the positive, optimistic reconstruction of the country, with the cleaning up of the oil wells and an apparently heroic fresh start. What the Kuwaitis wanted to portray on film and broadcast to the rest of the world consisted only of heroic firefighters and rescuers, not the scarred victims. They objected to me going into the deepest wounds the war had inflicted on some people, and one afternoon I was handed a letter by the Ministry of Information stating very plainly that we were being wished a pleasant flight out of the country early the next morning. It was obviously an expulsion order. If I had insisted on continuing filming, they would have confiscated my footage, so I wrapped things up and left.

You show both the landscape from afar and the firefighters on the ground.

Lessons of Darkness belongs as much to British cameraman and co-producer Paul Berriff as me. There was the danger of two cooks preparing one meal, but Paul is a man of such calibre that our collaboration worked very well; ultimately I owe the film to him. I knew after watching CNN that I wanted to go to Kuwait, and found Paul by searching for someone – anyone – with a shooting permit. The massive oil fires were being extinguished unexpectedly fast, so I had to hurry. I met Paul in a hotel in Vienna. It turned out that although he had all the required paperwork, he wasn't entirely sure what he wanted to film. We talked for only twenty minutes before I said, "Do you have the nerve to step back as director of this film and be just the cameraman?" Paul stood up and bowed. "It would be an honour," he said. A courageous man, very physical, dogged in everything he does. He had already made several daring films about people such as sea rescuers, who pluck drowning people from the North Sea as they dangle down on a cable from a helicopter, and throughout the seventies shot several films for the BBC about the unrest in Northern Ireland. Paul himself has risked his life to save people in trouble and has received numerous awards for bravery.

A skilled helicopter pilot was imperative, and fortunately Paul had already contacted Jerry Grayson, an expert pilot who had worked on several Hollywood films. He understood the terrain and airflows around the burning oil wells, and was able to establish a pattern of flight that facilitated a sequence of travelling shots. I was lucky he had a true narrative intelligence and knew intuitively where to move next in terms of the story being told. I was never in the helicopter; the footage was shot two days before I arrived in the country. The cameraman, Simon Werry, is an expert aerial photographer who knew I wanted as many unbroken travelling shots of the landscape as possible. I would never have been able to direct every one of the shots even if I had been up there, where temperatures reached over a thousand degrees. If Jerry had flown across an area into which the heat might be suddenly blown, the helicopter would have exploded. When flying over the burning oil fields he had to make his own choices for safety reasons, and did an outstanding job in allowing Simon to hold the shots for as long as he possibly could.

I was initially advised to make a film about Red Adair and his efforts to put out the fires, but his working methods involved the heaviest imaginable machinery and every precaution in the book. He was extremely meticulous, cowardly and overly bureaucratic; he wanted the most expensive, state-of-the-art equipment put in place, which would have taken months, and predicted it would take four or five years to put out the fires, which it would have done if Adair had gone about things his own way. Very few people in Kuwait were actually in favour of how he was doing things. The job was eventually done within about six months, though the crews working on the ground were running high risks. The men in the film are, I think, American or Canadian. There were also Iranians, Hungarians and teams from all over the world. The Iranians were the most remarkable because they didn't have much equipment, so they fought the fires almost with their bare hands, so to speak. Everyone who worked with these men spoke of them with great respect.

One of the reasons my collaboration with Paul worked so well was because of this understanding of hearts we had, something that became obvious when we decided we didn't want to use long zoom lenses when filming on the ground. If something interested us, we physically moved in together, and wherever possible placed ourselves beside the firefighters. Paul did most of the camerawork himself, and we shot only on film, not video. Sometimes this was a problem because raw stock has to be acclimatised, which meant we couldn't just unpack the celluloid and expose it in the camera. We had to protect the magazines with aluminium foil and remove the film from the heat as quickly as possible once a roll had been shot. Whenever possible we tried to shoot with the wind from behind, so the heat was blown away from us. We had regular cameras and wore Nomex suits for protection, the kind used by Formula One drivers, which can keep you alive for about half a minute when you're engulfed in flames. We cut the tips of our flameproof gloves off to operate the camera and were hosed down by firefighters every forty-five seconds; the soles of our shoes would have melted away if we hadn't been careful. At one point Paul jumped out from behind the barrier where we were taking refuge from the heat because he wanted to film something, and the part of his face not covered by the camera immediately began to redden. I held my two hands over his face for protection, and within ten seconds my thick leather gloves were burning. One of our boom microphones melted away. The sound was actually the most impressive thing; you have to see the film in a cinema with Dolby stereo to really appreciate it. Geysers of fire shooting three hundred feet up into the sky with that kind of pressure sound like four jumbo jets taking off simultaneously. You could scream as loud as you wanted over this noise and still not be heard. There was something cosmic about the experience that went far beyond the politics of the events. It really was like filming on a different planet.

You have described Lessons of Darkness, *like* Fata Morgana, *as a science-fiction film.*

Calling *Lessons of Darkness* a science-fiction film is a way of explaining that it contains not a single frame recognisable as our planet, yet we know it must have been shot here. I used the voice-over to place the film – and the audience – in a darkened planet somewhere in our solar system.

When we talked about *Fata Morgana*, I spoke of embarrassed landscapes. The landscape you see in *Lessons of Darkness* isn't just embarrassed, it's completely mutilated. I set out to record crimes perpetrated against not just humanity, but Creation itself. Our entire world seems to be burning away, and because of the music I call the film "a requiem for an uninhabitable planet." Unlike *La Soufrière* – which tries to document a natural catastrophe – *Lessons of Darkness* shows a landscape that has been mutilated by a man-made one. The film plays out as if aliens have landed on an unnamed planet and are observing the world around them. There is a line I speak in the voiceover when one of the firefighters makes a signal: "The first creature we encountered tried to com-municate something to us." This idea becomes more explicit with the shot of the firefighter lighting up a plume of gushing oil. The voiceover explains that these men have been seized by madness and are reigniting the flames because they can't imagine life without fire; having something to extinguish makes them happy again. In reality, the gush of oil had created a lake that was approaching other burning fires. If it had ignited, there would have been an even bigger problem, so there was a practical reason for the lighting of this plume. I asked the firefighters to let us know when they were going to take action so we could be there with a camera.

How did you select the music?

It fell into place very easily. During editing I watched the film and put on a piece of music, and knew within fifteen seconds if it fit. I didn't need more than two or three attempts for each sequence of the film. The title of *Lessons of Darkness* comes from a piece of music by François Couperin, *Leçons de ténèbres*, which was one of my earliest musical discoveries. In *Fata Morgana* there is a beautiful early recording of the piece performed by Hugues Cuénod, a Swiss tenor. I immediately had the feeling it should be the title of this film.

Bells from the Deep: Faith and Superstition in Russia *features an array of characters from Siberia.*

I engaged some Russian collaborators and asked them to scour the land for the most impressive Jesus Christ they could find; there were about a hundred of them roaming Siberia at the time, competing with each other. Eventually they came up with Vissarion, an ex-policeman who one day realised he was, in fact, Jesus. He lived an ascetic life in a tiny apartment in Krasnoyarsk in Siberia and actually had an agent in Moscow, but this didn't bother me because I had the feeling there was real depth to him. The faith healer in the film, Alan Chumack, used to be a well-known media figure on Russian television who would re-enact alien abductions. One day, after discovering he was wildly popular with audiences, Chumack decided he had psychic powers himself.

My favourite character in the film is Yuri Yurevitch Yurieff, the orphaned bell ringer who used to be a cinema projectionist. I flew out of the country the day after we filmed him tolling the bells. It was only months later, while I was editing, that the cameraman Jörg Schmidt-Reitwein said, "After you left we had dinner with Yuri and he told us his life story. He's an orphan and went in search of his lost family." I rushed back to Russia, brushed the snow away from the church tower, put Yuri in the same costume, framed the camera so we couldn't see the frozen landscape, and asked him to tell us his story. He spoke about his search for his parents, a story that mirrors the tragedy of Russia, with the Stalinist repressions and Hitler's invasion, when so many people died or disappeared. When he was found as a child and asked for his name – first, middle and family – all he would say was "Yuri." For me the man is a true musician; the way he strung up the ropes in the tower is incredible and the sound he gets from tolling the bells has real depth to it. My plan was to start the film at a monastery with a single monk playing a single bell, then show bigger and bigger bell-ringing orgies throughout. Yuri would have been somewhere in the middle. I also spent time looking for a hermit. Advertising for such people probably isn't the most useful way of going about things, but I did eventually find one. He wasn't actually a textbook hermit, just a convicted murderer who had built himself a small monastery within a prison compound near St Petersburg, next to the football pitch, where he lived a monastic life. I looked hard for a genuine hermit and had so many knowledgeable people engaged in the search that I can't imagine there are any left. Very few anyway, and well hidden at that.

Do you speak Russian?

I understand some words and more or less the subject of a conversation. The key to *Bells from the Deep* was Viktor Danilov, an interpreter I met during the shooting of Peter Fleischmann's *Hard to Be a God*, in which I played a small role. Viktor helped with the on-camera conversations and always knew in which direction I wanted the encounters with these people to move. Sometimes, when I would sense things were going off topic, he would look at me and signal with his face, as if to say, "Don't interrupt!" I wouldn't have made the film without him.

Is anything invented?

It depends on what you mean by "invented." A woman stands on a hilltop explaining that the locals call it "The Seventh Hill of Jerusalem," that the hill once opened up and revealed to visiting pilgrims a singing choir and cathedral consecrated to the fourteen thousand children killed in Bethlehem by Herod. Then she crawls on her hands and knees and touches the stump of a pine tree a man once chopped down, after which he immediately went blind and died. "Nobody is allowed to chop trees down on this sacred hill or harm them in any way," she explains, adding that the stump has miraculous powers and can heal the sick. Then she turns to me and asks if she should crawl around some more. I nodded from behind the camera. There is another old woman in the film – the one with a bandaged hand – who told me about her pig that had escaped from the sty. It went berserk and attacked a cow, so she grabbed a stick and yelled at it, at which point the animal turned on her and bit her hand. What does any of this have to do with "faith and superstition"? It's like in school, when I would write essays on German literature and apparently totally miss the point. "You were meant to write an essay about Hölderlin," the teachers would tell me, "but what you wrote is completely off topic." Today, having left school behind me, I can now take these apparent liberties and include the story of this rabid pig, which obviously has to do with faith and superstition. It's in the film, after all.

Bells from the Deep doesn't strive to report facts about Russia as an ethnographic film or book might do; that would be like reading a Hölderlin poem in which he describes a storm in the Alps and insisting it's a weather report from 1802. The best of the film is fabricated. It begins in the Tuvinian Autonomous Republic, northwest of Mongolia. An old man is throat-singing about the beauty of a mountain. Later in the film there are two boys – one twelve, the other fourteen – singing a love song. What does this have to do with a film about faith? Yet it belongs; just by dint of declaration this becomes a religious hymn. Later we see what appear to be people deep in prayer. We were driving to a location when I stopped the bus because in the distance I saw a frozen lake with dozens of people on it; they had drilled holes in the ice and were sitting, quietly fishing. It was so cold they were crouching down with their backs against the wind, all facing the same direction, as if they were in deep meditation, so the film declares them pilgrims in prayer.

In the final moments there are two speed skaters moving through the shot. I spotted them from a distance and whistled to catch their attention, then explained I wanted them to be in the film, passing in and out of the frame, gently in between the people on the ice. They agreed, but were anxious to show how good they were and started dashing around like madmen; one of them used to be in the Soviet Olympic skating team and wanted to show off. I had a specific piece of music in mind for this sequence, so the images had to correspond with the rhythms in my head. I told the skaters to go much slower and float majestically into shot with a certain gravitas and magnificence. We shot it several times before they understood exactly what I wanted. Watch the scene again and look at the precision with which they move.

Is the legend of the Lost City of Kitezh real?

Bells from the Deep is one of the most pronounced examples of what I mean when I say that through invention, fabrication and staging you can reach a more intense level of truth. I took a fact – that for many people this lake was the final resting place of this lost city – and explored the truth of the situation to reach a more poetic understanding. I heard about the myth while I was out there; it's a very real belief of these people. As recounted to me, the legend is that the city was systematically ransacked and demolished by hundreds of years of Tartar and Hun invasions. The inhabitants called on God to redeem them, and He sent an archangel who tossed the city into a bottomless lake, where the people live in bliss, chanting their hymns and tolling the bells. During the summer, pilgrims crawl around the lake on all fours, saying their prayers. I was also there at the beginning of winter because I wanted shots of them looking through the ice, trying to catch a glimpse of the lost city. Unfortunately there was no one around, so I hired two drunks from the nearby town and asked them to play pilgrims. One of them has his face on the ice and looks as if he's deep in meditation. The accountant's truth: he was fast asleep.

You can find a sister to this image in *Encounters at the End of the World*, which I filmed years later. The sound designer Douglas Quin gave me a series of extraordinary recordings of underwater seal calls – what one physiologist in Antarctica describes in the film as "inorganic sounds" – and I asked the scientists to get on their hands and knees, as if they were trying to listen through the ice for these noises, which sound like early electronic music. It was all precisely staged because I wanted the shot to be perfectly balanced; of course, none of these people would do such a thing for real. I asked them to repeat it a couple of times, to the point where the ear of one woman froze to the ice. I was immediately profuse with my apologies. While we were shooting *Encounters* I noticed that the divers who went under the Ross Ice Shelf, a bay in Antarctica the size of Texas, didn't speak much. To me, it seemed as if they were priests preparing for Mass. When under the ice, the divers find themselves in a separate reality in which space and time acquire a strange new dimension; Henry Kaiser, who filmed down there and whose footage appears in *The Wild Blue Yonder*, speaks about his dives being consciousness-altering experiences. In the film I say that those who have experienced the world under the frozen sky often talk of "going down into the cathedral." I made up that line, though there is something almost religious about being down under the ice, as if confronted by the essence of Creation itself.

Is what we see in Bells from the Deep *representative of the general attitudes and feelings in Russia today?*

Many Russians – including my wife – are philosophical when it comes to beliefs and superstitions. The depth of the Russian soul is unique, and the border between faith and superstition is often blurred for them. The question is: how do you depict the soul of an entire nation in only sixty minutes? The scene of the drunken city-seekers somehow represents Russia; the entire country is secretly searching for the Lost City of Kitezh. Russians who have seen *Bells from the Deep* consider this sequence the best in the film. They understand the devout passion and religious fervour of people who stare so intently, face down, with unwavering concentration, into the depths below.

Florian Fricke wrote the music for several of your films.

I first met him around 1967, at the home of an industrialist, the man whose wife took me to Africa to make *The Flying Doctors of East Africa*. I would play football with him on the lawn of this enormous house. He was classically trained, a fine pianist who had studied at Freiburg University until injury forced him to quit, so he became a composer instead. For decades he was a trusted collaborator and wrote the music for many of my films, including *The Great Ecstasy*, *Fitzcarraldo*, *Nosferatu* and *Heart of Glass*. He also appears as the pianist in both *Signs of Life* and *The Enigma of Kaspar Hauser*. We worked closely together, and often I would tell him the story I had in mind before there was even a written screenplay. We wouldn't talk about music; we spoke instead about the inner drama of the story, or about some sort of vision I had. He was a poet first and a musician second, and his feel for the inner narrative of a cinematic story was infallible. Florian never failed to create music that has forever given us an entrée into otherwise inaccessible dimensions. It's what I was saying earlier about the music in *Fata Morgana*. Florian's compositions add dimensions to a film that we never knew existed and enable us to shift our perception; they make visible what would otherwise remain mysterious and forever hidden in my films, and also what lies buried in our souls. Although when seen alongside Florian's music an image remains the same projection of light, it is somehow transformed, like the cliff faces and peaks of *The Dark Glow of the Mountains*, which appear to possess a sacred aura and cast a strange spell when we look at them while listening to music by Popol Vuh, Florian's one-man band.

I described to Florian what I wanted for *Aguirre* – something full of human pathos and the surreal – and what he came up with wasn't real singing, nor was it completely artificial either; it sits uncomfortably between the two. I wanted choral music that would sound out of this world. Florian used a strange instrument called a choir-organ, which is similar to a mellotron and contains three dozen different tapes running parallel in loops. Each tape would be a voice of a single pitch. Put together it sounds like a human choir, but the music has an artificial, eerie quality to it. He was always full of ideas like this, though towards the end we moved in different directions; he drifted into New Age pseudo-culture and the style of his music changed. I used to joke with Florian, telling him, "You must never grow old. You have to die young and beautiful." I can still hear those words in my mind today. After his death in 2001 I asked his widow if she had any music of his I had never heard, and she gave me a piece I used in *Wheel of Time*. Not only does this music somehow help transport the images, it's also a bow in the direction of my dear friend.

Has sound design always been important to your films?

On practically my first film I came to understand that sound decides the outcome of many battles, that the texture and subtleties of a film often come from its soundtrack. I encounter many young directors who manage to make their first film – after overcoming problems of finance, organisation and everything else – but fall down because of their neglect of sound. Almost all my films have been shot with direct sound, which inevitably takes more time and energy than recording it months later in the controlled environment of a studio. Sometimes it takes more time to prepare the sound than it does to set up the shot. When it comes to post-production, for *The Wild Blue Yonder* soundtrack I took recordings of howler monkeys I made in Guyana when I was making *The White Diamond* and carefully added them to Henry Kaiser's underwater footage. Every bird noise you hear in *Aguirre* was intentional. Throughout the shoot we recorded as many birds as possible, then carefully mixed the film's soundtrack, which makes the jungle seem alive and dangerous. The silences were especially carefully designed; whenever you hear nothing there must be Indians around, and that means death.

The silences in all my films are important. I asked Jean Clottes, one of the scientists in *Cave of Forgotten Dreams*, to talk about how the silence inside the cave is so profound that you can hear the beating of your own heart. Ernst Reijseger's cello emerges out of the faint heartbeat I added to the soundtrack and the almost imperceptible drops of water you hear inside the cave. It reminds me of a moment in the Taviani brothers' film *Padre Padrone*, when the father says to his son, "Close your eyes and listen." All we hear is the gentle rustling of leaves on a tree. I will never forget the enormity of the impressive silence I heard in the Sahara and when, as an adolescent, I went with the fishermen of Crete on their small boats that dispersed into the night. With powerful carbide lamps they would attract the fish, which would criss-cross the water like streaks of silver amidst reflections of the stars burning brightly in the sky. No one ever spoke; everything was dead quiet. It's no coincidence that there is a noticeable absence of urban life in my films. I rarely shoot in big cities. I admire Robert Bresson's films, in which we hear so many silences, each one different. Compare these subtleties with a film like *Apocalypse Now*, where sledgehammer sound effects constantly hit you over the head. It's like watching early colour films, with their absurdly bright and garish images screaming at you.

Can you read music?

Although for years when I was young my mother struggled to get me interested in playing the flute and failed to teach me even the most basic melodies, and though I must be one of the few opera directors who can't read music, I know I'm a very musical person. I put my disconnect from music down to a childhood tragedy I experienced at the age of thirteen. The music teacher at school asked everybody to stand up in alphabetical order and sing a song. The whole thing had an ideology behind it; at the time ideas were floating around about everyone having innate musical talent, whether or not they were able to sing. When it came to my turn, I was asked to stand up. "I am not going to sing," I told the teacher. It quickly turned nasty. Bold as I was at that age, I insisted, "Sir, you may do a somersault forward and backward. You may run up the walls and on to the ceiling. I . . . am . . . not . . . going . . . to . . . sing." That annoyed him so much he brought in the headmaster. In front of the whole class, while I was standing there, they discussed whether I should be thrown out of school. It was that serious, but I was very stubborn. Then the bastards took the whole class hostage. "Nobody is going to leave until Herzog sings." Everyone started pressuring me, saying, "Don't worry, we won't listen to you. We just want to go outside during the break." The headmaster insisted there would be no break if I didn't sing. I stood my ground, but after forty minutes, for the sake of my classmates, I sang. While doing so I knew I would never sing again in my life. I told myself, "No man will ever break me again."

I disconnected myself entirely from music at that moment, a painful move that created a profound vacuum within me. Today I would give ten years of my life if I could play the cello with the same ease as breathing. The finest music has a quality of consolation you find nowhere else, with perhaps the exception of religion or being in contact with small children. During music lessons at school I became ever more autistic. I was on a different planet; I turned off my ears, and between the ages of thirteen and eighteen music didn't exist for me. When I left school I sensed a huge void, so I dug into music with a ferocious intensity but no guidance from anyone. I started with Heinrich Schütz, and from there to Bach, Orlando di Lasso, Carissimi, then Beethoven and modern composers. Later I encountered Gesualdo's *Sixth Book of Madrigals*, a moment of absolute enlightenment for me. I was so excited I called up Florian Fricke at three in the morning. "Everyone who is into music knows about Gesualdo," he said after half an hour of my raving. "You sound as if you have discovered a new planet." But for me that's exactly what it felt like, as if I had found something tremendous within our solar system. "Are you ready to take the insult that the director of the opera can't read music?" I ask the conductors I'm working with. "But I can listen very well."

The Transformation of the World into Music *was made at the Bayreuth Wagner Festival.*

I became fascinated with Wagner relatively late, and today consider his music as some of the greatest ever written. When I heard Wagner's *Parsifal* for the first time in Bayreuth during a rehearsal, the auditorium was almost empty. There was a moment in that particular staging when for twenty minutes Kundry is lying on the ground, hidden as part of a rock formation, then suddenly rises up and screams. It was such a shock for me, with my knees propped up against the chairs in front of me, that I was jolted so violently I tore my entire row of seats from its anchoring. Along with Wolfgang Wagner, the grandson of Richard Wagner, I tumbled backwards. Wagner got to his feet and rushed over to me. I thought I was going to be fired, but he bowed, took my hand and said, "Finally, an audience that knows how to respond to the music." I appreciate that Richard Wagner isn't a particularly attractive figure and am well aware of his anti-Semitism, though he is no more to be blamed for Hitler than Marx is for Stalin.

Wolfgang sent a telegram asking me to stage *Lohengrin* at the Bayreuth Festival. I replied immediately, answering his request with a single word: "No." He refused to take that for an answer and became like a terrier snapping at my heels, insisting I reconsider, even though I kept turning him down. Finally, after weeks of this, he became suspicious and asked whether I had even heard the opera. I told him I hadn't. "Would you please listen to my favourite recording, which I'm going to send you?" he asked. "Then, if your answer is still no, I'll never bother you again." Upon hearing the *Vorspiel* [overture] for the first time, I was completely stunned, as if lightning had struck. I knew this was something big and beautiful, so I accepted Wagner's offer. "Let's just do the *Vorspiel* and keep the curtain closed," I said to him. "When people eventually demand to hear the opera, we'll just play it again." Wagner, I think, started to like me. A few years before, when I was writing the script for *Fitzcarraldo*, I decided Fitzcarraldo should listen to Wagner in the jungle, but when I was next in Peru I distinctly remember listening to *Siegfried* and quickly realising that Wagner's music didn't connect to the landscape and story I wanted to tell. It's too Teutonic; just go down to the jungle and try it for yourself. The ending of the film – where Bellini's *I Puritani* is performed with a jungle backdrop – couldn't have worked any other way.

I directed *Lohengrin* at Bayreuth in 1987, where it ran for seven consecutive years until 1994, when I made *The Transformation of the World into Music*. You have to see the film in context, as a work serving a clear purpose; it's another one of my "utility" films. Over the previous few years operas staged in Bayreuth were being recorded for transmission on the French/German television station Arte. The plan was to screen all of Wagner's operas – something like forty hours of music – in the space of a month, and an introductory piece about the festival was needed. Arte suggested a rather dubious approach, something like "The Myth of Bayreuth," but I told them I would focus instead on the more practical aspects of the festival. I knew I wanted to stay away from the Wagner fundamentalists and mystification of Bayreuth, though there is a moment in the film when Plácido Domingo talks about the festival being a pilgrimage for many people, where performances are sacred rituals. What interested me was that at Bayreuth you find a climate and atmosphere like no other opera festival, a genuine appreciation of music, something made clear by the women, who don't wear jewellery – not like they do in Milan and Salzburg – because it would be out of place. I was fascinated by the craftspeople, who spend months every year preparing the productions. I made *The Transformation of the World into Music* during my final restaging of *Lohengrin*, when I had easy access to colleagues, musicians and singers. There were new and significant productions being staged at the time, like Heiner Müller's *Tristan und Isolde*, so my own work on *Lohengrin* is only a small part of the film. What's important to remember is that Richard Wagner designed Bayreuth as a workshop where the most important thing is craft and experimentation, not adoration. For two years after I initially staged *Lohengrin*, I kept modifying and improving the production. The whole thing was an important learning experience for me.

My own stylised contemplation of the reality of Bayreuth, and just how extraordinary and unique the place is, comes in *The*

Transformation of the World into Music when I head into the bombproof vault with a small torch. I could have switched on the light, but entering this darkened, sacred, underground room guided by a custodian makes the whole trip down there more mysterious. The vault contains Wagner's original manuscripts and *partituras*, which taken together are undoubtedly a monumental achievement of German culture.

Why a desire to start staging opera in the eighties?

I never had any such aspiration; I was literally dragged into it. Although I selected the music, the opera at the start of *Fitzcarraldo* – Verdi's *Ernani* – was actually directed by Werner Schroeter, not me. When I made the film I had never been to the opera. A few years later, after I had already turned her down a few times, the *intendante* at the opera house in Bologna somehow persuaded me to come down and take a look at the place, and I was immediately fascinated by the logistics and mechanics. I was standing on the stage when all of a sudden I found myself surrounded by forty stagehands, electricians and other personnel who gently formed a solid circle of bodies. The circle tightened and they locked shoulder to shoulder, entrapping me. "I have been selected as spokesman," one man said. "We have taken a collective decision that we are not going to let you leave until you sign a contract and agree to stage an opera here. We want you to be with us." I looked around at all these nodding Italians with such determined looks on their faces, and said, "Where is this contract?" We went to the office as a group, and I signed. I love the Italians for their gift of physical enthusiasm. They liked the idea that when it came to music, I was untouched by certain ideas and tendencies, and that beholden as I was to no particular kind of staging, I would inevitably take a different approach to the work. Soon after this meeting I watched an opera at Bologna to get an idea of the space and its technical possibilities.

I staged my first opera, Busoni's *Doktor Faust*, in 1986. Busoni was born in Tuscany, but his mother was from Trieste. He lived most of his life in Germany and other German-speaking countries, so the Germans have never considered him German, and for Italians he was never a fellow countryman. He wrote *Doktor Faust* at a strange moment, when the world of music was somehow holding its breath, before it moved into twelve-tone. It's an unfinished work, full of gaps and inconsistencies, but I instantly felt comfortable and confident in what I was doing. There are some composers whose music I have no access to, like Schönberg's *Moses und Aron* or Berg's *Wozzeck*, though I quickly realised I can cope with the wildest and messiest of stories, even something like Verdi's *Giovanna d'Arco*, which was originally about a shepherd girl who falls in love with a king, but then – apparently with only a few days' notice – was rewritten as the story of Joan of Arc. The libretto really is *irrapresentabile*, as the Italians say. My opera work was appreciated with an immediacy by others, something I have rarely experienced with my films. Opera has brought me joy and inner balance, though I'm the first to admit that when I started I had little idea about what opera was supposed to look like and how it functions up there on the stage.

I never do research and have never read any of Wagner's books and essays. Before I started work on *Lohengrin* an assistant handed me a pile of literature and opera theory, none of which I looked at. The only thing I ever study – and I do it very carefully – is the libretto and the music. The truth is that apart from my own productions, I have watched maybe four or five operas in my entire life, though I have listened to lots of recordings. I know very little about the different stylistic approaches to opera or its trends and fashions; I just seize upon and work with what I see when I hear the music. I can construct the action, setting and entire architecture of an opera in my mind as I listen to it. Hardly anyone believes me when I tell them the first production I ever saw was at La Scala in Milan, two years after I made *Fitzcarraldo*. The key to my opera work is my love of music.

What does it mean to transform a whole world into music?

That's what opera is about. The idea of staging an opera seemed a strange thing for me to do, until I realised that since my earliest days as a filmmaker I have sought to transform every action, every word into images, so I thought, "Why shouldn't I try at least once in my life to do the same with music?"

Opera is a universe all its own. On stage an opera represents a complete world, a cosmos transformed into music. I love the stylised performances and grandeur of human emotions – whether love, hate, jealousy or guilt – being acted out. Do humans really recognise these archetypes of emotional exaltation? Of course we do. The fantastical situations we see in opera are almost like mathematical axioms: condensed and concentrated, speaking to audiences without appeal to realism or psychology. It doesn't matter that so many of the stories are implausible and most of the libretti are bad. Many plots aren't even within the calculus of probability; it would be like winning the lottery jackpot five consecutive times. Yet when the music is playing, no explanations are required; primordial feelings suddenly reverberate within us. The stories make sense and audiences are shaken. Strong inner truths shine through, and the veracity of facts no longer matters. Everything is possible. Working within these artificial worlds, with no representation of reality as such, and with music always dictating what's happening on stage, it's more a case of "staging" than "directing." An opera staging mustn't be so elaborate or extreme that it detracts from the music. For too long German opera was dominated by the so-called *Regietheater*, the "director's theatre," where *Lohengrin* is set in Auschwitz, Rigoletto enters on a Harley-Davidson, and Fidelio frequents S&M parties with a martini in hand.

Just as I don't like to over-rehearse scenes before I shoot them, I dislike rehearsing opera too much, otherwise it gets stale. Four weeks is enough for everything; anything longer and people start getting bored. I try to be quick at the job, though the practicalities of the opera world mean this isn't always possible, and it can be a fragmented and disjointed process. The great singers are booked years in advance, and sometimes I have to rehearse a scene involving half a dozen characters with only one singer because the other five aren't around; then, two weeks later, I might get a chance to rehearse the same scene without that one singer but with the other five. Much of the time we'll have only a pianist, not an entire orchestra, and a chorus that can work only on specific days. It means we have to rehearse with a chorus as if the lead singers are on stage, even if at the time they are performing on another continent. Frequently there aren't even stand-ins. The whole thing is like making a series of prints where you first produce everything in red, then green, then blue, and only then is it pieced together and a single image created. Things are different at Bayreuth because everyone arrives more than a month before performances start. In less than a week I work with the singers and move through the entire opera, locating the big questions and problems, establishing the flow of things.

People surrender themselves to music and film in similar ways, which means cinema is closer to music than it ever will be to literature or theatre. The fact that so many filmmakers have gravitated towards opera over the years is some kind of proof of this. When I rehearse an opera I forget everything, including that I'm a filmmaker. Film and opera are like cats and dogs; they will never be truly married together. For one thing their concepts of narrative are completely different. In opera, characters take five minutes to answer a simple question, then sing the same thing three times over. That could never work on film. With opera there are two thousand different perspectives, but with a camera there is only one position at a time. The opera director has to be aware of what the stage looks like from every possible angle, from the corner of every last balcony in the auditorium. If a singer takes a step too far to the right, one whole side of the house is unable to see them. When I first started out I would move around the auditorium, trying out every seat, but these days can tell, while still standing on the stage with the singers, with my back to the auditorium, exactly what an audience will and won't be able to see.

How do you find working with opera singers?

Opera singing is a merciless profession. A film actor can make a dozen mistakes and continuously shoot a scene, while a theatre actor who gets lost can somehow improvise until he finds his way back into the text. But opera singers can do neither of those things. They remind me of gladiators thrown into an arena packed with thousands of people all screaming for blood. I'm amazed by the boldness needed to step out in front of so many people, all of whom will notice within a millisecond if the voices they are listening to are off-key. When you see singers taking their bows at the end of a performance and the curtain comes down for good, it truly is something to behold. The men are several pounds lighter; they literally lose that much weight during the performance. When I stand on the sidelines, hidden from the audience, watching the singers in profile as they sing, with the lights on them, I can see the power in their voices because of the spitting they do. They literally give themselves away to the audience during a performance. There is something awesome about them, and I have total and absolute respect for these artists. I also salute the prompters, who are always one step ahead of the music. Never before have I seen such precision and concentration.

I rarely feel truly comfortable in opera houses. If I'm sitting in the front row of the auditorium, I admire everything in front of me – from the orchestra pit through to the darkest corners back-stage – but everything behind me isn't the kind of world I belong to. Many opera houses need the threat of catastrophe and intrigue to get sufficiently energised. I was directing Plácido Domingo in a production of *Il Guarany* in Washington D.C. and the atmosphere was a little flat, so to create a little spark I casually mentioned to my assistant that Domingo wouldn't be singing on the opening night. Within twenty minutes there was a conflagration at every corner of the opera house; even the chefs were arguing about it. Suddenly everyone was alert and wide awake. It can sometimes be healthy to set the roof on fire at these places. What I really like is literally being in the middle of the music. There is a wedding march in *Lohengrin*. Walking with the choir – one of the best in the world – being right there amidst a hundred and twenty people singing, most of whom could be soloists in other opera houses, was absolutely stunning, and a great privilege.

Many scenes in Death for Five Voices, *your film about Carlo Gesualdo, are subtly stylised.*

Subtly stylised? No, in this case some of them are complete fabrications. The film runs amok, and most of the stories it tells are invented and staged, yet they contain the most profound truths possible about Gesualdo. No book or other film gives as much insight into the man.

Gesualdo was a sixteenth-century musical visionary, the composer who has astonished me more than anyone else, though I wanted to make a film about him because his life is as intriguing as his music. He was never financially dependent on anyone, so could pay for his voyages into the musical unknown. While his previous work is more within the context of his epoch, with the *Sixth Book of Madrigals* Gesualdo all of a sudden seemed to step four hundred years ahead of his time, composing music we hear only from Stravinsky onwards. It's no coincidence that Stravinsky made two pilgrimages to Gesualdo's castle near Naples and wrote an orchestra piece with the title *Monumentum pro Gesualdo*. There are moments in *Death for Five Voices* where we hear the five separate voices of a madrigal. Each voice sounds normal, but in combination the music is fantastically ahead of its time, even of our own time. I always liked those kinds of visionaries. Gesualdo, Turner – predecessor of the Impressionists – the Egyptian pharaoh Akhenaten, Hercules Segers: those four have long been my favourites. Akhenaten, who ruled in the fourteenth century BC, was the first monotheist and a thousand years ahead of his time. He abandoned polytheism, making Aten the sole god of Egypt and forbidding the worship of any other deity. After his death the capital city he built was abandoned and his name systematically erased from all monuments; the new style of art he created disappeared with him. Akhenaten was also monogamous, loyal to his wife Nefertiti, in an era when pharaohs were expected to have harems packed with hundreds of women.

As for stylisations in *Death for Five Voices*, there is a sequence of a boy being prepared for horseback riding where we meet the director of a mental institution in Venosa. He talks about how we aren't allowed to film certain things because he has to protect the privacy of his patients, including two who both believe themselves to be Gesualdo. The problem, he explains, is how to keep them away from each other. This is all invented; the man playing the director is actually my opera agent. In the scene filmed inside the museum in the castle of Venosa, we see a glass showcase that contains a clay disc with an array of enigmatic script-like symbols and ideograms on it. When I first saw this thing I was fascinated by it and immediately wanted to include it in the film. I wrote a monologue about this disc for the director of the museum, which he speaks while standing next to the showcase. He presents a letter from Gesualdo to his alchemist, enlisting his aid in deciphering the mysterious signs on the disc. "The prince spent sleepless nights trying to unravel the secret of these strange symbols," the professor says. "In the course of this activity he became lost in a labyrinth of conjectures and hypotheses.

He almost lost his reason in the process." The letter he reads from is a real handwritten letter from Gesualdo, but is actually nothing more than an invitation to a party at his castle. The spoken text is entirely invented, and the professor is played by the dean of the law school in Milan. The scene reflects the fact that Gesualdo became demented in the final years of his life. He single-handedly chopped down the entire forest around his castle because he was convinced it was closing in on him, and hired young men to flog him daily, something that gave him festering wounds and apparently led to his death. There is a scene in *Death for Five Voices* where we meet a woman running around the prince's ruined castle, singing his music and insisting she is the spirit of Gesualdo's dead wife. Her character emphasises the profound impact Gesualdo's music has had on people over the centuries. We hired Milva, a famous Italian actress and singer, to play the part.

What about the story of Gesualdo killing his child?

I invented the scenario of Gesualdo placing his two-and-a-half-year-old son – who he had reasons to doubt was his child – on a swing and having his servants push him for two days and nights until the child was dead. In some of the existing documents there is an allusion to him killing his infant son, but no absolute proof. Having a choir on either side of the boy on the swing singing about the beauty of death is also invented, though in one of Gesualdo's compositions there is a text about such things. Historical documents make absolutely clear that he murdered his wife and her lover in flagrante.

The last scene of the film was shot at a mediaeval tournament in Arezzo. I wanted to have the musical director talk about boldness and adventure in music, and as I was speaking with him I noticed a young man who was playing a footman to one of the knights. The whole scene with him on his cellphone to his mother was staged. He was actually talking to my brother, who was standing ten feet away and knew exactly when to make the call. I told the young man to act as if it were his mother calling him and that she wanted him to come home for lunch. I already knew it would be the last scene in the film. "Don't worry," he says, "I'll be there soon. The film about Gesualdo is almost over." I asked him to look straight into the camera after speaking the line and be deadly serious, no matter what. I was right next to the camera, joking around. There is a strange expression on his face because he didn't know whether to laugh or look into the lens with great intent. He stares directly to camera, and the film ends.

Little Dieter Needs to Fly *is a moving story told powerfully by Dieter Dengler.*

I was invited by a German television station to contribute to their series *Voyages to Hell* and immediately sensed it was my kind of thing. The television executive wanted me to make a film about myself, about being imprisoned in Africa and the problems on *Fitzcarraldo.* "That was difficult work," I told him, "but it wasn't a voyage into hell." I had read about Dieter in the sixties – though by now he was very much a forgotten figure – and tracked him down. Although his accent hinted at his Swabian background, Dieter's English was fluent, and he was the greatest rapper I ever met. He died some years ago of Lou Gehrig's disease, and the first thing the illness took was his power of speech. How scandalous that in his final days he was bereft of words. Being with Dieter was a constant joy; the man had such an intense enjoyment of life, something you sense throughout *Little Dieter Needs to Fly.* Even when he was no longer able to talk, we still managed to have long conversations together. He could tell dirty jokes and stories without a word, just using his face and hands. I remember looking at his feet and having no trouble believing he had run barefoot in the jungle for weeks, and that by the end maggots were crawling out of them.

Dieter's story is an extraordinary one. Born in Germany just before the Second World War, his earliest memory is of Allied aeroplanes diving down from the sky and bombing his village of Wildberg, in the Black Forest. One bomber came so close to the house where Dieter lived – firing as it flew – that when it whipped past the window where he was standing, Dieter's eyes locked with the pilot's for a split second. Rather than being afraid, he was mesmerised by these almighty beings swooping down from the clouds, and from that moment Little Dieter Needed to Fly. After his apprenticeship as a blacksmith and clockmaker, at the age of eighteen he emigrated to America. In New York he survived on pizza crusts until he enlisted in the army. After more than two years of peeling potatoes and another two years of changing tyres, and three years of college, Dieter eventually became a pilot. He was excited to head to Vietnam because he wanted to hang out with the go-go girls in Saigon. In 1966, during the early stages of the war, he was shot down over Laos forty minutes into his first mission. He started preparing to eject once he was hit by enemy fire; fragments of the engine were flying about his head. But then, because of an updraught, his aeroplane picked up altitude as he flew over a dense jungle ridge and he decided not to jump out. Dieter told me he didn't eject because he didn't want to abandon his first-ever aeroplane, so he ended up going down with it. He immediately buried his emergency radio because he knew the North Vietnamese might use it to lure rescue helicopters into an ambush. He was wearing civilian clothes under his flight suit and had his German passport with him, as well as his old certificate of apprenticeship as a clockmaker; the idea was that he could pretend to be a journalist from Germany. Pathet Lao guerrillas found him quick enough. Two days later he escaped, but was recaptured after almost dying of thirst, then subjected to a forced three-week march through the jungle, and eventually transferred to a prison camp run by the North Vietnamese, where two other Americans and three Thais were being held.

When he saw the state of these men – who had been held captive for more than two and a half years – Dieter immediately began making plans to escape. The camp was heavily guarded, but he saw that an opportunity arose every time the guards put their weapons down and went to eat in the kitchen. Eventually Dieter put his plan into action, which led to a gun battle that left five guards dead. The prisoners, split into two groups, ran barefoot into the jungle. Dieter ended up the only survivor. After his friend Duane was killed, he threw caution to the wind and set fire to an abandoned village, hoping to attract the attention of nearby aircraft. After a series of incredible coincidences he was finally spotted by an aeroplane and hoisted into a helicopter. The crew didn't recognise him as one of their own and, afraid they might have picked up a North Vietnamese soldier on a suicide mission, a huge marine threw himself on Dieter, nearly crushing him. The marine almost fell out of the chopper in horror when he pulled out a half-eaten snake Dieter had stuffed down his shirt. It had been five months since his aeroplane had been shot down; he was down to eighty-five pounds and probably had no more than a day to live. Dieter was the only American POW to escape from North Vietnamese and Laotian captivity, and remains one of the most highly decorated soldiers in American history.

While Dieter was still recovering in hospital, his mother was flown over from Germany; it was the first time she had been in an aeroplane. She brought a box of apples with her and handed out fruit to her fellow passengers, but when dinner was served by the airline staff she refused to eat because she had no money and thought she had to pay for it. When the admiral who met her at the airport realised what had happened, he immediately ordered some food be brought from the nearest canteen. Dieter's mother was allowed to stay in the admiral's house, but at five o'clock the next morning an alarm went off because she had lowered herself down on a rope to clean the windows. It was her way of showing thanks. The following morning another alarm went off because she was seen behind the house showering with a garden hose. She just wanted to save water.

How did Dieter handle home life after his experiences as a prisoner?

He developed certain safeguards, but never had to struggle for his sanity and wasn't consumed by the problems you see among some Vietnam veterans, men who returned home completely destroyed inside. Dieter was a unique man with extraordinary survival instincts, alongside great integrity and pride, and wasn't affected by his experiences as much as most other people would have been. He was tortured by having sharp pieces of bamboo put under his fingernails, and one of his arms was bound so tightly that it was unusable for six months, but he still refused to sign the propaganda declaration that denounced American military action, something almost every other POW did. "I love America," Dieter kept saying. "America gave me wings." During the war his grandfather had been the only person in his village who hadn't voted for Hitler, and because of this was dragged through the streets by an angry mob and accused of being a traitor. If his grandfather could endure such treatment, said Dieter, he could too. Although he was imprisoned and tortured, he never looked at his captors with disgust. He respected them, something I have always admired.

Being held prisoner was clearly the event that shaped him, but Dieter had such a difficult childhood amidst the devastation of post-war Germany that he was well prepared for his jungle ordeal. He possessed all the qualities that make America so wonderful: self-reliance and courage, a readiness to take risks, a kind of frontier spirit. He grew up in a remote area of the country, and as a child saw things that made no earthly sense. Germany had been transformed into a dreamscape of the surreal, which is what we see in the film, those endless images of bombed-out cityscapes. Like me, Dieter had to take charge of his life from an early age, and we connected because as children we had both experienced things that children shouldn't, like real hunger, though things weren't as bad for us as they were for him. Dieter – whose father was killed at Stalingrad – would peel wallpaper from the walls of bombed-out houses, and his mother would cook it because there were nutrients in the glue. Until the day he died, Dieter refused to see himself as a hero. "Only dead people are heroes," he would say. One time after he spoke in detail about the tortures he experienced during captivity, my wife asked him, "How do you sleep at night? Do you have nightmares?" "You see, darling," he said nonchalantly, "that was the fun part of my life." When we screened *Little Dieter Needs to Fly* at the Telluride Film Festival, Dieter flew over in his single-engine Cessna, and the first night slept in the cockpit. One evening I was with him from eight o'clock until two the following morning, and he proposed – I swear to God – to eight consecutive women in total exuberance. The women all loved him for his intense charm and joy, even if they turned him down flat. He took the eight refusals with grace, then proceeded to get completely drunk and slept outside the door to our apartment because he had forgotten his key and didn't want to wake us up.

I like the United States for embracing someone like Dieter, a quintessential immigrant who came to America not just to find a job, but as a man with a big dream. Not only did he fulfil that dream, he was punished for it, then finally redeemed. The day we filmed the sequence on the aircraft carrier, I asked him to wait on the pier because I wanted to put the camera up on the bridge and get a shot of him walking into the ship for the first time. I went to the bridge, told the captain who I was, and explained what film we were making. "Dieter Dengler?" he asked. "You can place your camera here, but please give me five minutes." Almost immediately every officer on board scrambled onto the gangway, formed a line and saluted Dieter as he walked up. This was more than thirty years after his escape from the jungle. He died of Lou Gehrig's disease a few years after *Little Dieter Needs to Fly* was released, having battled the disease like a warrior. I filmed his funeral in Arlington National Cemetery and included the footage as a postscript on the DVD of the film. What I continue to find wondrous is that Dieter emerged from his experiences without so much as a hint of bitterness; he was forever able to bear the misery with great optimism. Dieter had such an impressive and jubilant attitude to life, able to brush his experiences aside and deal with them, never making a fuss. He has been a role model for me, and even today when I am in a complicated situation I ask myself, "What would Dieter do?"

How is Little Dieter Needs to Fly *stylised?*

The substantial elements are real. The two thousand pounds of rice, two thousand pounds of flour, six hundred pounds of honey and one thousand gallons of drinking water in vacuum-sealed plastic barrels really were there under the floorboards of his house. Dieter slept easier knowing it was all stashed away. Even years after returning home he thought about opening a restaurant where he could eat all the food he wanted. Also true is that when he was half dead in the jungle, a bear who had followed him for days came so close he could smell its foul breath. I was careful about representing Dieter's reality on screen, but did ask him to become an actor playing himself. Everything in the film is authentic Dieter, but to intensify him some of the stories were scripted, rehearsed and carefully orchestrated. It was my job as director to translate and edit his thoughts into something profound and cinematic, which meant trimming away everything that didn't fit, however interesting. Sometimes during filming Dieter would focus on some little detail and miss the bigger picture; I had to push him to condense a story that rambled on for almost an hour into only a couple of minutes. "Please, Dieter," I would say, "you have to be more disciplined. Stick to the essentials. Cut away everything that isn't important." There are a couple of scenes in the film that were shot at least five times until we got it right.

The film starts with Dieter visiting a tattoo parlour in San Francisco and looking at an image of Death whipping a team of horses up from Hell through fire and brimstone. He tells the tattoo artist he could never put that design on his body because for him it was different. "It didn't look like that to me," he says. "It was the angels who steered the horses. Death didn't want me." Although he had hallucinations when he was near death in the jungle, Dieter never had any intention of getting a tattoo; the whole thing was my idea. Then we cut to him driving to the home that he built with his own hands on Mount Tamalpais, north of San Francisco. When he gets out of his car, Dieter repeatedly opens and closes the car door before walking to the front door, which he again opens and closes. Eventually he goes inside. This is a scene I created after he casually mentioned that his experiences in the jungle made him appreciate being able to open a door whenever he wanted. I was intrigued by the many images of open doors on the walls of his home, all of which were really his. "They were a bargain," he said, "only ten bucks each." I told him we had to shoot a scene and make this truth visible. "Open and close your front door a couple of times," I said, "then talk about the door as a symbol of freedom." He hesitated and said, "I'll look weird to my buddies." What finally convinced him was when I told him how charming the ladies would think it was. From this moment early in the film the audience is irrevocably with Dieter, very much on his side. In our conversations, whenever he would describe his dreams to me, the image of a jellyfish – dancing in a kind of slow-motion transparent movement – floated into my mind, so we went to the local aquarium and filmed the sequence where he explains what death looked like to him. These ethereal, almost unreal creatures express his dreams perfectly, though it was all my idea.

One of the best examples of stylisation in any of my films comes at the end of *Little Dieter*, the scene shot at Davis-Monthan Air Force Base near Tucson, Arizona, an aeroplane graveyard with tens of thousands of mothballed aircraft sitting in rows, as far as the eye can see; nothing but aircraft from horizon to horizon. Dieter talks about the nightmares he had immediately after his rescue, and how his friends would take him from his bed at night and pack him into a cockpit, where he would sleep. He says that inside an aeroplane is where he felt safe. All this is true, though I chose the base because of the stunning visuals. Dieter had never been to Davis-Monthan, and his line "This is heaven for pilots" was scripted by me.

Wasn't it a bit much to march Dieter back through the jungle with his hands bound behind his back?

Dieter loved Asia and its people, and had been back to the jungle many times since the war. Soon after we shot the film he even returned to the village near where he had crashed, and where the engine from his aeroplane was displayed on a pedestal, as some kind of trophy, a souvenir of his failed sortie.

The Laotian authorities weren't too happy about us filming in their country because apparently they're still grumpy about the fact that Dieter shot and killed five Laotians during his escape, so we filmed in jungle areas of Thailand at the border and on the Mekong River instead. By the time we made the film many of the metal panels of his aeroplane had long since been turned into cooking pots by local villagers, but some of the fuselage was still at the crash site; we knew exactly where to find it, and Dieter insisted on swimming across the Mekong to clandestinely film some scenes at the site. I planned to go with him, carrying a small digital camera, but in the end prudent members of the crew advised us against it. I did also wonder whether including images of whatever remained of the aeroplane in the film would provide us with any significant insights. The German television network wanted me to shoot re-enactments of the events Dieter was talking about with actors, but I knew it would more effective if Dieter did everything himself. He always exuded such sanity that it was never a problem for him to run through the jungle with his hands tied behind his back, led by a group of locals hired from the nearest village. The line "This is a little too close to home" was scripted. The scene was a safe and effective way of getting something special from him. He insisted on playing the part, and rushed off into the forest, surrounded by these gun-toting men, with the cameraman and me running behind. Perhaps it was his way of chasing the demons away.

I chose not to include anything overly violent in the film, and a few years later there were scenes we shot for *Rescue Dawn* – where

Dieter was portrayed by Christian Bale – that even during production I felt shouldn't be included. There is certain imagery I don't appreciate: that of graphic violence, stark naked as it sometimes appears in real life, especially when perpetrated against the defence-less; such things are easier to stomach in stylised, comic-book form. I say this not because I find onscreen violence a particular danger to our children's well-being and civilisation in general; it's just that having to look at such things on screen is my Achilles heel. I have a tendency to faint when giving blood, and once passed out while watching the scene in *The Passion of Joan of Arc* when prison guards draw blood from Joan's arm. As for censorship, I'm against it, though I would cut something from a film if it deeply offended the religious feelings of the majority of people in a country. I would never show the butchering of a cow in the release print of one of my films in India, but would never cut something if all it did was hurt the feelings of cat lovers in England.

Wings of Hope, *another tale of horror in the jungle, is a sister to* Little Dieter.

The film – which was dormant in me for many years – is the story of Juliane Koepcke, a seventeen-year-old German girl, the sole survivor of an aeroplane crash in the Peruvian jungle on Christmas Eve in 1971. Juliane's mother was killed, along with ninety-four others. The aircraft was travelling from Lima to Pucallpa when it disintegrated over the jungle – probably after having been struck by lightning – less than an hour after taking off, and she sailed to earth still strapped to a row of seats. It was almost as if she didn't leave the aeroplane; the aeroplane left her. There are several explanations of how Juliane's fall was cushioned and she managed to survive a fall of nearly three miles. During particularly serious storms there are powerful updraughts, one of which might have caught the row of seats and driven it upwards. The seats might also have spun wildly as they fell, like a maple seed, because Juliane was sitting at one end of the row, and this may have slowed her. The dense lianas, intertwined with the tall trees, also probably broke her fall as she hit the ground. What's astonishing is that after ten days the intensive search was called off, and on the twelfth day Juliane – who had survived on a pocketful of candies – emerged from the jungle. Her eyes were so bloodshot that local villagers thought she was a forest demon and fled when they saw her.

The fact that Juliane landed without being killed is a miracle, but her escape from the jungle was not; it was sheer professionalism. She was familiar with the environment because of time spent at the ecological station her parents had founded deep in the jungle. She must also have inherited some of her father's dogged willpower. He was a biologist who wanted to do research in the jungle. After the war, without a penny or passport to his name, he dug himself into a cargo of salt on a freighter bound for South America as a stowaway, and walked across the entire continent until he reached Peru, which is where Juliane grew up. After the crash, she followed the water rather than waiting for help, which is what most people would probably have done. Juliane knew that a small creek always leads to a larger one and eventually a river, and eventually human beings, and that if she followed the shrieks of the Hoatzin bird she would end up at a large body of water. She never panicked when crocodiles splashed violently from the sandbanks and disappeared into the river in which she was wading. Her parents had taught her how to survive under such conditions; she knew that these animals, when on land, always flee from human beings and hide in the water, never in the jungle. She did everything right; everyone else, including me, would have fled into the jungle and inevitably perished. *Wings of Hope* isn't just about Juliane's ordeal; it deals with something deeper, touching powerfully on our relationship with nature and how to survive it.

The other reason for my fascination with the story is that in 1971 I was in Peru working on *Aguirre*, and was booked on the very flight that crashed. The girl who played Aguirre's daughter was a fifteen-year-old schoolgirl I found in Lima. We had a chaperone for her, but a few days before the start of shooting her parents suddenly decided to withdraw their permission for her to be in the film. I flew from Cusco to Lima and eventually persuaded them otherwise, then found myself – alongside my wife, some actors and crew – in Lima. We had tickets to fly back into the mountains shortly before Christmas, but the flight was delayed by a day and a half due to repairs. More and more passengers were accumulating at the airport. I had to bribe an airline employee so I could get a boarding pass, but at the last minute my scheduled flight was cancelled. After a series of crashes the airline had only a single aeroplane left, which flew the inland routes in Peru, all in a single day. In the end, because it was already so late in the day, it was decided this aircraft would fly only to Pucallpa. I remember being in the departure hall surrounded by people who had made it onto the flight; there was jubilation because they knew Christmas would be spent at home. I had flown in that same aeroplane many times, back and forth into the jungle, and knew the crew who died on the flight. I would talk to the stewardesses and always sit by a window because I wanted to see the Andes and the beginning of the jungle. The airline was notorious for its crashes, and only months before two of the company's pilots – who didn't even have proper licences – missed the runway in Cusco and smashed into a mountain. One hundred and six bodies were retrieved from the wreckage, although the maximum capacity of the aeroplane was only ninety-six. An airline employee had sold an additional ten standing places in the aisle and pocketed the cash. It also turned out that the airline's mechanics had repaired only motorcycles. Only much later did I discover that we were filming *Aguirre* a few rivers away from Juliane as she was fighting for her life.

I always knew I would make *Wings of Hope* one day, but it took a while to locate Juliane, who today is an expert on Amazonian bats. There had been an unprecedented media frenzy following her rescue and return to Germany, with journalists even showing up at her hospital room dressed as priests or cleaning personnel and taking photographs. After this intense harassment she successfully covered her tracks, got married and changed her name. I managed to find her father, who immediately ranted at me, saying he would never give the name and address of his daughter to anyone. I had a suspicion Juliane would be in Peru because that was where she had grown up; I knew she loved the jungle and thought she might be working as a biologist in one of the ecological stations down there. I eventually found her through some old newspaper clippings about her mother's burial in a small Bavarian town. The local priest told me that one of Juliane's aunts lived in a nearby village. I went straight over there, but she wouldn't tell me anything, so I asked her to give Juliane my phone number. Not too long after that Juliane called me, and it turned out she lived in Munich, not Peru. I said it would be enough to talk for thirty minutes, not a minute longer, and that five minutes into our conversation I would offer to withdraw. When we met, I put my wristwatch on the table. Exactly 300 seconds into the meeting I stood up, picked up my watch and bowed. "That's the deal," I said, "unless you would like to continue for the next twenty-five minutes." Juliane took my arm. "Sit down and stay," she said. "We haven't finished yet."

Juliane had seen a couple of my films and liked them, which was helpful, but all those years later she was still somewhat traumatised by the media's treatment of her – something I touch on in *Wings of Hope* when mentioning the trashy feature film made about her experiences* – and it took a year for her to decide that she would co-operate. There were some personal things Juliane didn't want to talk about, and she knew I would respect her wishes, but once she finally agreed to make the film she really went for it. When we flew into the jungle from Lima, I asked her to sit in window seat F, row 19, the seat she had been in when the aeroplane fell apart over the Amazon.

Is anything stylised in Wings of Hope?

The beginning and end of the film, with the broken and disfigured faces of the mannequins, and my voiceover of Juliane wanting to reassemble and somehow resurrect the plane, then seeing herself, strapped to her seat, sailing through the dark abyss. This is all poetry. My decision not to introduce too many stylised elements probably has something to do with the fact that Juliane is rather straight-talking and clear-headed. The only reason she survived her ordeal was because of her ability to act methodically in the face of such dire circumstances, and I wanted these qualities to shine through in the film. Look at how much the mosquitoes bother her husband, while Juliane isn't in the least troubled by them. There is real grief in the film, but it's handled with tenderness and discretion. Not dwelling on the pain that Juliane went through back then means her story is more haunting for audiences. As usual, the television executives wanted re-enactments of her experiences and never expected me to take Juliane herself back to the jungle, but by doing this – just as by tying up Dieter Dengler and walking him

* *The Story of Juliane Koepcke* (aka *Miracles Still Happen*) (1974), directed by Giuseppe Maria Scotese.

through the trails where he almost perished thirty years before – we dug into a deeper reality. Once the executives saw the footage of Juliane in the jungle they immediately complained. "Why doesn't she break down when confronted with fragments of the aeroplane?" Some people don't understand that discretion is a virtue.

In recent years you have spoken about our shifting perception of reality.

There has, in the recent past, been a momentous and ferocious onslaught of new media, tools and instruments that have radically challenged our sense of reality. Think back to the mediaeval knights who for centuries, from ancient times on, fought on horseback with sword and shield, then all of a sudden found themselves confronted with gunpowder, firearms and cannons. Overnight the most fundamental notions of warfare were irrevocably altered. The entire world of chivalry was made obsolete; centuries-old rules fell away and, amidst such radical change, certain values and virtues cataclysmically collapsed. Apparently a group of seventeenth-century Samurai in Japan decided to forgo firearms and use only swords, but they didn't last long. Then the plague decimated a third of Europe's population within only a few years. History became porous and the first signs of a new world came into view. Fresh horizons were being explored and new inventions predominated. Europe was in crisis; it was a period of absolute insecurity involving the exploration of the unknown and a wholesale re-evaluation of moral codes. What I find fascinating is the emergence of writers like Philippe de Commynes, whose memoirs of the late mediaeval period in France are invaluable. Historiography in his time perpetuated the glory of chivalresque behaviour, though it had long since been uprooted. He was the single clairvoyant who watched everything with an uncompromising, relentless gaze.

There are signs that our own times are full of equally great insecurities and upheavals, of tremendous cruelty and violence, of enormous changes, of astonishing achievements. One of the most powerful forces in society today is the unprecedented explosion of tools that have given us the ability to alter reality and create some kind of pseudo-reality, including digital special effects – such as credibly rendered cinematic dinosaurs, as compared to the model animation of the fifties and sixties – virtual reality, video games and the Internet. You can't trust a photo these days because of Photoshop, which can all too easily be used to modify and falsify an image. These things have arrived almost at once, in a single torrent. Our sense of the real world today is massively challenged; I include here reality television, breast enhancement and the carefully choreographed, fake drama of WrestleMania, populated by larger-than-life characters with muscles that nature doesn't normally provide us with and who take pleasure in telling everyone how unbelievably evil they are. Wrestling matches are continually interrupted by commercials, but never those moments when the owner of the franchise comes out into the ring with two buxom, bikini-clad blondes on his arms, or when his long-suffering wife – allegedly paraplegic and blind – is wheeled out into the ring. His son then steps out into the ring and confronts his father, but not because of how his mother is being treated; he vents because his percentage of the franchise revenue isn't big enough. I love people like Jesse Ventura, who in his wrestling days played the real bad-ass, the California surfer with long blond hair, sunglasses and a bronze tan. He would climb into the ring and shout to the audience, "You assholes, working day in, day out for a few bucks!" A young boy sheepishly walks up to him to ask for an autograph. Jesse rips the notebook into shreds and tramples on it, at which point ten thousand people howl gloriously in unison against him. This is all a new form of spectacle, of mythology and storytelling, like the crude beginnings of ancient Greek drama, work that preceded Sophocles, Aeschylus and Euripides, eventually flowering into something extraordinary. It's fascinating to see how these archetypes function in modern-day culture.

These tectonic shifts require similarly radical changes in the way we handle reality on screen. The more technical tricks filmmakers bring to the screen, the louder the question of truthfulness will become. A new kind of cinema is needed that can help us readjust and once again trust our eyes. This is a heavy burden for filmmakers, but there is one thing we can be sure of: *cinéma-vérité*, which was a coherent response in the sixties, is no longer valid today, when everything can be so easily manipulated. Cinema has to find a new position from which to tackle these issues. I want to take audiences back to the earliest days of cinema, when the Lumière brothers screened their film of a train pulling into a station. Apparently some people fled in panic because they were convinced they were about to be run over. I can't confirm this; it might be a legend, but I like the story. At screenings of *Fitzcarraldo* I heard gasps from audiences at the moment the steamship is dragged upwards. They pointed at the screen after realising this was no trick, that it was a real boat and a real mountain. If I had ploughed on with the plastic solution and filmed it in a studio with a model ship, six-year-olds everywhere today would have immediately known it was a special effect. I've seen people in a small open-air cinema in Mexico talking back to the bad guy; one of them even pulled out a gun and opened fire at the screen.

When *Grizzly Man* came out, children – drowning in the manipulated digital images that surround them and invade their every moment – insisted there was no way that Timothy Treadwell's footage was real. Science-fiction films make it perfectly clear that what you are looking at has been artificially created in a studio with digital effects, but young people, attuned to the changes taking place around them, couldn't believe this man really walked up to a thousand-pound grizzly and stretched out his hand to touch the beast. By insisting that this kind of imagery must be the result of digital trickery, they reveal themselves to be disconnected from the real world. A few years ago my wife Lena took a series of photos of me standing next to a bear in rural Utah, one of which was used to publicise *Grizzly Man*. People immediately assume this image was pieced together with Photoshop. No one believes me when I tell them that's a real grizzly.

At a film festival one year I was witness to a "pitching session," a grotesque gladiatorial contest run by thoroughly debased people in which documentary filmmakers line up in public and attempt to raise money for their projects. The entire thing is detestable, a revolting circus. One of the organisers – an obese man who snorted about the place – waddled onto the stage wearing a cape and carrying a stick. There were beads of sweat dripping down his forehead from underneath the top hat he was wearing as he pranced. I wanted to vomit. I was on a panel discussion with other filmmakers who were talking about "reality" and how to capture it on film, how *cinéma-vérité* was the only way forward, that manipulation and staging in non-fiction cinema was a no-no. A young woman next to me kept raving about her own particular style, how she wanted to be as unobtrusive as possible, like a fly on the wall. It was just the kind of thin, trivial ideology I look upon with deep suspicion. Even if some of the most disturbing footage I have ever seen – the abduction of a toddler by two young boys from a shopping mall in England in 1993 – was unstaged, captured by a surveillance camera, I have no interest in blindly recording hours of nothing, waiting for a bank robber to show up once every ten years.

I say here to adherents of *cinéma-vérité*: I am no bookkeeper; my mandate is poetry. I want to be involved. I want to shape and sculpt, to stage things, to intrude and invent. I want to be a film director. I was the only person at the festival arguing against these morons. The subject was being so hashed to death that I couldn't take it any longer. I grabbed a microphone and said, "I'm no fly on the wall. I am the hornet that stings." There was an immediate uproar, so not having anything more to say, I shouted out, "Happy New Year, losers." And that was that.

10

Fervour and Woe

You have acted in several films over the years.

I enjoy working with Zak Penn, who contributed to the script of *Rescue Dawn*. His film *Incident at Loch Ness* is very intelligent; it's a hoax built upon a hoax upon a hoax, and its marketing campaign was yet another hoax. Press reports were circulated saying that I was going to make a film about the Loch Ness monster and that at the same time cameraman John Bailey was making a documentary about me called *Herzog in Wonderland*. Both were diversions. The film we actually made is a complex ruse that seamlessly blends digital effects with a group of people – most of whom are playing themselves – improvising. The result is clever and funny, subtly incorporating the strangest and silliest stories and rumours about me. I enjoyed the element of self-mockery my part involved, like having the audience watch me buying razor blades in the local supermarket and packing my bags before I leave for Scotland. I had a feeling that a dose of self-irony would do me good. Even the DVD commentary Zak and I recorded is one big joke, with me storming off halfway, completely miffed.

References to my films and me are hiding under every rock; look carefully and you'll see them throughout. Some are subtler than others; for example, I have never cooked yucca – which needs to be carefully processed to rid it of all toxins – for dinner guests, and "my" house in the film was actually Zak's home at the time. But you can hardly miss the moment when Zak has me at the point of an unloaded flare gun because I refuse to film the styrofoam Loch Ness monster bobbing in the water; it's some kind of homage to the tales of Kinski and me during the production of *Aguirre*. There are some amusing moments that didn't make it into the film, like Zak's assistant thinking I'm a vegetarian. I assure you that's the last thing I would ever be. Maybe people took no notice of the ideas behind *Loch Ness* because it's a comedy, which is unfortunate because it raises what I consider to be important and serious questions. What would an ocean be without a monster lurking in the dark? Like sleep without dreams. How is it that three million Americans claim to have had encounters with aliens, and three hundred thousand American women maintain they have been gang-raped by extraterrestrials? Why do almost all these women weigh over 350 pounds? Why have we never heard about such things happening in Ethiopia?

A couple of years later Zak directed *The Grand*, in which I play "The German," who always needs extra hand lotion in his hotel room, believes coffee to be the beverage of cowards and has to kill something every day in order to feel alive. It doesn't need to be big; squashing an ant is sufficient. He shows up at the hotel with a luggage cart full of caged animals, only to be told they aren't allowed in his room. "Don't worry," he tells the receptionist. "They won't be here for long."

Harmony Korine.

A few years ago he wanted me to play the father in *julien donkey-boy*. Originally he was going to act as my son in the film, but felt uncomfortable being behind and in front of the camera at the same time. Actually he just chickened out. Harmony didn't want me for the role just because I was the right age and looked the part; it was more significant for him than that. The deeper meaning to my being cast was that I have been something of an influence on his filmmaking over the years, and he wanted his "cinematic father" to be in the film. There was no real screenplay; much of *julien* was improvised, like my lines from *Dirty Harry*. I was sitting at the dinner table, surrounded by a crazed grandmother, a son who is a failed wrestler, a daughter who has been impregnated by her own insane brother Julien, and Julien himself, who has just committed murder. All I knew was that Julien was going to read a poem, and my job was to insult him. The red light on the camera started blinking, so I turned to Harmony and said, "Are we rolling?" He nodded, saying nothing. I asked him what the dialogue was. "Speak!" he said. It was all born out of the pressure of having to say something; everything I did was improvised on the spot. The character I play is completely dysfunctional and hostile. Let's face it, my scope as an actor is limited, though I love playing these vile and debased characters. Whenever it comes to these kinds of people I'm the first person they call. After *julien donkey-boy* opened in France my wife received a call from a friend. "Is that monster really your husband? We can offer you immediate shelter."

I played a missionary in Harmony's *Mister Lonely*. Originally I had a bigger part but was editing *Rescue Dawn* at the time, so couldn't spare the time. We were filming on an island off the coast of Panama, at the airport. I strolled over to a man who was muttering to himself and had a bunch of half-wilted flowers in his hand. I starting talking to him, and though he was quite incoherent I figured out that he was waiting for an aeroplane to arrive. His wife and three kids had bolted three years ago, and ever since then he had been hoping she would come home to him, so there he was, waiting patiently. I was wearing a priest's costume and told Harmony we should improvise a scene where this man could confess. "I can look into your heart!" I said out of the blue. "I know your wife left you because you fornicated with other women! Repent now!" He insisted it wasn't true. I looked him square in the eye and said, "I know what happened! It wasn't just one woman, it was at least five! You sinned! Down on your knees and repent!"

As for my role in the Tom Cruise blockbuster *Jack Reacher*, I was paid to be scary. As chief ideologue of the baddies, my particular method of intimidation is forcing my adversaries to chew their own thumbs off. I wasn't hired just because I have a funny accent; apparently they were having difficulties in casting a real bad-ass bad guy. Some actors look dangerous only when they come at you with a gun or when they scream and shout, but apparently the only person they could think of who is threatening even before he opens his mouth is Herzog. It isn't the first time this has happened. I'm always being stopped by customs officials at airports, and many years ago I played a deranged murderer in Edgar Reitz's film *Geschichten vom Kübelkind*.

You lent your voice to an episode of The Simpsons.

When they invited me to voice a character, I said, "What do you mean, my voice? Isn't it a newspaper cartoon strip?" They thought I was pulling their leg, but I had no idea the animated series existed. I played a German pharmaceutical industrialist called Walter Hottenhoffer who creates an LSD-style pill that makes everyone happy, in particular grumpy grandpa. It's my apotheosis within American popular culture.

Do you still play football?

Not too often since moving to California, though for years I was with a club in Munich called Black and Yellow [Schwarz/Gelb München]. It was a hopeless team but a great joy to play with those people. I pay tribute here to the late Sepp Mosemeier, the founder and president, a chubby pastry baker by profession. In a different life he would have been an opera singer or poet. He had a wonderful outlook on everything and managed to keep the team together – men from all strata of society – for years.

During the early years I was a goalkeeper, about which I have a strange story. I'm interested in how sometimes we do things completely contrary to our intentions, yet they turn to be the right thing after all. We were playing against a far superior team – a group of apprentice butchers from Munich – and were having a good day, keeping the game tied at 1–1. One striker on the other team was a bully, strong as an ox and with a ferocious shot. Seconds before the game was over there was a penalty against us, and though I prayed, "Please, not the bully," I saw him trotting to the penalty spot with absolute confidence. When your opponent is someone with such a relentlessly strong kick, a monster who can turn a football into a projectile, a goalkeeper has no choice but to pick a corner and hope it's the one the ball is going to fly into. But even if I picked the correct corner there was still little chance of stopping the ball. I saw him placing the ball on the spot and had the feeling he glanced for a split second into the right-hand corner of the goal. I said to myself, "Go for the right, go for the right." He took the run-up, and the second before he kicked I inwardly screamed to myself, "THE RIGHT! THE RIGHT!" For some reason I flew to the left, which turned out to be where he was aiming for. The ball hit my fist, pounded into the ground, soared high into the air and bounced away from the goal. It was a strange experience, not unlike what Peter Handke describes in his novel *The Goalkeeper's Fear of the Penalty*, though in his story the goalkeeper is so terrified that he ends up frozen dead centre between the posts.

My time in goal ended a few years later during a football game at the Cannes Film Festival, where there was a tradition that directors played against actors. Although some of the directors were near obese and totally inept, it was a hard-fought match one year. The actors would draw our team into their half, then kick the ball at the goal and sprint – three or four at once – towards me. Up until half-time I had managed to save all their attempts at goal, but at the beginning of the second half the ball flew wide into empty space near me. As I ran out of the penalty area to connect with it, I saw Maximilian Schell galloping towards me like a furious bison. I was certain I could get there first to kick the ball away, which I did, but a split second later Schell crashed into me and dislocated my elbow; it still bothered me a year later. After that I stopped playing in goal and moved to centre forward, where I got the reputation of being a kamikaze player. I was never the fastest person on the pitch, but I was the most dangerous, though you have to see all this in perspective. It was football at a very low level.

During pre-production on *Aguirre* in Peru, I met the legendary Rudi Gutendorf, who over the decades coached six first-division teams in Germany and countless others in nearly forty countries. At the time he was the coach of Lima's top club, and one day he invited me to participate in the team's fitness training. After that there would be a test game, team A versus team B. One of the B-team players had hurt his ankle, so Rudi told me to step in as a substitute. Before we started he asked me, "Who do you want as your opponent?" I said, "I want to play against the best in the world. I want Gallardo." Alberto Gallardo – famous after his performance in the 1970 World Cup – was extremely unpredictable, so fast that no one in the world could follow him. I was confident I could at least shake him up on the pitch. This was ridiculous, wishful thinking on my part; the whole thing was hopeless from the start. I had no idea how tough it was going to be, how fiercely the players fought for the ball. Even with my thirty-foot start, Gallardo would outrun me by twenty feet, and after only ten minutes I was so bamboozled that I couldn't tell in which direction my team was playing. I couldn't even have told you the colour of my team's shirt. After fifteen minutes I had terrible stomach cramps and crawled pathetically off the field on all fours. I ended up behind some bushes, vomiting. Rudi was good enough to pretend he hadn't seen anything.

Did you go to football matches as a child?

Until the age of about fifteen my brother and I would go see Die Löwen [The Lions] play. It was more of a working-class club than Bayern Munich and quickly disappeared from the first division. My father always objected to us playing football; it was much too primitive and proletarian a game for him. He didn't like us coming home with dirty knees and shorts, and preferred we do something classier instead, like fencing.

Albert Camus apparently said that much of what he knew about morality he learnt from the football pitch. Can the same be said of you?

No. Football is just football.

My Best Fiend *is about your relationship with Klaus Kinski.*

Kinski was one of the great screen actors, perhaps the last expressionistic performer in cinema. As an adolescent I watched him in the anti-war film *Kinder, Mütter und ein General*, in which he plays a lieutenant who leads schoolboys to the front. The mothers of the boys and the soldiers go to sleep for a few hours. Kinski is awakened at daybreak, and the way he stirs, raising his head from the table, will forever stay in my memory; I replay it several times in *My Best Fiend*. I'm sure it looks like nothing special to most people, but this one moment impressed me so profoundly that later it was a decisive factor in my professional life. Strange how memory can magnify things. Today I find the scene where he orders Maximilian Schell to be shot much more impressive.

Kinski was undoubtedly the ultimate pestilence to work with, but he also gave truly amazing – and in subtle ways very different – performances in each of the films we made together. He and I were like two critical masses that would explode when they came into

335

contact with each other, though thankfully I was able to transform this highly flammable mixture into a productive screen collaboration. He constantly threw tantrums, created scandals, broke contracts and terrorised actors, crews and directors. Every day it was my task to domesticate the beast and make these crazed energies productive for the screen. One of my achievements was to do this without clipping his wings, which would have made him harmless and uninteresting on screen. I was able to see through him like looking through water in the sink; I could always gauge his hysterical energy, and knew how to mobilise and articulate it in front of the camera. People think we had a love–hate relationship, but I neither loved nor hated him. At one point I did seriously plan to firebomb him in his home, though I confess with some embarrassment that my infallible plan, with its airtight alibi, was sabotaged by the vigilance of his Alsatian. It was all a farce, like those Italian comedies of the fifties where bank robbers drill through the wrong wall and accidentally find themselves in the local police station. Kinski later told me he had planned to murder me around the same time. We had a few drinks and a good laugh about it.

Kinski and I complemented each other in a strange way, and though it's true I owe him a lot, it's also fair to say he owed me something, even if he could never admit it. It was a fortunate situation for both of us: fortunate for me that he decided to be in *Aguirre*; fortunate for him I took him seriously as an actor. He was so reckless with his own possibilities. Look at all the films he made and you see what I'm talking about; in many of them he appears for only two minutes, which meant he was needed for only one or two days of shooting. No one could endure him for longer than that. When he and his Vietnamese wife – who I had never met before – arrived on the set of *Aguirre*, Klaus and I embraced one another, after which I went to shake his wife's hand. He immediately pushed me aside and with a menacing look stood two inches from my face for at least a minute, staring directly into my eyes, snorting and fuming and shivering, without saying a word. This book isn't the place for me to talk about the monstrous way Kinski treated the women in his life and abused his daughter Pola, who sought me out before she published her memoir.* Let me say that there were debates in

* See Bibliography, p. 500.

Germany about whether her allegations could be proved, but there isn't a shred of doubt in my heart that she is telling the truth. If I am on anyone's side, it's hers. All this may change the way people see Kinski in my films, but this shift of perspective won't last for ever. Long into the future audiences will see Kinski again as Aguirre. All these centuries later, the fact that Caravaggio was a murderer doesn't change the way we look at his paintings.

Did you learn anything from Kinski?

What was impressive about him was his knowledge of cinema, of lighting, stagecraft and the choreography of the human body in front of the camera. I shot a sequence for *Aguirre*, but two days later had the feeling I hadn't filmed it correctly and decided a wider angle was needed. On set and in costume, Kinski made precise inch-by-inch movements and turns with the exact same rhythms as he had two days before. There was no video footage to study. He had instant recall of the physical nature of that particular moment and his contribution to the scene. Then there's the "Kinski Spiral," something I demonstrate in *My Best Fiend* with photographer Beat Presser. When an actor enters the frame from the side, there is often no dramatic tension, so whenever there was a reason for it Kinski would make his appearance from directly behind the camera. If he wanted to spin into frame from the left, he would position him-self next to the camera, with his left foot next to the tripod. Then he would step over the tripod with his right leg, twisting his foot inward. The whole body would unwind before the camera, allow-ing him to spin smoothly into frame, which created a mysterious nervousness. There is also a move called "Kinski's Double Spiral," where the initial movement is followed by a counter-spin, but that's complex stuff and I could never explain it to you in words. I adapted the single spiral for a shot in *The Enigma of Kaspar Hauser*, when Kaspar is at the party with Lord Stanhope. Look closely and you see me doing it myself in *Incident at Loch Ness*.

Was there a particular reason you made My Best Fiend *when you did?*

When I first heard Kinski had died I understood it only acousti-cally. I registered the fact but it didn't really enter my heart until

337

months later, when I stood alongside his ex-wife and son, his ashes in my hands, which I emptied out into the Pacific Ocean. I always felt that the five films we made together needed something to bind them together, and planned to make a film about the two of us – our struggles, our work together – but for years after his death it was all too heavy to deal with. Time lightened the burden, made everything milder, and when I felt able to talk about Kinski with warmth and humour I realised I was ready. If I had made the film immediately after his death, I'm sure it would have been much darker. Today I can laugh about what happened between us; I see the bizarre side of everything and look back with some serenity. As it is, *My Best Fiend* has a feeling of utter weightlessness for me.

The film was easy to make, almost effortless. It appeared before my eyes, complete, in the same room as me. I had no script; I knew only that I wanted to go back to this or that place, where we had shot our films, and talk to the camera. I always felt the film is more than just a personal look at my working relationship with an actor; it's about the process of creation itself, and could just as easily have been about two other people. The themes it deals with go far deeper than Kinski and me. I was very selective when it came to the conversations I included in *My Best Fiend*; I'm speaking here primarily of Eva Mattes and Claudia Cardinale. I could have found untold numbers of people who had only terrible things to say about Kinski, that he was the ultimate scum, but I wanted to show another side, one that doesn't necessarily shine through in his autobiography. He truly could be full of humour and generosity. On one occasion I complimented him on his beautiful couture jacket, at which point he took it off and insisted I keep it. If something didn't go as I hoped when we were working together on *Woyzeck*, he would take my arm and say, "Werner, what we're doing here is important. Just striving for it will give it its appropriate size. Don't worry, it will fall into place." He worked hard on Büchner's text, and unlike so many other times generally knew his lines. It was truly a joy to work with him during those days, and I think back on that time with genuine fondness. I'm glad the sequence of the two of us embracing at the Telluride Film Festival is in *My Best Fiend*. In fact, I'm glad that footage exists at all, otherwise no one would believe we could be so good with each other.

Kinski always complained about the money he was offered to be in certain films. He refused roles in films by Kurosawa, Visconti, Fellini and Pasolini, and spoke of those directors as psychopathic assholes who never paid enough. But I always had relatively small budgets and paid him less than what he would have earned working with these other filmmakers, so it's something of a paradox. We had a rapport that meant money wasn't important. In public Kinski claimed to hate my films and me, but when I spoke to him privately it was obvious the opposite was true, that he was proud of the work we did together.

In his autobiography Kinski describes his ambivalent feelings towards you.

The book is a series of highly fictitious and entertaining rants, in which he uses the wildest possible expletives to describe me; at one point he writes about pushing me into piranha-infested water, then watching them shred me to death. On page after page he keeps on coming back to me, like an obsessive compulsion.* I had a hand in helping to invent particularly vile expletives and insults. "Nobody will read this book if I don't write terrible things about you," he told me. "If I say we get along well together, nobody will buy it. The scum only want to read about the dirt. Don't let the vermin know we collaborated on this." I came with a dictionary from which we pulled out the foulest invectives we could find. He needed money at the time and knew that by writing a semi-pornographic rant against everyone and everything it would get some attention. Kinski actually grew up in a relatively well-to-do middle-class pharmacist's household, but in the book he describes his childhood as one of such poverty that he fought with rats over the last breadcrumbs and worked in a morgue washing corpses. He even wrote about an

---

* "I hate that killer's guts. I shriek to his face that I want to see him croak like the llama that he executed. He should be thrown alive to the crocodiles! An anaconda should strangle him slowly! The sting of a poisonous spider should sting him and paralyze his lungs! The most venomous serpent should bite him and make his brain explode! No panther claws should rip open his throat – that would be much too good for him! No! The huge red ants should piss into his lying eyes and gobble up his balls and his guts! He should catch the plague! Syphilis! Malaria! Yellow fever! Leprosy!" See Bibliography, p. 499.

incestuous relationship with his mother, something that apparently infuriated his brothers. What's fascinating about his book is that to a certain extent it tells the story of the life Kinski wished he had. Although I helped him find new and interesting insults, I can't deny that he wrote about me with some degree of disturbing sincerity.

You lived with Kinski for a time when you were young.

It was a chain of coincidences. My mother – struggling to raise three sons on her own – found a room in a boarding house for the four of us in the Schwabing neighbourhood of Munich. It was cramped, with a dozen people clambering for the same bathroom every morning. The owner was Klara Rieth, an elderly lady of sixty-five with wildly dyed orange hair who had a soft spot for starving artists, as she had come from a similar background herself. Kinski had been living in a nearby attic. Instead of furniture he had filled it knee high with dry leaves and would sometimes come to the door stark naked to sign for a letter. Klara invited Kinski to stay at her boarding house, and as a thirteen- or fourteen-year-old boy I distinctly remember the first time I saw him. It was in the long corridor of the apartment as he fled from a young housemaid who was chasing him, furiously beating him with a large wooden tray. Apparently Kinski had tried to grab under her skirt. When we ate at the same table, he would throw his knife, fork and spoon on the floor and eat with his fingers, insisting that "*Fressen ist ein viehischer Akt. Wir müssen mit den Händen essen*" ["Eating is a beastly act. We should eat with our hands"].

From the first moment he arrived at the boarding house, Kinski terrorised everyone. He once locked himself into the bathroom and, in his maniacal fury, smashed everything to smithereens for forty-eight hours. The bathtub, the toilet bowl, everything; you could sift it through a tennis racket. I never thought it possible that anyone could rave for so long. One day he took a running jump down the long corridor in the apartment and smashed through into Klara's room; the door flew off its hinges. He stood there flailing hysterically and foaming at the mouth. Something came floating down like leaves – it was his shirts – and three octaves too high he screamed, "KLARA! YOU PIG!" His voice was incredibly shrill; he could break wine glasses with it. What happened was this poor woman who let him live there for free, feeding and cleaning for him, had failed to iron his shirt collars neatly enough. He pretended to be a genius who had descended from heaven with God-given gifts, though in reality he worked very hard to train himself. I would hear him doing voice exercises for ten hours non-stop in his tiny room.

One day a theatre reviewer was invited for dinner. He hinted that having watched a play in which Kinski had a small role, he would mention this performance as being outstanding and extraordinary. Kinski immediately threw two steaming potatoes in the man's face, before jumping up and screaming, "I was not outstanding! I was not extraordinary! I WAS MONUMENTAL! I WAS EPOCHAL!" I appeared to be the only person at the table who wasn't afraid, merely astonished. He entered my life, when I was thirteen, like a tornado, and three months later left like a tornado. Years later, when I decided Kinski was the only person who could play Aguirre, I knew what was in store for me.

Was he some kind of alter ego for you?

We were similar in many ways, and I suppose you might say he was my screen alter ego, but only because all the characters in my films are close to my heart. The reality is Kinski always wished he could direct, and envied me. He wanted to articulate certain things that were brooding inside of him, but was never fully able to.

Although we often kept our distance, we would seek one another out at the right time, and could often make ourselves understood without words, non-verbally, almost like animals or a set of identical twins. Whenever he got going, I would turn on the camera as quickly as possible, and often managed to capture something unique. Sometimes I would even provoke him so that he would scream and shout for an hour, after which he would be exhausted and in the right mood: silent, quiet and dangerous. I did this for the speech in *Aguirre* in which he calls himself "the Wrath of God." He insisted on playing the scene screaming with anger, but I wanted him almost whispering, so I purposely irritated him, and after a particularly vicious tantrum he was utterly exhausted and literally foaming at the mouth. I turned the camera on, and he did the speech in a single take. I knew how to trick him into giving the best possible performance, though he always believed he was doing everything himself. During production on *Fitzcarraldo* we did takes where everything was perfect; the camera and sound were flawless, the acting was excellent. "Klaus," I would say, "I think there is more to this," and somehow he knew what I was talking about. I would roll the camera again, and he would move things in a fresh direction. At other times, as the scene was coming to a close, I wouldn't cut because I could see he was up to something exceptional, that an idea had popped into his head. I knew when there was more to be wrung from Kinski. This was usually all done without a word spoken; he would look at me out of the corner of his eye, instantly sensing I wasn't going to stop the camera, and launch into something new and original.

How did the Indians react to Kinski's behaviour during production on Aguirre *and* Fitzcarraldo?

His ravings strained our relations with the locals. He was quite frightening to them, and because the Indians would solve their conflicts in a totally different way, he became a real problem. During Kinski's frequent tantrums they would huddle together and whisper to themselves. In their culture everything is softly spoken; there is never a loud word. One of the chiefs came to me towards the end of production on *Fitzcarraldo*. "You probably realised we were afraid," he said, "but not for one moment were we scared of that screaming madman, shouting his head off." It turned out they were actually afraid of me because I was so quiet.

Kinski's behaviour can be explained partly by his egocentric character. Egocentric perhaps isn't the right word; he was an outright egomaniac. Whenever there was a serious accident, it became a big problem because all of a sudden he was no longer the centre of attention. The locals usually clear a swathe of trees in the jungle without wearing boots, because more likely than not they will be sucked into the mud. But even with dozens of woodcutters in the jungle working barefoot, it's rare for one of these men to be bitten by a snake because the animals naturally flee from the noise of the chainsaw and smell of gasoline; it happens maybe once every three years. Unfortunately a lumberman working on *Fitzcarraldo* was bitten twice by a shushupe, one of the most poisonous snakes on the planet. It would have taken a few minutes for cardiac arrest to take place, so this man thought for five seconds, grabbed his chainsaw and cut off his foot. His colleagues immediately applied a crude tourniquet using lianas. It saved his life because the camp – where the serum was stored – was twenty minutes away. I knew that when news of all this reached Kinski, he would throw a tantrum and rave about something trivial because he was now a marginal figure. After the plane crash I described earlier, there were garbled reports on the radio; we were desperately trying to work out whether we could send out a rescue party into the jungle. Kinski saw he was no longer in demand and threw a fit, claiming his coffee was only lukewarm that morning and his mineral water wasn't cold enough. For hours he screamed at me, three inches from my face, as I explained the severity of the situation to him. As usual in such situations, I stood like a silent rock wall and let him crash against it. I finally walked to my hut, where for months I had successfully hidden one last piece of Swiss chocolate from the ants. We would all have killed one another for a taste of something like that. I went right up to his face, unwrapped this tiny piece of chocolate and ate it in front of him. All of a sudden he was quiet; it was beyond him. Towards the end of shooting the Indians offered to kill Kinski for me. "No, for God's sake!" I told them. "I still need him for shooting. Leave him to me." They were dead serious, and there's no doubt they would have done the deed. Occasionally I regretted not having given them the nod.

Kinski was a peculiar mixture of physical cowardice and courage. A wasp would cause him to scream for his mosquito net and a doctor, though on *Fitzcarraldo*, when it was proposed we get onto the boat as it went through the rapids, Kinski was encouraging. "If you sink," he said, "I shall sink too." Although he styled himself as a man of nature, he never actually liked the jungle, and everything he said about nature was a careful pose. He declared everything there erotic, but never set foot outside of our encampment and brought with him antidotes for every kind of poisonous snake imaginable. If Kinski wandered a few feet into the jungle to where a fallen tree lay, a photographer had to follow and take hundreds of photos of him tenderly embracing and copulating with this thing. The shots of him with the butterfly in *My Best Fiend* are out-takes from *Burden of Dreams*; the only reason it was sticking so close to him was because it was licking his sweat. There was no mystical, animal-like connection between the two of them. There is a moment in *Burden of Dreams* when Kinski, Thomas Mauch and I pull up to shore in a small boat, and Kinski is the one who leaps out and pulls us onto dry land. He was playing to the camera, plain and simple; he took pride in being physical when he knew such things were being documented. It was the same thing with that photo of him at my throat with a machete, which became the poster image for *My Best Fiend*. He saw Beat Presser standing with a camera and lunged at me. You don't need to look carefully to see that I'm grinning. I distinctly remember Kinski embracing a young homeless child on the set of *Cobra Verde* and giving him a $100 bill, but only because two journalists were watching; he would never have done something like that otherwise. Poses and paraphernalia were what mattered to Kinski. His alpine gear was more important than the mountains, and his camouflage combat fatigues – tailored by Yves Saint Laurent – were much more important than any jungle. Kinski, in this regard, was endowed with his fair share of natural stupidity.

Do you miss him?

Perhaps sometimes, though my relationship with him had ended some years before he died. There were moments in *Cobra Verde* I'll never forget. The final scene where he tries to pull the fishing boat out into the ocean – something that would normally take a dozen men – was the last day of shooting we ever did together. It was unrehearsed and was supposed to last less than a minute. I sensed something else was coming, so I let the camera run. Kinski knew I wasn't going to cut the scene, and it soon became a sequence of extraordinary despair as he collapsed with exhaustion into the water. I thought he was really drowning and my first reflex was to run over and help him; the crew had to hold me back so I wouldn't jump into the surf and get him out. I knew at the time we could go no further together, and told him so. There was nothing I wanted to explore with him beyond the five films we made together; anything else would have been repetition. He sensed it too. He died in 1991 at his home north of San Francisco. He had burnt himself out, like a comet. I regret not a single moment, and today judge Klaus only for his work done in front of the camera. The butterfly shot is the image I like to keep in my head, even if it goes against many of my memories. Maybe sometimes I do miss him, the swine.

The Lord and the Laden *and* Pilgrimage *are both about faith and religious worship.*

Both films were made for television. The network asked me to contribute to a series about two thousand years of Christianity; I told them I wanted to do something about the church in Latin America, but they shouldn't expect anything encyclopaedic because I wanted to go to a couple of specific places. The opening shots of *The Lord and the Laden* were taken in Antigua, Guatemala, and the main sequence was shot at a shrine in San Andrés Itzapa, also in Guatemala. There is nothing organised about this religious ceremony; it's in a private yard and is run by regular people who pay nothing to attend. The mixture of paganism and Catholicism is evident. The figure being worshipped – Maximón, an ancient Mayan god dressed up like a rich Spanish ranchero to demonstrate his power – is a mannequin in a glass case. Part of the veneration of this pagan god involves fumigating him with cigar smoke and putting cigarettes in his mouth, so lots of people are smoking. Worshippers also spit and spray alcohol over him and each other, part of a ritual of cleansing and purification in the presence of God. The Catholic Church, not knowing what to do with this phenomenon, has more or less adopted Maximón. They wanted a foot in the door to places like this, so squeezed in a Catholic saint – St Simon – though everyone ignores him. You would never see a Catholic priest there. The whole place is completely chaotic, with no hierarchy or dogma.

I went to the Bibliothèque nationale in Paris, where I filmed the *Codex Telleriano-Remensis*, one of the few pieces of Aztec history that survives in its original form, and was also allowed to film the *Codex Florentino* in the Laurentian Library in Florence. For me the *Codex* is one of the greatest and most honourable deeds of humankind, unquestionably a monumental achievement. Even as Aztec culture was being destroyed by the Spanish invaders, there was one man, Bernardino de Sahagún, who, with other monks, spent decades methodically collecting accounts from Aztecs who had knowledge of their history, language, culture and economic system. The result was a book that describes Aztec life, from religious rituals to botanical knowledge and educational systems. Amidst the carnage of the Spanish invasion, this far-sighted monk attempted to preserve as much of the Aztec world as possible, and even purposely mistranslated certain Classical Nahuatl accounts about religion and human sacrifices because otherwise the texts would have been burnt by the Inquisition. A translation was done into English, which in its magnitude is comparable to the King James Bible. Two scholars at the University of Utah spent a quarter of a century on the project. It has such power of language that I made a pilgrimage to see the surviving translator, Charles Dibble, in Salt Lake City. He was an unobtrusive man in his eighties, a professor emeritus, moved and surprised that a filmmaker was so interested in his work.

You worked with John Tavener on Pilgrimage.

At the time we made the film I considered Tavener one of the greatest living composers, and was initially uncertain whether a collaboration would work because he always refused to write music for films. But in this case it was neither about him writing music for a film, nor me making a film to accompany his music. The idea was to ensure that both elements found common ground; this was a project where music and images had equal value. I contacted Tavener and was surprised when he told me he liked my films and would be happy to meet. We had a good working relationship. People who have a certain greatness to them are easy to get along with. The mediocre are the troublesome ones.

The context Tavener and I worked within was a religious one. His conversion to the Greek Orthodox Church as a young man strongly influenced his music, while I feel I understand religious impulses because of the short and dramatic religious phase I experienced in my adolescence. It meant we approached the film from the same point of view, one that seemed obvious for both of us. I proposed our collaboration be about the prayers and hopes of pilgrims. "We shouldn't talk about making a film together," I said. "We should make a pilgrimage together." When we first met we had such an instant concordance of hearts that we didn't even discuss the music or the film. He immediately knew what I wanted, and after he played maybe twenty seconds on the piano I interrupted him and said, "John, stop. Just compose it."

The finished film is only eighteen minutes long, with no dialogue or voiceover. We see only landscapes, bodies and faces – all material originally shot for other projects – but for me it's an important work about basic human emotions and practices. Some of the footage features pilgrims I filmed in Russia for *Bells from the Deep*, and the images of the crashing waves are from Christmas Island in the Indian Ocean, where I shot the crabs for *Invincible*. The quote at the beginning is from Thomas à Kempis, the mediaeval mystic: "It is only the pilgrims who in the travails of their earthly voyage do not lose their way, whether our planet be frozen or scorched: they are guided by the same prayers, and suffering, and fervour, and woe." If readers have had their eyes on the previous chapters of this book, they will smell something the moment this text appears. Yes, the quote is my invention. I had something else in mind, but Tavener wrote a fine letter to me, full of passion. I immediately knew he was the *melior pars* and had the right to overrule me. It's a question of fairness. I always try to respect the wishes of collaborators in these kinds of situations, when they come at me with such intensity and conviction. Unless what Tavener had proposed contradicted my deepest knowledge of cinema, I was willing to accede.

Most of *Pilgrimage* was shot at the Basilica of Our Lady of Guadalupe in Tepeyac, on the outskirts of Mexico City. There was very little available light, so we made the film entirely on video. People were arriving from all over the country, some literally on their knees, exhausted, weeping, tormented, at the end of their physical strength. Whether en route to Santiago de Compostela or at the shrine of the Virgen de Guadalupe, pilgrims on the move are a metaphor for human life. We had very little room to manoeuvre because thousands of people were arriving every hour, drifting through the basilica on a mechanical conveyor belt that moves slowly, never stopping. This is the only way to maintain any level of safety because otherwise there would be serious pile-ups. In the film it appears as if everyone is floating past the camera, looking up in wonder. My original idea was to include a variety of sounds I had recorded in the basilica, but the moment I heard John's music it was obvious this would bring the film down to some pseudo-realistic level. It isn't important to show exactly who these pilgrims are, or who and what they are venerating. A man talks to the image of the Virgin while holding a photo of a woman. We know nothing about him, yet through this simple, stirring image we seem to have complete knowledge of his story.

Would you have shot films like Aguirre *and* Fitzcarraldo *digitally if the technology had been available?*

Under no circumstances, though I'm not one of those caught in the nostalgia of celluloid. Nothing can compare with the depth and force of film, and though digital imagery has improved over the years and will continue to do so, I plan to stick with film for as long as possible. One problem is that some high-tech cameras are designed and produced by computer engineers who don't fully understand cinema's century-old history of high-precision mechanics. We shot *My Son, My Son, What Have Ye Done* using what at the time was an innovative camera that looked like a gigantic computer. It took me more than four minutes just to turn it on. That's an eternity for me when I'm on a film set. The more technologically advanced your equipment is, the more potential problems there are.

Although the relatively low cost of video means filmmakers can be more self-reliant, it provides an unhealthy and misleading pseudo-security, because you can instantly replay the images you have just captured. What I like about film is that you never immediately know what has been shot. When I feel in my guts we have the best we can possibly get, I stop. I don't want to be able to push a button and check there and then what we've been working on. This is why you won't find video-assist monitors on my set. I feel the same way about dailies, which I always found dangerously misleading and discouraging. Material fresh from the laboratory can be useful to look at if you want to check certain technical things, but when you take a shot out of context – not only from the scene but also the story as a whole – there is no way of knowing just how good it really is. Filming on celluloid naturally forces you into a much more intense relationship to whatever you're shooting. Careful deliberation is required; you have only a few minutes on a single reel to get what you need. On video, by comparison, you can pick up hours of material very easily, though most of it will likely be of mediocre quality, and you can never make a single extraordinary minute of cinema with mediocre material.

How much of Invincible *is based on historical fact?*

It was inspired by the true story of Siegmund "Zishe" Breitbart, a young Jewish blacksmith who became a famous strongman in the variety world of Vienna, Berlin and even Broadway in the early twenties. The Nazis, who were rising to power at the time, were dismayed that a Jew, not an Aryan Siegfried, was being hailed as the strongest man in the world. Zishe was fiercely proud of his Jewish heritage, called himself the "New Samson" and died after an absurd accident when a rusty nail scratched his knee.

One of Zishe's descendants, Gary Bart, had in his possession thousands of related photos, letters, newspaper reports and other documents. I also saw thirty seconds of a newsreel about him. There was a screenplay in existence that Gary had commissioned, but it was about Zishe's fairground exploits, and after reading it I called Gary and said I thought there was something big in the story, something everyone had overlooked. There was a fire on my roof almost instantly and I had to scramble up with a bucket. I asked Gary if he had the nerve to throw away his investment, telling him I would write a screenplay myself. As I already mentioned, I shifted the entire story ten years into the future, closer to the Nazi era. *Invincible* is a story that shows the Jewish people as strong and confident, and ends on 28 January 1933, two days before Hitler takes power. I also added things like the character of Zishe's nine-year-old brother Benjamin. Their relationship is an important one because it serves to show the power of family life in condensed form. I see Zishe and Benjamin as Moses and Aaron: the prophetic strongman heavy of tongue and his little brother having to speak for him. What really touched a nerve with me was the idea of someone so strong also being so vulnerable.

Zishe reminds me of Mike Tyson, who I have met a few times. Tyson appears to be a person of absolute violence and madness, an almost prehistoric type from the underbelly of society, but there is another side to him. He read a lot of books in prison; the man has the soul of Mozart and carries with him great intelligence and tenderness. You couldn't imagine talking to Mike Tyson about

Machiavelli, the Roman Republic and early Frankish kings like Clovis, Pepin the Short and Charles Martel, but that's what happened to me. He's a genuinely fascinating character.

Did you consider not casting a real strongman in the part?

Never. When I look around at actors with rippling muscles, they seem totally inauthentic and pumped up with steroids. The genuine strongest of the strong look very different, and I knew there would be a serious credibility gap with the film unless I found a real strongman. If audiences see Zishe in that early circus scene and don't absolutely believe his strength, *Invincible* instantly fails. When we shot the film, Jouko Ahola – who played the part and is a carpenter by trade – was in fact officially the strongest man in the world, an absolute colossus, able to drag a fire truck behind him. When he lifts nine hundred pounds in the film, that really is him lifting nine hundred pounds. Actually, it's slightly under nine hundred because Jouko knew that an injury would put him out of commission for months. He always stood out when compared to other strongmen, not least because he has such a boyish innocence about him, something made clear the second you see him on screen. What I liked was that he was so soft-spoken but had such charisma. He's the kind of person you want as your big brother, someone to look out for you. His good-heartedness was also something I saw women respond to immediately, which is another reason I cast him. Jouko was resistant to accepting the role, but I told him, "I know my job, and I know how to make you into a good actor."

This question of authenticity and attention to detail was important to me not just in the casting, but also when filming on location. At the time I was finishing up another film and staging an opera, so I asked my production designer Ulrich Bergfelder to go to eastern Poland and take photos of various landscapes and towns. He came back with a useful set of images, though I immediately sensed it wasn't the right place to film because so much had been destroyed during the Second World War and many of the beautiful wooden buildings had been replaced with concrete eyesores. I decided we had to film elsewhere, so on the advice of Volker Schlöndorff, who suggested I go to Latvia and Lithuania, a decision was taken rather quickly. For the market sequence, which was shot in Vilnius, we

made a real effort to create as historically authentic an environment as possible. All of a sudden, in the middle of the shot, after
having blocked off several streets and stopped traffic, an elderly
lady walked by carrying a big yellow shopping bag. She refused to
believe we were making a film and just wanted to do her shopping.
At that moment I had the feeling we were doing a good job. It
took us weeks to negotiate with the Jewish community in Vilnius
because we wanted to film in the local synagogue, the only one
out of more than a hundred that had survived the Nazi onslaught.
The locals were initially resistant to the idea. Could a German
filmmaker really depict Jewish life and rituals in a dignified way?
Eventually we were permitted to shoot there, and many of the
extras in *Invincible* are genuine congregants of the synagogue.

The father of Jacob Wein, who played Benjamin, gave me a book
of Jewish legends in which I found the story of the "unknown just."
In every generation, so the legend goes, there are born among the
Jews thirty-six men who God has chosen to bear the burden of the
world's suffering, and to whom he has granted the privilege of mar-
tyrdom. These men are indistinguishable from mere mortals, and
they themselves often don't know they are one of the thirty-six. I
realised the story embodied the soul of the film, that of an ordinary
man with an extraordinary gift who finds the courage to accept
and fulfil his destiny. I knew it had to be included in *Invincible*, as
spoken by the character of Rabbi Edelmann, and once the script
was written I asked Herb Golder, my assistant director, to read
it to Gary Bart. I instantly knew Herb had to play the part. We
had searched everywhere for a real rabbi – including Tel Aviv and
London – but with deadlines approaching I realised no one was as
convincing as Herb. I told him he would be playing the rabbi and
insisted he not shave for a few weeks.

The character of Hanussen figures prominently in the story.

While Zishe influences people by the strength of his body,
Hanussen manipulates audiences through the power of imagination, and the collision of these two makes for a strong dramatic
clash. Hanussen's character in the film is actually based more on
historical reality than Zishe's is; a fair amount is known about
him because he published his own newspaper and wrote a book

entitled *Mind Reading and Telepathy*, as well as an autobiography. Hanussen was an expert hypnotist and illusionist who claimed to be a genuine psychic, and stepped into the role of a clairvoyant because the climate of the early thirties demanded a seer, someone able to offer some perspective amidst the political chaos and turmoil of the times, with its bank collapses, unemployment and attempted coups. He reinvented himself as a Danish aristocrat with the stage name Erik Jan Hanussen, though he was actually a Czech Jew called Hermann Steinschneider. Hanussen said he predicted the burning of the Reichstag in 1933 and Hitler's electoral victory the year before; in the film he talks about "the figure of light that has come among us." In reality he did something all cheats and con men do: he bet on every horse, predicting the victories of Von Schleicher, Brüning and Von Papen as well. After the election he pointed only to the paragraph he had written about Hitler, who he knew personally. In the film the courtroom scenes between Zishe and Hanussen become more than just a legal battle, because Hanussen's true identity is revealed. He had compromised too many high-ranking Nazi party members, which seems to be why he was abducted and later found riddled with bullets in a forest outside Berlin, half eaten by wild boar.

Hans Zimmer wrote the music.

I like Zimmer because he is talented, self-made, has a true understanding of cinema and is unable to read music. It turns out he was inspired to become a film composer after seeing *Fitzcarraldo*, and immediately quit his band, moved into a sleazy hotel in Los Angeles and started a new career. I asked if he would write something for *Invincible* but made clear the budget wouldn't stretch to his normal fee, so he offered to write something for free and also pay for the choir and orchestra out of his own pocket. His attorneys advised him that this would have resulted in certain tax implications, so we agreed on a fee of $1. The transfer of music rights was originally to be in perpetuity, which is an unnerving concept for me, so I changed it to "perpetuity minus one day." When Hans saw that he insisted on having one day subtracted as well, so the contract we both signed read "in perpetuity minus two days."

You contributed to the compilation project Ten Minutes Older.

I was invited to make a film of exactly ten minutes on the subject of time. It was a challenge, an exercise in narrative discipline, like writing a Japanese haiku; everything not absolutely essential was put aside. I tell the story of a native Stone Age Indian tribe that lived deep in the Amazon rainforest of Brazil, the Uru Eu. They were the last significant group to come into contact with the rest of humanity and technological civilisation, though there are probably several tribes – perhaps some on the Andaman Islands in the Indian Ocean and tiny groups in the Amazon and New Guinea – that remain untouched. The tribe had shot arrows at anyone who approached, so in 1981 the Brazilian government decided to make controlled contact with this group because it was inevitably going to happen eventually, especially with the increasing encroachment of gold, lumber and petroleum companies. The encounter between these two cultures took only ten minutes, but in that time the Uru Eu society was dragged into modernity, thrust forward ten thousand years, from a Neolithic Stone Age existence into the twentieth century. Within days some of them were being flown to cities, driven in cars and exposed to television and prostitutes. The story of the Uru Eu is a profound tragedy because, with no immunity to chickenpox and the common cold, diseases the rest of humanity had developed resistance to, 75 per cent of the tribe died within a year. I found the only competent speaker of their language who also spoke Portuguese and, alongside the Brazilian cameraman who in 1981 had recorded the first contact, filmed with some of the few surviving members of the tribe. The film is called *Ten Thousand Years Older*.

Not many filmmakers have been invited by the Dalai Lama to film a Buddhist rite.

Which is one reason why I made *Wheel of Time*, though I could never claim to be very connected to Buddhist culture. At the time my understanding of the religion was rudimentary. A group of Buddhists in Graz, Austria, were planning to hold the Kalachakra initiation ceremony there. Every few years the Dalai Lama settles on one place where he invites the Buddhist world to celebrate this event with him. I was initially hesitant because I can't stand crowds of Western

Buddhists crammed together in one place; there's something about seeing them in multitudes that looks wrong to me. Besides, I had no desire to be a cultural tourist, slipping into a religion I knew little about. Then I watched an amateur video from an earlier Kalachakra ceremony in Ladakh, in the Himalayas, and was impressed. The plan was also to hold the ceremony in Bodhgaya, a small village in India, where – after years of wandering as an itinerant – the historical Buddha had experienced his enlightenment under a tree.

I was still undecided about the project, but the Dalai Lama sent an envoy who asked me to reconsider and make the film, starting in Bodhgaya. Apparently he's a big fan of cinema, especially vampire films, and enjoyed *Nosferatu*. It isn't easy to say no when the Dalai Lama summons you; the man is charismatic, warm-hearted and deeply philosophical, with an astoundingly clear worldview, able to articulate complex ideas, and one of the best laughers I have ever met. I decided to move forward with the project and read as much as I could about Buddhism, though made the film very much as an outsider, keeping to my own culture, an approach to the subject that I feel comes through in the film. The Dalai Lama has spoken of the importance of studying religions other than our own, but at the same time staying within our own faith. Explore Buddhism, but don't leave your own religion behind.

In Bodhgaya we were confronted by the vast makeshift tent-city constructed on the outskirts of town to cater for the half a million pilgrims expected for the Kalachakra event, an eagerly awaited ceremony for the faithful. Some people arrived hanging on to battered, overflowing trucks, some by train from Delhi, others travelled thousands of miles on foot. One had even come nearly two thousand miles, prostrating himself at each step by lowering his body, arms outstretched, touching the ground with his forehead, then standing up and moving to where his head was. The journey had taken him three and a half years. Although he had protected them with wooden clogs, the bones in his hands had grown nodules, and there was a permanent wound on his forehead that came from touching the ground a couple of million times. Yet this man radiated the placidity of a statue. It's the kind of devotion that one can't help but be respectful of, regardless of what religion – or otherwise – is being honoured.

You seem comfortable representing spirituality on film.

I felt the best way to represent the beliefs, intensity and dignity of Buddhists was simply to show what we found in India, Tibet and Austria, the wonderful physical side to the spirituality there. In Bodhgaya we participated in the frenzy by jumping into the crowd and immersing ourselves in the mayhem. The pilgrims piled themselves up as they scrambled for little symbolic gifts, and more than once I was nearly trampled underfoot.

Strictly speaking, the sequence of the circumambulation of Mount Kailash in Tibet by the faithful doesn't belong in the film because Kailash isn't part of the Kalachakra ceremony. What connects the mountain to the rest of *Wheel of Time* is that Kailash is considered the spiritual and physical centre of the universe, which is exactly what the sand mandala of the ceremony symbolically depicts. Kailash is a mountain of the highest significance not only for Buddhists, but also Hindus, Jains and the shamanistic Tibetan Bon-Po religion, which dates back to pre-Buddhist times. It's a sacred landscape for them, as well as being a barren and solitary place with no trees and vegetation. When a nomad walks away in the morning, you can see him at midday; the next day, through binoculars, he's still a dot in the distance. I did most of the shooting there myself. The Chinese authorities wouldn't issue us with a shooting permit, but at the last minute I managed to get a tourist visa. I was in Bangkok, which is at sea level, then flew from Thailand to Kathmandu in Nepal, and from there by truck into Tibet. Within a short time I was at an altitude of 16,000 feet. Not having had time to acclimatise myself made the whole thing difficult; I was panting and puffing. Truckloads of people were showing up daily at the encampment at the base of the mountain. In an average year you would find only a handful of pilgrims, but this was a particularly auspicious moment and more than a hundred thousand people arrived. The trek around the base of the mountain takes three days to complete. The path rises so high that while I was there a handful of people from the lowlands of India died because of altitude sickness.

I used a small, hand-held digital camera and looked like a tourist. *Wheel of Time* is the first occasion I've ever given myself a cameraman credit. I always find it embarrassing to take credit for too many things, so with several films in the past I asked a cameraman friend of mine to put his name in the credits, even though I had done all the filming myself. "Is it good work?" he would ask. "Of course," I said. "You won't be ashamed." It meant the television stations producing these films paid this man's salary, which was money I could use for other things directly related to the production. There are phantoms populating the credits of some of my films going back decades.

Did you feel a divine presence at Mount Kailash?

No, but I could tell everyone else did.

What is the wheel of time?

The centrepiece of the Kalachakra ceremony is an initiation rite comprised of teachings and prayers, with the aim of activating the seed of enlightenment dormant in all of us. The central ritual revolves around the creation of a highly symbolic sand mandala, the wheel of time, a complex vision of a sacred cosmography. As far as I know, five books of instruction are required to complete it and there are more than two hundred volumes of commentary and exegesis. The symbolic image of the mandala is deeply embedded in the eidetic memory of the Buddhist world. The artist monks come from the Dalai Lama's monastery in Dharamsala; they sit on the four sides of the platform and work with the utmost concentration, trickling extremely fine sand of different colours with pinpoint precision to create the mandala, all while wearing face masks, because to breathe or sneeze on their work would spell disaster. It's all extremely physical work, yet stunningly placid at the same time. Once the monks have finished, thousands of devout people move around the platform in prayer. Eventually the Dalai Lama disperses the image with a few strokes of a broom, then throws the sand into a nearby river, which symbolises the impermanence of things.

In The White Diamond *Graham Dorrington tests a prototype airship in the jungles of Guyana.*

The project was brought to me by my son Rudolph, who had the feeling I should do it because – with its themes of flight and hovering in the air – the story has such an intense connection to my feelings about flying. The film is the tale of aeronautical engineer Graham Dorrington, who once pedalled an airship from Southampton to the Isle of Wight, a distance of about a hundred miles. He was about to embark on a trip to the giant Kaieteur Falls – more than four times the height of Niagara Falls – in the heart of Guyana, hoping to float his helium-filled airship above the treetops. The purpose of the journey was to study the biosphere and wildlife high up in the canopy of the jungle, terrain which remains mostly unexplored; even the bottom of the ocean is better understood than the biodiversity you find up there. A helicopter would create an enormous amount of noise and wind, while a balloon would just float away wherever the wind takes it. A dirigible airship, the kind of subdued and contemplative form of flight that has always fascinated me, was the solution for this kind of exploration.

It was always a risky venture, something made clear by the fact that in 1993 a similar expedition in Sumatra had ended in disaster when German cameraman Dieter Plage perished on the maiden flight of a one-man airship that Dorrington had designed and built. He fell two hundred feet to his death, landing at Dorrington's feet. Plage appears in archival footage in *The White Diamond* only briefly, but his presence somehow casts a shadow over the entire film. Dorrington's story reminds me of a Greek tragedy about a man who dreams of flying. Until today, he hasn't fully redeemed himself; he will have to cope with his friend's death until the end of his days. Dorrington shied away from telling Plage's story on camera for weeks, but I kept pushing him. One day I cornered him. "This is the moment," I said, "otherwise it will never happen." He reluctantly agreed, acknowledging it would be a key sequence in the film. I told him the only witnesses would be a cameraman, me recording the sound, and my fourteen-year-old son. I sensed that the key to Dorrington opening up was having him speak not to a camera or a crew, but a young boy.

Behind the waterfall is a gigantic cave.

It's home to one and a half million nesting swifts. After diving down vertically at more than a hundred miles an hour, faster than a small aeroplane, they fly past – and some even through – this curtain of water. I stood on the edge of the cliff as they swept right past me

357

like bullets but wasn't hit once; even at that speed they somehow avoid everything in their way. I spoke to one of the tribal leaders and asked him what was inside this dark cave. He said that according to ancient beliefs, great monsters and gigantic snakes are back there, guarding treasure. We lowered one of the crew – an expert mountain climber who was carrying a camera – on a rope to shoot behind the waterfall, but the tribal leader implored me not to show the footage to anyone, which is why I didn't include it in the film.

What I like about *The White Diamond* is that the heart of the film imperceptibly shifts, midway, from Dorrington to Marc Anthony Yhap, one of the local Rastafarians, then again to Yhap's magnificent and beloved rooster Red Man. Moving from protagonist to protagonist wasn't my original plan, but as I looked at the cast of characters around me during filming, the storyline and centre of attention naturally drifted. By the end of *The White Diamond* we are following Red Man, who has become the film's new leading character. Kleist does something similar in *Michael Kohlhaas*, with the narrative moving from Kohlhaas to Martin Luther, then finally to a gypsy woman.

Do you ever think back on all the people you have filmed with over the years?

Of course. You would never say being the head of a family is a man's profession. For me it's the same thing. Making films isn't my profession, it's my life. The films and people in them aren't just characters; they are a vitally important part of me as a human being. Many are part of the family inside me, even if they probably mean something different to me today than when I made those particular films.

Fini died a few years after we made *Land of Silence and Darkness*, and I haven't had any contact with Steiner for several decades. I was last in touch with him when he was the trainer of the American ski-flying team in Colorado. Bruno S. died in 2010. Years before he had made his full name known to the public, so for the record and in his honour let me state it here: Bruno Schleinstein. He was a genuinely inventive man, and was proud of being a self-taught pianist. He would squeeze my fingertips when we watched *The Enigma of Kaspar Hauser* together and he heard music. "This is feeling strong in *Der Bruno*'s heart," he would say. I ended up writing some scenes for him in *Stroszek* where he could play the piano. He painted what I suppose would be called "naive" art, and one day showed me a great discovery he insisted was worth submitting to the Deutsche Akademie der Wissenschaften [German Academy of Sciences]. His apartment was full of found objects because he was always rummaging around city garbage cans. He collected dilapidated ventilators, a couple of which still worked, and painted one blade yellow, one blue, one red, and so on. Bruno was convinced he was the first person to discover that when they spun around, all of a sudden the colours would vanish and appear white. In his later years he published a book of aphorisms, had an exhibition of his art and released a CD of his music. For many people my hiring a man like Bruno was too far out of the ordinary. There was a very weak film about him a few years ago that suggests I used, abused, then dropped this innocent and defenceless man. It was directed by such a puny dimwit that I have nothing to say in response, other than: I know I did the right thing. I prefer my opponents to be more formidable. Although years passed between our meetings, I always kept one eye on Bruno from afar, and would have immediately done something had I discovered he was in trouble.

The short-range commitment of filmmaking means there's a deficit of deep personal connections in this job. If I made a film every five years, it would be easier to maintain contact with people, but that's never been the case. I lead a rather nomadic existence, and in any given year might travel to a dozen countries. I'm like a late-mediaeval mercenary; once a battle is fought, I move on. I can't feel guilty about not staying in touch with all the people I have worked with over the decades. However intense it might be, time spent with someone on a film is inevitably a fleeting alliance. These relationships always come to a natural end, and sustained contact rarely develops once our work together is completed. Everyone moves on to the next project, often thousands of miles away. I count myself lucky, however, because my oldest and dearest friends are those I met while making my early films; for a time it was the only way I made contact with people. Fortunately, over the decades I have been able to call upon many of the same trusted collaborators whenever I make a film. This includes my wife, who is a photographer and travels as widely and as intensively as I do.

She sometimes works as the set photographer on my films, which means we move about the world together.

Many of my collaborators over the years haven't strictly been people of cinema, though they have all brought much to the film-making process with their wildly divergent approaches. Tenacious men and women, singular, imaginative, dedicated and trustworthy, with great faith, all as agitated as I am. Ulrich Bergfelder, the set designer on several of my films, is a specialist in old Provençal languages and troubadour literature. Claude Chiarini, who died a few years ago, was a doctor and neurologist in a Parisian lunatic asylum, once of the French Foreign Legion and formerly a dentist. He joined us on the set of *Heart of Glass* in case one of the hypnotised actors didn't wake up, and also to take production photos. Cornelius Siegel, a mathematician and master carpenter, is an ingenious man who can build anything. If a battery fails in the middle of the jungle, he could take some bark and resin from a tree and make it work again. Herb Golder, the assistant director on several productions, is a professor of Classics at Boston University and a martial artist. It's important for the people working on a film to know they aren't just employees, rather an invaluable component part of a team, with a vested interest in doing the best work possible. On *Fitzcarraldo* one of the technicians at the processing lab had read the screenplay and looked at the footage we were sending him just as a filmmaker would, to the point where one time I got a message from him asking, "Where are the close-ups?"

You had a moustache for many years. Is the tattoo still there?

The moustache was a good one, some kind of defensive barrier to hide behind. Amidst the travails of life I got rid of it. It was actually the victim of a lost bet. Anyway, life has been good to me and perhaps I no longer need it. As for the tattoo, I don't think about it any more. It's there, on my arm, the image of Death, wearing a tuxedo and a bow tie, singing into an old-fashioned ZDF [Zweites Deutsches Fernsehen] microphone. I haven't noticed the thing for years. I was thirty-six, in San Francisco, accompanying my friend Paul Getty, who was getting a tattoo. The tattoo artist fascinated me, and while I was waiting I got one myself.

You once gave a talk at the New York Public Library entitled "Was the Twentieth Century a Mistake?"

The Polish author Ryszard Kapuściński and I worked on a science-fiction project together. Kapuściński was one of the few people who had survived the chaos of the eastern Congo in the early sixties; within a year and a half he had been arrested forty times and condemned to death four times. I asked him what his worst experience had been, and in his soft-spoken voice he told me it was when they threw dozens of poisonous snakes into his tiny cell with him. "My hair turned white in five days." He was a tremendously forceful personality, full of serenity and insight. The idea behind our proposed collaboration was simple: technology is something we all rely on, yet will be the first casualty. For Kapuściński and me, science fiction doesn't mean the projection of our technological possibilities into the future, rather the loss of such things. There will come a time when we lose our grasp on technology and will never be able to recover it.

Both of us would regularly encounter computers in airports with jungle weeds growing out of the keyboards; one look at those and you knew you weren't flying anywhere. We often found ourselves standing in front of terminally inoperative elevators, which meant taking the stairs. We encountered soldiers who would cut the water supplies of cities, then return a week later with huge water trucks and sell their cargo to the thirsty population. We stayed in hotels where the bellboy would show you to your room and produce a lightbulb from his pocket. The moment you left – even for an hour – the bulb would be unscrewed from the socket and taken away. A bicycle is easily repaired with basic tools, but a car without gasoline is useless. Imagine a worldwide electricity outage for a full fortnight; the chaos and distress it would cause is unfathomable. Having fundamental skills – starting a fire without a match, constructing a primitive shelter, knowing which berries are poisonous and which aren't – would become life or death. That was our science fiction.

The hubris that human beings display fascinates me. Look at certain forms of architecture, those grandiose follies that represent the point at which our attempts to construct vast objects alongside nature became too delirious; they touch dangerously upon taboos. The dam at Vajont in northern Italy, in the Dolomite Alps, is a fantastical structure, something like five hundred feet high, the largest in Europe when it was built. The lake that the dam created had steep slopes on either side, and a small number of dissident geologists spoke of the potential for catastrophe. In 1963 came the largest landslide since Neolithic times. In one cataclysmic event, nearly a billion cubic feet of rock crashed into the lake at incredible speed, creating a tsunami almost eight hundred feet high. It swept down over several villages, killing nearly two thousand people. The dam withstood this monumental onslaught completely intact; at its base the wall is nearly ninety feet thick, made of the finest steel and concrete, which is why it will probably still be around in five hundred thousand years. Vajont is one of the follies that will outlive the human race.

While the fundamental analysis of environmentalists is correct, the whole thing took a turn for the worse when tree-huggers entered into the equation. They are so blindly concerned with the wellbeing of tree frogs, panda bears and salad leaves, yet while we have been sitting here it's entirely possible a human language has died out. We can't overlook those kinds of irreversible losses to human culture, which are taking place at a staggering speed. The extinction of a language is beyond tragic. Imagine if the last Italian vanished and took with him Dante and Virgil, or if the Russian language disappeared and we no longer had Tolstoy or Pasternak. Ninety per cent of the languages spoken today will likely be dead within a hundred years. There is a new moral and cultural imperative out there, one we unfortunately haven't absorbed into our common thinking yet. Two centuries ago in Australia there were something like six hundred languages. Today there are less than one-tenth that number. When I made *Where the Green Ants Dream* I met an old Aborigine, the last surviving speaker of his language, living in a retirement home in Port Augusta, southern Australia. They called him "The Mute," but the only reason he didn't talk was that there was no one left on earth with whom he could communicate. I watched him walk up and down the corridors, lonely to the world, dropping change into an empty soda machine and putting his ear up to it so he could listen to the rattle of the coins as they settled at the bottom. He would do this all afternoon. At night, while he slept, the employees of the retirement home would take the money out of the machine and put it back in his pocket. With this man's death we lost part of our collective human knowledge.

We can actually identify the moment when things started to go awry. It was Petrarch who committed a "sin" by being the first to climb a mountain just for the sake of climbing. In a letter written in Latin, he speaks of a shudder he experienced; it was probably a premonition of the mass tourism that would soon strip the mountain of its dignity. An earlier arch sin, from prehistoric times, one which we can't date quite so exactly, was the breeding of the first pig. In the Palaeolithic era there were only hunter-gatherers. Breeding the first dog helped maintain that way of life because dogs would travel as companions with nomadic hunters. The same applies to horses, which were a means of transport. But the breeding of the first pig in Neolithic times was a true act of original sin. With agriculture came settlements and eventually cities, making humanity sedentary. This is where our real problems began. It's too late to turn the clock back.

Be under no illusions. Try to subdue this planet at your peril. Humanity is unsustainable. Trilobites and ammonites disappeared from this planet after hundreds of millions of years of existence, and later the dinosaurs became extinct. It never bothered me that the universe doesn't care about us, that we will all eventually disappear from the face of the earth. Crabs, urchins and sponges have a better chance of survival; they have been around for millions of years, and probably have millions more to go. We on land are more vulnerable than the cockroaches. Nature has always regulated mankind's existence. The microbes will get us in the end. Martin Luther was asked what he would do if the world were coming to an end that same day. There is a wondrous serenity to his response. "I would plant an apple tree," he said. Me, I would make a film.

11

Blowing the Fuses

During an interview a few years ago someone shot you. You told the world: "It was not a significant bullet."

Winston Churchill said that being shot at unsuccessfully is an exhilarating moment in a man's life. I was at the top of the Hollywood Hills near my home, recording an interview, when I heard a loud bang. I assumed the camera had exploded because it felt as if I had been hit in the stomach by a chunk of glowing metal, but it was intact. Then, some distance away, I saw a man with a gun, ducking out of sight on a veranda. We had already heard him shouting obscenities about the fact that yet another film star was being interviewed in public. In that respect, it was something on a par with road rage. Although the bullet – small calibre, probably 22mm, or a high-powered airgun – went through my leather jacket and a folded-up catalogue, it didn't perforate my abdomen, which would have been unpleasant. For this reason, the entire incident is nothing to speak of. I would have continued with the interview, but the cameraman had already hit the dirt. The miserable, cowardly BBC crew were terrified and wanted to call the cops, but I had no interest in spending the next five hours filling out police reports. When you dial 911 because of a burglary, the police take hours to check in on you, but when you report someone shooting, the helicopters start circling within five minutes, and soon after that a SWAT team moves in. The entire incident was more a piece of American folklore than anything else, though I'm glad it was caught on tape. No one would have believed me otherwise.

You live in Los Angeles, home of sun, surf and vitamins.

I leave such things – including gyms, exercising in public and tanning salons, all the idiocies of modern urban life – to Californians. I have been down to Venice Beach, where the musclemen congregate, only a couple of times, and that was to show it to some curious friends. What I like about Los Angeles is that it allows everyone to live his or her own lifestyle. Drive around the hills and you find a Moorish castle next to a Swiss chalet sitting beside a house shaped like a UFO. There is a lot of creative energy in Los Angeles not channelled into the film business. Florence and Venice have great surface beauty, but as cities they feel like museums, whereas for me Los Angeles is the city in America with the most substance, even if it's raw, uncouth and sometimes quite bizarre. Wherever you look is an immense depth, a tumult that resonates with me. New York is more concerned with finance than anything else. It doesn't create culture, only consumes it; most of what you find in New York comes from elsewhere. Things actually get done in Los Angeles. Look beyond the glitz and glamour of Hollywood and a wild excitement of intense dreams opens up; it has more horizons than any other place. There is a great deal of industry in the city and a real working class; I also appreciate the vibrant presence of the Mexicans. In the last half century every significant cultural and technical trend has emerged from California, including the Free Speech Movement and the acceptance of gays and lesbians as an integral part of a dignified society, computers and the Internet, and – thanks to Hollywood – the collective dreams of the entire world. A fascinating density of things exists there like nowhere else in the world. Muslim fundamentalism is probably the only contemporary mass movement that wasn't born there. One reason I'm so comfortable in Los Angeles is that Hollywood doesn't need me and I don't need Hollywood. I rarely involve myself with industry rituals and am rarely on the red carpet.

Of course, California is also where some of humanity's most astonishing stupidities started, like the hippie movement, New Age babble, stretch limos, pyramid energy, plastic surgery, yoga classes for children, vitamins and marijuana smoking. Whenever someone wants to pass on "good vibes" to me, I look for the nearest empty elevator shaft. There are a lot of well-educated people doing very silly things in Los Angeles, like a man in my neighbourhood who one day casually mentioned his cat was in some sort of a frenzy, so he called the cat psychic. He put the receiver to his pet's ear and for $200 the animal's problems were solved. I would rather jump off the Golden Gate Bridge than visit a psychiatrist. Self-scrutiny is a strong taboo for me, and if I had to stop and analyse myself, there's no doubt I would end up wrapped around the next tree. Psychoanalysis is no more scientific than the cranial surgery practised under the middle-period pharaohs, and by jerking the deepest secrets out into the open, it denies and destroys the great mysteries of our souls. Human beings illuminated to the last corner of their darkest soul are unbearable, the same way an apartment is uninhabitable if every corner is flooded with light. The Spanish Inquisition was a similar mistake in human history, forcing people to disclose the innermost nature of their religious faith. It did no good to anyone.

But ranting about cultural decay isn't very useful. The poet must not avert his eyes. When you look at the cultural shifts that have taken place over the centuries in the representation of female beauty, for example, someone as uncouth as Anna Nicole Smith becomes fascinating. The earliest representations of females are small statues from forty thousand years ago, like the *Venus of Willendorf*, with no face but a massive belly and breasts; this is apparently an idealised version of fertility and fecundity. Greek antiquity has its own well-known Venuses, and in late-mediaeval paintings we see fragile Madonnas, with porcelain-like skin and small breasts. Rubens's *Three Graces*, by comparison, are real porkers. With Anna Nicole Smith, the ideal of femininity was transformed into comic-book proportions. When combined in one person, breast enhancement, Botox and lip augmentation make for a walking art installation. However vulgar she was, there was something of great enormity and momentousness about Anna Nicole. I wish I had made a film with her.

Grizzly Man is about bear-lover Timothy Treadwell, *who was eaten by his furry friends.*

Treadwell was a celebrity because he spent thirteen summers living with bears in the Alaskan wilderness. He was killed and eaten in 2003, but not before he had filmed his final years among bears with a video camera. *Grizzly Man* is cut together from material he shot of himself with the animals amidst the extraordinary landscapes of Alaska, alongside the footage I filmed a few months after his death.

Treadwell's story is a dark and complex one, and his cause – though noble – was ill conceived. He saw a mission he wanted to fulfil and, by doing so, somehow wrestle meaning from a life he had already lost. As he says himself, "I had no life. Now I have a life." Although he tried to protect bears from poachers and other imagined dangers, it's fair to say he needed the animals more than they needed him; they were some kind of salvation for him. Treadwell was a haunted man, perhaps even with a death wish, who was forever trying to overcome his demons, which included a serious drug and alcohol problem. Out in the wilderness he was able to experience moments of both dazzling elation and utter dejection. In his footage one minute he's full of joy, exuberance and pride; the next he's weeping, feeling dejected and utterly downhearted, overwhelmed by paranoia. But whether you sympathise with Treadwell or not is irrelevant. *Grizzly Man* is a unique document about humanity's relationship with the wild and a glimpse into the deep abyss of the human soul. For me this is a story about the human condition, the misery and exhilarations that haunt us, the contradictions within. This was definitely a personal project for me, even if so much of the film is comprised of Treadwell's own footage. We owe him our admiration because of his courage and single-mindedness; it doesn't matter how wrong his basic assumptions were and how much he romanticised nature. No one holds out for thirteen summers living amongst grizzly bears without having a deep conviction within. Whether that conviction is right or wrong doesn't matter. There is something much bigger in his story.

It would be easy to denounce Treadwell because of the games he played with danger and his sporadic moments of paranoia, as well as the posture he had of an eco-warrior, but we have to separate his occasionally delusional acts as an individual from what he filmed, which is powerful indeed. I think everybody who has an instinct about cinema would acknowledge there is something out of the ordinary and of great depth in Treadwell's footage. Probably unbeknownst to him, he created unique images of extraordinary beauty and significance that Hollywood would never be able to reproduce, even with all the money in the world.

How did you discover that materal existed?

I went to pay a visit to a producer friend of mine, who took me on a tour of his office. We sat down at his desk – which was covered with paper, drawings, DVDs and empty FedEx boxes – and when I got up to leave realised I had misplaced my car keys. I glanced at the table and knew they were there somewhere, but my friend thought I had noticed something that interested me. He handed over an article, one of the first published about Treadwell. "Read this," he said. "We're making a film about it." I went out to my car, but ten minutes later, after having stood reading these few pages without taking my eyes off them, I walked back into his office and said, "How far along is this project? Who is directing it?" He answered, "Well, I'm kind of directing." When I heard his casual "kind of," I looked him in the eye and said, "No. I will direct this film!" I knew this was big, even before I had any notion of Treadwell's footage. I never look for these characters. I just stumble into them, or they into me.

Treadwell left behind almost a hundred hours of footage, though much of it was of kitsch landscapes and fluffy bear cubs. In his unedited footage we see how he staged and directed things, how he did one take after another and erased the ones he disliked. We know he did at least fifteen takes of certain shots because what survives in his footage are takes two, seven and fifteen. He was extremely selective and methodical, keeping only those images that made him look like Prince Valiant in the wilderness, protecting the bears against evil poachers. I give him great credit as a filmmaker; he was no amateur, and seemed to be preparing some big production with himself as the star. Treadwell was a failed actor who claimed he almost got the role of the bartender in *Cheers*. With *Grizzly Man* I wanted to give him the chance to be a real hero, and even gave him the most glorious soundtrack possible, written and performed by Richard Thompson.

Production took twenty-nine days from the first day of shooting – in Alaska, Florida and Los Angeles – to the delivery of the final film. Although I was aware of Treadwell's hundred hours of material, I went to Alaska before I had looked at a single frame. After shooting, I was able to create the essential structure of the film and record the voiceover in only nine days. Everything fell into place with such clarity and blind certainty that all I had to do was follow a single direction, as if a star were guiding me. As I watched the footage it became instantly clear what was needed for the film and what should be left out. Just viewing all of Treadwell's material would have taken me at least ten days, but I had four assistants who went through everything, melting it down to about twelve hours of footage. I gave them precise instructions about what I was looking for, but sometimes scrutinised what they had put aside and found extraordinary moments they had dismissed. The shots of the fox paws on the tent had been discarded because they were too shaky, but I thought it was very beautiful imagery. I think even Treadwell himself would have overlooked it. At certain moments, when he was in his *Starsky and Hutch* mode, sporting his bandanna, Treadwell would jump down in front of the camera and start talking. Then he would disappear for twelve seconds and jump down again; he would do take after take. But that "dead" footage of reed grass flowing and bending in the wind, in between takes, demanded to be seen. Even without Treadwell in shot, this empty and apparently useless material was extraordinarily powerful. To this day I have watched perhaps only 15 per cent of what Treadwell shot.

A key moment in Grizzly Man *is when we watch you listening to the audio recording of Treadwell's death.*

When the bear attacked Treadwell and Amie Huguenard, his girl-friend, their video camera was switched on. The lens cap was still attached, but the microphone continued to record for six and a half minutes. As I understand it, no one has heard the tape except for the coroner and a few park rangers, who discovered the camera. I stupidly told Jewel Palovak – a close friend and collaborator of Treadwell, and heir to his archives – that she should destroy the tape, but she was wise to lock it away in a safety-deposit box instead. To this day she has never listened to it.

Everyone knew of the tape's existence, so there was some pressure on me to address the issue. There is always a boundary that mustn't be crossed, and playing that tape in public would have been a gross intrusion into two people's right to a dignified death. Once again I found myself facing the question of limits, something I have carefully navigated from the start of my professional life. There is a difference between voyeurism and filmmaking. Voyeurs have a psychological sickness and would have jumped to include the tape in the film, but not me. This was no snuff movie. I explained that if anyone on the production insisted the recording be included in the film, I would quit. *Grizzly Man*'s producer and distributor asked me to film myself listening to it, but I thought it would be more effective to film Jewel as she watches me, trying to read the echoes from my face. She was worried that the screams would leak out of the earphones I was wearing and be picked up by the microphone, but I promised her that if I detected even the slightest sound, I would erase it. The camera is behind me, and what the audience is focused on at that moment is her anguish as she imagines what I'm hearing, which was horrible beyond description. The advancement of a medium is often driven by certain transgressions. Values change from one generation to the next, and perhaps my grandchildren will find it ridiculous I chose not to include the tape in *Grizzly Man*. But I doubt it.

The film contains few details about Amie Huguenard.

All I can say is she was very brave. She chose to stay and attack a thousand-pound bear with a frying pan, which was found next to her remains. These are animals that can run as fast as a racehorse, drag a huge moose up a steep mountain, decapitate with one blow of a paw and kill a human with a single crunching bite. Loud metallic bangs can be heard on the tape. Hardly anything was left of her. What's interesting is that though Huguenard had spent the last three summers with Treadwell, in her diary she described him as being "hellbent on destruction" and made it clear she was about to leave him for good and return to California. Treadwell seemed to hide Huguenard's presence out there; there is less than a minute of her in the hundred hours of his footage. He stylised himself as a lone warrior, and having his girlfriend with him in Alaska clearly didn't fit this image. I would have liked to talk to people who knew Huguenard; her sister was prepared to speak on camera, but the family decided against it. There is something deeply heroic and tragic about her, and she remains the great unknown of the film.

You said earlier that throughout the film your voiceover takes issue with Treadwell's views of nature.

He considered nature to be wondrously harmonious, but for me, the world is overwhelmingly chaotic, hostile and murderous, not some sentimental Disneyesque place. Treadwell overstepped a boundary; perhaps because he grew up so far from the wilderness he had no understanding of the place. We all know bear cubs are cute, but where there is a cub there must be a mother, and there is a ferocious instinct in these creatures to protect their little ones. When I look at Treadwell's footage I see someone who felt strangely privileged, constantly crossing this line. In his quest to be close to the bears he would actually act out being one, going down on all fours and adopting the nature of a wild beast. For Treadwell, stepping outside of his humanness into this ecstasy was an almost religious act. But there were many facets to the man, and I could never reject him out of hand. Despite his stupidities he had a vigorous joy of life, and there was a genuine warmth about him. I also admire him for the impact he had on education – he addressed tens of thousands of schoolchildren over the years – which means the argument I have with Treadwell is similar to one I might have with my brother, someone I love and respect.

I found it ridiculous that everyone thought Treadwell was so courageous. "Any idiot can walk up to a bear," I thought. After hibernation, the animals graze like cattle for a few months, and at the end of the summer, when the salmon run starts, converge in large numbers along the riverbanks. While filming at one of the creeks in Alaska where Treadwell had lived, I walked up to a sleeping bear, one of the biggest I could find, one we know Treadwell filmed. I slowly moved in until I was about thirty feet away, then started speaking Bavarian. The bear heard me coming, woke up and stared into my face, but didn't bother to get up. Grizzly bears are basically uninterested in human beings as objects of prey; many more people in the United States die from wasp stings than bear attacks. The truly dangerous bear is the polar, which will usually head straight towards you because it's accustomed to hunting mammals the size of human beings. Two days after my encounter I spoke to an Aleutic – a local native – who was the curator of the museum on Kodiak Island. He made it clear how inconsiderate Treadwell had been, and I realised how foolish I had been and how misplaced was my bravado. "Bears need to be respected," he explained, "and the only way to do this is from a distance. You have to know their boundaries." The National Park Service has certain rules, one of which is that you have to remain three hundred feet from any bear at all times, and a minimum of four hundred and fifty feet from a female bear with cubs. What I did by getting so close to these creatures was a gross transgression and outright stupidity, not because it was dangerous but because it was disrespectful. Don't love the bear. Respect the bear.

Had you been back to Alaska since shooting Heart of Glass?

About twenty years ago I spent a summer there with my son, at the end of his childhood. We were dropped on a lake beyond the Alaska Range with some tools and a large tarpaulin, but no tent, and immediately set about building a shelter. We had some basic food, like rice, noodles and salt. I'm not a hunter but I forage, so we searched for berries and mushrooms, and fished for salmon and trout. We lived off the land for six weeks, and from our encampment would venture out for day trips. It was so wonderful that we repeated our visit out there the following summer. I love Alaska for its solitude and space. It's one of the very few areas with a truly primordial nature. Much of the place is unchanged since humans started roaming the planet.

It can be quite sobering to return, years later, to certain places. The deserts and jungles where I filmed were fantasy locations, but seeing them again can make everything seem so banal in my mind. When I went back to the jungle, to the locations we used for *Fitzcarraldo*, two decades later while working on *My Best Fiend*, I remember wondering why it seemed such a grandiose place for me all those years before. Everything was completely overgrown; there was no trace of us ever having been there, and even if you had known where we shot the film, you wouldn't have recognised it. The mountainside where we cut the hundred-foot-wide path from one river to the other looked just as it did before we arrived to make the film, which is a humbling reality. There was absolutely nothing there, not a single nail or scrap of wire left, which is bizarre seeing as there are traces of prehistoric man still to be found on our planet. We were actually asked by the locals to leave certain things behind once production on the film was complete because they wanted every fragment they could find. It all had a use for them. Only Machu Picchu retained its power, though no one likes having to line up for a ticket among those throngs of tourists. The most sobering are the lava fields in Lanzarote, where I made *Even Dwarfs Started Small*. Back then the landscape was completely black and white, with barely any vegetation, but today the fields are swarming with hotels. The ten thousand windmills in *Signs of Life* were replaced by electric pumps years ago.

The Wild Blue Yonder *contains an array of footage, some archival, some shot by yourself.*

The film emerged from my fascination with the troubled *Galileo* space probe. After fourteen years drifting in space, the danger was that the probe would crash into one of Jupiter's moons, which apparently contains ice and shows signs of microbiotic life. To avoid contamination, scientists decided to use the last few ounces of the craft's energy to catapult it out of the moon's gravity and send it on a suicide mission: a premeditated immersion into Jupiter's atmosphere, where it would become a superheated plasma and vanish. The probe was sending messages back until its last moments; for the final fifty-two minutes – which is the time it takes for radio signals to reach Earth – it was actually already dead but still communicating with NASA scientists. Some of them were ecstatic and popping champagne corks; others were sad that the mission had been sent to its death. When I discovered the expedition was being orchestrated from Mission Control in Pasadena, only half an hour away from my home, I told myself I needed to be there to film it. I was ready to jump the fence and forge an ID to get inside, but had a stroke of luck because I spoke to someone from NASA in Washington who had seen some of my films, and he got me access.

Then, some time later, in a dusty old warehouse also in Pasadena, I discovered a NASA archive comprised of documents, photos, videos and film footage shot by astronauts. This staggering collection of material represents the history of our space explorations, like El Archivo General de Indias in Seville, the archive of the discovery and conquest of the New World, where you can find Columbus's personal diaries and Cortés's letters to the king of Spain. This NASA archive had been underfinanced and understaffed for years, and the archivists there were surprised to have a visitor. One of them took me around and pulled out a box full of 16mm footage shot in 1989 by the astronauts on the space shuttle *Atlantis*, which transported the *Galileo* spacecraft. The material had come directly from the lab and was still sealed; no one had ever looked at it. What they filmed on that mission – probably the last time celluloid was shot in space – has an extraordinary beauty. The television stations wouldn't have touched it because there are shots that go on, uncut and uninterrupted, for nearly three minutes, which for them is an eternity. But there was real beauty in these images precisely because they roll on and on, as we move from the cargo bay in the command module and drift past any number of weird and wonderful objects.

The other starting point for the film was when I saw some otherworldly footage that Henry Kaiser – who produced the music for *Grizzly Man* – had shot under the Ross Ice Shelf in Antarctica. Throughout the austral summer the sun penetrates the ice and illuminates everything, making it look as though there are frozen clouds up above. During the *Grizzly Man* recording sessions with Richard Thompson I looked, out of the corner of my eye, through the soundproof glass into the control booth and saw Henry and my editor Joe Bini, thirty feet away, staring at a laptop. I caught a two-second glance of something extraordinary on the screen. "Stop everything!" I said, and immediately rushed over to Henry, who insisted it was uninteresting amateur footage, shot with a single-chip digital camera. But to my eyes it contained some of the most profoundly beautiful images I had ever seen. With underwater shots of air bubbles pushing against the ceiling of ice and endless ice crystals floating towards the camera, it was as if a poet had descended deep below the surface of the planet. The divers are exploring and retrieving monocellular creatures under the ice, but taken out of context these images are unique. To me, they looked like astronauts floating in space, and I immediately knew they should be part of a bigger film. It was pure science fiction without a technical trick, as if shot on a foreign planet, something not from this earth, the kind of fantasy landscape we usually see only in our dreams. Suddenly here it was for real. "Believe it or not," I say when asked where the scenes were shot, "those really are images from the Andromeda Nebula." They remind me of the late-mediaeval painter Albrecht Dürer, who dreamt of columns of fire raining down from the sky. I asked Henry to let me use the material and to go back to Antarctica and do more filming, because I needed a series of long, flowing shots.

The film is a poetic mix of science fiction and documentary reality.

Which means it has a strong connection to *Fata Morgana* and *Lessons of Darkness*. More than ever with *The Wild Blue Yonder* I ignored the "rules" of cinema. This is where I blew all the fuses.

I wanted to explore certain ideas that had long fascinated me, like the fact that there are no friendly, inhabitable planets out there that we could ever colonise, and even if there were, we would never reach them. Jupiter is out of the question because it's gaseous, and other planets are either too hot or their gravitational pull is too strong. The Earth's moon and Mars are too barren, and even if some of Jupiter's moons contain frozen water, how would human beings survive any significant length of time out there? What would happen if we left our solar system and set out for some of the stars within the Milky Way? Insurmountable problems would immediately arise; for example, the maximum speed at which we could travel. Even if we could accelerate to velocities close to half the speed of light, we would need thousands of years to reach our destination, and centuries just to slow down upon arrival. The stark reality is that if twenty thousand years ago astronauts had set out travelling at the highest speed ever reached by a rocket, hoping to reach Earth's nearest neighbour outside our solar system, as of today they would have covered barely 15 per cent of the distance. To achieve only 10 per cent of the speed of light would mean lift-off with an amount of fuel on board equivalent not only to the mass of all the gasoline on Earth, but equivalent to the mass of everything in the entire visible universe, including the Sun and every star in every galaxy. Other exotic theoretical ideas – like entering a black hole and accessing a separate reality – have to be discarded; it would take us millions of years just to reach the nearest black hole. And how would you even survive one? They exert such unbelievable force that an entire galaxy would be squeezed into the size of an orange. Life on board the cramped spacecraft wouldn't be easy. After extended periods in space our bones develop osteoporosis, and exposure to radiation would eventually cause leukaemia or other forms of cancer. The number of coups, rebellions and insurrections, and the inbreeding and general discontent, that would have to be averted – over hundreds of generations – if a fleet of craft full of human beings set off from Earth means the whole idea is completely fanciful. Just getting to bed every night in a wall-mounted sleeping bag would be difficult enough.

In *The Wild Blue Yonder* I used anything I could find from whatever source that looked strange or seemed to come from outer space, including footage of two astronauts emerging from a water tank, which I filmed at the Johnson Space Center in Houston and immediately wove into the story of aliens arriving on Earth. I jumped at some spectacular footage from the National Archives of early aviators and material I found in the NASA archive of scientists and engineers piecing together the *Galileo* probe. I ignored shots of the actual assembly of the craft, using only instances of standstill, when they study the machinery and seem perplexed, even frightened. All these bizarre images were tied into a story of deadly microbes having polluted Earth and a group of astronauts being sent out to find a hospitable place for human habitation. I filmed several lengthy conversations with NASA scientists but didn't use most of this material because it pulled things too much in the direction of a traditional documentary, though I did include Ted Sweetser and his colleague Roger Diehl in the film. Roger works at NASA's Jet Propulsion Laboratory and is an expert in ballistic-trajectory designs for the delivery of spacecraft to the outer solar system. The plan was originally to send the *Galileo* probe directly towards Jupiter, but shortly before the launch the *Challenger* space shuttle disaster occurred, so the project was delayed for a few years. The probe was supposed to be transported into orbit on the shuttle, but the problem was finding a way to supply it with enough kinetic energy to propel it all the way to Jupiter. Roger came up with the idea of launching the probe in the opposite direction to Earth's motion around the Sun so it would fall in towards the Sun and fly by Venus. This provided a gravity assist that pumped energy into the probe's path so it could come back to Earth and fly by it, which in turn gave another gravity assist, putting it into an even bigger orbit around the Sun and setting up a second Earth gravity assist two years later that finally pumped the heliocentric orbit up big enough so the probe could reach Jupiter. I love those mathematicians and their imaginations.

The soundtrack is as important as the images.

The music was created by Ernst Reijseger, an astonishingly talented Dutch cellist who also worked on *The White Diamond*. I always asked him to be barefoot when recording; he plays even better without shoes. I can show him a film sequence he has never seen, or recite him a text he has never heard, and he can play along beautifully, never failing to create amazing music and truly capture the right mood, though neither of us knows exactly in which direction we are moving. Over two evenings in 2012 he and I put on a show at the Volksbühne in Berlin entitled *Eroberung des Nutzlosen* [*Conquest of the Useless*], with me reading from my *Fitzcarraldo* journals and him playing on his cello, alongside other musicians. There was a hammock on stage to which I would retire, in full view of the audience, when the music took over.

As with *The White Diamond*, where cameraman Henning Brümmer listened to the music before we left for Guyana, I anchored *The Wild Blue Yonder* in music that was recorded months earlier, then played the recordings to everyone involved before we started filming. It meant the music really did dictate the rhythm and flow of the narrative. Ernst brought to the *The Wild Blue Yonder* recording session the unlikely combination of a group from the mountains of Sardinia who sing prehistoric-sounding shepherd chants, and Mola Sylla, a Senegalese singer who sings in Wolof, his native language. When we put it all together, over a two-day period, the result was extraordinarily strange and beautiful. The musicians had never played in this combination before; every piece was unrehearsed and recorded in a single take. We ended up with two and a half hours of music. I was with them in the studio as they were performing, and would sometimes stretch out my arms and perform gentle floating movements, to mimic the images of astronauts in my mind, so the musicians would get a sense of the rhythms I wanted. It was similar to how I worked with Richard Thompson. At one point, when he was recording the piece that opens *Grizzly Man*, I asked him to stop. "This doesn't sound like the statement it needs to be," I said. "It has to start very strongly. Set your foot down! Your music establishes the law of the land."

The alien in The Wild Blue Yonder *is incompetent.*

His people have to escape their dying planet, deep in the outer reaches of Andromeda, in a galaxy far beyond our own, so they send out a huge armada of spacecraft, a few of which make it to Earth. It's a long and tedious journey for them, and though their ancestors were great thinkers and scientists, the group that finally arrives many generations later are a bunch of homesick and neurotic deadbeats. They have big plans and want to make an impression, but the capital city they construct to rival Washington D.C. is a grand failure. Nobody shows up either to live there or visit the Great Andromeda Memorial or shop in the enormous mall, which is full of unsold merchandise. The aliens might have wanted to destroy New York City in two minutes – as technically advanced superbeings from other planets usually do – but in this film they suck. I couldn't have picked a more credible alien than Brad Dourif to play the part. He's especially wonderful when explaining why everyone from his planet is such an abject failure and when he complains that the CIA won't listen to what he knows about the UFO that crashed near Roswell, which was actually a probe sent by his planet ahead of the armada.

There was no budget for *The Wild Blue Yonder*; I used money earned from *Grizzly Man* to produce the film. One project fed another, just as they always have done. Brad learnt his part in not much more than a day, and we spent a few hours filming him. I wrote an ad hoc text, a long monologue which he wanted to perfect down to the last comma. "I'm more interested in your train of thought," I told him. "It doesn't matter if you forget a few words. What's important is that you get the context right." The mall sequence was shot at Niland, California, close to Slab City, a rather bizarre place, what they call an "unincorporated community." Although federal law applies, there is no mayor, no tax board or anything like that, no sewerage system, water supply or electricity. This is a small corner of anarchy, a semi-lawless zone, a focal point for renegades and drop-outs, the kind of people who forever talk about arming themselves, marching to Washington and taking over the government. While we were filming, an intimidating fellow with a big fuzzy beard, dark glasses and a rather large belly gave us a threatening "time-out" sign, suggesting we should immediately stop what we were doing, pack up and get the hell out of there.

Rescue Dawn *is a fictional version of Dieter Dengler's escape from a prison camp.*

It was always clear to me that Dieter's story should become a feature film, but for various logistical reasons – not least because it took so long to find the money and actors – I made *Little Dieter Needs to Fly* before *Rescue Dawn*. There were also things Dieter didn't want to talk about when we made *Little Dieter*, like the fact that there was real animosity between him and some of the other prisoners, to the point where they would have strangled each other if they hadn't been cross-handcuffed and chained together. With everyone bound together for two years in mediaeval foot blocks, in the humidity and suffering from diarrhoea, it's completely understandable. "We'll make so much noise the guards will notice you," everyone said to Dieter when he told them about his escape plans. "We have to stay here. The war will be over in a few weeks anyway." Dieter was also embarrassed about the vicious beatings he had received at the hands of the blacksmith he apprenticed for as a child. "The old man is still around," he would say. *Little Dieter* is the version of the story I was bound to at the time for practical reasons. When I watched the film for the first time with Dieter, the lights went up and he turned to me. "Werner," he said without missing a beat, "this is unfinished business." The story of Dieter and Duane was always one I wanted to tell in a feature film, a tale of friendship and survival. Although *Rescue Dawn* came second, in spirit it really was the first film. *Little Dieter* was strongly influenced by a feature film that hadn't been made yet.

Is Rescue Dawn *based on Dieter's autobiography?*

Not really, though the hard core of his story is intact and the principal figures are the cast of characters Dieter encountered in the jungle. The published version of his story – *Escape from Laos* – was

379

rewritten and issued by a military press, which streamlined the text and removed many interesting details, leaving only the bare-bones tale of the prisoners. Everything inspiring about Dieter's original, rambling manuscript was simplified in the book, which is devoid of all imagination. He never learnt to read and write English properly, so articulated himself in what is essentially phonetic English. The misspelling and creation of new words are wild; he spells "machete" as "muchetty." I have always compared Dieter's prose to Joyce's *Finnegans Wake*, a book I don't much care for and which I feel drove English literature into a cul-de-sac from which – to this day – it has struggled to emerge. The learned poet Joyce attempted to push language to a certain limit in a rather calculated way, but the resulting book is an artificial and cerebral calculation, an experiment with language, a detour from true storytelling. Dieter plays with language in the same kind of way, but with genuine innocence, believing this actually is English. I can already feel the whacks from Joyce scholars for saying such sacrilegious things, but I'm convinced that Dieter's original manuscript – which truly brims with life – is an authentic *Finnegans Wake*.

The production of Rescue Dawn *was difficult.*

For four and a half years nobody wanted to invest in the project, until all of a sudden two producers came along willing to finance the film. The first was a hugely overweight man who had fulfilled his dream of becoming a foosball world champion, and who years before had made his money in the trucking business. He moved into the nightclub business, and from there to film production. Unfortunately I didn't look into his background; it turned out he had an extensive rap sheet. The second producer was a basketball star with no experience in filmmaking, which in a way was a blessing because he more or less left us alone. However, there were perpetual financial troubles and no money in place when it was most badly needed. The transportation department had no money for gas, one day more than thirty Thai crew quit because they hadn't been paid, and I was paid with cheques that bounced. I fought hard to make something out of this disaster, and even managed to finish the film two days ahead of schedule. The crew – most of whom I had never worked with before – were a group of technicians from

Hollywood, Europe and Thailand. They needed time to get used to the situation and each other, which eventually they did, but at the start it wasn't easy co-ordinating so many cultures of filmmaking into a single unit. The Americans were always nervous, telling me I wasn't shooting sufficient coverage. I took my assistant aside and asked, "What do they mean by coverage? I have insurance coverage for my car, but coverage when making a film?" They wanted me to get a range of intermediate shots, close-ups and reverse angles, all for safety's sake. But I have always filmed only what I need for the screen, and nothing else. When you do open heart surgery you don't go for the appendix or toenails, you go straight for the beating heart.

Once shooting was completed we had to wait six months to edit because there was no money for post-production. Some of the film's other producers ended up in prison, and a couple of years after *Rescue Dawn* was released I was arrested at the airport in Bangkok and handcuffed to a chair because the authorities thought I was one of the producers who had fled the country leaving a bundle of unpaid bills. It took some persuading to convince them I was only the director. But, as usual, this is all inconsequential. I have experienced these kinds of roadblocks on almost every one of my films; it's the nature of the business, and when I speak of these two producers I do so without complaint. I merely state the facts. They were, after all, the only people who took on the challenge of making *Rescue Dawn*. It didn't bother me that one was a nightclub owner; don't forget that Sam Goldwyn started out as a glove salesman, and Jon Peters was a hairdresser. The real question is whether I was forced to compromise, and the answer is no. One achievement of *Rescue Dawn* is that it is exactly the film I set out to make, especially the look and feel of the jungle.

Encounters at the End of the World *was filmed in Antarctica.*

I was drawn to the area when I saw the footage Henry Kaiser shot under the Ross Ice Shelf, which appears in *The Wild Blue Yonder*. After seeing the images I told him I wanted to go diving in Antarctica myself, and he proceeded to explain how dangerous it is. The water temperature is below freezing, compasses are useless because, being so close to the magnetic pole, needles always point straight up or down, and the divers – who explore under a twenty-foot ceiling of ice – are at constant risk of being swept away by tidal currents. Regardless, they swim untethered without safety lines, as such things might impede their work, which means they have nothing to assist them in finding the exit holes at the surface. It's fatal if they aren't able to orientate themselves quickly enough. You can't expect valuable resources to be spent rescuing some amateur trapped under the ice, so it was clear I would never have a chance to dive down there myself.

Henry told me about the Antarctic Artists and Writers Program of the National Science Foundation, to which anybody can apply. This was fortunate, as not being a pilot, scientist, mechanic or chef I had little to contribute to the community in Antarctica. I made a strange, wild application, explaining that though I was curious about insanity among mammals and, specifically, derangement in penguins, I wasn't going to make a film about the animals. My application made no secret of the fact that I was interested in certain species of ants that keep flocks of plant lice as slaves, milking them for droplets of glucose, and wondered why a sophisticated animal like a chimpanzee doesn't utilise inferior creatures, for example straddling a goat and riding off into the sunset. To my surprise, the National Science Foundation invited me down. There are Nobel Prize winners lined up hoping to go to Antarctica, so I have no idea why my application was successful. Once I finished the film, but before I screened it to anyone, the Foundation told me they hoped it could be used as an educational tool. I told them perhaps in a poetry class, but probably not a science one. I later learnt that James Cameron applied to make a film about Antarctica, though we'll probably never know what his plans were because his application was turned down. It seems that the minimum number of people in his crew would have been something like thirty.

Maintaining a single person per day in Antarctica costs about $10,000. Every piece of equipment has to be flown in from New Zealand, eight hours away by aeroplane, and every drop of water has to be produced through the desalination of ocean water; a single glass requires an equal amount of gasoline. Then there is transportation, heat, food, logistics and electricity to take into consideration. Knowing this, the plan was to fly down with the smallest crew possible: cameraman Peter Zeitlinger and me as sound recordist. Our base was McMurdo Station, the scientific centre and logistical hub that provides fixed laboratory facilities for research, which sits on an island in the Ross Sea, a bay the size of France, on a continent as big as North America, where a thousand men and women – all in pursuit of cutting-edge science – live together. From there, Peter and I travelled to different satellite camps, like the one from which the divers operate, collecting organisms for study. At least three new species were discovered while we were there.

Did you plan anything before you left for Antarctica?

Nothing. There was no testing of the waters; we were tossed down there and had to come back six weeks later with a film. I was flying into the unknown and had no idea who I was going to meet or what sort of film I was going to make. I looked at some photographs and read a little about Antarctica before we left, but knew that as soon as we arrived I had to keep my eyes open, act fast and follow my instincts.

The moment Peter and I stepped out from the aeroplane on the ice runway, he turned to me and said, "How, for God's sake, are we going to explain an entire continent to an audience back home?" I had a flash of an idea. I was forced to learn Latin for nine years, and ancient Greek for six, none of which I ever really enjoyed at school, though today I'm always digging into the literature of antiquity. Homer's epics have sunk in so deep that I could speak German in hexameters if I wanted to. One of my all-time favourites is Virgil's *Georgics*. Virgil grew up as a farm boy in northern Italy, and in his book he writes about agriculture, country life and working the land. The book is an incantation of the magnificence of the beehive and the horror of a pestilence in the goat stables. He writes about tree pruning and cattle in the field; he names the glory of the clouds moving across the land and the oxen moaning. My immediate response to Peter's question, after we had touched down in Antarctica, was, "We'll do it like Virgil in his *Georgics*. He never explains anything, he just names the glory of the land. Let's do the same."

Encounters at the End of the World – which was edited down from about sixty hours of footage – is an invocation of all that is wonderful on the planet, an articulation of my amazement and wonder at the Antarctic landscape, a celebration of the continent. Virgil gave me great consolation while I was there, which is why at the end of the film I use music from a Russian Orthodox church choir with a basso profundo, one octave lower in pitch than a regular bass, an incredible voice that establishes the glory of one saint after another merely by naming them. One of my targets was Mount Erebus, which is more than twelve thousand feet high and of particular importance for scientific study because the inner Earth is directly exposed inside the crater. Only two other such volcanoes exist on the planet. The glowing magma continuously spits out lava bombs, some of which are the size of Volkswagens. There is a strange curiosity we humans have for the power of volcanoes, perhaps because they are capable of wiping out entire species.

Was it a difficult film to make?

Not particularly. Everyone seems caught in the cliché of human toil that Amundsen, Scott and Shackleton had to endure, but McMurdo is an ugly mining town, full of noisy construction sites, earth-moving machinery and climate-controlled housing facilities with warm beds, a cafeteria and bar, and an ATM machine, plus an aerobic studio and yoga classes. Out in the field, of course, it gets a little harder. We were there during the summer, in November and December, but if you stay throughout the austral winter – five months of permanent darkness – evacuation is impossible, so your wisdom teeth and appendix have to be removed as a precaution, even if they're perfectly healthy. Adapting to weeks of permanent daylight can be difficult. You have to wear serious protection when the sun is out, otherwise snow blindness sets in within hours.

We weren't allowed to bring our own boots and parkas; everyone is issued with these things upon arrival. If you use regular boots, you might be able to hold on to your toes down to about −25°C, but after that frostbite sets in. We were sure to test our camera and sound recorder in a facility in Los Angeles at temperatures of around −20°C. I took two recorders with me to McMurdo, but almost immediately had to abandon the more sophisticated one because it had tiny buttons and was impossible to operate while wearing gloves. As soon as we arrived at McMurdo we lost about a week because we were obliged to undertake a mandatory survival course – which involved learning to build trenches and igloos – a course in radio communications, and one in snowmobile riding. I found the authorities there too concerned for my personal safety, and resented having to spend so much time on these things; it was a little excessive for my liking. Having said that, three days after arriving I had an accident on a steep slope when an eight-hundred-pound snowmobile rolled over my body. For weeks afterwards I was sore everywhere and could barely bend down to tie my shoelaces.

The film benefited greatly from the spirit of the Antarctic Treaty, which came into force in 1961 and which I consider to be one of the finest documents of the civilised world. It banned military activity on the continent and established the area as a scientific preserve, committing an entire landmass to the principles of peace and knowledge. There is also an unequivocal ban on nuclear testing or dumping of radioactive waste. The treaty is one of the most potent manifestations of civilised behaviour among nations in modern history. I remember a time when at least a dozen countries claimed segments of the continent as their national territory, but Antarctica has no government as such; it belongs to no one, and while making the film I was witness to the extraordinary international co-operation you find there. In the film you see the mysterious, surreal, frozen sturgeon, which sits under the mathematically true South Pole, stashed away in some kind of shrine, surrounded by garlands of popcorn, in a tunnel that is permanently –70°C. Russian scientists from the Vostok Station – which is particularly inaccessible – had run out of basic provisions and made it to the Amundsen-Scott Station asking for badly needed food. As a gift, they brought the fish and some caviar to barter for noodles.

If Antarctica represents anything, it's stark realism. Sam Bowser, a scientist and diver who works at the field camp, is a fan of sci-fi B-movies, and is always showing his colleagues films full of monsters and extraterrestrials, like *Them!*, starring giant ants that have mutated because of atomic-bomb tests in the middle of the desert. But this is kindergarten compared to the real world under the ice, the slimy blobs with ensnaring tendrils and ferocious mandibles that tear their prey apart. No wonder the mammals of prehistory retreated from the oceans to get on with their evolution in the relative sanctuary of dry land.

You filmed with a wonderful array of people.

The vast landscape of the continent is unique, but *Encounters at the End of the World* is more about the inhabitants of Antarctica than anything else. There is significant science being done there, which attracts a certain kind of person, and behind every door at McMurdo is an extraordinary character. With no indigenous population, no one there has anything in common other than a shared attraction to this immense, unspoilt and untouched area of the earth. Someone told me that everybody who isn't tied down falls to the bottom of the globe.

Some of the people in *Encounters* I met only a few minutes before I filmed with them, and in some instances our conversation lasted not much more than the time you see them on screen. I encountered Doug MacAyeal, an American glaciologist, thirty minutes before his flight for New Zealand was due to leave, and found what he was talking about so interesting that I insisted he film with us. It was warm in that room, but I asked him to keep his enormous red parka on because it would have been ridiculous having him talk about ice floes if he had been wearing a T-shirt. We talked about this and that, but there was a lot of noise coming from a nearby group of Italians, who were celebrating and drinking Chianti because their national football team had just won a match. Once I had quietened them down only twelve minutes remained before MacAyeal's flight took off. I looked him in the eye and said, "I don't want to hear from the scientist. I want to hear from the poet." He nodded and started talking about how he had come to Antarctica to study an iceberg, and soon realised this particular iceberg wasn't just bigger than the one that sank the *Titanic*, it was bigger than the country that built the *Titanic*. The sheer size of the continent is awe-inspiring. Perceptions of scale need to be recalibrated.

A utility mechanic who had escaped from behind the Iron Curtain was still too traumatised to talk about his experiences. His rucksack, containing a sleeping bag, a tent, clothes and cooking utensils, was by his side at all times; he was prepared to leave McMurdo at a moment's notice and explore new horizons. Then there was Stefan Pashov, a Bulgarian philosopher who operates heavy machinery at McMurdo. From the age of five his grandmother would read to him from *The Iliad*, *The Odyssey* and *The Argonautica*, literature that sparked something powerful within. "It's when I fell in love with the world," he explains. That really struck a chord with me; it was wonderful to discover such a kindred spirit so far from home. He found it perfectly logical that we met in Antarctica because it's where professional dreamers end up. Another young man, a linguist, was thriving in an environment where people with doctorates were washing dishes on a continent with no indigenous languages.

In interviews you claimed no knowledge of Abel Ferrara and his original Bad Lieutenant.

Until this very day I haven't seen his film, nor any of his work. A few years after my *Bad Lieutenant* came out I met Ferrara for the first time, at a film festival, and though we sat down to talk, we didn't do it over a drink because apparently he has problems with alcohol, and I had no desire to provoke anything. It was actually wonderful that even before I started making the film there was accompanying thunder from this man, who said he hoped I would rot in Hell for remaking his film. It was good music in the background, like the manager of a baseball team running out to the umpire, standing five inches from his face, yelling and kicking up dust. That's what people really want to see. At that meeting with Ferrara we laughed so much I barely recall what we talked about.

I agreed to do *Bad Lieutenant* only after the screenwriter, William Finkelstein, gave me a solemn oath his script wasn't a remake. The only thing that connects my film to Ferrara's is that one of the producers owned the rights to the title and was interested in starting a franchise; it was never a question of different "versions." The two films have nothing to do with each other, and the title – which was forced upon me, and which I told the producers would waft after the film like a bad smell – is misleading. Calling it a remake is like saying Mel Gibson's *Passion of the Christ* is a remake of Pasolini's *The Gospel According to St Matthew*, though practitioners of "film studies" will surely be ecstatic to find a reference or two in my film to Ferrara's. I call upon the pedantic theoreticians of cinema to chase after such things. Go for it, losers.

The producers sent the script to my agent, but when it comes to negotiating contracts I prefer doing things myself, and chose to face them and their henchmen man to man. At our first meeting I sat with five people from the production company. My first question was, "Are any of you legal counsel for the production?" One of them identified himself. I asked him to stay in the room but not participate in the discussion, then said, "What I have to say here isn't the invention of some industry agent who is trying to sound important. I represent myself here. If you want to be in business with me, I need certain indisputable prerequisites. I decide who the cameraman, editor and composer of this film will be." They quickly accepted this, then asked me for my rate. "What do you mean by 'rate'?" I said. "How much do you get for directing a film?" they said. "What's your price?" My response to such a ridiculous question was the most coherent I could muster: "I'm priceless." How can I answer a question like that in any other way? With a film like *The Wild Blue Yonder* I paid myself virtually nothing and used mostly my own money, but with *Bad Lieutenant* I quoted them an exorbitant figure, immediately adding, "I guarantee you I'll finish this film under budget, so in effect you'll be saving money." The main producer wanted to shake on it immediately, but I resisted. I prefer the overnight rule. "If I have a contract in my hands at eight o'clock tomorrow morning," I told them, "we have a deal." I have a general understanding of Hollywood: if you don't have a deal in two days, you won't have it in two years either. The next morning a messenger was at my house with a signed contract, which I looked at carefully for a few minutes, signed without telephoning a lawyer, then handed back for delivery to the producers.

I appreciate the value of money and know how to keep costs down because I've been my own producer for so many years. If it's your own money, you had better learn to look after it. I demanded a say on the size of the crew and asked for daily access to the cash flow, which the producers acceded to. I needed to know if I could afford another half a dozen police cars in this shot or twenty more extras in that sequence. People often throw money at problems, but I have always preferred to use vigilance and flexibility in advance, diffusing situations that have a tendency to become problems. I put an end to things like having duplicate costumes for actors with only a few lines and waived my right to a trailer, a personal assistant and – that awful status symbol – a director's chair. "I just saved you $65," I told the producers. The completion-bond guarantor visited the set during production to see how things were going. "You charge hundreds of thousands of dollars to guarantee that this film will be completed, which makes you a complete waste of money," I said to him. "I am the guarantee that this film will be delivered on time and on budget."

I met with Eva Mendes in a New York hotel and won her over by joking about her not bringing her dog's psychiatrist to the set. Eva eventually showed up with only two people: a make-up woman and a chauffeur, who doubled as her bodyguard. Nicolas Cage's entourage was similarly small. I had very little time for pre-production, and in three weeks scouted forty locations, cast thirty-five speaking roles, put together a crew and production office, and did the required set design. Every penny of the budget showed up on the screen. I know what I want and shoot only that, and on most days we were finished at three or four o'clock in the afternoon. I would do a couple of takes, then move on. The crew weren't used to my method of working and at the start of the shoot suggested I get more shots so I would have more editing options, but I told them we didn't need any of that. "Finally," said Nicolas, "somebody who knows what he's doing." We finished two days ahead of schedule and $2.6 million under budget. That's unheard of in Hollywood, and it meant I earned a bonus. I delivered the finished film two weeks after principal photography was completed. The producer wanted to marry me, and immediately offered me half a dozen other projects.

The film was shot in New Orleans.

The original script was set in New York, but the producer called me, quite embarrassed, apologetically explaining that New York was too expensive, and laying out the financial advantages of filming in post-Katrina New Orleans because of tax incentives. It was a move I immediately welcomed, as from the start I had the feeling we should make the film in a city genuinely in crisis and transition. At the time New Orleans was still recovering from Hurricane Katrina. It was as if every one of America's problems was located there, not least the crisis of government credibility, so as far as I was concerned it was the perfect place to set this story. I didn't know Nicolas Cage also wanted to go to New Orleans because he appreciates the culture down there, especially the music. I suggested we drop *Bad Lieutenant* and name the film *Port of Call New Orleans*, though in the end a rather clumsy compromise was struck.

The spirit of New Orleans is phenomenal; even a hurricane couldn't wipe it out. The police department read the script and, to my surprise, offered assistance. The city is more than just a backdrop to the story; it's almost a leading character, though in the film you don't see the usual postcard clichés, like the French Quarter, Mardi Gras and late-night smoky jazz clubs. There is latent danger on every corner. It wasn't only the levees that were breeched, it was civility itself. A highly visible breakdown of good citizenship and order took place in the aftermath of the hurricane. Looting was rampant and a number of policemen failed to report for duty; some of them stole brand-new Cadillacs from abandoned dealerships and vanished onto dry ground in neighbouring states. One of our locations was a street corner where two people had been shot dead the night before. We tried to incorporate this malaise into the story. The city was the perfect place to create a new form of film noir, the kind of cinema that erupts during periods of insecurity. Sometimes cultural history coincides with economic history, like the books of Raymond Chandler and Dashiell Hammett, which are children of the Great Depression and which in turn spawned the best of film noir, the cinema of Humphrey Bogart and Edward G. Robinson.

It turns out that *Bad Lieutenant* took the temperature of the time, of the imminent financial crisis. In the months leading up to the making of the film I sensed a breakdown was coming. When attempting to lease a car for my wife I was confronted with the news that I had no credit score, and so had to pay a much higher monthly rate. I questioned why this was, seeing that I have always paid my bills and have never owed money to anyone. But this was exactly my problem. I had never borrowed money, hardly ever used a credit card, and my bank account was in the black. The system penalises good housekeeping and encourages us to spend money we don't have. My immediate reaction was to withdraw my savings from Lehman Brothers, even while my bank manager frantically tried to persuade me to put even more money in. A few months later came Lehman's bankruptcy and the ensuing financial collapse.

We had almost finished shooting in New Orleans when Hurricane Gustav began to approach and whole areas of the city were evacuated. Nicolas Cage, cameraman Peter Zeitlinger and I decided we were going to stay behind. Once the storm hit, our plan was to crawl out and get some shots of a real hurricane, but we wrapped production a week before it arrived and left town. Gustav eventually ended up daintily hitting the city, like an old spinster's fart.

What contribution did you make to the screenplay?

The script is Finkelstein's, but as usual it kept shifting, demanding its own life, and I invented several new scenes full of what we might call "Herzogian" moments. The opening sequence was originally a man jumping in front of a New York subway train and the lieutenant saving him, but New Orleans has no subway. I wanted the story to start in the most debased way possible, and came up with the new beginning of the two detectives placing bets on how long it will take for the prisoner to drown. In that scene – for which Finkelstein wrote the dialogue – we initially used fresh water, but it looked too clean, so the set designer added dye, but that turned the water toxic. Someone had the idea of using instant coffee, but that would have been dangerous for the actors because caffeine seeps through skin and would probably have induced cardiac arrest. In the end we dumped two and a half thousand pounds of decaffeinated coffee powder into the water.

I added other moments, like the dancing soul and the alligator lying, run over, in the middle of the road with a nylon fish line attached to its leg, which I tugged on from off screen, so it looks as if the creature is still twitching. The iguanas, which the bad lieutenant sees thanks to the drug haze he is under, were my idea. There is nothing more wondrous than seeing Nicolas Cage and a lizard together in one shot. I was walking through the city and saw one of these creatures sitting up in a tree. "I need two of them," I told one of the producers. I filmed them myself in a thoroughly demented way, using a tiny lens at the end of a fibre-optic cable. Everyone on set asked me what the meaning of the shot was. "I have no idea," I said, "but it's going to be big." One of these little monsters bit into my thumb; its jaws were a steel vice. I struggled to shake it off as the entire crew laughed hysterically.

In the original script the relationship between the Nicolas Cage and Eva Mendes characters was based purely on sex and drugs, but

I wanted a love story with some depth, so I invented the sequence with the silver spoon. He talks about how as a child he thought that pirates travelled up the Mississippi river and buried their treasure under a tree near his home. Towards the end of the film he finds this spoon – which is actually a rusty little thing – and gives it to her, as if handing over his childhood dreams. The relationship between the two of them immediately becomes more profound. I cut several scenes of drug-taking involving the two of them because I have no connection to drug culture. This isn't moralising; I'm just telling you how things are. My most serious vice is fiendishly strong espresso. I've never taken drugs, though was accidentally stoned once, when Florian Fricke served me a pancake with some home-made marmalade. It was very tasty, but I had no idea it was laced with hashish. In the car, later that evening, I circled for half an hour around the block where I lived because I couldn't find my apartment. On *Bad Lieutenant* we had a prop man who would dish out harmless white powder, and when Nicolas sniffed this prop cocaine he instantly transformed into someone else. For a moment I thought it was the real stuff.

Cage gives a wonderful performance.

I first met him when he was an adolescent, at his uncle Francis Coppola's winery in the Napa Valley, during production on *Fitzcarraldo*. Then, soon after he won an Academy Award, we spoke about him playing Cortés in the conquistador film I was planning. By the time of *Bad Lieutenant* we had been eyeing each other's work for decades and wondered how we had managed to elude each other for so long. Once I brought Nicolas the script and told him I thought we could do something completely wild and hilarious with this story, it was clear this was the project we had to work on together. He called me from Australia, and within sixty seconds we were in business. Neither of us was prepared to sign a contract unless the other was on board, which put the film on solid ground from the start.

Bad Lieutenant isn't a film noir where an oppressive climate permeates; the whole thing is full of menacing humour. There's a light touch throughout, with a leading character who isn't in the least bit guilty about being so ferociously evil. On the second day of shooting Nicolas timidly said, "I hate to ask about 'motivations,' but why is this man so bad? Is it the drugs? Is it the destruction of the city? Police corruption? The hurricane?" My answer was, simply, "There is such a thing as the bliss of evil." Nicolas liked the physical comportment I wanted him to have throughout the film, with a slanted shoulder and his head sticking slightly out. "Your shoulder line should be slightly slanted," I said, "preceded by your gaze." He knew that sometimes, after we finished shooting a scene, I wouldn't turn the camera off because I sensed there was more to it. At the end of the film, after having committed innumerable evil deeds, the bad lieutenant takes refuge in a cheap hotel room, where he has an unexpected encounter with the former prisoner he rescued from drowning at the start of the film. The young man sees there is something wrong and offers to get him out of there. Both actors spoke their lines, but I kept the camera rolling, and after a full sixty seconds of silence Nicolas said to me, "What more should I add?" Without missing a beat I told him, "Do fish have dreams?" We shot the scene again with that line, and I added the final shot of them leaning up against the glass of a huge aquarium, where sharks and fish move as if caught in the dreams of a distant and incomprehensible world. I love the mysterious chuckle the lieutenant gives at the end. Who knows where such things come from? It reminds me of those final self-portraits by Rembrandt and Goya, of toothless old men laughing at who knows what.

Do you consider yourself to be politically engaged?

I'm certainly not apolitical. I have always been keenly aware of the forces that control the world, and am probably more informed than most people. Although I have never been a member of a political party, I have no problem with organised political movements, though prefer to formulate my own opinions, which means I often find myself on the other side of commonly embraced arguments. I appreciate Brutus, for example, who defended the Roman Republic against an emerging empire but is remembered primarily as the vile assassin of Julius Caesar. Caesar overextended the reach of Rome when he crossed over into Britain, and by doing so weakened the foundations of the Republic. Brutus had plenty of valid reasons to murder Caesar, and I can appreciate his farsightedness.

He didn't want the cult of the emperor to dominate, which came to pass after Caesar, with figures like Nero and Caligula.

I made *Even Dwarfs Started Small* at the height of the student protests, amidst the infighting on the Left, when the Maoists were attacking the Trotskyists, and vice versa, with more vitriol than they ever heaped on the Establishment. When it comes to a successful rebellion, timing, patience and clearly defined goals are the most important things, but the dwarfs in the film – a bunch of unprofessional revolutionaries – have none of those things. It isn't real damage they cause; these are more gestures of provocation and anarchy. A revolution for its own sake, without the necessary momentum behind it, is pathetic. Sometimes you have to wait fifty years for the right moment. The result was that the simpletons accused me of ridiculing worldwide protest rather than embracing it, which is probably the one thing they were right about. They were yearning to change the world, and insisted that whenever a filmmaker portrays a revolution, it has to be a successful one. There were very few reviewers of the period who didn't use wild revolutionary jargon and put ridiculous political demands on filmmakers. They were the kinds of people who felt that cinema has only one purpose: to serve the movement and contribute to the struggle of replacing the democratic order with socialism.

I told the agitators they were blinded by zealousness, that if they looked at *Even Dwarfs Started Small* in forty years they might see a more truthful representation of what happened in 1968 than in most other films. Let's face it, the hippie movement had a certain charm, but it was part of the gross stupidity that pervaded the era. No one ever prevented anything – let alone a war – by putting a flower in the barrel of a gun. Nightmares and dreams have never followed the rules of political correctness. I've outlasted more trends than I can remember. The radical ideologies of 1968 weren't for me because, contrary to most of my peers, I had already been much further out into the world. The analysis of West Germany as a repressive and fascist police state that needed to be overpowered by a socialist utopian revolution, and those in charge quelled, never looked right to me. Young men and women from well-to-do families insisted we had to take up arms on behalf of the working class and liberate the impoverished and exploited peoples of the Third World from the yoke of imperialism. I asked if any of them had been to Africa or worked in a factory. None of them had. I had done both those things, but still I was anathema for these people.

Ten years after *Even Dwarfs Started Small* I made my version of *Nosferatu*. Murnau's version seemed to sense what was going to happen in Germany a few years later; the film is the work of a visionary artist who felt the encroachment of real terror, even if he couldn't define it precisely. It's a kind of premonition, with the plague of rats as a prefiguration of the Nazi pestilence that soon swarmed over Germany. The legend of the vampire blossoms more freely in the face of external menace, so it's no surprise that the genre has never gone away. But though it might somehow have reflected the emotional and political temperature of the time, *Nosferatu* can't be simplified down to a sociological level because there was no looming political cataclysm in West Germany. The country was marked instead by stagnation; we were moving slowly but steadily towards boredom and obesity.

Twenty years after *Nosferatu*, with *Little Dieter Needs to Fly*, I was criticised for not denouncing American aggression in Vietnam and asked repeatedly why the film made no political statement about the war. But I never saw either *Little Dieter* or *Rescue Dawn* as films about Vietnam; the war takes place in the margins of both films. These are tales in the tradition of Conrad, about the trials and tests of man, about loyalty, survival and friendship. It was never Dieter's aim to go to war; he just wanted to fly, and as a German the only chance to do this was to go and live in the United States. Once on the ground – before the war had found its true magnitude and horror, before napalm was dropped on civilians – Vietnam suddenly wasn't an abstract grid on a map. Dieter's attitude changed; he came to understand that there was great suffering taking place in this country he knew so little about. His story cuts across all ideological lines, taking audiences to a more profound level than mere politics or sloganeering. In the course of a single week I received a call from the United States Naval Academy wanting to know if they could show *Little Dieter* to a class of naval cadets, and a fax from the Fajr International Film Festival in Tehran asking for permission to screen it as "an international film of special distinction." The mullahs must have approved the film otherwise it would never have passed the censors.

Does political cinema make a difference?

Film is capable of shifting our perception and understanding of things, and mobilising our fantasies. But though cinema and politics do occasionally meet, film isn't the right soil for political activity. Someone with a microphone or a rifle has always been a more powerful way of effecting change, though we shouldn't dismiss a handful of great films with a solid political core, like *The Battle of Algiers*, *Dr Strangelove* and *Salt of the Earth*. I'm not on any kind of mission. If I had one, I would be a missionary.

After watching eight minutes of unedited footage, I knew that Joshua Oppenheimer's surreal *The Act of Killing*, about the genocide in Indonesia that started in 1965, was an unprecedented work, more than just a piece of political agitation. I encouraged him during editing, insisting he not be a coward and leave anything out, including the final scene, which he was thinking of shortening or cutting completely. "Your life is worth nothing if you remove that ending," I told him. Outside Indonesia, *The Act of Killing* became an important catalyst; the historic, legal and philosophical issues were taken up and debated at length throughout the world. Within the country, the film – in which various individuals happily confess to their role in many instances of torture, rape and murder – made something of an impact; a number of long-overdue newspaper and magazine articles were published that described the regime of corruption and fear, one built on the basis of the genocide, thus exposing generations of young Indonesians to the truth for the first time. But several perpetrators of crimes committed fifty years ago still wield power today – people viewed by many as heroes – and the far-reaching changes that the film might have instigated have yet to materialise. Compare this to Marcel Ophüls's *The Sorrow and the Pity*, which became a wake-up call for French society, creating a ripple across the entire country, opening eyes to the fact that not everyone had been in resistance against the Nazis, that collaboration wasn't uncommon. To answer your question, art doesn't make a difference until it does.

You planned a contribution to the 1978 collective film project Germany in Autumn.

I became involved with a group – including Kluge, Reitz and

Schlöndorff – who were making a spontaneous film. It was an interesting idea, and I was actually in Fassbinder's apartment in Munich when he shot some of his sequence. The idea was to create a feature-length project comprised of various short films that would each comment on the activities of the Red Army Faction, including its kidnapping and murder of Hanns-Martin Schleyer, a German business leader, and the hijacking of a Lufthansa flight by a group wanting the release of various imprisoned RAF members, both in 1977. I had no sympathy for the RAF because I knew their analysis of the political landscape was wrong and I also disapprove of murder; it was clear I could never find anything worthwhile in their means and ends. My idea for *Germany in Autumn* was to film with Rolf Pohle, one of my few school friends, who had been politically active as a youth and was leader of the student council of Munich University. He became a member of the Baader-Meinhof Group and was sentenced to six years in prison, then along with other RAF members exchanged for a kidnapped politician and flew to South Yemen. Pohle ended up in Greece, where he went into hiding. He was eventually arrested, extradited to Germany and imprisoned in Straubing, the most severe of all Bavarian prisons, where he served out his sentence.

I visited Pohle there and found him in bad shape because he had been in isolation for a year and a half, unable to receive regular visitors. As a gift I brought him one of those small rubber balls that bounce wildly. They shoot with incredible speed in all directions; like a goalkeeper, you need quick reactions in response. I knew Pohle would want something to occupy his mind and remembered how fond he had been of these toys, but almost immediately it was confiscated by guards under the pretext of safety. What was so disquieting was that for the first twenty minutes Pohle spoke very loudly across the table. We had two guards sitting right there with us, listening to everything we were saying, but at arm's length he spoke as if he were talking to someone a hundred feet away. He had no feeling for intimacy because it had been so long since he had interacted with anyone. Pohle was eventually released and returned to Greece, where he died a few years later.

Was it around this time you tried to establish a utopian state in Guatemala?

No, that was long before, probably around 1964. By naming it a utopian state, you already name the stupidity of it. I wanted to go down to the Petén area and assist the locals because they clearly had a natural right to their own nation. They had their own language, culture and history, and lived in a special district that would have been perfect for a separate, independent country. I even wrote a constitution. The idea was to create a sovereign state, an independent republic, not just a makeshift community. The whole idea was a figment of my fantasies and is too embarrassing to talk about in detail. I had no right of belonging; I was an outsider to these people, and you can't build a state if you don't have the historical and cultural right. No viable nation can be constructed so abstractly. I never even made it to Guatemala because at the time there was a military regime in power and I couldn't get a visa. I reached the border with Mexico and discovered that the only way to get into the country was by swimming across the border river. Using a football as a floating device, I drifted towards the riverbank on the Guatemalan side. Suddenly I saw two sets of eyes on me, those of a couple of soldiers brandishing assault rifles. They clearly didn't have a clue what to do. I waved cautiously at them, then slowly, rather forlornly, paddled back to Mexico. My utopian community failed – rightly so – even before I crossed the border.

Around that same time I found myself in a small village in Mexico called Xichú. I was walking when the road disappeared underneath my feet, and I descended on solid rock, eventually encountering a remote community. An old man was sitting outside on a big chair that resembled a throne, surrounded by people. Someone explained to me that he was the father of 111 children, that the youngsters and women all around us were either his offspring or their mothers. This patriarch had created his own civilisation. It's a wild enough idea to have eleven children and form your own football team, but this man had created an entire league.

12

The Song of Life

Have you ever doubted your abilities?

Never, which is probably why I have achieved certain things. I'm aware that I possess an almost absurd self-confidence, but why should I doubt my abilities when I see all these films so clearly before my eyes? My destiny was somehow made clear to me at an early age, and I have shouldered it ever since. There was never any question as to what I should do with my life. None of this is anything to brag about. Anyone who raises children has at least as much courage as someone who follows his "destiny," whatever that means. It's an utterly pretentious word.

Most film-production companies have a half-life, normally not beyond six or seven years, but mine still exists fifty years after I established it. I have persevered, having learnt from the struggles and defeats and humiliations. My hunger as a child helped define me, as did seeing my mother desperate and furious while struggling to feed us. Something terrifying I will never forget is playing basketball at school one day and having a violent collision with another player. An hour later I began seeing black spots and was blind for nearly an hour. There is nothing wrong with hardships and obstacles, but everything wrong with not trying. I think about the original trip I made down several Amazon tributaries before I filmed *Aguirre*, not having the faintest idea what might be around the next corner. It's some kind of metaphor for my life, which has been lived on a tightrope, even a slalom. I couldn't tell you what has prevented me from slamming head first into a brick wall at a hundred miles an hour. I count myself lucky to have avoided the trapdoors.

I don't do anything on anyone else's terms and have never felt the need to prove anything. I don't have the kind of career where, once a project is finished, I check the *New York Times* bestseller list to see about buying the next big thing, or wait for my agent to send me scripts. I have never relied on anyone to find me work. The problem isn't coming up with ideas, it is how to contain the invasion. My ideas are like uninvited guests. They don't knock on the door; they climb in through the windows like burglars who show up in the middle of the night and make a racket in the kitchen as they raid the fridge. I don't sit and ponder which one I should deal with first. The one to be wrestled to the floor before all others is the one coming at me with the most vehemence. I have, over the years, developed methods to deal with the invaders as quickly and efficiently as possible, though the burglars never stop coming. You invite a handful of friends for dinner, but the door bursts open and a hundred people are pushing in. You might manage to get rid of them, but from around the corner another fifty appear almost immediately.

As we sit here today there are half a dozen projects lined up waiting to be ejected from my home. I would like to be able to make films as quickly as I can think of them, and if I had an unlimited amount of money could shoot five feature films every two years. I have never had much choice about what comes next; I just attend to the biggest pressure. I basically have tunnel vision, and when working on a project think of little else. It's been like this since I was fourteen years old. Today, finishing a film is like having a great weight lifted from my shoulders. It's relief, not necessarily happiness.

But you relish dealing with these "burglars."

I am glad to be rid of them after making a film or writing a book. The ideas are uninvited guests, but that doesn't mean they aren't welcome. As a soldier who holds a position others have long since abandoned, I have always accepted the challenges and am prepared for the worst. Rest assured I will never beat a cowardly retreat. I shall continue as long as there is breath in me.

You have never started a film you didn't finish. One also gets the feeling there are very few unproduced scripts in the drawers of your desk.

No sleep has been lost over the fact that I have written a small handful of screenplays that I haven't yet made. There are too many new ideas to spend time with for me to feel sorry for myself. One unproduced script of mine is the story of the conquest of Mexico, from the arrival of Cortés in Veracruz to fall of the city of Tenochtitlan, seen through the eyes of the Aztecs, for whom it must have felt like aliens landing on their shores. There are only three or four narratives in the history of mankind that have the same depth, calibre, enormity and tragedy. Joan of Arc, Genghis Khan, Akhenaten and Jesus Christ are the obvious examples. When I first started work on the project, my idea was to reconstruct Tenochtitlan, which would have meant sets five times bigger than those built for *Cleopatra*. Even with computerised digital effects, those pyramids, palaces and twenty thousand extras would cost a fortune. The rules of the game are simple: if one of my films is a box-office hit that brings in at least $250 million, the Aztec project might conceivably be financed. While researching I studied the primary sources, including lawsuits filed against Cortés after the conquest. I wanted to make the film in Spanish and Classical Nahuatl – which I even started to learn – though at the time it was unthinkable to make a film like this in anything other than English.

Have you ever taken a holiday?

It would never occur to me. Perhaps I should disappear for a while, though at this point I don't feel under any stress. I work steadily and methodically, with great focus. There is never anything frantic about how I do my job; I'm no workaholic. A holiday is a necessity for someone whose work is an unchanged daily routine, but for me everything is constantly fresh and always new. I love what I do, and my life feels like one long vacation.

It isn't easy to survive in this business. After my first ten years of making films – during which I made something of an impact, but only with small audiences – I was exhausted. This is when Lotte Eisner helped me by pointing out my duties, giving me courage for the next decade. Not long ago I watched *The Enigma of Kaspar Hauser* for the first time in years and was thrown back to those early years in Germany. I saw Hombre from *Even Dwarfs Started Small* and Bruno and Walter Steiner, and remembered that when making the film I was convinced it would be my last. It wasn't that I was discouraged or knew I wouldn't be able to continue, but that I was sure I wasn't going to live much beyond the age of thirty-two. I thought a metaphorical stray bullet would hit me, that my life wouldn't be a long one. I remember being convinced of this at the age of twenty-four, and feeling that each film would be my last. I knew I had to be careful about how I used my time, that I couldn't waste a single second or allow myself to be afraid of anything or anyone. Fear no longer exists for me. The man who frightens me has yet to be born.

Nothing frightens you?

A few years ago I was on an aeroplane that had to make an emergency landing. We were ordered to crouch down and push our faces into our knees. I outright refused, so the co-pilot came out from his cabin and ordered me to assume that undignified position. "If we're all going to perish," I told him, "I want to see what's coming at me. If we survive, I also want to see it. I'm posing no danger to anyone by sitting upright." In the end, the landing gear deployed correctly and we had a safe landing, but I was banned from the airline for life, which I'm happy to tell you went out of business a couple of years later. Being scared or not is only a question of the way you choose to deal with your own mortality. Once you're reconciled with that, it isn't an issue. When I made *Fitzcarraldo* I was a captain ready to go down with his ship. Death has never impressed me.

Strangely enough, one thing that does worry me – and has done for years – is the first hours of shooting a new film. It's the same every time: I arrive on set and look around, see myself surrounded by a group of exceptionally competent people, and desperately hope one of them is going to take charge. I wonder who is actually going to be making this film, then quickly realise there's no escape. That person is me. It's like a kid who steps into the classroom when he and his friends all know that the teacher is going to shout at him. Over the years I have tackled this feeling with a primitive ritual. As some kind of protection, the assistant cameraman places a piece of bright yellow gaffer tape over my heart and across my back, as if I am now plainly visible as the person in charge. This protective shield helps me settle in and get through the first hour.

Do you feel pain?

That's a ridiculous question. Of course I feel pain. I just don't make a fuss about it.

Your next project was a four-minute film based on a duet from a Puccini opera.

It was one of three films commissioned by the English National Opera; they had a new season starting and wanted to promote English-language opera. I was approached late in the day and was required to deliver the film – which had to be exactly the length of "O soave fanciulla," from *La Bohème* – in two weeks. I told them I wanted to go to the remotest corner of Africa and immediately left for Ethiopia, on the southern border near Sudan, a volatile area where the Mursi tribe lives and every six-year-old boy has a Kalashnikov. André Singer, the film's producer, was trained as an anthropologist and twenty-five years earlier had spent time in Ethiopia working on his thesis. The structure of the film is simple. I placed four sets of couples in front of the camera. They both stare at us, turn and face each other, then walk away in different directions. Between each couple I cut a shot of a group of armed men. The result is a series of stylised images, each of a man and a woman. This is an archetypal situation: boy meets girl. All you need feel is that each couple will never see each other again.

You wrote My Son, My Son, What Have Ye Done *with Herb Golder.*

Herb stumbled across a real criminal case in San Diego about a young man named Mark Yavorsky. He was a published poet, award-winning actor, outstanding athlete and basketball player with a near-genius IQ, and had performed in a theatrical production of the *Oresteia* as Orestes, the character who murders his mother. At one point Yavorsky converted to Islam and travelled to Pakistan, where he was arrested as a lunatic and thrown in prison. On his return home his behaviour became increasingly erratic, and he murdered his mother with a prop sword. Yavorsky was locked away in a maximum-security facility for the criminally insane, and was released after nine years. Herb was fascinated by this case of matricide; he became entangled in the story and collected thousands of pages of courtroom transcripts and material relating to the investigation. I could instantly tell there was something intriguing here, but Herb never got around to writing the screenplay, so I proposed that he and I hide out in the Austrian countryside. "You aren't leaving until the script is finished," I told him, "and you aren't staying more than a week."

The hard core of *My Son, My Son* is based on reality. Some of the strangest dialogue in the film is taken verbatim from Yavorsky's real statements and other sources, including his psychiatric evaluations, police forensic reports and Herb's interviews, though the hostage-taking of the flamingos and God as a box of Quaker Oats are my inventions. For the rehearsal scenes in the theatre, Herb pieced together dialogue by cherry-picking from Sophocles, Euripides and different choruses of the *Oresteia*. He offered up many profound lines from the original Greek texts, but we had to brush most of it aside. When you encounter abstract ideas on the page you can stop and ponder their meaning at leisure, but in a film they can overtake you and reverberate too loudly, and I felt the audience would be overloaded.

Yavorsky believed that by sacrificing his mother, he could save the planet.

He had obsessive ideas about being crucified live on national television, and ten minutes into his trial the prosecutor, defence attorney and judge all agreed that Yavorsky was unfit to stand trial by reason of insanity. He was locked away, but because his crime was directed towards his own mother and no one else, he was eventually deemed to be no threat to society and released. Herb spent time with Yavorsky while he was researching the case and introduced me to him one time in the decrepit trailer park where he lived near Riverside, California. I walked into his place, which was full of strange memorabilia; the walls were covered with religious quotes and pornographic images. One of the first things that caught my eye was a poster for *Aguirre*, in the corner surrounded by burning candles. I looked at this makeshift shrine and the crazed expression on Kinski's face, and immediately wanted to get out of there. The whole encounter was a big mistake; sometimes it's best to keep a distance from your sources. The screenplay had already been written by that point, so my trip was made more out of curiosity than anything else. You won't be surprised to hear that I chose not to maintain contact with Yavorsky.

There aren't many actors around of the calibre required to play the lead role in *My Son, My Son*. Although I only watched him for less than sixty seconds in a film, Michael Shannon was immediately at the top of my list. The moment I saw him, I trusted in him. Michael wanted to listen to the tape recordings we had of Yavorsky and even imitate his voice and the way he rambled when he spoke, but I discouraged this. Before we made *Rescue Dawn*, I advised Christian Bale not to get too caught up in imitating Dieter Dengler; I wanted Dieter's spirit to emerge through Christian's own particular way of talking and moving. The end result was so powerful that even Dieter's two sons, who showed up in Thailand during production, kept calling Christian "Dad." I took the same approach with Michael Shannon and Yavorsky; I wanted him to invent and shape the character himself. Generally it's bad enough that a screenwriter is overloaded with material, but even worse if an actor is too. The only legitimate reason to study a real person before playing them in a film is if that person is Muhammad Ali. Learning to move and rap like him would be imperative.

David Lynch helped produce the film.

David and I have a close affinity, and respect each other deeply. I appreciate his work, and though our films are very different, at times they touch each other. I first met him when I was working with Twentieth Century Fox on *Nosferatu*. I was in Hollywood when I ran into Mel Brooks and starting talking about David's extraordinary film *Eraserhead*, which I had just seen. I was in Mel's office, raving and ranting about the director's obvious talent. I didn't even know his name. Mel kept grinning, and after letting me exhaust myself said, "Do you want to meet him?" Three doors down David was working on *The Elephant Man*.

My Son, My Son fell dormant for several years because we

couldn't find any money, then one day I went to meet a producer who had worked with David for years, and all of sudden he walked in. We spoke about the state of cinema in general, about spiralling production and marketing budgets, about the fact that the average Hollywood feature costs tens of millions of dollars. "We should make films with a maximum budget of $2 million," I said. "Real stories, and the best actors. Not superstars." He asked if I had an idea for a film and when could I start. "Tomorrow," I said. David was immediately enthusiastic, but he didn't produce *My Son, My Son* as such. He left us alone during shooting and only saw the film once it was completed, so though he was involved, what he really did was throw a match onto a powder keg, giving the project the spark it needed.

My Son, My Son is one of the most concise pieces of filmmaking I have ever produced. The storytelling is disciplined from start to finish, with one scene blending into the next. A good part of the narrative is told in flashbacks, but audiences don't even notice because the transitions from past to present and back again are woven in so seamlessly. It all involved the kind of high-precision filmmaking I usually avoid. The story takes place somewhere with the appearance of absolute serenity, a well-ordered American suburb with a beautiful ocean, clean beaches, quiet parks and palm trees blowing in the wind, but also some kind of slowly advancing fear and horror. We filmed in San Diego. Nothing is as it seems or fully explained; we never see Yavorsky actually killing his mother, only the aftermath of the act. He makes a strange theatrical gesture with a sword, but the final horror of his crime lies only in the audience's imagination. What I like about the story is that it's a horror film, but without chainsaws and axes flying at you. There is a menace that creeps up on the audience anonymously; you never know from which direction it will appear. Sometimes the things you can't quite put your finger on are the scariest. The leading character is extremely dangerous, and there is some kind of existential terror about him, though this is revealed only through almost imperceptible signals here and there. He finds a basketball in a park and places it up in the branches of a tree, saying he wants to keep it there for a future basketball player. You sense he's either suicidal or homicidal. It isn't easy to nail down what makes him so frightening.

Why did you make Cave of Forgotten Dreams?

The film is about the Chauvet-Pont-d'Arc cave in the south of France, which was discovered in 1994 and contains what is the earliest-known human cave art, from thirty-two thousand years ago. My first intellectual awakening, my first real cultural fascination, independent of peers and family, came at a bookstore in Munich when I was twelve years old. On the cover of one of the books in the window was a painting of a horse from the prehistoric Lascaux cave. It shook me to my core; I felt a deep turmoil in my heart, an indescribable excitement that remains to this day. I had to have the book, and would walk past the store every week, heart pounding, to make sure no one had bought it. It seems I thought there was only a single copy in existence. I worked as a ball boy in a tennis club for more than half a year before I had enough money to pay for it. I still remember a shudder of awe when I first looked through its pages. Early fascinations rarely leave us. I still have the book, which turned out to be quite superficial.

When I was first allowed into the cave, some time before I made the film, I was struck by the freshness of everything. Cave bears became extinct twenty thousand years ago, but there are clearly bear tracks on the cave floor. In a recess is a footprint of a boy, next to one of a wolf. Did a hungry wolf stalk the child? Did they walk together as friends, or were their tracks made thousands of years apart? There are images of reindeer painted by someone and left incomplete, then finished by someone else. The stunning fact is that radiocarbon dating shows us that these additions came five thousand years later. Can we ever truly understand what was going on in the minds of these artists across such an unfathomable abyss of time? With the gorge of the Ardèche river, bridged by the Pont d'Arc, a two-hundred-foot-high natural rock arc, the landscape in the vicinity of the cave is equally extraordinary. The fact that it reminds us so much of Wagner and Caspar David Friedrich connects us to the artists who worked at Chauvet thirty thousand years ago; the landscape doesn't belong only to the Romantics. Stone Age man might have had a similar sense of its power, and it's no surprise that Chauvet is surrounded by a cluster of other Palaeolithic caves. I spoke to one of the primary scientists involved in the project, who suggested that Pont d'Arc wasn't just a physical landmark for the inhabitants of thirty thousand years ago, but most likely also played an imaginative part in their mythology.

Is it clear what purpose the paintings serve?

There are configurations of crouching bison in different caves, so perhaps travelling artists moved from cave to cave. But we don't even know if they were meant as art; perhaps they were used for target practice. The mysteries of Chauvet will likely linger for ever. We can only take an educated guess by looking at cultures that until recently were living a Stone Age existence, like Australian Aborigines or Kalahari bushmen. Through carbon dating we know that twenty-eight thousand years ago a torch was swiped against the cave wall to rekindle the flame. But when we see an altar-like rock that has a bear skull carefully placed upon it, nobody can definitively explain its meaning. Everything points to a religious ceremony, though it might just have been a child playing with a bear skull. When we see palm prints at different points on the walls, all clearly made by someone with a crooked little finger, we assume it's the work of the same person.

Much is known to us because of the modern-day archaeological instruments that we have at our disposal; every grain of sand on the cave floor has been measured with laser mapping. But even so, with no full and definitive answers to our questions about the cave paintings, we're forced to use our intelligence and capacity for vision. I admire the scientists working inside the cave; they are cautious in their declarations about Chauvet and have no time for spiritual, New Age interpretations. At the same time I appreciate people like Julien Monney, who tells us in the film that scientists are working to present a new understanding of the cave through scientific methods, but adds that their main goal – or at least his main goal – is to formulate stories about what happened in the cave thousands of years ago. Like me, Julien has a tremendous respect for both empirical science and the human imagination, and I was intrigued by him from the start of our conversations, not least because he was a circus performer before he became an archaeologist, someone able to walk parallel paths.

These aren't primitive scribblings on the cave walls, like the first attempts of young children. Art emerged fully accomplished, tens of thousands of years ago; Greek, Roman, Renaissance and modern art never got any better. This is the true origin of art, even of the modern human soul, and there is something wonderfully confident about it. At a time when most of Europe was covered with glaciers and ice, when the sea level was three hundred feet lower than it is today, we have on the wall of a cave in France the figurative and symbolic representation of the world. What's fascinating is the distant cultural echo of several cave images resonating through time, those innate visual conventions stretching from Chauvet until today, many millennia later. The only human representation in the cave is a painting of a bison embracing the lower part of a naked female body. We should ask ourselves why Picasso – who at the time had no knowledge of Chauvet – used the same motif in his series of drawings of the Minotaur and the woman. Another visual convention that has somehow lived through the ages is the galloping bison on the cave wall. In Norse mythology, Odin's horse Sleipnir is able to run so fast because it has eight legs, the same number as the Chauvet bison.

In the film you talk about the "proto-cinematic" elements in the cave.

There is charcoal evidence that fires burned on the cave floor, but no humans ever lived in the cave, and among the four thousand bones found inside there are no human remains. It means the fires were probably used for illumination, not cooking. There might have been light penetrating into the recesses before the cataclysmic rockslide hermetically sealed the cave for tens of thousands of years, but the paintings start some distance from the entrance, which means people must have stepped in front of a flickering fire to create and then look at the images on the walls. In doing so, their shadows would have become part of those images, and with a fire burning in the middle of the cave the animals on the walls would have appeared to move. All this brought to mind one of my favourite sequences in all of film history: Fred Astaire dancing with his own shadow in *Swing Time*. Three huge shadows are cast on the white wall behind him and mischievously become independent, dancing without him, before Fred eventually catches up with them. When you guess how the sequence was done, it becomes even more awesome. They must have filmed Fred earlier, created the shadow image, projected it on the wall, then had him dance with the utmost precision to match it. Today this would all be created digitally.

How did the French feel about a Bavarian making a film inside their cave?

I did wonder how I could hope to gain access to the cave. After all, the French are rather territorial when it comes to their patrimony. As I see it, the cave belongs to the French, but at the same time to the entire human race. I had the feeling that I – and no one else – should make this film, and was fortunate because when I met with the French minister of culture he insisted on having the first word, and spent ten minutes explaining how much my films meant to him. It turned out that decades before, as a young journalist, he had even interviewed me once for French television, though I had no memory of this. Additional permits were needed from both the regional government where the cave is situated and the council of French scientists involved. What probably won them over was the fire burning within me.

Once the permits had been issued, I asked if I could see the cave before the shoot and explore the technical possibilities, and two months before we made the film I was allowed inside for one hour. When I got the green light I felt like an impoverished little girl in a fairy tale who wanders out into the cold, starry night, holds open her apron, and stands there as gold coins rain into it. I might be the first person to have gone into the cave who wasn't strictly a scientist. I went in as a poet, hoping to activate the audience's imagination. If *Cave of Forgotten Dreams* were full only of scientific facts, it would be instantly forgettable. My idea was always to step aside and let the art do the talking. Of all my films, *Cave of Forgotten Dreams* probably comes closest to the definition of a documentary as we are accustomed to using the word. It was my duty to document as clearly as possible the work of people who lived thirty two thousand years ago.

You filmed in 3D.

When I saw photos of the cave, it looked as if the walls were flat or maybe gently undulating. Fortunately I made that trip inside before filming because the walls actually have dramatic concave niches, which were skilfully and expressively utilised by the artists for their paintings; for example, a protruding bulge of rock as the neck of a bison. It was instantly clear that the film had to be in 3D, especially because I knew we would be the only filmmakers ever allowed inside. 3D doesn't really interest me; I hadn't used it in the sixty films I had already made and have no plans to use it again. But shooting inside the cave in 3D was beyond legitimate. It was imperative. "We should be completely casual with 3D," I told Peter Zeitlinger, "as if we weren't trying to impress everyone with its scope." The intensity of the paintings comes through in the film because of the 3D imagery, and when audiences emerge they rarely speak about having seen a film. They talk instead about having actually been inside the cave.

From the minute Chauvet was located, the authorities understood the importance of this time capsule and did everything they could to preserve it. Today it's categorically closed to everyone, with the exception of a few scientists. None of this was a caprice on the part of the French. Scientists went in with great caution because at Lascaux in the Dordogne and Altamira in Spain the tourists' breath has caused irrevocable damage in the form of mould. I was allowed in the cave for four hours a day, for six days of shooting, with a crew of three people. Every minute counted. No matter what happened, we had to perform. We were permitted to bring only what we could carry in our hands, which meant no heavy equipment and only lights that emitted no heat. We weren't allowed to step off the two-foot-wide metal walkway, and at times I would hold Peter by his belt so he could lean over as far as possible, with the camera in his outstretched arm, and shoot into a dark corner. There is a fairly high level of gas in the cave at all times – both carbon dioxide and radon – and there was always a guard with us to measure levels. As if that weren't enough, 3D cameras are large and clumsy, full of high-precision mechanics, and have to be specifically reconfigured for different shots – close-ups, for example – so we were forced to piece the camera together on this walkway, in semi-darkness and with no technical support from outside, since the doors were always closed behind us to preserve the cave's atmosphere. We weren't even allowed to sneeze in there. One time our digital data recorder stopped working the minute we got inside, so we tore our battery belts apart and within fifteen minutes had created a special battery for this machine.

Some of the scientists told me that when they heard the sound of a beating heart inside the cave, they couldn't be sure if it was their own they were hearing. Several spoke of feeling eyes upon them, as if they were being observed from the darkest recesses. People ask me if being at Chauvet was like a religious experience. The answer is no; we were too busy being professionals. But once, after everyone else had left, I stood there for a few seconds in the darkness. It was truly awesome.

Tell me about the crocodiles.

In the postscript to the film I explain how I stumbled across some mutant albino crocodiles. My voiceover tells us they live a few miles from Chauvet in enormous greenhouses, vast tropical biospheres warmed by coolant water pumped in from a nuclear power plant, one of the largest in France. I avoid explicitly saying they had mutated because of radioactivity, but audiences can draw their own conclusions. I wanted to speculate on how these animals might perceive the world around them and look upon the paintings on the walls at Chauvet if they ever escaped from the greenhouse and made their way inside the cave. The crocs have nothing to do with the rest of the film, but this epilogue wasn't explicitly for the sake of invention; it has to do with perception, about how our great-great-grandchildren might look back on our present-day civilisation. We obviously bring a different cultural context to Chauvet than that of the people who created the paintings. I'm curious about how we perceive the images on the walls of the cave more than thirty thousand years after they were created, and how they will appear to people a hundred generations from now. Perhaps we're the albino crocodiles of today. They fit beautifully in the film, even though, had I proposed to a Hollywood studio that I include albino crocodiles in a film about Palaeolithic cave paintings, I would have been escorted from the premises by security guards. I just really wanted to film some crocodiles, though it turns out I got it wrong. Months later someone told me they aren't crocodiles. Those are actually alligators.

You re-edited some found footage about Siberian hunters into Happy People . . .

While driving in Los Angeles one day I noticed how close I was to a friend's place. Usually it's impossible to park outside his house, but that day there was a space, so I knocked on his door. When I walked in, he went to switch off his gigantic plasma screen, but I noticed something that interested me immediately. It turned out to be four one-hour-long films made by Dmitry Vasyukov, a young Russian filmmaker. They were about hunters and professional trappers in the forests of the Siberian taiga. Dmitry had shot his films over a full year, with each segment representing a single season. I found the images quite extraordinary; to my eyes these men looked almost prehistoric. But as a whole the films were too long and the music was poorly done, so I casually mentioned there should be an international version with a new soundtrack and a fresh voiceover, and suggested the film should be no longer than ninety minutes. Dmitry was delighted, and within a few weeks I had edited the material down, written and recorded a commentary, and incorporated Klaus Badelt's new score. I can't say much more about the project other than that I love these Russians and their dogs, the way they survive by living off the land in their tiny cabins miles from anywhere. They are truly free and happy people, unencumbered by rules, taxes, government, law, bureaucracy, telephones and radios. Whether making a set of skis or carving a dugout canoe from a tree, these are men equipped only with their expert survival skills and individual values, standards of conduct and rules. They live according to the dignity of nature, and despise commercial hunters who arrive in their territory and over-hunt and over-fish. One of the men in the film got a message to me saying he was worried that audiences would feel pity for him and his colleagues. But these are clearly proud people, and I respect and envy them. My ideal would be to spend a whole year out there, in the solitude of Siberia, a territory one and a half times the size of the continental United States.

. . . then made a short film called Ode to the Dawn of Man *during the recording of the music for* Cave of Forgotten Dreams.

I was in a seventeenth-century Lutheran church in Haarlem, a few miles outside of Amsterdam, recording the soundtrack with Ernst

Reijseger and the Netherlands National Choir, when I suddenly realised the session had to be filmed. I was about to run out and buy a camera when someone handed me a rather unsophisticated single-chip one. There is no narrative, no commentary; it's just music, plus Ernst describing the new cello he recently had made. I used a seven-minute shot of him from *Ode to the Dawn of Man* in "Hearsay of the Soul," my fourteen-minute multi-screen installation first seen at the 2012 Biennial at the Whitney Museum in New York, which features images by Hercules Segers. I was initially reluctant to participate in a contemporary-art event, but it turns out there are a few things in me that go beyond my regular work and that I'm unable to express through cinema or literature alone.

What made you produce the feature-length Into the Abyss *and the eight-part* On Death Row, *which contain conversations with men and women all of whom have been sentenced to death?*

Into the Abyss could have been the title of several of my films. Walter Steiner, Fini Straubinger, Reinhold Messner, Timothy Treadwell and the men on death row are somehow all part of the same family. They belong together. Wherever I look I seem to be peering into a dizzying, dark abyss, whether that of the human condition or, as with *Cave of Forgotten Dreams*, the recesses of human prehistory. By doing so, I've always tried to give audiences short flickering moments of illumination, some kind of understanding of who we are. When James Barnes tells us in *On Death Row* that he dreams about washing the filth from his body and spends most of the time wishing for things he doesn't have – like swimming in the ocean on a hot day and the sensation of rain on his face – we learn something about human beings everywhere. When Hank Skinner describes the ecstasy of a washing machine because for seventeen years he has washed his clothes in a sink, leaving both his little fingers permanently crooked, and when Blaine Milam talks of how he was caught fermenting prunes in his cell to make what he calls wine, we learn something about ourselves.

What interested you about the crime you detail in Into the Abyss?

The murderer Jason Burkett might be intimidating, but he never frightened me. However, I have met some dangerous people in dangerous situations, and though he looks like a pleasant, friendly young man, even a lost kid, no one – according to my instincts – was as deadly as the other perpetrator, Michael Perry. He's the last person I would want to meet at night under murky circumstances. When Perry and Burkett knocked at the door of their friend's mother, they had no plan beyond stealing her car and taking off. Then they realised she was alone, baking cookies, and Perry spontaneously decided it would be easier to kill her. They dumped the body in a pond before discovering they couldn't get the car beyond the gates of this private residential community, so waited until the woman's son returned home, lured him and his friend into nearby woods, shot both teenagers and used the electronic key to escape with the car, which was in their possession for only seventy-two hours. The fact that they ended up on death row is irrelevant, because even if both men had gotten away with life in prison, I would still have been intrigued by their crimes.

The story of *Into the Abyss* was so incomprehensible that I knew it was the basis of a full-length film, not just an hour-long television programme. The utter nihilism of this triple homicide, with all its ramifications and resulting emptiness and pain, was so staggering that it caught my eye. A bank robber shooting a teller for cash is within the boundaries of comprehension, but the facts of this case were mind-boggling, and I felt there was an epic film to be made, the story of a group of people – perpetrators and victims – that touched on the deepest, darkest recesses of what lies inside us all. The killings were the epicentre, after which came numerous aftershocks that caused profound damage to many people in the community. The programmes I made as *On Death Row* are different from *Into the Abyss* in that they focus on individual perpetrators rather than a complex crime involving two perpetrators, three murder victims and four crime scenes. With *Into the Abyss*, my interest spread to the chaplain, the former captain of the tie-down team, whose job it was to strap down the inmates for execution, and the victims' families. I quickly realised an entire tapestry could be woven around these senseless murders. Who are the perpetrators and the survivors? Who were the victims? What were the responses of the homicide detectives and lawyers? What did the crime scenes look like? How did the families react? When I started to investigate, all kinds of people on the periphery of the story edged towards the centre, and it became clear this was an American gothic tale of major proportions.

How did you end up choosing the eight perpetrators you filmed for On Death Row?

For each film there was a selection process not dissimilar to the casting I would do for a feature film. The website of the Texas Department of Criminal Justice contains basic details of every inmate on death row, including a summary of the crimes they were convicted for. I picked what I felt were the most interesting ones, leaving out things like bank robberies and acts of lawlessness that are relatively easy to comprehend. I was looking for an array of cases, and didn't want, for example, four rapists. The crimes were all different in nature, and the eight films include a child murderer, a wife killer, a kidnapper and someone who randomly killed two people because he was angry that day. One of the perpetrators in the first season of *On Death Row* is a woman.

These individuals inevitably led to a wider circle of people, from family members to law-enforcement representatives, coroners and attorneys, and certain questions relating to these surrounding characters emerged when it came to deciding who to pick for these hour-long films. How eloquently could the prosecution state its case? How coherent was the perpetrator's mother? The victims' and perpetrators' families often refused to talk, and occasionally I felt that a person I wanted to speak with wouldn't be articulate enough on camera. For *Into the Abyss* I filmed a conversation with a former girlfriend of Michael Perry that I didn't use because she was rather boring; everyone else we recorded appears in the film. For *On Death Row* I contacted the defence attorneys of every perpetrator I wanted to film with, and in one case a lawyer asked me not to meet with his client because it might jeopardise his chances in an upcoming hearing. "He has a tendency to say stupid things," the lawyer told me, "and it's only going to be to his detriment." I immediately cancelled our meeting, only twenty-four hours before we were due to film. Also important was the existence of police videos and audio recordings, and whether ongoing appeals might prevent me from using them in the film. If I were able to include this material, was it presentable? In the case of Blaine Milam, who appears in the second season of *On Death Row*, I never wanted to see photographs of the young child he tortured and murdered, but they were accidentally projected on a wall in front of me. My response was similar to when I saw photos of the remains of Timothy Treadwell and Amie Huguenard in the coroner's office. Not even my worst enemies should see what I saw that day.

Is there a particular technique to filming interviews like these?

These aren't interviews, they are conversations. In situations like these you have to be open to whatever comes at you and move in whatever direction is necessary, so the starting point is never a catalogue of questions I bring with me, which is how a journalist functions. I would never want to talk to anyone with the aim of denouncing them; I want to show everyone at their best. That said, if you're filming a conversation with someone and they are clearly lying, gently encourage them to be ever more outrageous and wild. Audiences will spot the insincerity all the more easily.

What's important is the intense concentration involved. Learn how to listen carefully to whatever is said to you, and consider how the tone of your voice can impact directly on the responses to your questions. A question asked softly will often draw the same emphasis and inflection from whomever you're talking to. Also vital is knowing how to endure the silences – those instances of quiet introspection – for as long as possible. I nudge the conversation along in a particular direction, towards moments of great magnitude, then stop talking. It takes nerve to sit silently in front of someone you have invited to have a filmed conversation with, but you must learn to absorb the silences that inevitably arise, as you sit behind the camera, holding eye contact with the person you're talking to. By staring into the abyss, somehow I'm able to encourage them. This is never an obstinate silence; there is always empathy and understanding with the person, which is somehow manifested in my physicality and the attention I give with my eyes, even the way I sit and hold my head. Lingering silences often have more weight, emotion and tacit horror than things that could ever be said. The silences in my films go on for about as long as it's possible to hold such moments of quiet before an audience starts shuffling in its seats.

The case of Blaine Milam involved the murder of a little girl who was killed in a crazed exorcism. The damage inflicted on her body was so beyond all imagination that a well-seasoned homicide detective with thirty-eight years' experience fell mute when trying to articulate the facts. His five colleagues at the crime scene had accumulated more than a hundred years of expertise, but they had never seen anything like this. When I filmed him talking about the case, it was as if he had lost the power of speech. The camera holds on him for what feels like an eternity. The image appears to be frozen, but then you see one of his fingers twitching.

Shooting on *Into the Abyss* was spread out over several months because of issues of access, but editing was relatively fast, in part because I shot less than ten hours of footage for the entire film, which is almost two hours long. Even if I had more time, I wouldn't have gathered much more material. Working through everything with editor Joe Bini was extraordinarily intense, much more so than during filming. There was no time to think deeply about what these people told me during the fifty minutes I spent with them, and little of what they were saying affected me at the time; I was completely immersed in our conversations. It hit me only later, when I was able to sit back, stop the film, rewind it and slowly absorb what was being said. It was as if Joe and I had been run over by a truck. This was an important moment for me, as I realised I don't necessarily have to fully understand the ramifications and meaning of something when I'm filming it. In situations like these it's legitimate for such realisations to come only later. Joe and I had both quit smoking, but every few hours we rushed out into the daylight to hang on to a cigarette. Usually we work eight- or nine-hour days together, but couldn't take more than five hours a day working on this material. That had never happened to me before. It was a feeling that followed me all the way home, and in the evenings I watched Fred Astaire films.

What was it like filming inside those prisons?

The state of Texas – which at the time had something like three hundred inmates on death row – is exceptionally media-friendly because the politicians are so convinced of their righteousness when it comes to capital punishment. But permission from the warden can still be denied without any explanation, and there were stringent rules imposed upon us, including security checks of our equipment, a crew limit of two or three people, and filming through two-inch-thick bulletproof glass. Thankfully, the guards placed radio microphones on the inmates, otherwise we would have had to record their voices via telephone. I was told that after exactly fifty minutes the guards would pull our plug from the electricity socket, but in most cases they gave us a few minutes more. One hundred and twenty seconds before our time was up I would feel a hand on my shoulder. It was an advance warning, a non-verbal way of telling us our time was coming to an end.

My experiences with the inmates were some of the most intense of my filmmaking life. I had done my homework by going through each individual's case file – sometimes hundreds of pages of police reports, witness interrogations, photographs and court transcripts – and was familiar with the crimes themselves, but I had never met the perpetrators before. The first time I ever laid eyes on these people is captured in the films; every conversation was a voyage into the unknown. Once they sat down in front of the camera, I had to settle in immediately and engage with them. The short time available meant instantly finding the right tone; I had to deliver. The one exception was Melyssa Burkett, the pregnant wife of Jason Burkett, who had some suspicions about the film, so I met with her beforehand. I always wore formal suits when filming in prison; there is a certain amount of respect that needs to be paid to a human being who is going to die in a few days. Visiting death row means meeting people whose lives are precisely structured around rituals and protocols, and more than that, who know exactly how and when they are going to die. At six o'clock sharp they will be led into the death chamber and strapped down. At 6.03 p.m. a lethal concoction will be injected into them. Less than ten minutes later they will be pronounced dead. When you sit opposite a man who is going to be killed by the state in eight days' time, most things become insignificant.

The balance and tone in these conversations was essential. My way of dealing with the inmates was risky because I spoke very directly with them, and it could have been all over in two minutes. Someone on death row can see a phoney coming a mile off, so in the first two minutes I looked Michael Perry in the eye and said, "The fact that destiny didn't dish out a good deck of cards to you doesn't exonerate you, and it doesn't necessarily mean I have to like you." For a moment he was taken aback, but ultimately liked me for being straightforward. In fact, every prisoner I filmed for *Into the Abyss* and *On Death Row* seemed to like me, and every one wrote to me saying they would gladly meet with me again. They all knew in advance – because I had written to them, explaining my position – that these films weren't going to be a platform for them to prove their innocence, which meant I took a fundamentally different approach to Errol Morris when he made *The Thin Blue Line*, the purpose of which was to exonerate a man. At the same time, this wasn't an opportunity for me to reiterate their guilt. Michael Perry insisted he had nothing to do with the murders, that he had merely been caught in the company of the real killer. I purposely left out of the film anything that made it absolutely clear he was without question one of the two murderers, that he was apparently the one who shot the mother. I chose not to mention that Perry's girlfriend was an eyewitness to the killings of the two boys lured into the forest; she testified in court, which meant immunity from prosecution. I even gave Perry a chance to lie to the camera and insist he wasn't involved in the murders. He seemed to believe what he was saying, perhaps because of the ten years he had spent talking to himself. He was somewhat disconnected from reality, and reiterating his innocence became like a mantra to him. Some of the people I filmed for *On Death Row* readily admitted their crimes to me, and James Barnes even confessed to two more murders while talking on camera. I immediately handed copies of the tapes to the authorities.

There was never any fake upbeat journalistic enthusiasm from me, no false sentimentality or commiseration, no activist's zeal. Above all, there was an understanding that these are human beings, alongside a genuine sense of solidarity with inmates concerning their appeals and legal battles to have their execution delayed or commuted to a life sentence. Their crimes are monstrous, but I didn't make these films to try and humanise these men and women. They already are human, and remain so no matter what.

You clearly have thoughts about capital punishment.

The majority of people in Texas are pro capital punishment, and legislation reflects this, but it doesn't mean I have to agree with the practice. I made my position clear to everyone, and strongly disagree with the people I met in rural Texas who said, "Why do we even give them a trial? Just hang 'em high." The state should never be allowed to kill anyone, under any circumstances. In the worst cases, life in prison without possibility of parole is still better than execution. Even if my own child were killed, I wouldn't demand the execution of the perpetrator. Justice is a strange beast that attempts to settle the travails, tribulations and complexities of human exchanges, and the due process of law is one of the most invaluable achievements of civilisation. Capital punishment taps into the ancient concept of retribution, something we see in the history of almost every civilisation on the planet; in this respect America isn't exceptional. The most populous nations on the planet still have capital punishment: China, India, Pakistan, Japan, Indonesia, Egypt. The only exception is Russia, which recently abolished it. But statistics make it clear that the death penalty has consistently failed to deter anyone from committing a crime; it's a feeble instrument when it comes to controlling the chaos of human life. A shift in the use of capital punishment can come only through a change in collective thinking. No film alone has sufficient power.

When it comes to my own convictions, I have no intellectual argument, only a story, that of the barbarism of Nazi Germany. There was a systematic programme of euthanasia during the Third Reich, the industrialised extermination of six million Jews in a genocide without precedent in human history, as well as thousands of cases of capital punishment; you could be executed for telling a joke about Hitler. The argument that innocent men and women on death row have died is, in my opinion, secondary. As a German, I would be the last person to tell the American people how to handle their criminal justice; I don't have voting power here and am a guest in this country. But as I say in *Into the Abyss*, when it comes to a foreigner like me commenting on how things are done in the United States, I respectfully disagree. There have been public executions for thousands of years, but I would never attend one, and if you offered me a million dollars to film an execution, I would throw the money back at you. The chaplain in *Into the Abyss* suggested I go see one, adding that he hoped it wasn't botched. It sounded absolutely horrific to me. A legitimate question to Christians in the United States – particularly fundamentalists – is whether Jesus, who was crucified in public, would have been an advocate of capital punishment. Lisa Stotler-Balloun, whose mother and brother were murdered, says something important in *Into the Abyss* that I have to accept, because I haven't gone through the same experiences she has. She talks of feeling a weight being taken off her shoulders when she witnessed Michael Perry's execution. I asked her if she would have been satisfied if Perry had received a sentence of life imprisonment without the possibility of parole, and she said it would have been a credible alternative, adding that some people don't deserve to live. I appreciated her honesty.

A few days before the first season of *Death Row* was screened on television, George Rivas – who appears in one of the films – was executed. Before his conviction for capital murder, he had already received eighteen consecutive life sentences for robbing a series of stores and locking away their employees. Rivas was a gentleman thief, dressing up as a security guard, going into a store, calling everyone together and explaining he had been sent over by head office. Then he would pull a gun, apologise, explain he was there for the cash and lock everyone away in a back room. One man even insisted on being shot because he was having a bad day, and Rivas spent time dissuading him. For every employee he locked away, Rivas was given a life sentence. Then, with no prospect of ever gaining his freedom, he concocted an ingenious plan of escape. With six other inmates he took thirteen guards and maintenance workers prisoner, using their clothes and IDs, and escaped from a maximum-security facility. A couple of weeks later, on Christmas Eve, the group robbed a sporting-goods store for weapons and money, and Rivas shot a policeman to death. In addition to capital punishment for this murder, Rivas got a life sentence for every one of the guards and workers he had captured during his escape. All in all, together with his death sentence he had to serve thirty-one life sentences, and on top of all that another ninety-nine years for utilising the pickup truck of the maintenance workers, which he abandoned after less than thirty minutes. I could never condone the murder of a police officer – which is as bad as it gets – but the disproportionality of Rivas's punishment defies my sense of justice. In the film he explains that what they call the death penalty he calls freedom.

The full title of the film is Into the Abyss: A Tale of Death, A Tale of Life.

Again and again the urgency of life seeped out of the footage. That *Into the Abyss* is a life-affirming film was unexpected. Somehow this eluded me during shooting, and revealed itself only during editing.

Hank Skinner was twenty-three minutes away from execution, having received the last rites and eaten his final meal, when he was reprieved. Death row is in the Polunsky Unit in Livingston, Texas, but the unit has no death house, so prisoners are transported forty-three miles away to Huntsville for execution. Skinner hadn't seen the outside world for seventeen years, and all of a sudden he was shackled, placed into a van and surrounded by armed guards, who told him, "If somebody tries to free you, we are under orders to shoot you dead." He could see the world through the windows during this drive. "It was magnificent, it was glorious," he told me. "Everything out there looked like the Holy Land." Curious, I made the trip myself. All of a sudden, amidst this forlorn and drab area of Texas, I saw the glory of the world in all its magnificence, joy and beauty. There was something wondrous at every turn, from the abandoned gas station to the ramshackle little hut with the "Happy Worm Bait Shop" sign. It truly was the Holy Land.

Lisa Stotler-Balloun talks about her father dying and how one uncle hanged himself and another shot himself because he had cancer; this is in addition to her mother and brother being murdered. Yet her appreciation of life shines through. And how does a woman become pregnant when her husband is in a maximum-security prison? Burkett's wife was a paralegal working on his case when she fell in love with him, which itself raises questions about love and destiny. They married over the telephone, with bulletproof glass between them, and now she can meet him at a table with a guard sitting with them. They are allowed only to touch hands, so how did she become pregnant? Clearly there is contraband that enters prisons, but could there be contraband going the other way? Shortly after we filmed with her, a healthy baby boy was born.

Perhaps the most important scene in the film comes towards the end. After 125 executions, Fred Allen, the captain of the tie-down team, talks about how, out of the blue, just before an execution, he started to cry and shake violently. He had been an advocate of the death penalty for a long time, but being the last person to look into the eyes of those about to die gave him an insight into the process that he couldn't entirely explain. This man of extraordinary dignity and stoicism turned his back on the job literally overnight, and by doing so forfeited his pension. In the film he talks about "living your dash", the dash between the dates on your gravestone, everything from the time you're born to the moment of your death. When I look at Fred Allen, I see the best America has to offer. His story is a powerful argument against capital punishment. With his integrity and experience, Fred is a national treasure, as trustworthy as anyone on this planet. He talks about sitting quietly, watching nature around him. "I have time to watch the ducks and the birds," he says. "I watch the hummingbirds. Why are there so many of them?" I couldn't have found a better ending to any of my films. I nearly fainted when he said that, and told him there and then he would have the final word. I'm blessed Fred offered up such a mysterious and profound question. It doesn't get any better.

Into the Abyss might also be a tale of God, because He is invoked by almost everyone in the film. The real question is: why wasn't He there to protect the innocent victims? The same question was asked by Pope Benedict XVI during his visit to Auschwitz in 2006. "Where was God in those days? Why was He silent?"

Your first film project was about people in prison, and one of your most recent too.

In the early sixties there was much discussion in West Germany about ensuring that the penal system became more about rehabilitation and resocialisation than punishment per se; it was an unrealistic dream, even if I do still think such attempts are worthy. This was the subject of an early project of mine – before even *Herakles* – that thankfully never came to pass. I had gone to Straubing prison as a seventeen-year-old and met several men serving life sentences, but eventually dropped the idea. It was a well-meaning but immature project and I'm glad the film never materialised, though I did remain in touch with the prison warden for a while. My fascination with maximum-security facilities – where the most violent of all offenders end up, and where seemingly all traces of civilisation have disappeared – has clearly never left me.

424

Into the Abyss points to the decay and lack of cohesion in families today, which means the fundamental issues of the film go far beyond the criminal case. Jason Burkett's father Delbert is also in prison, where he will almost certainly spend the rest of his life; he knows his son is never going to make it out either. It's powerful to hear him talk about how we should raise our children, about the baseball games and birthdays he missed, about how he should have encouraged his own children to finish high school – all the things that constitute the healthy upbringing of a child – and what he did wrong. Delbert testified on Jason's behalf at his son's trial, explaining that his children never had a chance, that their mother had to bring up all four of them on her own, that none of it was Jason's fault. He even said he wished he could do Jason's time for him, that he blamed himself for everything. When you hear Michael Perry talking about happier times – about a canoe trip in the Everglades he took as a thirteen-year-old, surrounded by alligators and monkeys – he seems oblivious to the fact that he's on death row. "I haven't felt this free in ten years," Perry told me at the end of our conversation. "While we were talking, I never felt I was in a cage." He spoke about the joyous moments he had experienced and what went wrong, about how close he was to a better life. Thirteen days before I met Perry, his father died. Perry was executed eight days after I filmed with him. I wanted to find out more about his family and upbringing, but his mother declined to appear on camera.

Perhaps by including Delbert Burkett in the film – a truly tragic figure – I'm asking audiences to assess themselves and think about how they live their own life. Over the years I had become somewhat dismissive of the kind of "family values" you see on television and in films, which is easy to do because they always prevail, with revolting regularity, in Hollywood happy endings. It was all too petty bourgeois for me. But today, as the father of three grown children out in the world living their own lives, and after talking with Delbert, I see things with fresh eyes. I don't think this kind of change necessarily happens with age; it's more about insight and actively dwelling on such things. Delbert reminded me that family loyalty is a priceless gift, that a parent must never abandon their child no matter what, that a parent's primary duty is to stand up to injustice on behalf of their child. Delbert was mature enough to admit what he did wrong as a father, even if his deep insights came too late.

Jared Talbert talks about learning to read while in prison.

I recorded a conversation for *Into the Abyss* with a woman who had worked in a bar in Cut and Shoot, a town near Conroe, where the murders had taken place, and who had known Michael Perry and Jason Burkett. She had a young man in tow and introduced me to him, saying, "This is Jared Talbert. You might be interested in talking to him because he also knew the murderers." I asked Jared to step aside while I filmed with this woman, then turned the camera ninety degrees – we didn't even move the tripod – to record a conversation with him. The second I shook Jared's hand I felt his callouses and knew he was a working man; I had those same callouses on my hands when, as a youngster, I worked as a welder. We connected immediately, and I said, "Now it's your turn to talk, welder to welder." He told the story of being stabbed through his chest with a fifteen-inch screwdriver, and of his friend throwing him a knife so he could defend himself. But Jared wanted to see his children that night, so he chose not to pick up the weapon and fight back. Half an hour after the attack on him he was at work, roofing a house. He spoke of how proud he was of his skills as a mechanic and his work in the local body shop, and told me how he had learnt to read only recently.

For me Jared is truly heroic, the best of the best. I have always been fascinated by the eloquence of illiterate people; some of the most enthralling conversations I have ever had were with people unable to read. How do you orientate yourself in a city when you can't read the street signs? How do you involve yourself in the most basic daily routines when you can't look at your address book? Memory becomes ever more important for such people. Jared and I had spoken with each other for only fifteen minutes, after which he needed a ride home so he could pick up some tools and get to work. I drove him back to his place. For ten minutes we rode silently in the car, though I felt he wanted to say something to me, and I know I wanted to say something to him. When he stepped out of the car, I turned to him and said, "Jared, wait a second." I walked around and stood in front of him. "I would like to tell you something," I said. "People always ask me whether spending time with death-row inmates is a life-changing experience. My answer is always no, it doesn't change my life. It might change my perspective, but it doesn't change the course of my life. Having met you doesn't change the course of my life either. But it does make it better." He paused for a second, hugged me briefly, almost in embarrassment – a hard quick hug – then turned around and walked off. I never saw him again.

In the cafeteria at McMurdo Station, when we were making *Encounters at the End of the World*, I met a journeyman plumber and welder called David Pacheco. It wasn't easy to establish a rapport with him, so instead of shaking his hand when he left, I turned to the side and gently elbowed him. He loved this and did the same. We knocked elbows together and were immediately in business; it was an instant, non-verbal form of communication. A few years before that I was watching a Thai film and noticed a man in the background with an intense, intimidating look. I immediately decided I wanted him for *Rescue Dawn* as the mute. His name was Chorn Solyda, and it turned out he spoke only a Cambodian dialect that nobody else understood, so on set we jokingly called him Walkie Talkie. Although no one could actually have a conversation with Chorn, I directed him anyway, without words, using my body to describe what I wanted. Decades before that, when I was making *The Great Ecstasy of Woodcarver Steiner*, something interesting happened. It was difficult to get Steiner to open up in front of the camera because he was embarrassed about being the focus of attention. One evening the crew and I grabbed him, hoisted him up onto our shoulders and ran through the streets. At that moment, because of this immediate physical sensation with the man, the film suddenly became quite clear to me. Only then did I know how to respond to the shots we had of Steiner flying through the air and really understand how to use them properly. At the same time, he became more comfortable talking on camera, as if he had reacted to this physical contact himself. It still wasn't easy to dig into him with words, but I felt a newfound connection.

These encounters with Jared, David, Chorn and Walter – these tactile experiences – are the story of my life, of all the people I have met and places I have visited, of my love of life and of moving around the earth. I feel most comfortable when it comes to physical contact, to being able to handle rolls of unexposed celluloid or a camera I can balance on my shoulder, to landscapes where I can touch the ground or grapple up a mountain or climb through the trees and vines of a jungle, where I can drive through the sand dunes of a desert or steer a boat through raging rapids. I spot these ideas, places and people and engage fully, without hesitation. When making a film, whenever possible, I serve as the actors' stand-in in front of the camera while the shot is being framed and the lights are set up, and I always do the slateboard myself because I like being the last person between the crew and the performers. It gets me closer to the action and also helps me know when everyone is ready; sometimes I stall and pretend to deal with some technical issue because I sense an actor needs a few more minutes to prepare. I never use a megaphone when directing; I prefer to gravitate physically towards the person I'm talking to, rather than shout from a distance. A grown man should have a good whistle, which is the most professional signal you can give a crew. Mine is vicious.

Would you ever make a television commercial?

I would rather work as a taxi driver. I don't want to make a moral issue out of this, so let me remind you what I said earlier about television and how the world of consumerism fragments our gift of storytelling. I have turned down many offers to direct television commercials over the years, though I did make a film called *From One Second to the Next*, part of AT&T's "It Can Wait" anti-texting-and-driving campaign. AT&T explained that because of my death-row films, and because they wanted somebody who was able to look into the emotional depths in a raw and direct way, they thought of me. What they proposed immediately reverberated. From the start I knew that showing wrecked cars and mangled bodies wasn't the way to make this film. What I wanted to do instead was reveal the inner effects of the catastrophes. It was also important to make clear that deep and lingering wounds were experienced by both victims and perpetrators.

AT&T wanted four thirty-second spots. I knew that the moments of great suffering, of silence, would be of vital importance, and that I needed more time to tell the stories properly. Audiences had to get to know the real-life people involved in these tales, which couldn't be done in only thirty seconds. I explained to AT&T that as well as making the four spots, I would shoot a longer film, for no extra money and within the same period of time. This wasn't particularly welcome, but I took the initiative anyway. *From One Second to the Next* contains four separate stories, each about how a catastrophic event invades a family. Entire lives are either wiped out or irrevocably changed in a single second, and in the case of those drivers who caused the accidents, they will forever carry with them a profound sense of guilt that pervades every action, every dream and nightmare. The film is more a public-service announcement than a commercial per se, and has nothing to do with consumerism. The whole AT&T campaign was actually about trying to dissuade people from excessive use of a product, not about selling anything to the public. It was about raising awareness, and within three weeks of the film being released more than two million people watched it on the Internet, in addition to it being screened at thousands of high schools and hundreds of safety organisations and government agencies across the United States, which means millions more people saw it within a very short period of time.

There was an immediate reaction to the film; hundreds of emails came in from children and their parents. One teenage girl told me she sat her mother down and said, "You text when you're driving me to school. That's not going to happen again." At the time the trend was shocking: something like a million accidents every year because of cellphone use, compared to almost none just a few years before. I heard about some mind-boggling cases, like a young man who killed a child because he was texting his girlfriend, who was sitting next to him in the same car. This is a phenomenon that represents a profound shift in our civilisation. I appreciate what the cowboy says at the end of the film: "Why don't they just talk to each other?" One thing that surprised me when I made the film was an almost complete absence of legislation relating to texting and driving; there were no relevant laws in many American states. If you ran over someone because you were texting, all you had to fear was a ticket. Just imagine, the same as for parking in the wrong space!

Spoken like a true grandfather.

The purpose of *From One Second to the Next* was simple: to make people aware of the consequences of their actions, which means the best evidence of its effectiveness is if the film correlates with a

429

noticeable drop in fatalities on the roads. Many people told me it will help save lives, but I haven't checked the statistics. All I can say is that if there is only one accident less because someone has watched the film, the whole enterprise will have been worth the effort. There's an interesting philosophical question here. You can quantify certain events – such as the number of accidents and fatalities every year – but how can you quantify things that haven't happened? How can we quantify the number of people not texting while driving? How many wonderful wives have you never met in your life because they left the plaza fifteen seconds before you got there?

Time *magazine declared you one of the hundred most influential people on the planet in 2009.*

I've never been ambitious for anything, be it a career, social status, wealth or fame; none of those things have ever particularly impressed me. In fact, I find the very idea of ambition completely foreign. It has always been noticeably absent in my thinking and actions. I would never describe myself as being influential and was genuinely surprised when the magazine told me I was being included. I immediately wrote back saying I didn't belong, that I would rather be counted as one of the anonymous three hundred Spartans, those foot soldiers who fought and perished with Leonidas at Thermopylae against the Persians. However, allow me to say one thing. When we were talking about the Rogue Film School, I said about how it has become clear over the years that young people see me as some kind of alternative to a certain kind of filmmaking, that I have developed tools to cope with the obstacles we all encounter when making films, that I have become some kind of beacon in the distance that gives people a sense of direction. They recognise that, against all odds, I have managed to make film after film despite the usual industry constraints. I seem to be a sign of hope for young people. Whenever I introduce one of my films, there is always a crowd of people wanting to talk to me; it's been like this everywhere I go for nearly forty years. A young man or woman might tell me how they quit their job or dropped out of school and started making their own films after seeing one of mine. In that respect, me being on the *Time* magazine list isn't completely grotesque.

Perhaps this book has helped contribute to that feeling amongst your admirers.

I couldn't say.

What people seem to respond to in these pages isn't necessarily the talk about specific films, more your methods of functioning in the world and how you have gone about producing your work over the past fifty years.

Perhaps, yes.

It's been more than ten years, and never have I heard you say whether this book is in any way important to you.

You are as much a prisoner of this project as I am.

True. There's little enough dignity in this work. Years ago you even told me you cursed the day you decided to co-operate.

True.

Are you happy we worked on this together?

I live my life with as little reflection as possible, but recognise that this book is the only competent comment on my work out there, and that there is ever likely to be. In that respect, I'm glad it exists.

You wouldn't lose any sleep if A Guide for the Perplexed *didn't exist?*

No.

How do you think the book would read if we had met regularly over the decades and discussed your approach to filmmaking?

Some of the basics probably haven't changed; my fundamental perspective on the world is the same. There's a tone I might recognise if I listened to forty-year-old recordings. People occasionally tell me I have "reinvented" myself over the years. Untrue. I leave that to someone like Madonna; she doesn't have much of a self, so has adopted a variety of roles throughout her career. I'm basically the same person I was when I was fourteen, with my shifting fascinations and way of looking at the world, even if I'm open to new ideas and have cast aside certain attitudes I had when I was younger. I try to live in my time, though I would have made a competent Palaeolithic hunter, bow and arrow or atlatl in hand. When I think about what animal I would have gone after if I had been around back then, the horse stands out. Their flight pattern is fairly predictable, which means they could be steered into a trap, like a pit dug in the ground and covered by leaves and branches. A stag would zigzag and most probably escape, while a bison would attack instead of running. It actually turns out I'm not entirely correct about this. When I spoke to various scientists during production of *Cave of Forgotten Dreams*, I discovered that after sifting through Palaeolithic garbage heaps, it was determined that reindeer – not horses – were a primary source of meat back then. Regardless, I would have been a good Neanderthal. I can always get a fire started when needed.

I'm glad we didn't have those regular meetings you talk about. It's good we take a step back and don't see each other, sometimes for years at a time. You do your work, I do mine, then we collide again. It would be a triumph of everything pedantic about the world if we met regularly. And I will deny the world that triumph. After having ploughed through so many hundreds of pages of these interview transcripts no one will believe me, but I have never particularly liked talking about myself, to you or anyone else. My films are the rewards for the struggles over the years; they have always been more important than the person sitting here today. The focus should be on the work, not me. I prefer to keep a low profile, in part because, on occasion, I attract certain people I would rather keep my distance from. I'm not talking about the kind of stalkers who want to sleep in my bed and take a pillow home as a souvenir. Years ago a woman identifying herself as Barbara made thirty frantic calls in a single hour to my apartment. I thought she was the former girlfriend of one of the crew of *Fitzcarraldo*. "If it would help," I told her, "why don't you come by?" When she arrived, I realised it wasn't the person I was expecting. She was very confused, in a real crisis, and insisted I was at the heart of a worldwide conspiracy to destroy and exterminate her. As she reached into her handbag, she said, "You see, sir, my only salvation is that I slaughter [*schlachten*] you first." I'm a friendly man, but at that moment felt obliged to lunge across the room and grab her bag, in which I found a loaded pistol. These days I prefer to sit with my back to the wall in restaurants.

I do the press junkets only because there's a necessity to build bridges to audiences, which might in turn make the next film easier to produce. Talking to journalists is part of the job; my way of keeping sane when having to say the same thing twenty times in a single day is to go into autopilot. I might be talking about a film I made last year, but in my mind I'm developing stories and ideas for films I'll be making next year. I always try to be gracious with the press, and have never been one of those directors who thrash about, exclaiming, "I absolutely hate interviews, but ask your questions anyway . . ." Whoever this "self" is, sitting in front of you here, is unimportant. Who cares about me? The only thing that counts is the work and what audiences see on the screen. At the end of the day only the films remain. They are the tracks in the sand as I move through life. Everything else dissipates.

Have there been any big disappointments in your career?

Not really. Things are good for me. When you're in Siberia and get into your car in the morning, you have to warm up the engine. Once warm, it works just fine. For years now, having learnt to cope with the disasters and struggles, I've been very warmed up. You won't ever see me hanging around licking my wounds.

I never sit and write a script about something that interests me, then feel detached from what I've just written as if having freed myself from it. For me, these two procedures – being fascinated by something, then processing it into a film – are simultaneous and inextricably linked. Perhaps there are a couple of my films that aren't as close to me as others, but I really do like them all, maybe with the exception of the first two. There is something fundamentally wrong with a director saying he dislikes his latest film. I want to grab him by the collar and ask, "So why did you make it in the first place? Why didn't you stop making it when you realised it was pushing against your instincts?" I love my films as I love my children. I'm like an African tribesman who needs only to cast a glance at his herd of fifty cattle to know whether one is missing, or a mother of six who, a second after entering a room, can tell if all her children are there. She doesn't even need to count them.

As a young man I discovered something that filmmakers need to learn as early as possible: a perfect film doesn't exist. No matter how much you tinker away at this scene or that frame, you have to accept there might be defects in your work. As a filmmaker, you have to learn to live with this, even if these flaws are amplified a thousand times when screened to an audience. It's the same way a parent has to live with his children. A new film is like a child that needs help when taking its first steps. Children are never perfect; one might have a limp, another might stutter. They all have their weaknesses and strong points. I actually love the most defective films even more than the others because they need my constant support and have to be protected from the world. It doesn't matter that every one of my films is flawed in some way; what's important is they are all alive. Like a child, a film grows up, finds a life of its own and learns to stand on its own two feet. At a certain point you have to unchain the boat, give it a gentle kick and let it float out into the middle of the lake. All my films have developed their own relationship with audiences, even those one or two that demand the same effort a mountain demands of a climber. At the summit we sit and bask, with drunken pleasure, in the view of a rarely seen landscape.

As you might have guessed, I look upon my profession with a certain suspicion. Cinema might give us insights into our lives and change our perspective on things, but there is much about it that's absurd. From a certain point of view cinema is nothing other than a projection of light, an illusion. It's utterly immaterial. And, of course, filmmaking can easily turn you into a clown. The careers of many directors have ended badly, even the most powerful and strongest among us; the fiercest of animals were eventually brought to their knees, even those with true vision, unafraid to deviate from the fashions of the day. Look at what happened to Orson Welles or Buster Keaton. Both were strong as an ox, both faded away and crumbled. These are most definitely cautionary tales. John Huston – who in his youth had been a high-ranking amateur boxer and literally died on set at more than eighty years of age – is an exception to the rule.

However vigilant we are, there is something destructive and disillusioning about the film business. Few filmmakers ever retire of their own free will, but the moment I feel I'm becoming an embarrassment, I shall walk away. I don't want to become like an ageing sportsman who should have quit years ago. In terms of careers, Buñuel is an interesting example. He made surrealist films in France, then went to Spain and the United States, then Mexico, where he made *Los Olvidados*, which is a very fine film, and from there back to France, where he made a handful of features very different to anything else he had already done. Although they are so diverse, every one of Buñuel's films is recognisable as his work. He never stopped opening himself up to new experiences and ideas. It's something I respect him for. His vision stayed constant. Watch Buñuel's films from start to finish and see a life's evolution.

If a filmmaker has no other legs to stand on, he can be easily broken. When someone knows how to milk a cow, there is something solid about him. A farmer who grows potatoes or breeds sheep is never ridiculous; nor is a cattle rancher or a chef able to feed a table full of hungry guests. The eighty-year-old man who brought me a bottle of wine from his vineyard before my first opera opened in Bologna could never be an embarrassment, but the film producer who takes to the red carpet at every opportunity and keeps his awards polished will always look foolish. I have seen dignified ninety-year-old cello players and photographers, but never filmmakers. My way of dealing with the inevitable is to step out of my job whenever I can. I travel on foot, I stage operas, I raise children, I cook, I write. I focus on things that give me independence beyond the world of cinema.

Cooking?

I'm good with meat – steak and venison – but lousy with soup and sweets. A man should prepare a decent meal at least once a week. I'm convinced it's the only real alternative to cinema. I was once asked if I felt most alive when filmmaking. "No," I said without hesitation. "When I'm eating a steak."

As you get older, does it become more difficult to exercise the required discipline?

I've actually always been a lazy bum. Yesterday I sat down and rewrote a script I've been working on for a while. I should have done it a couple of days ago but got caught up in the football matches from Europe I have beamed into my living room. The only reason I did the rewrite yesterday is that the person who is producing the film was due at my place just after lunch, so at eleven o'clock I grudgingly turned off the television, stopped fiddling around with God knows what, and sat down at my computer because I couldn't put it off any longer. I work best under pressure, knee-deep in the mud. It helps me concentrate. The truth is I have never been guided by the kind of strict discipline I see in some people, those who get up at five in the morning and jog for an hour. My priorities are elsewhere. I will rearrange my entire day to have a solid meal with friends.

Any final advice?

I once saw a film celebrating the life of Katharine Hepburn, who I like as an actress. It was some kind of homage to her, but unfortunately it turns out she had these vanilla-ice-cream emotions. At the end she sits on a rock by the ocean and someone off camera asks her, "Ms Hepburn, what would you like to pass on to the young generation?" She swallows, tears are welling. She takes a lot of time, as if she were thinking deeply about it all, then looks straight into the camera and proclaims: "Listen to the Song of Life." I was cringing so much it hurt, and still smart just thinking about it. It really couldn't get any worse. Hearing these words was such a blow that I wrote it into the Minnesota Declaration, Article Ten, which I repeat here and now for you. I look you right in the eye and say, "Don't you ever listen to the Song of Life."

Ten Poems
by Werner Herzog

Translated by Presley Parks
Originally published in *Akzente: Zeitschrift für Literatur*
June 1978

Jede der hellen Nächte lagen Mann und Weib
Im Ringen, und auf dem Dächern im Fächeln
Des Monds übten die Katzen wilde fremde
Begattung. Die Bäume reichten über die
Dächer, über die Bäume die Berge und
Über den Bergen zogen die Sterne hinter
Der Nacht her.

Da sprach der König: meine Kinder,
Habt Geduld. Warten wir ein paar Jahrhunderttausend,
Bis dahin wandern die Steine im Feld
Und vielleicht weint sogar einer einmal.

Every bright night lay man and woman struggling,
And on the roofs, fanned by the moon,
The cats practised wild fornication.
The trees extended above the
Roofs, above the trees the mountains, and
Above the mountains the stars followed
After the night.

So spoke the King: My children,
Have patience. We shall wait a few
   Hundred Thousand years,
Until then the stones will wander in the field
And perhaps someone will weep even once.

DER MUHLENFRENZEL

Drüben, jenseits des Teichs
Lebt der Mühlenfrenzel.
Mit Forschung im Auge sitzt
Da ein Frosch vor der Fliege.

Manchmal ist dem Frenzel sein
Einziger Freund der Sturm-Sepp.
Der hat sein Lebtag lang
Nur Bärendienste geleistet.

Aus Angst vor dem Reden schlägt
Der Frenzel die Hand auf den Mund.
So geht alles seit Jahren
Den Richtigen Weg.

Und jeden Abend in den Monaten
Ohne den Buchstaben R
Stellt sich unverzüglich am Teich
Eine Stimmung ein.

Over there, beyond the pond,
Lives Little Franz from the Mill.
With a searching eye, a frog sits
In front of the fly.

Sometimes Franz's only friend is
Sepp born by a Storm.
His whole life long he has
Only done bears' work.

Scared of speaking, Franz slaps
His hand over his mouth.
Thus, for years now,
Everything goes the right way.

And every evening in the months
Without the letter R
A festive mood appears, at once,
By the pond.

Die Stühle stehen leer
Und Farbe blättert von den Wänden
Schon wieder schmilzt der Schnee
Noch gleicht der Stuhl dem Stuhl
Das Zimmer einem Zimmer.

Nichts ist rot als der Fuchs
Nichts ist schwarz als die Raben
Dem Kampf zweier Schlangen
Gibt es nichts Gleiches.
Und die Reiher, heisst es
Zielen immer zuerst aufs
Auge des Gegners.

Ich fürchte mich davor,
Dass es sehr hell wird, dass
Türen und Fenster sich öffnen
Und hundert Gäste sich drängen
Ganz ungeladen.

The chairs are empty
And paint flakes off of the walls
Once again the snow is melting
The chair is still like a chair
The room like a room.

Nothing is red like the fox
Nothing is black like the raven
Nothing is like two snakes fighting.
And herons, so it is said, always aim first for
Their opponent's eye.

I fear that it will become very bright, that
Doors and windows will open,
And hundreds of guests will pour in,
All uninvited.

Ein wildfremdes Mädchen schrieb mir,
Sie sähe ständig Krokodile
Mit einem Brikett quer im Maul.
Sie schrieb: draussen auf dem
Himmelhoch heiligen Feld
Gäbe es Schatten vom Bäumen
Und Schatten von Menschen.
Nicht ohne Grund habe ein Rabe gehrächzt.
Die Erde erzeuge die Leichen
Und diese lägen fieberfrei.
Sie sitze kauend am Fenster
Und meine, sie kenne das Land.

A wildly strange girl wrote to me that
She keeps seeing crocodiles
Each with a brick sideways in its mouth.
She wrote: Outside, on the holy field
That is as high as heaven,
There are shadows of trees
And shadows of people.
Not without reason a raven crowed.
The earth produces corpses
And they lie there without fevers.
She sits ruminating by the window,
And thinks, she knows this land.

Man kann nicht verlangen,
Dass keiner nichts sieht:
Ist den nicht ein entlaufenes Schaf
Ein schlechtes Tauschobjekt?
Und da auf den Feldern
Liegen nur Steine wie Stein.
Auch die Bettler haben kein Geld.
Wenn nämlich einer vor Hunger stirbt,
Ist das oft ein Zeichen von Armut.

You can't wish
That no one doesn't see nothing;
Isn't a runaway sheep
A poor thing to barter?
And on the fields there lie only stones like stone.
The beggars also have no money.
Whenever one of them dies of hunger,
It is, in fact, often a sign of poverty.

An einer erschossenen Sau
Sogen sechs Ferkel nach Milch.
Auf gemeinsamen Beschluss hin
Stellten die Kinder jegliches Spiel ein.
Blindekuh und Sackhüpfen gab es
Von da an nur noch in Büchern.
Jemand stieg auf einen Turm
Und blickte lange nach Süden.
Das alles ist lange schon her,
Seitdem hat sich nichts mehr geändert.
Im Haus des Gehenkten
Spricht man nur noch vom Strick.

A sow that has been shot dead,
Six piglets suckle for milk.
With a group decision,
The children stop playing all games.
Blind man's bluff and sack-jumping
Were from then on only in books.
Someone climbed up a tower
And stared south for a long time.
All that was long ago,
Ever since then nothing has changed.
In the house of the hanged
They only speak of the rope.

Durch nassgeregnete Hecken
Regnet der Regen, regnet
Die Bergwand in Not.

Im Nebel steigen die Männer zum Berg
Und rufen sich laut.
Kalter Rauch weht um die Häuser herum.
Am Baum sind die Äpfel gefroren.

Wenn die Nacht sinkt,
Stirbt gas Gesicht.
Regen fällt neimals nach oben.

Through rain-wet bushes
Rains the rain, the face of the mountain
Rains in need.

In the mist the men climb the mountain
And yell loudly to each other.
Cold smoke blows around the houses.
The apples on the tree have frozen.

When the night sinks,
The face dies.
Rain never falls upward.

So zeigt sich der Nutzen der Fenster:
Ach, und hier, hier wächst ja ein
Bäumchen am Dach, und hier, im
Zwanzigsten Stock zeigt sich Gebüsch!

Vor einem Wald hat man alle Reden
Noch einmal gehalten.
In allen Gesichtern hat man geforscht
Jeden Stein umgedreht, dem Gelb
Selbst misstraut.

Lieber sich gar nicht mehr umsehen!
Da sind nur Gesichter im Kreis.
Hier, vor einem Kreidestrich
Geraten seltene Tiere ins Stocken.
Auch von den Hühnern in unserem Topf
Wissen wir wenig.

So, in this way, the use of windows reveals itself:
Ah, and here grows a
Little tree on the roof, and here on
The twentieth floor there is a bush!

In front of a forest they gave all the speeches
Once again.
In all the faces they searched,
Turned every stone, mistrusted
The colour yellow itself.

Better not to look around any longer!
There are only faces in a circle.
Here, in front of a chalk line
Rare animals come to a standstill.
And of the chickens in our pot
We also know little.

RAIN-IN-THE-FACE

Mit zweiundsiebzig, nach einem Joghurt
Legte mein Grossvater den Löffel beiseite
Und verlor den Verstand.
Im Garten sang er Lieder für Käfer
Und nannte sich Rudolf der Bär.
Er lernte sanfte Bärenlieder.

Früher trug er Anzug und Stock
Und trat oft für Recht und Ordnung ein.
Seine Kollegen hiessen nämlich
Nagel, Illemann, Muhr.

Zu der Zeit lebte schon mein
Liebster Indianer nicht mehr.
Er hiess Rain-in-the-Face
Und starb am Little Big Horn.
Sein Vater heiss Tretender Bär
Und seine Mutter Weisse-Kuh-Sieht.

RAIN-IN-THE-FACE

At age seventy-two, after eating a yogurt
My grandfather put aside his spoon
And lost his mind.
In the garden he sang songs for the beetles
And called himself Rudolf the Bear.
He learned sweet bear songs.

Before he had a suit and cane
And often stood up for law and order.
His colleagues were called
Nagel, Illemann, Muhr.

At that time my favourite Indian
Was no longer alive.
He was called Rain-in-the-Face
And died at Little Big Horn.
His father was named Kicking Bear
And his mother White Cow Sees.

Gestern Nacht wurde es
Ganz plötzlich still.

Under dem allerschwärzensten
Reglosen Himmel standen
Reglos die Bäume.
Nur unser Hund benagte leise
Die Fransen des Teppichs.

Am nächsten Morgen
Lag überall Reif.

Last night, all of a sudden,
it became utterly silent.

Under the blackest
Motionless sky, the
Trees stood dead still.
Only our dog nibbled quietly
On the frayed edges of the carpet.

The next morning
The land was covered with hoarfrost.

Thinking about Germany
by Werner Herzog

SACHRANG, 15 JUNE 1982

From the Mount of Olives chapel, just by the customs post, went the path through beautiful, tall, damp forest towards Sachrang, which I rapidly lost sight of as I climbed up via Mitterleiten. A construction machine was grinding heavy gravel next to the shell of a brick house they will never finish building. At Mitterleiten, I was overtaken by a farmer on his motorcycle. I knew who he was, but he didn't recognise me when I greeted him. Only hesitantly and with difficulty did I manage the first few strides. At the spot where the builders' rubbish was being dumped in the forest, where the lorries drive in over a bed of crushed roofing tiles between the trees, where the damp wind threatens to wrench off to the mountain plastic tarpaulins, held down by stones and looking like plundered corpses, where timid ducks fled before me from the ugly gravel ponds of the never fully completed building site, at this spot – after wandering around my past in my thoughts for a long time – I took leave of my beloved Sachrang, the scene of my childhood, and set off in great haste in the cool rain and through the dripping grass and yarrow up the mountainside. The fields smelt of mown grass, and I cast a glance across the valley at the Geigelstein, via which I would return after my long journey on foot. At this moment, I was filled with a sense of courage and certainty, stretching from border to border and from horizon to horizon. As I climbed up to the Spitzstein mountain hut, a loneliness increasingly settled on the countryside below me, very gently, much as a big strong animal might settle on the ground. For almost a whole hour, the innkeeper of the hut stared fixedly at me through a big telescope as I climbed the slopes towards him.

*

Steep descent to the Bavarian Alps. Several ugly alpine houses in an insignificant basin. This is the start of the woodland track to Wildbad Kreuth. At a stroke, after it had started to rain for a while on the way down, darkness descended as if heralding something biblical. For safety's sake I took refuge on a bench under the projecting roof of a hut, and didn't have long to wait before a violent storm arose, raging along the narrow valley and sweeping white and grey patches of mist in amongst the groaning trees. When it got worse and worse and I thought the rainstorm was at its most violent, something else occurred that made what had happened so far seem like a paltry beginning. Everywhere foaming white cataracts came rushing down from the steep wall opposite, then everything was shrouded in raging white clouds. These clouds broke up, revealing the treetops, and then fled away along the slopes in panic-stricken files. Like a curtain, the whole scene was then torn open, making visible raging cataracts of white foam and rivulets that hadn't existed before. The rain struck me just as a divine punishment strikes evil-doers. Waiting a long time until the worst was over, I gazed into this strange frenzy, knowing that no one else was witness to it apart from me. Given the curiously depressed state of mind I found myself in, I couldn't bear the thought of leaving the border and going down into some inhabited place in the valley, so I elected to head west and then steeply uphill in a somewhat southerly direction into the massif, though the rain had not ceased but merely stopped coming down at full force. The steep ascent took me at first alongside a raging waterfall. The stony path itself had been transformed into a swollen stream that got worse and worse further up. I was soon totally surrounded by cloud. When I arrived up on the Wild Man's col, the whole horizon suddenly opened up before me, permeated with a yellowish-orange glow in the rain. Deep into the heart of the massif, I could see mountaintops, valleys and forests shining for one glorious fleeting moment. It was like a sign of great promise for a whole thirsting nation. Meanwhile, behind me a billowing white curtain of mist was

459

shooting upwards from the abyss, immediately afterwards closing off the scene behind me with a theatrical gesture. Then, by the side of an alpine hut marked by the ravages of time, I came upon two shiny, brand-new signs, one for the free state of Bavaria, the other for the Federal Republic of Germany. The Austrian sign was badly dented and merely said: "Attention, National Border."

I spent the evening up in the hut in conversation with the nine-teen-fifties German champion in canoeing and wild-water racing, who told me about his life as a sportsman in the post-war period. He had often been so hungry, he said, that he had cried. On arrival in Wildbad Kreuth next morning I was tempted to go as far as the house of F. J. Strauss and invite myself in for a sandwich to keep me going. But then I simply didn't have the nerve to sit there chewing food in his company, with Germany's core ripped apart by barbaric absurdities. A farmer in rubber boots had tied a limping bull to the back of his tractor and was pulling it behind him along the main road. The bull was advancing reluctantly, snorting as it went, and when I looked upwards I saw the mountain peaks quite clearly bow to him.

The solemn sound of church bells from the valley. The fighting, strangling and murdering action of the forests also proceeds with silent solemnity. A pensioner, sitting on a bench, was asleep in the afternoon sun. "Good, good," he said in his sleep, and a little later, "Oh yes, good." On a sign next to the bench, indicating the border, written in felt pen and already almost worn away by the elements, stood the words: "Germany is bigger than the Federal Republic." In the forest the birds were starting to curse the forest. In the hut at the top of the Krinner Kofl I talked for a long time to a retired teacher from the Münster area. In response to my enquiries, he told me how the war had ended for him. In Holland, when the Canadians were advancing with their tanks and were only a few hundred feet away, he had – acting under orders – been taking prisoners at a farm beyond the advancing line of enemy tanks. By turning his weapon against his own superior officer, he'd prevented him from having the prisoners shot in the Dutch farmhouse. Then, together with the Dutch captives and the superior officer he'd now also taken prisoner, he had so to speak followed the enemy cur-rent, below the level of the raised road along which the Canadian tanks were advancing, under the cover of just a few bushes. But in attempting to overtake the enemy and get back to his own lines, he himself had been captured, together with his prisoners.

The innkeeper of the hut had mounted the silhouette of a chamois made of plywood up on the rock face, and it stood out against the sheer walls of the Karwendel range that were glowing in the rays of the setting sun. Lots of tourists, he told me, took it to be real. In an enclosure next to the hut there is a tame stag. A tourist, sitting only a hundred feet away, enjoying his afternoon coffee and cakes in the cafe for day trippers, picked it up in the viewfinder of his telescope and shouted to his wife, "Mum, Mum, look, there is a deer!" Taking the telescope from him, his wife, after studying the beast for some time, ticked him off, saying, "Egon, that's not a deer, it's a buck." The mentally retarded son of the forester living in the house near by came up and, emitting peculiar sounds from deep within his strange being, started to tug at me and then at a clever-looking hunting dog. The two of us patiently let him have his way. Later the boy followed me across to the hut of the alpine club, where I was just collecting my belongings together, and helped himself to my last piece of chocolate. I let him have it because he was making a move as if to take my binoculars and notebook too. As I had sacrificed such a small portion of my worldly goods without putting up any resistance, he seemed clearly content to put an end to his thieving spree there, merely lying down on the other articles which he would certainly have liked to have.

Just before Mittenwald, I saw a woman sitting on a bench by the educational nature trail and weeping. At a loss as to how to get myself past her, I greeted her cautiously. Looking at me through her tears, she returned my greeting without interrupting her weeping. Then I came to the barbed-wire fence of the Alpine Regiment's barracks, which seemed to go on for ever. There were signs warning of shooting practice. I left Mittenwald almost at a run. I never saw such commercial exploitation of the countryside anywhere. Paths spread with sand as in the grand parks of spa towns, educational nature trails and, walking on them, people who were themselves just as stunted. The Watzmann stood there in the wan light of evening, its rocks appearing to get colder and colder with their whitish-grey hues. It's a dogged mountain, the Watzmann. The woods became quite still, without a breath of wind. Two wild ducks were floating on a marshy pond, silently, like primeval dreams. Above them, doggedly, towered the Watzmann, while beyond the trees, the mountain slopes and the rocky crevices reigned an immense, quite transparent stillness. Walking around a large game fence, I came upon a big, almost factory-like site for the feeding of game animals, with great rakes for hay, salt licks, observation stands and one of those unimaginative huts too. In the field towards the forest two young deer were grazing together with a hind. When I appeared, they observed me closely for a while, trying to sniff out who this was that had come. "Herzog's my name," I said quietly and confidentially, and they set off at a majestically springy trot, disappearing into the wood.

Yesterday I lost an election I had put myself forward for as a candidate with no hope of winning. The whole thing took place in Hamburg, the victor being Leisler-Kiep, which struck me as strange. The various losing candidates, all members of parties except for me, were invited out onto a balcony high above the Elbe harbour. The balcony, though totally frozen over, had been deemed an appropriate enough backdrop for the television broadcast because of the spectacular view it afforded of the arctic ice fields stretching from here to the icy peaks of Spitzbergen. When it came to the congratulations, I, as the only non-party candidate, was last in line, waiting for the moment when the cameras would be switched off, and I had to hurry because the election winner was already turning to go. In the process I lost my footing, slid under the handrail of the frozen balcony and plunged into the yawning depths of the glacial tongues that fell away abruptly before me into the river Elbe. Filled with a sudden horror, I realised this was the end of me, but I had the presence of mind while still in the air to spread out my arms like a parachute jumper drifting diagonally into formation with his comrades below him, and thus to steer my fall in such a way that I plunged into the icy water of the river hundreds of feet downstream, just beyond the sharp edge of the broken-off ice floes. And since on this day the river was one of mercury, not water, this helped to cushion my breakneck fall. For a long time, presumably unconscious, I lay on the shore of the iced-up Elbe, and my memories of the subsequent period are only blurred. I can recall seeing a big ocean liner turn away after giving up the search for me. I can see the colour of the water it left in its churned-up, icy wake, a broad ribbon disappearing into the depths of the Spitzbergen archipelago. Lightning flashes in the distance brought some comfort. A band of rain lay firmly and resolutely over Germany. In an abandoned lift shaft there dwelt only despair beyond measure. On the ground, between rain-soaked nettles and in the fragments of broken tiles, a new faith in Germany begins to grow. I took out the tiny mouth organ I had been given, only the size of a thumbnail. It only has four notes, not enough to play the national anthem.

*

In Balderschwang people had set up their garden swing chair precisely so as to get the best view of the meadow. So there they sat, as on a summer holiday, taking a look at the cows. I climbed to the right, higher and higher into the mountains. It was already late, and light rain set in. Two cows followed me for a long time, as if expecting to hear the message to end all messages from me. "You're no cows," I said to them, "you're princesses," but even that didn't stop them. Only when I crossed a rain-soaked, blotchy snow field did they stay behind. On top, by the cable-car station, I had a vast, far-reaching view over Germany. Stretching out as far as the hazy, orange-tinted horizon I could see valleys and hills, becoming gentler and dotted with farms and hamlets as the land grew flatter in the far distance. To the west, bathed in a silver that slowly turned to reddish gold, lay Lake Constance. Pale, storm-laden clouds hovered over the whole scene, and far to the west, as in Old Master paintings, oblique reddish-orange rays of the setting sun were breaking through shafts of rain. Without casting a shadow, a subdued light settled evenly on silvery dark woods and silvery bright fields. In this shadow-free sheen, Germany looked as if it were submerged under water. It was a submissive country. I sat down. In chaotic flight, swallows were darting just above the hilltop away into the evening light. As if numbed, Germany lay there indecisively. In concert halls, you get this second of indecisiveness and silence when, listening to some little-known orchestral work, nobody is quite sure whether the piece has ended or not. In a whole hall full of people, everyone is waiting for everyone else, until the applause starts, bringing release to the audience. It is just such a second of dread, of fearful, frozen expectation, only extended over a long period lasting for decades, that Germany is inescapably caught up in. There it lay, this un-land, just as things unlucky and unloved exist; this un-territory, then, that clings tight with its broken limbs to the name Germany. It lay before me, visible from frontier to frontier.

A big bough came crashing down to the ground from a tall tree. My country lay there in the middle of Europe, of all countries the only one that had remained in the very core of its being barbaric. A country filled with longing, lost amidst aims that were not identifiable, unredeemed, obliged to admit that it had become homeless within its own territory. Having eaten their fill, people were going to bed. On Lake Constance, a swan was swimming from this shore to that.

Germany has given away all its secrets in two world wars.

*

Everywhere there is the smell of hay. The countryside is heavy with cherries. In Stein am Rhein elderly women, a whole busload of them, were passing through the city gate from a car park outside it and advancing in the direction of the town hall. "About turn, about turn," shouted a tour guide, wearing a small, brightly coloured checked hat, and since the file of women had already spread out considerably, the command was passed only hesitantly down the line, before eventually even those at the very front turned round in order to take photos of the half-timbered gateway from the inside. Beyond the town, I took a look at the Rhine's strong current, the swans, the wooden rowing boats. What I was looking at was another century. I dipped my arms deep into the water, bent over it and drank. You can drink the Rhine. I ate some bread with it. On the paths there are either brusque commands addressed to walkers, such as, "Keep out! Mortal danger!" "No entry, automatic firing devices!" or the most stupid of verses involving spoonerisms. There appears to be no kind of language in between. By the Freiwald chapel there is the start of a wildlife reserve. The sign saying so would, in fact, be enough, but underneath it you then have the following on a plaque: "Bear in mind, walker, that you're passing through nature, where there lives many a poor creature.

We therefore entreat you to remain on the marked paths, for in order to live the dear animals need their peace. Do your bit to help protect both wildlife and woods. Please stick to the paths."

Later on I saw in front of me the brush of a fox disappearing round a bend in the path, but the way the bushy tail vanished did not suggest flight. Quickening my steps and moving really quietly, after the bend I suddenly found myself standing directly behind the fox. He whirled halfway round, looking to my mind as big as an Alsatian dog. Given the extreme astonishment with which he contemplated me, he was only half able to cower down, and he remained standing like this for a moment without further reaction. He seemed to be listening to find out whether his heart, having stopped, was starting to beat again. Then, with an agile turn, he was off, running steeply down through the wood. From down below I could still hear the snapping twigs of fear some time afterwards. Then the peace of nature was restored in Germany. Basically, however, it was only an ostensible peace, nothing more than naked indifference.

The first person I encountered in the valley was a little girl on a plastic tricycle that wouldn't steer properly any more. She gave new names to all things. The dreams she had at night she called "films in her pillow."

Up in the mountain ranges with their massive farms and in the valleys below – I had the increasingly intense impression – there is nobody left alive. No dogs, no cattle, no hens, no human beings; all is totally still. Now a few birds are singing, quite tentatively, in the woods. So far, fortunately, I have been under tree cover during the day. The sun would be the death of me. I wish I could join a circle of monks, be their godless guest. A friendly notice in the woods, painted on a sign, said that all things born in the forest had met face to face with the great Lord God, and that you yourself were blessed by God if you remained dutifully silent.

I hope, if only on account of this sign, that the first atom bomb falls on the Black Forest!

*

The railway station in Offenburg was full of French recruits with their short back and sides. Obviously they are allowed home over

465

the weekend, and their mood was correspondingly high-spirited. When a girl walked by in tight white trousers, two of them turned on their heels to salute her. All day long the air was full of swallows going about their business. What can anyone do to protect me against the Black Forest? I succeeded in doing something extraordinary, something I discovered myself more by chance than anything else. I managed to describe a gathering of roughly a hundred women in such tiny writing that you needed a microscope to have any chance of deciphering the scribbles that crossed the paper like strings of beads. It then transpired that with this miniature handwriting I had not only described the gathering in the form of a text, but that the fine lines and loops also actually yielded a sketch of the women, sitting there in distinct rows on the benches and looking out attentively from the sheet of paper. Even shadows round the eyes and fleeting glimpses of facial features were identifiable because of the varying strength of pressure from my drawing pen, yet on the other hand it was clearly a piece of handwriting. Taking a handy microscope with me, I went to the cafe where Einstein was sitting with colleagues in the open air eating cake. At that time he was younger than he normally looks in the photos one knows of him, and his name had not yet become a household word. I showed him my writing, and he was astonished. We talked about information storage. At one point he choked on a piece of cake, and I slapped his back hard between the shoulder blades until his face returned to its normal colour.

Then I got held up in Strasbourg. Unable to leave, I was living in a ground-floor room that opened onto a narrow, park-like garden. The reason why I had to stay was, I think, that I was ill. During the endless afternoons, I liked most of all to take a cushion and lie across the threshold of the door on the garden side, gazing up into the big, wide-spreading tree that stuck doggedly to its position there in the sultry heat of the day. An oppressive breeze started to blow, causing all the leaves to tremble, flicker and shimmer like those of a boundless aspen. I could see the movement of every single one of the millions upon millions of leaves as something separate and unique, and yet at the same time I saw the collective movement of them all, as when a wind ruffles the smooth surface of a gigantic lake. All at once the lake now becomes old. Earlier periods of its history come and go. Dwellings built on piles emerge and vanish; quiet, peaceful prehistoric reptiles laze in the swamps by the shore; and finally the lake grows flat, the ruffling of the trees in the forest merging with a bashful ruffling of its reeds. Right at the end, pterodactyls circle over the reeds, their jerky flight paths not at all like those of birds but resembling those of powerful bats. There are as many of them as one sometimes sees gulls over the sea. However, when I return to the flickering of the leaves and can see it all simultaneously, my whole life, lying there so ill on the threshold, starts to quiver finely. An extraordinarily imperious North African man strides past, then a stocky, ugly woman with a Great Dane the size of calf. I can feel the oak doorstep under me, bleached by the sun and full of grooves made by the rain. A coating of dry algae was growing in the grooves of the wood's grain like a film of plaque on bad teeth. Two men are stepping solemnly and quietly into the open from a farm. Everything has an air of morning about it, still sleepy, as on Sundays. During the night the men have been helping out with the birth of a foal, and one of them still has a blade of straw in his hair.

*

In Strasbourg I was sitting on a bench, and after a while an Algerian came and sat down politely beside me. Soon afterwards another Algerian came up, carrying a white plastic bag. He shook the hand of his friend next to me, then, as if it was the most natural thing in the world, shook mine too, which I found deeply moving. I had switched over to the French side of the border. Germany lay beyond the Rhine like an invention of the imagination. The fact that I'm walking is also more of an invention than anything else, only it's a bad one because something horrific is dogging my steps. Lots of people were crossing the bridge to Germany, slowly, their movements stretched out as in slow motion, while beneath them the Rhine was flowing at an even slower, more crippling pace. The grasses under its surface were swaying immensely slowly in the turgid flow of the currents. Everything, it seemed, was about to come to a definitive standstill. In Strasbourg Minster, bikers were walking quietly through the silence of the church, only their tight-fitting leather suits making slight creaking noises. They were carrying their helmets under their arms like mediaeval knights. At night, out in the open fields where I was sleeping, the cows groaned in their dreams right by me. In the morning, very early, I woke up with a fright I had never known before. I was totally numb. Germany had gone, everything had gone. It was as if I had suddenly lost something entrusted to my special care the evening before. Or perhaps it was like being expected to take over guard duty for a whole army one evening, only to discover that one has in a mysterious way suddenly gone blind, and the troops are thus without protection. Everything had vanished, leaving me totally empty, without pain, without joy, without longing, without love, without warmth and friendship, without anger and hatred. Nothing, nothing remained. I was like a suit of armour without a knight in it. Slowly I at least began to experience something like fright. I only awoke fully when the sun, filled with hate, was shining in my face. I saw black swans. Heavy boughs were falling in the deadly still forest. For every five fish there are eighty anglers. Even on Sundays they make steel. The River Saar is unfortunately burnt out. Near a slag heap, four workers were running after an injured pheasant. I am collecting wheat fields for my dreams. At night the valleys and villages became empty. I slept out on a hillside under the open sky, my shoulder aching strongly, which caused me to just lie there motionless in the silence. Hours later in the night, caught in distress between the lights of the valley and the stars above, I got up, and was sick. Towards morning I managed to get some sleep, but it was already getting light and soon the sun rose. Above me on a branch I heard a bird first shake itself and tidy up its plumage before eventually starting to sing.

When it is all up with Germany, when human beings cease to exist, and ants and cockroaches have taken over, and subsequently algae in the oceans that have started boiling; when the earth is then extinguished and the universe goes dark, collapsing in on itself to nothing, it is possible that something abstract will remain behind, perhaps something akin to a state of happiness. But I have a deep fear inside me that what will fill the darkness and the space that no longer exists will be a form of stupidity. It does not need a particular place, it is everywhere. Happiness, at least, requires open space.

*

In Waldkirch I ended up on a road very busy with traffic that I avoided by walking along parallel to it in the forest. However, the path changed quite abruptly into a woodland nature trail with signs, serving at the same time as a fitness trail equipped with sets of rings, horizontal and high bars. Instructions for the use of these were posted on boards. On one of the high bars I encountered a muscular, very young man in white karate trousers. Swinging his legs wildly, he was kicking out in all directions into the air, then immediately afterwards doing pull-ups. I left this terrible path as quickly as I could, and since Waldkirch itself gave the impression of being one great town-size fitness trail, I steadfastly refused to pay it attention, practically not seeing the place at all. I lay down in a field of beet where, since big green leaves sprouted from my ears, I was well camouflaged. Then I grew electricity pylons in place of my arms and, using these steel tongs as hands, I fetched down low-flying aeroplanes from the sky, often two at a time. Then a black dog ran along the isolated tarmac road at full gallop. It had leapt straight from a Hieronymus Bosch picture, directly from hell, in fact. A man wanted to get rid of his Alsatian because it was always moulting too much on the carpet. Taking the dog with him on a business trip, he released it at the service station on a motorway. Weeks later the animal turned up at home again, emaciated but whimpering with joy. The beast's instinct and loyalty had led it home over a distance of a several hundred miles. Thereupon, its owner put an end to it by mixing rat poison into the starving dog's first meal.

Low-lying clouds, a gentle wind, the fields have wings and raise themselves towards the sky. The people here seem like albinos turned in on themselves, aseptic, free of pain, without sins, without vices, without joy. The leaves were trembling in the wind, and I knew they were whispering to one another, so I listened closely. Although I understood only a little, about this much I was clear: in the Hürtgenwald, in the Hürtgenwald, all hell had broken loose. The countryside, however, lies flat, bored. The maize fields are bored as they slowly ripen, and the cows are lying around bored too. Above me, low-flying jet fighters are pursuing each other. What with all the flies, it's impossible to think, even of something evil or stupid. For days now, a line of poetry I made up has been beating with gnawing intensity in my brain, ringing with every step I take, impossible to blot out. What I had written was: "The Watzmann's racing, the Watzmann's racing, hey-de-ho, my wooden leg is blazing!" And now I'll never get it out of my mind again. It's the same to this very day, by the way. Whenever I'm walking, the verse comes into my head and simply won't go away. It's a terrible thing. "The Watzmann's racing, the Watzmann's racing, hey-de-ho, my wooden leg is blazing!" May God protect you from this poem! Meanwhile, the hawks are entering their names in eternity.

*

A loving couple, country dwellers, were looking at each other for ages without exchanging a word. They did so for as long as the money they had put in the fruit machine lasted. At one point, a few coins came rattling out into the dish, but they didn't turn to look at them. Crouching, as if ready to leap, mean-looking park benches made of faded plastic were waiting for me to arrive. I sat down on one of them, under the dripping branches of a weeping willow. I saw mechanical heathers, arranged military-fashion in pots. Then I saw mechanical hens. When one of them started to run after seeds, they all took to running.

Today is a grey, cold, wet and motionless day. By a miserable field I had seen an abandoned fire engine surrounded by nettles and clumps of grass, and in retrospect I couldn't rid myself of the idea that a fireman must have committed suicide in the derelict vehicle. I saw lots of toads lying as if crucified on the edge of the road, their bright, spotted bellies turned upwards. They hadn't made it right across, yet lying there stretched out, they looked as if nothing at all was the matter with them, except that their entrails had come out through their mouths.

For a long time during my misty walk through the woods, I, the misty, solitary wanderer, was called after by a buzzard who was probably even more solitary. Thus I find myself walking over the Eifel range, taking short, very hurried strides. Totally unprepared for it, I suddenly came upon an American airforce base. Surrounded by a fence, it looked very strange. There were lorries mounted on concrete plinths, carrying radar screens that turned ceaselessly in circles. There were warning signs, strong electricity generators, a baseball pitch and broken-down American cars behind the fence, while in the damp mist the radar screens circled ceaselessly on the camouflaged lorries. All the way along the fence, I peered closely into the base and into the open windows of the barracks, but I didn't spot a human soul. I took it that the Americans stationed here must long since have fled. When rain began to fall heavily, I turned off into a forest clearing, suspecting that there might be a raised hide there. And indeed I soon found one, well roofed over. At the foot of a ladder was a metal sign, indicating that according to such-and-such a paragraph it was forbidden to enter these forestry premises. Diagonally opposite, on the other side of the clearing, is another such hide, no doubt bearing the same sign. I see more hides than human beings. Human beings are increasingly taking refuge in the mine works, in crevasses and in the earth's interior because it's warmer there, as the earth's core is still glowing a little, whereas the universe is freezing. The raised hides are staring at one another out of their empty rifle slits. The foresters smoking their pipes up there in them are the only people left throning over the land, like high priests. As I walked up the track to Rescheid, the rain stopped. At the edge of the track, there are dark wild roses. Emerging from the forest, I found the hills full of lapwings. They flew away listlessly as I came a bit nearer. To the west the view disappears deep into the haze of Belgium. Wide ranges of hills, lined with dark hedges; little wooded hillocks; the hamlets darkly scattered. To the right, the land drops away for a long distance; you can see the steam rising from the valleys, no more. There lies Germany. What on earth am I doing in this area, forsaken by both God and man? Astonished at myself, I paused by a stop for the "motor vehicle post bus." When there is serious flooding, of course, the motor vehicle post gets delivered by motor vehicle barque instead. O God, who art not, take me to the last of all countries, and you human beings – since that would bring more comfort – please put me in the last of all villages!

*

The first thing the farmer did that raised people's suspicions was to sell his hens one day and to keep peacocks from then on. After going to church on Sundays, he would crouch down on the floor in a corner of the pub with his beer, no longer recognising anyone. He ordered a telephone connection for the little hut on his allotment because he wanted to phone God from there, but he was worried about the right dialling code.

Walking down the Rhine, I found the greyish-brown river under a gloomy sky full of rain clouds. The lines of jet fighters were compressing the already flat scenery more profoundly and depressingly, making it appear thin. The ferry that according to the map should be here no longer exists. Everything else is still in place: the landing stages on both sides, the ferry's inn, a West German flag, chairs made of red and white plastic. At the landing stage, a man was standing holding a dog on a lead that unreeled mechanically. Next to him was a girl with Down's syndrome, keeping one eye almost shut. She had very bad teeth. "Ship, ship," she said to me, stressing the words strangely and looking at me as she did so. I nodded to her because there were lots of ships. One, a pleasure boat, was passing by quite close, going up the Rhine. It pulled by us like a strangely stressed word. The people on board in their deckchairs, with sunglasses on, had an unreal air about them, like sentences producing no meaning. Orderly thinking, which is not without its ugly side, is only to be found hiding in the geometrical fields. In the evening, Bocholt died away very quickly. There was nothing, I mean absolutely nothing left in the town. On discovering a few helpless schoolboys who were helplessly groping helpless schoolgirls – and taking care in the process that their mopeds shouldn't fall over – my heart beat, and I was what you might call relieved to have encountered living creatures. Increasingly, instead of being a matter of walking in a circle round a country, walking round Germany is turning into a circling round into myself. Often I don't notice at all now that I'm walking, and then I'm startled because I seem to have been walking around myself as one walks around a hill.

Most of the time I was walking along avenues of tall deciduous trees with very smooth black tarmac between them. Birds sing; peaceful, noon-day aircraft above the extensive countryside; ivy on tall beech trees. I stumbled upon a sheep, a triangular wooden yoke fastened round its neck. Things dreamt up in scarlet settle upon me. I don't recall having passed through Wrede, though I know I did. I found a flat cola can that must have lain there flattened for two winters because it was a faded whitish yellow rather than red.

And then the people vanished. You couldn't see how it happened. All at once they simply were not there. There was nobody in the supermarket; the shelves were full, the fruit fresh and the milk had a new date stamped on it, but no one was buying, and there were no girls at the checkouts. The houses were empty, their doors open.

Had something occurred that had been announced on the radio? Had a war broken out and people taken flight? Was I, walking and without a television set, the only one not in the know? Then it struck me that heavy curtains had been drawn everywhere and indoors, in the houses, all the furniture – tables, chairs, sofas – had been covered up with sheets to protect them against dust, the light and the elements. Then I realised something else. What was lying there motionless under the sheets, without ever a hope of change or liberation, was not the furniture at all, but the people themselves.

The last thing to be done was that a group of ladies resolved at a ripe old age to learn collectively the butcher's trade. In order to demonstrate that their intentions were serious, they set fire to a moped outside the nearest inn. Schoolchildren walked by, talking in low voices as if something had happened, about which I was the only person to know nothing. A girl was cautiously carrying a plastic cup filled with a Madeira cake. In the dry bark of a pine tree a fishing hook was sticking, together with a neatly coiled-up line, but there is no water to fish in for miles around here. With expert skill, one of the schoolchildren squashed a large beetle underfoot. Somebody was trying out a power saw. Someone else was looking for a station on the radio. One was smoking, one sleeping, one sharpening a scythe. Pine needles are blowing down out of the trees. Even when reflecting upon it, I wasn't at all clear why a rope should have been stretched in a dramatically tight diagonal between two trees. When a bird abruptly stopped singing, a profound silence struck me like a heavy blow. There it lay totally silent, the country. Germany was holding its breath, for a terribly long while. A black bird fluttered away between the trees, sounding like a badly reproduced sound effect in the cinema, so unreal was it, but this was because the silence was so bottomless. With the most horrific of silences, the whole universe had alighted gently and lethally on Germany. From the border on which I was standing, I looked to my right across the hills, that's to say on Germany, which seemed to be suffering the silence as in a fit of cramps and painful convulsions.

473

To my left, I listened across the border, longing deeply to be able to hear at least the snorting of invaders or the frenzy of heathen hordes. I could not manage to walk any further; I was rooted to the spot on the line of the border. Yes, there were things there worth recording: the horror of the silence, the heat of the summer in the extensive pine woods, the smell of resin, the dried-out needles. At night, the stars are too many in number. And one could also mention the word "bliss," the word "yolk," no-man's-land, kicking the bucket, ninety-one. Today, the refugees are no more than part of a bill to be paid. A schoolchild who had painted a watch on their wrist with a biro wrenched me from my stupor. And with that, my Germany started to move again too.

*

I then almost reached the North Sea, but fell ill and made my way back from there. This is now the last journal entry. At night the moon ought to have risen, but it did not appear again. The nocturnal earth grew large, gigantic when measured against its usual dimensions. In fear, by the light of my cigarette lighter, I wrote my name on the inside of my wristwatch's strap. In the dawn light, when the mist slowly lifted, Germany lay there before me as in a haze like an unwritten novel. Right by a fence there lay a torn-open bag of cement. It had been left there heedlessly for a long time in the rain and had now turned into a grey lump of stone with cracks in it. A pig was standing there, sniffing in a baffled manner for a long time at the chunk of cement, and not moving. I raised my eyes. I knew, I had to admit to myself that I couldn't go on, that I had fallen ill and had to go home. But where was that? To move back, I had to get away from the border, go diagonally through the interior of the country. Looking to the south, I saw Germany lying there, just as a tall woman may lie, beautifully and peacefully, her right leg stretched out, her left slightly bent at the knee, her head and body in a pool of bright-red blood, her face looking up at the sky, eyes wide open. Both her hands were stretched out, palms turned upwards, as if she wanted the whole universe to fall on her like a gentle rain. For the rest of the day, Germany lay there like that, as though the blood had been drained from it. I didn't go home, I stood guard. So it – Germany, the country – lay there in orderly fashion, its facial features composed, totally at peace, all its inner storms having blown themselves out. Everything nasty and hateful, all the detritus and terrible fear that the universe is filled with, are now at an end as far as Germany is concerned. It lies there before me, its fields ripped open, gazing at the universe above it and only tentatively hoping for its rebirth. Everything has dissolved, producing the most pointless state of affairs imaginable: a void frozen in symmetries. Into the outstretched, upturned hands, into the meadows and fields, into exhausted nature and into the opened eyes there now fell a light rain. Then I saw the blades of grass straighten up as the rain dripped from them. Against my better knowledge, something forced its way inside me. Very carefully, I ran my fingers over it. It felt like a ray of hope.

Translated by David Horrocks
Originally published in *Frankfurter Rundschau*
22 December 1984

The Minnesota Declaration
Truth and fact in documentary cinema

LESSONS OF DARKNESS
by Werner Herzog

1. By dint of declaration the so-called Cinéma Vérité is devoid of vérité. It reaches a merely superficial truth, the truth of accountants.

2. One well-known representative of Cinéma Vérité declared publicly that truth can be easily found by taking a camera and trying to be honest. He resembles the nightwatchman at the Supreme Court who resents the amount of written law and legal procedures. "For me," he says, "there should be only one single law: the bad guys should go to jail." Unfortunately, he is part right, for most of the many, much of the time.

3. Cinéma Vérité confounds fact and truth, and thus plows only stones. And yet, facts sometimes have a strange and bizarre power that makes their inherent truth seem unbelievable.

4. Fact creates norms, and truth illumination.

5. There are deeper strata of truth in cinema, and there is such a thing as poetic, ecstatic truth. It is mysterious and elusive, and can be reached only through fabrication and imagination and stylisation.

6. Filmmakers of Cinéma Vérité resemble tourists who take pictures amid ancient ruins of facts.

7. Tourism is sin, and travel on foot virtue.

8. Each year at springtime scores of people on snowmobiles crash through the melting ice on the lakes of Minnesota and drown. Pressure is mounting on the new governor to pass a protective law. He, the former wrestler and bodyguard, has the only sage answer to this: "You can't legislate stupidity."

9. The gauntlet is hereby thrown down.

10. The moon is dull. Mother Nature doesn't call, doesn't speak to you, although a glacier eventually farts. And don't you listen to the Song of Life.

11. We ought to be grateful that the Universe out there knows no smile.

12. Life in the oceans must be sheer hell. A vast, merciless hell of permanent and immediate danger. So much of a hell that during evolution some species – including man – crawled, fled onto some small continents of solid land, where the Lessons of Darkness continue.

Walker Art Center
Minneapolis, Minnesota
30 April 1999

Shooting on the Lam
by Herbert Golder

I. THE LAST NOMADS

My first experience of working with Werner Herzog was on his short film *Les Gauloises*, about the champion French rugby squad. We drove from Bayreuth to Frankfurt, where Werner wanted to record the cry of hammer throwers at the German National Athletic Championships for the soundtrack of the film. He wasn't satisfied with the sounds of rugby players that he had originally captured on the playing field. Despite their fierce combat, the roars of the combatants did not express the real inner force of their struggle, their true inner life. He wanted something deeper than the grunting, groaning and panting he had recorded, something more like the bellow of a bull, the kind of deep exhalations that mark strenuous athletic competition as a true test of life. He waxed enthusiastically about these rugby players, who were men, he said, like the heroes in Homer. They are much too proud to play for money. They play as a matter of pride. They perform fierce rituals through which they prepare themselves for their matches, exercising and taking meals and drinking large quantities of beer together, like warriors preparing for a battle.

For *Les Gauloises*, Werner wanted a sound worthy of the men he knew. He was looking for a sound he had once heard that had made a deep and indelible impression on him: the cry of the hammer thrower, the roar emitted by these leonine creatures at the moment they burst out of their wind-up spin and the iron hammer leaves their hands with thousands of pounds of pressure behind it. Later, as the television producers were preparing our passes so we could be on the field close to the competitors, Werner told them that they miss something essential in their coverage of live sports when they omit the vital in- and exhalations of human breathing, which, he said, express the inner spirit and strength of a man. He pronounced their sports coverage sterile and inadequate, that they scanted something fundamental about such competitions: the inner sounds of powerful exertion, struggle and pain that signal athletics as a true test of life.

Before we left for Frankfurt, Werner and I paused in the small parking area to watch a ceremony being performed by an ancient shooting club, men in traditional Bavarian costumes armed with rifles and sporting colourful sashes and assorted badges signifying their various accomplishments. They were honouring a young man who had proven the best marksman. The whole procedure was highly ritualised. Werner – who at the time was directing a production of Wagner's *Lohengrin* at Bayreuth – told me I was witnessing something absolutely authentic and indeed very ancient, as such confraternities of marksmen had protected Bavaria for centuries. These ceremonies, he told me, reinforced an ancient code of conduct and values essential to survival. By contrast, he found the whole bourgeois, touristic culture of Bayreuth – the pretentiousness of the aesthetes drawn to the world of opera and the cult-like worship at the shrine of Wagner – suffocating and oppressive. I sensed he felt relieved and liberated to get away. The ancient ceremony somehow augured a rite of passage to something more real.

As we drove off, he insisted we first stop in town and pick up a few essentials. I was, of course, keen to know what Werner Herzog considered essential. First, he needed a part for the exhaust of his van, as it had started making strange noises. After we took care of that, he insisted we make one more stop, at a bookstore. As we entered he asked me pointedly if I had read Büchner's *Lenz* – this, he said emphatically, I must read – the short stories of Kleist, the poetry of Hölderlin, the *Nibelungenlied*, the Icelandic Eddas, the *Götterlieder*, but more importantly the *Heldenlieder*, and above all, *The Saga of Grettir the Strong*. Before I could answer (some I knew, some I didn't), he pulled several volumes off the shelves (those compact little German Reclam editions), bought them for me, and we were on our way. As we drove off he told me he regretted he had so little time to read, but that when he did it was things like books about lion taming.

It was a grey day, and it started to rain as we drove through the Bavarian countryside, hilly greenswards dotted with villages, with more distant and formidable mountains always in view. Because *The Saga of Grettir the Strong* did not appear to be in the little volume of Eddas he had purchased for me, Werner told me the story, one of his favourites. Set in the eleventh century, Grettir's story is that of an Icelandic strongman who lived on into a newly Christianised era, where a rugged individual like him increasingly had no place. He carried on the brave fight against ogres and ghouls and revenants and monsters, even as the rest of the world was on the verge of "enlightenment" and believed its salvation lay in the laws of civil society and faith in Christ. Grettir, of course, knew otherwise. He knew the beast didn't just go away, it merely assumed other forms. To this day I remember the way Werner told the story, with his particular emphases. More sinned against than sinning, Grettir's fate was to become an outcast and an outlaw, a man whose strength was so great that his good deeds often backfired on him. He would shake someone's hand and rip it from his socket. He scratched his father's back and tore off the skin. He would slap a man on the shoulder and kill him. A man whom no one could control, and who naturally fell afoul of those who endeavoured to do so, they made him an outlaw and hunted him down like some kind of beast. He was forced to live in remote mountains and caves, driven to ever lonelier and more desolate places. Sometimes he even took in bounty hunters, men whom he knew were there to kill him, just to ease his loneliness. Although stronger than any twenty men and afraid of nothing, human or supernatural, Grettir was nonetheless afraid to be alone in the dark, where he was haunted by the eyes of Glam, the most terrible monster he had slain. Living atop the isolated isle of Drang, a rocky crag in a deep fjord opening up into the Northern Sea, he died treacherously, murdered by his enemies. Werner told me that a line in *Aguirre* – "Long arrows are coming back into fashion," spoken by one of the doomed Spaniards on Aguirre's fleet of rafts as he is struck in the chest, just before pitching into the water – is taken from *Grettir*. Pierced through the stomach by one of Grettir's enemies, his brother Atli utters the words "Broad spears are the fashion these days" as he dies.

His eye always on the horizon and attuned to the landscape, its contours as well as its inner story – which so often becomes an expression of the inner landscape of the characters in his films – Werner told me about the geological and then early history of the region we were passing through, revealing almost matter-of-factly a vast and impressively detailed knowledge. His best stories had to do with men being outwitted by the terrain, the unending undulation of mountains and valleys, as if lost in their own fever dreams. He regaled me with detailed accounts of battles in antiquity and the Middle Ages that never took place because the two armies, on the march and determined to fight, were simply unable to find one another. In the silence that followed the thoughts settled. The road had been mostly empty of traffic. Then at one point, as if out of nowhere, we found ourselves completely surrounded by a German motorcycle gang. Grizzled, broad-backed, rough-looking men, on big bikes in full biker regalia, rode up alongside us, and then finally passed us on either side. They really did look like ancient Vikings or a lost warrior tribe. Werner lit up. "Look at that," he said. "The last nomads."

II. KNEES AND THIGHS

My Best Fiend was made in the immediate aftermath of *Wings of Hope*, as we were already in Peru, even though no budget for the film had been formalised. We were all free to leave if we wished – Werner would understand and pay anyone's way home – or to pick up the camera and our gear and head straight back into the jungle from which we'd only just emerged to make another film for which none of the details had yet been worked out and nothing was as yet planned. I remember our pre-production meeting at the hotel in Lima. Werner said there was no money yet and thus no contracts of any kind for anyone, and asked who was in. I think everyone assented. I wrote the following in my journal, which gives, I think, something of the flavour of what it is like heading off into the jungle to make an inspired and serendipitously impromptu film with Werner.

At lunch we discussed our options. Werner drew a map and rehearsed the alternatives. First we go to Cusco then Machu Picchu where the opening sequence of *Aguirre* was shot. Then we can either backtrack to Lima and fly back to Pucallpa, then south to the city nearest Rio Camisea with an airport. Or, part of the team – Werner, someone, either Peter or Eric to operate camera, and possibly me to do sound – might float by raft from Machu Picchu to Rio Camisea where *Fitzcarraldo* was shot. We would have to pass through the Pongo. It's dry season, but this could still be quite dangerous. Plus there would be nothing to eat between Machu Picchu and Rio Camisea. We might find a few scattered huts with Indians cooking bananas, but that's about it. Once through the Pongo there is no way back, unless the others have met us by boat coming from the south. We would take only a skeleton crew on the raft because there would be no way to feed the whole group. And we don't even know if we can find rafts or people to make them on the river below Machu Picchu . . .

And so it went, along these lines, though we ultimately decided to make our way across the Andes first by train, till the tracks ended, then by van, climbing up through winding passes on cliff-edge dirt roads to nearly five thousand metres, level with a great glacier. There were three days of travel before we would even reach the river, to places with virtually no way in and no way out, to small towns of only seven huts, vast mountain meadows stretching across the horizon with grazing llamas and alpacas, and finally down into the Urubamba Valley, where the jungle suddenly thickens and takes over, as if swallowing the mountain, getting tangibly deeper with every minute. From this point travel was entirely by river, just as Werner had described, with massive rocks, cascading waterfalls and the jungle seeming to pour itself in steeply from every side. But all this was quite tame and leisurely compared to what Werner must have been up against when making *Aguirre* and *Fitzcarraldo* under the most challenging circumstances. In the bustling port of Pucallpa on the Ucayali, which is an unimaginable sight, with the boundless energy of the whole of Amazon life teeming ubiquitously around it – hundreds of shirtless, muscled, sun-baked men loading and unloading ships, carrying heavy loads, even massive wooden crates, up a steep embankment on their backs with a binding strap gripping their foreheads, women cooking chicken and fish and yucca and bananas standing behind small carts, fishmongers and butchers hawking their bloody wares, merchants at makeshift stalls selling everything from high rubber boots to medicinal barks from deep in the jungle to engine parts and electrical equipment, people lazing and in animated conversation and drinking, life everywhere, men, women, strong-featured with powerful expressive eyes – Werner looked out across the port to the Ucayali and then, pointing to the chaotic bustle of virile, sweating, swearing, pulling, hoisting men, turned to me and said, with a feeling of deep fondness for the place, "Imagine trying to organise this into *Fitzcarraldo*. This is pretty much how it was and how we lived for three years."

Because it was necessary that Werner appear physically in *My Best Fiend*, we decided to film atop Huayna Picchu, as this was a mountain of destiny. The opening shots of *Aguirre* were filmed here, the army of men descending the narrow defile we were about to ascend. The climb is an almost vertical four-hundred-metre ascent to an altitude of nearly four thousand metres, up steeply pitched and well-worn stone steps carved by the Incas hundreds of years ago. The four of us took turns carrying the heavy 16mm camera. Some steps were worn down almost completely in places, and the stones underfoot – sometimes slick from rain – made it difficult at times to keep from slipping. In places the path narrows and one has to hug a boulder as one inches along a slender ledge. The drop is, needless to say, sheer. When we reached the summit we filmed Werner looking off into the hovering clouds, made more dramatic that day by the strong sun they were hiding. On the way down, along the steep steps, we got a few shots of Werner running up the steps towards us from a lower elevation and then disappearing into a passageway. Half joking, I told Werner that his brisk ascent had looked too leisurely and wasn't very convincing. Suspecting I might be right, Werner decided on another take. This time he literally bounded up those treacherously steep steps like a mountain goat, taking an astonishing ten seconds off his previous time. I was absolutely certain I could not have matched this feat. It was not merely the speed, but the balance and footing. It brought back to me the very first time I climbed a flight of stairs with Werner in an office building in Munich. He bounded two at a time. The alacrity with which he attacked the stairs took me by surprise. I really had to strain to the utmost to keep up.

Werner wanted some shots taken of him standing on top of the giant boulders on the upper stretch of the Urubamba river. It had rained all morning, and the giant boulders – smooth as glass from a thousand years of raging water of unimaginable force exploding over and around them – were especially slippery. As it was the dry season, the river was low, and the boulders, completely submerged when the river is high, protruded some thirty or forty feet above the river below. A fall, needless to say, would be fatal. The cameraman Peter Zeitlinger was harnessed and tied to someone else who was also roped. Because our stills photographer had refused to venture out onto the slippery rocks, Werner directed me to climb a rock higher than all the others, where I could shoot stills without obstruction. I could barely keep my footing, so tried to stay low, hugging the slick rock, but Werner walked nimbly across these vitreous surfaces and then bounded from boulder to boulder, sometimes leaping across crevices several feet wide, with a straight drop into an abyss of raging river below. He moved with the sureness of a mountain goat. I watched in amazement as I looked at the others roped and harnessed. (I did, somehow, manage to take one of the best photos of Werner, in mid-leap over the abyss, that I have ever taken.) He wasn't showing off or taking some unwarranted risk; he was merely making his way through this landscape – this river and these rocks of destiny where he had filmed both *Aguirre* and *Fitzcarraldo* all those years before – with absolute self-assurance.

As gravity would have it, what goes up must come down. On what was one of our first trips together to the Telluride Film Festival, we attended a picnic at the top of one of the ski lifts. We had intended that afternoon to see a screening of a film, but had lost track of time and suddenly realised it was starting in only a few minutes. There was a huge line for the chairlift and we knew if we waited, we would miss the film. One of the event organisers offered us the next chair, as Werner is always a special guest – even patron saint – at Telluride, but Werner didn't want to jump the line. Instead, he turned to me and said, "Let's just run down." And, with that, he bolted down the mountain.

III. DANCING SOUL

In the fall of 2001 I published a translation from the ancient Greek of Euripides' play *The Bacchae*. I conceived it as a text for performance – just as Euripides had intended it to come to life on a stage – and worked my version out through readings and rehearsals with actors and dancers. My goal was to be true to the spirit of the original and to capture something not only of Euripides' complex tone and heightened poetic language (alternating as always in Euripides with colloquial speech), but also something of the play's structured dramatic power and scenic forms, something you cannot render by merely translating words (or writing learned endnotes). Naturally I sent Werner a copy. Around that time he was scheduled to reprise his production of Wagner's *Tannhäuser* for the Houston Opera Company and suggested I meet him there. I asked him if there was anything he needed me to bring, as I always did whenever we were to meet up. Once he needed me to meet him in Vienna – from where we were flying to Thailand for *Little Dieter Needs to Fly* – with three pairs of handcuffs we would need for the film. (They sent up a red flag at security and I almost missed the plane. I had to surrender them to the captain upon boarding, and they were given back to me when I arrived in Vienna.) This time Werner said, "Bring only one thing: a Greek text of *The Bacchae*." He added that he had questions about some of my renderings.

By the time I arrived, Werner had already marked in my version the passages he had queried, and we spent much of the afternoon prior to opening night in his hotel room reading these passages against the Greek original, which he read aloud as fluently as if he were a professor of Greek, even though he probably hadn't studied the language since he was sixteen years old. There were any number of things he queried, but he was particularly focused on my translation of the lines from the opening chorus of the play: θιασεύεται ψυχὰν/ ἐν ὄρεσσι βακχεύων/ ὁσίοις καθαρμοῖσιν (ll. 75–77). The expression is, admittedly, not easy to put into English. The chorus is singing of the glories of the god Dionysus. The lines literally mean something like, "the one who joins his soul with the Bacchic holy throng, inspired with Bacchic ecstasy in the mountains, in sacred purifying rites." As I was composing my version in sprung rhythms to be sung or chanted by a chorus moving to the words, the lines broken into tercets to indicate rhythmical phrases, I rendered it as "so wholly there/ on the mountain/ dancing his soul/ over and into/ the pack of Bacchus." "Wholly" is a homonym of "holy" and so does the double duty I wished it to, but Werner

485

wasn't entirely convinced. He liked the "dancing soul" but thought it didn't go far enough in expressing the mysterious notion in the Greek.

The rapt Bacchae dance in the thrall of the god of ecstasy, Dionysus. They are not merely dancing *on* the mountain; their souls have become one *with* the mountain ("wholly/holy there"). Throughout the play, the landscapes through which the Bacchae move are described as alive, wild with god. At one point, the whole mountain is said to explode into an ecstasy when the Bacchic throng moves. Their dancing souls and the inspirited landscape fuse. The world they pass through merges with their dreams. When I think about it now, the passage Werner questioned is about as vivid an evocation of experiencing "ecstatic truth" – the mundane transformed into the miraculous – as any to be found in the whole of Greek literature. How uncanny that Werner – whose spirit is, like that of the Bacchae, consecrated to the ecstasy of truth and whose vision transforms landscapes into ecstatic dreams – should, of all the passages in the play, hone in on these lines and the difficulty, indeed near impossibility, of rendering them.

IV. THE HUNT, OR WHAT IS INCIDENTAL

One thing that always strikes me about Werner's work is the nobility of human passion found there, a passion in no way invalidated by the impossibility of the quest or dream. The miracle at the heart of his films is mankind's relentless struggle to find meaning, despite the indifference and hostility of the universe. However barren and parched the wasteland, however ice-encased and sheer the mountain, however fathomless the abyss, however dense and overgrown the jungle, the human spirit digs in, sends up its flare and ultimately – like Stroszek and his fireworks in *Signs of Life*, the existential flight of Walter Steiner, the scientists studying neutrinos in the upper atmosphere in *Encounters at the End of the World*, the painters inside the Chauvet cave – writes its will across the sky in stars. The physical and metaphysical (the latter often arising in the fierce struggle to overcome the crushing gravity imposed by the former) are of a piece in Werner's work.

I always marvel at the way Werner manages to wring the sublime from the banal. He has a poet's vision, one that arises from a stark, almost scientifically disciplined view. He admires Virgil's *Georgics* because of the poet's objective and rigorous attention to the minute particulars of life's details, requiring the keenest powers of observation like those of a scientist, but combined with a poet's sympathy. For Werner, like Virgil, a physical sense of place – a felt connection to the landscape over which one sweats – is essential to the full realisation of a human life. Virgil's didactic poem on the dignity and meaning of working the earth is rich in close observation and study of the wonder and hostility of nature: its beauty, mystery and abundance, but also its savagery and horror; its indifference to us, but also its uncanny, incomprehensible power; its seasons of life, death and renewal, but also man's tragic isolation; nature's implacability and general law of inhumanity, but also those rare moments of *anagnorisis*, or recognition, when something like a familiar spirit – man fused with, mirrored by, implicated in nature's exuberant larger pattern of existence – can be glimpsed. In *Grizzly Man*, Werner speaks in the voiceover narration of a moment of strange beauty, a deserted scene with reeds swaying in the wind, which we watch as he describes it. Treadwell had walked out of frame, having finished filming his staged scene, but had left his camera on, and this simple image of the wind blowing through the reeds – a found moment of unabashed nature just being nature, gusting, rustling, a wind suddenly out of nowhere mysteriously stirring, without regard to human intentions or framed by a cameraman's eyes – was accidentally recorded. Robert Graves described such moments in poetry as the very essence of it, epiphanies of "things," ordinary and yet mysterious, that make the hair on the back of the neck stand on end: "an apparently unpeopled or eventless scene . . . when owls hoot, the moon rides like a ship through scudding cloud, trees sway slowly together above a rushing waterfall, and a distant barking of dogs is heard, or when a peal of bells in frosty weather suddenly announces the birth of the New Year."

Werner is not beholden to modern sentimentality, or notions of propriety, or pleasing nostrums like political correctness, or any of the politely observed decorums and petty pieties of people not in the habit of saying what they really mean, think or feel. Like the horseman whom Yeats bids from the grave to pass him by, Werner casts a sober eye, on life, on death. When a mutual friend informed us he had been diagnosed with cancer and that there was a change of plan, Werner responded with fatal lucidity, "That is the plan." But by saying Werner looks at reality with a kind of objective detachment, I do not thereby mean that he stands apart or remains aloof from it. I know of no one more in love with the world, more full of the capacity for wonder and awe, or more connected to what he sees. He looks at the world around him, takes it all in, the beautiful and the ugly, the good and the bad, and transforms it into an experience in cinema. Seeing the trees – one by one, for what they actually are – for the forest is as important to Werner as the other way around. This is the nature of Werner's engagement with what he sees, an intensity of observation on the verge of fusion with his subject.

Werner's landscapes in film may be, as he calls them, fever dreams or inner landscapes, but their power comes from his genuine ability to dream them, to ensoul them with visionary power. In his essay that closes this book, physicist Lawrence Krauss defines genius as the ability to create something out of nothing. I would only add: to create something so utterly remarkable, wondrous and original that no one could ever have imagined it being created out of that nothing, even if one had been given a full breakdown of the original elements.

Werner is more a predator than a grazer. The senses are always working the horizon for sustenance, the strategy for the chase being wrought minutely by instinct, the whole being braced for the struggle leading to the kill. Like a predator, he takes his spoils quickly and his rest at whatever hideaway happens to be near by and convenient. The hunt – his creative activity – is everything, and all else (possessions, meals, accommodations, social life) incidental to it.

Herbert Golder is Professor of Classical Studies at Boston University, and the Editor-in-Chief of *Arion, A Journal of Humanities and the Classics*. He has worked with Werner Herzog since 1988 on films such as *Little Dieter Needs to Fly*, *Wings of Hope*, *My Best Fiend*, *Invincible*, *The White Diamond* and *The Wild Blue Yonder*. He played Rabbi Edelmann in *Invincible* and co-wrote the script for *My Son, My Son, What Have Ye Done*.

Afterword
by Lawrence Krauss

I will always remember the first time I met Werner Herzog. It was an incredibly disappointing experience. I was not disappointed in him, but rather in myself.

As a graduate student in the late seventies and early eighties, movies provided much-needed respite from the combination of long hours and the constant feeling of insecurity that arose from being surrounded by a community of overachievers, each of whom was eager to relate their brilliance and accomplishments at the slightest opportunity. Being a graduate student at MIT, I frequented art-movie houses, I admit in part because of social pressure from my peer group, but also because the movies were generally much better and more interesting than American films.

It was here that I first fell in love with Werner Herzog's films. They were like nothing I had ever seen before, a visual feast combined with raw emotion, and sometimes, it seemed to me, celebrating the edge of madness. The first one I remember seeing was *Aguirre, the Wrath of God*, in 1977, around the time I started graduate school. It was also the first collaboration between Herzog and the unforgettable Klaus Kinski. I later learnt that the madness portrayed on screen mirrored the manic volatility of Kinski the man. At that time I could only assume this was balanced by an equal volatility in Herzog the director.

Next for me was *Fitzcarraldo*, which came out in 1982, just after I had completed my PhD, staying in Boston to move from MIT to Harvard, and much closer to the movie theatre I frequented. My own situation had changed, and I felt like a big deal, no longer a lowly graduate student but a real person with an important enough job that I could now hold my own during cocktail-party conversations. However, when I learnt that for *Fitzcarraldo* Herzog had actually not only moved a real steamboat up and over a mountain deep in the Amazon, but had also essentially shot the film twice, in two equally remote locations, having lost Jason Robards and Mick Jagger in the process and replaced them with the unstable Kinski, my own accomplishments during the period seemed far less inspired, or demanding.

Which brings me to my disappointment upon first meeting Werner. I had been asked to be a judge at the Sundance Film Festival in 2005, not because of my film expertise, but rather, I think, because I had written a book called *The Physics of Star Trek*, and the Sloan Foundation was sponsoring a prize for the best feature film incorporating scientific themes or characters. Since I knew science, and *Star Trek* was drama, I suppose they decided I had sufficient expertise to judge the combination of the two in a feature film. As it turned out, the twenty or so movies we had to judge were terrible. None fit the bill. If there was a realistic scientific character, the rest of the plot or cinematography was miserable. If the plot was scintillating, the science was awful. We judges ultimately met as a team and decided to enlarge the competition beyond pure fiction, and to include documentaries with a narrative theme, ones that hinged on a story. That year Werner's gripping documentary *Grizzly Man*, about Timothy Treadwell, who spent thirteen summers filming and living with grizzly bears in Alaska before he and his girlfriend were killed and partially eaten by one of them, was in competition.

The movie was visually riveting, and highly unusual. It was based for the most part on over a hundred hours of footage shot by Treadwell himself, material that Herzog praises for its visual quality during the film, which he narrates. What made *Grizzly Man* so memorable for me was not the visual background, but rather Werner's remarkable narration. It would have been easy to present Treadwell as a two-dimensional character, a nut who felt a Disneyesque kinship with bears. But Werner clearly felt some real kinship with the loner Treadwell, who scorned human companionship in favour of time with these wild creatures.

One scene captured for me the vital message of the film, and was the reason I was so pleased we awarded our prize to it at Sundance.

There is a moment near the end with some of the last footage taken by Treadwell, perhaps of the very bear who killed him. The camera pans in for a close-up of the bear's face and eyes, staring at the camera, and Werner narrates: "What haunts me is that in all the faces of all the bears that Treadwell ever filmed, I discover no kinship, no understanding, no mercy. I see only the overwhelming indifference of nature." The message is clear: don't mess with Mother Nature. Nature is neither good nor bad, nor does it care about us or our desires. The natural world is violent, and most of it is not suited for our existence. Our whims, our imagination and our happiness reside within us, and shouldn't be imposed on a natural world that would carry on just as well without us. I still find this message profoundly moving, and I have never seen this commentary on our pitifully vain anthropocentric view of the universe expressed so pithily and in such a haunting context anywhere else.

The reception honouring the prizewinner was where I first met Werner and his wife Lena. They walked in the door together, hand in hand, seeming larger than life, and at the same time as if they were prepared to endure the event for the sake of the film, and then escape as quickly as politeness could allow. But my biggest surprise was the discovery that Werner was not the old man I had expected. All the time I had been watching his films while a graduate student and young postdoc he was not that much older than I was, and had already established his reputation as one of the most prolific, energetic and inventive filmmakers on any continent. He had done all this while I had taken the easy and traditional route towards a PhD and an academic career. So much for having felt so full of myself at the time.

I have since been privileged to spend many hours with Werner. On one occasion he encouraged me to skip a physics meeting at Caltech to be a guest speaker at his highly coveted Rogue Film School, where he interviewed me about what it might be like to film in four dimensions. In turn, Werner was my guest at an Arizona State University Origins Project event, where we screened his 3D film *Cave of Forgotten Dreams*, and later had an on-stage discussion about early modern humans with one of the world's leading palaeontologists. Werner had earlier explained to me, as only he could, without an ounce of inappropriate vanity, that it was the first film that really required 3D filming. As he described it, the detailed Palaeolithic cave paintings, which the film focused on, incorporated the curvature and shape of the walls to embellish the animal figures. Without 3D, that feature would have been completely lost. To achieve this Werner had built his own cameras and reassembled them on the spot, all while restricted to a thin metal railing in the dark, inside a cave in which fewer people have stepped than have walked on the moon, with just six days to film the entire project. I have often insisted to Werner that it seems he doesn't like to make a film unless it is difficult, but he insists equally strongly that this is nonsense.

Werner is a genius. I say this without intending hyperbole. I have worked with some very talented people in my own field, including numerous Nobel Laureates, but I would call only a few of these colleagues geniuses. It is not a matter of intelligence alone. It is the ability to create, out of thin air, stories, explanations and images in ways that could not have been anticipated by others. Often, when presented with a completed work – for example, Einstein's special relativity – it's possible to imagine how, if one had had the initial idea, one could have puzzled through to the end. Yet for some creations – like those of Newton, for example – the road from beginning to end seems as remarkable after the fact as before it. I feel that way when I talk to Werner, listen to his plans and watch the end results.

Ultimately, the Werner Herzog I have come to know is not the wild man of his press clippings. He is a caring, thoughtful, playful and essentially gentle human being. Possessing a restless mind, with a fertile and creative imagination, he is a man interested in all aspects of the human experience. Self-taught, he is widely read and deeply knowledgeable. I like to think that one of the reasons we enjoy each other's company is that we both share a deep excitement in the human experience. I particularly enjoy listening to the child-like wonder with which he expresses his insights and ideas, something many other people lose early on. In this sense, I think that if Werner had chosen a different road to travel, he could easily have been a scientist – an experimental one, I am certain, because of his desire to experience directly the phenomena he imagines – and his career might easily have taken him to the wilds of the Amazon or the Antarctic end of the world. Maybe in a parallel universe that is precisely what he is doing. I only hope that in that universe I am making films. At the same time Werner possesses attributes I can only admire and wish I shared, including deep bravery. He is fascinated by the dark side of life, and recognises the universe is a deeply inhospitable place, and that to imagine otherwise is foolishness. But he runs headlong into the fray to capture every aspect of this universe that he can on film. He is not foolhardy. He always knows what the possible consequences are, but he finds a way to do it anyway.

Werner has a unique way of answering questions, without pretence or worries about the possible reception of his words. He speaks his mind directly and to the point. Moreover, without being cloying in any way, in conversation he reveals the unexpected challenges and sometimes completely fortuitous circumstances that colour the end results, and that have resulted in some of the most remarkable films of the last century. I think a particularly illuminating aspect of the real Werner was on display during the same weekend we screened his 3D film in Arizona. In what was the most amazing hour of radio I have ever participated in, Werner joined me and another friend, the remarkable writer Cormac McCarthy, along with *Science Friday* host Ira Flatow, to talk about early modern humans, their culture and technology. I will never forget as these two icons discussed the science in detail and with authority, demonstrating to everyone that to be cultured in the modern world doesn't mean shying away from science, and moreover that you don't have to be a scientist either to be interested in the natural world or to gain some expertise. The programme ended with Werner reading aloud from McCarthy's novel *All the Pretty Horses*. It was a magical moment, and a magical connection between two creative artists willing to explore sides of the world that many would otherwise be glad to pretend don't exist.

Lawrence Krauss is Foundation Professor of Physics in the School of Earth and Space Exploration at Arizona State University, and Director of the Origins Project. His books include *Fear of Physics*, *The Physics of Star Trek* and *A Universe from Nothing: Why There Is Something Rather than Nothing*. In 2012 he was awarded the National Science Board Public Service Award and Medal.

Bibliographic Essay

The primary focus of this short essay – merely a starting point for those studying Herzog's work – is Werner's own output. Those seeking more detailed information on the reviews, articles, chapters, doctoral theses and other ephemera about Herzog's life and work are encouraged to access his official website (http://www.wernerherzog.com) for Professor Herbert Golder's expansive (though by now somewhat out of date) bibliography. Several of the academic titles mentioned below also contain substantial bibliographies.

Herzog's own publishing house Skellig produced two volumes of his prose screenplays (in German) in 1977. Volume one contains *Lebenszeichen*, *Auch Zwerge haben klein augefangen, Fata Morgana*; volume two (also published in English by Tanam, in 1980) contains *Aguirre, Der Zorn Gottes, Jeder für sich und Gott gegen alle, Land des Schweigens und der Dunkelheit*. Over the years Carl Hanser Verlag has published several Herzog scripts in German: *Stroszek* and *Nosferatu* (1979), *Fitzcarraldo* (1982; also Knaur, 1982), *Wo die grünen Ameisen träumen* (1984) and *Cobra Verde* (1987). In 1987 Verlag Volk und Welt issued *Fitzcarraldo* and *Wo die grünen Ameisen träumen* together in one volume. *Cobra Verde Filmbuch* was published by 1987 by Edition Stemmle and contains a German translation of Bruce Chatwin's essay "History in the Making," Herzog's short piece about the background to the film ("Die Geschichte des Films"), the transcript of Steff Gruber's interview recorded during production, nearly eighty pages of Beat Presser's colour photographs of the film, and several pages of his black-and-white production shots.

There exist several books of Herzog's screenplays in other languages, notably French. *L'Avant-scène cinéma* published *L'énigme de Kaspar Hauser* in 1976 and *Aguirre, la colère de dieu* in 1978. In 1981 Hachette P.O.L. issued *Scénarios*, which contains *Signes de vie, Les nains aussi ont commencé petits, Fata Morgana* and *Aguirre, la colère de Dieu*. *Le pays où rêvent les fourmis vertes* was released by P.O.L in 1985, and *Cobra*

Verde by Jade-Flammarion in 1988. Two Herzog volumes have appeared in Italian (*La ballata di Stroszek* and *Nosferatu, il principe della notte*, Ubulibri, 1982; and *Fitzcarraldo*, Guanda, 1982) and one in Spanish (*Kaspar Hauser*, Elias Querejeta Ediciones, 1976). *Cobra Verde* was translated into Catalan and published in 1988 by Laia Libros.

Heart of Glass (Skellig) was published in 1976, and contains Herzog and Herbert Achternbusch's prose script of the film, intercut with Alan Greenberg's interviews with Herzog and his thoughts compiled on the set of the film. The book is an important, early representation of several of the ideas in *Herzog on Herzog*. Greenberg issued a slightly different version of the book in 2012 as *Every Night the Trees Disappear: Werner Herzog and the Making of Heart of Glass* (Chicago Review Press), with colour photographs. Paul Monette's novelisation of *Nosferatu*, based on Herzog's script, was published in 1979 (UK: Picador; US: Avon), and in 2004 the British Film Institute published S. S. Prawer's monograph on *Nosferatu* in its Modern Film Classics series (reissued in 2013 with an introduction by Brad Prager).

Herzog's *Fitzcarraldo* has spawned several books. The English edition of his original script (which differs substantially from the completed film, it being the basis of the original Robards/Jagger version) was published by Fjord Press, the Dutch by Uitgeverij Bert Bakker, the Italian by Guanda, the Polish by Państwowy Instytut Wydawniczy, and the French, alongside *Nosferatu* and *La Ballade de Bruno* (*Stroszek*), by Mazarine (all 1982). The Greek edition, published by θεμελιο, followed in 1984. Schirmer/Mosel published *Fitzcarraldo Filmbuch* the same year, which contains a foreword by Herzog and the dialogue transcript (both in German), followed by more than a hundred pages of colour still frames taken from the film. The volume also includes ten pages of extracts from Herzog's diaries written during production. In 2004 Herzog published these journals in full as *Eroberung des Nutzlosen* (Carl Hanser Verlag). Various foreign editions exist, including Italian (*La conquista dell'inutile*, Oscar Mondadori, 2007), French (*Conquête de l'inutile*, Capricci, 2008), English (*Conquest of the Useless*, HarperCollins, 2009) and Spanish (*Conquista de lo inútil*, Blackie, 2010). Short extracts from Herzog's jungle diaries also appear in *Burden of Dreams* (North Atlantic Books, 1984), edited by Les Blank and James Bogan, a book that contains a collection of journal extracts by Blank and his fellow filmmaker Maureen Gosling written on the set of *Fitzcarraldo*, as well as reviews and photographs, plus a dialogue transcript of the film *Burden of Dreams*. (Blank's film was issued on DVD in 2005 by the Criterion Collection, a release which also contains his 1980 short *Werner Herzog Eats his Shoe* and an eighty-page booklet with edited extracts from the Blank/Gosling journals. Herzog, alongside Blank and Gosling, contributed a commentary to the release, as well as a thirty-eight-minute filmed interview.) The booklet *Der Fall Herzog* is a partisan collection of documents and essays about the production of *Fitzcarraldo*, edited by Nina Gladitz. Gerhard Kaiser's *Fitzcarraldo Faust*, a monograph on *Fitzcarraldo* (Carl Friedrich von Siemens Stiftung), was published in 1993.

Herzog's prose book *Of Walking in Ice* was first published by Carl Hanser Verlag in 1978 (reprinted 1995, then re-released by Fischer Taschenbuch Verlag in 2009 and Hanser in 2012). The English translation followed in 1980 (Tanam) and was reprinted by Jonathan Cape (UK) in 1991 and Free Association (US) in 2007. The French edition, entitled *Sur le chemin des glaces* (Hachette), was published in 1979 (re-released by Editions Payot & Rivages in 1996), and Italian (*Sentieri nel ghiaccio*, Guanda), Japanese (Orion Literary Agency) and Swedish (*Att gå kylan*, Norstedt) translations appeared in 1980. A Dutch edition (*Over een Voettocht door de Kou*, Uitgeverij Bert Bakker) appeared in 1981 (reissued 2006 by Prometheus). A Spanish edition (*Del caminar sobre hielo*, Muchnik/Alphaville) was published in 1981 and re-released by Tempestad in 2003. The Brazilian edition (*Caminhando no gelo*, Paz e Terra) was issued in 1982 (reissued by Tinta-da-China in 2011), the Finnish (*Jäinen matka*, Like) in 1990 and Danish (*Om at gå i is og sne*, C&K Verlag) in 2014. An audio recording of the original German text, read by Herzog, was released on CD in 2007 by Winter & Winter.

Herzog has published a small number of articles, essays and reviews over the decades, and a fairly comprehensive list can be found on his website. These include two articles from 1964: "Rebellen in Amerika" and a review of Mikhail Romm's 1962 film *Nine Days of One Year*, both published in German film magazine *Filmstudio*. In 1968 Herzog wrote a short piece that also appeared in *Filmstudio* called "Mit den Wölfen Heulen," about the politics of the German film industry and his refusal to allow his short film *Last Words* "to be used as a political instrument" at the Oberhausen Film Festival (this article is quoted from in the essay "Visionary Vehemence" above). He wrote reviews of the Taviani brothers' film *Padre Padrone* (see page 68) and Peter Schneider's book *Der Mauerspringer* in 1978 and 1982 respectively. In 1986 Herzog published a magazine article about ski flying in *Der Spiegel*, and four years later one about the Wodaabe in *Stern*. He wrote the foreword to his wife Lena's book *Pilgrims*, describing the environment in which he filmed *Wheel of Time*, and in his foreword to Lena's volume of photographs shot on the set of *Bad Lieutenant* (Universe, 2009) offers a vivid, brief account of the film's production. His review of Wolfgang Buscher's book *Berlin–Moskau: Eine Reise zu Fuss* ("a journey on foot") appeared in 2003. Herzog published two articles – one long, one short – in *Arion, A Journal of Humanities and the Classics* in 2010 and 2012. The first, which can be found on both the *Arion* and official Herzog websites, is entitled "On the Absolute, the Sublime and Ecstatic Truth." The second is "On Pope Benedict's Address to the Bundestag."

Other miscellany worth mentioning are *Und die Fremde ist der Tod*

(MaasMedia, 2004), a dual-language book of "Excerpts and Drawings by Bruno S," and Miron Zownir's film about Bruno, *Die Fremde ist der Tod* (2003). Beat Presser's book of photographs *Werner Herzog* (Jovis, 2002) contains production shots taken on the sets of *Fitzcarraldo*, *Cobra Verde* and *Invincible*, as well as photographs taken during the staging of two operas in the mid-eighties. (The book also includes the testimonies of several Herzog collaborators over the years, including Volker Schlöndorff and Herbert Achternbusch.) A summary of Herzog's work up until 1978 was issued by Filmverlag Autoren. Entitled simply *Werner Herzog*, it's a useful collection of approximately a hundred pages, and includes articles, interviews, reviews and photographs. Herzog's translation of Michael Ondaatje's *The Collected Works of Billy the Kid: Left-Handed Poems* was published by Carl Hanser Verlag in 1997, and again by Deutscher Taschenbuch Verlag in 1999.

Herzog has never been shy about talking to the world's media, especially if doing so will help sell his films to the public. There are three lengthy interviews of note. Andrea Rost edited *Werner Herzog in Bamberg: Protokoll einer Diskussion*, a conversation in German from 1985. Grazia Paganeli's interview, originally conducted in English, appears in Italian in her book *Segni di vita: Werner Herzog e il cinema*, an illustrated catalogue published in 2008 by the Museo Nazionale del Cinema to celebrate a retrospective of Herzog's work. (The book includes a number of critical essays, alongside a selection of photographs from Herzog's archive, and was also issued in Portuguese and Greek by, respectively, IndieLisboa and the Thessaloniki International Film Festival.) In 2008 *Manuel de survie: entretien avec Werner Herzog*, a short interview book by Emmanuel Burdeau and Hervé Aubron, appeared in French (a Spanish translation was released in 2013). A collection of previously published interviews with Herzog, edited by Eric Ames, appeared in 2014, released by the University Press of Mississippi. The first iteration of this book (2002, as *Herzog on Herzog*) has been published in numerous foreign-language editions.

Herzog has by now been fully integrated into the cross-currents of university departments and presses worldwide, and several of the following books are full of impeccable academic prose. Timothy Corrigan's *Between Mirage and History, The Films of Werner Herzog* (Methuen, 1986) contains eleven essays about the films, and was for many years the only full-length study in English. Two books in English – Brad Prager's *The Cinema of Werner Herzog: Aesthetic Ecstasy and Truth* (Wallflower, 2007) and Eric Ames's *Ferocious Reality: Documentary According to Werner Herzog* (University of Minnesota, 2012) – have appeared more recently. Prager also edited a six-hundred-page collection of essays entitled *A Companion to Werner Herzog* (Wiley-Blackwell, 2012). In German, Chris Wahl's *Lektionen in Herzog: Neues über Deutschlands verlorenen Filmautor und sein Werk* (Text und Kritik, 2011) is an assembly of essays about Herzog's reception in Germany, Italy, France and the United States. There are three full-length studies of the films in French: Emmanuel Carrère's *Werner Herzog* (Edilig, 1982), Radu Gabrea's *Werner Herzog et la mystique rhénane* (L'Age d'Homme, 1986) and Valérie Carré's *La quête anthropologique de Werner Herzog: documentaires et fictions en regard* (Press Universitaires de Strasbourg, 2007). There are two studies in Italian, one by Paolo Sirianni (Scambio Editrice, 1980), the other by Fabrizio Grosoli (La Nova Italia, 1981), and one in Hungarian by Muhi Klára and Perlaki Tamás (Mùzsák Közmüvelödési Kiadó, 1986). Lucia Nagib's 1991 book *Werner Herzog: O cinema como realidade* was published in Portuguese and includes a twenty-four-page interview. Antonio Weinrichter's *Caminar sobre hielo y fuego: los documentales de Werner Herzog* appeared in 2007. In 1979 Carl Hanser Verlag published *Werner Herzog*, which contains a lengthy interview in German and commentaries on the films (up to *Woyzeck*). The relevant chapters in the same publisher's *Herzog/Kluge/Straub* (1976) are similarly structured. *Postscript: Essays in Film and the Humanities* (Jacksonville University and Georgia Institute of Technology) devoted much of its summer 1988 issue to Herzog's films. The German magazine *Film-dienst* published several articles about Herzog's documentaries in its summer 2010 issue. Moritz Holdfelder's "unauthorised" biography of Herzog was published in German (LangenMüller) in 2012. While Holdfelder did not interview the subject of his book or have access to Herzog's archive, he did conduct interviews with several of Herzog's collaborators, including Jörg Schmidt-Reitwein, Beate Mainka-Jellinghaus, Eva Mattes and Alexander Kluge.

Apart from the two Les Blank films mentioned above, there are a small number of worthwhile documentaries about Herzog. Thomas Mauch's short film from 1972 *Der Welt zeigen, dass man noch da ist* [*Show the World We're Still There*] features footage shot on the set of *Signs of Life*, *Even Dwarfs Started Small* and *Aguirre*, and audio of Herzog and Kinski. *I Am My Films*, parts of which were filmed in Herzog's Munich apartment by Erwin Keusch and Christian Weisenborn in 1979, includes a conversation between him and Laurens Straub, footage shot on the set of *Stroszek* and of Herzog listening to a recording of Kinski screaming at him during the production of *Aguirre*. (Its lacklustre sequel, *I Am My Films: Part 2 . . . Thirty Years Later*, filmed in Herzog's Los Angeles home by Christian Weisenborn, was produced in 2010.) In 1982 the British arts programme *The South Bank Show* produced Jack Bond's hour-long film, which was broadcast to mark the release of *Fitzcarraldo*. It includes Herzog reading the Robert Walser poem featured at the end of *The Great Ecstasy of Woodcarver Steiner*, driving around the menhirs of Carnac, showing us his home town of Sachrang, football training alongside his Schwarz/Gelb München teammates, and in conversation with Lotte Eisner. Herzog's own half-hour *Werner Herzog: Filmmaker* (1986) – which recycles its best moments from *The South Bank Show* and *Burden of Dreams* – includes footage of him drinking beer at the Oktoberfest. *To the Limit and then Beyond* is an hour-long "film essay" by Peter Buchka containing good interview material, produced in 1989 by Bayerischen Rundfunk.

In 1993 Milan released *Best of Popol Vuh: Werner Herzog*, which contains Florian Fricke's music from *Aguirre, Nosferatu, Fitzcarraldo, Cobra Verde* and *The Dark Glow of the Mountains*. A 2010 box set, released by SPV, entitled *Popol Vuh: The Werner Herzog Sountracks*, contains a pamphlet with photos and liner notes, and five CDs: music from *Aguirre, Heart of Glass, Nosferatu, Fitzcarraldo* and *Cobra Verde*. Winter & Winter released Ernst Reijseger's soundtracks to *My Son, My Son, What Have Ye Done* (2010), *Cave of Forgotten Dreams* (2011) and, on a single CD entitled *Requiem for a Dying Planet, The Wild Blue Yonder* and *The White Diamond* (2006). In 2013 Winter & Winter released *Eroberung des Nutzlosen*, a recording of Herzog and Reijseger's performances in Berlin. Cooking Vinyl issued Richard Thompson's music for *Grizzly Man* in 2005.

For more in English on modern German cinema, Sabine Hake's *German National Cinema* (Routledge, 2001) is a good summary, though for specifics on New German Cinema, James Franklin's *New German Cinema* (Columbus Books, 1986) and Thomas Elsaesser's *New German Cinema* (Rutgers University Press, 1989) are more substantial. Elsaesser and Michael Wedel's *The BFI Companion to German Cinema* (BFI, 1999) is also a solid alphabetical listing, while Eric Rentschler's *West German Filmmakers on Film, Visions and Voices* (Holmes and Meier, 1988) is a useful collection of writings by West German directors (including Kluge, Straub, Syberberg, Achternbusch, Schlöndorff, Wenders, Fassbinder and Herzog), and also contains the texts of the Oberhausen, Mannheim and Hamberg Manifestos. There is a longer German edition, edited by Helmut Prinzler and Eric Rentschler, entitled *Der alte Film war tot* (Verlag der Autoren, 2001).

In recent years there has been an explosion of all things Klaus Kinski. His crazed autobiography, of which there exist two versions, is a grotesque and sensational rant. *Ich bin so wild nach deinem Erdbeermund* (the opening line of a François Villon poem; literally: *Lusting for your Strawberry Lips*) was first published in 1975 (Rogner & Bernhard), with a French edition the following year (*Crever pour vivre*, Belfond). Two English editions were released as *All I Need Is Love* (Random House, 1988) and *Kinski Uncut* (US: Viking, 1996; UK: Bloomsbury, 1997), both shorter versions of the German *Ich brauche Liebe* (Wilhelm Heyne Verlag, 1991). *Kinski* (Parthas, 2000) is a collection of photographs by Beat Presser. *Ich, Kinski*, published by the Deutsches Filmmusem in Frankfurt, and *Klaus Kinski "Ich bin so wie ich bin"* (Deutscher Taschenbuch Verlag) (both 2001) are collections of essays and photos. *Fieber: Tagebuch eines Aussätzigen*, a collection of Kinski's own poetry (with photographs), was published by

Eichborn Verlag (2001). Two biographies exist in German, one by Peter Geyer (Suhrkamp, 2006), the other by Christian David (Aufbau, 2006). Kinski's *Jesus Christus Erlöser* (Surhkamp, 2006) is a book detailing his 1971 performance in Berlin. A recording of the event was released in 2006 (Random House Audio) and a DVD issued in 2009. *Kinski Vermächtnis* is a mammoth scrapbook, edited by Peter Geyer and O. A. Krimmel, published by Edel in 2011, and contains a wealth of writings, documents and photographs. Many of Kinski's audio recordings (all in German) have been released over the past few years, notably the twelve-CD set *Kinski Spricht: Werke der Weltliteratur* (Deutsche Grammophon, 2003). In 1990 Amadeo released a CD of Kinski readings entitled *Ich bin so wild nach deinem Erdbeermund*, and in 2001 Deutsche Grammophon published *Klaus Kinski*, a single CD of readings from, among others, Dostoyevsky and Nietzsche. Klaus Kinski Productions produced an audio version of Kinski's book *Fieber*, with Ben Becker reading the poetry (2001). In 2002 Random House Audio released *Klaus Kinski: Hörspiele*, readings from the archives of Hessischen Rundfunk, and in 2006 issued a 1956 recording of Kinski playing the title role in *Henry IV*. Three DVDs of filmed interviews with Kinski (entitled *Kinski Talks*) were released between 2010 and 2012 by Klaus Kinski Productions, and his film *Kinski/Paganini* is available on DVD. Kinski's daughter Pola published a memoir entitled *Kindermund* [*Child's Mouth*] in 2013 (Suhrkamp), in which she details the decade-long sexual abuse she suffered at the hands of her father.

The following is an incomplete list of DVD/Blu-ray editions of Herzog's films. Most titles in the Anchor Bay Entertainment (US) DVD box sets from 2004 (one with the five Kinski features plus *My Best Fiend*, the other containing *The Enigma of Kaspar Hauser*, *Even Dwarfs Started Small*, *Fata Morgana*, *Lessons of Darkness*, *Heart of Glass*, *Stroszek* and *Little Dieter Needs to Fly*) include audio commentaries recorded by Herzog. The two box sets issued by Opening (France) in 2006 contain a selection of features and documentaries alongside a two-hour filmed interview. A six-disc set was released by Arthaus (Germany) in 2007, four of which (*Kaspar Hauser*, *Fata Morgana*, *Stroszek* and *Signs of Life*) include commentaries by Herzog in German. In 2011 Werner Herzog Filmproduktion published the thirteen-disc box set *Documentaries 1962–2005*, and the following year from StudioCanal (Germany) came the five Kinski films on Blu-ray. The British Film Institute's eight-disc DVD/seven-disc Blu-ray sets from 2014 consist of eighteen digitally remastered features and shorts (some of which include audio commentary), plus a few extras, including *The South Bank Show* (see above). A slimmed-down version was issued (Blu-ray only) by Shout! (US).

Acknowledgements

Truman Anderson for his perceptive comments; Ian Bahrami for his patience and diligence; Ramin Bahrani; John Bailey; Jeremy Belinfante; Joe Bini; Ryan Bojanovic; Michael Chaiken, for being such a discerning sceptic; Michel Ciment; Jem Cohen; the Cronins of NW5 and N19; Victoria Dailey; Roger Diehl; Sam Di Iorio for those nuances; Walter Donohue at Faber and Faber for his unstinting faith; Graham Dorrington for opening up that one particular story; Sarah Ereira; Snorre Fredlund for his Nordic sensibility; Todd Gitlin; Herb Golder for helping me reach a deeper understanding; Alan Greenberg; Ulli Gruber for her enthusiasm; Marie-Antoinette Guillochon and Remi Guillochon for translation assistance; Simon Hacker; Lena Herzog for her hospitality and images; Rudolph Herzog for those arcane details; Paul Holdengräber for being so good at doing it in public; Gus Holwerda; Neil Hornick; the late David Horrocks; Christoph Huber; Ricky Jay; Harmony Korine for those addled evenings spent at his grandma's house in Queens; Daniel Kothenschulte; Lawrence Krauss; Bruce "Pacho" Lane; David LaRocca for his insights; Martina Lauster for her graciousness and excellence as a translator; Tom Luddy; Grazia Paganelli; Presley Parks for always being around; Zak Penn; Doris Perlman for her sharp eye and knowledge of opera; Rory Pfotenhauer; Thom Powers and Raphaela Neihausen for their unrelenting spirit; Alexandra Proulx; Denis Reichle for his sense of history; Blanche and Bruce Rubin for their long-standing Northridge hospitality; Volker Schlöndorff; John Sorensen for his way of seeing; Lucki Stipetić for being such a benevolent custodian; Ted Sweetser; Gabrielle Tenzer for allowing all those stacks of books; Justin Van Voorhis; Chris Wahl; Damon Wise; and – at the Deutsche Kinemathek in Berlin – Julia Pattis, Julia Reidel, Sandra Schieke and Werner Sudendorf.

Thanks to those interviewers who don't sell their work as being "in depth," who never describe a published piece as being "edited and condensed," and are steadfast about conducting Q&As rather than "masterclasses." Also to a number of Roguistas whose names I have long forgotten and with whom over the years I discussed – often saturated with alcohol, sitting in a hotel bar, into the early hours – the preceding day's events. If even a single one of them decides to break out, to wander the desert with a handful of carefully chosen books, to bask in the solitude, as they smile at the infinite delight and mystery of it all, everything will have been worthwhile. Sometimes it's best not to live quite so relentlessly in the real world. Wrote Emerson: "A man should learn to detect and watch that gleam of light which flashes across his mind from within, more than the lustre of the firmament of bards and sages."

Filmography

"I have worked with the same crew now for fourteen years, and some of them are among the best there are in the world today. They are the real authors of my films; we have a similar outlook and sensibility. I decide on the subject matter, and we do everything else together."

Werner Herzog
Cinéma, October 1979

1957
A Lost Western [unreleased]
Fiction, 6 minutes, 8mm, b/w
Director: Werner Herzog
Screenplay: Werner Herzog
Location: Munich

1962
Herakles
Fiction, 12 minutes, 35mm, b/w
Director: Werner Herzog
Screenplay: Werner Herzog
Producer: Werner Herzog
Camera: Jaime Pacheco
Editor: Werner Herzog
Sound: Werner Herzog
Music: Uwe Brandner
Production Company: Cineropa Film
Featuring: Mr Germany 1962

1964
Spiel im Sand (Game in the Sand) [unreleased]
Non-fiction, 14 minutes, 35mm, b/w
Director: Werner Herzog
Producer: Werner Herzog
Camera: Jaime Pacheco
Editor: Werner Herzog
Sound: Werner Herzog
Music: Uwe Brandner
Production Company: Werner Herzog Filmproduktion
Location: Austria

1966
Die beispiellose Verteidigung der Festung Deutschkreuz (The Unprecedented Defence of the Fortress Deutschkreuz)
Fiction, 15 minutes, 35mm, b/w
Director: Werner Herzog
Screenplay: Werner Herzog
Producer: Werner Herzog
Camera: Jaime Pacheco
Editor: Werner Herzog
Sound: Uwe Brandner
Production Companies: Werner Herzog Filmproduktion, Arpa-Film
Location: Burgenland (Austria)
Cast: Peter Brumm, Georg Eska, Karl-Heinz Steffel, Wolfgang von Ungern-Sternberg
Premiere: April 1967, Oberhausen Short Film Festival

1967
Letzte Worte (Last Words)
Fiction, 13 minutes, 35mm, b/w
Director: Werner Herzog
Screenplay: Werner Herzog
Producer: Werner Herzog
Camera: Thomas Mauch
Editor: Beate Mainka-Jellinghaus
Sound: Herbert Prasch
Music: Folkmusic of Crete
Production Company: Werner Herzog Filmproduktion
Locations: Crete, Kos (Greece)
Premiere: April 1968, Oberhausen Short Film Festival

1968
Lebenszeichen (Signs of Life)
Fiction, 87 minutes, 35mm, b/w
Director: Werner Herzog
Screenplay: Werner Herzog
Producer: Werner Herzog
Camera: Thomas Mauch
Editor: Beate Mainka-Jellinghaus
Sound: Herbert Prasch
Music: Stavros Xarchakos
Production Company: Werner Herzog Filmproduktion
Locations: Crete, Kos (Greece)
Cast: Peter Brogle (Stroszek), Wolfgang Reichmann (Meinhard), Athina Zacharopoulou (Nora), Wolfgang von Ungern-Sternberg (Becker),

Wolfgang Stumpf (Captain), Henry van Lyck (Lieutenant), Florian Fricke (Pianist)
Premiere: June 1968, Berlin Film Festival

1969
Massnahmen gegen Fanatiker (Precautions against Fanatics)
Fiction, 12 minutes, 35mm, colour
Director: Werner Herzog
Screenplay: Werner Herzog
Producer: Werner Herzog
Camera: Dieter Lohmann
Editor: Beate Mainka-Jellinghaus
Sound: Werner Herzog
Production Company: Werner Herzog Filmproduktion
Location: Munich
Cast: Petar Radenković, Mario Adorf, Hans Tiedemann, Herbert Hisel, Peter Schamoni
Premiere: March 1969, Oberhausen Short Film Festival

1969
Die fliegenden Ärzte von Ostafrika (The Flying Doctors of East Africa)
Fiction, 45 minutes, 35mm, colour
Director: Werner Herzog
Producer: Werner Herzog
Executive Producer: Eleonore Semler
Camera: Thomas Mauch
Editor: Beate Mainka-Jellinghaus
Sound: Werner Herzog
Production Company: Werner Herzog Filmproduktion (for the African Medical & Research Foundation)
Locations: Kenya, Uganda, Tanzania
Participants: Dr Michael Wood, Dr Ann Spoery, Betty Miller, James Kabale
Premiere: March 1970, ZDF (German television)

1970
Auch Zwerge haben klein angefangen (Even Dwarfs Started Small)
Fiction, 96 minutes, 35mm, b/w
Director: Werner Herzog
Screenplay: Werner Herzog
Producer: Werner Herzog
Camera: Thomas Mauch, Jörg Schmidt-Reitwein
Editor: Beate Mainka-Jellinghaus, Maximiliane Mainka
Sound: Herbert Prasch

Music: Florian Fricke (Popol Vuh) and folk songs of Côte d'Ivoire, West Africa, Canary Islands
Production Company: Werner Herzog Filmproduktion
Location: Lanzarote (Canary Islands)
Cast: Helmut Döring (Hombre), Gerd Gickel (Pepe), Paul Glauer (Erzieher), Erna Gschwendtner (Azúcar), Gisela Hertwig (Pobrecita)
Premiere: May 1970, Cannes Film Festival

1970
Fata Morgana
Non-fiction, 79 minutes, 35mm, colour
Director: Werner Herzog
Producer: Werner Herzog
Camera: Jörg Schmidt-Reitwein
Editor: Beate Mainka-Jellinghaus
Sound: Hans von Mallinckrodt
Music: Leonard Cohen, Blind Faith, Couperin, Mozart, Handel
Production Company: Werner Herzog Filmproduktion
Locations: Southern Sahara, Cameroon, Canary Islands
Participants: Wolfgang von Ungern-Sternberg, James William Gledhill, Eugen des Montagnes
Premiere: May 1970, Cannes Film Festival

1971
Behinderte Zukunft (Handicapped Future)
Non-fiction, 43 minutes, 16mm, colour
Director: Werner Herzog
Producer: Werner Herzog
Camera: Jörg Schmidt-Reitwein
Editor: Beate Mainka-Jellinghaus
Sound: Werner Herzog
Production Company: Werner Herzog Filmproduktion (for North Rhine-Westphalia)
Locations: Munich, Hannover, Los Angeles
Participants: Adolph Ratzka

1971
Land des Schweigens und der Dunkelheit (Land of Silence and Darkness)
Non-fiction, 85 minutes, 16mm, colour
Director: Werner Herzog
Producer: Werner Herzog
Camera: Jörg Schmidt-Reitwein
Editor: Beate Mainka-Jellinghaus
Sound: Werner Herzog

Music: Bach, Vivaldi
Production Company: Werner Herzog Filmproduktion (for North Rhine-Westphalia)
Locations: Munich, Niederbayern, Hannover
Participants: Fini Straubinger, Else Fährer, Ursula Riedmeier, Joseph Riedmeier, Vladimir Kokol, Heinrich Fleischmann, Resi Mittermeier
Premiere: October 1978, Mannheim Film Festival

1972
Aguirre, der Zorn Gottes (Aguirre, the Wrath of God)
Fiction, 93 minutes, 35mm, colour
Director: Werner Herzog
Screenplay: Werner Herzog
Producer: Werner Herzog
Camera: Thomas Mauch
Editor: Beate Mainka-Jellinghaus
Sound: Herbert Prasch
Music: Florian Fricke (Popol Vuh)
Production Companies: Werner Herzog Filmproduktion, Hessischer Rundfunk
Location: Peru (Urubamba Valley, River Huallaga, River Nanay, Cusco)
Cast: Klaus Kinski (Lope de Aguirre), Helena Rojo (Inez de Atienza), Del Negro (Carvajal), Ruy Guerra (Ursúa), Peter Berling (Guzman), Cecilia Rivera (Flores), Daniel Ades (Perucho)
Premiere: December 1972, Germany

1973
Die grosse Ekstase des Bildschnitzers Steiner (The Great Ecstasy of Woodcarver Steiner)
Non-fiction, 47 minutes, 16mm, colour
Director: Werner Herzog
Producer: Werner Herzog
Camera: Jörg Schmidt-Reitwein
Editor: Beate Mainka-Jellinghaus
Sound: Benedikt Kuby
Music: Florian Fricke (Popol Vuh)
Production Company: Werner Herzog Filmproduktion (for Süddeutscher Rundfunk)
Locations: Oberstdorf and Garmisch-Partenkirchen (Germany), Planica (Slovenia)
Participant: Walter Steiner
Premiere: November 1974, Munich

1974
Jeder für sich und Gott gegen alle (The Enigma of Kaspar Hauser)
Fiction, 109 minutes, 35mm, colour
Director: Werner Herzog
Screenplay: Werner Herzog
Producer: Werner Herzog
Camera: Jörg Schmidt-Reitwein
Editor: Beate Mainka-Jellinghaus, Martha Lederer
Sound: Haymo Henry Heyder
Music: Florian Fricke (Popol Vuh), Mozart, di Lasso, Albinoni,
Pachelbel
Production Companies: Werner Herzog Filmproduktion, Zweites
Deutsches Fernsehen
Location Dinkelsbühl, Ireland, Spanish Sahara
Cast: Bruno S. (Kaspar), Walter Ladengast (Daumer), Brigitte Mira
(Kathe), Hans Musäus (Unknown man), Willy Semmelrogge (Circus
Director), Michael Kroecher (Stanhope), Henry van Lyck (Cavalry
Captain), Enno Patalas (Vicar Fuhrmann), Florian Fricke (Florian),
Clemens Scheitz (Scribe)
Premiere: November 1974, Dinkelsbühl

1976
Herz aus Glas (Heart of Glass)
Fiction, 97 minutes, 35mm, colour
Director: Werner Herzog
Screenplay: Werner Herzog, Herbert Achternbusch
Producer: Werner Herzog
Camera: Jörg Schmidt-Reitwein
Editor: Beate Mainka-Jellinghaus
Sound: Haymo Henry Heyder
Music: Florian Fricke (Popol Vuh), Studio der Frühen Musik
Production Companies: Werner Herzog Filmproduktion, Zweites
Deutsches Fernsehen
Locations: Bavaria, Skellig Rock (Ireland), Graubünden (Switzerland),
Alaska, Monument Valley, Yellowstone National Park, Niagra Falls
Cast: Josef Bierbichler (Hias), Stefan Güttler (Factory Owner), Clemens
Scheitz (Adalbert), Volker Prechtel (Wudy), Sonja Skiba (Ludmilla),
Brunhilde Klöckner (Paulin), Wolf Albrecht (Sam), Thomas Binkley (Lute
Player), Janos Fischer (Ägide)
Premiere: November 1976, Paris Film Festival

1976
Mit mir will keiner spielen (No One Will Play with Me)
Non-fiction, 14 minutes, 16mm, colour

Director: Werner Herzog
Producer: Werner Herzog
Camera: Jörg Schmidt-Reitwein
Editor: Beate Mainka-Jellinghaus
Sound: Haymo Henry Heyder
Production Companies: Werner Herzog Filmproduktion, Institut für Film und Bild in Wissenschaft und Unterricht
Location: Munich

1976
How Much Wood Would a Woodchuck Chuck . . .: Beobachtungen zu einer neuen Sprache (How Much Wood Would a Woodchuck Chuck . . .: Observations on a New Language)
Non-fiction, 45 minutes, 16mm, colour
Director: Werner Herzog
Producer: Werner Herzog
Camera: Thomas Mauch
Editor: Beate Mainka-Jellinghaus
Sound: Walter Saxer
Music: Shorty Eager and the Eager Beavers
Production Companies: Werner Herzog Filmproduktion, Süddeutscher Rundfunk
Location: New Holland, Pennsylvania
Participants: Steve Liptay, Ralph Wade, Alan Ball, Abe Diffenbach
Premiere: June 1976, Hof International Film Festival

1976
Stroszek
Fiction, 108 minutes, 35mm, colour
Director: Werner Herzog
Screenplay: Werner Herzog
Producer: Werner Herzog
Camera: Thomas Mauch
Editor: Beate Mainka-Jellinghaus
Sound: Haymo Henry Heyder
Music: Chet Atkins, Sonny Terry, Tom Paxton, Beethoven
Production Companies: Werner Herzog Filmproduktion, Zweites Deutsches Fernsehen
Locations: Berlin, New York, Wisconsin, North Carolina
Cast: Bruno S. (Stroszek), Eva Mattes (Eva), Clemens Scheitz (Scheitz)
Premiere: May 1977, Munich

1977
La Soufrière: Warten auf eine unausweichliche Katastrophe (La Soufrière: Waiting for an Unavoidable Catastrophe)
Non-fiction, 30 minutes, 16mm, colour
Director: Werner Herzog
Producer: Werner Herzog
Camera: Jörg Schmidt-Reitwein, Ed Lachman
Editor: Beate Mainka-Jellinghaus
Sound: Werner Herzog
Music: Rachmaninov, Mendelssohn, Brahms, Wagner
Production Company: Werner Herzog Filmproduktion (for Süddeutscher Rundfunk)
Location: Guadeloupe
Premiere: March 1977, Bonn

1979
Nosferatu – Phantom der Nacht (Nosferatu the Vampyre)
Fiction, 103 minutes, 35mm, colour
Director: Werner Herzog
Screenplay: Werner Herzog
Producer: Werner Herzog
Camera: Jörg Schmidt-Reitwein
Editor: Beate Mainka-Jellinghaus
Sound: Harald Maury
Music: Florian Fricke (Popol Vuh), Wagner, Gounod
Production Companies: Werner Herzog Filmproduktion, Gaumont, Zweites Deutsches Fernsehen
Locations: Czech Republic, Netherlands, Mexico, Slovakia
Cast: Klaus Kinski (Count Dracula), Isabelle Adjani (Lucy Harker), Bruno Ganz (Jonathan Harker), Jaques Dufilho (Captain), Roland Topor (Renfield), Walter Ladengast (Dr van Helsing)
Premiere: January 1979, Paris

1979
Woyzeck
Fiction, 81 minutes, 35mm, colour
Director: Werner Herzog
Screenplay: Werner Herzog (from the play by Georg Büchner)
Producer: Werner Herzog
Camera: Jörg Schmidt-Reitwein
Editor: Beate Mainka-Jellinghaus
Sound: Harald Maury
Music: Fiedelquartett Telč, Rudolf Obruca, Benedetto Marcello, Vivaldi
Production Companies: Werner Herzog Filmproduktion, Zweites

Deutsches Fernsehen
Location: Czech Republic
Cast: Klaus Kinski (Woyzeck), Eva Mattes (Marie), Wolfgang Reichmann (Hauptmann), Willy Semmelrogge (Doctor), Josef Bierbichler (Drum-Major), Paul Burian (Andres)
Premiere: May 1979, Cannes

1980
Glaube und Währung (God's Angry Man)
Non-fiction, 44 minutes, 16mm, colour
Director: Werner Herzog
Producer: Werner Herzog
Camera: Thomas Mauch
Editor: Beate Mainka-Jellinghaus
Sound: Walter Saxer
Production Company: Werner Herzog Filmproduktion (for Süddeutscher Rundfunk)
Location: Glendale, California
Participant: Dr Gene Scott
Premiere: May 1981, ARD (German television)

1980
Huie's Predigt (Huie's Sermon)
Non-fiction, 43 minutes, 16mm, colour
Director: Werner Herzog
Producer: Werner Herzog
Camera: Thomas Mauch
Editor: Beate Mainka-Jellinghaus
Sound: Walter Saxer
Production Company: Werner Herzog Filmproduktion (for Süddeutscher Rundfunk)
Location: New York
Participant: Bishop Huie L. Rogers
Premiere: June 1981, ARD (German television)

1982
Fitzcarraldo
Fiction, 137 minutes, 35mm, colour
Director: Werner Herzog
Screenplay: Werner Herzog
Producers: Lucki Stipetić, Werner Herzog
Camera: Thomas Mauch
Editor: Beate Mainka-Jellinghaus
Sound: Jaurez Dagoberto Costa, Zezé d'Alice

Music: Florian Fricke (Popol Vuh), Verdi, Bellini
Production Companies: Werner Herzog Filmproduktion, Zweites
Deutsches Fernsehen, Filmverlag der Autoren
Locations: Iquitos, Río Camisea (Peru), Manaus and Iquito (Brazil)
Cast: Klaus Kinski (Brian Sweeney Fitzgerald), Claudia Cardinale
(Molly), José Lewgoy (Don Aquilino), Paul Hittscher (Captain),
Huerequeque Enrique Bohórquez (Huerequeque)
Premiere: March 1982, Munich

1984
Wo die grünen Ameisen träumen (Where the Green Ants Dream)
Fiction, 100 minutes, 35mm, colour
Director: Werner Herzog
Screenplay: Werner Herzog
Producer: Lucki Stipetić
Camera: Jörg Schmidt-Reitwein
Editor: Beate Mainka-Jellinghaus
Sound: Claus Langer
Music: Fauré, Bloch, Wagner, Klaus-Jochen Wiese, Wandjuk Marika
Production Companies: Werner Herzog Filmproduktion, Zweites
Deutsches Fernsehen, Filmverlag der Autoren
Locations: Melbourne, Coober Pedy (Australia)
Cast: Bruce Spence (Hackett), Wandjuk Marika (Miliritbi), Roy Marika
(Dayipu), Ray Barrett (Cole), Norman Kaye (Ferguson), Colleen Clifford
(Miss Strehlow)
Premiere: May 1984, Cannes Film Festival

1984
Ballad of the Little Soldier (Ballade vom kleinen Soldaten)
Non-fiction, 45 minutes, 16mm, colour
Director: Werner Herzog
Producer: Lucki Stipetić
Camera: Jorge Vignati
Editor: Maximiliane Mainka
Sound: Christine Ebenberger
Music: Folk songs performed by Isidoro Reyes and Paladino Taylor
Production Company: Werner Herzog Filmproduktion (for Süddeutscher
Rundfunk)
Locations: Nicaragua, Honduras
Participants Miskito Indians of Nicaragua
Premiere: October 1984, Hof International Film Festival

1984
Gasherbrum – Der leuchtende Berg (The Dark Glow of the Mountains)
Non-fiction, 45 minutes, 16mm and Super 8, colour
Director: Werner Herzog
Producer: Lucki Stipetić
Camera: Rainer Klausmann
Editor: Maximiliane Mainka
Sound: Christine Ebenberger
Music: Florian Fricke (Popol Vuh), Renate Knaup, Daniel Fichelscher
Production Company: Werner Herzog Filmproduktion (for Süddeutscher Rundfunk)
Location: Karakorum, Pakistan
Participants: Reinhold Messner, Hans Kammerlander
Premiere: June 1985, ARD (German television)

1987
Cobra Verde
Fiction, 110 minutes, 35mm, colour
Director: Werner Herzog
Screenplay: Werner Herzog (from the novel *The Viceroy of Ouidah* by Bruce Chatwin)
Producer: Lucki Stipetić
Camera: Viktor Růžička
Editor: Maximiliane Mainka, Rainer Standke
Sound: Haymo Henry Heyder
Music: Florian Fricke (Popol Vuh)
Production Companies: Werner Herzog Filmproduktion, Zweites Deutsches Fernsehen
Locations: Dahomey (Benin), Elmina, Tamale (Ghana), Cartagena, Cali and Guajira (Colombia), Juazeiro do Norte, Bahia (Brazil)
Cast: Klaus Kinski (Francisco Manoel da Silva), King Ampaw (Taparica), José Lewgoy (Don Octavio Coutinho), Salvatore Basile (Captain Fraternidade), Peter Berling (Bernabé), Guillermo Coronel (Euclides), His Royal Highness King Nana Agyefi Kwame II of Nsein (Bossa Ahadee)
Premiere: December 1987, Munich

1988
Les Français vus par . . . les Gauloises
Non-fiction, 12 minutes, 16mm, colour
Director: Werner Herzog
Camera: Jörg Schmidt-Reitwein
Editor: Rainer Standke
Sound: Bernard Aubouy
Production Company: Erato Films

Locations: Paris, Toulouse
Participants: Claude Josse, Jean Clemente, the rugby team of Stade Toulousain and the Sporting Club of Graulheit

1989
Wodaabe, Die Hirten der Sonne (Wodaabe, Herdsmen of the Sun)
Non-fiction, 52 minutes, 16mm, colour
Director: Werner Herzog
Producer: Patrick Sandrin
Camera: Jörg Schmidt-Reitwein
Editor: Maximiliane Mainka
Sound: Walter Saxer
Music: Gounod, Mozart, Handel, Verdi
Production Company: Werner Herzog Filmproduktion (for Süddeutscher Rundfunk)
Location: Southern Sahara (Republic of Niger)
Participants: Members of the Wodaabe
Premiere: June 1989, Südwest 3 (German television)

1990
Echos aus einem düsteren Reich (Echoes from a Sombre Empire)
Non-fiction, 93 minutes, 16mm, colour
Director: Werner Herzog
Producer: Werner Herzog
Camera: Jörg Schmidt-Reitwein
Editor: Rainer Standke
Sound: Harald Maury
Music: Bartók, Prokofiev, Lutoslawski, Schubert, Shostakovich, Bach, Esther Lamandier
Production Companies: Werner Herzog Filmproduktion, SERA Filmproduktion, Films sans Frontières
Locations: Central African Republic, France, Venice
Participants: Michael Goldsmith, François Gilbault, Augustine Assemat, Francis Szpiner, David Dacko, Marie-Reine Hassen
Premiere: November 1990, Paris

1991
Cerro Torre: Schrei aus Stein (Scream of Stone)
Fiction, 105 minutes, 35mm, colour
Director: Werner Herzog
Screenplay: Hans-Ulrich Klenner, Walter Saxer, Robert Geoffrion (from an original idea by Reinhold Messner)
Producers: Walter Saxer, Henry Lange, Richard Sadler
Camera: Rainer Klausmann

Editor: Suzanne Baron, Anne Wagner
Sound: Christopher Price
Music: Heinrich Schütz, Wagner, Ingram Marshall, Sarah Hopkins, Alan Lamb, Atahualpa Yupanqui
Production Companies: Sera Filmproduktions GmbH, Molecule, Les Stock Films International, Zweites Deutsches Fernsehen, Canal+
Locations: Patagonia (Argentina), Munich, Australia, Grenoble (France)
Cast: Vittorio Mezzogiorno (Roccia), Stefan Glowacz (Martin), Mathilda May (Katharina), Donald Sutherland (Ivan), Brad Dourif (Fingerless), Al Waxman (Stephen)
Premiere: September 1991, Venice Film Festival

1991
Das exzentrische Privattheater des Maharadjah von Udaipur (The Eccentric Private Theatre of the Maharaja of Udaipur)
Non-fiction, 85 minutes, 16mm, colour
Director: Werner Herzog
Producer: Werner Herzog
Camera: Rainer Klausmann
Editor: Michou Hutter, Ursula Darrer
Sound: Herbert Giesser
Production Company: Neue Studio Film GmbH (for Zweites Deutsches Fernsehen and Österreichischer Rundfunk)
Location: Udaipur (India)
Participants: André Heller, Manipuri Jagoi, Deb Des Baul, Pusekhan Hayatm, Huyel Lallong, Devi Bhakta, Pazur, Damodara Marar, M. Mariyan Pillai, Raghu Presed, V. P. Paul
Premiere: November 1991, ORF (Austrian television)

1991
Film Stunde (Film Lessons)
Non-fiction, 4 × 60 minutes, Betacam, colour
Director: Werner Herzog
Producer: Gerda Weissenberger
Camera: Karl Kofler, Michael Ferk
Editor: Albert Skalak
Production Company: Österreichischer Rundfunk
Location: Vienna
Participants: Michael Kreihsl, Jeff Sheridan, Peter Turrini, Volker Schlöndorff, Kamal Saiful Islam, Philippe Petit, Ryszard Kapuściński
Premiere: December 1991, ORF (Austrian television)

1992
Lektionen in Finsternis (Lessons of Darkness)
Non-fiction, 52 minutes, Super 16, colour
Director: Werner Herzog
Producer: Lucki Stipetić
Camera: Paul Berriff, Simon Werry, Rainer Klausmann
Editor: Rainer Standke
Sound: John G. Pearson
Music: Wagner, Grieg, Prokofiev, Pärt, Verdi, Schubert, Mahler
Production Companies: Werner Herzog Filmproduktion, Canal+,
Premiere Medien GmbH
Location: Kuwait
Premiere: February 1991, Berlin Film Festival

1993
Glocken aus der Tiefe (Bells from the Deep: Faith and Superstition in Russia)
Non-fiction, 60 minutes, Super 16, colour
Director: Werner Herzog
Producers: Lucki Stipetić, Ira Barmak
Camera: Jörg Schmidt-Reitwein
Editor: Rainer Standke
Sound: Vyacheslav Belozerou
Music: Choir of the Spiritual Academy, Saint Petersburg, Choir of the
Zagorsk Monastery, Choir of the Pühtica Dormition Convent
Production Company: Werner Herzog Filmproduktion
Location: Siberia (Russia)
Premiere: November 1993, Stockholm Film Festival

1994
Die Verwandlung der Welt in Musik (The Transformation of the World into Music)
Non-fiction, 90 minutes, Super 16, colour
Director: Werner Herzog
Producer: Lucki Stipetić
Camera: Jörg Schmidt-Reitwein
Editor: Rainer Standke
Sound: Ekkehard Baumung
Music: Wagner (Choir and Orchestra of the Bayreuth Wagner Festival)
Production Company: Werner Herzog Filmproduktion (for ARTE and
Zweites Deutsches Fernsehen)
Locations: Bayreuth, Linderhof Castle
Participants: Wolfgang Wagner, Sven Friedrich, Yohji Yamamoto, Plácido
Domingo, Dieter Dorn, Heiner Müller, Waltraud Meier, Siegfried Jerusalem
Premiere: July 1996, ZDF (German television)

1995
Gesualdo, Tod für fünf Stimmen (Death for Five Voices)
Non-fiction, 60 minutes, Super 16, colour
Director: Werner Herzog
Producer: Lucki Stipetić
Camera: Peter Zeitlinger
Editor: Rainer Standke
Sound: Ekkehard Baumung
Music: Gesualdo, Wagner
Production Company: Werner Herzog Filmproduktion (for Zweites
Deutsches Fernsehen)
Locations: Ferrara, Castel Gesualdo, Arezzo, Venosa, Naples
Participants: Pasquale D'Onofrio, Salvatore Catorano, Angelo Carrabs,
Milva, Angelo Michele Torriello, Raffaele Virocolo, Vincenzo Giusto,
Giovanni Iudica, Walter Beloch, Principe D'Avalos, Antonio Massa,
Alan Curtis, Gennaro Miccio, Silvano Milli, Marisa Milli, Gerald Place,
Alberto Lanini, Il Complesso Barocco, Gesualdo Consort of London
Premiere: November 1996, ZDF (German television)

1997
Little Dieter Needs to Fly (Flucht aus Laos)
Non-fiction, 80 minutes (theatrical), 52 minutes (English/German televi-
sion), Super 16, colour
Director: Werner Herzog
Producer: Lucki Stipetić
Camera: Peter Zeitlinger
Editor: Joe Bini
Sound: Ekkehard Baumung
Music: Bartók, Carlos Gardel, Glenn Miller, Kongar-ol Ondar, Wagner,
Dvořák, Bach, folk music of the people of Sayan Altal and the Ural
mountains
Production Companies: Werner Herzog Filmproduktion, Café
Productions (for Zweites Deutsches Fernsehen, BBC and ARTE)
Locations: Thailand, San Francisco, Tuscon, San Diego, Wildberg (Black
Forest)
Participant: Dieter Dengler
Premiere: February 1998, Portland International Film Festival

1999
Mein liebster Feind (My Best Fiend)
Non-fiction, 95 minutes, Super 16, colour
Director: Werner Herzog
Producer: Lucki Stipetić
Camera: Peter Zeitlinger

Editor: Joe Bini
Sound: Eric Spitzer
Music: Florian Fricke (Popol Vuh)
Production Companies: Werner Herzog Filmproduktion, Café
Productions, Zephir Film
Locations: Peru, Netherlands, Czech Republic, Munich, Paris, San
Francisco
Participants: Klaus Kinski, Eva Mattes, Claudia Cardinale, Beat Presser,
Guillermo Rios, Andres Vicente, Justo Gonzalez, Benino Moreno Placido,
Baron und Baronin von d. Recke, José Koechlin von Stein
Premiere: May 1999, Cannes Film Festival

1999
Gott and die Beladenen (The Lord and the Laden)
Non-fiction, 43 minutes, digital video, colour
Director: Werner Herzog
Producers: Martin Choroba, Joachim Puls
Camera: Jorge Vignati
Editor: Joe Bini, Thomas Staunton
Sound: Francisco Adrianzén
Music: Gounod, di Lasso
Production Company: Tellux Film
Locations: Antigua, San Andrés Itzapa (Guatemala)
Premiere: January 2000, ARD (German television)

2000
Julianes Sturz in den Dschungel (Wings of Hope)
Non-fiction, 70 minutes (theatrical), 42 minutes (German television), 49
minutes (English television), Super 16, colour
Director: Werner Herzog
Producer: Lucki Stipetić
Camera: Peter Zeitlinger
Editor: Joe Bini
Sound: Eric Spitzer
Music: Wagner, Stravinsky
Production Companies: Werner Herzog Filmproduktion, Zweites
Deutsches Fernsehen (ZDF), BBC
Location: Peru
Participants: Juliane Koepcke, Moisés Rengito Chavez, Juan Limber
Ribera Soto, Richard Silva Manujama, Ricardo Oroche Rengite, El
Moro
Premiere: February 2000, ZDF (German television)

2001
Pilgrimage
Non-fiction, 18 minutes, 35mm, colour
Director: Werner Herzog
Camera: Jorge Pacheco, Jörg Schmidt-Reitwein, Erik Söllner
Editor: Joe Bini
Sound: Neil Pemperton
Music: John Tavener (*Mahámátra* performed by BBC Symphony
Orchestra, conducted by Leonard Slatkin, performed by Parvin Cox and
the Westminster Cathedral Choir)
Production Company: Werner Herzog Filmproduktion (for BBC)
Locations: Mexico, Siberia
Premiere: March 2001, London

2001
Invincible
Fiction, 130 minutes, 35mm, colour
Director: Werner Herzog
Screenplay: Werner Herzog
Producers: Gary Bart, Werner Herzog, Christine Ruppert
Camera: Peter Zeitlinger
Editor: Joe Bini
Sound: Simon Willis
Music: Hans Zimmer, Klaus Badelt
Production Companies: Werner Herzog Filmproduktion, Tatfilm
Produktion
Locations: Germany, Latvia, Lithuania, Netherlands, Christmas Island
(Australia), Black Island Studios (London), Monterey Bay Aquarium
Cast: Tim Roth (Hanussen), Jouko Ahola (Zishe Breitbart), Anna
Gourari (Marta Farra), Jacob Wein (Benjamin Breitbart), Max Raabe
(Master of Ceremonies), Gustav Peter Woehler (Landwehr), Udo Kier
(Count Helldorf), Herb Golder (Rabbi Edelmann), Gary Bart (Yitzak
Breitbart), Renata Krössner (Mother Breitbart)
Premiere: September 2001, Venice Film Festival

2002
Ten Thousand Years Older [part of Ten Minutes Older: The Trumpet]
Non-fiction, 10 minutes, Super 16, colour
Director: Werner Herzog
Producer: Lucki Stipetić
Camera: Vincente Rios
Editor: Joe Bini
Sound: Walter Saxer
Music: Paul Englishby (performed by Hugh Masekela)

Production Company: Werner Herzog Filmproduktion
Location: Brazil
Premiere: May 2002, Cannes Film Festival

2003
Rad der Zeit (Wheel of Time)
Non-fiction, 80 minutes, Super 16, colour
Director: Werner Herzog
Producers: Werner Herzog, André Singer
Camera: Peter Zeitlinger
Editor: Joe Bini
Sound: Eric Spitzer
Music: Prem Rana Autari, Sur Sudha-Autari, Vaidya Bihaya, Lhamo Dolma, Florian Fricke (Popol Vuh), Shresta Surendra
Production Companies: Werner Herzog Filmproduktion, Café Productions
Locations: Graz (Austria), Bodhgaya (India), Mount Kailash (Tibet, China)
Participants: Dalai Lama, Manfred Klell, Tenzin Dhargye
Premiere: March 2003, BBC Television

2004
The White Diamond
Non-fiction, 87 minutes, Super 16, colour
Director: Werner Herzog
Producers: Werner Herzog, Annette Scheurich, Lucki Stipetić
Camera: Henning Brümmer, Klaus Scheurich
Editor: Joe Bini
Sound: Eric Spitzer
Music: Ernst Reijseger
Production Companies: Marco Polo Film, NDR Naturfilm, Nippon Hoso Kyokai, BBC
Locations: Bedford (England), Guyana
Participants: Graham Dorrington, Marc Anthony Yhap, Jason Gibson, Jan-Peter Meewes
Premiere: November 2004, Halle (Germany)

2005
Grizzly Man
Non-fiction, 103 minutes, Super 16, colour
Director: Werner Herzog
Producer: Erik Nelson
Camera: Peter Zeitlinger
Editor: Joe Bini
Sound: Ken King

Music: Richard Thompson
Production Company: Real Big Productions (for Lionsgate Films and Discovery Docs)
Location: Katmai National Park (Alaska)
Participants: Timothy Treadwell, Amie Huguenard, Jewel Palovak, Carol Dexter, Val Dexter, Sam Egli
Premiere: January 2005, Sundance Film Festival

2005
The Wild Blue Yonder
Non-fiction, 81 minutes, HDCAM, colour
Director: Werner Herzog
Producer: Werner Herzog
Camera: Henry Kaiser, Tanja Koop, Klaus Scheurich
Editor: Joe Bini
Sound: Joe Crabb
Music: Ernst Reijseger
Production Companies: Werner Herzog Filmproduktion, West Park Pictures
Locations: Niland (California), McMurdo Station (Antarctic)
Cast: Brad Dourif, Michael McCulley, Ted Sweetser, Roger Diehl, Donald Williams
Premiere: September 2005, Venice Film Festival

2006
Rescue Dawn
Fiction, 126 minutes, 35mm, colour
Director: Werner Herzog
Screenplay: Werner Herzog
Producers: Steve Marlton, Elton Brand, Harry Knapp
Camera: Peter Zeitlinger
Editor: Joe Bini
Sound: Paul Paragon
Music: Klaus Badelt
Production Company: Top Gun Productions
Location: Thailand
Cast: Christian Bale (Dieter Dengler), Steve Zahn (Duane Martin), Jeremy Davies (Eugene DeBruin), Chorn Solyda (Walkie Talkie)
Premiere: September 2006, Toronto Film Festival

2007
Encounters at the End of the World
Non-fiction, 99 minutes, HDCAM, colour
Director: Werner Herzog

Producers: Henry Kaiser, Erik Nelson
Camera: Peter Zeitlinger
Editor: Joe Bini
Sound: Werner Herzog
Music: Henry Kaiser, David Lindley
Production Companies: Discovery Films, Creative Differences
Location: McMurdo Station (Antarctic)
Participants: Scott Rowland, David Ainley, Stefan Pashov, Doug MacAyeal, Ryan Andrew Evans, Kevin Emery, Olav T. Oftedal, Regina Eisert, Clive Oppenheimer, Libor Zicha, Karen Joyce, Sam Bowser, David Pacheco
Premiere: September 2007, Telluride Film Festival

2009
Bad Lieutenant: Port of Call – New Orleans
Fiction, 122 minutes, 35mm, colour
Director: Werner Herzog
Screenplay: William M. Finkelstein
Producers: Stephen Belafonte, Nicolas Cage, Randall Emmett, Alan Polsky, Gabe Polsky, Edward R. Pressman
Camera: Peter Zeitlinger
Editor: Joe Bini
Sound: Jay Meagher
Music: Mark Isham
Production Companies: Millennium Films, Edward R. Pressman Films, Saturn Films, Polsky Films
Location: New Orleans
Cast: Nicolas Cage (Terence McDonagh), Eva Mendes (Frankie Donnenfield), Val Kilmer (Steve Pruit), Alvin "Xzibit" Joiner (Big Fate), Fairuza Balk (Heidi), Jennifer Coolidge (Genevieve), Tom Bower (Pat McDonagh), Brad Dourif (Ned Schoenholtz), Irma Hall (Binnie Rogers), Michael Shannon (Mundt)
Premiere: September 2009, Venice Film Festival

2009
La Bohème
Non-fiction, 4 minutes, HDCAM, colour
Director: Werner Herzog
Producer: Andre Singer
Camera: Richard Blanshard
Editor: Joe Bini
Music: Puccini
Production Companies: Sky Arts, English National Opera
Location: Ethiopia
Premiere: September 2009, Venice Film Festival

2009
My Son, My Son, What Have Ye Done
Fiction, 93 minutes, HDCAM, colour
Director: Werner Herzog
Screenplay: Herbert Golder, Werner Herzog
Producer: Eric Bassett
Camera: Peter Zeitlinger
Editor: Joe Bini
Sound: Greg Agalsoff
Music: Ernst Reijseger
Production Companies: Defilm, Paper Street Films
Locations: San Diego, Kashgar (China), Tijuana (Mexico), Peru (Urubamba Valley)
Cast: Michael Shannon (Brad Macallam), Willem Dafoe (Detective Hank Havenhurst), Chloë Sevigny (Ingrid Gudmundson), Udo Kier (Lee Meyers), Michael Peña (Detective Vargas), Grace Zabriskie (Mrs Macallam), Brad Dourif (Uncle Ted), Irma Hall (Mrs Roberts)
Premiere: September 2009, Venice Film Festival

2010
Cave of Forgotten Dreams
Non-fiction, 90 minutes, 3D, colour
Director: Werner Herzog
Producers: Erik Nelson, Adrienne Ciuffo
Camera: Peter Zeitlinger
Editor: Joe Bini
Sound: Eric Spitzer
Music: Ernst Reijseger
Production Companies: Werner Herzog Filmproduktion, Creative Differences, ARTE
Locations: Chauvet-Pont-d'Arc Cave, Vallon-Pont-d'Arc, France
Participants: Jean Clottes, Julien Monney, Jean-Michel Geneste, Michel Philippe
Premiere: September 2010, Toronto Film Festival

2010
Happy People: A Year in the Taiga
Non-fiction, 90 minutes, Video, colour
Director: Dmitry Vasyukov
Co-Director: Werner Herzog
Producers: Christoph Fisser, Vladimir Perepelkin, Nick N. Raslan, Charlie Woebcken
Camera: Alexy Matveev, Gleb Stephanov, Arthur Sibirski, Michael Tarkovsky

Editor: Joe Bini
Sound: Robert Getty
Music: Klaus Badelt
Production Company: Studio Babelsberg
Location: Siberia, Russia
Premiere: November 2010, Germany

2011
Ode to the Dawn of Man
Non-fiction, 30 minutes, Video, colour
Director: Werner Herzog
Camera: Werner Herzog
Editor: Maya Hawke
Sound: Werner Herzog
Music: Ernst Reijseger
Production Company: Werner Herzog Filmproduktion
Location: Haarlem, The Netherlands
Participants: Ernst Reijseger, Sean Bergin, Harmen Fraanje
Premiere: September 2011, Telluride Film Festival

2011
Into the Abyss: A Tale of Death, a Tale of Life
Non-fiction, 107 minutes, HDCAM, colour
Director: Werner Herzog
Producer: Erik Nelson
Camera: Peter Zeitlinger
Editor: Joe Bini
Sound: Steve Osmon
Music: Mark De Gli Antoni
Production Companies: Creative Differences, Werner Herzog
Filmproduktion
Location: Texas
Participants: Michael Perry, Jason Burkett, Richard Lopez, Lisa Stotler-
Balloun, Jared Talbert, Damon Hall
Premiere: September 2011, Toronto Film Festival

2012–13
On Death Row
Non-fiction, 8 × 52 minutes, HDCAM, colour
Director: Werner Herzog
Producer: Erik Nelson
Camera: Peter Zeitlinger, Dave Roberson
Editors: Joe Bini, Marco Capalbo
Sound: Steve Osmon

Music: Mark De Gli Antoni
Production Companies: Creative Differences, Werner Herzog
Filmproduktion
Locations: Texas, Florida
Participants: James Barnes, Joseph Garcia, George Rivas, Hank Skinner,
Linda Carty, Blaine Milam, Darlie Routier, Douglas Feldman, Robert
Fratta
Premiere: February 2012, Berlin Film Festival; August 2013, Locarno
Film Festival

2013
From One Second to the Next
Non-fiction, 35 minutes, HDCAM, colour
Director: Werner Herzog
Producer: George Sholley
Camera: Peter Zeitlinger
Editor: Joe Bini
Sound: Steve Osmon
Music: Mark De Gli Antoni
Production Companies: AT&T, Verizon Communications
Locations: Wisconsin, Indiana, Vermont, Utah
Participants: Xzavier Davis-Bilbo, Reggie Shaw, Debbie Drewniak,
Chandler Gerber
Premiere: August 2013, Locarno Film Festival

OPERA STAGINGS

1985 *Doktor Faust* (Busoni), Teatro Comunale, Bologna
1987 *Lohengrin* (Wagner), Richard-Wagner-Festspielhaus, Bayreuth
1989 *Giovanna d'Arco* (Verdi), Teatro Comunale, Bologna
1991 *Die Zauberflöte* (Mozart), Teatro Bellini, Catania
1992 *La donna del lago* (Rossini), Teatro La Scala, Milan
1993 *Der fliegende Holländer* (Wagner), Opera Bastille, Paris
1994 *Il Guarany* (Gomes), Bonn Opera
1994 *Norma* (Bellini), Arena di Verona
1996 *Il Guarany* (Gomes), the Washington Opera
1997 *Chusingura* (Saegusa), Opera Tokyo
1997 *Tannhäuser* (Wagner), Teatro de la Maestranza, Sevilla
1997 *Tannhäuser* (Wagner), Opera Royal de Wallonie, Liège
1998 *Tannhäuser* (Wagner), Teatro di San Carlo, Naples
1998 *Tannhäuser* (Wagner), Teatro Massimo, Palermo
1999 *Tannhäuser* (Wagner), Teatro Real, Madrid
1999 *Die Zauberflöte* (Mozart), Teatro Bellini, Catania

1999 *Tannhäuser* (Wagner), Teatro Real, Madrid
1999 *Fidelio* (Beethoven), Teatro La Scala, Milan
2000 *Tannhäuser* (Wagner), Baltimore Opera Company
2001 *Giovanna d'Arco* (Verdi), Teatro Carlo Felice, Genua
2001 *Tannhäuser* (Wagner), Teatro Municipal, Rio de Janeiro
2001 *Tannhäuser* (Wagner), Grand Opera, Houston
2001 *Die Zauberflöte* (Mozart), Baltimore Opera Company
2002 *Der fliegende Holländer* (Wagner), Domstufen Festspiele, Erfurt
2003 *Fidelio* (Beethoven), Teatro La Scala, Milan
2008 *Parsifal* (Wagner), Palau de les Arts, Valencia
2013 *I due Foscari* (Verdi), Teatro dell'Opera, Rome

Index

530

responses to Herzog's films, 77–8;
responses to hypnotised actors,
137–9; responses to *Into the
Abyss*, 425; responses to *Land
of Silence and Darkness*, 85;
responses to *Lessons of Darkness*,
292–3; responses to *Nosferatu*,
174; size, 244, 401; theatre, 149;
views and interviews, xv
auto-didacticism, xxvi, 212, 492
ballet, 150
Bavarian dialect, 37, 38–9, 117, 371
boredom, 13, 16, 310
capital punishment, 420–2, 424
Catholicism, 1, 3, 73, 256
character motivation, 222–3
characters, xxiii–xxvi, xxxix, 79–80,
85, 132, 161, 210, 289, 341, 358,
481
childhood, 1–3, 7–16, 340, 407
cinéma-vérité, xxxi–xxxiii, 179,
286–9, 327–9, 476
collaborators, xxvii, 246, 282–3,
294, 296, 298, 302, 346–7,
359–60
communication, xxx, 40–1, 427
cooking, 180, 202, 251, 435
dance, 146, 150, 409–10, 486
deserts, 59–64, 96, 270–1
disappointment, 149, 150, 433–5
discipline, 243–4, 353, 435–6, 487
documentary cinema, xxxi–xxxii,
286–9, 476–7
dreaming, 61, 74–5, 255, 261
drugs, 392
ecstasy/ecstatic: Bacchic, 485–6;
concept, 117; Herzog's position,
xxvii–xxviii, xxxi–xxxiv; filmmaking, xxxiii; landscapes, 50, 139,
277; ski flyers, 117–18, 289; truth,
287–8, 476; Wodaabe tribesmen,
270, 271
editing, 28–9, 65, 242, 248, 280–4,
389, 396, 423
environmental destruction, 82,
361–2
ethnography, 269–70
exploration, xix, xxxvi, 210–11, 357
facial hair, 279, 360
family of characters, 79, 358, 414
fear, 231, 244, 402–3, 468, 474–5
film crews, 70, 108, 112, 163, 172,
224–5, 241, 380–1, 428
film festivals, 147–8

film-going, 16–17, 18–19, 226–7
film preservation, 284–5
film schools, xix, 28, 212–13,
229–31, 241
films (as director), *see under individual titles*
finance and money: *Aguirre* budget,
92; attitudes to film finance,
179, 220–1, 247–8, 328–9, 378;
awards, 31, 44, 53; editing, 280–1;
expenses, 21, 31, 388–9; film preservation, 284–5; film production
company, 20–1, 244–5; financial
crisis (2008), 390; *Fitzcarraldo*,
24; lifestyle, 246–7; *My Best Fiend*
funding, 481; *My Son, My Son*
financing, 406; paying extras,
264–5; projects, 400; publishing
screenplays, 245–6; raising money,
22–4, 244–5; *Rescue Dawn*
financing, 380–1; subsidy system,
44; trade unions, 24–5; Twentieth
Century Fox, 21
foolishness of filmmakers, 328–9
football: assessing players, 159;
childhood interest, 1, 335; favourite players, 101; film director as
football coach, 219; goalkeeping,
333–4; imaginary match, xvi;
injuries, 164, 254; playing for
Munich team, 103, 114–15, 333;
playing in Peru, 334–5; thinking
about, 255; understanding of,
xi–xii; watching matches on television, 435
forgery, 231, 232–3, 234, 373
God, 3–4, 109, 142n, 424
gravity, 118, 143, 189, 226, 376–7,
486
gun-runner story, 35
happiness, 39, 400, 468, 491
health: altitude sickness, 210; antibiotics, 165, 193; broken leg, 35;
cacti spines, 70; childhood illness,
12–13; football injuries, 164, 254;
illness on the Nile, 5–6; malaria
and bilharzia, 62–3; pain relief,
xxxvi, 165; rodeo injuries, 36;
snowmobile injury, 385; whiplash,
26
hobbies, 152
hotels, 152, 230, 361
house-breaking, 2
humour, xli, 42

533

537